BRIEF CONTENTS

THE MACROECONOMY

Private Choices, Public Actions, and Aggregate Outcomes

Michael B. McElroy
North Carolina State University

PRENTICE HALL
Upper Saddle River, New Jersey 07458

Library of Congress Cataloging-in-Publication Data

McElroy, Michael B.
    The macroeconomy : private choices, public actions & aggregate
outcomes / Michael B. McElroy.
      p.   cm.
    Includes bibliographical references and index.
    ISBN 0-02-378801-1
    1. Macroeconomics.   I. Title.
HB172.5.M376 1996
339—dc20

95-40085
CIP

Acquisitions editor: Leah Jewell
Assistant editor: Teresa Cohan
Design director: Patricia Wosczyk
Interior design: Donna Wickes
Cover design: Lorraine Castellano
Cover image: Pamela Hamilton/The Image Bank
Manufacturing buyer: Marie McNamara
Production supervision: Progressive Publishing Alternatives

© 1996 by Prentice-Hall, Inc.
A Simon & Schuster Company
Upper Saddle River, New Jersey 07458

Printed in the United States of America
10 9 8 7 6 5 4 3 2 1

ISBN 0-02-378801-1

Prentice-Hall International (UK) Limited, *London*
Prentice-Hall of Australia Pty. Limited, *Sydney*
Prentice-Hall Canada Inc., *Toronto*
Prentice-Hall Hispanoamericana, S. A., *Mexico*
Prentice-Hall of India Private Limited, *New Delhi*
Prentice-Hall of Japan, Inc., *Tokyo*
Simon & Schuster Asia Pte. Ltd., *Singapore*
Editora Prentice-Hall do Brasil, Ltda., *Rio de Janeiro*

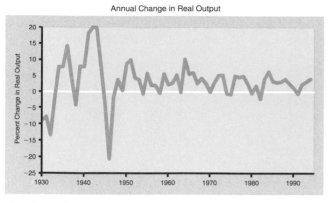

Annual Change in Real Output

■ FIGURE 4

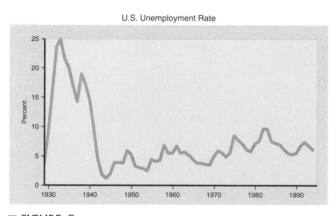

U.S. Unemployment Rate

■ FIGURE 5

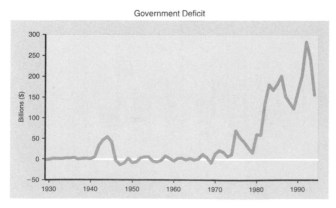

Government Deficit

■ FIGURE 6

limiting it with very few exceptions to *rule-maker and enforcer* rather than *active player* in the game. Keynes saw the stagnation of the Great Depression as proof that the classical theory did not apply to "the economic society in which we actually live." He argued for **active government involvement** to supplement the important but, in his view, limited ability of market forces to maintain full employment.

Much of what has been learned about the workings of the macroeconomy since 1936 can be usefully viewed as an extension of this initial clash between *Keynesians* and *classicals,* subsequently joined by *monetarists, new classicals, new Keynesians, real business cycle theorists* and many others whose scientific research spans or resists these labels. Although controversy continues over the broad question of what the government can (and cannot) do to smooth the ups and downs of the business cycle, the area of disagreement has been considerably narrowed and refined. Research is now focused on a few key questions: (1) What is the primary **source of output fluctuations** (instability in private spending, erratic fiscal or monetary changes, or supply-side shocks from innovations and new technologies)? (2) How quickly do our **perceptions and expectations** respond to changing information? (3) To what degree do **market frictions** slow down the automatic market-clearing process of the price system? and (4) How long and predictable is the **time lag** between policy action and its impact on the macroeconomy?

Though the dispute continues, there is no doubt that macroeconomic policy-making has become far more responsive (too much so, some think) to changing economic events than it was in the 1930s. There has also been a substantial **increase in the economic size of the Federal government,** from about 3% of total spending in the 1920s to over 20% today. This dramatic growth in public spending—reflecting higher military as well as social expenditures—has been accompanied by increased reliance on *public borrowing* to supplement the traditional mainstay of public finance, *current taxes.* Continued **deficit spending** (Figure 6) and its

(Continued inside the back cover)

To Elzbieta and Philip, with Love

CONTENTS

PART II. BASIC MACROECONOMIC ANALYSIS 61

6 Monetary Policy   165

7 International Trade   199

PART III. SMOOTHING BUSINESS CYCLES AND CONTROLLING INFLATION   235

8 Macroeconomic Fluctuations   237

9 Stabilization Policy and the Phillips Curve 273

10 Inflation 299

11 Unemployment 327

PART IV. LONG-RUN DYNAMICS: SAVING, INVESTMENT, AND GROWTH   347

12 Consumption, Saving, and Investment   349

13 Capital Markets   375

14 Economic Growth   395

PART V.   MODELS, MEASUREMENT, AND PERFORMANCE   425

15   Models and Measurement   427

16   The Macroeconomy: Choices, Policies, and Outcomes   457

APPENDIX   NATIONAL AND INTERNATIONAL MACROECONOMIC DATA   471

Whatever the mind does is done by constructing, constituting, grasping, not just by "taking in" or receiving or containing or retaining. . . . Good college teaching is the kind that promises to make the teacher finally superfluous, the kind that leads students to *want* to continue work in the given subject and to be *able* to, because they have the necessary intellectual equipment to continue to work at a more advanced level. [Each] course should be viewed not primarily as a preparation for some future course or future experience but *as an end in itself*. If you hope for a future that includes your subject, you must not teach to that future but to a delight in learning *in the present moment*.
   —Wayne C. Booth, *The Vocation of a Teacher: Rhetorical Occasions 1967–1988*

   Although the underlying story of macroeconomic events, theories, and policies told in these pages is very much in the mainstream, I have taken great care *not* to follow the well-worn expository path that I believe typifies intermediate textbooks in macroeconomics. Though many do a fine job of keeping the topics and techniques and controversies up to date, they continue what I see as a stubborn and damaging tradition of writing to the wrong audience—to economists rather than to students. Their structure, content, and voice are based on the presumption that our students' interest in and uses of macroeconomic knowledge differ little from our own. The result is that by semester's end most students view macroeconomics as an intricate and technical subject, filled with subtleties, traps, and fundamental disagreements. Even the best come away with varying degrees of discouragement and confusion, unsure about "which model to use when" and, most damning of all, thinking it was a course about "models" rather than "issues." We have failed to convince them that a careful analytical framework is a prerequisite to any *practical* understanding of the macroeconomy. When they address these issues in the future it is not likely to be with tools or insights from past courses but with the slogans that so dominate and limit popular discussion of macroeconomic policy.

   So this book reflects my conviction that our textbooks themselves pose a major obstacle to the learning of macroeconomics. It is the outgrowth of more than twenty years of teaching macroeconomics to a large and varied audience—undergraduate majors in economics, business, and accounting and graduate students in economics, business, and public policy—at North Carolina State University and, for the past seven years, also at Duke University. My overriding goal has been to develop a text that will help the *actual* students sitting in our classes experience the excitement and satisfaction of grappling with and, finally, understanding the key macroeconomic issues. This means ending the implicit fiction that the representative reader is a precocious and dedicated economist-to-be, eager to assimilate the jargon and concerns of the experts. It means addressing an array of students of differing backgrounds and interests whose initial curiosity about macroeconomic topics is easily discouraged by needlessly complex or stylized presentations that seem to disregard their perspective and concerns.

   Our students' interest in topics like inflation, unemployment, economic growth, international trade, interest rates, taxes, deficits, and public debt is very real but also very different from ours. It has shallower roots that require nourishment, not just transplanting. My goal has been to write a book that will help instructor and student cultivate this interest into a practical and durable understanding of macroeconomic events and policies. Because I want to spend considerable class time discussing current issues (with readings from the *Wall Street Journal*, the *Economist, Business Week*, and so on), I have worked hard to create a text that is sufficiently interesting and accessible to the student that it doesn't have to be "redone" in class. Although we'll always need class time to develop and reinforce the basic mechanics, I want a book that allows ample time for doing economic analysis with the students, not just showing them what others have done. Testing successive versions of the manuscript on perhaps a thousand students over the past four years has convinced me that it is possible to create such a text, one that works substantially better for our students in both the short run and the long run—better at holding their interest throughout the semester and better at improving their macroeconomic understanding once the theoretical superstructure has been forgotten.

There is little in this book that has not been thought out carefully—the sequencing of topics; the reinforcement of important results at various points and in different contexts; the development and use of models, of course, but also the transformation of their key insights into more lasting formulations and metaphors; and, most important, the use of a unified framework that maintains analytical continuity across chapters and topics. A major challenge, one that I think few texts take seriously, is to provide an appealing and useful analytical mechanism without letting the machinery overwhelm the story. In the end, what is perhaps most distinctive about the present text is its determination to address the economic sophistication of students who will *not* become professional economists. My ambitious, but I believe realistic, goal is for them to reach a basic understanding of macroeconomic issues that will not evaporate soon after the final examination, but will become part of an economic common sense to be drawn on one, three, or ten years hence. I think such a solid grounding in basic macroeconomic analysis will also prove highly beneficial to those who continue on to the Ph D in economics. The common lament that too many of our graduate students acquire technique without economic intuition may partly reflect their failure to get a strong and balanced analytical foundation at the intermediate level.

To be more specific, the following topics are among those in which I believe existing texts fail to serve the interests of our students.

(1) THE IMPLICATIONS OF *PUBLIC DEFICITS AND DEBT* FOR A COUNTRY'S CURRENT AND FUTURE STANDARD OF LIVING. Despite the massive visibility of this topic, our textbooks continue to treat it obliquely and incompletely. They offer no satisfactory middle ground to help students relate abstract conditions on "primary deficits" or "perfect tax discounting" to the slogans with which deficits are actually discussed and decided on by voters and politicians. I believe this reflects a wider failure of the profession to alert the public to the substantive issues that lie beneath the sound bites on a "balanced budget." The economic consequences of various alternatives are poorly understood because economists have not insisted on the kind of careful analysis of costs and benefits in which we usually take so much pride.

I devote most of Chapter 5 ("Fiscal Policy") to a careful but accessible discussion of the various *economic* dimensions of the "deficit issue." After a look at the problems of measuring the deficit and separating structural from cyclical changes, the aggregate demand/aggregate supply (*AD/AS*) framework is used to examine the impact of changes in the structural deficit under various assumptions about tax discounting. I then turn to the crucial "day-of-reckoning" part of the story by starting with private borrowing decisions—specifically the circumstances in which such borrowing is and is not sustainable. This takes the focus away from *whether we borrow*, privately or publicly, and redirects it to *how we use the borrowed funds.*

At this point I make a simple but, I'm convinced, very useful distinction among three types of borrowing: (1) "self-financing" (used for investment activities), (2) "consumption smoothing" (used for consumption but in the context of a rising expected future income stream), or (3) "consumption draining" (used for consumption when expected income is constant or declining). This is an easy way to see the boundary between sustainable and unsustainable, and makes it clear that although a (cash flow) deficit means spending beyond the limits of our *current* income, it does not necessarily mean spending "beyond our means" in an intertemporal context. This helps to counter knee-jerk reactions in which pure semantics ("balance = good"; "deficit = bad") masquerades as analysis. It also allows us to examine specific costs and benefits when continued borrowing falls in either of the sustainable categories. But just because we *can* borrow without courting disaster doesn't mean we *should*, and this approach offers a commonsense "now or later?" framework in which students can appreciate the intertemporal costs and benefits of the timing of taxes and the timing of government benefits. They can readily see why a balanced *cash flow* budget is neither necessary nor sufficient for "fiscal responsibility" in any meaningful sense and can thereby look at the issue of a Balanced Budget Amendment without falling into the simplistic slogans that have dominated the popular discussion. In the process they become aware that fiscal responsibility is more about "*how we spend* our public dollars and *how we tax* to raise those dollars" than about "*when* we tax."

(2) THE IMPACT OF *TRADE RESTRICTIONS, EXCHANGE RATE FLUCTUATIONS,* AND *CONTINUING TRADE DEFICITS* ON THE MACROECONOMY. Most students are very much drawn to international trade issues and will acquire a solid analytical grounding so long as the presentation keeps in reasonable contact with what they see in the daily news. Some texts try to do so much on this topic that the student drowns in theorems, institutional detail, or both. Others continue to treat the foreign sector as an appendage and fail to make a satisfactory integration of trade topics with the other issues, policies, and events in the course.

My choice has been to put trade into the analysis from the very beginning. Chapter 1 examines external borrowing, and Chapter 3 incorporates net exports into the aggregate demand model. Once they have been through the basic mechanics of the *AD/AS* framework (Chapter 4), and several applications of fiscal and monetary policy (Chapters 5 and 6), I then devote a full chapter to why and how international trade affects our economic lives. I arrived at this presentation through trial and error, a gradual process of finally hearing what my students were telling me. It turns out to be a perfect time and setting in which to reinforce their understanding of economic fundamentals by relating (briefly) the notions of mutual gains from trade and comparative advantage, thereby laying the foundation for *why* we care about exchange rates, trade restrictions, and capital flows across international borders. As they come to see that trade across nations is economically identical to any other trade, students develop a unified and intuitive appreciation of the workings of the macroeconomy that is a strong foundation for the short- and long-run dynamics of the remaining chapters.

(3) THE INFLUENCE OF MONETARY AND FISCAL POLICY ON OUTPUT, EMPLOYMENT, AND INTEREST RATES, AND THE PROSPECTS AND DANGERS OF *STABLIZATION POLICY.* Many texts do a good job on the mechanics of short-run dynamics, but fail to leave students with a clear view of how all this relates to what is being played out around them in day-to-day events and policy decisions. I cover the basic analytics but complement this by also presenting the main results in a way that does not depend on remembering the intricacies and variations of the theoretical models. I emphasize that activist/nonactivist differences over what the government can do to smooth the ups and downs of the business cycle turn on four main issues, each of which is characterized by a substantial gray area in terms of current empirical knowledge: (1) the underlying *source of cyclical fluctuations* (demand side or supply side; private or public sector); (2) the *speed at which expectations adjust* to changing events and policies; (3) the *degree of price* and *wage stickiness;* and (4) the *extent of policy lags.* This gives students a handle on what is involved in the controversy over short-run stabilization policy without extinguishing their interest and understanding in a flood of theoretical, ideological, or historical detail.

(4) THE IMPORTANCE OF *AGGREGATE SUPPLY* IN UNDERSTANDING POLICY OPTIONS. The trend toward an early emphasis on the role of aggregate supply can only be applauded. It is a long-needed counterweight to presentations of aggregate demand that obscure the presence of scarcity and encourage the crudest of "Old Keynesian" habits of thought. But the way in which this is usually done—through growth models—is a classic example of the failure to write to our audience.

My experience is that the early introduction of a steady-state growth model is not a useful way to develop a student's analytical or intuitive understanding of basic supply-side constraints. Its rarified setting is disorienting and confusing to most students. I introduce aggregate supply in Chapter 1 and in the simplest possible way—through the production function and the production possibility frontier. I then return to these concepts in later chapters to supplement the aggregate supply curve whenever a warning about underlying constraints seems especially important for the topic at hand. This means that the reader gets periodic reminders that scarcity lies at the heart of every choice between "this or that?" and "now or later?"

A solid understanding of the main issues of economic growth, in my view, is best built on a foundation in comparative statics and short-run dynamics and should, therefore, come toward the end of the text. Chapters 12 to 14 ("Consumption, Saving, and Investment"; "Capital Markets"; and "Economic Growth," respectively) develop both the mechanics and the intuition of the "now or later?" choice underlying growth. In contrast to standard treatments of long-run dynamics that are almost entirely detached from the rest of the course, I present growth as a continuation of the earlier analysis that now delves further into the consumption/saving choice, the investment decision, the workings of capital markets, and the production function to analyze the issues and policy options underlying the process of economic growth.

(5) INTRODUCING THE STORY. The usual opening chapters—filled with statistical portraits, a barrage of definitions, and synopses of major results—may be revealing to *us* but can have little meaning for our students until the end of the course. Not only do these chapters use precious time on material that belongs later, but they reduce our chances of enlisting the student's enthusiasm at the start. Simple definitions of a few key concepts are enough for the initial analytics that can stimulate their interest in macroeconomic issues. After students have a solid analytical base, they'll be able to appreciate the significance of measurement problems for public and private decision making. For example, the central issue of gaps between many of the *concepts* in our models and their real-world *measures* is entirely missed when definitions are consigned to the opening chapters. By obscuring the point that theory logically precedes measurement, this only reinforces the all-too-common "let the facts speak for themselves" fallacy. I cover measurement, estimation, and forecasting in Chapter 15, "Models and Measurement."

These are a few examples of the many choices I've made in the way the text addresses the student. I want to invite our students into a substantive macroeconomic "conversation" without requiring them to mimic the professional economist. I am convinced of the wisdom of Wayne Booth's dictum that "If you hope for a future that includes your subject, you must not teach to that future but to a delight in learning *in the present moment*."

PREFACE

Most of our information about macroeconomic events and policies comes from the news media. Radio and TV news programs, magazines, and newspapers can be informative and entertaining, but they do not and cannot provide a reliable foundation for understanding complex relationships and events. Their focus is on issues of immediate political interest and emphasizes controversies and personalities. By frequently blurring the boundary between political disagreement and scientific dispute, they can leave us with the impression that the careful use of logic and facts is relatively unimportant. Why put time and effort into learning a subject about which so little seems to be known even by so-called experts and so much seems to be simply a matter of opinion? This book will show you why this view of macroeconomic events and policies is quite incorrect. It will take you beneath the contentious and often confusing surface of economic policy discussions to a straightforward and practical analytical framework for understanding basic cause-and-effect linkages in the overall economy.

This is a course in macroeconomic analysis—the process of combining clues from the past with logic and intuition to determine the likely impact of events and policies on our overall economic well-being. Put another way, it's about building and then applying a macroeconomic model that mimics the actual cause-and-effect network linking our private and public choices to aggregate outcomes. Economic models, by design, are simplified and, thereby, manageable representations of complex processes. The fact that they are only a *representation* of reality leads some to dismiss them as "only theories," especially if the model's predictions don't support their own beliefs or preconceptions. This common but very damaging attitude implies that a better alternative exists—some simple, direct way to get insights without having to think very long or very hard. Unfortunately, but not surprisingly, easy answers are seldom found to important economic questions. So-called practical approaches—slogans, rules-of-thumb, the more primitive varieties of common sense, and just plain wishful thinking—are also statements of cause-and-effect. In other words they're "models" too, but usually so over-simplified as to provide only a very incomplete and distorted representation of the underlying economic mechanism. The analytical framework developed in this book takes a little time and patience to understand. But once learned it offers a flexible, practical, and durable framework for thinking clearly and carefully about the big issues in macroeconomics. By the end of this course I hope you'll see why a favorite slogan among economists is that "there's nothing as *practical* as good theory!"

ACKNOWLEDGMENTS

It has been my good fortune over the years to have received guidance and encouragement from many talented teachers and friends. I am especially indebted to Ralph Beals, George Daly, Robert Eisner, Harry Landreth, Art Treadway, Bob Vaillancourt, Terry Vance, Donald Walker, and Bob Wallace. Each has each helped me to learn and inspired me to help others learn.

I offer a large collective thanks to my students, scattered over many years and, now, many places. Those who have made specific and helpful contributions to various parts of this project are Nihal Ergun, Michael Gordon, Donna Grieco, and E. C. Sykes. Many more have participated, unsuspectingly, through their questions and answers in class and, not least, their struggles with my exams. They have taught me much about what is difficult and important and fun in macroeconomics.

A number of colleagues at North Carolina State University and at Duke University have taken the time to discuss issues of exposition as well as to read and comment on drafts of the manuscript. I am especially indebted to my colleague and friend John Lapp for his unfailing helpfulness and patience during untold hours of conversation over many years about the learning and teaching of macroeconomics. I am also grateful to Neil DeMarchi, John Dutton, Tom Grennes, Duncan Holthausen, Dale Hoover, David Hyman, Doug Pearce, John Seater, Wally Thurman, and Ed Tower for comments and discussion on this material. Terrie Rouse provided prompt and careful secretarial assistance at several important stages.

Two senior editors were vital to the development of this book. Jill Lectka had the initial enthusiasm and commitment that got the project going; Leah Jewell then provided the encouragement and final orchestration that saw the manuscript through the production process. I am very grateful to both of them and also to assistant editor Teresa Cohan, a constant source of help and guidance through the entire process. Elaine Lynch of Prentice Hall and Donna King and Suzanne Mescan of Progressive Publishing Alternatives were helpful and understanding in overseeing the production process. Others at Prentice Hall who played an important role in making this a satisfying experience include Kristen Kaiser, Patricia Morris, and Bill Wicker.

I wish to thank the following reviewers who made many useful comments at various stages of the evolving manuscript and often shared their own classroom experiences of what works and what doesn't in the teaching and learning of intermediate macroeconomics.

David K. Backus	*New York University*
Scott Bloom	*North Dakota State University*
Fred Joutz	*George Washington University*
Ed Gamber	*Lafayette College*
Michael J. Gootzeit	*Memphis State University*
Yoon Bai Kim	*University of Kentucky*
John Lapp	*North Carolina State University*
William S. Rawson	*University of South Carolina*
Michael R. Redfearn	*University of North Texas*
Malcolm Robinson	*University of Cincinnati*
John Shea	*University of Wisconsin*
Calvin D. Siebert	*University of Iowa*
Vincent H. Smith	*Montana State University*
Case Sprenkle	*University of Illinois*
Michael K. Taussig	*Rutgers University*
Philip Wiest	*George Mason University*
Jeffrey Zimmerman	*Methodist College*

PART I

Mapping the Territory

The two chapters in this section provide an overview of the main concerns of macroeconomics and a basic framework for addressing key issues like unemployment, inflation, and economic growth. Both chapters are introductory in nature and need no introduction themselves. But this is a good time to draw your attention to two analytical techniques used throughout this book: "aggregation" and "metaphor."

Aggregation is the familiar process of combining many elements into a single one, like your grade-point average (GPA), an index of prices, or a nation's gross domestic product. It's much simpler to use such averages or totals instead of all the individual, disaggregated data from which they are calculated. Your GPA is far easier to remember and communicate than your entire transcript, and provides useful information for many purposes. In the same way, aggregates like "income per capita," the "federal deficit," and the "rate of economic growth" convey important insights in a direct, understandable way. In the act of simplifying, however, aggregation also hides information. For example, suppose you have As and Bs in economics, mathematics, and statistics and Ds and Fs in literature, history, and foreign languages. To say that you have a C average is probably not very useful information. Similarly, an average family income of $20,000 a year tells us nothing about the distribution of income around this average, which may be wide or narrow, and is crucial to a reliable picture of a nation's economic well-being. Aggregation is a powerful and essential analytical tool. But any aggregate can also be a tool that breaks in our hands when used carelessly or improperly.

Macroeconomics, as the name suggests, deals with sweeping, economy-wide events, such as unemployment, inflation, and economic growth. So it cannot escape doing much of its work with aggregate measures. We will see situations in which aggregates hide information in a way that distorts our understanding and can lead to costly mistakes in policy making. Avoiding this common aggregation problem is, in good part, a skill that comes with practice. We can also get some help from an area called the "microfoundations" of macroeconomics, which has become quite important in recent years. In the early chapters, however, aggregate concepts are used freely and unquestioningly to capture the spirit and basic power of macroeconomic analysis. As we later sharpen our view and refine the analysis, more attention will be paid to what's hidden beneath the aggregates.

The use of **metaphor** (and its close relations "analogy" and "simile") is another common technique in economics. Familiar as a rhetorical device for enriching language ("Shall I compare thee to a summer's day?") or attracting interest ("This book is a veritable gold mine for those wishing to . . ."), metaphor also helps us perceive, analyze, and draw conclusions about how things work ("All the world's a stage and all the men and women merely players: They have their exits and their entrances; and one man in his time plays many parts."). The function of a metaphor—to connect one thing with another that is similar but more easily understood—is simple, but its consequences are sometimes profound. It enables us to use our everyday knowledge about "this" to describe, analyze, and even experience "that."

We use comparisons of "this" with "that" frequently and, often, unknowingly. Even the most obvious metaphors, with repeated use, become so ingrained in our thinking that we may forget that we are using one thing to talk about something very different. For example, "The government deficit is *Public Enemy Number 1*" or "The Federal Reserve needs to *put on the brakes* before inflation gets *out of control*." Sometimes we even mix very different metaphors without realizing it. For example, "I've *invested too much time* in this already and I still don't *have a handle* on it" or "Attempting to *fine-tune* the economy may make it even more *unstable*." Don't worry about trying to figure out why the italicized phrases are metaphors and not "reality itself." At this point, the important thing is just to be aware that we habitually, often unconsciously, use a metaphor to apply our understanding (or misunderstanding) of one thing to another.[1] A world without metaphors would be a drab and colorless place indeed. Not only would our descriptions and even perceptions of reality suffer, but our knowledge of how things work would be quite primitive. Lessons learned in one area would not be extended to another.

To be more specific, a well-chosen metaphor helps us understand a complex event or process by directing attention toward the essential elements and away from the less important. It acts like a filter. Like aggregation, the use of metaphor has the power to conceal as well as simplify. An inappropriate metaphor can hide otherwise obvious connections by focusing our attention in the wrong place. A particular metaphor may seem intuitively appealing, even irresistible—especially if it happens to agree with our preconceptions. Yet it may turn out to be decidedly misleading in its implications and end up serving as a barrier to understanding. Equally important,

---

[1] For those interested in learning more about the importance of metaphors, see George Lakoff and Mark Johnson, *Metaphors We Live By* (Chicago: University of Chicago Press, 1980).

A SAMPLING OF METAPHORS IN ECONOMICS

Medicine and Health

- "The best prescription is a strict fiscal diet that eliminates all unnecessary fat from the government's budget."
- "The federal budget continues to hemorrhage red ink."

Warfare

- "International trade is an ongoing economic battle—for every winner there must also be a loser."
- "Our policy makers need to wake up to the fact that the United States is in head-to-head competition with other nations. Every effort should be made to enhance our competitive edge in the global community."

Engineering

- "The marvelous engine of economic growth that worked so smoothly and powerfully until the 1970s continues to sputter."
- "It's time for the government to do some good old-fashioned pump priming to get the economy moving again."

Transportation

- "If the economy doesn't respond soon, the government will have to "jump-start" it with a quick tax cut or an increase in the supply of money."
- "The government's job is to steer the boat, not to row it."
- "A rising tide lifts all the boats—except those that have already sunk."
- "That loud sucking noise you'll hear will be the sound of our jobs heading for the Mexican border."

Fantasy

- "The economy is lead automatically to maximum efficiency, as if guided by an invisible hand."
- "Deficit spending is like sneaking into the future and stealing from our grandchildren."

Mathematics

- "Tax revenues are the big unknown in the deficit equation."
- "Because $y = c + i + x + g = c + s + t$, it must be true that $i = s + t - g - x$. So if we want investment to rise we must either save more, tax more, slash government spending or borrow from foreigners."

metaphors can also create an illusion of understanding where there is little or none. Politicians often resort to them in response to the expectations of the public and the media that they appear instantly knowledgeable on all issues. The danger for policy making is that they may fool even themselves and end up equating a too simple metaphor with a complex reality.[2]

We use metaphors constantly in trying to describe and interpret economic events. The preceding examples are only the tip of the iceberg (an overworked but still helpful metaphor). The profusion of metaphors in economics raises the obvious question of which one to use in a particular situation. It's important to be aware that there can be no simple answer to this because economics is *not* medicine, physics, mathematics, sailing, or anything else. Many in the preceding list fall into the category of inappropriate metaphors, as you will discover by the end of this book. Others may be useful in some circumstances but not in others.

Although many metaphors are valuable in particular situations or at certain times, the most generally useful one in economics has proved to be mathematics. Perhaps a more accurate way to say this is that the dominant metaphor in modern economics is that of an equilibrium system, borrowed directly from the celestial mechanics of Newtonian physics. An **equilibrium system**—a balance of many interacting forces—can be very complicated. It turns out, however, that these systems (whether in physics, engineering, meteorology, or economics) can be usefully described and analyzed if we treat them as if they were a system of simultaneous equations.

Within the economics profession, communication is increasingly carried out in a highly specialized, largely mathematical language. This has the great advantage of allowing economists to work through their ideas more carefully and rapidly, and to communicate them more readily to their colleagues. But it has also become a major barrier to communication outside the profession. Mathematics is simply not a meaningful metaphor for the general public or for most political decision makers.

This book attempts to establish a middle ground in which basic mathematics is one of several useful metaphors for the workings of an economic system. Mathematics is not economics, nor is it a substitute for economics. But it happens to be an astonishingly valuable tool for understanding complex events in many areas, including economics. Basic algebra and geometry will be an important ingredient in the process by which you learn macroeconomics. I hope you will come to see mathematics as an ally in understanding the complex but very *practical* issues that determine our individual and collective levels of economic well-being.

The thoughtful use of both aggregation and metaphor can make complicated events easier to visualize, understand, and communicate. Metaphor can also breathe life into otherwise tedious topics. It is in this spirit that this first section of two introductory chapters has been titled *Mapping the Territory.* The metaphor of "exploration and discovery" is one that I hope will come alive for you throughout this book.

[2] In Jerzy Kosinski's novel *Being There* (made into a movie with Peter Sellers and Shirley MacLaine), a simple, illiterate gardener speaks of the change of seasons, and its effect on the length of the day and the growth of plants. His statements are so child-like that his new acquaintances assume he must be speaking metaphorically rather than literally. They interpret his unsophisticated observations as subtle and wise, and, one thing leading to another, he soon becomes a valued adviser to the president of the United States.

CHAPTER 1

SCARCITY, BOUNDARIES, AND CHOICES

⚭ 1.1 INTRODUCTION

Every economy—past, present, or future; rich or poor; industrial or agricultural; capitalist, socialist, or totalitarian—exists for a single, powerful reason: to cope with the problems created by **scarcity.** Scarcity means we can't have everything we want, forcing us to face unwelcome questions like "which goods to produce?" and "who gets them?" For individuals and nations alike, scarcity is the inescapable fact at the root of the "economic problem." And, unfortunately, this problem is not the kind we can "solve." Scarcity is a *condition,* inherent in nature, that we must endure. **Resources** (or inputs) such as land, labor, and even "time" are required to produce **output,** such as food, clothes, houses, and haircuts. These goods and services are scarce because the resources needed to produce them are limited in supply. This simple fact has enormous and inescapable consequences for each of us and ensures that the economic problem is a permanent and universal condition of mankind.

Scarcity has many faces, its cruelest shown in the suffering and indignities inflicted by poverty. For the poor of any time or any place, the struggle with scarcity is unrelenting. The slightest disturbance to their economic environment has tragic potential. The expectation of a rising standard of living, so natural to us, is as incredible to many hundreds of millions of the world's people as their plight is to us. In spite of unprecedented growth in the average standard of living of many countries over the past century or more, the dream of eliminating poverty through the vast powers of industrialization and capital accumulation remains unrealized. The disparity of incomes around the world is apparent in Figure 1.1. But hidden in these figures are variations around the average that reflect serious poverty within even the richest nations. A significant frac-

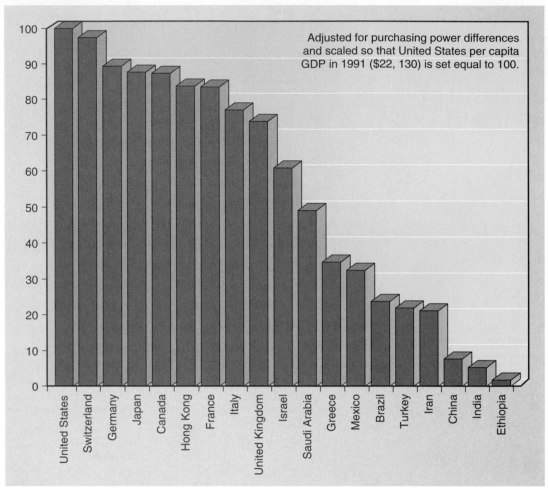

World Per Capita Incomes
(% of U.S. Gross Domestic Product/Head in 1991)

Adjusted for purchasing power differences and scaled so that United States per capita GDP in 1991 ($22, 130) is set equal to 100.

■ FIGURE 1.1

The World Bank, *World Development Report 1993: Investing in Health* (Oxford: Oxford University Press, 1993 pp. 296—97).

tion of the world's inhabitants continue to live abbreviated lives under appalling conditions.[1] For them, scarcity is literally a matter of life or death.

For those of us safely above a subsistence level of income, scarcity presents a different face. We don't "struggle" in the same sense, but we "work." That is, we undertake activities that we would not pursue, at least to such an extent, if scarcity did not exist. The *degree* to which scarcity impinges on us depends partly on how well rewarded our work is. But it also depends on the level of our desires and expectations.

---

[1] According to The World Bank, "More than 1 billion people, one-fifth of the world's population, live on less than one dollar a day—a standard of living that Western Europe and the United States attained two hundred years ago" (The World Bank, *World Development Report 1991: The Challenge of Development.* Oxford: Oxford University Press, 1991, p. 1).

For example, if we could be content with the standard of living of our great-grand-parents, scarcity would still be present but as a much less powerful force in most of our lives, absorbing far less of our attention and energy. We could satisfy our relatively modest material wants with fewer weeks of work per year.

But we have chosen not to transform our tremendous advances in productivity into leisure time. Even in the wealthiest nations there is no evidence of rising productivity catching up with our desire for goods and services. The carrot seems to move at least as fast as productive capacity, always dangling just beyond our reach. As we get more, we desire more, which prompts some to question whether economic growth really is such an important goal for those comfortably above the poverty level. Our willingness to make the sacrifices that a high and growing level of economic activity requires is the best evidence that, for most of us, the prospect of a higher standard of living for ourselves and our children is a *very* important goal.

Work continues to be the central activity in most of our lives. Social, political, and religious reformers have had little success in convincing people in industrialized economies that happiness is to be found by substituting humanistic, spiritual, or communal goals for material rewards. Scarcity absorbs our energies as much in the richest nations as in the poorest, even though the average levels of economic well-being are poles apart. Nearly all of us continue to want more than scarcity will allow. *Economics* studies the nature and implications of our varied attempts to satisfy these wants and to expand our productive boundaries.

With its focus on the inevitability of scarcity, economics has long been dubbed the "dismal science." Scarcity is indeed a bitter pill to swallow. But having done so, the study of economics can then be seen as inherently optimistic, as a search for ways to raise our standard of living through specialization, innovation, and exchange. Though we tend to emphasize the competitive aspects of economic systems, **mutual gain** is an equally important characteristic of an efficient economic organization. When adverse events or policies interfere with these "gains from trade," repercussions are felt throughout the economy.

There is an ever-present temptation to ignore what economic analysis has to tell us. Its complexity and limitations can be frustrating, and its inevitable refrain of costs, limits, and alternatives is never welcome. In later chapters we'll see many examples where careful economic analysis was sacrificed to much simpler slogans, ideology, or so-called common sense. These include policies that deepened the Great Depression in the guise of curing it, policies that dramatically increased a budget deficit under the banner of eliminating it, and policies that fanned the flames of inflation in the name of price control. To the extent that economic theory can help us avoid such mistakes, it is obviously valuable. Hence, the underlying theme of this book—there is nothing as *practical* as good theory.

1.2 SCARCITY AND THE PRODUCTION POSSIBILITY FRONTIER

The **production possibility frontier** (PPF) is a simple but very useful map of the boundaries that scarcity imposes on us. It will be used throughout the book to provide an overview of the economic landscape under a variety of different economic events and policies. The PPF starts from the concept of a **production function** in which the production of goods and services is viewed as a process of transforming one set of objects (inputs or resources) into another (output). For now, we aggregate the many different kinds of inputs into just three broad categories: *labor* (*n*); *capital* (*k*) (which includes machinery, structures, natural resources, and technology); and *social, political, and economic institutions* (i^{nst}).

This last input—the *institutional structure*, for short—is a catch-all for the rules and traditions within which economic transactions occur. This structure is so much a part of our lives that we tend to take it for granted and neglect its crucial role.[2] Two important examples are *property rights* (such as private versus public ownership) and *laws limiting or prohibiting certain kinds of economic transactions* (like zoning restrictions, child labor laws, environmental protection laws, or illicit goods and services).

The institutional structure is critical to productive efficiency. Certain institutional restrictions, such as in "planned" economies of the old Soviet type, can doom a nation quite rich in labor and natural resources to a relatively low standard of living. Easing such restrictions will ultimately increase output but, as the postcommunist countries are so painfully learning, institutional change can be a slow and difficult process. The clumsy symbol i^{nst} is perhaps appropriate for this diverse and unwieldy category. It represents an *index of institutional efficiency*, so that an increase ($+ \Delta i^{nst}$) indicates an improvement in the institutional environment (hence, an increase in potential output), whereas $- \Delta i^{nst}$ means a deterioration. We'll explore the decisive role of institutions in the final chapters of this book. Until then the focus will be on the other inputs, taking the institutional framework as given and constant.

The production process transforms these three inputs—labor, capital, and the institutional structure—into *output*, denoted by the symbol *y*. "Output" includes all the *final* goods and services that are produced within the economy in a given period, usually a year.[3] This transformation of inputs into output can be represented algebraically by the *production function*

$$y = F(n,k,i^{nst})$$

with the functional notation $F(\ )$ representing, in very general terms, the production process. What characteristics of actual production should we include in this functional relationship? For now, to keep it simple and clear, we specify only the basic fact of scarcity: more output requires more inputs—more labor, more capital, or more efficient institutional arrangements. Economists often express this in the easily remembered refrain, "There's no such thing as a free lunch."

To move from the production function to the PPF we assume that the levels of the inputs (*n*, *k*, and i^{nst}) are fixed, and that we now want to produce either or both of *two* types of outputs, x_1 and x_2. The graph of the PPF (see Figure 1.2) is downward-sloping and bowed out from the origin, and shows the maximum combinations of the two outputs that can be produced with the given amount of inputs. We cannot pro-

---

[2] A more ambitious and engaging definition is provided by Douglass North, economic historian and Nobel Prize winner. "Institutions are the humanly devised constraints that structure political, economic and social interaction. They consist of both informal constraints (sanctions, taboos, customs, traditions, and codes of conduct), and formal rules (constitutions, laws, property rights). Throughout history, institutions have been devised by human beings to create order and reduce uncertainty in exchange. Together with the standard constraints of economics they define the choice set and therefore determine transaction and production costs and hence the profitability and feasibility of engaging in economic activity. They evolve incrementally, connecting the past with the present and the future; history in consequence is largely a story of institutional evolution in which the historical performance of economies can only be understood as a part of a sequential story. Institutions provide the incentive structure of an economy; as that structure evolves, it shapes the direction of economic change towards growth, stagnation, or decline" (Douglass C. North, "Institutions," *Journal of Economic Perspectives* 5[winter 1991]: (97–112).

[3] A useful measure of output must exclude *intermediate* goods and services. For example, we don't want to count the output of the automobile industry and the output of the iron ore mines, transport services, and steel production that eventually become part of the car. To avoid such double-counting, we restrict our measure to *final* goods and services, because their value already includes that of the intermediate products.

■ FIGURE 1.2

An economy producing two kinds of output, x_1 and x_2, from a fixed amount of inputs can produce only those combinations shown on or inside the PPF. The region beyond the curve is unattainable given the available inputs.

Starting at point A, where all inputs are producing x_1, we can begin to produce x_2 only by freeing resources from x_1. The best we can do is move along PPF from A to B to C if we choose to have more x_2. Point Z and all others beyond the PPF are unattainable. Point U is attainable but inefficient because we can get more of either or both goods by moving from U to a point on the PPF.

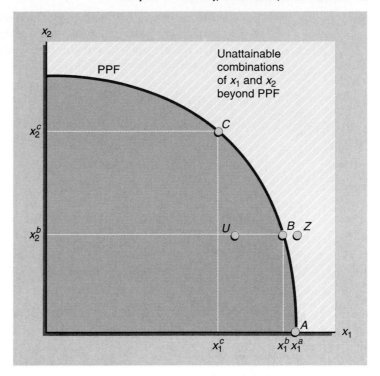

The Production Possibility
Frontier (PPF)

duce beyond the curve, hence the term "frontier." In other words, the PPF is a portrait of the boundaries set by scarcity. To produce more of one good we must take resources (inputs) out of the production of the other. Hence, the downward slope of the PPF tells us that the **opportunity cost** of producing more of one good is the amount of the other good that must be sacrificed.

To illustrate this, suppose the economy represented in Figure 1.2 puts all its inputs into the production of the output x_1, resulting in a maximum production level of x_1^a. Because no resources go into making x_2, this economy will be operating at point A, $(x_1^a, 0)$. If we decide to increase the amount of x_2 from 0 to x_2^b, we must transfer some inputs from the production of x_1 to x_2. The result is shown in the graph as a reduction of x_1 (from x_1^a to x_1^b) and a corresponding increase in x_2 (from 0 to x_2^b), as the economy moves along its PPF from A to B. The opportunity cost of producing x_2^b for this economy is the amount of x_1 given up—the distance $(x_1^a - x_1^b)$.

Clearly we'd prefer to go straight up from point A to Z, increasing the production of x_2 with no loss of x_1, that is, with zero opportunity cost. Scarcity denies us any chance of producing beyond the frontier. We could, of course, move to a point *inside* the PPF like U, but this is obviously less desirable than B because it requires the sacrifice of even *more* x_1 to produce the same level of x_2. In other words, moving from A to U involves a higher opportunity cost than is mandated by the slope of the PPF. To produce x_2^b, the *best* we can do is move along the PPF from A to B.

What if we want to increase x_2 again by the *same* amount, raising it to x_2^c? We will have to transfer additional inputs from the production of x_1 to x_2 as we move from B to C in the graph. Will the decrease in x_1 be the same as before? For reasons that are not of direct concern at this point, the second increment in x_2 is likely to require a *larger* sacrifice of x_1 than did the first. So the distance $(x_1^b - x_1^c)$ will be larger than the previous increment, $(x_1^a - x_1^b)$. Put another way, *the opportunity cost of x_2 rises as we produce more of it.* This is reflected in the concavity of the PPF.[4]

IN SUMMARY . . .

The Production Possibility Frontier

The PPF is a useful and easily remembered map of the boundaries imposed by scarcity. Specifically, the PPF shows that

1. With a given amount of inputs, our options lie along (or inside) the curve. Points beyond the curve are beyond our production capabilities.

2. To get more of one good requires us to sacrifice another good to free up the necessary inputs. This is shown as a movement along the PPF. Thus, the downward slope of the PPF captures the important (and inevitable) principle of "no free lunch."

1.3 SCARCITY MEANS CHOICE

A world of scarcity is always a world of choice. It's "this *or* that?" not "this and that"; "now *or* later?" not "and later." With scarcity, there's "no free lunch," and "we can't have our cake and eat it too." We've seen that the basic "this or that?" decision is embodied in the PPF trade-off between x_1 and x_2 (see Figure 1.2). The insights from this simple two-dimensional map apply even in the "real world" of many kinds of goods. The underlying facts of *scarcity* and *opportunity cost* and *choice* remain at the heart of our models and of the reality these models seek to imitate.

Perhaps the most controversial of our many choices is between "public" and "private" output, the process that determines the economic size of government. The tension between "this or that?" is intensified here because it happens amid all the clamor and compromise of the political process. Each and every unit of output provided through the public sector (such as police and fire protection, national defense, highways, sewage systems, and schools) requires the use of scarce inputs. In other words, the opportunity cost of spending on government goods and services is the amount of private sector output (cars, clothes, computers, and so on) that could have been produced instead. As you'll see later in the chapter, the PPF emphasis on "this or that?" is ideal for viewing the **public/private choice** and, hence, the **cost of government.**

---

[4] The underlying reason for this concavity is diminishing marginal product of inputs as we produce more and more of any one good. More precisely, this happens because the productivity of the inputs differs, depending on which output they are producing. Starting at point A (in Figure 1.2), diminishing marginal product tells us that because *all* inputs are used in the production of x_1 their marginal productivity will be relatively low. As we transfer some of them to the production of x_2 (where their marginal products will be much higher) there will be a relatively larger $+\Delta x_2$ compared with the $-\Delta x_1$ that made it possible. But as we continue this transfer of inputs, increased production of x_2 brings about diminishing marginal productivity there, whereas reduced production of x_1 results in increasing marginal productivity in that good. Hence, successive increments will bring smaller and smaller $+\Delta x_2$'s for given $-\Delta x_1$'s. Because this ratio of the change in one to the change in the other $(\Delta x_2 / \Delta x_1)$ defines the slope of the PPF, it will be diminishing (in absolute terms) as we move up the curve from point A.

Equally important is our choice between "now or later?" In fact, this decision—taken by individuals, businesses, and governments—is the key determinant of a nation's rate of **economic growth.** The PPF curve in Figure 1.2 represented the economy's productive capacity for a fixed amount of labor and capital inputs, and a given institutional structure. But when the amount of inputs changes over time, the PPF shifts accordingly. For example, an increase in the size of the labor force will raise potential production of both x_1 and x_2, shifting the frontier outward from PPF to PPF′ as shown in Figure 1.3. For an economy initially at point C, this increase in resources enables a movement to any point on the higher PPF′. Once on this higher frontier, of course, it again faces the "more of this means less of that" problem in deciding among alternative points, such as D, E, or F.

Economic growth is clearly welcome insofar as it enables us to expand our productive limits. But we must be aware that it comes with a price. We can choose to "produce" more of it, but only at the cost of giving up something else. For now we want to focus on the role of investment and capital accumulation to make a crucial point—more output requires more (or better) inputs, and this entails a cost to society. In other words, economic growth is an "economic good" like any other—it yields benefits, but it has its price as well. We attempt to balance the tension between costs and benefits in our decisions about how much of this (or any other good) to purchase.

To illustrate this, we divide the economy's total output (y) into two categories—consumption (c) and net investment (i)—so that $y = c + i$. **Consumption** goods and services are defined as those providing *current benefits* only, such as food, transportation, and entertainment. **Investment,** conversely, refers to currently produced goods and services that are expected to yield a stream of *future benefits* over time. Expenditures on plant and equipment, education, and research and development are familiar and important types of investment activity. A positive level of cur-

■ FIGURE 1.3

More inputs (labor, capital, and institutional efficiency) allow increased production of any combination of the two outputs, shifting the PPF curve outward to PPF′. Once on the higher PPF, we will still face the problem of choosing among points, such as *D, E,* or *F.*

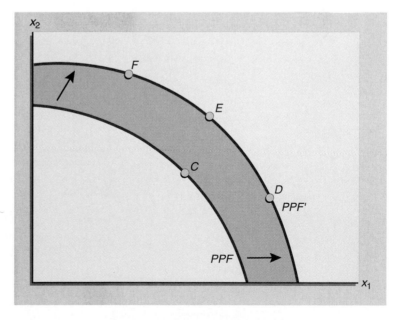

Economic Growth and the PPF

rent net investment ($i > 0$) increases the economy's total capital stock ($+ \Delta k$), increases its potential output level (via $\uparrow y = F(n,k\uparrow,i^{nst})$)), and thereby expands the boundaries of its PPF.

Turning to Figure 1.4, we start at point A with an economy putting all its resources into the production of consumption goods. But suppose there is a second economy with exactly the same PPF that chooses point B, putting some of its inputs into the production of investment goods. We can see that the first economy's current consumption is higher ($c_a > c_b$) because it is doing no net investment spending ($i_a = 0$). The second economy has chosen to use some of its current resources to increase its capital stock through net investment ($i_b > 0$). This net investment increases its capital stock and shifts its production possibility frontier out to PPF_B. The first economy, making the zero growth choice at point A, will remain on the original PPF.[5]

This illustrates a simple but easily overlooked point. The *cost* of economic growth is a loss of current consumption as we transfer resources into the production of investment goods. Because growth comes with a price tag, we cannot say which of these two economies made the "wisest" choice. Most people would probably say that point B (see Figure 1.4) is the better choice. But it is neither wrong nor irrational for someone to prefer the zero-growth choice at point A. Those who choose point A

■ FIGURE 1.4

Point A is a "zero-growth" choice, whereas point B and higher points reflect an increased willingness to sacrifice current consumption to investment so that the resulting rise in the capital stock will bring higher consumption in the future.

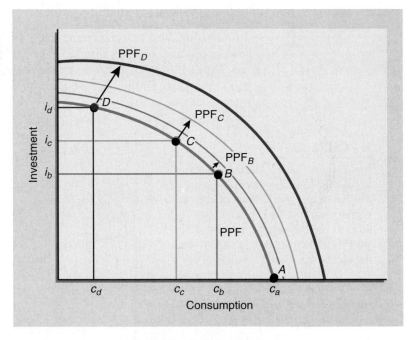

Consumption, Investment, and Economic Growth

place a higher value on current than on future consumption compared with those who choose point *B*. They are said to have a high **rate of time preference** relative to those who choose point *B*.

To see that there is no "correct" or "best" choice between consumption and investment, we note that if point *B* is "better" than point *A* wouldn't it be better still to move on up the PPF to point *C* or even point *D*? Remember that the choice is not just "more growth or less?" That would be easy. The decision is between "more growth and less current consumption," or "less growth and more current consumption." Because investment is a means to increased future consumption we can also say that the choice is really about *when* to consume.

More growth requires that we move up the curve, sacrificing current consumption as we go. Where do we stop sacrificing "now" to "later"? Different individuals make different choices. For misers, it's one extreme; for spendthrifts, the opposite. Most of us find a balance somewhere between the two that reflects our individual response to the tension created by the following two basic facts:

1. Capital is productive, so any resources taken out of consumption today will give us that amount plus *more* tomorrow.

2. We're mortal and live in an uncertain world, which may shorten our horizon and push us to consume sooner rather than later.[6]

Consciously or not, each of us strikes a bargain between the *productivity of capital* and our *economic horizon* that reflects our personal rate of time preference. This is our individual response to the inevitable tension between "now or later?"

Another aspect of this "now or later?" theme should be noted. When we delay consumption by setting aside part of our income as **saving,** most of us do not engage in the direct purchase of capital goods that constitutes investment. We may turn to a **financial intermediary** (like a bank or credit union) to find a user for our savings and also to assume some of the risk should that borrower eventually default on payments. This presents still another option. We can choose to be on the "borrowing" rather than the "lending" side of the financial intermediation process, to *dis*save rather than save.

In later chapters we'll have much to say about how financial intermediation and **capital markets** allow us to change the "timing" of our consumption. For now, the important point is that it adds another dimension to our available choices. Not only must we decide between "this or that?" and between "consume now or consume *more* later?" but, because of the widely available borrowing/lending services of financial intermediaries, between paying now or postponing payment until later. These **borrowed funds** may be used for current consumption or for investment now that will yield consumption in the future. Either way, the borrower—whether consumer, business, or government—agrees to repay principal plus interest to the lender. Hence, it's not a simple "now or later," but the more perplexing choice between "pay now or pay *more* later."

---

[6] To the extent that we consider the economic well-being of our children, this horizon may extend well beyond our own mortality. This and other issues relating to our lifetime consumption and investment choices are examined in Chapter 12.

A CRUCIAL DEFINITION— WHAT IS "INVESTMENT"?

The concept of "investment" in economics is a bit different than the everyday usage of the term. Both include the purchase of tangible and intangible capital goods (e.g., buildings or education). But the purchase of stocks and bonds, popularly termed "investment," is *not* by itself investment in an economic sense. The reason is that buying a stock or bond is just a "paper exchange"— bonds or stocks go one way, and "green" pieces of paper (in the United States) go the other. There's no overall creation of *new* capital goods, hence, no net real investment in the economy. For example, if AT&T sells a share of stock and you buy it, no new capital has been produced. Only when AT&T takes that money and purchases the actual capital goods does investment in our sense occur.

The reason we don't just go along with the common definition of the word is that it could lead to an overestimate of capital formation in the economy because stocks and bonds change hands many times after their original issuance. For example, suppose you decide to sell your share of AT&T to me. Although I might think of this as an "investment" in the everyday sense, it does not represent the creation of new capital goods. You and I have just traded pieces of paper. The country's stock of productive capital hasn't budged.

If you took this money from selling me your share of stock and purchased new capital goods, *then* investment would occur—but it would be yours, not mine. If, instead, you used the money to pay for a vacation (or some other consumption item), no new capital has been created. Although my purchase of the stock is a form of "saving" for me, it is offset by your "dissaving" (converting an asset into current consumption). There would be no net investment and no change in the economy's stock of capital.

IN SUMMARY . . .

Scarcity and Choice

1. Scarcity forces us to make choices between "this or that?" as illustrated in the downward slope of the PPF curve. The opportunity cost of "more of this" is an inevitable "less of that."

2. Another dimension is added by the choice between consumption (benefits now) and investment (benefits later). Because of the productivity of capital, the choice is really between "consume now or consume more later?" For the economy as a whole, our collective answer to this question is a key determinant of the rate of economic growth. The more we put into investment rather than consumption, the faster the PPF will grow.

(Continued)

Scarcity and Choice (Continued)

3. Once we think in terms of investment as an ever-present alternative to consumption, it's tempting to think that investment is somehow "better" and consumption "worse." Try to avoid this connotation because it is at best a half-truth. It obscures the fact that the primary goal of all economic activity is consumption. Investment offers a mechanism to trade some consumption now for *more* consumption later. But it's still consumption we seek.

4. Because it has a *cost*, more economic growth is not necessarily better than less. This depends on a subjective evaluation as to whether it's worth the cost and, therefore, differs across individuals. How much growth we choose depends on both the *rate of return* we get from the investment and on our individual *rate of time preference*—our willingness (or lack of it) to delay some consumption now in return for more later.

5. The presence of *capital markets* and *financial intermediaries* allows us to postpone payment for consumption or investment goods by borrowing from someone else. Because we must pay an interest premium to get others to postpone consumption and lend to us, this gives us the additional choice of "pay now or pay *more* later?"

1.4 THE OPEN ECONOMY

This overview of "scarcity" has so far omitted an ingredient of increasing importance in the U.S. economy—economic exchange with other nations. International trade turns a "closed economy" into an **open economy,** creating an array of new opportunities as well as threats. Later chapters will have much to say about the specific benefits and costs associated with international trade. But this is a good time to take a look at how the flow of borrowing and lending across economies can extend our range of choice.

We saw earlier that the borrowing/lending option allows us to "pay now" or "pay *more* later." As long as this occurs inside the economy, its impact nets out in the aggregate. Every dollar *borrowed and repaid* is also a dollar *loaned and received* within the economy. The interest payment by the borrower becomes the interest income that compensates the lender for postponing consumption and for risking the possibility of default. As long as our indebtedness is internal, we essentially "owe it to ourselves."

Now suppose that foreign lenders offer us a loan at a lower rate of interest than we can get internally, perhaps because they have a lower rate of time preference and hence are "better savers" than we are. What impact would such **external borrowing** have on our macroeconomy? To answer this let's start with a country that uses all its resources for current consumption, as shown at point *A* in Figure 1.5. Unwilling or unable to postpone benefits, it has little hope for a rising standard of living. If this is a nation of shortsighted spendthrifts, we'll probably have little sympathy for them. We might even find some satisfaction in seeing them reap the consequences of their actions.

■ **FIGURE 1.5**

An economy starting at point *A* can move outside its PPF through external borrowing. If the borrowed resources are channeled into investment, as shown in the movement from points *A* to *I*, the result can be increased economic growth (not shown in the graph) that will allow it to repay the loan and still be better off. But if an external loan is used to pay for consumption (as shown in the movement from points *A* to *C*), when it comes time to repay the loan the economy will be forced to consume inside its fixed PPF (point *Z*) until both principal and interest are repaid.

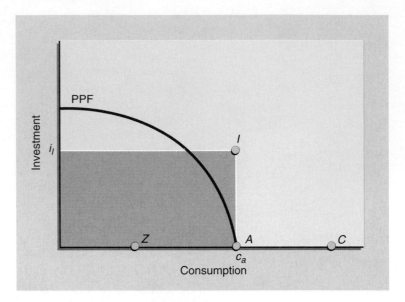

External Borrowing

But what if it's a very poor economy, living at bare subsistence and unable to free resources for capital formation without immediate hardship, perhaps even starvation, for many of its people? If this is also a closed economy, there's little more to be said. Its inability to reduce consumption means it simply can't generate the saving and investment needed to achieve economic growth. But by opening its economy to transactions with other nations, an impoverished nation creates the potential for breaking out of this cycle of poverty. By attracting resources from abroad, it can actually move *outside* the confines of its closed-economy PPF by drawing on the output of other economies. This option is shown in Figure 1.5 as a movement from points *A* to *I*. Note that moving beyond the PPF is not a violation of scarcity and the "no-free-lunch" principle. A nation (or individual or firm) that can draw on external resources can move beyond its PPF as long as other nations are willing to donate or loan their goods and services.

So an open economy permits the proverbial situation where we can "beg, borrow, or steal" from others to enhance our well-being. Setting the first and last options aside for now, let's look more closely at external borrowing. The initial effect of adding borrowed resources to our own is to move us—temporarily—beyond our domestic PPF. Once the loan ends, of course, we must return to its boundaries. And then, although we keep producing on our PPF, part of this output must go to repay principal and interest on the loan. The result is that we must consume at a point inside our domestic PPF while the external loan is being repaid. Thus, the *benefit* of external borrowing is that it allows an economy to move temporarily beyond its PPF, giving it more of some goods without sacrificing others. But the *cost* of external borrowing is that repayment of principal plus interest outside the economy forces it to consume inside its PPF. In contrast, internal borrowing doesn't force us inside during repayment, because one person's payment is another's receipt. But neither does it allow the initial movement outside the PPF.

To determine whether external borrowing is a blessing or a curse for an economy (or individual or firm), we must know two things: *how much was paid for the borrowed funds*, and *how were these funds used?* To illustrate, let's start with an extreme case and suppose that the borrowed resources are spent entirely on consumption goods, moving the economy from points *A* to *C* in Figure 1.5. With net investment staying at zero, there can be no economic growth, hence, no expansion of the PPF. When the loan ends, the economy must return to its PPF. But to pay off past borrowing, it must now reduce its consumption by the amount of the original loan (the distance between points *C* and *A*) *plus* an additional amount for interest. The result is a temporary consumption "binge" (points *A* to *C*) followed by a bigger repayment "hangover" (binge *plus* interest) as we move to a point like *Z*. When the loan is finally repaid, the economy will find itself back at its original predicament at point *A*.

But suppose the borrowed funds were used entirely for investment projects, moving the economy initially from points *A* to *I*? This increase in the capital stock will result in an *expansion of the PPF* (shown earlier in Figure 1.4 but, for clarity's sake, not added to Figure 1.5). Repayment again requires principal plus interest, but the crucial difference now is that because the borrowed resources went into investment instead of consumption, the economy will end up on a higher PPF. Will the result be a gain or a loss to this economy? If the project returned 15% and the country borrowed at 10%, then it clearly struck a good bargain and made a net gain. But if it realized only a 5% return, it has paid too dearly for economic growth. Even though the PPF will have shifted out because of the new investment, the country has suffered a net loss because it gave up more in repayment than it earned from the use of the borrowed funds.

IN SUMMARY . . .

Pay Now or Pay More Later?

Internal and External Choices

1. Those eager to consume now are said to have a high rate of time preference and will seek to borrow funds from those more willing to postpone consumption (with lower rates of time preference). The borrowing/lending process offers borrowers the *benefit of postponed payments* at the cost of added interest expense when the repayment is finally made. It is this interest payment that provides the incentive for lenders to postpone consumption (save) and to risk possible default by the borrower.

2. Unlike the "consume/invest" choice that underlies economic growth, borrowing and lending *within* the country represents an internal transfer of resources with little direct impact on overall macroeconomic performance because we owe it to ourselves.

3. But when a country borrows *externally* it reaches beyond the limits of its own PPF. Once the loan has ended and repayment begins, however, this economy will be forced to consume inside its PPF as it transfers principal plus interest back to the lender. The net outcome will depend on *how the borrowed funds are used and the rate of interest paid for these funds.*

4. So when all is said and done, how things turn out depends on how the borrowed funds are used (the consumption-investment choice), not on whether we have borrowed from inside or outside the economy.

⌾⌾ 1.5 *UNEMPLOYMENT*

Our discussion of scarcity and choices and opportunity costs has implicitly assumed *full employment* of existing resources. In reality, of course, economies suffer recurrent bouts of **unemployment** of labor and capital that show up as periodic movements inside their PPF. The cost of unemployment is a loss of goods and services such as that shown at point *U* in Figure 1.6. Unemployment pulls the economy below its productive potential and thereby reduces its standard of living. This problem of idle resources only compounds the unavoidable frustrations of scarcity and choice. Such a downturn in economic activity, termed a **recession,** involves a sacrifice of output that can never be erased from the past *or* the present. Although the return to full employment and the given PPF—termed **economic recovery**—will end the recession, the goods and services that were not produced during the downturn will never be recaptured. To the extent that some of this lost output is investment goods, recession lowers the economy's rate of growth. It thereby imposes some of its costs on the future, dictating a lower future standard of living than if the episode of unemployment had been avoided.[7]

■ FIGURE 1.6

An economy that fails to use its available resources fully sacrifices potential output and remains inside its PPF, as shown at point *U.* By putting its idle resources to work it could produce more of either good (or more of both if it moves to the northeast from point *U*). The cost of this **recession** is a standard of living even lower than that dictated by the fact of scarcity.

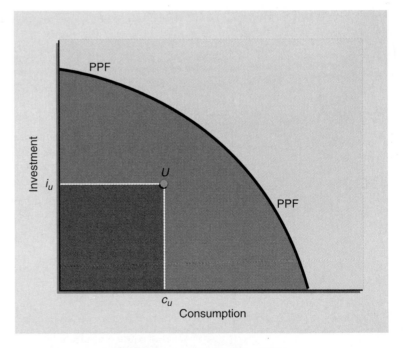

Unemployment and the PPF

---

[7] As an economy recovers from recession and moves from point *U* out to its PPF, it might seem to be getting "something for nothing" and violating the dictates of scarcity. Although it can get more of one good without sacrificing another as it returns to a point on its PPF, this obviously isn't a victory over scarcity. As it returns to its PPF, it can produce more of one good without giving up the other only because it had already made the sacrifice by having unemployment. As long as we remain inside the PPF, we are paying a premium over and above the inevitable costs imposed by scarcity.

The search for the causes and cures of unemployment has been the dominant theme in macroeconomics since the Great Depression of the 1930s, the deepest and most prolonged downturn in our history. Since World War II, episodes of unemployment and recession have been far less severe, and their ebb and flow is described as the **business cycle.** Earlier hope of virtually eliminating these cyclical ups and downs in macroeconomic activity has given way to various strategies for moderating their amplitude through **stabilization policy.** Although the PPF framework offers a useful way to portray the problem of unemployment it gives us no insight into its causes or its remedies, a task we'll begin to address in Chapter 2.[8]

✂ 1.6 SCARCITY AND CHOICE IN THE PUBLIC SECTOR

We have seen how scarcity and choice confront us at every turn. Every day brings, for each of us, a stream of decisions not only about how to spend our money but also about how to spend our time. It's constantly, "this *or* that?" and "now *or* later?" Failure to make a choice is a choice itself. One of the most significant and far reaching of our many choices is made through the political process rather than through markets. This is our choice of how to balance private and public activities in the overall economy. Which of our economic choices should be made individually through the **private sector,** where households and businesses operate within certain "rules of the game" defined by a given institutional structure? And which should be made collectively through the **public sector,** where political votes supplement dollar votes, and the government becomes an active "player" in the economic game?

Different nations have made very different choices about the split between public and private output as shown in Figure 1.7. This choice is usually a contentious one that reflects a compromise among different attitudes toward government and also among divergent views of how the economy works. Some see government as the best hope for a better economic life, a cushion against the rough edges of the market system. For others, its concentrated power represents a continual threat to economic freedom and market efficiency. Most of us see both sides and struggle with a complex love/hate attitude toward government's economic role. For all of us, government can act as a lightning rod for our hopes and fears, and become a convenient scapegoat for the endless economic and other frustrations in our lives.

Our reactions sometimes make it difficult to see the obvious—*our public choices are subject to exactly the same laws of scarcity as our private decisions.* Throughout this book you will find examples of policy actions that ignored the basic facts of scarcity and common sense, promising enormous benefits at little or no cost. And you will also see the opposite—policy *in*action defended with mistaken arguments about the prohibitive costs and uncertain benefits of *any* policy change. An understanding of what can and cannot be expected from government policy must begin with a clear view of the public-sector counterparts to the issues already examined in this chapter: "trade-offs," "economic growth," and "borrowing and lending."

---

[8] We have portrayed unemployment and the business cycle as recurrent movements from the PPF to points inside the curve. Another way to categorize economic fluctuations is as fluctuations in the PPF curve itself. In this view (called "real business cycle theory") the instability is not related to ups and downs in unemployment, but to volatility in our full employment capacity to produce. The two approaches have very different implications for economic policy that will be considered carefully in later chapters. For now, we adopt the standard view that the most useful way to picture the business cycle is as temporary deviations from the economy's PPF.

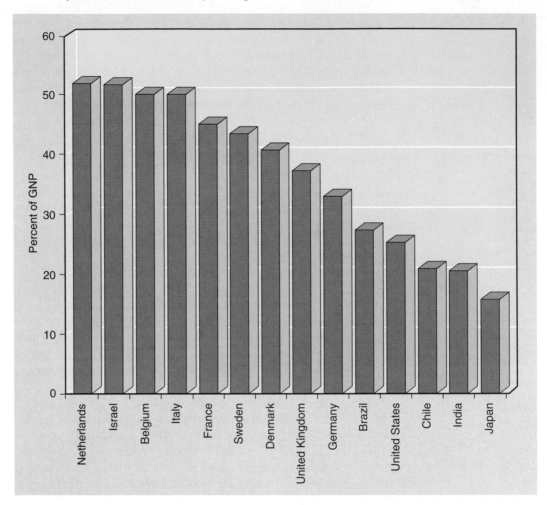

Government's Economic Size
(Central Government Spending as % of Gross National Product, 1990)

■ FIGURE 1.7

From World Bank, *World Development Report 1992: Development and the Environment* (New York: Oxford University Press, 1992).

SCARCITY AND THE PUBLIC SECTOR

1. "No Free Lunch"

> *Because every unit of output—public or private—uses scarce inputs, the opportunity cost of more government output is less private output. The common name for this cost is* **taxation.** *This sacrifice of private goods to get more public (government) goods is shown in the downward slope of the PPF in Figure 1.8. It tells us that the inevitable tension between "this or that" applies equally to private and public actions. We can't escape the chains of scarcity by simply letting the government do it.*

■ FIGURE 1.8

To get more public output $(+\Delta g)$ in a fully-employed economy, we must sacrifice private output $(-\Delta(c+i))$ as we move from points J to K.

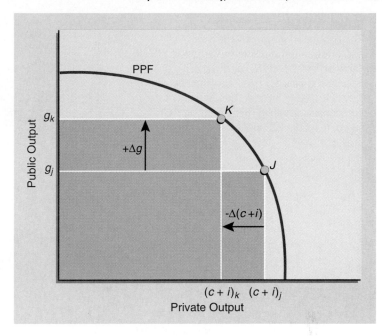

Public vs. Private Spending

2. *"Consume Now or Consume More Later"*

Current government spending can be divided between public consumption (g^c), yielding immediate benefits, and public investment (g^i), with returns spread over many years. Public net investment, like its private counterpart, represents an addition to the nation's capital stock and results in an outward shift of the PPF. As shown in Figure 1.9, the more we put into public investment rather than consumption, the faster the rate of growth. The tension between "consume now or consume more later" afflicts our public as well as our private choices.

3. *"Pay Now or Pay More Later"*

While we can't escape the taxes that transfer resources from private to public use, we can (within limits) postpone them by making a "borrow now/tax later" choice. Whether we do this by borrowing individually (using a loan to cover current tax payments) or collectively (with the U.S. Treasury borrowing in our name by running a deficit), the cost is the added interest charge.

*Suppose we decide to increase government spending as shown in the movement from points J to K in Figure 1.10. Tax financing, by reducing after-tax incomes, forces private spending to fall so resources can be transferred to public uses. If, instead, this transfer is done by **internal borrowing**, the lenders willingly reduce their spending now in return for more spending (principal plus interest) when the loan is repaid. In either case, financing an increase in public spending by taxes or by internal borrowing, the result is a direct movement along the PPF. As we saw earlier, **external borrowing** would allow an initial movement outside the PPF (from points J to J' in 1.10). But it would force us to consume inside our PPF later as the loan was repaid.*

■ FIGURE 1.9

The consumption-investment choice is also present in the public sector. It is a "now or later" decision with respect to reaping the benefits from government spending. As we increase the investment component of public spending (point Q to point R), the PPF will grow more rapidly.

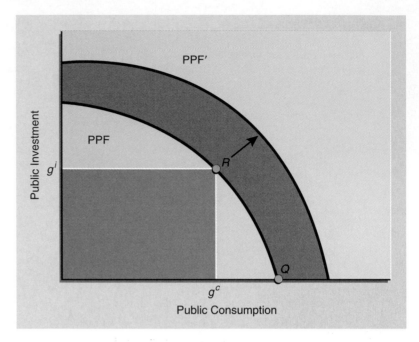

Public Consumption,
Public Investment, and Growth

■ FIGURE 1.10

In a fully-employed economy any increase in public output $(+\Delta g)$ must come at the cost of reduced private output $(-\Delta(c + i))$, illustrated as the movement from points J to K. This is true regardless of whether the $+\Delta g$ was paid for by tax financing or borrowing (deficit financing). External borrowing allows an initial movement to J', but this "bonus" is counterbalanced when the loan plus interest is repaid. The economy must return to its PPF (e.g., points J or K) but reduce its consumption to a point inside the curve until repayment is complete.

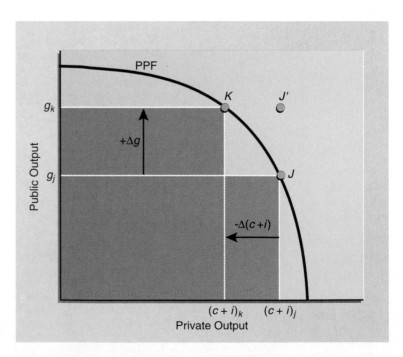

Cost of Public Spending

ᖇᖇ *1.7 PAYING THE PRICE FOR PUBLIC GOODS*

One of the most controversial issues in macroeconomic policy making in recent years has been how we should pay for our public spending. We will analyze this topic carefully in later chapters, but even at this point you should see that the basic choices are straightforward. A country that wants to raise its current level of public output *must* reduce its private output.[9] Short of stealing from other countries, there is *no* alternative. **Taxation** accomplishes this by directly "coercing" resources from private to public use. **Internal borrowing** gets the same result, but postpones the coercion at the cost of added interest (paid and received internally). **External borrowing** permits an initial move outside the PPF, but then forces us inside during repayment. Eventually it ends up at the same place as the other two mechanisms.

Perhaps you're wondering why the public discussion of taxes and government deficits is so acrimonious and unsettled if the basic issues are so apparent? We'll discuss several reasons later, but one is simply that our emotional reactions to government actions can make it difficult to see some points that would be obvious in a different context—in this case, that the true cost of more of "this" (public output) is less of "that" (private output). The *only* way to lower the cost of government ("taxes" in the broadest sense) is to lower government spending. Put another way, a pledge of "no new taxes" can be fulfilled only if it starts without a legacy of postponed taxes from the past and if it includes a pledge of "no new spending." Focusing on financing (taxes or deficits) rather than on spending puts the horse behind the cart. Once the expenditure is made, the taxes *must* follow. At that point our choices can only be about "when to tax?" and "who to tax?" not *whether* to tax.

To make this more concrete, let's work through an example of a country that decides to increase its public spending but refuses to raise taxes to pay for it. As we've seen, this can be done by borrowing the funds (internally or externally), a practice popularly known as **deficit financing.** But borrowing, unlike raising taxes, is only a *temporary* transfer from private to public use. Let's now go a step further and suppose that having chosen deficit over tax financing, when it comes time to pay back the previous borrowing (plus interest), taxpayers are still unwilling to accept a tax increase (or an expenditure cut). Both incumbent politicians (not wanting to become ex-politicians) and would-be politicians may show great enthusiasm for this "no new taxes" crusade. If so, they will soon discover that it leaves them with just three remaining options for dealing with the postponed taxes from previous deficits: *default*, *borrow more*, or *print money*.

Default, the public equivalent of private bankruptcy, would certainly allow us to eliminate the earlier borrowing without raising tax rates or cutting government spending. But this "free lunch" for taxpayers is obviously being paid for by those who made the loans in the first place. Those unfortunate lenders will be the victims of what is essentially the government's newest tax program—the "100% Tax on All Holders of Government Bonds." Any government practicing such "financing" (more accurately "theft") will find it difficult to attract lenders in the future.

But why default when, having borrowed once to avoid higher taxes, we can just borrow again? This option of **continued deficit spending** (or "rolling over the debt") will be analyzed carefully in a later chapter. We will discover that it can be prudently done *within certain limits* defined by the amount borrowed, the interest rate

---

[9] Although we're assuming full employment and zero economic growth here, the insights from this simplified analysis carry over to more complicated settings.

on the loan, the level of public investment, the rate of economic growth, and some other factors.[10] For now, however, your intuition will tell you that we could easily get outside those "certain limits" if we weren't careful. Let's compare a government deficit with a student loan. Suppose you have borrowed substantially to finance your investment in education, with payments postponed until graduation. But having worked so hard and sacrificed so much to get through college, you want to enjoy your newly acquired income rather than use it for loan repayments. Ruling out default ("theft") you decide to just extend your personal "deficit financing" a bit further by getting a new loan to cover the payments on the previous loans.

The arithmetic of compound interest dictates that your total indebtedness will grow exponentially from month to month and year to year. You will have to increase your borrowing so you can make not only the original student loan payments but also the payments on the amount you borrowed to postpone those original loan payments. In the following year, you will have to increase your borrowing further to pay still more interest on the amount borrowed to pay previous interest, and on and on. Assuming your income growth is not keeping pace with this exponential increase in total indebtedness, you become an increasingly risky borrower, and lenders will charge you higher and higher interest rates. As you reach the limits of your credit, you'll find your alternatives still more limited—either a drastic cut in your standard of living (so you can repay out of your current income) or bankruptcy.

"Excessive" public deficits—those that threaten to outrun our public income (the tax base)—create similar threats to the public sector. Recognizing this, suppose taxpayers now insist that the government end these continued deficits, but are still unwilling to accept either a tax increase or a cut in public spending. With these options ruled out, what's left? The only remaining choice is for the government to turn to its "power of the mint" to simply print new money.[11]

Money creation is a time-honored device for raising taxes while pretending not to. It works by reducing the purchasing power of private-sector money holdings as this new money pushes up the price level. Because it transfers resources from private to public use just like ordinary taxes, money-financed increases in public spending are said to impose an **inflation tax.** This method of taxation is widely regarded as an unfair and unwise practice.[12] But it continues to be used at various times and places because it is a very easy tax to administer. It allows weak governments, unable to enforce tax laws or find buyers for their bonds, to stay in business.[13] To the extent that it circumvents the ordinary tax structure set through the political process, it also invites the explosive label of "taxation without representation."

Where does all this leave our hypothetical economy that initially financed an increase in public goods and services by borrowing, but then refused to raise taxes or cut spending when the loan came due? Note that the increased public output has already occurred, so the only choices left are "when to tax?" and "who to tax?";

---

[10] Anticipating your negative reaction to continuing deficits, note that just because a continued federal deficit *can* be run without (under certain conditions) causing economic collapse, it does not necessarily follow that it *should* be done.

[11] Some economies, including the United States, have taken the control of the money supply away from the political arena and created a Central Bank (the Federal Reserve System in the United States) that is relatively immune to political pressures. In many countries, however, the Central Bank (controlling the money supply) and the Treasury (paying for government spending, collecting taxes, and issuing government bonds to cover the difference) are either a single unit or work very closely together, creating the possibility of paying for government spending by simply printing more money.

[12] Inflation not only erodes the value of money but also the value of outstanding bonds. Assuming the inflation was not anticipated when the bonds (public and private) were issued, it acts as a tax on bondholders as well as on anyone who holds money.

[13] Compared with direct taxes, however, the inflation tax is also very inefficient—requiring large increases in inflation to raise relatively small amounts of revenue, as we'll see later.

"whether to tax?" was decided when public spending was increased. There's no question that the tax will be paid; it's as inevitable as death, as the saying goes. The only suspense is whether the tax will be paid through the *tax system* (by raising tax revenues somewhere, sometime, from someone), by *money creation and the inflation tax* (indirectly and inefficiently), or by *bondholders* (should the government default on its promises).

IN SUMMARY . . .

The Cost of Public Goods

The public sector is bound by the limits of scarcity in exactly the same way as the private sector. Our collective decisions—carried out through government—must also be choices between "this *or* that?" and "now *or* later?" This similarity between public- and private-sector choices may be obscured by the fact that we grant the government two unique powers—*to tax* and *to print money*. This can lead us to think that the government can do pretty much anything it wants. It can do much, but the powers to tax and print money are primarily ways to *transfer resources* from one place (or group or person) to another. They cannot defy the laws of scarcity.

To put taxation and money creation in perspective, note that when these exact same activities are carried out in the private sector, their names change to "theft" and "counterfeiting." This is not to question the importance and legitimacy of taxation and money creation by a duly elected, representative government. It's merely to stress the point that the government cannot produce "something for nothing," no matter how much we hope or pretend otherwise. If we pressure our elected representatives to use these two great powers in ways that *seem* to give a "free lunch"—for example, a substantial cut in tax rates without a decrease in government spending—it will only force the tax to show up at another time (with interest) or in another guise (default on bonds or inflation tax), causing potential confusion and instability in the process.

The "true" level of taxation is always the one shown on the PPF—the amount of resources that must be transferred from the private sector to finance a certain amount of public spending. A true tax cut can occur only if fewer resources are transferred from private to public use. That is, it must be accompanied by a cut in government spending.

1.8 ECONOMIC ANALYSIS: FROM CHOICES TO CONSEQUENCES

Scarcity and choice lie at the heart of all economic issues. The PPF provides a simple, easily remembered map that reveals the boundaries imposed by scarcity and gives a clear picture of the inevitable choices between "this or that?" and "now or later?" We've seen that the PPF can also portray economic growth, external borrowing, and unemployment, all important issues in macroeconomics.

Useful as it is, however, the PPF is just a beginning. It cannot answer most of the important questions that these issues raise. Although the PPF graph is a very handy visual reminder of limitations, it gives little help in understanding how the economy operates and how we might work within the constraints of scarcity to alter certain outcomes. For this we must venture further into **economic analysis**—a world of theory and models—to explore questions like the following:

1. Why does economic growth seem to come so easily to some economies, sporadically to others, and so sparingly to the most impoverished?

2. What does it mean to say that the U.S. economy went from the largest creditor to the largest debtor nation in the world during the 1980s? Is the inevitable result a substantial transfer of U.S. assets to other countries?

3. How can one economy borrow and apparently thrive, whereas others borrow and end up still deeper in crisis?

4. Why does a drop in investment or consumption spending trigger a serious recession or even depression at one time but result in only a mild and temporary downturn at another?

5. If we make significant cuts in the size of certain government programs won't we push the economy into recession? Can we be confident that the resources released from the public sector will be absorbed in the private sector? How long will this take?

6. Will the massive federal deficits of the 1980s and early 1990s mean a substantial drop in the U.S. standard of living in the coming years? Will the young of today be forced to bear the burden of their parents apparent shortsightedness?

7. What impacts, immediate and longer term, will a ban on deficit spending have on the economy?

8. What would happen if we went even further and tried to pay off the national debt that represents all the accumulated deficits from the past?

9. Why doesn't the government do a better job of moderating the recurrent economic ups and downs? Are bouts of "boom or bust"—recession and inflation and sometimes both together—inevitable?

10. Why does inflation seem to cluster in certain regions at certain times? Can it spread from country to country through international trade?

11. Why doesn't the Federal Reserve use its power over the money supply to keep interest rates at low levels to stimulate investment and, hence, economic growth?

Such practical questions are among the central concerns of macroeconomic analysis. By the end of this course you will be able to give clear, thoughtful answers to these and many other questions. This requires a basic understanding of the main cause-and-effect linkages across the macroeconomy. So you will need to first develop a good *theoretical model* of how the economy works before you can answer the practical and relevant questions that lie at the heart of macroeconomics. The basic elements of such a theoretical structure are introduced in the next chapter.

1.9   OVERVIEW

1. **Scarcity** is the term used to define the underlying premise of economics—our material wants far exceed our capacity to satisfy them. We live in a world of **choices.** Though we'd all prefer "this *and* that," scarcity makes it "this *or* that." An

economic system is a set of rules, laws, and traditions—built into the nation's institutional structure—that help organize, enact, and, in some cases, limit our set of choices.

2. **Economic analysis** is our attempt to understand the individual and social consequences of alternative choices under a variety of different circumstances. *Macroeconomic* analysis explores how these many decisions combine to determine the overall performance of the economy—the depth and duration of its recessions and the vigor of its recoveries, its rate of inflation, and its long-term rate of growth.

3. Economists (like lawyers, proctologists, and used-car dealers) are often regarded with suspicion, even distaste. Their message of inevitable costs, limits, and trade-offs is never welcome. But the alternatives to a careful, systematic analysis of choice and its consequences—such as slogans, dogma, or sheer fantasy—can lead to an enormous and sometimes tragic waste of already scarce resources.

4. Even with the unprecedented economic growth of the past two hundred years, a large portion of humankind still live at or near bare subsistence, face to face with scarcity every day of their lives. Inside even the richest nations are heartbreakingly long lists of economic misfortune. Poorly designed economic policies, perhaps responding to the well-intentioned but simplistic slogans of the moment, frequently worsen these economic problems. Inept economic policies can waste resources just as effectively as the most destructive of wars. To the extent that economic theory can help us foresee the consequences of our actions, it is an immensely *practical* undertaking.

5. The **PPF** is a useful way to picture scarcity and choice—particularly the notion of **opportunity cost.** Its downward slope is a manifestation of the "no-free-lunch" principle that makes economics so frustrating but so important. **Economic growth** can be illustrated as an outward shift in the PPF in response to an increase in one or more of the basic inputs—labor, capital, and institutional efficiency. An economy can experience rapid and sustained output growth only through rapid and sustained growth of these inputs.

6. The **costs of economic growth** are no less real than its benefits. A larger pie pleases everyone at the table. But too easily we forget that scarcity applies here, as everywhere. It takes more ingredients, and someone has to bake it. Specifically, more consumption in the future requires that we sacrifice consumption now to transfer resources into capital formation via the investment process. Choice shows up again, this time as "now *or* later?" denying our desire for both.

7. Because investment now means *higher* consumption later, we tend to think of consumption spending as "inferior" or even "wasted" because it could have been invested "productively." This is incorrect. Remember what it is that investment is productive *of*—consumption. Investment is a means for altering the *timing of consumption.* But the basic goal of economic activity is still consumption, not investment.

8. Just as consumption can be moved from now to later, payments can also be delayed through **borrowing and lending.** But the cost of this postponement is an interest charge, a payment needed to induce someone else to postpone their consumption and essentially make the payment for the borrower. Because borrowing (and, of course, its flip side—lending) is a procedure that occurs across time—borrow now, repay later—it inevitably involves elements of uncertainty and risk. If we borrow to pay for current pleasures (consumption now), we are es-

sentially exchanging future income for current returns. The obvious threat to the lender is that our future income might not be sufficient to cover these payments, hence the interest rate will reflect an allowance for the risk of default by the borrower.

9. Economic growth can be in the negative direction too. When some of our productive capital stock is lost or destroyed through acts of God (such as earthquake, hurricanes, or droughts) or acts of man (wars, restrictive laws, or shortsighted practices that damage the environment), the PPF shifts inward. Such losses *must* show up as a lower standard of living, either now or later, depending on the nature of this "supply shock" and our response to it.

10. Output can fall because a negative supply shock contracts the PPF. But it can also fall without any change in the PPF if the economy goes into a **recession** and experiences **unemployment.** This loss of output results in a reduction in our standard of living as we move to a point *inside* our PPF. It represents an economic cost beyond that dictated by scarcity, making this underutilization of available resources all the more regrettable because, unlike scarcity, it is not inevitable.

11. It's important to distinguish between **economic growth** and **economic recovery.** "Economic growth" refers to changes in the full employment level of output regardless of whether the economy happens to be producing at full employment or below it. "Economic recovery" refers to a movement from a point of unemployment toward a given full employment level of output. In other words, economic recovery means an economy in recession moves toward a point on its given PPF; economic growth means the PPF itself shifts out.

12. The economic activity of government is said to occur in the **public sector,** as opposed to **private-sector** actions of individuals and businesses. This is a useful distinction for many purposes but must not be allowed to obscure the fact that the public sector is not just some impersonal, monolithic "it" or "them." It's "us!" Through the political process, we make decisions to provide certain goods and services to ourselves as a community and to pay for those, through taxes, as a community as well. We also give our public sector two exclusive and very great powers—the right to **tax** and the right to **print money.** We cannot, however, confer immunity from the laws of scarcity upon our public sector. "No free lunch," "pay now or pay more later," "consume now or consume more later" follow us wherever we go. No matter what means of financing public spending we may choose—taxing, borrowing, or printing money—the underlying outcome is the same: resources are transferred from the private to the public sector. The controversy over taxes and deficits is really just a struggle over **who pays?** and **when?**

13. **Economic theory** is the attempt to identify the paths leading from *choices* to *consequences.* More simply, it tries to discover the main cause-and-effect relationships in the economy. Such a theory or hypothesis is embodied in an **economic model** that expresses and explores these interdependencies in words, equations, graphs, or other symbols. Testing our models, and thereby choosing among competing theories, requires careful use of information from past experience. This combination of economic model with statistical analysis is called an **econometric model.**

ᙅᙅ 1.10 REVIEW QUESTIONS

1. Define the following basic concepts:

Aggregation	Opportunity cost	Unemployment
Macroeconomics	Economic growth	Economic recovery
Metaphor	Consumption	Recession
Economic model	Investment	Business cycle
Scarcity	Saving	Stabilization policy
Mutual gain	Financial intermediary	Private and public sectors
Resources (inputs)	Capital markets	Taxation
Output	Borrowing	Deficit financing
PPF	External borrowing	Money creation
Production function	Rate of time preference	Economic analysis

2. Explain how the PPF illustrates scarcity and, especially, the fact that in a world of scarcity choices are unavoidable. Be specific.

3. Explain what it means to say that economic growth is primarily a matter of choice, not luck or good fortune.

4. Use the PPF diagram to illustrate the following events:

   a. Josef Stalin institutes the "Five-Year Plan," asking citizens to sacrifice now to promote industrialization, which will usher in a new era of prosperity and economic justice in the near future. (Why do you think this was followed by a series of Five-Year Plans?)

   b. A poor country borrows externally as part of an ambitious plan of economic development. Somehow these new resources get diverted from their intended use and end up as consumption by a few top members of the government and their close friends and families.

   c. "The U.S. economy was devastated by the severe unemployment of the Great Depression. After such an ordeal and such damage, it is surprising that the country was able to mobilize for World War II with relatively little hardship." Use the PPF to evaluate this statement and, especially, the contention that it was surprising.

5. Illustrate each of the concepts listed below using the PPF diagram. For example, for a negative supply shock you would show the PPF shifting inward. For scarcity you would show a movement along the PPF. Note that some of these events may leave no trace whatsoever in terms of the PPF.

   a. Unemployment

   b. Borrowing externally to finance an increase in government spending

   c. An increase in taxes to finance an increase in government spending

   d. Borrowing internally to finance an increase in government spending

   e. An equal cut in both government spending and taxes

   f. A tax cut with no change in government spending

   g. An increase in net investment spending

   h. A continued increase in the average rate of time preference

   i. A major breakdown in the ability of government to carry out its basic functions

6. Suppose a country puts *all* its resources into consumption and doesn't even undertake replacement investment as its capital stock wears out. How can you portray this situation of negative net investment ($i < 0$) and its aftermath in terms of the PPF curve?

7. Evaluate and explain the following statements.

    a. "The *best* way to finance any government spending is through taxes."

    b. "The *only* way to finance government spending is by taxes—direct or indirect, now or later."

8. "The problem with borrowing outside the United States is that we end up making interest payments outside our economy. If we've got to borrow, it's best to do it internally because then we make the interest payments to ourselves and keep more total resources inside the country." Evaluate and explain.

9. In the Civil War, the North began the war with the greater amount of resources. Both sides attempted to transfer production to military output as quickly as possible. In the North this was accomplished in good part through taxes and borrowing. The southern states had no established system or even tradition of taxation and were able to raise relatively little money in taxes. The South was also unable to find many buyers for its bonds. By the end of the war the North had experienced total inflation over four years of about 180% and the South more than 9000%.

    a. Portray as much of the preceding information as you can in terms of the PPF. Assume full employment in both economies and put military spending on the vertical axis and all other spending on the horizontal axis.

    b. Assuming that potential lenders had no idea who would eventually win the war, why do you think the South found it so difficult to borrow funds? (There could be many factors, but just consider the information given earlier to keep this simple.)

    c. Why do you think the transformation of resources was accomplished with so much inflation on the one side but relatively little on the other?

10. An oil-rich nation discovers that its usable petroleum will be virtually depleted in 20 years.

    a. Use the PPF framework to portray what will happen to it during the next 20 years if it simply ignores this information and continues "business as usual."

    b. If you were chief economic adviser to the prime minister, what policies would you advocate to avoid the scenario in part a? Explain.

1.11 FURTHER READING

Todd G. Buchholz, *New Ideas from Dead Economists: An Introduction to Modern Economic Thought* (New York: Penguin/Plume, 1989).

Rondo Cameron, *A Concise Economic History of the World: From Paleolithic Times to the Present*, 2nd ed. (New York: Oxford University Press, 1993).

Robert L. Heilbroner, *The Making of Economic Society*, 9th ed. (Englewood Cliffs, N.J.: Prentice Hall, 1993).

George Lakoff and Mark Johnson, *Metaphors We Live By* (Chicago: University of Chicago Press, 1980).

JAMES M. MCPHERSON, "How Lincoln Won the War With Metaphors," in *Abraham Lincoln and the Second American Revolution* (New York: Oxford University Press, 1991).

DOUGLASS C. NORTH, *Institutions, Institutional Change, and Economic Performance* (Cambridge: Cambridge University Press, 1990).

MICHAEL WALDEN, *Economic Issues: Rhetoric and Reality* (Englewood Cliffs, N.J.: Prentice Hall, 1995).

THE WORLD BANK, *World Development Report 1991: The Challenge of Development* (New York: Oxford University Press, 1991).

CHAPTER 2

THE CLASSICAL MODEL OF THE MACROECONOMY

✂ 2.1 INTRODUCTION

The PPF is a handy reminder that economic choices confront us whichever way we turn. It's always "this or that?" and "now or later?" When we forget or ignore this message, unwanted consequences often follow. But the PPF framework itself tells us little about these consequences because it doesn't reveal the underlying causes of unemployment, inflation, the business cycle, dwindling productivity growth, volatile foreign exchange rates, soaring levels of indebtedness, and other economic disorders. So our next step, a big one that will concern us through most of the book, is to turn to **economic theory** for some insights into the linkages between our economic *choices* (private and public) and the resulting *outcomes*.

An economic theory, embodied in an **economic model,** becomes a device for predicting the consequences of alternative economic paths without having to actually journey along them. Such models are simplified representations of the much more complicated "real" world. As you will see throughout the book, a careful analytical model, intelligently used, can help us avoid the costly trial-and-error approach to economic policy making. You'll also see examples where a "bad" model turns out even worse than trial or error. It can act as a set of blinders that prevents us from understanding or even perceiving some of the consequences of our actions.

It's a common mistake to view "theory" as something exotic, mysterious, impractical, or inherently complicated. Economic theory is the "bridge" from choices to outcomes. It connects *if* with *then* and *cause* with *effect*. Therefore, it is exactly the same kind of process that we engage in every day just to get through the ordinary business of life—looking for *connections*, *patterns*, and *interrelationships*. Those who claim to dislike "theory" probably misunderstand it. Avoidance of theory and models is often defended as a way to be "practical," "let the facts speak for themselves," and "get to the bottom line." But this so-called commonsense attitude ensures a superficial understanding of complex situations and often leads to decisions and policies that waste scarce resources. The many examples and discussions of economic policy throughout this book should convince you what is merely asserted now: Effective choices—private or public—must have a foundation in an understanding of cause-and-effect linkages. In other words, good practical choices *start* with a good theory.

But what happens in situations where two or more theories seem to make sense? How do we choose among them? What if the available evidence is consistent with several different explanations? Do we then pick according to hunch or other subjective criteria, flip a coin, or just remain agnostic? We'll explore this important issue later when you have a solid working knowledge of basic macroeconomic analysis. In this chapter we take a first look at the two major theoretical bridges between choices and outcomes in macroeconomics: the **Keynesian** and **classical** models. Though similar in most respects, they differ in a few telling ways. These differences, examined with increasing precision in later chapters, have created most of the controversy and stimulated much of the progress in macroeconomics over the past sixty years.

୧୧ 2.2 MACROECONOMICS AND THE KEYNESIAN TRADITION

It was not until the 1930s that macroeconomics emerged as a separate field within economics. Befitting its birth during the depths of the Great Depression, it has remained decidedly policy oriented. The prominent British economist **John Maynard Keynes** (it rhymes with "brains," he would say) identified *unemployment* as a vital issue about which mainstream economics of that time, which he called Classical economics, had too little to say. In his influential book, *The General Theory of Employment, Interest, and Money* (1936), Keynes claimed to have discovered a policy mechanism for ending unemployment and stimulating overall economic activity.

The "Keynesian Revolution" means different things to different people. But even its critics have agreed that Keynes's *General Theory* triggered a series of analytical innovations and policy experiments that resulted in dramatically higher expectations about the government's ability to favorably influence overall economic performance. More than half a century later the very practical, applied focus of **Keynesian economics** remains strong. Keynes's vision of an active policy role for government in guiding and stabilizing the economy is now so widely accepted in practice that it's difficult to imagine how radical it was in 1936. Most of us take it for granted that the federal government should respond quickly and appropriately to signs of a weakening economy, though we may disagree over the specifics and extent of that action. Our perspective is reflected in and reinforced by the news media's close attention to macroeconomic issues. Inflation, recession, and the latest rumors of depression; taxes, deficits, and the national debt; interest rates, Federal Reserve policies, the international value of the dollar, and growth of output—all are newsworthy items for which we hold our governments accountable. Candidates for public office are expected to tell a convincing story about how they will use government power to improve the situation, whereas their opponent's plan will only make things worse.

The appeal of **policy activism** is powerful even though experience has shown that the government's ability to control the macroeconomy is probably much more limited than is popularly believed. This tendency to look to the government for solutions to macroeconomic issues is due, in part, to some dramatic past successes but perhaps also to a need to believe that we can control our economic destiny. It has fostered levels of government involvement in the U.S. economy that would have been unthinkable in earlier decades and has also created strong resistance from those who fear such concentration of power. Reaganomics and Thatcherism, for example, were movements to reverse the activist influence that is in part a legacy of the work of John Maynard Keynes. The Republican party's takeover of Congress in the 1994 elections was another reaction against a large public sector. Were he alive today, however, this change in the role of government and the controversy it has generated would not surprise the man who wrote that

the ideas of economists and political philosophers, both when they are right and when they are wrong, are more powerful than is commonly understood. Indeed the world is ruled by little else. Practical men, who believe themselves to be quite exempt from any intellectual influences, are usually the slaves of some defunct economist. Madmen in authority, who hear voices in the air, are distilling their frenzy from some academic scribbler of a few years back.[1]

In alerting us to our dependence on ideas and slogans from the past, Keynes was also foretelling the future of Keynesian economics. Many of his ideas, even some that have not held up to careful scrutiny, continue to hold us in their grip.

⊗⊘ 2.3 THE CLASSICAL TRADITION IN MACROECONOMICS

Though macroeconomics as a separate branch of economics is relatively young, there is a long history of theories and policies about such vital issues as prosperity and depression, inflation, and the economic role of government. The most prominent and enduring of these earlier theories is known as **classical economics**—the focus of Keynes's attack in *The General Theory*. The policy implications of classical economics are in stark contrast to the activism of Keynes and his followers. For more than 150 years following the publication of **Adam Smith's** masterpiece, *The Wealth of Nations* (1776), most political economists, moral philosophers, and policy makers held the belief that the workings of private enterprise and the market system, unfettered by much direct governmental involvement, was the best prescription for overall economic health. Smith's famous "invisible hand" metaphor describes how individual self-interest is translated by a competitive market system into a coherent, efficient, and stable outcome for the whole nation.[2] There was no need, in the classical view, for a distinct field concerned with aggregate or *macro*economics.

---

[1] John Maynard Keynes, *The General Theory of Employment, Interest, and Money* (London: Macmillan Publishing Company, 1936), p. 383.

[2] "As every individual . . . endeavours as much as he can both to employ his capital in the support of domestic industry, and so to direct that industry that its produce may be of the greatest value; every individual necessarily labours to render the annual revenue of the society as great as he can. He generally, indeed, neither intends to promote the public interest, nor knows how much he is promoting it. By preferring the support of domestic to that of foreign industry, he intends only his own security; and by directing that industry in such a manner as its produce may be of the greatest value, he intends only his own gain, and he is in this, as in many other cases, led by an invisible hand to promote an end which was no part of his intention. Nor is it always the worse for the society that it was no part of it. By pursuing his own interest he frequently promotes that of the society more effectually than when he really intends to promote it. I have never known much good done by those who affected to trade for the public good" (Adam Smith, *An Inquiry Into the Nature and Causes of the Wealth of Nations*, Glasgow ed. of the *Works and Correspondence of Adam Smith*, [Oxford: Oxford University Press, 1976 (1776)], 1:456).

At the onset of the Great Depression, the classical perspective dominated economic thinking in Western industrial nations. It advocated a limited but still very important role for the public sector. First, and most important, the government must set up and enforce the basic **institutional structure** (such as private property, enforcement of contracts, and prevention of monopoly power) around which a market-oriented economy revolves. This vital role has become increasingly appreciated as we watch the nations of the former Soviet bloc struggle to lay institutional foundations consistent with a market system. Second, the classical tradition envisions the government as **provider of a *limited* number of public goods and services** (national defense, highways, and education made Adam Smith's list) to be paid out of *current* taxes except in national emergencies (namely wars) when temporary borrowing was acceptable.

This limited direct role for government had deep roots in the abundant historical evidence of abuse of concentrated political and economic power by governments. That this power would typically be used to reward friends and punish enemies was taken as self-evident. In fact, deep mistrust of government remains widespread and often coexists in our minds side by side with its opposite—a naive faith that government action can and should solve all our economic problems. It's no wonder that we find the "role of government" issue so perplexing and so frustrating.

This general aversion to direct economic participation by the government is echoed and reinforced by the classical theory of how a market economy functions. With only a small handful of exceptions (national defense, highways, etc.), public-sector actions to promote economic prosperity are doomed to failure according to the classical analysis. At best, government involvement is ineffective; at worst, it can impede the "engine of economic growth" that resides in the private sector and is powered by the incentives of private property and competitive markets.

This classical theory of limited government effectiveness, reinforced by abuses of public power throughout recorded history, came to dominate economic policy making in the industrialized countries for most of the nineteenth and early twentieth centuries. Though the classical model was often criticized, most notably and

WHO'S RIGHT? KEYNES OR THE CLASSICS

The two views differ markedly in their picture of how the macroeconomy functions and what the government can and cannot accomplish. It would seem that we could simply look at the facts and decide who's right and who's wrong. Is it the Keynesian or the classical view that best describes economies at the end of the twentieth century?

This seemingly straightforward question turns out to be both too involved and too important for us to tackle in a responsible way at this point. By the end of this chapter you should begin to see why. By the end of Chapter 15 you will have the background and analytical skill to carefully assess the two central and distinct questions defining the Keynesian and classical traditions: What *can* the government do? and What *should* the government do?

severely by Karl Marx, it was never seriously challenged until the publication of Keynes's *General Theory*. Keynes and his followers were the first to provide a substantive and careful counteralliance of facts and theory to rival the authority of the orthodox classical view.

The *General Theory* was written in the midst of the Great Depression, a time when many were proclaiming the fulfillment of Karl Marx's prediction that class conflict would lead to the inevitable destruction of capitalism and the abolishment of private ownership of economic resources. Keynes rejected the Marxian diagnosis as well as the passive optimism of the classical tradition. The abolition of private property in favor of state ownership was repugnant to Keynes. But, in his view, the mechanism underlying the classical "invisible hand" was much too weak to sustain prosperity in a growing industrial nation. Keynes thought that an expanded and active economic role for government was needed to maintain a healthy macroeconomic environment within which free enterprise and a market economy could flourish. A fair and thoughtful assessment of this view requires us to begin with a clear understanding of the classical model.

⊗⊙ 2.4 ELEMENTS OF THE CLASSICAL MODEL

To speak of *the* classical model is an obvious distortion because no single framework can encompass all economists working in the classical tradition for more than two centuries. Variations continue to arise, and sometimes the differences are significant enough to warrant a new label like "neoclassical," "Austrian," or "new classical." But from our present vantage point, what is most striking is the *similarities*, not the differences. There is a remarkable continuity in the classical tradition that extends over the centuries right down to the present. It is these similarities that are embodied in the representative classical model of this chapter.

Any model of a market-oriented economy must go beneath all the noise and commotion on the surface of economic life to the underlying forces that power and guide the system. The classical model is built around two basic elements: the process of **market clearing** in competitive markets and the **Quantity Theory of Money.** Together they define a set of activities and interactions designed to represent (i.e., simulate or approximate) the workings of a real world, market system.

The classical system describes a process in which *competition* and *self-interest* "control" economic activity in much the same way that a thermostat controls temperature. A smoothly operating classical world is one in which "market clearing" ensures that the thermostat is set on full employment. Moreover, the "Quantity Theory," as we'll see, yields a clear and simple policy for price stability: let the money supply grow at approximately the same rate at which the full employment level of output is expected to grow. These two characteristics—automatic full employment and a simple rule for achieving price stability—make this model sound almost irresistible. The obvious question is whether the "model" bears much resemblance to the "real world" in which we live.

The classical tradition contends that such a model presents a reliable picture of the actual workings of the macroeconomy and that its policy conclusions follow logically from its analytical insights. Keynes, as we have seen, believed the classical model to be a *mis*representation of reality. Its thermostat, in his view, was unreliable, and the government had both the ability and the obligation to alter the setting or override the mechanism altogether. To understand the Keynesian remedy (and its limitations) we must first understand the classical theory (and its limitations).

Market Clearing

The adjustment process of a market system, called "market clearing," lies at the heart of the classical model. The emphasis is on the interplay and resolution of market forces through price and quantity adjustments in competitive markets. The familiar graphs in Figure 2.1 portray hypothetical supply and demand curves, representing the preferences and interactions of buyers (demanders) and sellers (suppliers). The downward slope of the demand curve (D) reflects the observation that when the price (p) of the commodity falls, other things the same, quantity demanded (q^d) will rise as individuals increase their purchases of this now relatively cheaper good. Any other event that changes the amount purchased—such as a change in income or in consumer preferences—will shift the entire curve, leaving the slope unchanged. The upward-sloping supply curves (S) in Figure 2.1 show that as the price of the good rises (other things the same) quantity supplied (q^s) increases as sellers step up production of this now relatively more profitable good. Any other event that changes the amount produced—such as a change in the cost of inputs, new taxes, or environmental restrictions—will shift the entire curve. *In short, all factors that affect buyers are incorporated either in the slope or the position (intercept) of the demand curve* (D); *all factors that affect sellers are captured in either the slope or intercept of the supply curve* (S).

The basic supply and demand diagram essentially brings buyers and sellers together, and demonstrates how their ensuing interactions can lead to a resolution (equilibrium) of conflicting interests. For example, in Figure 2.1(a) the price of the commodity is p_0, and the quantity traded is $q^d = q^s = q_0$. This is the only point at which the two curves intersect, meaning that it's the only market price at which the decisions of buyers and sellers are consistent. It doesn't mean that either party is necessarily pleased with the price. Buyers will always like it lower, sellers higher. But this is the only price that is acceptable to both. When there is neither **surplus** ($q^s > q^d$) nor **shortage** ($q^d > q^s$) at the prevailing price, the market is said to be **cleared.**

■ FIGURE 2.1

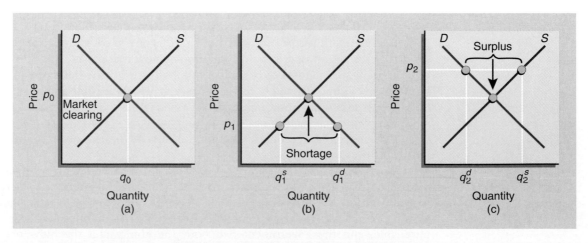

Basic Mechanics of Supply and Demand

Suppose the initial price is *below* the market clearing level, such as at p_1 in Figure 2.1(b). Compared with the first picture, buyers will now demand more than q_0, but sellers will supply less. Therefore, p_1 results in a *shortage* of the amount $(q_1{}^d - q_1{}^s)$. As long as there are no restrictions (legal or otherwise) fixing the price at p_1, this shortage will create an upward pressure on the price. Buyers unable to get as much as they want at this price will, in effect, bid up the price to entice sellers to increase their production—both sides merely following the dictates of their own self-interest. As p_1 rises, some buyers drop out of the market at the same time as some sellers are expanding production. Together these reactions reduce the gap between the quantities demanded and supplied. With stable (nonshifting) supply-and-demand curves, this upward pressure continues until the price has risen to its equilibrium level. Only at p_0 will the shortage disappear.

What if the price is *above* the market clearing level, as shown by p_2 in Figure 2.1(c)? Suppliers respond by producing $q_2{}^s$, whereas buyers demand only $q_2{}^d$. As long as prices are free to adjust, the resulting *surplus* $(q_2{}^s - q_2{}^d)$ generates downward pressure on the price as sellers compete for buyers. As the price falls, suppliers cut back on production levels and the surplus diminishes and, finally, disappears when the price reaches p_0, and the market is again cleared.

This framework—supply, demand, and market clearing—is the most basic and frequently used of all economic models. It offers a simple, reliable way to describe and predict market events and interactions. For example, suppose we're at point *A* in Figure 2.2(a) when an increase in demand for this good occurs. *D* shifts to *D'* and the initial price (p_0) no longer clears the market. This demand shift has created a shortage that forces the price upward as more buyers compete for the available supply. Only when the price reaches p_1, at point *B*, will the market again clear. Figure 2.2(b) shows how a positive supply shift (*S* shifts out to *S'*) creates a surplus. Market clearing is restored only when the price falls to p_1, as the economy adjusts from points *A* to *B*.

■ FIGURE 2.2

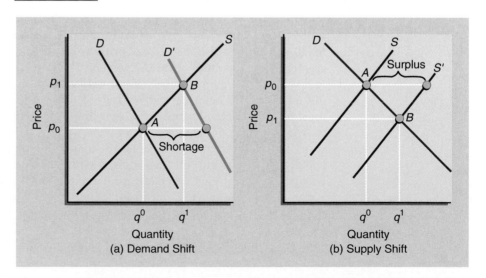

Market Adjustments to Shifting Demand and Supply

IN SUMMARY . . .

Market Clearing

Three simple assumptions—demand curves slope down, supply curves up, and prices adjust automatically until markets "clear"—lie at the heart of much economic analysis. They form our most basic model of prices and quantities and the conditions under which they change.

The market clearing price can change only in response to a shift in demand or supply. Moreover, the market clearing price represents a stable equilibrium. Any disturbance of price from p_0 will set in motion events that, for given supply and demand curves, return price to its original market clearing level. The market mechanism—responding to the dictates of self-interest of its participants—works automatically (as if controlled by an "invisible hand") to maintain or restore the equilibrium price.

We assume for now that when a shift in demand or supply occurs, the price adjusts "quickly" to its market clearing level. The actual speed of price adjustment is an extremely controversial issue that will be examined carefully in later chapters.

From Labor Market
Clearing to Aggregate Supply

Much of the appeal of supply and demand analysis stems from its remarkable versatility. It can be usefully applied to virtually any type of exchange. Though never the "whole truth," it almost always yields important insights that are difficult to see in any other way. Our present interest in the classical view of the automatic functioning of the macroeconomy leads us to examine the workings of supply and demand in the so-called **labor market.** The demand for labor services by employers and the supply of these services by workers are brought together by market forces, thereby determining the real wage ("price" of labor) and the number of hours worked ("quantity" of labor).

Starting with supply, we ask what happens to the *quantity of labor supplied* (denoted by n^s) as the *real wage* rises? Letting W denote the "money wage" (such as $7.50 per hour) and P the average price of goods and services (as measured, for example, by the consumer price index), then W/P represents the purchasing power or real value of the money wage. As this **real wage** rises, some potential workers who did not seek jobs before are now attracted to the labor market by the higher earnings. In addition, the higher real wage will induce some currently employed workers to work overtime or take a second job.[3]

This is illustrated by the upward sloping labor supply curve, n^s in Figure 2.3, which says that as the real wage rises, total hours worked also increase. Note that a change in the real wage can come from either a change in the money wage (ΔW) or a price level change (ΔP). But if, for example, both the price level and the money wage rate double, there is no change in labor supply because the *real* wage is unchanged (that is, $W_0/P_0 = 2W_0/2P_0$). This characteristic of the labor supply curve is sometimes described as the absence of "money illusion" by workers. They respond to

---

[3] At the same time, some workers may decide to work *fewer* hours, essentially taking this pay raise in the form of more leisure rather than higher income. Statistical evidence confirms that the *net* economy-wide effect is a relatively small increase in total labor supply when the real wage rises.

■ FIGURE 2.3

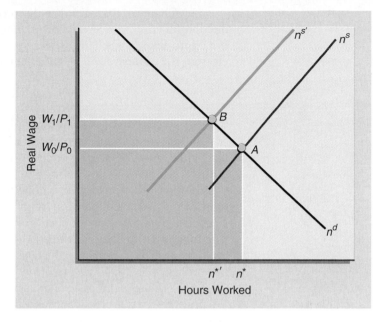

Supply and Demand in the Labor Market

changes in the purchasing power not just the nominal value of their wages.[4] In macroeconomic policy making—especially prospects for smoothing the ups and downs of the business cycle—a lot depends on *which* specific events do and do not influence the labor supply relationship. Our initial working hypothesis of an *upward sloping labor supply curve with no money illusion* is the classical benchmark from which later variations depart.

On the demand side, the downward sloping labor demand curve, n^d in Figure 2.3, embodies the well-established and commonsense notion that a rise in the real wage (other things the same) leads firms to cut back employment as they substitute capital for labor. Again, we assume that it is the *real* wage, not the money wage, that matters—this time to the firm, earlier to the worker. One way to think about this is that P represents the average price of output in the economy. So the typical firm will be concerned with changes in the money wage it *pays* (W) relative to the price it *receives* (P) for its output. If both W and P should double, this firm is assumed to continue to demand the same amount of labor.[5]

For given labor supply-and-demand curves, a market clearing real wage occurs at their intersection, such as point A in Figure 2.3. **Full employment,** in this context, means that all who want jobs at the going real wage (as shown by the labor supply curve) will be hired (demanded) by firms. Assuming that real wages adjust to clear the labor market, shifts in labor supply or demand lead to new market clearing levels of the real wage and hours worked. For example, a decrease in labor supply will shift labor supply to $n^{s'}$ in Figure 2.3 and create a new market clearing, full employment equilibrium at point B.

---

[4] But what if some workers actually *do* respond solely to changes in the money wage (ΔW) and ignore, at least initially, what's happening to the price level (ΔP)? They are said to have *money illusion,* an "affliction" that has played a large role in the debate between classicals and Keynesians. This issue will be explored in Chapter 8.

[5] As with labor supply, further discussion of the factors underlying the slope and shifts of the labor demand curve is postponed to Chapter 8.

In Chapter 1 we said that the production process, as summarized in the production function, converts labor (n) and capital (k), for a given institutional structure (i^{nst}), into final goods and services (y). When the labor market is in equilibrium (or cleared) the economy will be at full employment, and we can write this as follows:

$$y^* = F(n^*, k_0, i_0^{nst})$$

where k_0 is the fixed level of capital (including natural resources, technology, as well as plant and equipment, among other inputs), i_0^{nst} refers to a given institutional structure while n^* and y^* are, respectively, the full employment levels of employment and output.

Suppose we want to determine how a change in the price level will affect the level of real output in an economy with a fixed capital stock and given institutional structure. The previous production function makes it clear that the only remaining way for output to change is through a change in the labor input (n). If a change in the price level is to influence the level of real output it will have to be through the labor market.[6]

So let's use some basic market mechanics to see what effect, if any, a change in the price level has on the labor market. The initial impact of a price level change is to change the real wage, which, in turn, will affect *both* labor demand and supply. Turning to Figure 2.4, suppose we start at the full employment, market clearing equilib-

Starting at point A, a doubling of the price level will reduce the real wage ($W_0/P_0 \rightarrow W_0/2P_0$), creating a temporary labor shortage. The resulting excess demand for labor (at $W_0/2P_0$) puts upward pressure on the money wage until the shortage is eliminated ($W_0 \rightarrow 2W_0$).

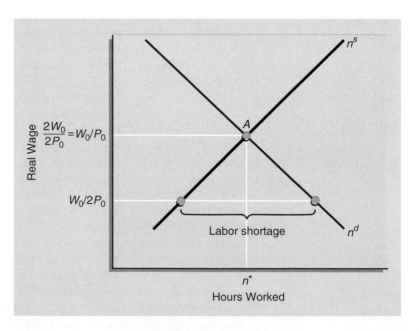

Temporary Labor Shortage from an Increase in the Price Level

---

[6] Holding the levels of the nonlabor inputs (capital and the institutional structure) constant not only simplifies the analysis but seems to be realistic for a good many macroeconomic issues. But when we turn to longer run issues (such as economic growth) we will allow all the inputs to vary with whatever events or policies are being considered.

rium of point A. If the price level were to suddenly double, the real wage would fall from W_0/P_0 to $W_0/2P_0$, as shown. The declining real wage means a reduction in the quantity supplied of labor, moving us down the labor supply curve. At the same time it will stimulate the demand for labor, moving us down the labor demand curve as well. The result is a labor shortage, portrayed as the gap between the two curves at the lower real wage, $W_0/2P_0$.

This shortage—just like the one shown earlier in Figure 2.1(b)—puts upward pressure on the price (W/P in this case). So assuming the price level stays at $2P_0$ this forces a rise in the *money* wage, $+\Delta W$. In fact, market clearing insures that the money wage must *also* double to eliminate the labor shortage. So the real wage will have returned to its original level ($2W_0/2P_0 = W_0/P_0$), and we'll be right back at point A with a higher price level, a proportionately higher money wage, but the same real wage and quantity of labor (n^*).

The end result is that a doubling of the price level does *not* alter equilibrium in the labor market because neither suppliers nor demanders of labor had "money illusion." They focused on the real wage, not the money wage, in making their labor market decisions. And because changes in the price level don't change the level of employment in the classical model they will have *no* impact on the level of real output. This is captured in the **classical aggregate supply curve (AS*)** shown in Figure 2.5. It is this curve—vertical at the full employment level of output—that *defines* full employment in the classical model. It plays the same role of portraying the limits imposed by scarcity that the PPF did in our earlier setting.

■ FIGURE 2.5

For a given capital stock and institutional structure, the process of market clearing keeps the equilibrium level of real output always at full employment. Changes in the price level will be met by equiproportionate changes in the nominal wage, leaving the real wage, employment (hence, real output), unchanged. Equilibrium real output is said to be invariant with respect to changes in the price level.

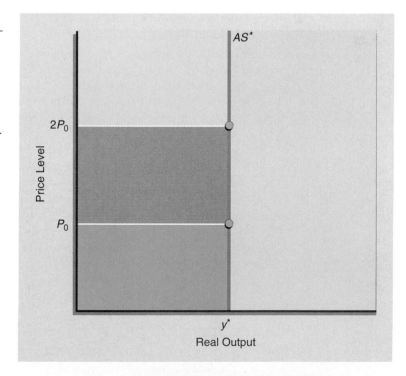

Classical Aggregate Supply Curve (AS*)

IN SUMMARY . . .

Aggregate Supply

The classical aggregate supply model applies basic supply-and-demand analysis to a competitive labor market with flexible wages and no "money illusion" to tell the story of an economy that adjusts automatically to full employment. A situation in which actual output (y) deviates from its full employment level (y^*) is viewed as exceptional and short-lived. This is because flexible wages and prices allow market clearing to keep employment close to its full employment level, n^*. It is this mechanism that makes the classical aggregate supply curve (AS^*) vertical.

The "thermostat" of market clearing is set to keep the economy at full employment and, therefore, on its PPF. This is the "invisible hand" idea, and the classical presumption is that whichever metaphor you choose—hand, thermostat, magnetism, or gravity—it is strong enough to keep the economy from straying very far or for very long from full employment. No government action, other than ensuring competitive markets, is required.

and in prospect . . .

Aggregate Demand

While the labor market and aggregate supply determine *employment* and *output*, they have told us nothing about what determines the *price level*. For this, we need to supplement the analysis with a theory of aggregate demand.

From the Quantity Theory of Money to Aggregate Demand

If market clearing is the cornerstone of classical aggregate supply, the **Quantity Theory of Money** plays the same role in classical aggregate demand analysis.[7] The Quantity Theory relates the price level to the quantity of money circulating in the economy. It leads to a theory of aggregate demand (AD), which, combined with the market clearing model of aggregate supply (AS^*), tells the classical "story" of the workings of the macroeconomy. The classical AD/AS^* model, as we'll refer to it, is an explanation of the levels of output, employment, and the price level in a market system. This section presents the demand side, and the next will combine it with supply to complete the classical macroeconomic model.

Aggregate demand is another name for total spending on goods and services. And spending can change either because of a change in the *quantity* (or *real value*) of goods we purchase (denoted by y^{AD}) or a change in the *average price* (P) we pay for these goods. This definition of total spending, also called *nominal* aggregate demand, can be written as follows:

$$\text{Total spending} = \text{nominal aggregate demand} = Py^{AD}$$

---

[7] Although hints of the Quantity Theory go far back in history, it is most often associated with the work about 250 years ago of the Scottish philosopher, David Hume. The American economist Irving Fisher gave it its present form early in this century, and Milton Friedman is largely responsible for its modern revival among monetarists.

Note that if we divide all three parts of this expression by the price level (P), real demand (y^{AD}) equals nominal aggregate demand (or total spending) *deflated* (divided) by the price level. The point here is to separate changes in total spending, $\Delta(Py^{AD})$, into price change (ΔP) and quantity change (Δy^{AD}).

Because spending entails the use of *money*, this gives us a second and equivalent way to express total spending or nominal aggregate demand. Total spending is equal to the available **money supply** (M), the number of dollars in circulation, *times* the **velocity of money** (V), the number of times that the *average* dollar changes hands during a particular period. Combining these two equivalent measures of total spending, we have

$$Py^{AD} = \text{total spending} = MV$$

The preceding equation states that the total amount spent on goods and services (Py^{AD}) must equal the amount of dollars available (M) times the average speed at which they circulate through the economy (V) during, say, a particular year. It provides the foundation for an explanation of the real demand for output, y^{AD}. Dividing both sides by P, we have

$$y^{AD} = MV/P$$

An equation can be thought of as a sentence about relationships and balance. This one says that aggregate real demand for output varies *directly* with changes in either the amount of money or its speed of circulation (M and V, respectively) but *inversely* with the average level of prices (P). Most of us find it easier to remember short equations than sentences like the last one. So one important use for mathematics in economics is as a convenient shorthand for describing and remembering key relationships like the Quantity Theory of Money: $y^{AD} = MV/P$.

Let's first focus on the inverse relationship between the real demand for output and the price level. As the price level falls (other things the same), y^{AD} will rise—a result that is simply common sense. If we spend a given amount of money (M) at a constant rate (V), a fall in the average price ($-\Delta P$) must increase the total amount ($+\Delta y^{AD}$) we can buy. This relationship between the demand for output and the price level (geometrically, a rectangular hyperbola) is captured in the downward slope of the **classical aggregate demand curve** (AD) in Figure 2.6. As the price level changes, we move along the aggregate demand curve. So by design we're building the impact of a changing price level into the *slope* of the aggregate demand curve. Anything else that changes aggregate demand must *shift* the entire curve in or out. From the demand equation, $y^{AD} = (MV)/P$, we see that only two events can cause shifts in the aggregate demand curve—a change in the supply of money (ΔM) or a change in its velocity (ΔV). We assume for now that the money supply is completely controlled by the Central Bank. In other words, M is a **policy instrument** that could become a source of instability in aggregate demand only if the Central Bank (the Federal Reserve in the United States) chooses a volatile, stop-and-go time path for the money supply. Let's presume, for now, that they do not.

What about the stability of the velocity of money? Unlike the money supply, velocity is not controlled by policy makers. The rate at which dollars change hands is

■ FIGURE 2.6

For a given supply of money and velocity of money, the demand for real output must vary inversely with the price level— $\uparrow y^{AD} = MV/P \downarrow$ —shown as the movement from points A to B.

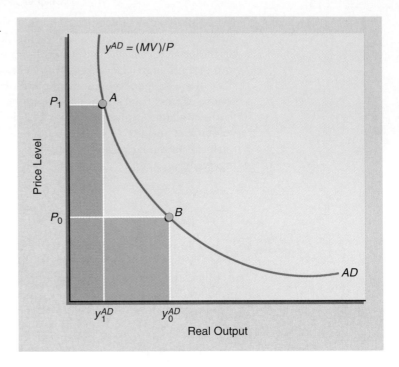

Classical Aggregate
Demand Curve

the outcome of literally trillions of economic decisions each year, by anyone, anywhere in the world, who uses dollars—individuals, businesses, and governments alike. To discuss even the relative handful of most important determinants of velocity could obviously prove lengthy and involved. It is highly convenient, then, that the basic *long-run* facts about movements in velocity can be captured with a very simple, almost superficial, theory. The classical Quantity Theory of Money typically assumes that velocity can be considered a constant over relatively long periods of time. Is such a strong assumption reasonable? Statistical evidence is generally clear on this point—while velocity often fluctuates substantially from year to year, these ups and downs have usually offset one another over longer periods. In a later chapter we will look more carefully at long run trends in velocity. For now we'll just accept the classical approximation that the velocity of money can be treated as a constant.

The classical tradition contends that the assumption of constant velocity, when combined with actual monetary actions of central banks and the market-clearing adjustments that lead to a vertical aggregate supply curve, paints a faithful, broad-brush picture of observed economic activity in market-oriented economies. Specifically, this portrait is one of *long-run equilibrium at full employment*, overlaid with *short-lived, disequilibrium fluctuations* around full employment, and punctuated by the *occasional panics and crises*, attributable either to irresponsible central bank manipulation of the money supply or the inevitable acts of God or man (like earthquakes or wars) that take their toll on any economic system.

IN SUMMARY . . .

Aggregate Demand

The classical aggregate demand curve displays an inverse relationship between the price level and the real demand for output in an economy with a given money supply and constant velocity of money. Changes in *M shift* aggregate demand; changes in *P* are *movements along* the curve.

and in prospect . . .

The Full Classical Model

The complete classical *AD/AS** model looks past day-to-day and, on occasion, even year-to-year changes, toward those forces thought to be the enduring determinants of overall economic activity and prices. The classical tradition contends that volatile and haphazard factors in short-run events tend to distract our attention from the fundamental forces and relationships that dominate economic activity and emerge only in the longer run. On this basis, it justifies the twin assumptions of market clearing and constant velocity of money.

Put another way, a model seeking to explain **short-run events** will face two substantial challenges: (1) it must provide a theory of observed *short-run changes in velocity* in a world in which (2) *markets are not always cleared.* We'll see in the next chapter that such short-run models become considerably more complex than the long run classical model.

2.5 FOUR IMPLICATIONS OF THE CLASSICAL MODEL

Remember that a model, no matter how crude or sophisticated, is always a representation of something else. It's a *reflection* of the "real" thing and is of interest only if it is *simpler and more manageable* than its real-world counterpart and if it is a *good mimic* of the original. In this section we use the classical macroeconomic model to predict consequences of hypothetical macroeconomic events or policy changes. We ask "*What if . . . ?*" and let the logic of the model respond with "*Then. . . .*" More specifically, we now look at four major implications of the classical model: (1) Full employment prevails; (2) aggregate demand has no impact on output or employment; (3) supply is the key to economic growth; and (4) inflation is a result of the actions of the monetary authority. The section following this will then consider, in an informal and preliminary way, how faithfully these implications echo the sound of the real world.

1. Full Employment Prevails

Classical theory combines the vertical *AS** curve (which assumes market clearing) with the downward-sloping *AD* curve (derived from the long run Quantity Theory) to form a model of output and the price level. Output in this model can be in equilibrium only at full employment (y^*). If the price level is too high for market clearing, there will be *excess supply* (a surplus) that leads to price cutting until an equilibrium

HOW MUCH UNEMPLOYMENT AT "FULL" EMPLOYMENT?
The Natural *Rate of Unemployment*

Not mentioned in our discussion so far is the fact that there is unemployment at "full employment." This **natural rate of unemployment** (denoted by U^*) has two broad categories. The first is frictional unemployment and refers to those who are temporarily between jobs and will soon fill an available job vacancy. The second is structural unemployment and includes the long term or "hard core" unemployed. These groups are discussed carefully in Chapter 11, "Unemployment." Even an economy operating at full employment will have a certain percentage of its labor force out of work. For the U.S. economy today, U^* is thought to lie in the 5 to 6% range.

A "natural rate of unemployment" greater than zero is inevitable in any economy in which workers are free to quit and firms are free to fire them. In fact, a very low U^* is most typical of rigid and inefficient economies in which poor economic performance shows up in a very low standard of living rather than a high rate of unemployment. In these situations, even "full employment" may be at a point well-inside the country's potential PPF, reflecting a state of "hidden" unemployment.

What about those who don't fall in the frictional or structural categories, but are unemployed because the economy is currently operating below capacity? This gap between actual unemployment (U) and the natural rate of unemployment (U^*) is called cyclical unemployment and will play a central role in coming chapters.

price level is reached and the market clears. A similar story holds for an *excess demand* (shortage) when the price level is below equilibrium. The "thermostat" is in control, ensuring that the economy stays at or near its full employment level of output, as shown in Figure 2.7.

There is nothing subtle about this implication. The model is obviously constructed (contrived, some would say) to yield equilibrium only at full employment. How does it explain periods of recession ($y < y^*$) when the economy is inside its PPF? In a nutshell: as unfortunate, inevitable, but thanks to automatic market adjustments, temporary. Unemployment is said to be a "disequilibrium phenomenon" in this model.

There have always been doubts and misgivings about this implication. It's an obvious target for criticism and even parody. Keynes's critique of automatic full employment equilibrium is certainly the best known as well as the most forceful, and we'll examine it in the next two chapters. But there is a long history of earlier theories (including one by Thomas Robert Malthus of population dynamics fame) that were variously termed "overproduction," "underconsumption," or "oversaving" hypotheses. Although differing in specifics, they all concluded that in a market system total demand may not be large enough to buy the entire full employment level of

■ FIGURE 2.7

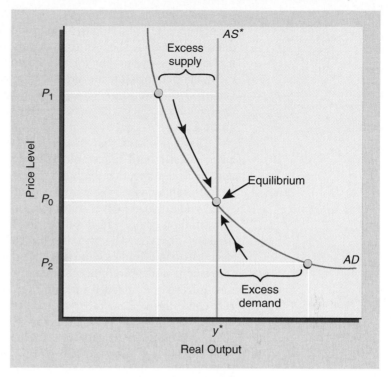

Equilibrium Is Always at
Full Employment

production. According to these theories there may be too much saving (too little spending) to purchase the full employment amount of goods and services. The result of this overproduction is a subsequent cutback in output levels so that some workers will be fired and unemployment will rise. Loss of jobs means a further drop in income—and spending—and the situation continues, perhaps even worsening. The automatic adjustment of prices and wages, stressed by the classicals, cannot correct the underspending problem because falling wages only reduce spending further. Consequently, unemployment cannot just be dismissed as a short-lived disequilibrium phenomenon.

Such criticisms strike at the heart of the classical proposition that the interplay of market forces guides the economy surely and smoothly to the efficient use of its scarce resources. The classical response has typically followed the reasoning of the French economist Jean-Baptiste Say (1767–1832). **Say's Law of Markets,** often compressed to the cryptic "supply creates its own demand," insists that in a system of competitive markets there will always be enough purchasing power generated at full employment to purchase all goods produced. The production process itself creates exactly enough income to ensure its purchase, because every dollar spent on output must also be a dollar received as income by someone. No dollars are thrown away or left lying around unclaimed.

Say's law is far more than a footnote in the history of economic thought. It identifies a process that is critical to the success of any market system, yet is virtually invisible to the untrained eye. In nations that have forsaken planning in which most jobs were created by the government, there is understandable anxiety about turning job creation over to an "invisible hand." Where will the millions and millions of jobs needed to reach full employment come from if no agency or commissar is there to define and include them in the budget officially? And when the budget is tight, isn't it both necessary and fair for these planners to force older workers into early retirement to open jobs for new graduates of the high schools, technical schools, and universities? In a world of economic planning, this discarding of willing and able workers seems perversely reasonable because, after all, there are only so many jobs to go around.

Say's law says that in a market economy the job of "job creation" occurs automatically until full employment is reached. More specifically, market clearing and Say's law together define a process by which jobs and incomes are balanced at full employment. What makes you think there will be a job available for you when you graduate? After all, millions of new graduates went into the job market last year, millions more will flood the market this year, and so what will be left for the millions like you who will be graduating in the coming years? Where will the new jobs come from? Some space at the entry level will result from the process of retirement and promotion. But this will account for only a small fraction of the new jobs that are needed to keep the economy at full employment. Where will the rest come from? Remember the millions of people who have entered the job market over the past few years? They have been receiving income for their services, and their consumption expenditures have risen notably since they were students. In buying cars and furniture and clothes and cribs, they are essentially transforming their newly acquired incomes (generated by their supply of labor) into additional demand for goods and services. Hence, in Say's terms, supply creates its own demand.

Say's law effectively silenced the view that people would consistently be unable to purchase the full employment volume of goods and services. Though the often stubborn dissenters from the classical orthodoxy weren't about to surrender, they were forced to modify their attack. Their response was that even though there may be enough income generated to purchase all the output produced at full employment, there's no reason to expect that it will all be spent on output. Specifically, there is no guarantee that all saving (nonconsumption) will flow smoothly into investment or other spending.

This view points the finger at the "capital market" as a weak link in the chain connecting decisions of savers with plans of investors. We'll have more to say about this issue in coming chapters. For now we simply note that this restructured criticism does *not* invalidate the classical "equilibrium only at full employment" proposition. But it raises the possibility that such an equilibrium may be relatively slow in getting established (or re-established after a demand or supply shock) because of "frictions" in capital or other markets. In other words, this argument questions the *strength* of the magnet drawing the economy to equilibrium at full employment but not its existence.

2. Aggregate Demand Has No Impact on Output or Employment

A second implication of the classical model is that an aggregate demand shift changes the market-clearing price level but *not* the equilibrium level of real output. This is shown by the movement from points A to B in Figure 2.8. Put another way, the overall standard of living (y^*) stays constant even though the cost of living (P) rises. De-

■ FIGURE 2.8

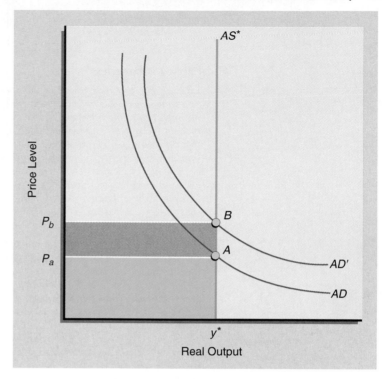

Demand Shifts Change the Price
Level, Not Real Output

mand shifts are said to have no "real" effects in this model, meaning that the equilibrium levels of output and employment are unchanged.[8]

This simple but important implication can be stated in a variety of ways, including three common macroeconomic slogans.

"Money is a Veil"

Because an increase in the money supply shifts aggregate demand (but not supply), it follows that monetary expansion or contraction will alter only the price level, not real output. With the money supply having no impact on the standard of living, it is said to be a "veil" that is merely draped over the economy, leaving the underlying market conditions (supply and demand), and, hence, real economic activity undisturbed. **Monetary neutrality** *is another term used to express this classical implication that monetary events do not influence "real" events. In equilibrium, expansionary monetary policy cannot raise the standard of living nor can contractionary monetary policy drive us into unemployment and recession. Note that it is a short step from this result to the policy recommendation that price stability should be the primary goal of monetary policy.*

"Only Money Matters"

It may seem contradictory to say "money is a veil" in one breath and "only money matters" in the next, but both are important implications of the classical model of the macroeconomy. "Only money matters" simply says that with long run constancy of velocity,

---

[8] Certainly the effects on the price level are "real" enough in every other sense of the word. But this definition of "real," which excludes price-level changes, is widely used in economics and finance, and, increasingly, among business journalists.

aggregate demand ($y^{AD} = MV/P$) can shift only through a change in the money supply (as we saw in Section 2.4).

"Fiscal Policy is Powerless"

Like the dogs that didn't bark in the Sherlock Holmes story "Silver Blaze," the significant thing about government spending and taxing (together, fiscal policy) is that they have no impact on equilibrium output or prices in the classical model. If it seems obvious to you that an increase in government spending can't increase total productive potential (y^*), that's a good sign.[9] For an economy at full employment, the adage that "you can't spend your way to prosperity" is certainly valid. Scarcity, the root of all economics, intervenes. To be more specific, we saw in Chapter 1 that an increase in government spending at full employment just transfers resources from private to public use. More public goods "crowd out" an equal value of private goods, leaving total output unchanged. Similarly, a permanent cut in taxes increases our personal spending and ends up transferring resources from other uses, typically investment, to consumption.

But what should be surprising to you is that neither an increase in government spending ($+\Delta g$) nor a reduction in taxes ($-\Delta t$) has any effect on the price level, according to the classical model. In discussing "money is a veil" we saw that printing more money didn't alter output, but definitely did push aggregate demand out and prices up. Why wouldn't an expansionary fiscal policy also shift AD to the right? There are several ways to answer this. The simplest is to note that government spending simply doesn't show up in the aggregate demand curve, $y^{AD} = MV/P$. Your next question should be: "Why not?" Isn't there something wrong with the classical model if it implies that expansionary monetary policy shifts aggregate demand out and increases the price level, but fiscal policy has absolutely no effect on either? Keynes certainly thought so, and we'll see why in the next few chapters. But for now just note that as long as we confine our attention to long-run implications, the observed constancy of velocity ensures that neither fiscal policy nor anything else except a change in the money supply can shift aggregate demand. In this sense, then, fiscal policy is said to be powerless.

3. Supply is the Key to Economic Growth

Within a given institutional framework (i^{nst}_0), capital accumulation and technological innovation ($+\Delta k$) and growth in the quality and quantity of the work force ($+\Delta n^*$) are the only forces driving long-run economic growth ($+\Delta y^*$). According to the classical model, economic stagnation comes from failure or inability to expand these inputs. So economic growth comes solely from shifts in aggregate supply, such as that illustrated in Figure 2.9. The outward movement of AS^* forces equilibrium from points A to B as the price level falls, real output increases, and the PPF expands.

In the classical view, then, a higher level of real output is a "supply-side" issue and demand stimulus simply won't help. For example, expansionary monetary policy shifts aggregate demand out, but cannot change the full employment level of output. Put another way, producing pieces of paper and naming them "money" doesn't increase our potential to produce goods and services. If it did, all nations would simply "print" their way to prosperity. Expansionary fiscal policy can have no impact on output (or even *total* demand) because it merely shifts inputs from one sector or use to another (e.g., private to public). In short, neither monetary nor fiscal policy, the two major weapons of macroeconomic policy making, have any impact whatsoever on our

---

[9] To the extent that the increase in government spending is spent on public *capital* goods there may be an effect on both AS^* and PPF. This will be relatively small and slow in coming, and may be offset by other factors. Linkages between demand and supply will be discussed in later chapters.

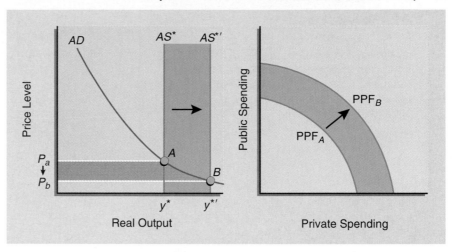

Supply Shifts Change
Both the Price Level and Real Output

■ FIGURE 2.9

standard of living because they do not alter aggregate supply. Slogans and epigrams being easier to remember than theorems or models, think of this result as a reminder that "there's no such thing as a free lunch" or that "you can't spend or print your way to prosperity."

4. Inflation is Caused by the Central Bank

Defining **inflation** as a *continued* rise in the overall price level, we see that in the classical framework this could come either from a continuing leftward shift in aggregate supply, a continuing rightward shift in aggregate demand, or some combination of the two. Negative supply shocks do cause supply to shift left and thereby push up the equilibrium price level. Fortunately, however, we do not live in a world of negative economic growth with *continuing* leftward shifts in supply. Negative supply shocks are occasional events and often are more than offset by the capital accumulation that underlies positive economic growth.

If we can't find the continued leftward supply shifts that would cause inflation, the classical model leaves but one choice—continued growth of the money supply is the only thing that can cause an ongoing long-run rightward shift in aggregate demand. In other words, *inflation is always caused by the failure of the government to control the rate of growth of the money supply.* This is a remarkable conclusion and, if true, a serious indictment of central bankers throughout the world, past and present.

Viewed another way the classical model provides a simple policy prescription for price stability. In the long run, if the money supply increases at the same rate at which aggregate supply is growing, the equilibrium price level will not change. In other words, the central bank needs to control the money supply so that $\%\Delta M = \%\Delta y^*$. This would ensure that both aggregate demand (AD) and aggregate supply

■ FIGURE 2.10

For the price level to stay at P_a as supply grows ($AS^* \rightarrow AS^{*\prime}$), aggregate demand must grow at the same rate (i.e., $\%\Delta AD = \%\Delta AS^*$). In the classical model ("only money matters"), this requires that $\%\Delta M = \%\Delta y^*$.

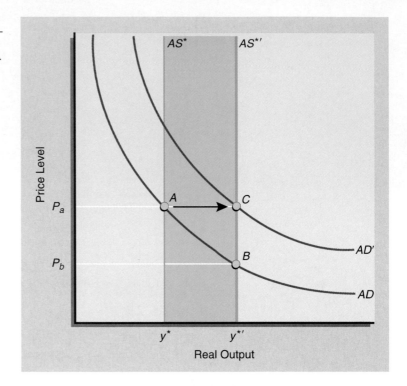

Price Stability
in a Growing Economy

(AS^*) shift at the same rate, leaving the equilibrium level of prices unchanged. Such a result is illustrated in the movement from points A to C in Figure 2.10.

2.6 SUMMARY AND ASSESSMENT

Chapter 1 used the simple notion of the PPF to display some of the ways that scarcity presents itself in the overall economy. Though useful in characterizing the many *choices* that confront us, the PPF said little about the *consequences* stemming from different choices. The present chapter began with a general discussion of "theory" as the indispensable bridge between choices and outcomes. Economic models embody that theory and provide a tool to address important policy questions. We usually think of a model as a scaled-down or simpler version of the real thing. Or it might be a purer, ideal version of reality (as in fashion models). Another metaphor may be even more useful at this point—think of a model as a device for converting questions (What if . . . ?) into answers (Then . . .).

Following a brief survey of the two major theoretical bridges in macroeconomics, Keynesian and classical, this chapter explored the workings of a macroeconomic model that captures the spirit of the classical approach. It's important to appreciate that while the classical tradition has quite a long history, our interest in it is definitely *not* as an early artifact of primitive macroeconomics. It is very much alive today and continues to be revitalized with each successive generation of scholars. Much of the most innovative and technically sophisticated research in macroeconomics in the past quarter century has come from within this tradition. The relatively simple classical model of this chapter is merely a starting point from which to develop the Keynesian alternative and the subsequent advances of both the new classical and new Keynesian economists. So one goal of this chapter has been to serve as a transition from the descriptive material in Chapter 1 to the more specific and precise reasoning that lies at the heart of macroeconomic analysis.

In the classical model we found that full employment of all resources is assured so long as prices and wages are free to adjust to their market-clearing levels. We also determined that the long-run position of aggregate demand in the classical model is firmly in the hands of the central bank ("only money matters"). Because of the vertical aggregate supply curve, however, this control translates into power over the price level rather than real output ("money is a veil"). This result, called "monetary neutrality," is central to the classical view. Rapid growth of the money supply cannot enrich the economy, it tells us. Monetary policy is neutral with respect to real output (y^*), though definitely anything but neutral with respect to the level of prices (P). The responsibility for inflation in a classical world lies squarely with the Central Bank.

Changes in the level of government spending or taxes (fiscal policy) also leave equilibrium real output unchanged at y^*. Unlike monetary changes, however, fiscal policy has no impact on aggregate demand or the price level. Once we are at full employment, any increase in public spending will just reduce private spending by an equal amount, leaving total demand constant. This phenomenon is called "total crowding out" and will be explained carefully in Chapter 4.

What *can* enrich or impoverish the economy in the classical model is a rightward or leftward shift in aggregate supply, which can occur only with changes in capital (Δk) or labor (Δn^*), or a changing institutional structure (Δi^{nst}) that alters the "rules of the game" within which capital and labor operate. For a given institutional structure and fixed capital stock, the market clearing process ensures full employment in competitive labor markets, moving the economy persistently toward AS^*. Whether growth in AS^* is steady, erratic, or absent is entirely independent of events on the demand side of the model.

This model is clearly consistent with the "limited government" attitude of the classical tradition in economics. It is based on the presumed ability of individual markets, working together, to organize economic activity and also to propel and guide the economy to its productive capacity without public intervention. This is the first of many instances in which we'll see a model apparently serving two very different functions at once. The classical macroeconomic model represents a **scientific investigation**—what *can* the government do? But it is often interpreted as a **political conclusion**—what *should* the government do? At this point, we simply note that there is no reason why "can" and "should" must be in agreement. For example, it could be the case that the classical model underestimates the actual power of the government to influence the overall economy. This need not change one's personal preferences about what role the government should play. Just because they "can" do more than the classical structure suggests doesn't mean they "should." Alternatively, to the extent the classical model is correct about the limited powers of government in the overall economy, someone who is predisposed toward using government policy to improve economic well-being can obviously make better policy proposals by understanding these limitations on public actions. Just because you think the government "should" doesn't mean it "can."

This leads to the central question—which model presents the most accurate portrayal of the "real world"? As noted earlier, Keynes believed that the classical model was flawed in its emphasis on long run results and particularly its faith in the powers of the market clearing process to keep an economy from coming to rest below full employment. "It may well be," said Keynes, "that the classical theory represents the way in which we should like our Economy to behave. But to assume that it actually does so is to assume our difficulties away." [10]

Those who have followed in the Keynesian tradition have always focused on unemployment as the Achilles heel of classical economics. Its preoccupation with market clearing seems to prevent it from explaining cyclical unemployment that can persist month after month and even year after year. This dispute is obviously crucial to policy making, and we'll turn to it in detail in later chapters. However, don't let this controversy obscure the equally important fact that the classical model continues to be a very useful and blessedly simple guide to understanding both *inflation* and *long-run economic growth*, as we'll also see in later chapters.

ᏫᏨ 2.7 *OVERVIEW*

1. **Economic theory** is the framework we use to express our opinions about cause-and-effect connections in the economy. It can be as casual as "*if* we do _____, *then* _____ will happen." Or it can be stated more formally and precisely in terms of equations or graphs.

2. Either way, the point is the same—we try to use good sense (logic and whatever clues we can glean from the past) to discern important and continuing relationships within the economy. We want to see if there are some basic, preferably simple, patterns that we can count on in making decisions and policies.

3. Our theories are often embodied in **economic models**—simplified representations of reality that capture essential economic patterns and interactions. A model that works well for one purpose (say, understanding inflation) may not work well for another (forecasting economic growth), so there can be a number of models. In addition, there are often alternative models of the same thing reflecting different judgments as to what are the "essential" variables and relationships and yielding different readings of past experience. "Reality" seldom reveals itself neatly and simply. Much of the appeal of being an economist is to be engaged in the process of trying to combine ingenuity with hard work to discover additional evidence in favor of some models and against others.

4. These models are then used to ask questions ("What if . . .") in the hope that the answers will give us a reasonable picture (simulation) of what would happen if we conducted actual experiments on the actual economy. There are a depressingly large number of ways in which a model can be biased, incomplete, and misleading. But it's important to remember that the alternatives to using a carefully designed model suffer from even more weaknesses and are far less reliable guides to policy. Slogans, dogma, and wishful thinking are poor and costly substitutes to careful analysis.

5. Two basic perspectives dominate current thinking and policy making in macroeconomics and these are embodied in the **classical** and **Keynesian** models. Among their differences, which will emerge more fully in coming chapters, are:

---

[10] Keynes, *The General Theory of Employment, Interest, and Money*, p. 34.

a. Different judgments as to the speed and reliability of **market clearing** in the overall economy.

b. Different views of the appropriate time horizon for policy making, leading to disagreement over the relevance of observed long run (but not short run) regularities in the **velocity** of money.

c. Different individual judgments about the desirability of giving an active economic role to the government rather than putting primary reliance on competitive market forces for attaining our macroeconomic goals, particularly full employment and economic growth.

6. Modern macroeconomics is very much a reaction to the Great Depression of the 1930s, in which industrial economies throughout the world experienced unprecedented levels of unemployment for an extended period. This event led many economists to question the dominant classical model, which had evolved from the framework and tradition of Adam Smith's monumental *Wealth of Nations* (1776). In 1936, John Maynard Keynes (in *The General Theory of Employment, Interest, and Money*) offered an explanation for the crisis of the 1930s and a policy prescription that involved an expanded and active role for the government. Since then, macroeconomics has attempted to improve our understanding of the issue of "what the government *can* do" in a world in which decisions must constantly be made as to "what the government *should* do."

7. The ensuing controversies—some resolved, some not, some unresolvable because they involve personal preferences rather than scientific results—continue to define the activities of macroeconomists and their actions as policy advisers to presidents, legislatures, central banks, international agencies, and corporations. These are not issues that stay quietly within the ivied walls of academia. Like it or not, they affect each of us, every day of our lives. They are debated by experts and novices alike. Often the least informed and least thoughtful hold the strongest opinions on "What this economy needs is. . . !" And sometimes they are in high places and have important policy-making powers. It is often not clear whether disagreements are over objective facts or subjective preferences. Many people cling to theories that have no factual support. Economic analysis tries to create a structure within which these issues can be discussed with the care and responsibility they deserve.

8. Perhaps the most crucial element in the classical model is the reliance put on the process of market clearing. It assumes a quick, complete response of prices and wages to changes in underlying supply and demand factors throughout the economy. Price adjustments ensure that shortages and surpluses are rapidly eliminated. In the labor market, this process means that wage flexibility is sufficient to keep employment at or very near its full employment level. With individual self-interest working like an "invisible hand," the economy is guided quickly and surely to an equilibrium at full employment. All this is assumed and captured in the very simple **vertical aggregate supply curve,** AS^*.

9. The second key element in the classical model is the **Quantity Theory of Money,** which provides a framework for determining total demand in the economy. The Quantity Theory yields a relationship between the price level and total demand that is summarized in the downward sloping aggregate demand (*AD*) curve. Combined with the approximate long-run constancy of the "velocity of money" (roughly, the rate at which dollars change hands), it also implies that the only thing that can shift the *AD* curve is changes in the money supply.

10. Together, market clearing and the Quantity Theory yield a representation of reality called the **classical model.** Using this to simulate the possible effects of actual policy making, we find that our simple model yields the following predictions:

  a. The economy will automatically come to rest at full employment.

  b. The aggregate demand curve can be shifted by changes in the money supply ("only money matters"), but not by changes in government spending or taxes ("fiscal policy is powerless").

  c. Shifts in *AD* change the price level but not output or employment ("money is a veil").

  d. A rising standard of living can only come through events on the supply side, namely, changes in the quality or quantity of labor and capital inputs or a more effective institutional structure.

  e. Only the central bank has the power to cause (or cure) inflation.

✂ 2.8 REVIEW QUESTIONS

1. Define the following basic concepts:

Keynesian economics	Quantity Theory of Money	Policy instrument
Classical economics	Surplus	Say's Law of Markets
John Maynard Keynes	Shortage	"Money is a veil"
The General Theory	Labor market	"Only money matters"
Policy activism	Real wage	"Fiscal policy is
Adam Smith	Money illusion	powerless"
The Wealth of Nations	Aggregate demand	Monetary neutrality
Institutional structure	Velocity of money	Inflation
Market clearing	Price level	

2. Using the classical model of the overall economy, what impact would the following events have on the equilibrium values of the price level and total real output?

   a. An increase in government spending financed by higher taxes.

   b. An increase in government spending financed by printing money.

   c. A substantial increase in the nation's stock of capital.

   d. A simultaneous increase in the capital stock and in the money supply.

3. In Chapter 1 we used the PPF to profile an economy that raised government spending but refused to raise taxes to pay for it. Using the Classical *AD/AS** framework, what impact would such a policy have on the price level and real output? (Remember that there are *two* ways to finance the increase in government spending.)

4. Use the classical macroeconomic model to evaluate the likely impact of a substantial negative supply shock on output and the price level if the government:

   a. Does nothing in response.

   b. Runs an expansionary monetary policy.

   c. Runs an expansionary fiscal policy.

   d. Runs a contractionary monetary policy.

5. Explain how each of the three important slogans below describes an implication of the classical model. In other words, describe the meaning behind the slogan and demonstrate that it is a logical consequence of the assumptions of the classical model.

   a. "Money is a veil."

   b. "Supply creates its own demand."

   c. "Inflation is everywhere and always a monetary phenomenon."

6. Each graduation sees a flood of new job hopefuls entering the labor force. And while there are also retirements, they are usually many fewer. How can the economy keep absorbing this growing labor force year after year? Where will the new jobs come from? Have we just been lucky, or is there some systematic process going on which guarantees, more or less, that a market system will be able to handle a growing labor force?

   Use the classical framework to analyze this in terms of both the demand and supply sides of the model. That is, *will* the new jobs be created and if they are will there be enough *spending* to support this additional production? Explain.

7. Suppose the economy finds itself in a situation in which aggregate demand is well below aggregate supply, resulting in unsold goods and real output below its full employment level. How does the classical model explain the existence of such a situation, and what remedy, if any, would it propose?

8. A key assumption in the classical model is that wages and prices are perfectly flexible, responding quickly to any changes in market conditions. Suppose, instead, that the *money* wage (W) can move upward but not downward while the price level (P) remains flexible.

   a. With the addition of this minimum nominal wage assumption, derive the corresponding aggregate supply curve for this economy.

   b. Using this new supply curve, what impact would a decrease in the money supply have on real output and the price level in this economy?

   c. Some of the major implications of the classical model are listed below. Would the addition of this minimum wage assumption change any of these results? Explain your reasoning.

      • Money is a veil.

      • Full employment prevails.

      • Only money matters.

      • We can't print our way to prosperity.

      • Economic growth can only come from the supply side.

      • Inflation is everywhere and always a monetary phenomenon.

9. Suppose that flexible wages and prices hold, but that "constant velocity of money" is dropped from the classical assumptions. Which of the implications listed in the question above will remain true? Explain your reasoning.

10. Suppose we discover that the economy's aggregate supply curve is actually horizontal in the "short run." Which, if any, of the four basic implications of the classical macroeconomic model would be affected by this change in one of the underlying assumptions of that model? Explain your reasoning.

ভভ 2.9 FURTHER READING

TODD G. BUCHHOLZ, *New Ideas from Dead Economists: An Introduction to Modern Economic Thought* (New York: Penguin/Plume, 1989).

ROBERT HEILBRONER, *The Worldly Philosophers*, 6th ed. (New York: Simon & Schuster, 1986).

JOHN MAYNARD KEYNES, *The General Theory of Employment, Interest, and Money* (London: Macmillan, 1936).

DAVID LAIDLER, *The Golden Age of the Quantity Theory* (Princeton: Princeton University Press, 1991).

HARRY LANDRETH AND DAVID C. COLANDER, *History of Economic Thought*, 3rd ed. (Boston: Houghton Mifflin Company, 1994).

ADAM SMITH, *An Inquiry into the Nature and Causes of the Wealth of Nations* Glasgow ed. of *The Works and Correspondence of Adam Smith*, vols. 1 and 2 (Oxford: Oxford University Press, 1976 [1776]).

PART II

Basic Macroeconomic Analysis

As noted in the last chapter, the activist policy implications of the Keynesian tradition differ markedly from the classical reliance on the self-regulating adjustments of a competitive market system. One implies that it's irresponsible for the government *not* to intervene to improve overall economic performance, particularly during periods of recession in output and employment. The other says such intervention, however well intended, will prove ineffective or even harmful to macroeconomic activity.

Confronted with such a divergence of views, our instinct is to look for a quick resolution—pick one or the other or find a middle ground that incorporates the best of both. There are some good reasons not to make a hasty choice on this issue. You may discover in the coming pages that many of your current views on the government's ability to control economic activity are either wrong or only partially correct. To the extent that you can keep an open mind until you have acquired more knowledge and analytical skills, the process of learning macroeconomic analysis will not only be faster and more enjoyable, but you'll end up with a stronger foundation and a deeper understanding of the enduring issues.

You might find it helpful to think of the policy-making process as similar to a criminal case. It must begin with a careful **analytical investigation** of the evidence before proceeding to a **judgment** about guilt and appropriate punishment.[1] Before we can reach a responsible choice among policy options we must do a careful investigation of how the macroeconomy works. Ultimately, you will be chief investigator, judge, and jury. It will be your responsibility to make policy choices based on your knowledge of macroeconomic cause and effect and on your subjective preferences among various, often competing, economic goals.

The next five chapters provide your basic training as an investigator. They develop and begin to apply a macroeconomic model that incorporates both the short-run Keynesian concern with unemployment and the longer-run classical focus on issues of market clearing, inflation, and economic growth. Such a synthesis of Keynesian and classical models has taken various forms and been given many names over the years. We'll simply call it an "expanded macroeconomic model" to indicate that it provides a comprehensive framework that can encompass the Keynesian "activist" policy tradition, the "nonactivist" classical tradition, and many other positions along the policy spectrum.

---

[1] For those who like to combine economic analysis with murder mysteries, there are at least three novels to turn to—Kim Hill and Owen Dale, *Death on Demand*, rev. ed. (Sun Lakes, Ariz.: Thomas Horton & Daughters, 1988); Murray Wolfson and Vincent Buranelli, *In the Long Run We Are All Dead: A Macroeconomics Murder Mystery*, 2nd ed. (New York: St. Martin's Press, 1990); and Marshall Jevons, *Murder on the Margin* (Sun Lakes, Ariz.: Thomas Horton & Daughters, 1977).

CHAPTER 3

THE KEYNESIAN MODEL OF AGGREGATE DEMAND

⚭ 3.1 INTRODUCTION

The classical tradition provided an analysis of the determinants of output in which the supply side (capital, labor, and the institutional structure underlying the production process) predominated over demand (spending, money supply, and government fiscal actions) in explaining overall economic activity. This was a widely accepted framework that John Maynard Keynes initially embraced but came to scorn. His four-sentence opening chapter is blunt.

> *I have called this book the* General Theory of Employment, Interest, and Money, *placing the emphasis on the prefix* general. *The object of such a title is to contrast the character of my arguments and conclusions with those of the* classical *theory of the subject, upon which I was brought up and which dominates the economic thought, both practical and theoretical, of the governing and academic classes of this generation, as it has for a hundred years past. I shall argue that the postulates of the classical theory are applicable to a special case only and not to the general case, the situation which it assumes being a limiting point of the possible positions of equilibrium. Moreover, the characteristics of the special case assumed by the classical theory happen not to be those of the economic society in which we actually live, with the result that its teaching is misleading and disastrous if we attempt to apply it to the facts of experience.*[1]

What so many have believed for so long, asserts Keynes, holds true only under particular circumstances that no longer exist. He claims that the policy implications of this outdated model are destructive when applied to the economic reality of his day.

Keynes was just one of many to attack the classical view of the overall economy. Why his judgment was so much more influential than the others is a complicated question. Certainly a main factor was its innovative analytical

---

[1] Keynes, The *General Theory of Employment, Interest, and Money,* p. 3.

structure—one that focused on the significance of aggregate *demand* in the determination of the "wealth of nations." Disciples, opponents, and the undecided vote of his generation generally agreed that, whatever its merits, Keynesian economics was a distinct break from the past. Eventually a sizable majority of economists were joined by opinion leaders, policy makers, and the media in proclaiming the "Keynesian Revolution." With more than half a century of hindsight and, especially, with the resurgence of the classical tradition over the past 30 years, Keynes's work now seems less radical to most economists, less of a break from the classical path. But it is still a departure and his analytical framework continues to structure our thinking about the macroeconomy.

In the last chapter we saw that aggregate demand was quite unimportant in the classical system. Only changes in the money supply could alter demand ("only money matters" while "fiscal policy is powerless"), yet even this had no impact on output and employment ("money is a veil"), which stay at their full employment levels in equilibrium ("full employment prevails"). With demand playing such a minor role, little attention was paid to its underlying determinants. But as we adjust our focus from the longer run classical equilibria to short-run adjustments, we discover that velocity and, therefore, aggregate demand is not always the passive, domesticated creature of the Quantity Theory. Hence, the classical model's reliance on constant velocity may no longer offer the best route to understanding the determinants of aggregate demand. This chapter presents the elements of Keynes's alternative approach to the demand side of the macroeconomy, explained within the expository framework developed by another famed British economist, Nobel laureate John Hicks (1904–1989).[2]

✆ 3.2 WHAT IS "AGGREGATE DEMAND"?

Before beginning our search for a theory of aggregate demand, let's make sure we know what we're after. The concept of aggregate demand has four important characteristics:

1. *Aggregate demand includes only the demand for "final" goods and services during a certain interval of time, such as a year.* Because our focus is on the goods and services that make up our standard of living, we want to be sure to include each relevant item once and only once. This is an obvious point but requires some attention simply because the production process for most products occurs in a series of steps. We want to include the production of automobiles, computers, and bread, but not separately count the **intermediate goods** (steel, silicon chips, flour) that are already included in **final output.** By counting demand only at its final stage of production and sale,

---

[2] Hicks's interpretation of the General Theory ("Mr. Keynes and the 'Classics'; a Suggested Interpretation," *Econometrica*, 1937, Vol. 5, No. 1, pp. 147–159) was set in what he labeled the *IS-LM* model. Although this framework is exceedingly useful, it is important to remember that it is incomplete (e.g., it only looks at demand, not supply) and even when joined to a model of aggregate supply, makes some simplifications that limit its applicability. Like any approximation to the complex reality of macroeconomic events, it needs to be used carefully.

the value of intermediate products is automatically included and they must not be counted again as separate items.[3]

2. *Aggregate demand represents the demand for final goods and services produced in a particular economy.* Aggregate demand for U.S. output must include the demand for our exports by other countries but exclude our demand for their output. The way this is done in practice is to first count *all* spending by U.S. citizens, businesses, and governments on final goods and services regardless of where they were produced. Then we add in foreign demand for our exports but also subtract that portion of our total spending that went for imports. This is done through a **net exports** variable—exports minus imports, which we denote by the symbol x. To get *total* demand for U.S. output, then, we add net exports to total spending on consumption, investment, and government output. For the United States, net exports have been a large negative number for more than a decade.

3. *Aggregate demand is measured in monetary units such as dollars or francs or yen.* Money represents a common unit of measure that can be applied to such diverse objects as bushels of grain, gallons of milk, and miles of flight. But unlike other units of measure, monetary units change "length" over time because of inflation. As a result, comparisons across the years (e.g., comparing the federal deficit in 1990 with 1980) must be done in **constant dollars** if they are to have any economic meaning. This requires the use of a **price index** (basically the average level of prices denoted by P in the previous chapter) to adjust for changes in the unit of measure. It also raises a number of conceptual and practical problems in measurement that are better appreciated after you have a good grasp of the analytical issues. They will be discussed in Chapter 15, "Models and Measurement."

4. *Aggregate demand for final output is the same thing as aggregate income.* For the whole economy, every dollar spent on final goods and services must also be a dollar received by someone as income. No unclaimed dollars are left lying around. If we denote total spending and total income as $P \cdot y^{AD}$ and $P \cdot y$, respectively, this says that they are equal and, dividing (deflating) both by P, that *real* income equals *real* aggregate demand, $y = y^{AD}$. In the next chapter we will add the market-clearing condition that aggregate demand and supply must be equal, i.e., $y^{AD} = y^{AS}$. In anticipation of this, we can make things simpler by using the symbol "y" to represent all three concepts—total real income, total real demand, and total real supply of output. Note the adjective "real," reflecting the fact that for now we are correcting for any changes in the price level resulting from inflation and focusing on the underlying "quantities" of output that determine our economic well-being. In other words, we assume that purely "inflationary" changes in income or spending resulting from a changing price level have been eliminated.

---

[3] One qualification needs to be made. Total demand for final goods does include one type of "intermediate" output—investment spending. The value of these new capital goods will eventually show up in the future consumption goods and services that they produce. To avoid double-counting, we deduct a capital consumption allowance (often called depreciation) as this capital is used up and transformed into other final goods and services over the years. Ultimately, the original investment expenditure is completely offset by deductions for capital consumption. The net result of putting investment in now and taking it out later is simply to alter the *timing* of measured output to give a more accurate reflection of current economic activity year by year.

Having defined aggregate demand, we turn to the more difficult task of explaining its changes over time. In other words, we move from a definition to a theory of total demand. Following Keynes, we set aside the quantity theory of money approach to aggregate demand. Instead we formulate four hypotheses about what factors influence **planned** (or **equilibrium**) **spending:** one for each of the four categories of aggregate demand—consumption (c), investment (i), net exports (x), and government (g).[4] Aggregate demand, then, can be written as

$$y = c + i + x + g \qquad \text{(Equilibrium condition)}$$

Together, the hypotheses about the four terms on the right-hand side will form the basis of a model of equilibrium aggregate demand that is more powerful than the classical demand theory of the previous chapter but also more complex. To keep it from getting too complicated, too quickly, let's start with the simplifying assumption that three of the four components of total demand are constant. We'll focus on consumption spending (c) as we pretend that spending on investment, net exports, and government is fixed at the values i_0, x_0, and g_0, respectively. This pretense of constancy is dropped in just a few pages.

3.3 THE CONSUMPTION FUNCTION

A multitude of factors influence total consumption demand for the whole economy in a given year. To avoid becoming mired in details, we note that spending on current consumption is limited by our available purchasing power, which, in turn, depends on our lifetime income stream—our past, present, and future income. *Past income* can influence current consumption through accumulated savings (net worth), whereas *future income* can be used to the extent that we can borrow on it, consuming now and paying back later.

As important as past or future earnings might be in determining our current consumption spending, the Keynesian explanation of consumption puts the emphasis on the role of our *present* after-tax earnings, sometimes called "current disposable income." In a later chapter we will build on this lifetime view in which saving and borrowing, via **capital markets,** combine to moderate the influence of current economic events and policies on consumption spending. For now, though, we follow Keynes and emphasize the connection between *current* consumption (c) and *current* after-tax income ($y - t$), in what he termed the **consumption function:**

$$c = c_0 + c_1(y - t), \qquad \text{(Consumption function)}$$

where $c_0 > 0$
and $0 < c_1 < 1$

The c_0 and c_1 terms are called **coefficients** or **parameters** and are symbols that represent particular numerical values.[5]

---

[4] What if unanticipated events frustrate our *planned* levels of spending? For example, unexpectedly poor sales would leave businesses with an unplanned increase in inventories, a capital investment that was not desired. This deviation from the planned or **equilibrium** level of spending is assumed to lead to revised spending plans for the next year and, barring further unforeseen events, a return to equilibrium or intended levels. Therefore, $y = c + i + x + g$ is the equation for the **equilibrium level of aggregate demand** in the economy. For now we assume that such deviations from equilibrium are relatively small and quickly corrected.

[5] Specific values of c_0 and c_1 can be estimated from past data using techniques such as least squares regression. This process of converting our economic models into econo*metric* models is discussed in Chapter 15.

Like all equations, the consumption function is a sentence, expressed in the compact language of algebra. It emphasizes the relationship between current consumption and current after-tax income and their linkage through the parameter c_1, called the **marginal propensity to consume.** Other determinants of current consumption spending—past income, future income, and everything else—are all lumped together in the c_0 term. This is called **autonomous consumption,** "autonomous" in the sense that it stands by itself, independent of the influence of after-tax income. Keeping the focus on the short run for now, we assume that c_0 and c_1 are both constant so that the sole determinant of changes in current consumption spending is changes in current after-tax income.

To get an idea of the workings of the consumption function, note that if after-tax real income increases, real consumption will increase by the fraction c_1 times $\Delta(y - t)$.[6] The remainder of that increase in income, the fraction $(1 - c_1)\Delta(y - t)$, is defined as current real saving and denoted by the symbol s. For example, if the marginal propensity to consume (c_1) is .9 and after-tax income rises by \$100, then the change in consumption is given by $\Delta c = c_1 \Delta(y - t) = .9(\$100) = \$90$. A \$100 increase in current disposable income causes current consumption to rise by \$90. The remaining \$10 $[(1 - c_1)\Delta(y - t) = (1 - .9)100 = .1(100)]$ goes into current saving, making it available for future consumption. A lower value of c_1 would describe a weaker link between current consumption and current income, so that a smaller share of any increase in after-tax income would go into current consumption but a larger share into current saving.[7]

IN SUMMARY . . .

The Consumption Function

Current consumption demand depends on many factors, particularly *current income* (after taxes) as well as savings from the past and borrowing on the future. The Keynesian consumption function, $c = c_0 + c_1(y - t)$, captures the following four important characteristics:

1. Current consumption changes in the same direction as current after-tax income but not by as much because the two are connected by the fraction c_1.

2. Because consumption is assumed to depend on after-tax income, it responds identically to either a change in income or a change in taxes.

3. The part of any change in after-tax income that does *not* go into consumption is added to current saving. That is, $\Delta s = (1 - c_1)\Delta(y - t)$, where $(1 - c_1)$ is the fraction of after-tax income that is saved.

4. All determinants of consumption other than after-tax income are grouped together in the autonomous consumption term, c_0.

---

[6] Because $c = c_0 + c_1(y - t)$, then a change in after-tax income $[\Delta(y - t)]$ must alter both sides of the equation. We can write this as $c + \Delta c = c_0 + c_1[(y - t) + \Delta(y - t)]$. Multiplying out and canceling leaves us with $\Delta c = c_1 \Delta(y - t)$. Put another way, the first derivative of consumption with respect to after-tax income is equal to c_1, i.e., $dc/d(y - t) = c_1$.

[7] By convention, "saving" is the part of *current* income that we set aside, whereas the plural "savings" refers to accumulated saving over the years, e.g., from past saving. Saving in any particular year can, of course, be negative if we consume more than our current income by drawing on past saving or borrowing from future income.

🕮 *3.4 THE "MULTIPLIER" PROCESS*

We have seen that the equilibrium aggregate demand equation is $y = c + i + x + g$. This tells us that current income depends, in part, on current consumption spending ($+\Delta c \Rightarrow +\Delta y$), whereas the consumption function, $c = c_0 + c_1(y - t)$, says that current consumption spending depends, in part, on current income ($+\Delta y \Rightarrow +\Delta c$). This *two-way interaction* between consumption and income probably seems pretty obvious, and you may wonder why we have to substitute equations for ordinary common sense. The reason is one that will become increasingly apparent as we begin to make the analysis more realistic: When there are two or more interdependent events, understanding their cumulative effects can quickly exceed the important but quite limited powers of "common sense."

To see the significance of this mutual causality between consumption and income, suppose government spending is increased, and we want to predict what affect this will have on aggregate demand (y). Continuing the simplifying assumption that investment, net exports, government spending, and taxes are known and constant, we have the following information about aggregate demand:

$$y = c + i + x + g \qquad \text{(Equilibrium condition)} \qquad (1)$$
$$c = c_0 + c_1(y - t) \qquad \text{(Consumption function)} \qquad (2)$$
$$t = t_0 \qquad \text{(Taxes)} \qquad (3)$$
$$i = i_0 \qquad \text{(Investment demand)} \qquad (4)$$
$$x = x_0 \qquad \text{(Net export demand)} \qquad (5)$$
$$g = g_0 \qquad \text{(Government demand)} \qquad (6)$$

This is a six-equation model or, equivalently, a six sentence "story" about what determines the level of aggregate demand. Our focus is on the interaction between the first two equations, keeping the other four "constants" in the background for the moment.

A given increase in government spending ($+\Delta g$) will cause total demand to rise by the same amount ($+\Delta y = +\Delta g$), according to equation 1. But the consumption function tells us that this increase in income raises after-tax income and thereby increases consumption spending by a fraction (c_1) of the increased income, i.e., $\Delta c = c_1 \Delta (y - t)$. It is at this point that the feedback begins as the increased consumption spending causes another increase in income ($+\Delta y' = +\Delta c = c_1 \Delta (y - t)$) and raises income a second time. This boost in disposable income will, in turn, increase consumption again, then income, then consumption, and so on as the first two equations reinforce one another through what is aptly called the **multiplier process.**

The "multiplier" might be likened to a game of tag or a cat chasing its tail. Alternatively, we could emphasize its cumulative potential and portray it as an avalanche or even a nuclear chain reaction. Which, if any, of these images describes the final economic impact of the increase in government spending on aggregate demand? To see which pattern, or metaphor, we're dealing with here let's return to the primary metaphor in economics—algebra. Remember that metaphor works by treating an unfamiliar "this" as if it's a more familiar "that." Using the operations of algebra as an analogue ("that") for economic events ("this"), we solve this model of total demand by substituting the last five equations into the first.

$$y = c + i + x + g \tag{1}$$
$$c = c_0 + c_1(y - t) \tag{2}$$
$$t = t_0 \tag{3}$$
$$i = i_0 \tag{4}$$
$$x = x_0 \tag{5}$$
$$g = g_0 \tag{6}$$

Substituting and solving for aggregate demand/income

$$y = c_0 + c_1(y - t_0) + i_0 + x_0 + g_0$$
$$y = c_0 + c_1y - c_1t_0 + i_0 + x_0 + g_0$$
$$y - c_1y = c_0 - c_1t_0 + i_0 + x_0 + g_0$$
$$(1 - c_1)y = c_0 - c_1t_0 + i_0 + x_0 + g_0$$
$$y = [1/(1 - c_1)](c_0 - c_1t_0 + i_0 + x_0 + g_0)$$

More concisely, we can write the solution for y as

$$y = \mu_0(z_0 + g_0 - c_1t_0), \qquad \text{(Solution [IS] equation)}$$

where $\qquad \mu_0 = 1/(1 - c_1)$

and $\qquad z_0 = c_0 + i_0 + x_0$

This solution equation condenses all the information from the six-sentence "story" of aggregate demand into a single "sentence." It's traditionally called the **IS equation,** following the original derivation by John Hicks (1937), which used an equivalent framework that started from investment and saving, hence *I* and *S*. The text box on the next page shows the solution in numerical terms to reinforce the basic mechanics of this model.

Let's now use these equations to get at the multiplier process through which an initial increase in government spending touches off a series of interactions between consumption and income. Starting with the numerical values given in the text box, suppose there's an increase in government spending from $80 billion to $100 billion. What happens to the level of aggregate demand/income? Because of the interdependence embodied in the first two equations, the rise in government spending triggers a sequence of events in which the initial $+\Delta g = 20$ increases demand by 20, with 18 (.9 of 20) going into consumption and the remaining 2 (.1 of 20) to saving. This increase in consumption spending means another increase in income, this time by 18, which, in turn, will increase saving by 1.8 (.1 of 18), with the remaining 16.2 (.9 of 18) going to consumption. This increased consumption spending then increases income by another 16.2, which causes consumption to rise by 14.58 (.9 of 16.2), and on and on. The sum total of all the increases in spending/income will be the initial 20 plus a succession of increments that are each 90% (the part of income that goes into consumption) of the previous change: $20 + .9(20) + .9(.9)(20) + (.9)(.9)(.9)(20) + \ldots = 20 + 18 + 16.2 + 14.58 + \ldots$ and so on.

SOLVING THE SIX-EQUATION DEMAND MODEL: NUMERICAL SOLUTION

Suppose a statistical study reveals that aggregate consumption for the whole nation can be reliably, if not exactly, predicted as $10 billion plus 90% of current after-tax income. Also assume we can make good guesses at this year's level of tax revenues ($80 billion), investment spending ($30 billion), government spending ($80 billion), and net exports ($−8 billion). Incorporating this information into our model of aggregate demand, we solve for the equilibrium values of income and consumption.

$$y = c + i + x + g \tag{1}$$
$$c = 10 + .9(y - t) \tag{2}$$
$$t = 80 \tag{3}$$
$$i = 30 \tag{4}$$
$$x = -8 \tag{5}$$
$$g = 80 \tag{6}$$

Substituting into the first equation yields,

$$y = 10 + .9(y - 80) + 30 - 8 + 80$$
$$y = 112 + .9y - 72$$
$$.1y = 40$$
$$y = 400$$

This says that the only value of total demand (y) that satisfies all six equations is $400 billion. We can then solve for the value of consumption by substituting into the second equation:

$$c = 10 + .9(y - t)$$
$$c = 10 + .9(400 - 80)$$
$$c = 298$$

The obvious question is how to get to the end of this sequence of interactions to determine the size of the multiplier effect. This is where some basic algebraic results can be a welcome companion to common sense. Continuing the numerical example in the box above, let's solve the six equations together again, but this time with $g = 100$ rather than the initial 80. The result is

$$y = 10 + .9(y - 80) + 30 - 8 + 100$$
$$y = 132 + .9y - 72$$
$$.1y = 60$$
$$y = 600$$

When government spending was 80, we found that total demand was 400. The increase in government spending from 80 to 100 ($+\Delta g = 20$) has increased total income from 400 to 600 ($+\Delta y = 200$). So the cumulative effect of all those increments (20 + 18 + 16.2 + . . .) turns out to be 600 − 400 = 200. In other words, the initial change was magnified tenfold through the consumption/income interaction of the multiplier, telling us that the value of the multiplier is $\Delta y/\Delta g = 200/20 = 10$.

Referring back to our earlier list of potential metaphors for the multiplier process, it did not explode to infinity or chase its own tail forever. Instead, the size of the consumption/income interaction gradually dwindled away but left behind a siz-

A SHORTCUT TO THE MULTIPLIER

To determine that the multiplier in our example was 10, we had to solve the model twice, once with $g = 80$ and then with $g = 100$. Then we compared the resulting change in total spending/income (Δy) with the initial change in government spending (Δg). Fortunately, there's a *much* simpler way to find the size of the multiplier that doesn't require us to solve and then resolve the entire six equation model.

Remember that the general solution is given by the *IS* equation

$$y = \mu_0(z_0 + g_0 - c_1 t_0),$$

where $$\mu_0 = 1/(1 - c_1) \text{ and } z_0 = c_0 + i_0 + x_0$$

To see what happens to equilibrium income when government spending changes, we can just add Δg_0 to the original g_0 on the right-hand side, knowing that the left-hand side will then change by some amount Δy. Therefore,

$$y + \Delta y = \mu_0[z_0 + (g_0 + \Delta g_0) - c_1 t_0]$$

or $$y + \Delta y = \mu_0(z_0 + g_0 - c_1 t_0) + \mu_0 \Delta g_0$$

and canceling gives

$$\Delta y = \mu_0 \Delta g_0 \qquad \text{(Multiplier equation)}$$

hence, $$\Delta y/\Delta g_0 = \mu_0 \qquad \text{(Spending multiplier)}$$

What have we discovered here? Without using any specific numbers, we have derived a useful general result: *When government spending changes, the equilibrium value of income will change by the amount* $\mu_0 \Delta g_0$. Because $\mu_0 = 1/(1 - c_1)$ and $0 < c_1 < 1$, then μ_0 must take a value greater than 1, and it represents the value of the demand-side spending multiplier. Therefore, we need know only the value of c_1 to determine the impact of a given change in government spending on total spending/income. Applied to our numerical example, the initial $20 billion increase in spending will ultimately increase total demand by

$$\Delta y = \mu_0(\Delta g_0) = [1/(1 - c_1)](\Delta g_0) = [1/(1 - .9)](20)$$
$$\Delta y = (1/.1)(20) = 10(20)$$

able cumulative jump in the overall level of demand. A \$20 billion increase in government spending set off a series of events that eventually increased aggregate demand from \$400 billion to \$600 billion, a tenfold increase in the initial spending change.

The basic idea of the multiplier process should now be clear. The consumption/income interaction magnifies a given increase in spending because that spending becomes someone's income, a fraction of which becomes new spending, which, in turn, generates more income and so on. This was illustrated with a numerical example, followed by the general result that the size of the multiplier depends on the "marginal propensity to consume," the fraction (c_1) of a change in after-tax income that goes into consumption spending. We saw that for $c_1 = .9$, the size of the multiplier was 10. But if the marginal propensity to consume dropped to $c_1 = .8$, the multiplier would decline to $\mu_0 = 1/(1 - c_1) = 5$. If we consumed only half of any increment to our income, this $c_1 = .5$ would yield a multiplier of 2. As a smaller fraction of a change in our income goes into consumption (hence, more into saving) the consumption/income interaction is diminished and the multiplier reduced in size.

We've derived the multiplier in response to a specific question: What impact will an increase in government spending have on total income/spending in our six-equation model of aggregate demand? But the multiplier concept can be applied far beyond this particular example. Returning to the algebra (but remembering that it's just a tool for establishing *economic* results), let's look at three further implications of the multiplier.

■ THE MULTIPLIER WORKS IN *BOTH* DIRECTIONS

The multiplier equation $\Delta y = \mu_0 \Delta g_0$ makes no distinction between an increase and a decrease in government spending. This algebraic symmetry has a potentially very significant implication when applied to the macroeconomy. A cut in government spending, for example, will decrease total spending/income by a *multiple* of the initial change in demand. If, as Keynes believed, this drop in total demand causes a short-run decline in real output, then this model may be able to identify the causes and cures for periods of economic recession.

■ *ANY* CHANGE IN SPENDING WILL SET OFF THE MULTIPLIER PROCESS

In our example, the interaction between consumption and income was initiated by a change in government spending. But it could just as well have been a change in any of the components of *autonomous private spending*, i.e., Δc_0, Δi_0, or Δx_0. To see this, we return to the solution of the six-equation model of demand, shown in the *IS* equation.

$$y = \mu_0(z_0 + g_0 - c_1 t_0) \qquad \text{(Solution [\textit{IS}] equation)}$$

We previously derived the multiplier by asking what would happen to total spending (y) if we increased government spending by the amount Δg_0. Now let's ask what happens if there's a change in any of the three components of autonomous private spending ($z_0 = c_0 + i_0 + x_0$). We simply repeat the process of adding in something (this time Δz_0) on the right-hand side of the *IS* equation, then solving for the value of the balancing Δy on the left-hand side.

$$y + \Delta y = \mu_0[(z_0 + \Delta z_0) + g_0 - c_1 t_0]$$
$$y + \Delta y = \mu_0(z_0 + g_0 - c_1 t_0) + \mu_0 \Delta z_0, \text{ and canceling gives}$$
$$\Delta y = \mu_0 \Delta z_0,$$

where
$$\mu_0 = 1/(1 - c_1) \text{ and } z_0 = c_0 + i_0 + x_0$$

This tells us that the multiplier applies to *any* change in aggregate demand, public (g) or private ($c + i + x$). It also raises the possibility of a countercyclical increase in government spending ($+ \Delta g_0$) to offset the economy-wide consequences of a drop in private demand ($- \Delta z_0$). Remember that the potential for *countercyclical fiscal actions* never arose in the classical model where aggregate demand was determined entirely by the money supply and the supposedly constant velocity of money.

■ *TAX CHANGES* ALSO HAVE A MULTIPLIER EFFECT ON TOTAL DEMAND

The consumption function ($c = c_0 + c_1(y - t)$) assumes that changes in taxes alter after-tax income and, hence, consumption. Because this change in consumption also affects income ($y = c + i + x + g$), it also triggers a multiplier process. The algebra of this is again straightforward. In the solution equation (*IS*) we now ask what happens to total demand (y) if we change the level of taxes (t_0).

$$y = \mu_0(z_0 + g_0 - c_1 t_0) \qquad \text{(Solution [\textit{IS}] equation)}$$

Adding the amount Δt_0 to the initial level of taxes and balancing it with Δy,

$$y + \Delta y = \mu_0[z_0 + g_0 - c_1(t_0 + \Delta t_0)]$$

we then multiply through and cancel to get

$$y + \Delta y = \mu_0(z_0 + g_0 - c_1 t_0) - \mu_0 c_1 \Delta t_0,$$
$$\Delta y = -c_1 \mu_0 \Delta t_0 \text{ and} \qquad \text{(Tax multiplier equation)}$$
$$\Delta y / \Delta t_0 = -c_1 \mu_0 \qquad \text{(Tax multiplier)}$$

Routine algebra, unexciting at best, has revealed an important result that would otherwise be difficult to spot. The **tax multiplier** ($\Delta y / \Delta t_0 = -c_1 \mu_0$) turns out to be a fraction (c_1) of the expenditure multiplier (μ_0) and works in the opposite direction. For example, if $c_1 = .9$ so that the expenditure multiplier (μ_0) was 10, then a $10 billion increase in public or private spending (Δg_0 or Δz_0) will increase total demand by $100 billion. In contrast, a $10 billion increase in taxes will lead to a $90 billion drop in demand. The higher taxes *reduce* consumption and set off a downward multiplier process. But the total effect is smaller in absolute value ($90 rather than $100) because only a fraction (c_1) of the initial tax change goes into spending changes.

A word of caution is appropriate here. The discovery of a tax-multiplier lurking inside our model is correct and important. But don't forget that this is a quite simple, uncomplicated model compared with the reality it describes. In later chapters we'll see some good reasons to suspect that this model overestimates, perhaps greatly, the power of current tax changes to affect aggregate demand.[8]

ᏸᎾᏸ 3.5 REFINING THE MULTIPLIER

The multiplier process exists because a fraction of any increase in after-tax income is spent on consumption, which, in turn, increases income and so on in an interplay of forces between the first two equations in the demand model. The larger the marginal propensity to consume (c_1), the larger the multiplier. An increase in income in our model either goes into consumption, feeding the multiplier process, or it exits the "spending stream" and implicitly goes into saving. Saving, then, can be thought of as a "leakage" from the current flow of spending. The smaller the marginal propensity to consume, the larger this leakage and, hence, the smaller the multiplier.

In reality, there are other important leakages from the spending stream and the failure to include them results in a significant overestimate of the size of the multiplier. Like saving, they reduce the fraction of an increase in income that goes into current consumption (of domestic goods) and, thereby, lower the size of the multiplier. Two of these additional leakages are particularly significant—**income taxes** and **imports.**

We saw that each round of the multiplier adds an increment to income. Taxes (t_0) were assumed to be given and unchanging. So changes in income through the multiplier didn't alter the amount of taxes. In the "real world," the existence of an **income tax** means that each part of each round of the multiplier is diverted to taxes and, therefore, is a leakage from the consumption/income dynamics of the multiplier process. We incorporate this into our analysis by rewriting the tax equation as

$$t = t_0 + t_1 y, \qquad \text{(Tax function)}$$

where $\qquad t_0 > 0$

and $\qquad 0 < t_1 < 1$

As before, t represents this year's total tax revenues but is now divided into two parts. The t_0 term represents the level of all *nonincome taxes*, such as sales and property taxes. The $t_1 y$ term shows the amount of revenue generated by the income tax, because y is before-tax total income, and t_1 is the income tax rate.[9]

As the above tax function reveals, an increase in income raises tax revenues by $t_1 \Delta y$. For example, if the income tax rate is 20% ($t_1 = .20$), then an increase in income of $2000 will create $400 in additional taxes, leaving $1600, rather than $2000, to be split between saving and consumption. As each increment in consumption creates another increase in income, 20% will be siphoned off the top for taxes, reducing the multiplier accordingly.

---

[8] As a preview, remember from Chapter 1 that lowering taxes now simply means higher taxes later, assuming government spending is unchanged. If such a tax *cut* is viewed as just a tax *postponement*, people may not increase current consumption very much, if at all. Put another way, a cut in current taxes would stimulate consumption only if people were economically "nearsighted" and ignored the *fact* that a tax cut now must be paid back later plus interest.

[9] This equation embodies a constant income tax rate, called a *proportional* or *flat* tax. A *progressive* income tax system, in which the tax *rate* rises with the income level, is more realistic but also more complicated to handle. We keep the simpler assumption because it yields virtually the same analytical and policy conclusions.

In addition to generating taxes, an increase in income also results in more consumption of both domestic and *imported* goods. Because this last part is not a demand for U.S. output, it represents another leakage from the U.S. expenditure stream. It shows up in the first equation ($y = c + i + x + g$) as a reduction in net exports ($-\Delta x$). We can express this inverse relationship between net exports and income by expanding the net export equation as follows:

$$x = x_0 - x_1 y, \qquad \text{(Net export function)}$$

where x_0 can take any sign

and
$$0 < x_1 < 1$$

So x represents net export demand (exports minus imports), x_1 (sometimes called the "marginal propensity to import") is the fraction of an increase in our income that is spent on other countries' products, and x_0 ("autonomous" net exports) represents everything that influences net export spending other than current income. This equation shows that an increase in income reduces net exports, causing a further leakage from spending on U.S. goods of the amount $x_1 \Delta y$.

How can we adjust our multiplier to include these two additional leakages from the spending stream? Intuitively, the situation is not hard to understand. The interaction between changes in consumption and changes in income that comprises the multiplier is now diminished by leakages out of domestic consumption due to saving, income taxes, and imports. It takes only a little more work to find the actual size of this new multiplier. Adding the revised tax and net export equations into the six equations gives us the following more realistic model of the demand for output, y.

$$y = c + i + x + g \qquad (1)$$
$$c = c_0 + c_1(y - t) \qquad (2)$$
$$t = t_0 + t_1 y \qquad (3)$$
$$i = i_0 \qquad (4)$$
$$x = x_0 - x_1 y \qquad (5)$$
$$g = g_0 \qquad (6)$$

Again taking advantage of the relative simplicity of algebra (compared to handling all these interactions in words), we substitute the last five equations into the first and solve for total demand/income (y).

$$y = c_0 + c_1[y - (t_0 + t_1 y)] + i_0 + x_0 - x_1 y + g_0$$
$$y = c_0 + c_1 y - c_1 t_0 - c_1 t_1 y + i_0 + x_0 - x_1 y + g_0$$
$$y - c_1 y + c_1 t_1 y + x_1 y = c_0 - c_1 t_0 + i_0 + x_0 + g_0$$
$$y(1 - c_1 + c_1 t_1 + x_1) = c_0 - c_1 t_0 + i_0 + x_0 + g_0$$
$$y = [1/(1 - c_1 + c_1 t_1 + x_1)](c_0 - c_1 t_0 + i_0 + x_0 + g_0)$$

and, more concisely,

$$y = \mu(z_0 + g_0 - c_1 t_0), \qquad \text{(Solution [IS] equation)}$$

where, as before, we still have

$$z_0 = c_0 + i_0 + x_0,$$

but the multiplier is now

$$\mu = 1/(1 - c_1 + c_1 t_1 + x_1)$$

This is the solution of a more realistic model of aggregate demand, incorporating the dependence of taxes and net exports on the level of income. We have again condensed a six sentence story about aggregate demand into a single sentence. In other words, we have derived a new *IS* equation that incorporates a more complete and realistic treatment of taxes and imports.

Notice that the only difference between this new solution and the earlier one is that we now have μ rather than μ_0 for the multiplier term. How do they differ? Intuitively, we know that since two additional leakages have been added, the new multiplier must be smaller. A look at the algebra confirms this, because $\mu = 1/(1 - c_1 + c_1 t_1 + x_1)$ has a larger denominator than $\mu_0 = 1/(1 - c_1)$, thereby reducing its size.[10] To get an idea of how significant the inclusion of tax and import leakages can be in the multiplier process, let's put in some numbers. Recall that when $c_1 = .9$, the earlier multiplier was $1/(1 - .9) = 10$. But if $t_1 = .25$ and $x_1 = .075$, we now find a substantially reduced multiplier effect with $\mu = 2.5$.

IN SUMMARY . . .

The Multiplier Process

The multiplier reflects a two-way interaction between changes in income and changes in consumption. They feed one another, magnifying the overall impact of any change in aggregate demand on the economy. The ultimate size of this magnification depends on the size of the leakages from the spending stream that occur with each round of increased income—increased saving, higher tax payments, and more purchases of foreign goods and services. Specifically, the size of the multiplier is given by $\mu = 1/(1 - c_1 + c_1 t_1 + x_1)$. Its impact on total spending/income is captured in the expression $y = \mu(z_0 + g_0 - c_1 t_0)$, in which any change in private or public spending (Δz_0 or Δg_0, respectively) is multiplied by μ and any change in taxes is multiplied by $-c_1 \mu$.

The main implications of the multiplier for the macroeconomy are

1. The multiplier applies to both increases and decreases in any component of $(z_0 + g_0 - c_1 t_0)$.

2. The same multiplier applies to both public and private changes in demand, i.e., $\Delta y = \mu \Delta g_0$ and $\Delta y = \mu \Delta z_0$.

3. Tax changes have an indirect and partial effect on spending (via consumption) so the relevant multiplier is smaller by the amount c_1, i.e., $\Delta y = -c_1 \mu \Delta t_0$. Because higher taxes reduce after-tax income, the tax multiplier has the opposite sign of the expenditure multiplier.

⚭ *3.6 SOME WORDS OF ENCOURAGEMENT*

Do you have the unpleasant feeling that what looked like it might be an interesting and useful subject is rapidly losing its appeal? This is the point at which the common "economics is too abstract, too theoretical" syndrome usually sets

---

[10] If $t_1 = x_1 = 0$, the two multipliers would be identical, which means that μ_0 is a "special case" of the more general, more inclusive μ.

in. It looks like we've lost sight of the real world and the real issues that involve the lives of real people. We haven't, but for the moment you may need to take it on faith that this tedious algebraic discussion will turn out to be both important and practical. Part of the problem is simply that algebra is not a popular language in which to tell a story. But when the story is a complex one with lots of interrelationships, ordinary language will often tell it badly. For example, explaining the multiplier process in words could give us pages and pages of the following:

> *If government spending rises, this increases equilibrium income since every dollar spent is also a dollar received by someone else. This leads, in turn, to an increase in people's planned consumption spending, although not all the increase in income goes into consumption since some is put away for a rainy day as saving. Moreover, some of that increase in income is scooped off the top by Uncle Sam, while still another part of it is spent by consumers on foreign goods which, of course, is not received as income in the U.S. (But don't forget, of course, that foreign spending on our goods is received as income here.) The original increase in government spending, while over and done with now, continues to be felt because it has increased income which in turn increased consumption (after taking out some for taxes, saving, and imports), and it is precisely this increase in consumption which is now received as income by someone else. And out of this new round of income, part will go into saving, taxes, and imports, the remainder going to consumption spending which will increase income yet again and where this process all ends up is a bit hard to tell because basically it just keeps happening over and over, though each time it's a little smaller and so. . . .*

So many words; so little information. All this has barely scratched the surface. For example, it tells us nothing about the magnitude of the multiplier process. Is it moderate, small, huge, or trivial?

Trying to push such an analysis further would only add to the ambiguity and confusion, and we would soon abandon it. Where could we then turn? Most likely to some combination of political slogans and relatively primitive common sense. But there's always tea leaves and astrological signs for variety. Alternatively, we might try to clarify things by first defining shorthand **symbols** for the key concepts (e.g., y, c, i, etc.) and then trying to figure out the **relationships** among them. This response (symbols and their relationships) is *exactly* what our six-equation model does and the solution equation $[y = \mu(z_0 + g_0 - c_1 t_0)]$ is exactly the "bottom line" we seek. Ordinary language, rich and powerful in so many ways, is simply inadequate in situations of the "net-result-of-numerous-interactions" type. Interdependence and interaction characterize most of the important issues in macroeconomics and, therefore, complicate decision making at all levels—individual, business, and government. Without a little basic algebra to guide us, we're likely to end up making drastic oversimplifications that limit and distort our understanding.

You don't have to be a whiz-bang mathematician to be a good analyst and problem solver. High school algebra and geometry plus a little patience are all that's required. If you find this process tedious and distasteful, it may help to remind yourself that we're using mathematics as our metaphor *only* because it can give relatively clear, easy, and reliable answers to some difficult and very important questions. Yes, we're involved in mathematical operations on abstract symbols but only superficially. Underneath are the real issues of prosperity and recession, unemployment and inflation, and our hopes for improving our lives through thoughtful individual decisions and public policy making. Mathematics is a powerful and practical means toward attaining these important ends.

☯ 3.7 EXTENDING THE MODEL
OF AGGREGATE DEMAND

Remember that we're exploring the determinants of aggregate demand for two reasons: (1) the "quantity theory" approach of the classical model is limited by the assumption of constant velocity of money, and (2) we want to pursue Keynes's suspicions that changes in aggregate demand cause short-run fluctuations in real output and employment. So far we've focused on the multiplier process, the two-way consumption/income interaction moderated by leakages into savings, taxes, and imports. The next step toward a practical understanding of demand is to add the influence of the **real interest rate** on two of the components of aggregate demand—investment and net exports.

As with consumption earlier, many factors influence *investment demand* for the whole economy in a given year. Because spending on a capital good depends not only on the purchase price of these goods but also on the anticipated future returns over their lifetime, changing expectations about future events can have a decisive impact on the level of investment spending undertaken today. This sensitivity to changing expectations makes investment a much more volatile category than consumption. It also makes it more difficult for us to devise a good explanation of investment spending based on currently observable variables. A useful place to start, however, is with the impact of the *real rate of interest* (r) on current investment spending.[11]

Investment projects, by definition, yield a stream of returns over time. They are often financed by borrowed funds, which essentially spreads the cost of the new capital over its anticipated economic lifetime. An increase in the real interest rate makes it more expensive to borrow, raising the cost stream and, thereby, lowering the expected net return on investment spending. Projects that would have been undertaken with a real interest rate of 5% may be rejected at 7%. Hence, there is an *inverse* relationship between current investment spending and the real rate of interest.[12]

We focus on this connection between investment spending and the real rate of interest by putting all other factors that could influence investment in the "autonomous investment" category (i_0). We then have a **net real investment function,**

$$i = i_0 - i_2 r,$$ (Investment equation)

where $i_2 > 0$

Autonomous investment can have any sign, which means that total net investment (i) can be positive, negative, or zero.[13] Both i_0 and i_2 are parameters of the investment function and can be estimated statistically. The parameter i_2 shows the sensitivity of

---

[11] The real rate of interest (r) is an average of the various interest rates in the capital market, adjusted for anticipated inflation. In later chapters, we will discuss both the aggregation issue (using a single number to represent all interest rates) and the important distinction between the *real* rate (r) and the money or *market* rate of interest (R).

[12] Even if investment is financed through a firm's retained earnings (current saving) rather than by borrowing, the inverse relationship between the real rate of interest (r) and investment spending (i) remains. The reason is that a rise in interest rates in the economy increases the return a firm could get if it used its retained earnings outside the company to purchase, for example, government bonds. So an increase in the real interest rate increases either the *cost of borrowed funds* or the *opportunity cost* of internal funds, thereby making a given investment project more expensive and lowering its expected profitability.

[13] Zero net investment means that the economy is investing only enough to replace existing capital as it depreciates. So $i > 0$ represents positive net capital accumulation ($+\Delta k$, the key ingredient in economic growth and outward shifts in the PPF). An economy with negative net investment ($i < 0$) is "consuming its capital" ($-\Delta k$) and its shrinking capital stock means economic decline as shown by a contraction of the PPF.

investment to changes in the real rate of interest, i.e., $\Delta i = -i_2 \Delta r$.[14] A large value of i_2 would describe an economy in which a small change in interest rates sets off a relatively large change in investment spending.

The good news is that adding this new investment equation to our model of demand doesn't involve anything near as complicated as the multiplier interactions we've just done. The bad news is that it has introduced a new variable, the real rate of interest, whose level must be known before we can determine the value of investment and, hence, real output. Put a different way, by trying to make the story more realistic we have introduced an important but largely unknown character named r. Later in the chapter we'll add information that will clarify the identity of this mysterious stranger and help us bring the basic story of "What determines aggregate demand?" to a conclusion.

But changes in the real rate of interest alter aggregate demand not only through investment spending but also through the *net export* term. We saw earlier that imports represent a leakage from the spending stream that reduces the size of the multiplier. We must add to this the fact that both exports and imports are also altered by changes in the real rate of interest. This relationship will be discussed carefully in a later chapter. For now we'll just assert that a rise in the real rate of interest results in an increased demand for the U.S. dollar by foreigners looking for a good return on their savings. This increase in the demand for the dollar then pushes up its international value. The stronger dollar now buys more foreign currency, making imports less expensive to U.S. consumers and raising the price of our exports to foreigners whose currency has lost value relative to the dollar. The end result, which is all you need to know for now, is that *a rise in the real rate of interest, via events in the foreign exchange market, leads to a reduction in net exports.*

This expanded view of net exports is summarized in the following **net export demand function:**

$$x = x_0 - x_1 y - x_2 r,$$ (Net exports equation)

where $x_1, x_2 > 0$

All factors that might affect net exports other than income and the real interest rate, such as tariffs, are combined into the **autonomous net exports** term, x_0. The size of the parameters x_1 and x_2 show, respectively, the magnitude of the impact of changes in income and changes in the real interest rate on net exports. The actual size of these coefficients—x_0, x_1, and x_2—can be estimated statistically.

✂ 3.8 IMPLICATIONS OF THE "IS MODEL" OF AGGREGATE DEMAND

This chapter has developed a model of aggregate demand in the following three stages:

1. We started with a simple framework (the six-equation model of demand) that focused on the **consumption-income interaction** $(+\Delta y \Leftrightarrow +\Delta c)$

---

[14] Because $i = i_0 - i_2 r$, then a change in the real rate of interest must alter both sides of the equation. We can write this as $i + \Delta i = i_0 - i_2(r + \Delta r)$. Multiplying out and canceling, we get $\Delta i = -i_2 \Delta r$. Thus the value of $i_2 = -\Delta i / \Delta r$ represents the responsiveness (or first derivative) of net investment to a change in the real interest rate.

underlying the multiplier process. We discovered an expenditure multiplier of $\mu_0 = 1/(1 - c_1)$, where c_1 is the marginal propensity to consume. The tax multiplier was $- c_1\mu_0$ (see Section 3.4, "The 'Multiplier' Process").

2. We then modified this model in which saving was the only "leakage" from the spending stream, to include leakages to taxes and imports. Adding the **dependence of taxes and net exports on income** ($+ \Delta y \Rightarrow + \Delta t$ and $-\Delta x$) reduced the size of the multiplier to $\mu = 1/(1 - c_1 + c_1 t_1 + x_1) < \mu_0$ (see Section 3.5, "Refining the Multiplier"). This is the multiplier relationship that we'll use throughout the book.

3. We took next step toward realism by adding another important determinant of aggregate demand—the real rate of interest. Specifically, we added the observed **inverse relationship between the real interest rate and both investment and net exports** ($+ \Delta r \Rightarrow - \Delta i$ and $- \Delta x$) (see Section 3.7, "Extending the Model of Aggregate Demand").

Let's now put these modifications together and explore some of the policy implications of this **expanded model of aggregate demand.** As usual, there's too much happening to rely solely on ordinary language, so we turn to algebra for assistance.

$$y = c + i + x + g \tag{1}$$
$$c = c_0 + c_1(y - t) \tag{2}$$
$$t = t_0 + t_1 y \tag{3}$$
$$i = i_0 - i_2 r \tag{4}$$
$$x = x_0 - x_1 y - x_2 r \tag{5}$$
$$g = g_0 \tag{6}$$

This expanded model includes the basic multiplier ingredients (the interaction of equations 1 and 2), the additional leakages into taxes and imports that reduce the size of the multiplier (through the t_1 and x_1 coefficients), and the additional influence of the real interest rate on total demand via investment and net export spending (through the i_2 and x_2 coefficients).

To make it easier to trace the implications of this model, we find its solution (*IS*) equation. As before, we substitute the last five equations into the first and, rearranging and canceling, end up with an expression for the total demand for real output (y).

$$y = c_0 + c_1[y - (t_0 + t_1 y)] + i_0 - i_2 r + x_0 - x_1 y - x_2 r + g_0$$
$$y = c_0 + c_1 y - c_1 t_0 - c_1 t_1 y + i_0 + x_0 - x_1 y + g_0 - i_2 r - x_2 r$$
$$y - c_1 y + c_1 t_1 y + x_1 y = c_0 - c_1 t_0 + i_0 + x_0 + g_0 - (i_2 + x_2)r$$
$$y(1 - c_1 + c_1 t_1 + x_1) = c_0 - c_1 t_0 + i_0 + x_0 + g_0 - (i_2 + x_2)r$$
$$y = \frac{c_0 - c_1 t_0 + i_0 + x_0 + g_0}{(1 - c_1 + c_1 t_1 + x_1)} - \frac{(i_2 + x_2)}{(1 - c_1 + c_1 t_1 + x_1)}r$$

or, more concisely,

$$y = \mu(z_0 + g_0 - c_1 t_0) - \mu(i_2 + x_2)r, \qquad \text{(Solution [IS] equation)}$$

where $\quad \mu = 1/(1 - c_1 + c_1 t_1 + x_1)$

and $\quad z_0 = c_0 + i_0 + x_0$

The solution (IS) equation for this expanded model differs from the previous one (see Section 3.5) only in the addition of the last term, which captures the influence of the real rate of interest (r) on total demand (y) through the coefficient $-\mu(i_2 + x_2)$. The IS equation is six equations in one, a compact, self-contained version of the full model. With this as our foundation, we now use a combination of algebra, diagrams, graphs, and words to uncover the basic mechanics of aggregate demand.

We begin by noting that the IS equation has *two* unknown **variables,** r and y. All the other symbols in the equation are either **parameters** (that is, μ, i_2, x_2, z_0), that can be estimated statistically, or **policy instruments** (g_0, t_0, or t_1) that we take as given. So given a value for r, the IS equation tells us the value of y that satisfies the conditions of the model. (Or given a value of y, it gives the solution for r.) Plotting the IS equation on a graph with r on the vertical axis and y on the horizontal, we discover a linear relationship between the real rate of interest and aggregate demand. To see this, suppose we start with $r = 0$. This means that the second term on the right hand side of the IS equation drops out, leaving a specific value of $y = \mu(z_0 + g_0 - c_1 t_0)$. We plot this at point A in Figure 3.1 as the *horizontal intercept* of the IS curve.

Now suppose that the real interest rate increases from $r = 0$ to the positive value r_1, shown in Figure 3.1. The plot of the IS curve shows that the solution of the six equations now moves from points A to B. That is, as the assumed increase in the real interest rate works its way through the model, the equilibrium value of aggregate demand declines from y_0 to y_1. This inverse relationship between r and y ($+ \Delta r \Rightarrow - \Delta y$) can be viewed in several ways. Algebraically, we can see that a higher value of r increases the size of the right-hand-side term, $-\mu(i_2 + x_2)r$. This means that a larger number is being subtracted from the first term $[\mu(z_0 + g_0 - c_1 t_0)]$, lowering the equilibrium value of y by the amount of the change in the last term, i.e., $\Delta y = - \mu(i_2 + x_2)\Delta r$.[15]

It's important to learn the algebraic mechanics of this inverse relationship between aggregate demand and the real interest rate. But it's even more important to understand the underlying economic cause and effect that explains *why* this happens. An increase in the real rate of interest, as we saw earlier, leads to a reduction in investment spending (as shown in equation 4: $+ \Delta r \Rightarrow \Delta i = - i_2 \Delta r$) and in net export demand (equation 5: $+ \Delta r \Rightarrow \Delta x = - x_2 \Delta r$). The size of the parameters $-i_2$ and $-x_2$ represent the strength of these inverse relationships between r and i and r and x, respectively. The resulting fall in i and x as a result of the $+ \Delta r$ shows up in equation 1 as a drop in y. This, of course, then sets off a (downward) multiplier process, lower-

---

[15] To derive this algebraically, note that changing one of the variables on the right hand side of the equation (Δr) must result in some Δy on the left hand side. Multiplying through, rearranging, and canceling yields the solution below.

$$y + \Delta y = \mu(z_0 + g_0 - c_1 t_0) - \mu(i_2 + x_2)(r + \Delta r)$$
$$\Delta y = -\mu(i_2 + x_2)\Delta r$$

■ FIGURE 3.1

The graph of the *IS* equation—the solution to the six equations of aggregate demand—reveals an inverse relationship between the real rate of interest (r) and aggregate demand (y). Starting at point A with $r = 0$, an increase in the interest rate to r_1 leads to a drop in demand of the amount $\Delta y = -\mu(i_2 + x_2)\Delta r$ as the economy moves to point B.

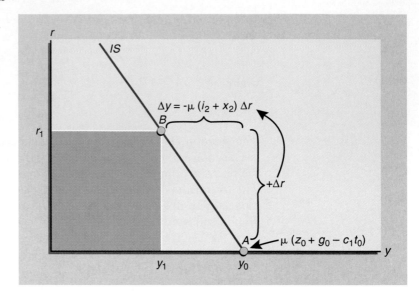

A Movement Along the *IS* Curve

ing c and y and so on through the multiplier, μ. The full impact of the $+\Delta r$ on demand will be the multiplier (μ) times the changes in i ($\Delta i = -i_2\Delta r$) and x ($\Delta x = -x_2\Delta r$). This sequence of events, as we move along the *IS* curve from points A to B, can be summarized as

$$+\Delta r \Rightarrow \begin{cases} \Delta i = -i_2\Delta r \\ \text{and} \Rightarrow -(i_2 + x_2)\Delta r \Rightarrow -\Delta(i + x) \Rightarrow -\Delta y \Leftrightarrow -\Delta c, \\ \Delta x = -x_2\Delta r \end{cases}$$

with this multiplier process ending in $-\Delta y = -\mu(i_2 + x_2)\Delta r$

Whether we present it with algebra, words, or arrows and symbols, *the end result is that an increase in the real rate of interest reduces both net investment and net exports and hence total spending, which is then magnified into a larger drop in spending/output/income through the multiplier interaction with consumption.* This inverse relationship between the real rate of interest and aggregate demand is built into the **downward slope of the *IS* curve.**

In our earlier versions of the demand model we saw that a change in either government spending or autonomous private spending changed aggregate demand by the amount $\mu\Delta g_0$ or $\mu\Delta z_0$ via the multiplier process. This result is unchanged in this expanded model and is illustrated in Figure 3.2. Starting with the *IS* curve intersecting the horizontal axis at point A, an increase in government spending ($+\Delta g_0$) moves the horizontal intercept out to point A', leaving the slope unchanged. The distance of this parallel shift in *IS* is $\mu\Delta g_0$, just as before.[16]

---

[16] Subtracting the value of the intercept at A' from its value at A, we find the horizontal distance (Δy) as

$$\Delta y = [\mu(z_0 + g_0 + \Delta g_0 - c_1 t_0)] - [\mu(z_0 + g_0 - c_1 t_0)] \text{ or}$$
$$\Delta y = \mu\Delta g_0$$

■ FIGURE 3.2

An increase in government spending $(+\Delta g_0)$ shifts the horizontal intercept of *IS* by the amount $\mu\Delta g_0$, where μ is the expenditure multiplier and has a value greater than 1.

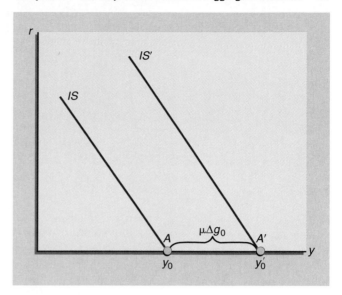

A Shift of the *IS* Curve

What impact does a change in taxes now have on the *IS* curve? The answer is again the same as before. A Δt_0 will alter the horizontal intercept of the *IS* curve by $-c_1\mu\Delta t_0$.[17] Because c_1 is a fraction between 0 and 1, we see again that the tax multiplier is slightly smaller than the expenditure multiplier and, of course, has the opposite sign.

IN SUMMARY . . .

The Expanded "IS Model" of Aggregate Demand

The most important thing to remember about this "story" of aggregate demand is that it is composed of very simple, commonsense assumptions, such as "consumption spending depends primarily on after-tax income," "because of the income tax, tax receipts rise with income," and "an increase in the real rate of interest makes it more expensive to borrow, which chokes off investment spending."

But because the *interaction* of these individually straightforward relationships gets a bit complicated, we take advantage of the power of our analogue (algebra and geometry) to determine a solution that makes a consistent whole

(Continued)

---

[17] The algebra is also the same as before. Finding the difference between the horizontal intercept before and after the tax change, we have

$$\Delta y = [\mu(z_0 + g_0 - c_1(t_0 + \Delta t_0))] - [\mu(z_0 + g_0 - c_1 t_0)] \text{ or}$$
$$\Delta y = -c_1\mu\Delta t_0$$

out of these individual parts. Mathematics can look complicated and forbidding. It's important that you appreciate that it is actually *far* easier than trying to capture the outcome of these interactions in ordinary language.

Algebraically we can portray our hypotheses about the various components of aggregate demand as

$$y = c + i + x + g \tag{1}$$
$$c = c_0 + c_1(y - t) \tag{2}$$
$$t = t_0 + t_1 y \tag{3}$$
$$i = i_0 - i_2 r \tag{4}$$
$$x = x_0 - x_1 y - x_2 r \tag{5}$$
$$g = g_0 \tag{6}$$

The solution of these six equations is the single *IS* equation, a compact and convenient "bottom-line" expression of all the interactions within the six equations.

$$y = \mu(z_0 + g_0 - c_1 t_0) - \mu(i_2 + x_2)r, \qquad \textbf{(IS equation)}$$

where $\qquad \mu = 1/(1 - c_1 + c_1 t_1 + x_1)$

and $\qquad z_0 = c_0 + i_0 + x_0$

The graph of this equation—the *IS* curve—reveals a linear relationship that is both easy to remember and easy to use in determining changes in aggregate demand.

THE "IS CURVE:" SLOPE & INTERCEPT

1. A *movement down the* IS *curve* reflects interactions in which a lower real interest rate stimulates investment and net export spending (according to the size of the parameters i_2 and x_2) and which is then magnified by the action of the multiplier (μ). So $\Delta y = -\mu(i_2 + x_2)\Delta r$ tells us exactly how much aggregate demand increases as the real interest rate declines.

2. A change in any of the variables in the horizontal intercept $[\mu(z_0 + g_0 - c_1 t_0)]$ results in a *parallel shift in the* IS *curve* by the amount of the change in that variable times the multiplier. That is, the horizontal distance of the shift would be $\mu\Delta z_0$ or $\mu\Delta g_0$. Because only a fraction (c_1) of a tax change goes into consumption, the tax multiplier shifts *IS* by the distance $-c_1\mu\Delta t_0$.

3. The *IS* model is an important but incomplete explanation of aggregate demand because it requires us to know the real interest rate (r) before we can determine the level of demand (y). Because the real interest rate is not a constant that we can take as given, we must now make one final addition to our demand model for it to become an explanation of *both* aggregate demand and the real interest rate.

✆ 3.9 *THE FINAL INGREDIENTS OF AGGREGATE DEMAND—MONEY SUPPLY AND DEMAND*

The classical model of the last chapter used a relatively simple theory of aggregate demand derived from the Quantity Theory of Money. With the assumption of constant velocity (turnover) of money, it implied that money supply drives aggregate demand while fiscal policy (government spending and taxing) has no impact on total demand whatsoever. The pendulum has now swung the other way as our present model of demand (summarized in the *IS* curve) implies that fiscal policy has a powerful demand-side impact, via the multiplier, whereas monetary policy has disappeared entirely.

To reach a balance between these policy extremes, we must add the missing monetary ingredients—**money demand and supply**—to our analysis. In economics, the "demand for money" has a more specific meaning than "something we'd all like more of." It refers to the choice to hold part of our assets in the form of *currency* and *checking accounts*.[18] The relative ease with which money can be exchanged for goods and services—its **liquidity**—is a central reason that we hold some of our wealth in the form of money rather than bonds, stocks, gold, real estate, or other assets.[19] *Our first hypothesis about money demand is that it rises with an individual's or nation's level of real income.* The higher our income, the more transactions we are likely to make and, therefore, the greater our demand for the medium of exchange, money.

An *un*appealing characteristic of money is that it earns little or no return relative to other assets like stocks and bonds. This means that the decision to hold (i.e., demand) money has an important cost in foregone earnings. In other words, holding more money gives us increased liquidity to facilitate exchange but it comes at the opportunity cost of foregone earnings. *So our second hypothesis about money demand is that as the overall interest rate rises, the resulting increase in the opportunity cost of holding money—the interest rate—will encourage us to demand less of it.*

Combining this two-part hypothesis of money demand with a given supply of money from the monetary authority gives us what we need to complete our "Keynesian" theory of aggregate demand. Once again the power and compactness of algebra turn out to simplify the analysis greatly.

$$L/P = M/P \qquad \text{(Equilibrium)} \qquad (7)$$
$$L/P = j_0 + j_1 y - j_2 r \qquad \text{(Money demand)} \qquad (8)$$
$$M = M_0 \qquad \text{(Money supply)} \qquad (9)$$
$$P = P_0 \qquad \text{(Fixed price level)} \qquad (10)$$

The top equation states that the *real* demand for money (L/P) must equal the *real* value of the money supply (M/P) in **equilibrium.** This assumes that the "money

---

[18] There is no single "correct" definition of money. The definition that includes just currency and checking accounts is usually called M_1. There are other assets that function very much like M_1 or can be easily converted into cash and might also be included. Broader measures of the money supply that include certificates of deposit and certain savings accounts will be discussed in later chapters.

[19] The degree of liquidity depends, of course, on the current "health" of the currency. American dollars may be widely accepted, not just in the United States but throughout the world. Russian rubles, conversely, may be losing value so rapidly (through inflation) that even in their native country they are avoided. Instead trades are made with more stable foreign currencies (such as the dollar) or on a barter basis to avoid the risk of holding rubles even for a very short time. Deteriorating currencies are like the proverbial hot potato—avoided if possible, otherwise passed on quickly.

market" (in the specific sense of money demand and supply) moves to an equilibrium point of market clearing, just like other markets. The dual hypothesis that the real demand for money (L/P) varies directly with income ($+\Delta y \Rightarrow +\Delta(L/P) = j_1\Delta y$) and inversely with the interest rate ($+\Delta r \Rightarrow -\Delta(L/P) = -j_2\Delta r$) is contained in equation 8, where it's assumed that the coefficients j_1 and j_2 are positive numbers. All other factors that could influence money demand are grouped together as **autonomous real money demand** and captured in the j_0 term. These three parameters of money demand (j_0, j_1, and j_2) are coefficients that can be estimated statistically.

On the supply side, the ***nominal* value of the money supply** (M) is assumed to be controlled by the Central Bank. In the United States this function is the responsibility of the Federal Reserve System. The nominal money supply is a **policy instrument** just as government spending (g_0) and taxes (t_0) were in the IS side of the model. As you'll soon see, it is significant that the Central Bank can control the *nominal* value of the money supply (M) but not its *real* value (M/P). For the moment, let's take the average level of prices as given at some value P_0, a simplification that is dropped in the next chapter.

In the same way that we converted the first six equations into a single relationship (the IS equation), we can compress these four equations into a single one, called the LM equation. (In the early Keynesian parlance, money demand was termed "liquidity preference," hence, L for money demand and M for money supply.) Substituting equations 8 to 10 into 7 yields

$$j_0 + j_1 y - j_2 r = M_0/P_0$$

which can be rearranged as

$$j_1 y = (M_0/P_0) - j_0 + j_2 r,$$

or
$$y = \frac{(M_0/P_0) - j_0}{j_1} + \frac{j_2}{j_1} r \qquad \textbf{(\textit{LM} equation)}$$

The LM equation is four equations (7–10) combined into one and is a convenient expression for exploring the implications of this model of money demand and supply for aggregate demand. LM, like the IS equation, is a linear relationship between aggregate demand (y) and the real interest rate (r). Given one we could find the value for the other that satisfies the four equations underlying the LM model. All the other symbols in the equation are either **parameters** (j_0, j_1, j_2) that can be estimated statistically or **policy instruments** (M_0), except for the price level that we temporarily assume to be known and constant (P_0).

The graph of the LM equation is shown in Figure 3.3. When the real rate of interest is zero, the second term on the right-hand side of the LM equation drops out, leaving $y = [(M_0/P_0) - j_0]/j_1$ as the value of the *horizontal intercept* of the LM curve. If the real interest rate rises from 0 to r_1, the economy will move from points A to B in the graph. That is, a given rise in the real rate of interest sets off a series of adjustments in the four-equation money market model that ends only when aggregate demand has risen from y_0 to y_1.

This direct relationship between the real rate of interest and aggregate demand (income) ($+\Delta r \Rightarrow +\Delta y$) can be viewed as a consequence of the fact that equilibrium requires an equality between money supply and demand, $L/P = M_0/P_0$. Because an increase in the real rate of interest ($+\Delta r$) causes us to *reduce* our money holdings (because of their higher opportunity cost), there must be an equal *increase* in money

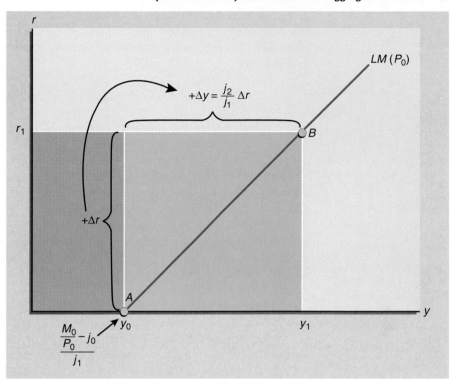

A Movement Along the *LM* Curve

■ **FIGURE 3.3**

The graph of the *LM* equation—the solution to the four equations of the "money market"—reveals a positive relationship between the real rate of interest (r) and aggregate demand (y). Starting at point A with $r = 0$, an increase in the interest rate to r_1 will reduce money demand, necessitating a balancing increase in income of the amount $\Delta y = (j_2 / j_1) \Delta r$ to restore real money demand (L / P) to equality with the fixed real money supply (M_0 / P_0) as the economy moves to point B.

demand via a rise in income ($+\Delta y$) to restore the equality between the fixed amount of money and total money demand.[20]

It's important to see how this direct relationship between r and y comes out of the basic algebra of the *LM* equation, but even more important to understand it in terms of economic cause and effect. One nicely intuitive approach starts with a rise in real income ($+\Delta y$). According to our money demand hypothesis (equation 8) this will increase money demand and create a temporary imbalance in which money demand exceeds the fixed money supply ($L/P > M_0/P_0$). As with any commodity, excess demand pushes up its price. Because the "price of money," loosely speaking, is its opportunity cost, the rate of interest must rise.[21] As the interest rate rises, it becomes more costly to hold money because alternative interest-bearing assets now yield a higher return. This will lead households and businesses to reduce their money

---

[20] Changing one of the variables on the right-hand side of the equation (Δr) results in a Δy on the left-hand side. The size of this Δy is given by $y + \Delta y = [(M_0/P_0) - j_0]/j_1 + [j_2/j_1](r + \Delta r)$, hence, $\Delta y = (j_2/j_1)\Delta r$.

[21] More carefully stated, the real rate of interest (r) is the cost of *borrowing* money or the "price of credit."

holdings, a process that continues until money demand and supply are back in balance (equation 7), and the upward pressure on the interest rate has disappeared. This sequence of events underlying the upward slope of the LM curve can be summarized concisely as

$$+\Delta y \Rightarrow +\Delta L/P \Rightarrow (L/P) > M_0/P_0 \Rightarrow +\Delta r \Rightarrow -\Delta L/P$$

What about the *intercept* of the *LM* curve? The *LM* equation, $y = [(M_0/P_0) - j_0]/j_1 + (j_2/j_1)r$, shows that the value of the horizontal intercept is $[(M_0/P_0) - j_0]/j_1$. Changes in any of these four variables can alter its value and shift the *LM* curve accordingly. For example, suppose there is an increase in the money supply by the Federal Reserve. The resulting rise in its real value, now $(M_0 + \Delta M_0)/P$, will cause a rightward shift in the curve as shown in Figure 3.4(a). $LM(P_0)$ shifts to $LM'(P_0)$, a parallel movement because the slope (j_1/j_2) is unchanged. The new curve tells us that a higher money supply results in a higher real demand for output at any given value of the real rate of interest. Therefore, expansionary monetary policy $(+\Delta M)$ shifts $LM(P_0)$ out while a contractionary policy $(-\Delta M)$ shifts it in.

How will a changing price level influence the four equation money market model and, hence, the *LM* curve? A rise in the price level $(+\Delta P)$, other things the same, will reduce the purchasing power of the nominal money supply. This decrease in the real money supply, $-\Delta(M/P)$, has exactly the same effect as a decline in *M*. It reduces the size of the horizontal intercept and shifts $LM(P_0)$ to the left to $LM(P_1)$ as shown in Figure 3.4(b). Note that while the Federal Reserve controls the nominal money supply, a variety of events in the overall economy combine to determine the price level. For example, the classical model of Chapter 2 showed that a doubling of the money supply resulted in a long-run doubling of the price level. In our four-equation model this would show up as a rightward shift in *LM* $(+\Delta M)$, exactly offset by a leftward shift $(-\Delta P)$, the *real value* of the money

■ FIGURE 3.4

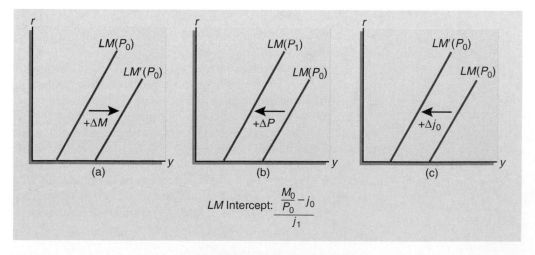

(a)   (b)   (c)

LM Intercept: $\dfrac{\dfrac{M_0}{P_0} - j_0}{j_1}$

Three Shifts in the *LM* Curve

supply remaining constant. With such a link between the nominal money supply and prices, the central bank would be powerless to cause a lasting shift in *LM* and would, therefore, have no ability to influence either the real rate of interest (r) or the real demand for output (y). We'll examine this and other policy situations in the following chapter.

Finally let's ask what happens if there's a *change in autonomous money demand* (j_0), i.e., a change in one of the determinants of money demand other than real income or the real rate of interest. Because an increase in j_0 reduces the value of the intercept (j_0 has a minus in front of it in the *LM* equation), the *LM* curve shifts to the *left* as j_0 rises. In other words, while an increase in money supply has an expansionary impact, an increase in autonomous money demand results in a *contraction* of the *LM* curve, as shown in Figure 3.4(c). If we decide to hold larger money balances it is equivalent to a reduction in the *velocity* of money, and the result is contractionary.

IN SUMMARY . . .

The **LM** *Model of Money Demand and Supply*

Like the six-equation model underlying the *IS* curve, this four-equation model of money demand and supply is a set of commonsense statements expressed algebraically. For example, our money holdings (currency plus checking accounts) rise with our income [$+ \Delta y \Rightarrow + \Delta(L/P) = j_1 \Delta y$] and diminish as interest rates on alternative asset holdings rise [$+ \Delta r \Rightarrow - \Delta(L/P) = - j_2 \Delta r$]. The basic structure of money demand and supply is captured in the following relationships:

$$L/P = M/P \tag{7}$$
$$L/P = j_0 + j_1 y - j_2 r \tag{8}$$
$$M = M_0 \tag{9}$$
$$P = P_0 \tag{10}$$

The solution of these four equations is the single *LM* equation, a shorthand expression that encompasses all the information in this model.

$$y = \frac{[(M_0/P_0) - j_0]}{j_1} + \frac{j_2}{j_1} r \qquad (LM \text{ equation})$$

The graph of this equation—the *LM* curve—is a linear relationship between real income and the real rate of interest and has the following characteristics:

1. A movement along the *LM* curve reflects real-world interactions in which a higher level of income increases the demand for money and, with money supply constant, drives up its "price," the rate of interest.

2. A change in any of the variables in the horizontal intercept, $[(M_0/P_0) - j_0]/j_1$, results in a parallel shift in the *LM* curve.

⚙ 3.10 *THE* **IS-LM** *MODEL*
OF AGGREGATE DEMAND

The introduction to this group of five chapters (of which this is the first) portrayed this material as your "basic training" in macroeconomic analysis. This was a warning that the material would be difficult but essential. The main challenge for most students is not the level of analysis but the level of tedium. The derivation of the two-part *IS-LM* **model of aggregate demand** seems mechanical and lifeless, apparently far removed from important issues of the real world. It may help you to know that the extensions and applications of subsequent chapters will breathe some life into this basic structure. This *IS-LM* model of aggregate demand will turn out to play a key role in your understanding of unemployment and the business cycle, stabilization policy, government deficits, monetary policy and interest rates, inflation, and international phenomena like trade deficits, exchange rates, and restrictions on trade.

This chapter, though long and involved, has explored just one question: "What factors determine the level of aggregate demand in the macroeconomy?" Chapter 2 gave a much simpler but more primitive answer that assumed both *market clearing* and *constant velocity of money*. Both assumptions imply a very long-run focus. Following the path blazed by Keynes, this chapter has implicitly dropped the constant velocity of money restriction to examine short-run issues of aggregate demand. But in the process it has also opened up what looks like the proverbial can of worms—consumption, investment, and net export equations; parameters and policy instruments; expenditure and tax multipliers; and money demand equations. All these creatures are interrelated, intertwined, and very uninviting. It's definitely more complicated than the classical long-run approach. But it will turn out to be far more useful and, with a little practice, not nearly as forbidding as it looks just now.

The answer to "What determines the overall level of aggregate demand?" is contained in the ten equations (or sentences) of the combined *IS-LM* model. Remember that the six-equation *IS* model was incomplete because it could determine the value of output/income (y) only if the real rate of interest (r) was already known. It gave a relationship *between* y and r (shown in the linear *IS* curve) but could not tell us where we were along that curve. It could tell us which events shift the *IS* curve ($\Delta z_0, \Delta g_0, \Delta t_0$) and by how much ($\mu \Delta z_0, \mu \Delta g_0, -c_1 \mu \Delta t_0$) but, again, not where we'd end up along the new curve. More information was needed to complete the model of aggregate demand, and this information was found in the four-equation model of money demand and supply summarized by the *LM* equation and curve.

Putting *IS* (equations 1–6) with *LM* (equations 7–10) yields a complete model of aggregate demand, in which both y and r are determined, as are c, i, x, and other variables that depend on either income or the real rate of interest. Remember that underneath the deceptively simple veneer of the *IS-LM* graph, shown in Figure 3.5, is the elaborate ten-equation structure of aggregate demand. Though each of the ten components is straightforward, together they are quite complex because of their interactions. Fortunately, with a little practice you will be able to use the compact *IS-LM* framework to get at some very important applications. In the following chapter, this model of aggregate demand is combined with a simple theory of aggregate supply to form the basic analytical framework used through the rest of the book.

■ FIGURE 3.5

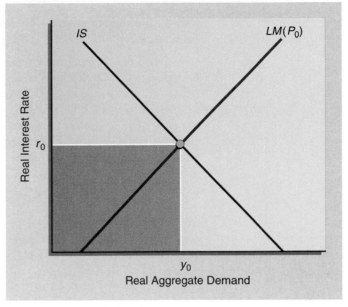

The *IS-LM* Model of Aggregate Demand

✆ *3.11 OVERVIEW*

1. This long and challenging chapter has led us from the simple, tranquil long-run world of the classical model to the more intricate and potentially stormy short-run world of the Keynesian model. To John Maynard Keynes, the classical dismissal of aggregate demand as a determinant of output and employment was absurd. He was especially critical of the contention that "fiscal policy is powerless" to influence output and employment. Keynes's response was to compose an alternative story (theory/model) in which demand played a significant, sometimes even dominant, role.

2. This chapter has developed an expanded model of aggregate demand based on Keynes's analysis. It requires some attention and patience. In your frustration, be careful not to slip back into the common view that "theory" is the opposite of "practical" and that models just make things more difficult than they really are. Economic models, however imperfect, are the most reliable maps we have. Without them, policy makers are destined to sail in uncharted waters—taking the economy and us along with them. Put another way, it is through models (and their embodied theories) that we attempt to decipher lessons from the past and transfer them to the present. It is not a choice between "theory" or "practice," or even between "theory" and "no theory." It's a matter of how carefully we use logic and past experience to understand the present and prepare for the future.

3. Aggregate demand (y), in Keynes's alternative to the classical Quantity Theory of Money, is divided into four categories—consumption, investment, net exports, and government spending. More concisely, $y = c + i + x + g$, from which we build a model of total demand from smaller models of each component, namely, $c = c_0 + c_1(y - t)$, $t = t_0 + t_1 y$, $i = i_0 - i_2 r$, $x = x_0 - x_1 y - x_2 r$, and $g = g_0$. Be-

cause total demand in equilibrium will be the same as total supply, we denote them both by the symbol y. This allows us to talk interchangeably of "income" or "output" because every dollar spent is a dollar received by someone.

4. The consumption-income relationship lies at the center of the process by which aggregate demand changes over time. A change in any of the four components of demand will initially change income by the same amount (because $y = c + i + x + g$). This stimulus will then be transmitted to consumption (because $c = c_0 + c_1(y - t)$), which, in turn, alters income (again, $y = c + i + x + g$), which changes consumption again, then income, and on and on. This interaction between consumption and income means that any initial change in income is magnified through a **multiplier process.** Where all this interaction ends up is relatively easy to discover with some algebra and almost impossible without it. But easy or not, the important thing is to understand *why* this expenditure multiplier exists and what it implies for our ability to influence total demand in the economy. Review Section 3.4 until you have a comfortable understanding of why "the multiplier works in *both* directions," why "*any* Δy sets off the multiplier process," and why "*tax changes* also have a multiple, though smaller, impact on total demand."

5. Once the basic logic of the multiplier is appreciated, it's not difficult to go beyond the consumption-income interaction ($+\Delta y \Leftrightarrow +\Delta c$) to see that because income taxes and imports rise with income, the size of the multiplier is reduced. In a nutshell, an initial rise in income starts the multiplier process through its impact on our consumption spending. But if part of that initial $+\Delta y$ goes to the tax collector ($+\Delta t$) and another part goes to purchase goods from other countries ($-\Delta x$), less of it is left for $+\Delta c$ in the United States. This, in turn, means a smaller subsequent increase in income, hence, smaller rise in consumption and so on, resulting in a smaller total effect on aggregate demand. Although these additional leakages reduce the size of the multiplier somewhat, it remains something to be reckoned with if we are to understand and attempt to control aggregate demand.

6. Another piece that must be added to our theory of aggregate demand is the fact that a change in the real rate of interest affects both net investment and net export spending. Specifically, there is an inverse relationship between the interest rate and these components of spending ($+\Delta r$ causes $-\Delta i$ and $-\Delta x$). Remember that because $y = c + i + x + g$, any change in i or x on the right-hand side alters income and is then magnified by the multiplier process (e.g., $-\Delta i$ and $-\Delta x \Rightarrow -\Delta y \Leftrightarrow -\Delta c$).

7. All these ingredients are incorporated in the expanded six equation model:

$$y = c + i + x + g \tag{1}$$
$$c = c_0 + c_1(y - t) \tag{2}$$
$$t = t_0 + t_1 y \tag{3}$$
$$i = i_0 - i_2 r \tag{4}$$
$$x = x_0 - x_1 y - x_2 r \tag{5}$$
$$g = g_0 \tag{6}$$

The solution of this model, called the *IS* equation, is

$$y = \mu(z_0 + g_0 - c_1 t_0) - \mu(i_2 + x_2)r, \qquad \text{(IS equation)}$$

where $\qquad \mu = 1/(1 - c_1 + c_1 t_1 + x_1)$

and $\qquad z_0 = c_0 + i_0 + x_0$

8. Three important characteristics of the *IS* equation should be noted:

   a. The algebra that gets us from six equations to a single solution (one equation) may look messy, but it's far easier and more practical than "common sense," "brute force," or other alternatives.

   b. The significance of this *IS* equation is that it is a true "bottom line." It takes into account the *multiplier process* (the interaction of equations 1 and 2, with leakages through equations 3 and 5) and the *inverse relationship of aggregate demand and the real interest rate* (equations 4 and 5). It tells us that, all things considered:

   i. A change in autonomous private spending (Δz_0) or public spending (Δg_0) affects income/output (y) through the expenditure multiplier (μ) according to $\Delta y = \mu \Delta z_0$ or $\Delta y = \mu \Delta g_0$.

   ii. A change in taxes (nonincome taxes for simplicity, Δt_0) affects income/output through the tax multiplier ($-c_1 \mu$) as described by $\Delta y = -c_1 \mu \Delta t_0$.

   iii. A change in the real rate of interest (Δr) affects income/output (y) through its impact on investment (Δi) and net exports (Δx) as summarized by the sizes of the i_2 and x_2 parameters. This is then magnified by the expenditure multiplier (μ) and the final impact of a change in r on y is captured by $\Delta y = -(i_2 + x_2)\mu \Delta r$.

   c. Once you get the general picture of what's going on in terms of the algebra (parts *a* and *b* above), you can move them to the background and concentrate on the geometrical representation of the solution, the **IS curve.** It's easy to remember and easy to use.

   i. The multiplier processes in parts *b*(i) and *b*(ii) above show up as *parallel shifts* of the *IS* curve by the amount of the Δz_0, Δg_0, or Δt_0 times the appropriate multiplier.

   ii. The role of the real interest rate is captured in the *downward slope* of the *IS* curve, with an increase in r causing y to fall because of both the i_2 and x_2 terms and the spending multiplier, as given in part *b*(iii).

9. Much of the information needed to understand aggregate demand is incorporated into the *IS* equation and curve.

$$y = \mu(z_0 + g_0 - c_1 t_0) - \mu(i_2 + x_2)r, \qquad \text{(IS equation)}$$

where $\qquad \mu = 1/(1 - c_1 + c_1 t_1 + x_1)$

and $\qquad z_0 = c_0 + i_0 + x_0$

Everything we need to know is either a *policy instrument* (values of which can be observed, forecast, or simulated) or is a *parameter that can be estimated statistically* except for one variable—the real interest rate. The real interest rate (r) is not a constant that we can take as given. It's a variable that can and does change in response to many of the same things that alter aggregate demand itself. So without more information we're left in a situation in which if we knew r then we could find y and vice versa. But we don't, so we can't (and vice versa).

10. The needed information comes from the supply of money by the Federal Reserve and the demand for money by everyone who uses it. This is captured in the relatively simple "money market" model of equations 7 to 10 and summarized in the single equation solution, called the **LM equation.**

$$L/P = M/P \tag{7}$$

$$L/P = j_0 + j_1 y - j_2 r \tag{8}$$

$$M = M_0 \tag{9}$$

$$P = P_0 \tag{10}$$

$$y = \frac{[(M_0/P_0) - j_0]}{j_1} + \frac{j_2}{j_1} r \qquad (LM \text{ equation})$$

11. Three characteristics of the *LM* equation should be noted:

a. The algebra that gets us from four equations to a single solution (one equation) is a bit messy, but easier and more useful than other alternatives.

b. The importance of this *LM* equation is that, like the *IS*, it is a "bottom line," considering the various factors influencing both money demand (namely, *y* and *r*) and money supply (the monetary authority).

c. Once you get the general picture of what's going on in terms of the algebra (parts *a* and *b*), you can push it into the background and concentrate on the geometrical representation of the solution, the **LM curve.** It is easy to remember and use.

   i. A *movement along* the *LM* curve reflects the fact that as income rises $(+\Delta y)$, the demand for money also rises. (Remember that we can equate "aggregate demand" and "income" because every dollar spent is a dollar received.) And with a constant money supply this $+\Delta y \Rightarrow +\Delta(L/P)$ puts upward pressure on the "price" of money. The result is that an increase in *y* leads to a rise in *r*.

   ii. A change in any of the variables in the intercept term results in a *parallel shift* in the *LM* curve. For example, a $+\Delta M_0$, $-\Delta P_0$, or a $-\Delta j_0$, shifts *LM* to the right, leaving the slope unchanged.

12. All this work has gone to answer a single but crucial question: "What determines the level of aggregate demand in the economy?" All the elements of the ten-equation model, summarized in the two solution equations/curves (*IS* and *LM*, see Figure 3.5) are necessary to give a reliable answer that, unlike the classical model, is applicable to the short as well as the long run. Chapter 4 will pull this model of demand together, add a simple model of aggregate supply, and begin the applications that are the only justification for going to all this trouble.

⚙ *3.12 REVIEW QUESTIONS*

1. Define the following basic concepts or terms:

Aggregate demand	Marginal propensity to consume	IS equation
Net exports		Expenditure multiplier
Price index	Autonomous consumption	Tax multiplier
Income = output		Tax function
Consumption function	Multiplier process	Net export function

Autonomous net exports	Policy instrument	Nominal money supply
Net investment function	Parameter	*LM* equation
Real rate of interest	Money demand function	*IS-LM* model of *AD*
Autonomous net investment	Autonomous money demand	

2. In the simplest model of aggregate demand, we find that income changes by a *multiple* of any change in government spending or autonomous consumption or investment spending. What basic *interaction* is built into that model that leads to this result? Explain how it works.

3. In the simplest model of demand there was neither an income tax nor an impact of changing income on net export spending. Once we add these two factors, the size of the multiplier declines. Show this algebraically and explain in common-sense terms.

4. Suppose the government decides to reduce its deficit by $100 billion by cutting government spending. What will happen to the *IS* curve? Would your answer change if they raised taxes by $100 billion instead of cutting spending? Explain.

5. "If the government starts off with a balanced federal budget and then increases spending by $20 billion, this will create a $20 billion deficit and shift the *IS* curve to the right. If the next year the government keeps its spending at this higher level and runs another $20 billion deficit, the *IS* curve will again shift to the right by the same amount." Evaluate.

6. Show that a change in autonomous money demand (Δj_0) and a change in the money supply (ΔM_0) both shift the *LM* curve, but in opposite directions.

7. Show that a change in money supply (M) and the price level (P) both shift the *LM* curve, but in opposite directions. Use the *LM* equation to explain.

8. Suppose that two nearly identical countries both use fiscal and monetary policy to keep output at the *same* full employment level, but that country A has higher taxes and a larger money supply than country B. Government spending is the same.

   a. On a single graph, show how the *IS* and *LM* curves of these two countries differ.

   b. Compare the levels of each of the following variables for the two countries, i.e., higher, lower, or the same: consumption, investment, net exports, and the federal deficit.

9. Suppose there is a sudden increase in autonomous investment spending ($+\Delta i_0$ in our model).

   a. What impact will this have on equilibrium y and r? Explain.

   b. Suppose the Federal Reserve reacts to this event ($+\Delta i_0$) by changing M so as to move r back to its original level. What will happen to equilibrium y? Explain.

   c. Instead, suppose the fiscal authorities react by changing g so as to move r back to its original level. What will happen to equilibrium y? Explain.

10. "The *IS-LM* model cannot be more than a partial explanation of economic activity, because it implies that monetary or fiscal policy (or both together) could be used to push y to any level we desired." Do you agree or disagree? Explain.

11. *a.* Suppose the economy is initially in short-run equilibrium below full employment and policy makers decide it's time to take strong actions to restore full employment (y^*). They decide to do this with fiscal policy, but want to do it in a way that causes the smallest increase in the already large government deficit. They ask you to devise a plan to accomplish this. What would you recommend? Explain.

    b. Your proposal is immediately attacked by an influential senator as short-sighted and irresponsible. She says that it might work, but only at the cost of a larger deficit and a smaller rate of capital formation hence slower long run economic growth. (*Note:* "Economic growth" refers to changes in y^*, and "economic recovery" is the return of y to a given y^*.) She advocates the use of monetary policy instead, arguing that this will not only restore full employment but actually *reduce* the budget deficit and *increase* economic growth. Evaluate her proposal and (if you can) defend your own.

    c. The chairman of the Descendants of Adam (Smith) Society attacks both you and the senator for your knee-jerk invocation of government policy. Your "visible fist," as he calls it, is neither needed nor welcome. He says you have forgotten that basic market mechanics ensure that $y^{AD} > y^* \Rightarrow + \Delta P$, $y^{AD} < y^* \Rightarrow - \Delta P$, and $y^{AD} = y^* \Rightarrow \Delta P = 0$. Adding this ingredient to the *IS-LM* model of aggregate demand, he concludes that we will not only return to full employment *automatically*, but also in a way that stimulates growth and reduces the deficit—*and* all without the use of any centralized policy manipulation. Evaluate his proposal.

12. In equilibrium in the Keynesian model, the real money supply (M_0/P) equals real money demand ($L/P = j_0 + j_1 y - j_2 r$). Equilibrium in the "money market" is then $M_0/P = j_0 + j_1 y - j_2 r$. Show that in the classical model (with constant velocity of money) the analogous money market equilibrium is $M_0/P = (1/V)y$ and graph this relationship in terms of (y, r) − space (i.e., with the same axes as for the *IS-LM* graph). In other words, what does the graph of the *classical LM curve* look like? Explain.

CHAPTER 4

AGGREGATE DEMAND AND SUPPLY

✆ 4.1 INTRODUCTION

This chapter continues a mathematical approach to macroeconomic interactions but marks the transition from algebra to a more intuitive geometric view. Mathematics is important to us because it is a convenient shorthand notation as well as a familiar "this" to help us understand an unfamiliar "that." Even if math hasn't been your favorite or best subject, you've been studying it for many years and surely know more about solving equations than about analyzing the macroeconomic consequences of interacting events and policies in a world of scarcity.

But don't forget that it is *economics*—scarcity, choices, and outcomes— that is our real concern. The equations and graphs of these models are useful only insofar as they can simulate the interactions of real people in the real world. As we continue working with the *IS-LM* model, converting it into an "aggregate demand curve" and then adding a theory of "aggregate supply," remind yourself that this is not just an algebraic exercise or a geometric puzzle. The lives of actual people, all of us, are affected by every major economic event and every policy success or failure. In the poorest economies, where so many live on the very edge of subsistence, unfavorable events and policy mistakes can have the most tragic consequences.

The classical model, introduced in Chapter 2, predicted that an economy organized around self-interest and markets, with a relatively passive role for government, would have many desirable characteristics, including a built-in "thermostat"—the process of market clearing—to guide it automatically to full employment. In the midst of the Great Depression, the assurance from economists that the downturn was a "temporary disequilibrium phenomenon" and, from politicians, that "prosperity was just around the corner" seemed increasingly mistaken and, finally, ridiculous. By 1933, with 25% of the labor force out of work, real output 30% below its 1929 level, and vast losses of wealth from the collapse of stock and bond markets and the (uninsured) failure of many banks, patience with the "invisible hand" was wearing thin.

This was a time of profound economic crisis in the industrialized economies of the West, not unlike the present situation in the nations of the former Soviet block.[1] The classical model appeared to offer little insight into either why economic performance collapsed during the early 1930s or how it could be improved. We seemed to be both "adrift without a rudder" and "taking on water rapidly." Policy makers were likened to cruise directors scurrying to find the optimal arrangement of deck chairs—on the Titanic. But neither nautical nor mathematical nor any other metaphors seemed able to guide us out of the storm to a safe harbor.

The *IS-LM* model of aggregate demand is a modern textbook embodiment and extension of the alternative theory proposed by John Maynard Keynes in *The General Theory of Employment, Interest, and Money* (1936). Keynes and his followers were convinced that a more realistic model was needed to explain the actual workings of the economy. Though considerably more intricate than the classical model—hence, all the algebra of Chapter 3—it seeks to understand what happens *in between* positions of classical long-run market clearing. The Keynesian structure considers "short-run" situations in which the velocity of money can change and markets can remain uncleared. The inevitable cost of this additional realism is more complexity. But the analytical simplicity of the long run classical model was purchased at too high a cost if it couldn't deal with economic distress of the magnitudes experienced during the 1930s.

✆ 4.2 *FROM* IS-LM *TO THE AGGREGATE DEMAND CURVE*

It is sometimes joked that economists see everything in pairs—supply and demand; "this or that?"; "now or later"; "on the one hand . . . , but then on the other . . ."; and so on. In large part, this duality is imposed by scarcity and the resulting competition for limited resources—more of X means less of Y. But another reason that so many things seem to come in two's in economics is the usefulness of geometry as an analytical and explanatory tool. The two-dimensional surface of the page (and blackboard and computer screen) focuses the spotlight on the relationship between whatever variables we decide to put on the two axes, leaving everything else in the shadows. For example, the six equations summarized in the *IS* curve are expressed as an explicit relationship between two variables, real output (y) and the real interest rate (r), even though we saw that many other variables and parameters are involved in determining the slope and intercept of that curve. The same is true of the four equations underlying the *LM* curve—y and r are explicit, whereas all the parameters and policy instruments that define the connections between money demand and supply remain implicit, defining the slope and intercept of the relationship.

While real output (y) and the real interest rate (r) are obviously important, suppose we want to bring a *third* variable into the spotlight—the price level (P). Instead of going to an awkward three-dimensional graph to look at (y, r; P) relationships, we can accomplish the same thing by linking *two* two-dimensional graphs, the

---

[1] An important difference is that the current crises in Russia and other formerly planned economies represent the failure of a large, obtrusive role for government in the economy. The hoped-for solution, ironically, is the same "invisible hand" that seemed to many observers to be the source of the problem in the 1930s.

■ FIGURE 4.1

In words, this says that an increase in the price level initially decreases the real value of the given nominal money supply, thereby shifting the LM curve to the left and raising the real rate of interest. This, in turn, reduces both investment and net export spending (equations 4 and 5), setting off a multiplier effect $(-\Delta y \Leftrightarrow -\Delta c)$ as we move up the IS curve. In sum, the $+\Delta P$ triggers a sequence of events that ends in $-\Delta y$, a relationship that defines the downward slope of the AD curve.

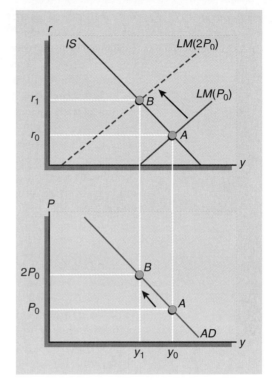

From *IS-LM* to *AD*

Why Does Aggregate Demand Slope Downward?
$$+\Delta P \implies -\Delta M/P \implies +\Delta r \implies -\Delta i \text{ and } -\Delta x \implies -\Delta y \Leftrightarrow -\Delta c$$

familiar *IS-LM* curves (in y and r) plus a new **AD curve** (in y and P). Both are a complete representation of the same ten-equation aggregate demand model of Chapter 3, differing only in which variables are explicit (on the axis) and which left implicit (in the intercept and slope). You might think of this as first looking at an elephant (the ten-equation model) from the front (*IS-LM* graph) and then going to the rear for another view (the *AD* graph). These different perspectives on the same creature can provide further clues as to the nature of "elephantness" (or aggregate demand).

Let's now derive and incorporate this twin view of aggregate demand into our analytical framework. We start with the *IS-LM* view of y and r, and transform it into a picture of an *aggregate demand curve* showing the underlying relationship between y and P. Starting at point A in the top graph of Figure 4.1 with a price level of P_0, suppose some outside event causes the price level to double to $2P_0$. What happens to the level of aggregate demand? We know from the last chapter that an increase in the price level lowers the *real value* (or purchasing power) of the given nominal money supply (that is, $+\Delta P$ leads to $-\Delta(M_0/P)$). This reduces the horizontal intercept of *LM*, shifting the curve from $LM(P_0)$ to $LM(2P_0)$ and sliding it along *IS*. Equilibrium is now at point B, with a higher real interest rate $(+\Delta r)$ and a lower level of aggregate demand $(-\Delta y)$.

Now move down to the bottom graph of Figure 4.1. It is simply another way to portray the underlying ten-equation model of demand and therefore tells *exactly the same story*. A doubling of the price level moves the economy from points A to B. The only difference is that we now see this movement in terms of the *price level* and aggregate demand (*P* and *y*) rather than the *interest rate* and aggregate demand (*r* and *y*). Plotting the initial values (y_0,P_0) at point *A* and the new equilibrium values (y_1,$2P_0$) at point *B* and connecting these two points reveals a familiar downward-sloping demand curve (*AD*).

But note that the negative slope of the *aggregate* demand curve has little in common with the income and substitution effects underlying the derivation of demand curves for individual commodities in microeconomics. Like its cousin the classical aggregate demand curve, this curve tells a story of declining demand for real goods and services as the average level of prices rises. But *un*like the classical curve, there is no presumption of constant velocity of money and, as you will see, fiscal policy is no longer "powerless" to alter aggregate demand. Anything that shifts *IS*, including changes in fiscal policy, will also shift this aggregate demand curve. In addition, anything that shifts *LM except changes in the price level*, shifts *AD* as well.[2]

ᏸᏸ *4.3 ADDING A SIMPLE MODEL OF AGGREGATE SUPPLY*

With so many moving parts in this ten-equation/two-graph model of aggregate demand, it's easy to get distracted by all the machinery and forget that it's a theory of *demand* only. It completely ignores the most fundamental economic fact of life— **scarcity.** Before going any further with our analysis, then, we need to remedy this by incorporating the process through which limited inputs are transformed into output. This is done by adding a model of **aggregate supply.**

In the earlier discussion of the classical approach to aggregate supply we found that constant market clearing implied a vertical aggregate supply curve, *AS**, that defined the full employment level of real output. Changes in the price level ($\pm\Delta P$) led to equiproportional changes in money wages ($\pm\Delta W$) that left the *real* wage, hence, employment and output, unchanged. Scarcity kept us from getting beyond full employment, whereas market clearing ensured that we wouldn't get stuck below it. Equilibrium only occurred at full employment and was achieved through automatic market clearing—the classical "thermostat" in action.

But the long run focus of this classical approach treats market clearing as an *event* rather than a *process of change and re-evaluation* that requires information, decision making, and, inevitably, adjustment through "time." In later chapters we'll explore the "time path" traveled by our variables during the process of market clearing, a topic termed "short-run dynamics." For now, however, we settle for a much simpler, cruder but still useful approximation to this process. Instead of trying to create a continuous movie of the adjustment process from one equilibrium to another (called "dynamics"), we'll just take a few snapshots along the way ("comparative statics") to get a rough approximation to the actual path.

We start by defining the *interval of time during which markets are not fully cleared* as the **short run.** This term is distressingly vague but nevertheless turns out to be a very useful first approach to issues of recession and depression that can't be captured in models focused only on long-run market clearing at full employment. Using a concept of short-run aggregate supply allows us to examine what happens to output

---

[2] The impact of the price level on the real demand for output is already built into the *slope* of *AD* ($-\Delta P \rightarrow . . . \rightarrow +\Delta y$). To also *shift AD* as the price level changes would be to double-count its impact.

■ FIGURE 4.2

Short- and long-run supply responses to an increase in aggregate demand. SR: *A* to *A'*; LR: *A* to *B*.

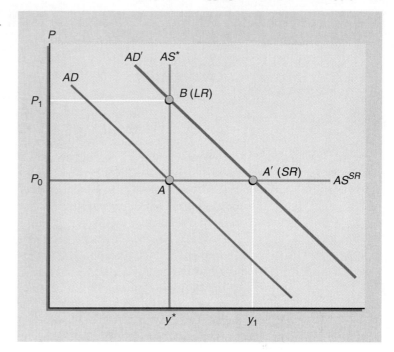

(and other variables) *after aggregate demand has shifted but before market clearing is complete.* In the classical model this was labeled "temporary disequilibrium" and left unexplored.[3]

In our first approximation to macroeconomic dynamics, let's do the opposite of the classical model by supposing that the initial adjustment occurs *entirely in output change* rather than price change. In terms of the *AD/AS* graph in Figure 4.2, an increase in aggregate demand now causes an initial movement from points *A* to *A'*. Shifts in aggregate demand ($\pm \Delta AD$), then, are assumed to move the economy in an "east/west" direction ($\pm \Delta y$) in the short run, but "north/south" ($\pm \Delta P$) in the long run. This is called **short-run price rigidity** (or "price stickiness") and we incorporate it into our graph as a **horizontal short-run aggregate supply curve, AS^{SR}**. How long this rigidity lasts is, of course, crucial for policy making and an issue we will examine in later chapters. For now, however, we suppose it continues long enough to account for business cycle deviations from full employment that last anywhere from a few months to a year or more.[4]

Is this short-run assumption of "flexible output" any more realistic than the "flexible prices" assumption of the classicals? The answer, most macroeconomists believe, is "yes," although there is *much* disagreement as to the underlying reasons

---

[3] This is not to say that there were no serious attempts to explain the business cycle until the arrival of John Maynard Keynes and the Great Depression. In fact, a considerable literature on economic fluctuations had developed within the classical framework throughout the nineteenth and early twentieth centuries. But it was the long-run classical model that predominated and which told public officials that "hands off" was the best policy in a market economy. Although there were many explanations of economic fluctuations put forth in the nineteenth and early twentieth centuries, they were never integrated into a coherent, careful model of the determinants of output and employment over time.

[4] In a later chapter we'll see that merely assuming rigidities in order to make the model more relevant has its limitations. The specifics of the price adjustment process between short and long run turn out to be both subtle and crucial to short run policy making.

"GROSS DOMESTIC PRODUCT"
REAL WORLD COUNTERPART
TO REAL OUTPUT

The equivalent terms "real output" and "real income," as represented by the symbol *y*, have been used without saying anything about the real world *numbers* that correspond to this fundamental *concept* of economic activity. **Gross domestic product** (GDP) is the official measure of total income and output for the overall economy. It is defined as the value of all final goods and services produced within the geographic boundaries of the nation, during a particular time period, usually a year.

GDP has now replaced *gross national product* (GNP) as the official measure in the United States to facilitate comparisons with other countries, nearly all of which have long used GDP rather than GNP. GDP measures production within borders regardless of the nationality of the workers or the owners of the firm, whereas GNP measures only output produced by U.S. residents, businesses, and government regardless of where they're located. So the output of a Japanese auto plant located in the United States is included in GDP but not GNP. The output of a U.S. textile firm in Mexico would be included in our GNP but not our GDP. For the U.S., the numerical difference between the two numbers is very small. For example, in 1990 GDP was $5.514 trillion, whereas GNP was $5.525 trillion, a difference of less than two-tenths of 1%.

Nominal GDP is measured in current dollars. To make a meaningful comparison across years it must be deflated for changes in the price level, converting it to a constant-dollar measure of *real* **GDP**, or *gdp* to continue our practice of using lower case letters for "real" values. It is this measure that most closely approximates the concept of **real output, *y*,** used in our model.

for these short-run output adjustments.[5] For now we simply assume that a decline in aggregate demand prompts businesses to cut back on production, reduce average hours of work per week, and perhaps lay off some workers. Similarly, an increase in overall demand is initially met by an increase in hours worked, perhaps through overtime by current employees or hiring temporary workers to meet the surge in demand. This yields a horizontal short run aggregate supply curve and also means a *temporary* movement beyond the economy's long-run production possibility frontier. *The PPF is still downward sloping, so scarcity and choice still rule. It simply means that the boundary has some elasticity to it so that even a fully employed economy can temporarily increase total output in the short run.*

This alteration of supply side assumptions leaves us with a model in which the initial impact of an increase in aggregate demand will be from points *A* to *A′* in Fig-

---

[5] The question of what causes these short-run adjustments in real output is at the center of one of the most controversial issues in macroeconomics—the nature of the business cycle. The disagreement is mostly over why, and for how long, real output can diverge from its full employment level. Our current assumption that this occurs temporarily (in something called a "short run") is consistent with several very different hypotheses about *why* it happens and *how long* it persists. Alternative stories of the business cycle and their policy implications are the subject of Part III, "Smoothing Business Cycles and Controlling Inflation."

ure 4.2, as *AD* shifts along the new short-run aggregate supply curve AS^{SR}. Then, as the market-clearing process works its way through the macroeconomy, output will eventually return to its long-run full employment level, but at the higher equilibrium price level at point *B*. Any further shifts in aggregate demand would initially move along a new horizontal short run supply curve through point *B* (not shown in the graph) as prices now become "sticky" at the higher price level, P_1.

With this combination of *short-run (SR) price rigidity* (horizontal AS^{SR}) and *long-run (LR) market clearing* (vertical *AS**) we have outlined a simple adjustment path (points *A* to *A'* to *B* in Figure 4.2) of a fully employed economy undergoing an increase in aggregate demand. This is a simple but significant step toward bringing our analysis closer to the real world. We can incorporate it formally into the model by specifying both short and long run responses in the following expanded version of equation 10.

$$P = P_0 \tag{10 SR}$$
$$y^* = F(n^*, k_0, i_0^{nst}) \tag{10 LR}$$

As before, k_0 is the fixed level of capital stock, i_0^{nst}) is the given institutional structure of the economy, and n^* and y^* are the full employment levels of employment and real output, respectively. We have restored scarcity to our analysis, yielding an *AD/AS* framework that will guide our thinking for the remainder of the book. The ingredients of this **expanded *AD/AS* model,** as we'll call it, are shown in Figure 4.3.

IN SUMMARY . . .

The Expanded AD/AS Model

As we discovered in Chapter 3, dropping the classical "constant velocity of money" assumption definitely complicates the aggregate demand picture by adding a number of interactions to the analysis. For example, we now need to consider the impact of **changes in real income** on consumption, money demand, tax revenues, and net exports. We must also consider the effect of **changes in the real rate of interest** on investment, net exports, and money demand. (These relationships are represented, respectively, in the parameters c_1, j_1, t_1, x_1, and i_2, x_2, and j_2.)

These interactions are all captured in the *IS* and *LM* equations and portrayed in the twin *IS-LM* and *AD* graphs. The result is a more complex picture, but also a more realistic and accurate one, in which aggregate demand can be altered not only by changes in monetary policy (ΔM_0), but also by changes in fiscal policy ($\Delta g_0, \Delta t_0$) or autonomous private spending (Δz_0).

Substituting short-run "sticky prices" for classical "market clearing" means shifts in *AD* now lead to temporary deviations of output from full employment along AS^{SR}. A recession, for example, doesn't have to be dismissed as a "temporary disequilibrium phenomenon" but can be modeled as the initial consequence of a sudden drop in aggregate demand. Long-run market clearing, sooner or later, brings the economy back to full employment along the vertical *AS** curve.

In short, the ten-equation expanded *AD/AS* model (shown in Figure 4.3) features "long-run market clearing" but also adds "short-run price stickiness" in which output rather than prices adjusts to changes in aggregate demand. With the velocity of money free to vary, shifts in aggregate demand can come from expenditure changes (public or private) as well as monetary changes.

The
Expanded
AD/AS
Model

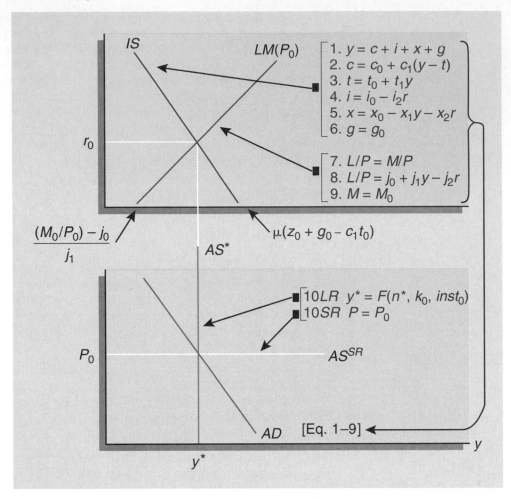

The equations shown in the figure:

1. $y = c + i + x + g$
2. $c = c_0 + c_1(y - t)$
3. $t = t_0 + t_1 y$
4. $i = i_0 - i_2 r$
5. $x = x_0 - x_1 y - x_2 r$
6. $g = g_0$

7. $L/P = M/P$
8. $L/P = j_0 + j_1 y - j_2 r$
9. $M = M_0$

$$\frac{(M_0/P_0) - j_0}{j_1}$$

$\mu(z_0 + g_0 - c_1 t_0)$

10LR $y^* = F(n^*, k_0, inst_0)$
10SR $P = P_0$

■ **FIGURE 4.3**

This model is "expanded" in the sense that it combines deviations from full employment (in a Keynesian short run, AS^{SR}) with a market-clearing return to full employment (in a classical long run, AS^*). The elements of aggregate demand are contained in the 6 equations underlying the *IS* curve and the three equations underlying *LM*. The *AD* curve contains all the information included in *IS* and *LM*, with the focus on y and P rather than y and r.

4.4 THREE APPLICATIONS OF THE EXPANDED AD/AS MODEL

Let's begin using the model by looking at three events—first a decline in autonomous investment spending ($-\Delta i_0$), then an increase in autonomous money demand ($+\Delta j_0$), and, finally, a sudden loss of capital stock ($-\Delta k_0$). These are important situations in their own right, but the main goal at this point is for you to learn the *AD/AS* model by using it rather than talking about it.

APPLICATION 1

A Decrease in Autonomous Real Investment Spending   Suppose there is a sudden drop in real private investment spending on plant and equipment by businesses, perhaps reflecting expectations of lower consumer demand and, hence, lower profits in the future. The expanded *AD/AS* model can help us trace the impact of this decline in investment spending on real output, the price level, and the real rate of interest, as well as on consumption, investment, net exports, tax revenues, and the size of the government deficit. More concisely, our model can reveal the effect of this $-\Delta i_0$ on y, P, r, c, i, x, t, and $b = g - t$.

With the economy initially at the corresponding points *A* in the twin graphs of Figure 4.4, this fall in investment spending will show up as a decline in *autonomous* investment expenditures ($-\Delta i_0$). Remember that we represented the three variables $c_0 + i_0 + x_0$ by the single term z_0 to streamline the *IS* equation to $y = \mu(z_0 + g_0 - c_1 t_0) - \mu(i_2 + x_2)r$. So our $-\Delta i_0$ means a $-\Delta z_0$ and, hence, a leftward shift from *IS* to *IS'* by the distance $\mu \Delta z_0$. Remember also that we added the money demand and supply relationships through the *LM* equation, which we write as $y = [(M_0/P_0) - j_0]/j_1 + (j_2/j_1)r]$. So as the inward shift in *IS* causes real output to fall it also decreases the demand for money and, finally, the real rate of interest as we slide down $LM(P_0)$ to point *B*.

The top graph shows that the real demand for output has fallen from y^* to y_1. This appears in the bottom picture as the movement from points *A* to *B* as aggregate demand shifts along the horizontal AS^{SR} curve. The full impact of this decrease in real investment spending on the economy is presented in the five steps below. This laborious and formal step-by-step analysis is used only in the three examples of this section. Once these basic mechanics are understood, many of the details can be dropped when using the model.

Step 1. Figure 4.4 shows that $-\Delta i_0$ leads to $-\Delta y$ and $-\Delta r$ at the given price level, P_0, as the economy adjusts initially along AS^{SR} and $LM(P_0)$ from points *A* to *B*.

Step 2. We now use the individual equations of the *AD/AS* model (restated below) to determine the short run change in all variables whose values depend upon y or r.

$y = c + i + x + g$	(1)		$L/P = M/P$	(7)
$c = c_0 + c_1(y - t)$	(2)		$L/P = j_0 + j_1 y - j_2 r$	(8)
$t = t_0 + t_1 y$	(3)		$M = M_0$	(9)
$i = i_0 - i_2 r$	(4)		$P = P_0$	(10 SR)
$x = x_0 - x_1 y - x_2 r$	(5)		$y^* = F(n^*, k_0, i_0^{nst})$	(10 LR)
$g = g_0$	(6)			

a. $+\Delta x$ **Net exports** (equation 5) rise because both y and r fell in step 1.

b. $-\Delta t$ **Tax revenues** (equation 3) decrease with the fall in income, even with no change in tax rates. The decrease in the tax base ($-\Delta y$) means a decline in tax revenues/payments.

c. $-\Delta(y - t)$ **Income after taxes** falls with the $-\Delta y$ but decreases with the $-\Delta t$. But because the income tax rate is less than 1 (i.e., $0 < t_1 < 1$), the fall in taxes is only a fraction of the drop in income. So the net effect must be to decrease $y - t$.

d. $-\Delta c$ The decrease in after-tax income, according to equation 2, decreases **consumption** spending by the fraction c_1 times the $\Delta(y - t)$.

■ **FIGURE 4.4**

The $-\Delta i_0$ shifts *IS* to *IS'* moving the economy from points *A* to *B* in the short run. As market clearing results in $-\Delta P$ in the long run, $LM(P_0)$ shifts to $LM(P_1)$ and the economy adjusts to point *C*.

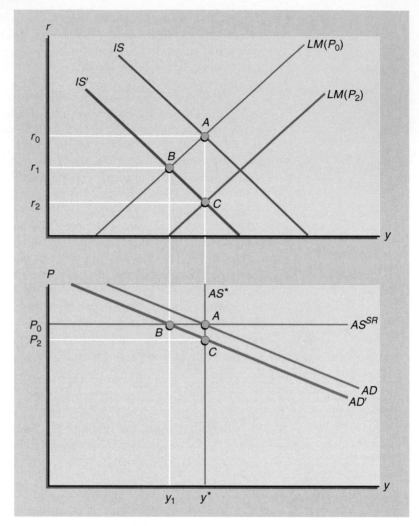

Impact of a Decline in Autonomous Investment

e. $+\Delta b$ Because of the decline in tax revenues, the **government deficit** ($b = g - t$) will rise because government spending is assumed to be unchanged. This is called a "cyclical change" in the deficit and is discussed further in the next chapter.

f. Δi?   **Investment spending** (equation 4) has two changes working in opposite directions. The initial fall in autonomous investment ($-\Delta i_0$) is followed by a decline in the real rate of interest ($-\Delta r$), which will induce additional investment spending of the amount $-i_2\Delta r$. Without further information we can't say which of these two effects is largest, so the short run change in real investment is unknown.

Step 3. As "sticky" short-run prices become flexible in the long run, the process of market clearing returns the economy to its vertical AS^* curve. This is shown in the bottom graph of Figure 4.4 as the movement from points

B to C along the AD' curve. The **price level falls** $(-\Delta P)$ and **output rises** $(+\Delta y)$ until the overall excess supply—the gap between AD', and AS^* at P_0—is eliminated at P_2.

Step 4. Because these are two pictures of the same economy, we can't leave the top graph stranded at point B while the bottom has adjusted to point C. We must include the impact of this falling price level $(-\Delta P)$ in the IS-LM graph by **shifting the LM curve** to the right as the decrease in P increases the real value of the money supply (M_0/P). The LM curve continues to shift until P has reached its long run equilibrium (P_2), returning real output to its long-run level (y^*). This shift from $LM(P_0)$ to $LM(P_2)$ causes the real interest rate to fall even further than it did in the short run. Thus, Figure 4.4 reveals that the net long run impact of the initial decrease in real investment spending $(-\Delta i_0)$ in a fully employed economy is $-\Delta P$, $-\Delta r$, but $\Delta y = 0$ as the economy moves from points A to C.

Step 5. The long-run story is completed by returning to the underlying equations as we did for the short run in step 2. The long-run impact (from start to finish, ignoring the temporary short-run adjustments) of the $-\Delta i_0$ on the underlying variables is

a. $+\Delta x$ **Net exports** (equation 5) have risen in the long run because of the fall in r.

b. $\Delta t = 0$ **Tax revenues** (equation 3) have remained unchanged since real income has not changed in the long run.

c. $\Delta(y - t) = 0$ Since neither income nor taxes has changed, real **after-tax income** is unchanged.

d. $\Delta c = 0$ With no change in $y - t$, **consumption spending** (equation 2) is unchanged.

e. $\Delta b = 0$ The **government deficit** $(b = g - t)$ is unaffected in the long run because neither public spending nor taxes have changed.

f. $-\Delta i$ This is a slightly tricky one because real **investment spending** (equation 4) has two factors working in opposite directions—the initial decrease in i_0 and the subsequent long-run decrease in the real rate of interest to r_2 which increases investment spending. How can we say that the net effect is a decrease in investment spending? We know that $y = c + i + x + g$ and also $\Delta y = \Delta c = \Delta g = 0$ in the long run. The long-run drop in r has caused a $+\Delta x$, so it must be true that the net effect on real investment is negative and equal, in absolute value, to the increase in net exports. If it weren't, equation 1 wouldn't hold true.[6]

---

[6] Note also that because the real interest rate has fallen even more than it did in the short run and Δi still ends up negative, then it must also be true that the short run Δi, which we called indeterminate back in step $2(f)$, was actually negative.

So the answer to the question "What macroeconomic impact will a decrease in autonomous real investment spending have in a fully employed economy?" is as follows.

Impact of $-\Delta i_0$ on	Short Run $(A \to B)$	Long Run $(A \to C)$
y	−	0
r	−	−
P	0	−
c	−	0
i	?	−
x	+	+
b	+	0

If autonomous investment were to rise instead of fall, the reasoning would be identical and the answer would be everything in reverse. *IS* and *AD* would shift to the right, all the pluses would change to minuses and vice versa. Because Δc_0 and Δx_0 work the same as Δi_0 (remember they all shift *IS* through the z_0 term), those changes would be similar in their impact on the economy. Moreover, because public spending works with the same multiplier as private spending, as we saw in the previous chapter, the results would be basically the same for a Δg_0 as for Δz_0.[7] Learning the mechanics of the analysis (not just the "right" answers) for this single example will, therefore, enable you to understand the short- and long-run impacts of *any* event that shifts the *IS* curve. The next example presents a similar analysis for shifts in the other segment of aggregate demand, the *LM* curve.

APPLICATION 2

An Increase in Autonomous Real Money Demand　Suppose there's a sudden increase in the demand for money, perhaps reflecting fears of a coming financial crisis and plummeting stock and bond prices. What will be the impact of this increase in *autonomous* money demand ($+\Delta j_0$ in equation 7, the part that's independent of current levels of income and interest rates) on the variables in our model of the macroeconomy, y, P, r, c, i, x, t, and b?

Starting at points A in the twin graphs of Figure 4.5, the $+\Delta j_0$ *reduces* the horizontal intercept of the *LM* curve, $y \downarrow = [(M_0/P_0) - \uparrow j_0]/j_1 + (j_2/j_1)r$, shifting it to the left to $LM'(P_0)$ in Figure 4.5. Equilibrium on the demand side has moved from points A to B in the top graph as the increased money demand raises the real interest rate and lowers aggregate demand. This drop in demand shows up in the bottom graph as the shift from *AD* to *AD'* and the movement from points A to B along the short run aggregate supply curve, AS^{SR}. So the short-run impact of this increase in real money demand can be summarized as

Step 1.　Figure 4.5 shows that the $+\Delta j_0$ leads to $+\Delta r$ and $-\Delta y$ at the initial price level, P_0, as the economy adjusts from points A to B.

Step 2.　We now use the individual relationships in the underlying equations of

---

[7] However, public spending is a little more involved because the government has three options for financing an increase in spending—an increase in taxes ($+\Delta t$), deficit spending ($+\Delta b$), or simply printing more money (ΔM). This is covered in Section 4.6.

■ FIGURE 4.5

The $+\Delta j_0$ shifts $LM(P_0)$ to $LM(P_0)'$, moving the economy from points A to B in the short run. As market clearing results in $-\Delta P$ in the long run, $LM(P_0)'$ shifts to $LM(P_2)'$ as the economy adjusts to point C. Note that the real rate of interest returns to its original level.

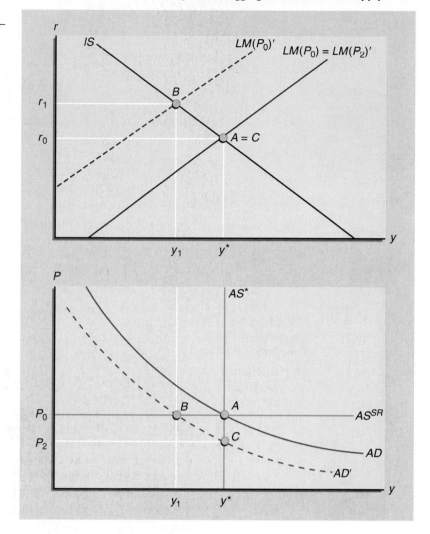

Impact of an Increase in Autonomous Money Demand

the *AD/AS* model to determine the short-run changes of the remaining variables.

$y = c + i + x + g$	(1)		$L/P = M/P$	(7)
$c = c_0 + c_1(y - t)$	(2)		$L/P = j_0 + j_1 y - j_2 r$	(8)
$t = t_0 + t_1 y$	(3)		$M = M_0$	(9)
$i = i_0 - i_2 r$	(4)		$P = P_0$	(10 SR)
$x = x_0 - x_1 y - x_2 r$	(5)		$y^* = F(n^*, k_0, i_0^{nst})$	(10 LR)
$g = g_0$	(6)			

a. $-\Delta i$ **Investment spending** (equation 4) declines with the rise in the real interest rate.

b. $-\Delta t$ **Tax revenues** (equation 3) will also decline as the tax base, y, falls.

c. $-\Delta(y - t)$ **After-tax income** has fallen because of the $-\Delta y$ but has risen because of the $-\Delta t$. Because the decline in taxes is a fraction (t_1) of the fall in y, the net effect must be a decrease in $(y - t)$.

d. $-\Delta c$ The drop in after-tax income leads households to lower **consumption spending** (equation 2).

e. $+\Delta b$ Because of the drop in tax revenues, the **government deficit** $(b = g - t)$ will increase as the economy slips below full employment. This is called a cyclical rise in the deficit because it's the result of a "cyclical" departure from full employment, i.e., $y \neq y^*$.

f. Δx?   **Net exports** (equation 5) have two changes working in opposite directions. The rise in the interest rate $(+\Delta r)$ lowers net exports while the decline in income works to increase them. Without further information about the magnitudes of the $+\Delta y$, $+\Delta r$, x_1, and x_2, we can't determine the final impact on net exports. So Δx is unknown.

Step 3. In the long run, price flexibility and market clearing return the economy to full employment (y^*), and we move to point C in the bottom graph of Figure 4.5. As the **price level** falls to P_2, the overall excess supply (the gap between AD' and AS^* at the initial price level) is eliminated.

Step 4. This drop in the price level $(-\Delta P)$ feeds back to the top graph by **shifting the LM curve** to the right as the *real* value of the money supply (M/P) rises. The LM curve continues to shift until P has reached its long-run equilibrium (P_2), returning demand for output to its long run level (y^*). This shift from $LM(P_0)'$ to $LM(P_2)'$ lowers the real interest rate back to its initial level. Thus Figure 4.5 reveals that the net long-run impact of the autonomous increase in money demand in a fully employed economy is $-\Delta P$, with $\Delta y = \Delta r = 0$.

Step 5. The story is then completed by returning to the underlying equations as we did for the short run in step 2. The long-run impact (from start to finish, points A to C) of an increased autonomous demand for money is

a. $\Delta i = 0$ **Investment spending** (equation 4) is unchanged because $\Delta r = 0$ in the long run.

b. $\Delta t = 0$ **Tax revenues** (equation 3) have remained unchanged since real income has not changed in the long run.

c. $\Delta(y - t) = 0$ Because neither y nor t has changed, there is no change in **after-tax income.**

d. $\Delta c = 0$ With no change in $y - t$, **consumption spending** (equation 2) is unchanged.

e. $\Delta b = 0$ The **government deficit** is unaffected in the long run because neither g nor t have changed.

f. $\Delta x = 0$ **Net exports** (equation 5) are also unchanged because neither y nor r has changed in the long run.

So the answer to the question "What impact will an increase in autonomous money demand have in a fully employed economy?" is as follows.

Impact of $+\Delta j_0$ on	Short Run $(A \to B)$	Long Run $(A \to C)$
y	−	0
r	+	0
P	0	−
c	−	0
i	−	0
x	?	0
b	+	0

A fall in autonomous money demand would be the mirror image of this. *LM* and *AD* would shift to the right, all the pluses would change to minuses and vice versa. Because a change in the money supply (ΔM) also changes the intercept of the *LM* curve, *monetary policy* will have similar effects as we'll see in Chapter 6.

APPLICATION 3

A Negative Supply Shock   The first two applications looked at events that originated on the demand or spending side and then spread their short- and long-run effects throughout the economy. Let's now turn to the supply side of our model, represented in the long run by the production function in equation 10 [$y^* = F(n^*, k_0, i_0^{nst})$]. Suppose there's a sudden loss or destruction of our capital stock ($-\Delta k_0$), perhaps from an economic embargo (e.g., oil), a war, or a natural disaster. Unlike the two earlier applications, the initial impact of this **negative supply shock** begins on the supply side of our model.

Figure 4.6 illustrates this loss of capital with the leftward shift of aggregate supply to AS*′, creating a situation at point *A* in which aggregate demand now exceeds the newly reduced level of supply, putting upward pressure on the price level. The short-run "price stickiness" assumption, embodied in the horizontal AS^{SR} curve, tells us that the economy remains at point *A* in the short run, despite the fact that the full employment level of output has fallen. But as price rigidity loosens and the market clearing process gets under way, the macroeconomy will adjust to the now lower full employment level of output ($y^{*\prime}$) at a higher price level (P_1) as it moves from points *A* to *B* in the graphs. The rising price level reduces the real value of the money supply, shifting $LM(P_0)$ to $LM(P_1)$ and results in a rise in the real rate of interest.

This example raises an important question. Is it realistic to assume that the degree of price stickiness following a shift in aggregate supply is the same as for a demand shift? Sources of price rigidity will be examined more carefully in our later discussion of business cycles. But let's suppose that while prices adjust sluggishly to demand shocks, they react much more quickly to supply shocks. Our present rule of thumb will be that for supply shocks the short run price rigidity is generally so brief that we can safely ignore it and focus on the long-run impact.

Without going through all the step-by-step detail, we see that the long run impact of a sizable loss of capital on the macroeconomy is to reduce real output ($-\Delta y$) and raise both the real interest rate ($+\Delta r$) and the price level ($+\Delta P$). Investment spending (equation 4) will then decline ($-\Delta i$) because of the higher rate of interest. Tax revenues (equation 3) will fall because of the lower tax base ($-\Delta y^*$), leading to a rise in the government deficit [$+\Delta b = +\Delta(g - t)$]. Both income and taxes have

■ **FIGURE 4.6**

The impact of a loss of capital stock $(-\Delta k_0)$ shows up initially as a leftward shift of AS^* to $AS^{*\prime}$, reducing the long-run full employment level of real output accordingly $(-\Delta y^*)$. As the price level rises, the real value of the money supply diminishes, and the economy moves to a new equilibrium (point B) with a higher interest rate and price level, and lower output.

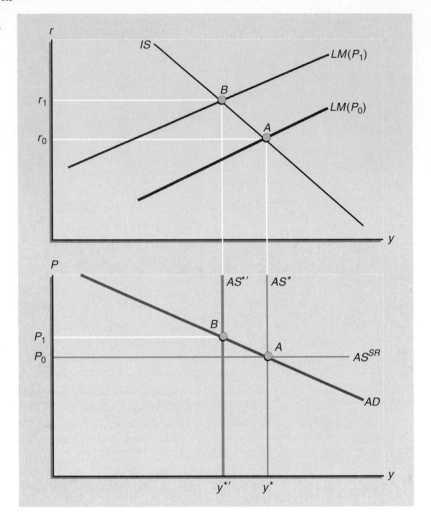

Negative Supply Shock

fallen, but because taxes are a fraction (t_1) of the change in income (equation 3), after-tax income will fall and so will consumption spending $(-\Delta c$, from equation 2). The impact on net exports (equation 6) is uncertain without further information on the actual magnitude of the changes in y and r as well as the size of the parameters x_1 and x_2.

Impact of $-\Delta k$ on	Short Run (A)	Long Run $(A \to B)$
y	0	−
r	0	+
P	0	+
c	0	−
i	0	−
x	0	?
b	0	+

A WORD ABOUT MODELS AND REALITY

These equations and graphs are a simplified (abstract) representation of the macroeconomy, to which we apply deductive logic to derive implications. A model can never be the "true" picture of the "real world" that we would like. It is just a window through which we hope to catch a partial glimpse of a complex and changing reality. When you begin to wonder whether such a quick peek is worth all this trouble, remember the alternatives. How else can we get at the connections between choices and consequences? Other approaches involve rules of thumb and slogans that are often just thinly disguised versions of wishful thinking or narrow self-interest.

It's not surprising that those less analytical approaches are far more prevalent than economic analysis. They offer quick, easy answers without requiring us to gather many facts or do much, if any, thinking. They fit nicely into media "sound bites" used by political candidates who have learned that a memorable phrase ("Read my lips, no new taxes"; "The loud sucking sound you'll hear is our jobs headed South to Mexico.") gets much more political mileage than a careful, responsible explanation of the various alternatives confronting economic policy.

Such shortcuts have their place, but so does a more painstaking and responsible attempt to understand how economic events and policy changes will affect our overall economy and our individual lives. We'll see many examples of popular economic programs, marketed through slogans, appeals to the crudest "common sense," patriotism, and so on, that turned out badly. We will also see how a little careful thought and enlightened common sense, guided by an analytical framework (model), can do dramatically better.

4.5 STABILIZATION POLICY—A FIRST LOOK

Let's take the three examples of the previous section a step further to get a first look at **macroeconomic stabilization policy.** The notion of using fiscal and monetary policies to counteract unwelcome shocks to the economy, so widely accepted today, is a legacy of the "activist" policy stance of Keynes and his followers. Simply put, the idea is to quicken the return to full employment with "countercyclical" policy stimulus rather than relying solely on the market-clearing process.

Viewed through the lens of our *AD/AS* model it's easy to see both the logic and appeal of such an approach. In the first example earlier, a decline in autonomous investment spending $(-\Delta i_0)$ set off a contraction of aggregate demand that pushed the economy into recession. This is reproduced in Figure 4.7(a) as the movement from points A to B. But rather than waiting for price level adjustments to slide us down to point C, suppose we ran an *expansionary fiscal policy* $(+\Delta g_0$ or $-\Delta t_0)$. This could shift IS' and hence AD' back to their initial levels and return the economy to its original position at point A. In the same way, the contraction triggered by increased autonomous money demand $(+\Delta j_0)$, as illustrated in Figure 4.7(b), could be

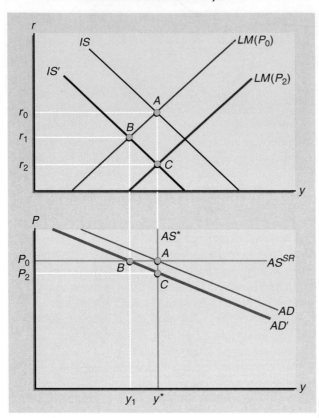

Drop in Autonomous Investment

■ FIGURE 4.7(a)

$(IS \rightarrow IS'$ and $AD \rightarrow AD')$ could be off-set by expansionary fiscal policy $(+\Delta g_0$ or $-\Delta t_0)$, returning the economy to point A instead of relying on the market-clearing process to move the economy to point C.

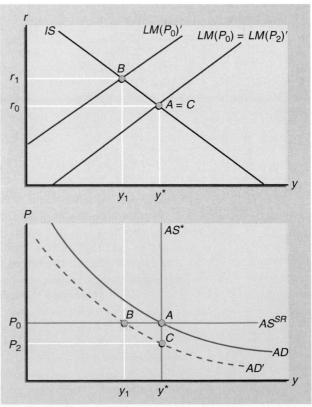

Increased Autonomous Money Demand

■ FIGURE 4.7(b)

$(LM(P_0) \rightarrow LM(P_0)'$ and $AD \rightarrow AD')$ could be offset by expansionary monetary policy $(+\Delta M)$, returning the economy to A instead of relying on the market-clearing process to move the economy to point C.

counteracted by an *expansionary monetary policy* $(+\Delta M_0)$ that shifts both the *LM* and *AD* curves back to their original positions.

In either case, the allure of using fiscal and monetary policy to stabilize the economy around full employment is obvious. Its potential to moderate if not eliminate the periodic ups and downs of economic activity that characterize the business cycle is just as appealing today as it was in the Great Depression. The difference between a mild and a severe recession in the U.S. in the 1990s can be measured in millions of workers who don't experience joblessness and in output and income differentials in the hundreds of billions of dollars.

Our *AD/AS* framework makes stabilization policy look easy. We apparently need only keep a close watch on current economic performance and at the first sign of trouble respond appropriately. In reality, of course, things are never so simple, and it's important to remind ourselves of the limitations of this first view of stabilization policy. Although the model now incorporates a short-run response that was missing in the classical analysis, it does so in a very primitive way. In particular, there is no explanation of how long this "short run" lasts before price flexibility returns us to "long-run" full employment. Nor is there any analysis of how long it takes for a policy response to be implemented and then to have its desired impact on aggregate demand. As it now stands, this model holds out the promise of effective countercyclical policy but withholds the details about timing that are crucial to an "appropriate" policy response.

When an economy has fallen into a very deep and prolonged recession, popularly called an economic "depression," the timing of a policy response is of little practical significance. This, of course, was the backdrop against which Keynes's policy views in the 1930s were set. But the post–World War II period has been one in which departures from full employment have been comparatively small and short-lived, making issues of timing and policy lags more important. We will have much more to say about this in later chapters. You may already know that the economics profession is divided over whether aggressive policy responses can or cannot moderate economic fluctuations. One view, associated with the so-called **Keynesian** and **new Keynesian** schools, is convinced that careful countercyclical policy actions can greatly reduce the inherent instability of the macroeconomy. They advocate what is usually termed an **activist** approach to macroeconomic fluctuations. At the other end of the spectrum we find the **nonactivist** views of the **new classical** and **monetarist** schools, which contend that attempts to reduce fluctuations in output and employment, however well intended, are doomed to failure. Either they will have minimal impact on real output and employment (new classical), or they may actually turn out to *de*stabilize overall economic activity and prices (monetarist).

In later chapters, we'll look carefully at the reasons behind such widely differing views. There's clearly no simple right or wrong answer revealed by past experience. We can find episodes in which activist policies surely prevented lost jobs and lost output. We can also find situations in which the impact of a policy change was felt only after economic recovery was substantially complete, causing overshooting and further macroeconomic instability. The key question, of course, is whether we can determine *in advance* whether an intended countercyclical policy is likely to be effective, inconsequential, or *pro*cyclical. This will be the focus of Part III (Chapters 8–11) "Smoothing Business Cycles and Controlling Inflation."

So far our discussion of stabilization policy has considered only situations in which the initial disturbance came from the demand side of the economy. What about our third example in which the decline in output came from a *negative supply shock?* Figure 4.8 shows how a loss in capital stock shifts aggregate supply to the left,

■ FIGURE 4.8

The initial $-\Delta k_0$ would move the economy from points A to B. But a prompt $+\Delta M_0$ might move it to point C. However, because this lies above the new full-employment level of output, $y^{*\prime}$, it is not sustainable. The rising price level and interest rate will move the economy up and back to point D.

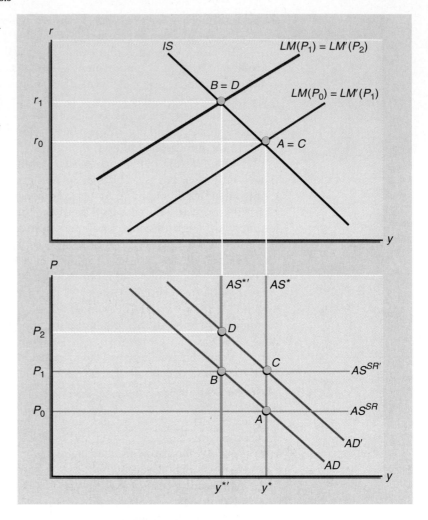

Negative Supply Shock with
Expansionary Monetary Policy

eventually causing output to fall and both the price level and real interest rates to rise. Suppose policy makers attempt to counter this falling output by increasing the money supply. At first glance such an expansionary response to a contractionary event may seem beneficial. As the negative supply shock shifts AS^* to $AS^{*\prime}$, moving the economy from points A to B in Figure 4.8, the increase in the money supply shifts LM and AD to the right along $AS^{SR\prime}$, pushing the macroeconomy to point C. This combination of negative supply shock $(-\Delta k_0)$ and expansionary monetary policy $(+\Delta M_0)$ has increased the price level but prevented output from falling.

Unfortunately, however, this is not the end of the story. The situation at point C is not sustainable. The leftward shift to $AS^{*\prime}$ means that long run output must end up at the lower level, $y^{*\prime}$. You should not be surprised that the attempt to offset a loss in productive inputs $(-\Delta k_0)$ with more "green" pieces of paper $(+\Delta M_0)$ is doomed to failure as market clearing pushes the economy to a lower level of output and an even higher price level as shown at point D. Repeated attempts to use monetary policy to offset a negative supply shock and return the economy to its initial level of real output (y^*) can only lead to continued increases in the price level. This last example is a useful reminder that our policy instruments work predominantly from the demand side and that no matter how ingenious or well meaning their use, they are no match for supply-side problems.

The possibility that at least some of the ups and downs of the macroeconomy originate on the supply side certainly complicates the use of stabilization policy. Implementation of an activist approach to the business cycle requires prompt responses to changing circumstances. But we may not be able to see at the outset whether a downturn in economic activity is coming from a negative demand shock, a negative supply shock, or some combination of the two. The likelihood that economic instability might originate on the supply side was given little attention until the Organization of Petroleum Exporting Countries (OPEC) oil embargo and subsequent price shocks of the 1970s. Since then, even the more activist-oriented economists have become more hesitant to recommend aggressive monetary or fiscal responses at the first sign of a downturn. Moreover, another school of nonactivists has arisen to argue that supply fluctuations are actually the *primary* source of the business cycle. This so-called **real business cycle** view, though certainly in the minority among economists, has been an important challenge to the earlier presumption of both activists and nonactivists that macroeconomic instability is inevitably a demand-side phenomenon.

4.6 A QUICK SKETCH OF THE GREAT DEPRESSION

The most costly economic lesson in U.S. history was undoubtedly the decade-long economic crisis known as the Great Depression. Between 1929 and 1933, for example, the price level fell by more than 20%, yet real output in 1933 was almost one-third below its 1929 level. Even the most rapid price and wage declines of the century were unable to bring about the market-clearing return to full employment predicted by the classical model.

There were many events that influenced economic performance in the 1930s, and there is still disagreement about their relative importance. But we need not go beyond a few basic events to understand a good part of why the U.S. economy suffered such devastation. There is general agreement that an initial recessionary decline in autonomous consumption and investment spending in 1929 and 1930 was then turned into a depressionary collapse by a powerful accomplice—the *government*. A rough characterization of the decisive years 1929 to 1933 would be a period of major declines in autonomous private spending ($-\Delta z_0$) followed by both contractionary fiscal policy in an attempt to balance the federal budget ($-\Delta g_0$ and $+\Delta t_0$) and severely contractionary monetary policy ($-\Delta M_0$) as the Federal Reserve stood by while bank closings and other monetary events resulted in almost a 33% drop in the nation's supply of money.

Putting all this together in Figure 4.9 paints a somber portrait of a deep and partly self-inflicted economic wound. After the initial drop in autonomous spending ($-\Delta z_0$) shifted IS to IS', subsequent attempts at budget balancing caused a further drop in aggregate demand as higher taxes ($+\Delta t_0$) and reduced government spending ($-\Delta g_0$) shifted IS' to IS'', moving the economy from points B to C. Monetary contraction then reduced demand still further as the $-\Delta M$ caused $LM(P_0)$ to shift to

■ FIGURE 4.9

An initial drop in autonomous consumption and investment spending moved the economy from points *A* to *B*. This was then followed by contractionary fiscal and monetary policies that continued the contraction to points *C* and *D*.

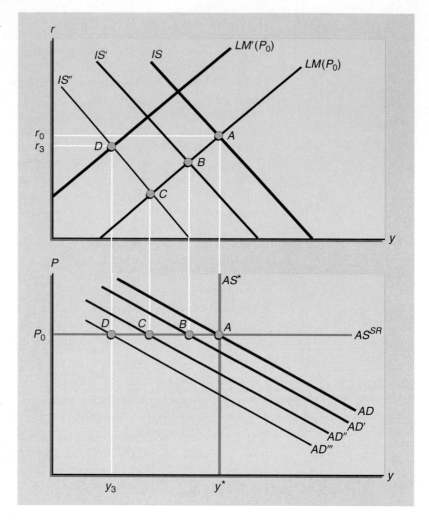

Scenario for the Great Depression

$LM'(P_0)$.[8] The combined effect is to shift aggregate demand all the way to AD''', moving the economy finally to point D in the graphs. Whatever decline in the price level was occurring (not shown in the graph) was obliterated by the continuing leftward shift of aggregate demand.

In hindsight, viewed through the lens of our expanded *AD/AS* model, it's difficult to resist the conclusion that a significant recession was prolonged and deepened by the actions of bewildered policy makers following the advice of a confused economics profession. The orthodox classical analysis at the time, which could do little more than proclaim a continuing "temporary disequilibrium in the economy" and prescribe "patience" as the treatment, became increasingly ridiculed. Market clearing was supposed to ensure that such "temporary" events would not continue year after year after year. In the absence of an alternative analysis, policy was guided by slogans

---

[8] If you're wondering how *far* to shift the *IS* and *LM* curves, don't worry about it. Without specific values for this model all we can know is the *direction* of the changes, not their magnitude. This is sometimes called a "qualitative" as opposed to "quantitative" analysis. Of course, if we had chosen a larger shift in *LM*, the real interest rate would have risen further. So this qualitative analysis does have its limitations. But for the present case our concern is with the change in real output from all these shifts. It is unambiguously *negative!*

and wishful thinking. Tragically, but not surprisingly, this only deepened and extended the crisis.

The Great Depression was a watershed event not only in the lives of hundreds of millions of people across the world, but also in the study of macroeconomics and the practice of economic policy making. It led Keynes and a flood of followers to the kind of short-run analysis now embodied in our *AD/AS* framework. This model reveals that contractionary aggregate demand policies are powerful enough to plunge a nation into an extended period of stagnation. But it also implies that such policies in reverse can be used to hoist it out. This lesson is now fully incorporated into the mainstream of economic science.

A POLICY FANTASY FOR THE 1930s

Policy making in the 1930s was guided by a model that focused on relatively distant, long-run outcomes by *assuming* both market clearing and constant velocity of money. It was unable to address the tragic short term consequences of the contractionary events and policies of the early 1930s. How might things have been different if the expanded *AD/AS* model had been available to policy makers?

Returning in a time machine, suppose we convince President Hoover and Congress that however laudable their "balance the budget" program might sound, a recession is not the time for *contractionary* policies. We caution them that their hopeful "Prosperity is just around the corner" campaign is little more than empty propaganda.

Suppose they're persuaded by our arguments and agree to run a neutral fiscal policy that is neither contractionary nor expansionary. Equally important, suppose we convince decision makers at the Federal Reserve to offset the rapid decline in the money supply with an unprecedented infusion of funds into the banking system so that they will at least be running a neutral monetary policy.

In the absence of sharply contractionary fiscal and monetary policies, our expanded *AD/AS* model predicts that the Great Depression would not have occurred. Economic history would instead tell a story of a serious downturn that might have been called the "Long Recession." But it would not have produced the deep economic devastation that was actually experienced.

Unshackled from the Great Depression, what directions the energy and creativity of that decade might have taken can never be known. For most people, the struggle with a falling and then stagnant standard of living was at the center of their lives, every day, month after month, year after year. For those not directly affected, the uncertainty as to how long it would last and how far it would spread meant endless anxiety. If macroeconomics does no more than keep us alert to the kinds of policy mistakes made in the 1930s, it can prevent a fall in living standards that would reach well into the trillions of dollars. Try to keep this in mind the next time you become frustrated with the conflicting advice of distinguished economists on how to cope with the latest economic "crisis." As serious as many of our current economic issues may seem, they pale in comparison with the reality of the Great Depression.

⑤ⓒ *4.7 A COMPARISON OF TWO MODELS*

A useful way to reinforce the main results of these last three chapters is to contrast the major implications of this Keynesian-inspired expansion of the *AD/AS* model with those of the classical model of Chapter 2.

1. Full Employment

    Classical Model: Full Employment Prevails

    > The market-clearing process keeps the "classical thermostat" set at full employment. Deviations from full employment are assumed to be relatively short-lived, provided that price flexibility is not limited by monopoly power or government policies.

    Keynesian Model: Full Employment Is a Long Run Outcome

    > Markets don't clear instantly. Short-run price "stickiness" following demand shifts can explain the departures of actual from full employment output that define the "business cycle."

2. Importance of Aggregate Demand

    Classical Model: Aggregate Demand Has No "Real" Effects

    > *Money is a "veil."* Changes in the money supply alter the price level but leave real output, employment, and the real rate of interest unchanged.

    > *Only money matters.* Under the assumption that the velocity of money is constant over time, only ΔM can shift aggregate demand.

    > *Fiscal policy is "powerless."* Changes in government spending and taxes don't alter aggregate demand, hence have no impact on real output or the price level.

    Keynesian Model: Aggregate Demand Has "Real" Effects in the Short Run, But Not in the Long Run

    > Because price rigidity permits real output to deviate from full employment, shifts in aggregate demand cause short run changes in output (and employment). Moreover, because the velocity of money can vary, aggregate demand can be shifted by fiscal policy or by changes in private spending, as well as by monetary policy. Hence fiscal policy is not powerless to shift aggregate demand and money is not all that matters. Money is still a "veil" but only in the long run.

3. Importance of Aggregate Supply

    Classical Model: Supply Is the Key to Economic Growth

    > Output is determined solely by the vertical *AS** curve. It can increase only with growth in the inputs—with increases in labor or capital or improvements in the institutional structure.

    Keynesian Model: Supply Remains the Key to Growth

    > In the short run the economy can deviate from its long run *AS** curve, moving along the horizontal short run supply curve. But ulti-

mately, real output is determined by the vertical aggregate supply curve, just as in the classical world.

4. Inflation

Classical Model: Inflation Comes from "Too Much" Money

Continued increases in the price level are typically the result of a too rapid growth of aggregate demand, specifically $\%\Delta M > \%\Delta y^*$. With velocity assumed constant, it is only continued increases in the money supply that can cause demand to grow. In other words, the central bank is the only possible source of inflation and, therefore, its only cure.

Keynesian Model: Inflation Can Come from Anything that Keeps Aggregate Demand Growing More Rapidly Than Aggregate Supply

Whether or not the central bank is the culprit becomes an empirical question (a matter for statistical testing) rather than a foregone conclusion based on the logic of the model.

These last two chapters have introduced the basic analytical framework underlying macroeconomic thinking since Keynes's *General Theory*. Developments in macroeconomic theory and policy making since that time can be usefully viewed as either extensions of this model or as reactions to its perceived limitations. Coming chapters will continue to apply the expanded (Keynesian) *AD/AS* model to major policy issues. Let's reiterate some important policy insights already uncovered.

1. An **economic depression** is not something that happens frequently or easily. In the 1930s, a recession was turned into prolonged decline and stagnation by contractionary actions of both the fiscal and monetary authorities.

2. The *AD/AS* model provides a framework for understanding **cyclical fluctuations** in output but can sometimes prove to be an unreliable guide to stabilization policy unless analysis of the time dimension—that is, time lags in policy formulation as well as in the multiplier and market-clearing processes—is carefully included.

3. **Supply shocks** create a special situation in which prices adjust more rapidly than with demand shifts. Hence a negative supply shock quickly leads to falling output and rising prices. Attempts to offset it with demand stimulus may temporarily prevent output from falling but will cause lasting price-level increases.

☯ *4.8 OVERVIEW*

1. This chapter began by translating the information from the *IS-LM* model of aggregate demand into an explicit relationship between total real output (y) and the overall price level (P), called the **aggregate demand curve (AD).** Using this ten-equation model, we found that a change in the price level alters the real value of the money supply (M_0/P) changing the intercept of the *LM* curve. This shift in *LM* means a movement along the *IS* curve until new equilibrium levels of y and r are established for the new level of P. The result is that an increase in P sets off the following process: $+\Delta P \Rightarrow -\Delta(M_0/P) \Rightarrow +\Delta r \Rightarrow -\Delta i$ and $-\Delta x \Rightarrow -\Delta y \Leftrightarrow -\Delta c$. This

inverse relationship between the price level and real output $(+\Delta P \Rightarrow \ldots \Rightarrow -\Delta y)$ is contained in the **downward slope of the *AD* curve.**

2. Changes in the price level, which shift *LM* along *IS*, are therefore built into the slope of *AD*. Anything else that shifts either *LM* or *IS* will **shift** the entire *AD* curve. For example, expansionary fiscal policy $(+\Delta g_0$ or $-\Delta t_0)$ shifts both *IS* and *AD* to the right. So does any increase in the components of private autonomous spending $(+\Delta z_0)$. Expansionary monetary policy $(+\Delta M_0)$ shifts *LM* and *AD* to the right. So does a decrease in autonomous money demand $(-\Delta j_0)$.

3. Intricate as the twin *IS-LM* and *AD* graphs may seem, they only address half the issue—demand, not supply. They reveal nothing about the production process, nothing about how many goods will actually be supplied in the economy. In other words, the central frustration that defines economics—**scarcity**—has been left out. This is easily amended by adding a familiar relationship, the production function $[y^* = F(n^*, k_0, i_0^{nst})]$. This now defines a vertical aggregate supply curve at full employment, AS^*. This curve represents essentially the same boundary that we encountered with the PPF and is identical to the supply curve of the classical model.

4. But to capture the Keynesian belief that shifts in aggregate demand cause short run changes in real output, the classical aggregate supply curve must somehow be relaxed. An easy way to do this is with the subsidiary assumption that the price level is fixed ("sticky prices") in the short run. The resulting **horizontal short run aggregate supply curve, AS^{SR},** allows this model to explain short run deviations of output from its full employment level. As time passes and markets clear, we return to the long run, vertical aggregate supply curve and full employment (y^*).

5. With all this apparatus in place—*IS-LM as the foundation for AD* and *price stickiness underlying short-run deviations from AS**—substantive economic analysis of short-run events is finally available to us. We applied this expanded **Keynesian AD/AS model** to some basic situations and saw that it could be used to address several important questions, including the following:

a. A decrease in investment spending contracts output in the short run. But a decrease in money demand would work in the opposite direction to expand the economy. Precisely why is this?

b. Countercyclical policy is designed to "calm the waters" of the business cycle. What insights does the classical framework yield on such a plan? How does the expanded *AD/AS* model differ on this issue?

c. In what ways might the expanded *AD/AS* model not be a reliable guide to smoothing the business cycle? What implications do you think this would have for the activist policy position associated with the Keynesian tradition?

d. Why may an antirecession policy that makes sense for a negative demand shock not be appropriate if the downturn is due to a negative supply shock?

e. The classical model predicts that extended periods of high unemployment are prevented by the process of market clearing. But it could not offer a convincing explanation of the economic crisis of the 1930s. How can the expanded *AD/AS* model explain the Great Depression?

f. If we could go back to the early days of the Great Depression, taking this new and improved *AD/AS* model with us, what policy recommendations are we likely to make? How does this compare with the actual policy choices made at the time?

g. Why did the U.S. economy spring back to life so buoyantly with the coming of World War II?

6. The questions above might seem to have been mistakenly put in the Overview section instead of with the Review Questions. Actually, they belong in both. The reason for putting questions here is to encourage you to learn to derive your own answers to whatever issues may arise. Rather than memorizing answers to many hundreds of potential questions, it is more sensible as well as much simpler (with a little practice) to use the mechanics of the model to generate your own answers. As the parable says: Give me a fish and I will eat for a day. Teach me to fish and I shall eat for a lifetime.

✆ *4.9 REVIEW QUESTIONS*

1. Define the following basic concepts or terms:

Aggregate demand curve	Gross domestic product	Monetarist
Short-run aggregate supply	Negative supply shock	Nonactivist
Short-run price rigidity	Stabilization policy	Recession
Long-run market clearing	Keynesian	Economic depression
Keynesian (expanded) *AD/AS* model	Activist	Cyclical fluctuations
	Classical	

2. In the classical tradition, the direct economic role of government is highly circumscribed and the conclusion that this does not hinder economic performance is embodied in the classical macroeconomic model. In the Keynesian tradition, government action is viewed as a response to the supposed failure of actual economies to achieve the optimal results of the classical model.

a. What are the alleged shortcomings of the classical analytics, and how does the Keynesian model "correct" these?

b. Discuss the similarities and differences in the policy predictions of the classical and Keynesian models.

3. Following many long years of happiness and prosperity in her kingdom, the queen responds quickly to the first rumors of a coming economic downturn by asking the three wisest persons in the land for their diagnoses and remedies. Evaluate each of their responses in terms of the *AD/AS* model.

a. "The problem is that we have become too used to prosperity, and it has led us to borrow and spend too freely for our own good. Right now the kingdom is borrowing beyond what it is investing, and the result must be economic stagnation, falling incomes and a declining standard of living. An end to the royal deficit will restore prosperity."

b. "The problem is a temporary supply shock, caused by events beyond our control. They will end eventually. In the meantime we should contract our money supply a bit to be sure that we don't end up with both a recession (unavoidable) and inflation (avoidable)."

c. "Periodically the animal spirits of our citizens combine with the alignment of the heavens and lead to feelings of anxiety and pessimism. This, in turn, causes them to reduce investment spending, and thus begins the cyclical downturn. A slight fiscal or monetary "goose" will provide the necessary economic stimulation to restore our fabled prosperity."

4. Suppose that rising fears of a coming inflation lead many people to decrease their money holdings and that this results in a significant decrease in autonomous money demand $(-\Delta j_0)$ for the whole economy.

   a. What short run impact will this event have on P, y, and r? Explain.

   b. According to the activist view, what sort of monetary policy change, if any, would be appropriate? Explain.

   c. What is the long run impact of $-\Delta j_0$ on the economy? Explain.

   d. Suppose the Federal Reserve responds by adjusting M so as to keep the real value or purchasing power of money (M/P) at its original (preshock) level. What impact would such a policy have on the economy? Explain.

5. Suppose a statistical analysis finds that money demand does *not* depend on the real rate of interest and that the j_2 coefficient equals zero. Explain why this economy would be better described by the classical macro model than by the expanded Keynesian model. Explain your reasoning.

6.

   a. Suppose the economy is in short run equilibrium well-below full employment. If no policy changes whatsoever are made, what is the cause-and-effect process that is alleged to bring the economy back to full employment in the long run? Be specific and explain.

   b. What information would you need before you could conclude that changes in fiscal or in monetary policy would return the economy to full employment more rapidly than market clearing? Explain.

7. "In the long run, assuming flexible wages and prices, real output/income is determined entirely by factors on the supply side. Similarly, the real interest rate is determined entirely by factors on the demand side." Do you agree or disagree with this statement? Explain your reasoning.

8. John Maynard Keynes argued that fiscal policy could alter aggregate demand with a multiplier effect and that the remedy for the devastating unemployment of the Great Depression was expansionary fiscal policy. His critics asserted that this expansionary policy would have no impact whatsoever on aggregate demand, income, or employment. Which of these two diametrically opposed views is embodied in the *AD/AS* model that we've been using? *Explain.*

9. In terms of the expanded *AD/AS* model, what is the short- and long-run impact of an increase in the money supply on y, P, r, c, i, and x? Explain your reasoning.

10. Suppose a careful statistical study shows that the real interest rate does *not* influence either investment or net exports at all.

    a. How would this change the *IS* equation, the *IS* curve, and the *AD* curve? Explain.

b. Would this new information alter our conclusions about the impact of fiscal and monetary policy on aggregate demand? Explain.

11. "For all its sounds of revolution, the Keynesian model is really quite tame and ultimately very much like the classical model of the macroeconomy. It retains the basic classical insights that 'We can't spend our way to prosperity,' 'We can't print our way to prosperity,' 'Economic growth depends on the supply side,' and 'Inflation is everywhere and always a monetary phenomenon.'"

Do you agree with this statement? Explain why or why not?

12. Suppose we increase government spending but refuse to raise taxes to pay for it.

a. According to the classical model of the overall economy, what consequences, if any, would this have for the economy?

b. According to the Keynesian or expanded *AD/AS* model, what *SR* and *LR* consequences, if any, would this have for the economy?

Use the Following Model to Answer the Questions Below:

$$y = c + i + x + g \qquad\qquad L/P = M/P$$
$$c = 50 + .9(y - t) \qquad\quad L/P = 387.5 + .1y - 1000r$$
$$t = 200 + .2y \qquad\qquad\quad M = 500$$
$$i = 300 - 1000r \qquad\qquad P = 1$$
$$x = 100 - .12y - 500r$$
$$g = 730$$

13. *a.* What is the equation for the *IS* curve for this economy? Put it in terms of the specific quantitative values that describe this economy.

b. Calculate the value of the expenditure multiplier, $\mu = 1/(1 - c_1 + c_1 t_1 + x_1)$.

c. If government spending rises by \$100 (billion), what will happen to this equation and to the *IS* curve? Be specific. (*Suggestion:* Use the multiplier from above instead of resolving the entire set of equations.)

d. Calculate the value of the tax multiplier, $-c_1\mu$.

e. If taxes (t_0 for simplicity) fall by \$100 billion, what happens to this equation and to the *IS* curve? (*Suggestion:* Use the tax multiplier instead of resolving the equations.)

f. If both public spending and taxes rise by \$100 billion, what happens to this equation and to the curve?

14. *a.* What is the equation for the *LM* curve, again with specific values?

b. If the money supply rises by \$100 billion, what happens to this equation and to the *LM* curve? Be specific.

c. With the money supply still at this higher value, suppose the price level rises to 1.20. What happens to this equation and the *LM* curve?

15. Suppose this economy is initially in both short-run and long-run equilibrium in terms of the complete *AD/AS* model. Find the specific equilibrium values of $r, y, c, i, x,$ and $b = g - t$.

16. What happens to equilibrium r, y, and b if government spending rises by $110 (billion)?

17. Several former presidents optimistically predicted that we could "grow" our way out of the deficit without raising tax rates or cutting spending. Without any change in tax rates or government spending, how high would real output (and income) have to grow in this economy to bring about a balanced government budget?

18. To stimulate economic growth, we need to get resources out of consumption and into saving. To help this along, suppose that we eliminate taxes on income earned from saving accounts, and that the effect of this is to increase saving hence decrease autonomous consumption by $110 (billion). What will be the short- and long-run impacts of this policy on r, y, c, i, x, and b in this model?

CHAPTER 5

FISCAL POLICY

⊗⊚ 5.1 INTRODUCTION

We now have an analytical framework that combines the short run analytics of Keynes with the long run market-clearing analysis of the classical tradition to provide a general model of macroeconomic interactions. After two demanding chapters in which the many pieces of the model were put together (ten equations' worth), it's time to see how all this apparatus can be used. This *AD/AS* framework underlies, explicitly or implicitly, all that we do throughout the rest of the book so it is important that you learn it well. This chapter and the next two are designed to strengthen your understanding of the model by applying it to major issues in **fiscal policy** (Chapter 5), **monetary policy** (Chapter 6), and **international trade** (Chapter 7).

We've seen that the combination of *variable velocity of money* (inherent in the *IS-LM* derivation of aggregate demand) and *short-run price rigidity* (yielding a horizontal short-run supply curve) creates a system in which a variety of events not only shift aggregate demand but, in the short run, cause a very unclassical change in real output and employment. This, of course, is the essential innovation of Keynes and the backbone of his explanation of why the "invisible hand" failed to restore economic prosperity during the 1930s even though wages and prices fell by more than 20% during the precipitous 1930 to 1933 period. The picture of the Great Depression painted by our *AD/AS* model is one of substantial declines in private consumption and investment spending followed by misguided fiscal and monetary contractions of such magnitude that the market-clearing process was simply overwhelmed.

The subsequent rapid return to full employment accompanying the massive expenditures of World War II seemed to offer hard proof of the Keynesian theory that aggregate demand plays an important role in determining the level of output and employment. The problems of the 1930s, seen from this new perspective, were the result of an immense and prolonged collapse in aggregate demand. With strong growth of the money supply and with government spending and the federal deficit soaring to unprecedented levels, the U.S. economy sprang quickly back to life during the war years.

This back-to-back experience of depression and prosperity left an indelible mark on our collective attitude toward policy manipulation of the macroeconomy. An early manifestation of this change was the **Employment Act of 1946,** a bill that committed the federal government "to promote maximum employment, production, and purchasing power." Though the act did not specify *how* this was to be done, other than staying within the boundaries of policies "calculated to foster and promote free competitive enterprise and the general welfare," it did establish some mechanisms for reviewing economic conditions and policies. These included the requirement that the president deliver an **Economic Report to Congress** at least once a year. The Employment Act of 1946 also established the **Council of Economic Advisers** to advise the president and the **Joint Economic Committee** of Congress to review the president's reports and present its own economic assessments to the lawmakers in the House and Senate.

Perhaps because it was filled with good intentions and lacked specific recommendations for how to achieve them, the Employment Act of 1946 was quickly and widely accepted as a commonsense commitment to effective economic policy. The deep distrust of central government action embedded in U.S. political tradition and practice before the 1930s was clearly diminishing. This changing attitude no doubt reflected the shock waves still radiating from the Great Depression. The most visible damage had been the loss of jobs and income, but a longer-lived casualty was the elusive but very real level of "economic optimism." The drastic loss of savings through the stock market crash and bank closings plus persistent high unemployment caused many to question the ability of a market economy to reward hard work and sacrifice. There was a very palpable fear that the depression would return with the end of the war-time stimulus. The Employment Act of 1946 was, if nothing else, a vow to try to learn from the policy mistakes of the 1930s.

Half a century later, the influence of the Employment Act of 1946 lives on. It marked a turning point in the popular perception of the macroeconomic role of government. By accepting public responsibility for the overall health and stability of the economy, it took on a job that had been left to the market system and the private sector in the classical tradition. Behind the Employment Act of 1946 lay two large, unstated presumptions that (1) the government has the *ability* to favorably influence and guide the overall economy, and (2) the political process is capable of *controlling* the use of this power in a way that is consistent with some reasonable and acceptable notion of general economic welfare.[1] Neither proposition is obviously and unambiguously valid or invalid. Both raise issues that lie at the heart of macroeconomic policy analysis and will be explored throughout the remaining chapters.

Over the past fifty years the pledge to use public policies to improve macroeconomic performance has been reconfirmed, time and again, in both economic and political actions. For example, the influential 1962 report of President Kennedy's Council of Economic Advisers argued that more active monetary and fiscal policies were essential for achieving the employment, production, and price stability goals of

---

[1] The classical tradition, remember, was firmly rooted in the *opposite* twin beliefs. The government was thought to have little or no ability to improve the overall level of economic activity, but all too much power to reward one group at another's expense, thereby increasing economic waste and inefficiency.

the Employment Act of 1946.[2] This was a period in which it appeared to many economists and policy makers that frequent policy adjustments in response to changing economic conditions—a strategy known as **discretionary "fine-tuning"**—could significantly reduce the size of macroeconomic fluctuations associated with the business cycle.

The high hopes of the 1960s were dashed by the realities of the 1970s, a decade of negative supply shocks, advancing inflation, and sluggish economic growth. But rather than bringing discouragement, this only spurred public policy makers to reiterate and even extend their commitment to improved macroeconomic performance. The **Full Employment and Balanced Growth Act of 1978** (popularly known as the "Humphrey-Hawkins Bill") expanded the government's macroeconomic goals to include "full employment and production, increased real income, balanced growth, a balanced federal budget, adequate productivity growth, . . . an improved trade balance . . . and reasonable price stability." Like the Employment Act of 1946, it is filled with admirable goals but leaves the means, the costs, and even the feasibility of achieving them unexamined.

Insofar as public policy makers were concerned, then, it appeared that little faith remained in the ability of the self-regulating powers of the market to keep the economy operating at or near full employment. A quiet revolution had occurred in our thinking about the proper role for macroeconomic policy making. But the unanswered question was whether macroeconomic policy could possibly achieve such ambitious goals. We begin a careful analysis of the prospects and limits of macroeconomic policy with *fiscal policy*—the spending, taxing, and borrowing choices made by the public sector.

5.2 FISCAL POLICY BASICS

Fiscal policy (from the Latin *fisc* for the public treasury of Ancient Rome) is a short term for a multitude of choices about **public spending**—*how much* to spend and on *what?*—and about **financing that spending**—*who* pays and *when?* In the United States, the president and Congress share responsibility for determining the level and types of federal spending and taxing. The U.S. Treasury then carries out those decisions, writing the checks and, through its Internal Revenue Service division, collecting the taxes.

When tax collections fall short of government spending the Treasury must turn to borrowing or **deficit financing** as it's usually called when done by the federal government. But whether the borrower is a consumer, a corporation, or the government, the process is the same—issuance of a promissory note (or security) in exchange for the borrowed funds. Federal borrowing in the U.S. is done through the sale of **Treasury bonds.** These IOUs are the liability of the Treasury but an asset to their holder. Because the Treasury's only source of funds for repayment is taxes, its bonds are really backed by taxpayers—by all of us! This may seem so obvious as to hardly need saying. Yet we'll see that it's a basic fact that is easily forgotten in discussions of economic policy. It is also the center of a lively debate among economists as to whether

---

[2] Both the 1962 (Kennedy) and 1982 (Reagan) reports of the Council of Economic Advisers have been reprinted with added commentary by several of the original participants. The result is a fascinating contrast in expectations for government activity in the macroeconomy. See James Tobin and Murray Weidenbaum, editors, *Two Revolutions in Economic Policy: The First Economic Reports of Presidents Kennedy and Reagan* (Cambridge: The Massachusetts Institute of Technology Press, 1988).

we actually make choices as if we're aware that current government deficits are a claim on our future incomes.

In the U.S. the government must finance all its spending by either taxes or deficits. The third option, printing money to finance public spending, is prohibited by the institutional framework that authorizes the largely independent Federal Reserve System to manage the nation's money supply.[3] So when the *inflow of current taxes* falls short of the *outflow of government spending* for a fiscal year, the only option is for the Treasury to sell bonds and thereby run what's properly called a **cash flow deficit** for that year. The cumulative total of these Treasury bonds currently outstanding, newly issued or preexisting, is called the **national debt.** So the 1995 federal deficit of about $200 billion raised the U.S. national debt to approximately $4 trillion by the start of 1996.[4]

Be careful not to confuse the current deficit with the outstanding national debt. The national debt is the total value of outstanding IOUs of the government at a particular time. The deficit is only the amount that is added to that total during a particular interval of time (usually a year). If we picture the national debt as a tree, the deficit will be its growth this year. So the current federal deficit is a new loan that is added to its outstanding debt, which is called the national or public debt. "Balancing the budget" means eliminating the current deficit, not the national debt. A zero deficit only yields a *constant* national debt. To actually *reduce* the total debt itself would require a negative deficit or budget *surplus* ($b = g - t < 0$ or $g < t$). To eliminate the entire U.S. national debt would take sizable surpluses in the budget for many years to come.

Though we usually think of fiscal policy as a tool for manipulating macroeconomic performance, this is only the tip of the iceberg or, some might say, icing on the cake. Either way, it's a metaphor that tells us to look underneath for the fundamentals. In the case of **fiscal policy** we discover an underlying **system for transferring resources from private to public use.** Fiscal policy is fundamentally about *how we choose and pay for our public goods and services.* Let's examine this transfer process with the *AD/AS* model, supposing that we wish to increase the level of real government spending ($+\Delta g_0$) in a fully employed economy ($y = y^*$). We've seen that the rise in government spending—by itself—sets off the multiplier process as rising income and consumption feed one another until leakages into saving, taxes, and imports eventually bring it to an end. The resulting rightward shift in *IS* and *AD* causes a short-run increase in the real rate of interest and output/income. This analysis is correct as far as it goes, but it is incomplete in an important way—it says nothing about *how this increased government spending is financed.* The only options, as we saw in Chapter 1, are **tax financing** ($+\Delta g_0 = +\Delta t_0$), **deficit financing** ($+\Delta g_0 = +\Delta b$), and **money financing** ($+\Delta g_0 = +\Delta M_0$, not used in the United States but prevalent in countries with weak tax systems). The impact of these three choices for financing a given increase in public spending is illustrated in Figure 5.1 and is outlined as follows.

---

[3] Fiscal and monetary authorities might conceivably act together, so that whenever there is a deficit-financed increase in federal spending by the Treasury, the Federal Reserve simultaneously increases the money supply by the same amount. Called "monetizing the deficit," this is equivalent in its expansionary impact on aggregate demand to a money-financed increase in government spending. This highly inflationary practice is common in countries that have limited ability to collect taxes and borrow, as will be discussed in later chapters.

[4] This is the figure for that part of the gross federal debt held by the public. It subtracts the amount the Treasury has borrowed from other government agencies (which becomes an asset to these other branches) to arrive at the amount of net public indebtedness to the private sector. These figures can be found in the annual "Economic Report of the President."

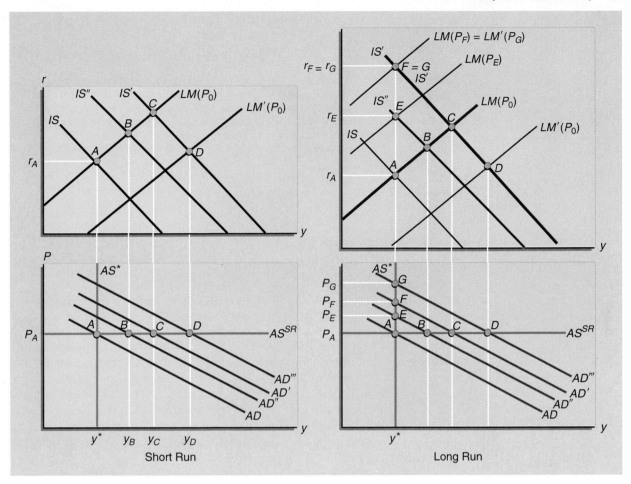

Short- and Long-Run Impacts of Increased
Government Spending When It's:
- Tax financed $+\Delta g_0 = +\Delta t_0$ $(A \rightarrow B \rightarrow E)$
- Deficit financed $+\Delta g_0 = +\Delta b$ $(A \rightarrow C \rightarrow F)$
- Money financed $+\Delta g_0 = +\Delta M_0$ $(A \rightarrow D \rightarrow G)$

■ FIGURE 5.1

1. A Tax-Financed Increase in Government Spending

$$(+\Delta g_0 = +\Delta t_0)$$

The $+\Delta g_0$ shifts IS to IS' while the $+\Delta t_0$ shifts IS' back to the left (to IS'') but by a smaller amount, because the tax multiplier $(-c_1\mu)$ is smaller than the expenditure multiplier (μ). The net result of a tax-financed spending increase is a relatively small rightward shift in both IS (IS to IS'') and AD (AD to AD'') and a movement along the short-run aggregate supply curve from A to B in Figure 5.1. As market-clearing proceeds, the rising price level contracts LM and the economy moves to point E in the long run.

2. A Bond-Financed Increase in Government Spending

$$(+\Delta g_0 = +\Delta b)$$

The $+\Delta g_0$ again shifts IS to IS', but deficit-financing (through the issuance of new bonds, $+\Delta b$) doesn't show up in any of the ten equations. What this means is that there is no further short-run change beyond the initial shift of IS and AD when we use bonds to finance new public spending. The net result of a bond-financed increase in spending is a rightward shift in IS and AD to IS' and AD' and a movement from A to C in Figure 5.1. The long-run market-clearing result is a rising price level and a movement to point F.

3. A Money-Financed Increase in Government Spending

$$(+\Delta g_0 = +\Delta M_0)$$

Once again the $+\Delta g_0$ is a fiscal expansion from IS to IS'. But now it is reinforced by a simultaneous monetary expansion, with $+\Delta M_0$ shifting LM(P_0) to LM'(P_0). The net result of this money-financed spending increase is thus a rightward shift of both IS and LM, resulting in a relatively large expansion of AD to AD''' and a movement from A to D in the graph. In the long run the economy ends up at point G.

As the graphs on the left-hand side of Figure 5.1 illustrate, this increase in government spending pushes the economy along the short-run aggregate supply curve and, temporarily, beyond its full-employment level. The distance of this shift in aggregate demand is smallest when spending is tax financed, largest when it's money financed. As this unsustainably high level of aggregate demand pushes against a fixed productive capacity, the consequence must be a rise in the price level until the economy reaches a sustainable long-run equilibrium as shown along AS^* in the graphs on the right-hand side.

To summarize these results, a tax-financed increase in government spending ($A \rightarrow B \rightarrow E$ in Figure 5.1) has the smallest impact on aggregate demand and, in the long run, on P and r. The relatively small rise in the real interest rate means that only a small part of the increased public spending comes from declines in investment and net exports (because both are inversely related to r). Most of the new public spending comes out of private consumption, as described by the consumption function ($c = c_0 + c_1(y - t)$).

A deficit-financed (bond-financed) increase in government spending has a stronger impact on aggregate demand ($A \rightarrow C \rightarrow F$), pushing the price level to P_F and the real interest rate to r_F in the long run. Because there has been no tax increase to reduce consumption, the entire increase in government spending must be squeezed out of investment and net exports by the rising real rate of interest. Therefore a deficit-financed increase in public spending requires a larger jump in the real interest rate than does a tax-financed increase, until it **"crowds out"** enough investment and net exports to make room for the increased government spending.

Because a money-financed increase in public spending also avoids a tax increase, it, too, must rely on the *crowding out mechanism* to transfer resources from private to public use. Therefore, as with deficit financing, the interest rate rises to r_F (A to $G = F$ in the long-run graph). But, not surprisingly, a money-financed spending hike has a stronger impact on aggregate demand than does deficit financing. The additional demand stimulus from the money creation ($+\Delta LM$) adds to that of the expenditure increase ($+\Delta IS$) to shift aggregate demand still further and to push the price level still higher to P_G.

IN SUMMARY . . .

Financing Government Spending Means *Moving Output From Private to Public Use*

The PPF in Chapter 1 made it apparent that in a fully employed, zero-growth economy more public output can be provided only at the cost of less private output in the long run, i.e., $+\Delta g \Leftrightarrow -\Delta(c + i + x)$. But the PPF didn't tell us *how* the cost of more government spending would be distributed across private consumption, investment, and net exports. This is an important issue because it determines whether the increased public spending is paid out of consumption now or consumption later. If an increase in public spending comes entirely from *current consumption* $(-\Delta c)$ then we say that the "coercion" is now and the price of the $+\Delta g$ has been paid. But to the extent that the $+\Delta g$ comes from a decline in investment or net export spending $(-\Delta i$ or $-\Delta x)$ the drop in private consumption is only postponed, not escaped. It will show up later as reduced *future consumption* because of either a lower rate of growth (remember that $-\Delta i$ means a reduced rate of capital formation) or repayment of external borrowing. (For simplicity it's assumed that $x < 0$ so that we are net borrowers from abroad. The conclusion would be the same even if we had a trade surplus rather than a trade deficit.)

The *AD/AS* model can show us how the cost of this increased public spending $(+\Delta g)$ is divided between reduced current consumption $(-\Delta c)$ and reduced future consumption $(-\Delta i$ or $-\Delta x$ now). Roughly speaking the difference depends on whether the transfer is accomplished through *taxes* or through *crowding out*. Suppose we raise public spending $(+\Delta g)$ but instead of raising current taxes we finance it by either a deficit $(+\Delta g = +\Delta b)$ or by printing money $(+\Delta g = +\Delta M)$. As shown in Figure 5.1, either way the transfer from private to public use occurs through the process termed "crowding out." This is a sequence of events in which the increased public spending causes the real interest rate to rise (a little in the short run, more in the long run) and thereby chokes off private investment spending $(-\Delta i)$ and net exports $(-\Delta x)$ to free the needed resources to produce the desired increase in government output $(+\Delta g)$. This is shown in the movement from A to $F = G$.

But if the increased public spending is instead financed by an increase in current taxes $(+\Delta g = +\Delta t)$, the resulting drop in current consumption $(+\Delta t_0 \Rightarrow -\Delta c)$ keeps *IS* from shifting out as far and thereby reduces the resulting rise in the interest rate and, hence, the extent of "crowding out." When real output returns to its long run level, the increase in public spending will have been paid primarily by reduced current consumption rather than by crowding out $(+\Delta r \Rightarrow -\Delta i$ and $-\Delta x)$. The part of the cost of increased public goods yet to be paid from future consumption is therefore smaller with tax financing than with deficit or money financing.

5.3 HOW LARGE IS THE GOVERNMENT DEFICIT?

Fiscal policy, the day-to-day getting and spending of money by the government, has moved from the business page to the front page over the past 15 years for one big reason—the continued use of large doses of *deficit financing*. Hardly a day goes by when the size of the government deficit or the national debt is not, in one way or another, a news item. Whether it's about accumulated deficits from the past or projected deficits of the future, the story can only cause anxiety about what lies ahead. Yet the much-predicted "day of reckoning!" still hasn't appeared and after more than a decade of apparently false alarms we may begin to wonder whether continued, massive public borrowing is really such a problem after all. Having lived in close quarters with these supposed monsters for so long, they come to seem less terrifying. When faced with unpleasant remedies like precipitous tax hikes or deep spending cuts, our collective decision has been to continue with the large deficits. Attempts to restrain deficit spending with laws (the Gramm-Rudman-Hollings bill in the 1980s) failed to overcome the reluctance of the American voter to accept the reality that higher taxes or lower government spending are the price that deficit reduction demands. Even if the much discussed Balanced Budget Amendment to the Constitution is passed by Congress and ratified by the state legislatures, it remains to be seen how or even whether a balanced federal cash flow deficit could actually be realized. If we fail to achieve a balanced budget, does economic catastrophe lie ahead?

Common sense and a wealth of anecdotes and aphorisms all warn us that excessive borrowing—personal, business, or government—is a threat that can't be ignored. We can find any number of metaphors to remind us of the dangers of going too far, such as "the straw that broke the camel's back," "what goes up must come down," or "another nail in our coffin." Many believe the U.S. has already reached the danger point and that each day of continued public deficits only digs a deeper and deeper hole in our economic future. They maintain that deficit spending must be stopped immediately and that failure to do so is irresponsible to the economic future, particularly that of our children and grandchildren. Others make less dire predictions, but are convinced that our heavy reliance on deficit financing is shortsighted and should be reduced gradually but steadily. Still others maintain that the deficit issue has been blown out of proportion and that there is no pressing economic reason to end or even reduce recent levels of deficit spending. A few even call for larger government deficits.

Such a wide range of disagreement on such a central issue is certainly disquieting. Why is there so much controversy? How much of it reflects the exaggerations of the political process and how much of it reflects economic reality? We begin our analysis with a close look at the *size* of the government deficit. In the next section we will return to the *AD/AS* framework to trace the *impact* of deficits on current economic activity—real output, prices, interest rates, and so on. Then, in the following section, we turn to the long-term issue of the conditions under which continued government deficits, feeding an ever-growing national debt, are *sustainable*.

How large is the government deficit? This is not as simple a question as you might think. The number that regularly grabs the headlines is for the federal government only and is an extremely crude measure. It includes both too much and too little. It's certainly an important part of the overall deficit picture but by itself this "gross federal deficit" figure can be very misleading. So before we begin an assessment of the economic impact of deficits, we need to be aware of the shortcomings in our measurements. A meaningful deficit figure requires the following adjustments to the basic figure: (1) exclude funds borrowed from other federal agencies, (2) include the deficits (or surpluses) of state and local governments, (3) modify the real value of outstanding public debt to reflect current inflation, and (4) include hidden liabilities that currently escape detection in the government's accounting system.

(1) Part of the amount borrowed by the Treasury each year comes from other government agencies who purchase the new bonds to hold as an asset. In these transactions the debt of the Treasury becomes the asset of another branch of the government (such as the Social Security Trust Fund or the Federal Reserve System). To count the new government debt but not the new government asset would obviously be a distortion. So this adjustment converts an overstated gross amount of Federal borrowing into a slightly slimmer net Federal deficit figure.

(2) Since our ultimate goal is to understand what determines whether we are borrowing "too much" through our public sector, we must include not only all branches of government but all levels of government—Federal, state, and local. In recent years, combined state and local budgets have actually ended up with budget surpluses—between $20 and $60 billion each year since the late 1970s. These two basic adjustments to a net total government deficit reduce the size of the gross deficit anywhere from 20% to 50% over recent years. Yet this is almost never noted by the media or by campaigning politicians, perhaps because we prefer simplicity as well as overstatement and sensationalism in our deficit stories.

(3) A less obvious but even more important correction is to adjust the net deficit measure for the loss in real value of existing government bonds through inflation. Since both principal and interest payments on bonds are fixed in dollar terms, inflation erodes their purchasing power. By the time the bond reaches maturity its purchasing power may be only a small fraction of its original value. Therefore a bond's real claim on our taxes falls as inflation works to transfer purchasing power from bondholders to taxpayers.

To take a specific example, the net public deficit for 1991 after making adjustments (1) and (2) was about $170 billion. But inflation during the year reduced the real value (purchasing power) of the pre-existing national debt by 3.3%. The national debt (again, net of intra-governmental holdings) at the beginning of 1991 was about $2,500 billion. Though we added $170 billion to the national debt over the next 12 months, at the same time inflation was subtracting about $82 billion (3.3% × $2,500 billion) of its real value. Therefore the real change in the national debt during 1991 was $170 − $82 = $88 billion. Still a large number, of course, but only one-third the size of the unadjusted $268.7 billion most often given as the official (gross Federal) deficit for that year.

Probably your immediate reaction, a healthy one in economics, is skepticism. This adjustment may seem artificial, an attempt to substitute fancy reasoning for common sense. But in this case such suspicions are unfounded, as the following example demonstrates. When you were born, let's say 20 years ago today for simplicity, your grandparents gave you a $10,000 20 year U.S. Treasury bond paying a 5% rate of interest. To further simplify, suppose you have been spending the $500 annual interest receipts each year as they arrived. (And you've no doubt noticed that $500 doesn't go as far these days as it used to.) This morning the bond reached maturity and you received the principal. How much is it worth? $10,000 obviously. But this is 10,000 1996 dollars, a far cry from the 10,000 1976 dollars that your grandparents loaned the government. In fact, the price level has almost tripled over those two decades, reducing the purchasing power of that original $10,000 to just 3,333 1976 dollars. But your loss is the taxpayers gain since they only have to repay one-third of the purchasing power of the loan. Inflation each year reduced the real value of your asset and, with it, the taxpayer's liability. As all victims of this "inflation tax" know, there's no smoke and mirrors here. It's a "real" change in the value of government bonds in every sense of the word.[5]

---

[5] This "inflation tax" is a bit more complicated than it may seem at this point. We'll discuss it carefully in Chapter 10. For now, just note that if the average annual inflation rate of about 5% had been *foreseen* by investors in 1975, the Treasury would have had to build an extra "inflation premium" of 5% into the interest rate in order to attract buyers for the bonds. With the inflation loss covered by this interest rate premium, there would no longer be a net loss to bondholders, hence no inflation tax. Periodically there are proposals for the U.S. Treasury to issue "inflation proof" bonds, offering investors the security of government-backed bonds without the threat of the inflation tax from unexpected inflation. This could be accomplished by indexing the interest rate on the bonds for the actual inflation rate, as is now done for Social Security payments and variable rate mortgages. The Treasury, however, has continued to oppose such plans.

(4) While the three adjustments above are necessary to transform a bloated gross Federal deficit into an economically meaningful real net government deficit, they can do their job only to the extent that the original, unadjusted deficit number was complete. Unfortunately the Federal accounting system ignores a sizable amount of government liabilities that don't show up explicitly as an increase in the amount of Treasury bonds outstanding. These hidden liabilities, sometimes called a "stealth budget," include future obligations to retirement programs for government employees and military personnel, as well as future obligations for Social Security and Medicare. They also include so-called "contingent" liabilities, such as loan guarantees or subsidized disaster insurance. These become claims on future taxes only in the event of loan defaults or natural disaster. An example of a contingency that became a reality is the deposit insurance paid out during the widespread failure of many Savings and Loan associations in the late 80s and early 90s.

These programs are current promises by the government to make future payments. In this respect, they are no different than Treasury bonds. Hence they're just as much a part of our true national debt as are outstanding government bonds. And as the government makes additional promises or "entitlements," as they are often called, this is every bit as much a part of our current deficit as the issuance of additional government bonds. Yet this sizable addition to our future taxes is excluded from the official deficit and debt calculations, primarily because, unlike Treasury bonds, it is impossible to make a precise assessment of its size. With a bond we know the exact amount of the interest and principal and when it will be paid back. But the timing and amounts of future costs of Medicare, for example, will depend on a number of things that we can't know right now, such as the cost of advancing medical technology as well as changing trends in major diseases. Similarly, the future costs of Social Security will depend on retirement ages and life expectancy, not to mention possible legislative changes by Congress.

While there has been some movement by the Treasury toward a so-called "accrual accounting" system that attempts to make reasonable estimates of these hidden liabilities, it is still in the experimental stage.[6] For the present we should be aware that a considerably larger share of our future incomes has already been claimed by the government than appears in our adjusted measures of government deficit and debt. This doesn't necessarily mean that we won't be able to afford these programs. Nor does it mean that our "net real government deficit" measure (with the first three adjustments) isn't important and useful. It is an accurate indicator of a key part of fiscal reality and it helps us understand how current fiscal decisions will affect our future well-being. But the existence of this stealth budget does mean that even our most careful measures understate total government indebtedness and that this needs to be taken into account in making fiscal choices.

The bottom line is that popular discussions of the size of the cash flow deficit are based on the wrong numbers. While a more careful estimate is possible for the government securities portion (the "net real deficit"), the unfunded liabilities of the "stealth budget" remain imprecise.

---

[6] In 1975 the accounting firm Arthur Andersen & Co. prepared a very complete set of financial accounting statements for the federal government as a pilot study. The conventional, unadjusted national debt figure was found to be only about 40% of their estimated "true" public debt. The Treasury continued this study on an experimental basis and estimated that the measured national debt of $1300 billion in 1984 was actually $3800 billion once "hidden liabilities" were included. A more recent estimate puts these hidden liabilities at $4 trillion as of 1989, compared to net outstanding government bonds of $2.2 trillion for that year. See Roy H. Webb, "The Stealth Budget: Unfunded Liabilities of the Federal Government," *Economic Review*, Federal Reserve Bank of Richmond (May/June 1991): 23–32.

THE SOCIAL SECURITY
TRUST FUND AND THE DEFICIT

In anticipation of the retirement of large numbers of "baby boomers" beginning around 2010, the Social Security program puts the amount by which current Social Security taxes exceed current Social Security payments into a "trust fund." If we did not set aside these funds, when the "pig in the python" age group reaches retirement there would have to be either an extraordinary increase in taxes on the working population or a sizable cut in benefits to retirees.

This Social Security surplus, currently running about $60 billion each year, is used to purchase federal bonds. So these bonds, the liability of the Treasury, become assets of the Social Security Trust Fund. Put another way, the current savings of the Social Security program are used to finance current borrowing by the government. But since the debt of one agency is offset by the other's asset, the Social Security surplus ends up reducing the measured net federal government deficit. For example, a measured net federal deficit of, say, $240 billion last year would mean that the Treasury actually borrowed $300 billion if $60 billion was purchased by the Social Security Trust Fund.

This adjustment is correct if we wish to know the net new borrowing through government bonds in a particular year. However, it can also be argued that we should not deduct these Social Security purchases of debt because they are going to be paid out to retirees in the future. In other words, the Social Security surplus has an offsetting "hidden liability" that should not be ignored. The true deficit in our example, they would argue, is $300 billion not $240 billion. Therefore, there is a good economic case for changing the current procedure in a way that would raise the measured deficit by the amount of the Social Security surplus.

Those who argue against this change point out that it singles out Social Security but ignores all the other "hidden liabilities" from an array of programs and entitlements. They maintain that our current practice of deducting the Social Security surplus from the current deficit is consistent with our treatment of other kinds of government entitlement programs.

5.4 THE IMPACT OF DEFICITS
ON CURRENT ECONOMIC ACTIVITY

Whatever the true size of the deficit may be, it is commonly blamed for everything from recession to inflation, including high interest rates, large international trade deficits, and sluggish rates of economic growth. Some of these charges, under certain conditions, may be justified; others are not. To find out just how government deficits are connected to overall performance of the macroeconomy, let's return to our AD/AS framework. Suppose we start with a balanced cash flow budget ($b = g - t = 0$), but then finance a $100 billion increase in government spending by borrowing. This $+\Delta g_0$, as we've seen, sets off a multiplier process that shifts both the IS and AD curves to the right as shown in Figure 5.2. The economy moves initially from points A to B and, as prices adjust and markets clear, finally to point C.

■ FIGURE 5.2

Starting with a balanced cash flow budget ($b = g - t = 0$) at point A, an increase in government spending ($+\Delta g_0$) shifts out IS and AD. The result is a movement to point B in the SR and to point C in the LR. Hence this *increase* in the cash flow deficit is an expansionary fiscal policy.

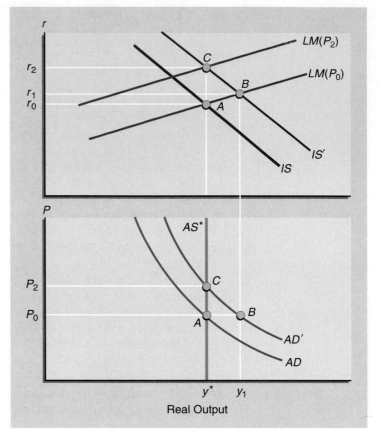

An *Increasing* Deficit Is Expansionary

So a deficit-financed increase in public spending has the expected *expansionary* impact on aggregate demand. But here's the part that may surprise you. Your intuition may tell you that if the government decides to continue this $100 billion deficit year after year, the IS and AD curves will continue to shift out each year. In fact this conclusion is wrong. Because there has been no further change in either government spending or tax rates, there is no further shift in IS or AD. The *increasing* deficit (from 0 to $100 billion) in the first year was expansionary because it reflected an increase in the horizontal intercept of the IS curve (via $+\Delta g_0$). But the subsequent *constant* deficit, reflecting no change in either spending or tax rates (g_0, t_0, and t_1 are all unchanged) is neutral. It has no further impact on any of the variables in our model. One deficit follows another and, though the national debt grows each year by the amount of this continued deficit, economic performance (measured by y, P, r, and the variables that depend on them, c, i, and x) remains unchanged.[7]

---

[7] The result that continuing, constant deficits are a neutral fiscal policy, leaving IS and AD unchanged from year to year needs some qualification. (1) A constant deficit could be slightly expansionary or contractionary if *both* g_0 and t_0 change in the same direction and by the same amount. If we start with a $100 billion deficit and increase spending and taxes by $10 billion the deficit remains unchanged. But because the expenditure multiplier (μ) is slightly larger in absolute value than the tax multiplier ($-c_1\mu$), there will be a small net rightward shift in IS and AD. Similarly, an equal cut in both government spending and taxes leaves the deficit constant but will be slightly contractionary. (2) Continuing deficits, even if constant, may have some additional impact on consumption (hence, IS) and money demand (hence, LM). These "wealth effects" along with the so-called balanced budget multiplier [of (1)] are sufficiently small that the generalization "a constant cash flow deficit is a neutral fiscal policy" is reliable, even if not precisely true.

We've discovered that to determine whether a given cash flow deficit represents an expansionary, neutral, or contractionary fiscal policy we need to know the *change* in the deficit from its previous level. A government may be running very large cash-flow deficits by historical standards, but if they are decreasing each year because of cuts in spending or tax rate increases, the impact of this fiscal policy on aggregate demand is *contractionary*.[8] The fact that fear of triggering a recession has been a primary impediment to deficit reduction in the U.S. is another way of saying that a declining deficit, no matter how large, is a contractionary fiscal policy.

It's crucial to see that it's the *change* in the cash flow deficit, not its level, that is important to current economic activity. But you also need to be aware of two exceptions to this general result. The first qualification is for **cyclical** changes in the cash flow deficit that arise purely from fluctuations of real output around its full employment level. For example, when an economy slides into a recession, the fall in real income means a declining tax base. Assuming tax *rates* (t_0 and t_1) are unchanged, this leads to a drop in the government's tax collections ($\downarrow t = t_0 + t_1 y \downarrow$) and, therefore, to a rising cash flow deficit ($\uparrow b = g - t \downarrow$). Such a *cyclical* rise in the deficit is not a reflection of underlying expansionary fiscal policy ($+\Delta g_0$, $-\Delta t_0$, or $-\Delta t_1$). So before we can determine the impact of a changing government deficit on aggregate demand we need to exclude this cyclical component to isolate what are called cyclically adjusted or **structural** changes in the deficit.

In other words, the actual change in the cash flow deficit (Δb) can be a combination of *cyclical* (from Δy) or *structural* (from Δg_0, Δt_0, or Δt_1), and we can write this more concisely as $\Delta b = \Delta b^{cyc} + \Delta b^{str}$. A changing structural deficit reflects a change in one or more of the fiscal policy instruments and therefore means a shift in *IS* and *AD*. But a cyclical change in the deficit is the consequence of anything that has altered the level of real income and *causes no further shifts in IS or AD*. Failure to make this distinction can cause much confusion about the connection between government deficits and economic activity. For example, it has been said that the "Keynesian" proposal to use deficit spending to stimulate the economy was disproved by the experience of the Great Depression. The existence of continued government deficits throughout the Great Depression, the argument goes, is clear evidence against their supposed expansionary powers. In truth, the rising government deficits in the early and mid-1930s were cyclical deficits brought on by the collapse of income as well as by misguided attempts to balance the budget with *contractionary* spending cuts and tax rate increases. When we separate cyclical from structural changes, we discover that fiscal policy was actually contractionary even though the cash flow deficit was rising (i.e., $\uparrow \Delta b = \uparrow \uparrow \Delta b^{cyc} + \downarrow \Delta b^{str}$).

This first modification—that to determine whether fiscal policy is expansionary, contractionary, or neutral we need to look at the change in the *structural* cash flow deficit (not just the actual change in the deficit)—is widely accepted by economists and policy makers.[9] This is in marked contrast to the controversy surrounding a second suggested modification of the link between government deficits and current economic activity. Our analysis has so far presumed that consumers simply ignore

---

[8] This assumes, however, that the Central Bank doesn't get into the act by "monetizing" the deficit, i.e., buying up these newly issued government bonds and thereby adding an expansionary monetary policy to the neutral fiscal policy. This can obviously have a significant impact on aggregate demand as we'll see in the discussion of inflation in Chapter 10.

[9] This approach was first suggested in an important contribution by E. Cary Brown, "Fiscal Policy in the 'Thirties' A Reappraisal," *American Economic Review* 46 (December 1956): 857–879. Measures of the structural deficit, officially called the "cyclically-adjusted deficit" or, sometimes, the "full employment deficit," are provided in the government's accounting system but tend to be ignored by the media.

the fact that current deficits mean higher taxes in the future. Those future taxes, we have supposed, will only affect future consumption in the year when the taxes are actually paid. This hypothesis is built into the consumption function relationship $(c = c_0 + c_1(y - t))$ that is a centerpiece of our model. An alternative approach, called the **tax discounting view,** assumes that consumers are generally aware that deficits only postpone the inevitable and, therefore, *treat deficits just the same as taxes when making consumption decisions.*[10]

If tax-discounting behavior is a better description of consumer decision-making, our conclusions about the impact of fiscal policy need substantial revision. For example, we saw earlier (see Figure 5.1) that a deficit-financed increase in government spending had a stronger impact on aggregate demand than if it had been tax financed $(+\Delta g_0 = \Delta t_0)$. But if the tax discounting hypothesis is correct, a deficit-financed increase in spending would have exactly the same, relatively small, expansionary impact as tax financing. In fact, the ability of fiscal policy to alter ag-

■ **FIGURE 5.3**

(A) A tax cut in our *standard model* (implicitly, with no tax discounting) shifts *IS* and *AD* outward as shown in the graphs on the right.

(B) But if consumers are *full tax discounters,* seeing lower taxes now as simply higher taxes later, they would feel no richer as a result of this tax "postponement." They would not increase their consumption spending and there would be no expansion of *IS* or *AD* in response to a cut in current taxes.

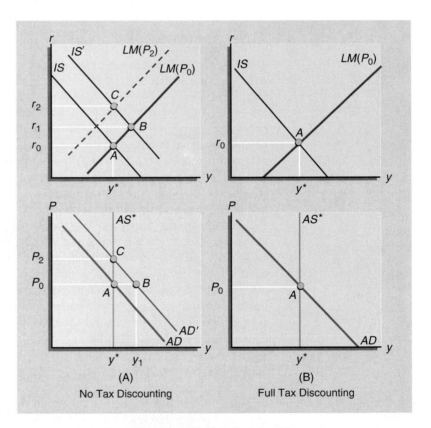

Impact of a Tax Cut $(-\Delta t_0)$
with and without Tax Discounting

---

[10] In the economics literature "tax discounting" is often referred to as "Ricardian equivalence" in reference to British economist David Ricardo's (1772–1823) recognition of the essential similarities of tax and deficit financing.

gregate demand would be much reduced, a result that calls into question the notion of using discretionary fiscal policy to offset unwanted shifts in aggregate demand.

To take another example, our standard *AD/AS* model tells us that a tax cut unaccompanied by a change in government spending, will shift *IS* outward (by the horizontal distance of the tax multiplier, $-c_1\mu\Delta t_0$) and expand aggregate demand, as shown in the left-hand graphs of Figure 5.3. But in a world of tax discounters the perception of higher future taxes from the deficit would counterbalance the fact of lower current taxes, leaving consumption unchanged. Hence, this cut in taxes would cause no shift whatsoever in the *IS* or *AD* curves. In a world of tax discounters, then, our predictions about the impact of an increasing structural deficit would have to be revised. If it increased because of a deficit-financed increase in spending ($+\Delta g_0 = +\Delta b$), shown in Figure 5.4, the effect would be the same as a tax-financed increase. If the structural deficit rose because of a cut in current tax rates ($-\Delta t_0 \Rightarrow +\Delta b$), there would be no impact whatsoever.

We will take a careful look at the tax discounting hypothesis and related statistical evidence in our discussion of consumption and saving behavior in Chapter 12. For now we just note that the existence of *complete* tax discounting is a minority view

■ FIGURE 5.4

A tax-financed increase in public spending ($A \rightarrow B \rightarrow C$) expands aggregate demand less than a deficit-financed increase in spending ($A \rightarrow D \rightarrow E$), unless consumers are "tax discounters," making deficit and tax-financed spending increases equivalent ($A \rightarrow B \rightarrow C$).

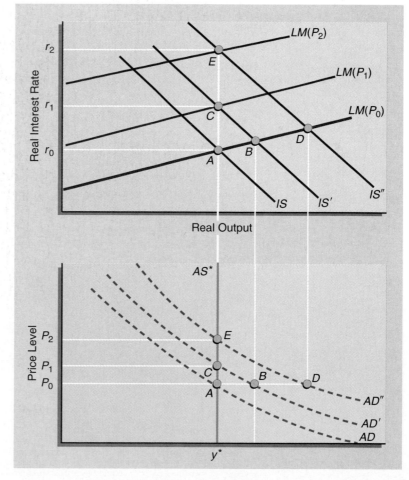

among macroeconomists. But the presence of *zero* tax discounting also seems improbable. So to the extent that *partial tax discounting* exists, the quantitative impact of changing structural deficits on aggregate demand is somewhat smaller than predicted by our *AD/AS* model.[11]

IN SUMMARY . . .

Government Deficits and Current Economic Activity

What impact does the current government deficit have on the macroeconomy? To answer this very important question requires us to answer four smaller questions.

1. *How large is the current deficit?* A meaningful cash flow deficit measure requires us to exclude intra-governmental holdings of debt, deduct state and local government surpluses, subtract the loss of real indebtedness due to current inflation, and, where feasible, include the hidden liabilities from current government promises (entitlements) to make future payments.

2. *What is the change in the current deficit?* To determine whether the impact of current fiscal policy on aggregate demand is expansionary, contractionary, or neutral, we need to know the *change* in the government deficit from last year's level.

3. *What part of the deficit change is "cyclical" and what part "structural"?* Cyclical changes in the deficit, by definition, reflect only the ups and downs of the tax base and do not stem from changes that shift the *IS* and *AD* curves. When we eliminate these purely cyclical changes what remains is the so-called structural changes that represent changes in government spending (Δg_0) or changes in tax *rates* (Δt_0 or Δt_1). Our expanded *AD/AS* model tells us that an increasing structural deficit expands aggregate demand, a constant structural deficit is neutral, and a diminishing structural deficit is contractionary.

4. *How prevalent is "tax discounting" behavior?* One final qualification must be considered. To the extent that consumers are forward looking and treat the *postponed* taxes represented by deficits as equivalent to *current* taxes, the impact of changing structural deficits on aggregate demand will be diminished. For example, when confronted by a tax "cut" unaccompanied by a cut in government spending, a tax discounter might reason that "This so-called tax cut just delays the inevitable. It certainly doesn't make me any wealthier in

(Continued)

---

[11] We'll continue with our current *AD/AS* model and the implicit assumption of no tax discounting. But we could readily alter this *AD/AS* framework to incorporate such behavior. If consumers view current deficits and taxes as equivalent, then the consumption function becomes $c = c_0 + c_1(y - t - b)$. And because all current government spending is paid either by taxes or deficits ($g_0 = t + b$), we can rewrite this as $c = c_0 + c_1(y - g_0)$. This more forward-looking consumption function hypothesizes that consumers don't just look at *current* taxes in deciding how much to consume. They realize that all government spending must ultimately be paid from taxes (now or later), so they use the level of current government spending (g_0) to determine their "true" after-tax income. Whether *actual* consumers are so farsighted is at the heart of the controversy.

any meaningful sense. What it gives me now it takes away later, plus interest. Therefore if I increase my consumption now I'll just have to reduce it later. Instead, I'll just hold my consumption steady and use this so-called tax cut to buy government bonds which will exactly pay for the higher future taxes." Do we live in a world of rational, forward-looking tax discounters or one of short-sighted, go-for-it-now consumers? We'll come back to this issue in Chapter 12, "Consumption, Saving, and Investment."

5.5 DEFICITS, DEBT, AND THE "DAY OF RECKONING"

We now come to the most provocative aspect of the deficit issue, the part that gives it the power to command headlines. Does continued government borrowing (and its accumulation in the form of an escalating national debt) necessarily undermine our long-term economic prosperity? Does the regular use of deficit financing represent a shortsighted and ultimately irresponsible fiscal policy that will mean a reduced standard of living in the future? The remainder of this chapter explores this crucial question of whether continued government deficits are *sustainable* or not.[12]

Although "deficit" has now become a household word, the essential ambiguity of this term is seldom discussed and, even then, poorly understood.[13] This is unfortunate but not surprising. Both the concept and implications of "public deficits" are somewhat involved topics. With the highly emotional and politicized atmosphere surrounding recent U.S. deficits, it's inevitable that popular discussions have been oversimplified and shallow. The easiest way to understand the "sustainability" issue is to analyze it first in another setting, one that is well understood and uncontroversial, and does not involve the government. Hence, we begin with a survey of the consequences of continued borrowing by households and businesses.

Private borrowing (and its mirror image, lending) is a logical and time-honored response to some basic economic facts: Individual circumstances and preferences often differ widely, creating situations in which two parties can *both* benefit from a temporary exchange of purchasing power (loan) at some price (interest rate) that compensates the lender for giving up alternative uses of these funds and for assuming the risk that the borrower might default. For example, consumers with high rates of time preference, eager to consume now, seek to borrow from those with lower rates of time preference who are willing to postpone consumption in return for principal plus interest later. Those with a taste for immediate consumption get what they want, as long as they are willing to pay the price—interest costs. And those who would rather have the extra money—interest receipts—for later consumption, also get what they want. Similarly, those with promising but somewhat risky investment opportunities

---

[12] Remember that one of the simplifying assumptions of our *AD/AS* model is a *fixed* long-run *AS** curve. That is, it represents a rather limited concept of "long run" that involves market clearing but allows neither economic growth ($+\Delta AS^*$) nor decline ($-\Delta AS^*$). Instead of making the analytically difficult conversion into a growth model (which we'll do in Chapter 14), we take a simpler but still useful approach to "sustainability" in this section.

[13] Herbert Stein, a former chairman of the Council of Economic Advisers, finds that "this public obsession with the deficit as unmitigated evil is amazing. I would guess that not more than one person in 10,000 has any very clear idea of the definition of the deficit, of the meaning of $100 billion, of the nature and probable magnitude of the effects of the deficit or of the steps that would be required to eliminate it. It is almost as if the American people were obsessed by the fact that everybody bears the burden of 15 pounds of atmospheric pressure per square inch" (Herbert Stein, "Deficits, Disaster and Ross Perot," *The Wall Street Journal*, June 17, 1992).

may seek funds from more risk-averse lenders, pledging existing assets (house or factory) as collateral to "secure" the loan. The result is that those who are willing to take risks are able to raise capital from those willing to accept a lower rate of interest in return for more security. In these and other ways, the borrowing-lending process helps to bring about a more efficient use of our limited resources and essentially expands the nation's productive capacity ($+ \Delta PPF$ and $+ \Delta AS^*$) beyond what it would be in the absence of such transactions.[14]

But we also know that there are circumstances in which "excessive borrowing" or "unexpected events" can result in one or both parties being made worse off and wishing they'd never entered into that particular deal. What are the conditions that distinguish prudent borrowing, beneficial to all concerned, from irresponsible borrowing that ends in loss and even bankruptcy? The general answer is surprisingly simple—it depends on how much has been borrowed relative to the future income levels from which the payments must come. Borrowing that is prudent and sustainable goes beyond the limits of current income, but stays within the boundaries defined by the expected future income stream. *Borrowing becomes unsustainable when, knowingly or not, it exceeds the limit defined by present and expected future income.* To make this a bit more specific, let's consider two circumstances in which you might reasonably choose to borrow now and make payments (principal *plus* interest, of course) out of future income.

1. You use the borrowed funds to buy a durable or investment good (for example, a house or a computer or a college education) that is expected to yield a stream of returns over a number of years. Instead of having to make all the payments now, this allows a closer match between the timing of your payments and the timing of the benefits. Taking out a loan on a house (termed a "mortgage") is a common and widely accepted, even respected, economic activity. Similarly, borrowing money to invest in a new plant or in new product development is standard business practice, allowing firms to match their payments stream with the expected flow of future returns. Assuming expectations are realized, both borrower and lender gain from such transactions, which we categorize as **self-financing** *because the loan is used to generate the future returns to make the future payments.*

2. Suppose you borrow to buy a good or service that yields all its returns now rather than over a number of years. Can such a "consumption loan" ever be justified? That, of course, depends entirely on the size of this loan relative to your future income levels. Suppose you expect your real income to rise over the coming years as you become increasingly skilled in your occupation. Or suppose you're in a cyclically sensitive industry (e.g., construction, sales, or agriculture) that is currently in a "down" phase of the cycle. In either situation, you may well choose to have a "smoother" consumption stream—not so low now and not so high later—by borrowing to pay for current consumption. This process, called **consumption-smoothing,** *essentially averages your higher expected future incomes with your current income to determine your present consumption level.[15]*

In short, borrowing that is either **self-financing** or **consumption-smoothing** is neither dangerous nor irresponsible since both categories, by definition, stay within the limits defined by our combined current and expected future income levels. This doesn't mean that borrowing for investment or consumption smoothing is necessarily a "good" thing to do. Whether you *should* borrow is an entirely different

---

[14] The main reason that borrowing and lending seem different from other kinds of transactions is the presence of the time dimension—borrow *now*, pay *later*—which adds both uncertainty and risk to the exchange. We will have much to say about the importance of time and uncertainty when we discuss consumption, saving, investment, capital markets, and economic growth in Chapters 12 to 14.

[15] This and other aspects of the *timing* of consumption (now or later?) are explored in Chapter 12, "Consumption, Saving, and Investment."

question that depends on subjective factors like your personal attitude toward risk and your individual rate of time preference. What's important here is that we've identified the conditions under which you *can* borrow, if you so choose, without jeopardizing your economic future.[16]

What happens when the limits of prudent borrowing are ignored? Borrowed funds that are neither put into productive investments nor based on smoothing a growing level of income will have to be repaid out of a future net income that is no greater than today's. We will have precommitted so much of our future income to making payments on principal and interest that the amount left for consumption will dwindle, forcing a decline in our standard of living. We will have pushed our borrowing into the unsustainable zone.

> *3. We can characterize such excessive borrowing as **consumption-draining** in the sense that its repayment forces future consumption below today's. "Belt tightening" is a common term for these situations. Such borrowing can be done but only up to a point. The further we go beyond "self-financing" and "consumption-smoothing" and into "consumption-draining," the deeper our future consumption must be cut, increasing the likelihood that we will not be able to make our payments.*

Default and bankruptcy are the likely consequences when borrowing is guided by a "life's short, grab for all the gusto you can get" attitude that glorifies today with little thought of tomorrow. The arithmetic of compound interest ensures that such **consumption-draining** behavior can't continue long. For one thing, who would provide continued loans in such circumstances? Those who specialize in making such risky loans are called "loan sharks," a metaphor that should give one pause. In rational anticipation of the level of risk, they charge very high rates of interest. To stay in business (as they have for millennia), what they lose from those who default must be covered by those who fulfill the bargain. Friends and relatives sometimes provide risky loans at much lower rates of interest and the frequent result is a painful lesson in the fundamentals of capital market risk. Whatever else they may be, loan sharks are rational in assessing the cost of risk.

> IN SUMMARY . . .
>
> *Private "Deficits"*
>
> - When individuals borrow to smooth a growing or fluctuating income stream or to invest in income-generating activities, future liabilities from the loan are matched, more or less, by higher future income. If expectations are fulfilled, future consumption levels will not decline below today's as the loan is repaid.
> - But if neither "smoothing" nor "self-financing" are involved, borrowing to pay for consumption now must be "consumption-draining" later. This
>
> *(Continued)*

---

[16] Of course, not all our income expectations come to pass, and there's always the chance that the most careful plans will be undone by unforeseen or uncontrollable factors. That's part of the inevitable risk associated with arrangements, such as borrowing and lending, that extend into an always unknowable future. But the existence of risk is *not* an argument against the economic legitimacy of the borrowing and lending relationship. Both parties can still benefit from the transactions even under highly risky conditions.

can be done within a fairly narrow range. Beyond this, however, repayment becomes increasingly difficult. Either the borrower will be forced to severely reduce future consumption or the lender will be left with a worthless piece of paper.
- In short, a careful evaluation confirms our common sense perception that private "deficits" (borrowing) can be prudent or reckless, depending upon underlying circumstances. Note, however, that "who we borrow from" is *not* one of these circumstances.

Can we extend these commonsense conclusions about private borrowing to public deficits? Despite their very different emotional connotations, the words "deficit" and "borrowing" describe precisely the same thing. In popular usage, households and businesses "borrow"—sometimes wisely, sometimes not. But the federal government is said to "run a deficit!" Semantics, alone, virtually stop us from considering the possibility that public borrowing could be done prudently. In fact, we go even further and characterize a public cash flow deficit as an "unbalanced" budget. It's difficult to imagine anything good coming from something that is unbalanced. But *all* borrowing, public or private, means an "unbalanced" budget in the sense that current spending exceeds current income by the amount of the borrowed funds. The connotations of popular terminology discourage us from drawing parallels between private and public borrowing.

Let's try to remove these semantic obstacles by viewing the government's continuing use of deficit financing as an ongoing borrowing/lending relationship identical in all essentials to such arrangements in the private sector. It's obvious that the viability of any "borrow now, pay *more* later" arrangement does not depend on the specific identities of the involved parties—*who* borrows and *who* lends—but on whether the payments on these continued loans stay within the limits defined by the borrower's stream of income. As we saw earlier for the private sector, borrowing that exceeds the bounds of present and future income falls into the "consumption-draining" category and is obviously not sustainable.

But borrowing to finance public spending could also be "self-financing" or "consumption-smoothing," a fact that is little appreciated in the popular discussion of the ultimate consequences of continued deficits. It is apparent that *public investment* can increase the nation's stock of productive capital in just the same manner as private investment and thereby generate future income ($+ \Delta y^*$) and, hence, future tax revenues ($+ \Delta t$) to repay the loan (via $\uparrow t = t_0 + t_1 y^* \uparrow$). As its name reveals, borrowing that is "self-financing" increases future tax revenues with no increase in tax *rates* and, therefore, no drop in future consumption spending.[17] The obvious question is whether there really *are* returns to public investment. The returns to private investment are far more obvious, showing up in the form of higher incomes, profits, dividends, share prices and so on to the owners of the new capital.

Identifying the returns to public capital is more difficult because, by definition, public capital is owned collectively. The returns show up in a variety of ways, most of which we barely notice until, perhaps, a cut in government spending makes us suddenly aware of the absence of specific public goods or services. For example, govern-

[17] See David Alan Aschauer, "Is Public Expenditure Productive?" *Journal of Monetary Economics* 23 (1989): 177–200, for an empirical study of the impact of public capital spending on overall productivity.

ment spending on transportation makes travel more convenient, faster, and cheaper. Without this spending we would either incur the higher costs of a more primitive transportation system or we would have to pay a higher cost to get comparable transportation services through the private sector (e.g., toll roads). The cost of highway travel, including the price of all goods shipped by truck, would rise to reflect these higher private costs as well.

So although the returns to public investment may not show up directly as higher money incomes, they can be every bit as real. When public investment spending is cut, we must either go without that particular good or service (an economic cost) or turn to the private sector to provide a substitute, again for a cost. It follows that a deficit-financed increase in government investment spending ($+\Delta g^i = +\Delta b$) is very similar to borrowing to finance private investment—both transactions yield a stream of returns (directly or indirectly) that acts to counterbalance the future liability of the additional debt. In other words, they fall in the "self-financing" category and are therefore not a step down the road to future impoverishment.

Alternatively, suppose that even without more public investment we expect rising incomes and hence increased tax revenues in the coming years. If our expectations are well founded, we'll be able to borrow now and pay the higher future taxes out of higher future incomes, even if we use the borrowed funds for public consumption rather than investment purposes. In a steadily growing economy such borrowing works to smooth public spending across time. Just as with private borrowing, it works to redistribute consumption from a wealthier future to the present. For example, in a cyclically fluctuating economy, we could borrow in the lean years of recession to keep government spending from falling with tax revenues, repaying the loans in more prosperous times when income and tax collections have risen. The result is a deficit in downturns that allows us to smooth our public consumption spending across the business cycle. By not cutting spending or raising tax rates in a downturn, we are actually postponing taxes until the recession has ended and our incomes have returned to "normal" levels.[18]

What all this says is both simple and important. Just as households and corporations can borrow unwisely—in circumstances that start a time bomb ticking—so can the government. Specifically, any borrowing that is not based on a realistic expectation of higher tax revenues from rising future incomes will cut into our future standard of living and be "consumption-draining." The more we borrow in such circumstances—privately or publicly—the harder it will be for us later. In the extreme, "national bankruptcy" or its usual precursor, "hyperinflation," could result. We will examine such possibilities in later chapters. For now the main point is to understand why the mere existence of a cash flow deficit, public or private, tells us nothing about its sustainability. Whether it is a threat to future well-being or not depends on the size of the deficit relative to the future income stream from which it must be paid. To put it another way, the only honest answer to the question "Won't continued government deficits lead to future economic decline?" is an unequivocal "It depends!" It depends on whether they fall into the self-financing, consumption-smoothing, or consumption-draining categories.

---

[18] To avoid a cyclical deficit we would need to increase tax rates or cut spending and either of these policies would contract IS and AD, slowing the economy's attempt to return to full employment through the market clearing process. (If this doesn't sound familiar, look back at Chapter 4's discussion of how contractionary fiscal policies helped deepen and prolong the Great Depression.) Tolerating a cyclical deficit, even though it is not in the "self-financing" category, is not a perilous economic act. It simply postpones costs from hard times to good times. Nothing good comes without its price, of course, and the cost of this postponement is interest on the debt.

IN SUMMARY . . .

Public Deficits

1. When the government borrows to make *public investments* or to *smooth a growing or fluctuating tax revenue stream*, future liabilities from the loan are more or less matched by higher future tax revenues. Repayment will not force us into a declining standard of living.

2. But if neither "smoothing" nor "investing" are involved, borrowing to finance higher public consumption will indeed bring forth the kind of consequences implied by the "day of reckoning" image. To repay our debts will require either higher tax rates or lower government spending. The higher tax rates reduce after-tax income causing lower private consumption. Either way, private or public consumption will eventually fall if deficits are "consumption-draining."

3. Once we take away the semantic confusion of calling the same thing by two very different names—deficit or borrowing—depending on who does it, common sense can handle the rest. Public deficits, like private borrowing, can be prudent or reckless. It depends on the underlying circumstances. Failure to apply the same standards to government deficits as we do to private borrowing causes much confusion and needless worry and can result in ill-advised and costly policy responses.

5.6 ARE U.S. DEFICITS OF THE 1990s SUSTAINABLE?

This brings us to the central question for U.S. fiscal policy today. Are the large and continuing cash flow government deficits sustainable or are we headed for a period of declining consumption from shortsighted, consumption-draining deficits of recent decades? Have these deficits remained within the limits of our future income prospects or not? Note that the question is not whether government deficits are a "good" idea or a "bad" idea. That's a much larger question involving issues to be developed in coming chapters as well as subjective preferences that lie beyond the domain of economic analysis. The question for now is simply whether our large government deficits are sustainable or whether they're moving us inexorably toward some painful "day of reckoning" when a falling standard of living will be the price we pay for past mistakes.

One obvious fact is that decades of prophecies of imminent collapse have proved false. On the surface, at least, there are few signs that the U.S. government has pushed its borrowing into the consumption-draining range. Aggregate consumption levels, private or public, have not declined. Investors from all over the world continue to buy U.S. government bonds at what are quite low rates of interest by recent standards. This suggests that lenders are not expecting the U.S. government to default on its IOUs or to undertake a policy of rapid inflation that will diminish the real value of these bonds. Were such events anticipated, investors would not purchase the bonds unless a much higher rate of interest was offered to compensate them for the perceived risk.

But what if expectations of investors are wrong? Perhaps the economic collapse is just ahead, a year or a month or an hour from now. For an issue of such potential significance we'd like more assurance than "it hasn't happened yet" or "financial markets aren't anticipating it." After all, the same things could have been said the day before the October 1929 stock market crash. Is there more tangible evidence that we're not committing an act that will cause future generations of students to marvel over the economic ignorance of the late twentieth century?

Let's start by returning to the distinction between cyclical and structural components of the deficit ($b = b^{cyc} + b^{str}$). In the recession of the early 1980s and the next one in the early 1990s, part of the actual deficit was the consequence of the reduced tax base from the downturn ($-\Delta y \Rightarrow -\Delta t \Rightarrow +\Delta b^{cyc}$). This cyclical component of the deficit is consumption smoothing because it postpones some of our taxes when aggregate income falls and thereby moderates the decline in our current after-tax income and, hence, current consumption. As we return to full employment the cyclical component of the deficit, by definition, disappears. This is clearly a reasonable and sustainable activity.

But the striking feature of U.S. deficits since the 1980s is that they have remained high even *after* the economy has returned to full employment. They go far beyond consumption-smoothing from good times to bad. We have chosen to run large *structural deficits* that must either fall in the self-financing or consumption-draining categories. Thus the "sustainability" issue can be narrowed down to whether or not these large structural deficits (b^{str}) are matched by public *investment* spending (g^i). If so, they're self-financing and sustainable. If not, we're borrowing to finance current public consumption (g^c), creating future obligations but not the future returns to match—a classic case of consumption-draining.

To find out if U.S. deficits have remained in the sustainable range, then, we need information on how government is dividing its spending between public consumption and public investment. In relating the amount of borrowing to how it's spent, we're following the widely accepted business accounting practice of using a **capital account budget** to determine the sustainability of current borrowing. This compares the size of the cash-flow deficit to current investment spending to see whether or not these *new liabilities* (promises to make future payments) are matched by *new assets* (reasonable prospects of future returns). If not, a firm is said to have a capital account deficit, an unsustainable situation that threatens to drain its future profits and reduce its net worth. Applying this notion to the public sector, we define the *government capital account deficit* as $b^k = b - g^i$, the difference between the cash flow deficit and spending on investment projects. If the cash flow deficit is larger than public investment, then the resulting capital account deficit ($b^k > 0$) means we have exceeded the limits of self-financing and are borrowing at a rate that will ultimately prove consumption-draining. To be sustainable, the capital account budget must be balanced or in surplus ($b^k \leq 0$).[19]

Suppose that the current cash flow deficit at full employment (i.e., the structural cash flow deficit) is $100 billion and that public investment spending is $120 billion. Is the government running a deficit? By one measure ($b = g - t$) the deficit is $100 billion, but by another ($b^k = b - g^i$) we have a $20 billion *surplus*. Which is correct? If our concern is in how much the public debt grew this year then the ap-

---

[19] This also presumes that the rate of return on these investments, on average, is at least as great as the rate of interest being paid on the bonds. Some investments, private or public, yield unusually high returns, some unusually low. The inevitable uncertainty accompanying any investment is obviously important, but something that applies to business as well as government investment spending. It does not justify a zero borrowing strategy in either sector.

propriate concept is the government's current cash flow deficit (adjusted, wherever possible, for the measurement problems discussed earlier). But if our interest lies in whether this additional indebtedness threatens a future "day of reckoning," the cash flow deficit is almost useless because it reveals nothing about how the borrowed funds were used. The capital account deficit, by comparing the amount borrowed with the amount invested, incorporates the additional information about public investment needed for a reliable indicator of sustainability.

So let's now return to the big question: Do continued government cash flow deficits threaten to impoverish us or not? Are they mountains or mole hills on the landscape of our economic future? We've learned that we need to move beyond the cash flow concept of the deficit to the government's *capital account deficit* ($b^k = b - g^i$). If this remains in balance or surplus our fears of a "day of reckoning" are unfounded and we might do well to turn our attention to more pressing issues. (For example, instead of worrying about *when* the taxes will be collected—another way to view the tax/borrow choice—we could focus on *how they're spent*.) But if the capital account budget is in deficit ($b^k > 0$) then we have borrowed beyond the limits of current and future income and endangered our economic future. Failure to eliminate a capital account deficit will force us to struggle with its consequences in the future. But as long as we pay attention to the capital account budget rather than the cash flow, there should be no mystery about where we're headed: either our borrowing is sustainable ($b^k \leq 0$) or it's not ($b^k > 0$).

As you've probably guessed from the fact that you've never heard anything about the government's capital account budget, a reliable measure of the Federal capital account deficit is not available, ending our hope of a simple "yes or no" verdict on the sustainability of current deficits. There are a number of reasons why such a measure has not been provided. We saw part of it earlier—official deficit figures include some fictitious elements but exclude some real but hidden ones, leaving us with only a rough idea of the real size of the cash flow deficit. The other part of the problem is that the federal accounting system does not distinguish between public consumption and public investment spending, forcing us to do still more guessing to estimate what part of a crudely estimated cash flow deficit may be matched by an even more approximate estimate of current government investment.[20] In short, the inadequacy of our measurements hinders our attempt to determine whether U.S. deficits have been self-financing or not.

Fortunately, however, there's an alternative. It won't give us the hard and fast evidence of a solid government capital account deficit measure but it provides some reliable indirect clues as to the sustainability of continued cash flow deficits. Let's return to the *analogy with private sector borrowing*. Suppose you continue to borrow beyond the limits of your future income, adding future liabilities without corresponding future returns. Will there be any overt signals that you've entered dangerous waters or will you only find out when it's too late to respond?

In fact, signs of danger are likely to be all around you. One is the continuing escalation in your monthly interest payments without a comparable rise in your monthly income. As your borrowing rises, a larger and larger fraction of your in-

---

[20] The conceptual and measurement problems of making such estimates are indeed substantial. But many other countries as well as most state and local governments do make the attempt to estimate both hidden liabilities and public investment spending. However tentative the figures might be, they would almost certainly be more informative than the present situation in which a precise estimate of the wrong thing—the gross federal cash flow deficit—gets all the attention.

come will be claimed by interest expense. Note that higher interest payments, by themselves, are not necessarily a danger signal because they reveal nothing about whether you're borrowing responsibly or not. The key is the **ratio of interest payments to income.** As this rise in the fraction of your income claimed by interest begins to impair your standard of living, you might turn to still more borrowing to further postpone any drop in consumption. But with every new loan and every new credit card, two additional signals will light up—the **ratio of new borrowing to income** and the **ratio of total borrowing to income.**

So even if you follow the federal government in failing to keep a capital account budget, your continued search for new loans to maintain your consumption will be a reminder of your precarious circumstances. In the absence of a reliable measure of the capital account deficit, then, we turn to three easily calculated indicators—*the ratios of interest payments, new borrowing, and total indebtedness to current income.* A shortsighted borrower engaged in continuing consumption-draining activities will find all three ratios rising at an accelerating rate. This will make it increasingly difficult and costly for such a borrower to obtain additional financing from anyone who is aware of the underlying circumstances. New loans are likely to come at the expense of a substantial interest premium that protects the lender against the risk of default. In short, there is no shortage of warning signals when someone pushes their borrowing beyond consumption-smoothing and self-financing into the consumption-draining territory.

Translating this from personal to public finance, we'd expect that a government exhibiting this same irresponsible fiscal behavior (running continued cash flow deficits to finance current consumption) will see early warning signs in the following ratios—interest payments to income (g^{int}/y), current cash flow deficit to income (b/y), and national debt to income (nd/y)—and in an inability to attract additional lenders without paying increasingly high rates of interest on bonds. The main difference, and a very important one, is that bankruptcy can be postponed and consumption-draining deficits pushed much further by governments than by individuals or business. One way to appreciate this is to suppose that your personal goal is to consume as much as possible now and postpone payment for as long as possible. As your ratios rise and your creditors refuse to make further loans, however, you try two additional schemes—*theft* (directly transferring resources from others to yourself) and *counterfeiting* (printing money to finance your consumption and indirectly transferring resources from others). Obviously this greatly expands your capacity to continue consumption-draining activities. Having spent to the limits of your own current and future resources you are now spending those of others, siphoning their consumption into your tank.

With a little exaggeration, we can see that the public counterparts to theft and counterfeiting are, respectively, *fiscal policy* (specifically the power to tax and transfer resources) and *monetary policy* (control of the money supply). Unrestrained "siphoning" from private to public uses is not just a theoretical possibility but historical reality. Time and again, from the earliest civilizations to the present, governments have abused fiscal and monetary powers to transfer resources in illegal or irresponsible ways from one group to another.

So there is certainly good reason to fear the possibility that government deficits could be pushed to levels that are consumption-draining. But it's also important to see that this is neither economically nor politically inevitable. The issue is an empirical one that, in the absence of a reliable measure of the government's capital account budget, sends us to the key ratios—interest payments to income, deficits to income, and national debt to income.[21] The three graphs in Figure 5.5 present these ratios for the U.S. economy since 1940. The visually most striking event during the period is surely World War II. The decision to finance the huge military expenditures largely by future rather than current taxes showed up in all three ratios. But even though there were continued Federal cash flow deficits in most subsequent years, it is apparent that the growth in GDP was outpacing the growth in the national debt. The conditions for an *un*sustainable deficit—that these ratios rise continually—are clearly not present.

Next to World War II, the ratios of recent decades look quite moderate.[22] Though the interest payments to income ratio has risen a bit in recent years, it shows no more sign of accelerating increase than do the other ratios. What this tells us is that the large government cash flow deficits of recent years have not been capital account deficits since they would have been accompanied by an acceleration in the growth of these ratios, not just an upward drift. In the absence of a government capital account deficit, the behavior of these ratios is the best evidence that our government deficits have been of the sustainable self-investment and consumption-smoothing types, not consumption-draining.

Be careful not to read too much into this conclusion. It does not mean that these deficits were therefore a "good thing" and it certainly doesn't mean that just because the economy isn't going to crash and burn that we successfully defied scarcity and got "something for nothing." The "something" we got is more government spending than we paid for out of taxes during this period. If we had not run a cash-flow deficit we would have had either higher taxes or lower public output than we actually did. But the price we must pay for this benefit is higher taxes in the coming years, reducing our after-tax income and, hence, consumption levels in those years below what they would have been had we tax financed rather than deficit financed in the earlier years. And, of course, these consumption levels will be lowered by the amount of the deficits *plus* interest payments on those deficits. Just as with private borrowing, we end up paying a premium when we choose to postpone costs.

Again, the fact that large government cash flow deficits have *not* been the clear prelude to bankruptcy that so many have assumed does not mean that such large deficits are a wise choice. In fact, there are some good reasons to be concerned with the recent performance of fiscal policy in the U.S. and its implications for the future. The text box, "Deficits and Crowding Out," considers one important issue and others will be raised at the appropriate time. What is important for now is that you see that consumption draining is *not* a likely consequence of the deficits of the 1980s and 1990s. You won't wake up one morning to headlines like "Day of Reckoning Is Here!"; "U.S. Economy Collapses Under Weight of Its Own Debt!"; or "Federal Government Proclaims Bankruptcy!" Removing this troll from beneath the bridge is the first step to understanding the government deficit situation facing us today.

---

[21] To get a long and consistent series of observations, we have to settle for data that are somewhat incomplete. For example, net interest payments are for the federal government only; the deficit measure is corrected only for intragovernmental holdings and state and local surpluses, but not for the inflation tax or hidden liabilities; the national debt only includes outstanding Treasury bonds so it, too, ignores state and local debt, and is uncorrected for inflation and hidden liabilities. These numbers are the conventional ones used in most popular discussions of deficits. We use them because they're readily available and because there's evidence that the size of what we're omitting hasn't changed much relative to the size of what's included. Therefore, movements in what we observe more or less parallel movements in what we'd like to but can't. Any troublesome trends would show up in both series.

[22] Though we hear so much about the troubling deficits in the U.S., many other nations have considerably higher and more rapidly growing ratios. For example, the nations of the European Union saw their average *b/y* ratio rise from 3% in 1989 to more than 7% in 1993. Their *nd/y* ratio rose from about 43% in 1980 to more than 66% by 1993.

■ FIGURE 5.5

Continued deficits that fall into the consumption-draining category would result in continued increases in these three ratios: (1) g^{int}/y, (2) b/y, and (3) nd/y.

The absence of soaring levels of these ratios in the 1990s implies that the large cash flow deficits of recent years have not exceeded the sustainable consumption-smoothing and self-financing categories.

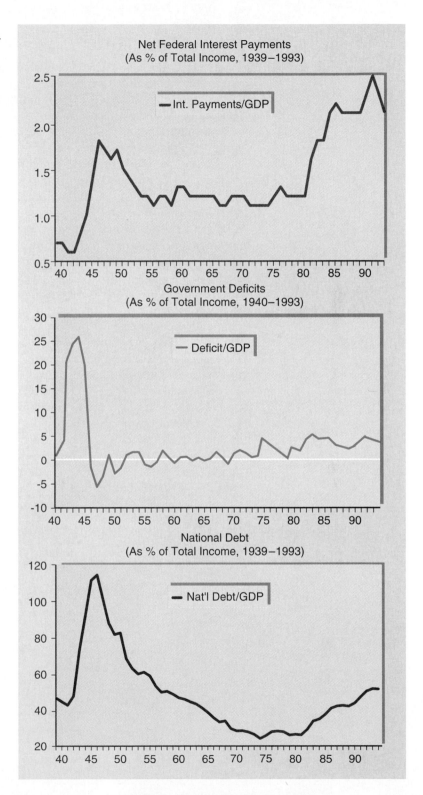

Three Key Ratios to Sustainability

IN SUMMARY . . .

How Much Longer Can These Deficits Continue?

In assessing whether we are borrowing "too much"—privately or publicly—the primary consideration must be whether the future payments threaten to outrun the limits imposed by our future incomes. Borrowing that is "self-financing" (invested with a return no less than the interest payments on the loan) or "consumption-smoothing" (transferring purchasing power from a richer future to the poorer present) is clearly within these limits and hence sustainable. Borrowing beyond these two categories must inevitably be "consumption-draining"—transferring purchasing power from a future that is *not* richer than the present, thereby draining that future to support the present.

The notion behind a "capital account" budget is central to business accounting practice because, unlike a "cash flow" concept of borrowing, it incorporates some measure of the *use* of borrowed funds. In this way borrowing that is self-financing shows up as a cash flow deficit but not a capital account deficit. Borrowing—public or private—that involves a capital account deficit, on the other hand, means that we are creating future liabilities without future returns to pay for them, a situation that cannot continue without some degree of economic disappointment for borrowers or lenders or both. This is the fear that most people have when they see large cash flow government deficits in the U.S. continuing into a second decade. They wrongly presume that a cash flow deficit necessarily has the same consequences as a capital account deficit.

Unfortunately there is no official measure of the capital account deficit—cash flow deficit minus government investment spending—available for the public sector. But we can turn to some indirect clues as to whether recent government cash flow deficits in the U.S. have also been capital account deficits and hence unsustainable. Three key ratios—interest payments, cash flow deficits, and the national debt to total output (GDP)—would all be rising continuously if these deficits had been capital account deficits and, hence, consumption draining. The data give no indication of any such problem. On bond markets, lenders continue to buy and hold U.S. Treasury bonds at relatively low rates of interest.

We conclude that the popular view that "the government simply can't continue to run such massive deficits" is mistaken. This is not to say that we *should* continue them, but only that we can if we so choose.

DEFICITS AND CROWDING OUT

Much has been said in this chapter about the common misperception that government deficits are *always* consumption-draining. It's crucial to understand that public borrowing, like private, can also fall in the self-financing or consumption-smoothing categories and hence be sustainable. But even if the large cash flow deficits of the 1980s and 1990s are sustainable, this does not mean that they are without adverse consequences.

Let's look at a situation, roughly descriptive of the United States over the past 15 years, in which a large deficit, though sustainable, reflects policy choices of dubious wisdom. Suppose the economy starts with a relatively small cash flow deficit of $50 billion and public investment of $150 billion. The government thus has a healthy capital account surplus ($b^k = b - g^i = 50 - 150 = -\$100$ billion) that ensures that the $50 billion cash flow deficit is well within the government's ability to pay without raising future tax rates.

Now suppose that a sudden craving for increased consumption results in a combination of tax cuts (causing an increase in private consumption) and increased spending on public consumption. Together they increase the cash flow deficit to $150 billion, causing the capital account surplus to disappear. While still sustainable, this increasing structural deficit means an outward shift in both *IS* and *AD* and a consequent rise in the real rate of interest ($+\Delta r$). This, in turn, means *crowding out* of both private investment and net exports, since both vary inversely with the real rate of interest. Assuming the economy was at full employment to begin, the net outcome is an **increase in total consumption** (as result of $+\Delta g^c$ and $+\Delta c$) offset by an equal **decrease in total investment and net exports.**

This change in the *timing* of consumption from future to present is an example of what we have termed "consumption-smoothing." It necessarily forces a decline in the rate of economic growth (a subject discussed carefully in a later chapter) and the mechanism is the crowding out of private investment by a growing public deficit. If this choice for more consumption had been made with the full understanding that the cost was slower growth of future consumption then it would simply reflect a particular outcome in the inevitable battle between "now" and "later." However, anyone who was under the illusion that this increased public and private consumption reflected a permanent increase in overall economic well-being and that future economic growth would not be diminished will be sorely disappointed.

✂ 5.7 *IF WE COULD START OVER . . . SHOULD WE TRY TO BALANCE THE CASH FLOW BUDGET?*

We've seen that much of the worry about continued Federal cash flow deficits ($b = g - t > 0$) stems from the misperception that their consequences are the same as those of large capital account deficits ($b^k = b - g^i > 0$). But logical error or not, the fact is that most Americans favor a "balanced budget" for the government sector and think in terms of a simple cash flow budget. Repeated attempts to move toward this goal through legislation (such as the Gramm-Rudman-Hollings bill in the late 1980s and a frequently proposed but still unconsumated fiscal amendment to the Constitution) leave no doubt as to the widespread appeal of a "balanced budget." One important barrier to its attainment is the fear that the cost of "getting there from here" could be extremely high due to the contractionary impact of a large decrease in the structural deficit. But there seems to be little doubt in most people's mind that the goal itself is worthy and that we should move gradually and steadily toward it.

So let's set aside the transition costs of getting there and look, instead, at whether a balanced cash flow budget is really as desirable as it seems. Suppose we could start from scratch with a brand new economy. Should we try to preserve our fiscal innocence and take the pledge to never ever run a government deficit? Or should we consider a more complicated plan that allows some public borrowing under certain conditions and within certain limits? Although economic analysis can never give a "correct" answer to what policy makers *should* do, it certainly can be used to explore the likely consequences of alternative choices.

Suppose our new economy adopts the simplest and most rigid balanced budget law requiring the government to spend every dollar of its tax revenues each year, not a penny more or less. Ignoring the mechanics of how this would be done in the presence of unforeseen changes in tax and spending streams, let's think about the general costs and benefits of such an approach. On the benefit side, the pluses are obvious—it's *popular* with the voters, *simple* to define and monitor, and obviously *safe* in terms of the important "sustainability" criteria. By always setting public spending equal to current revenues, we will be sure to stay well inside our ability to pay in a growing economy. Resistance to the imposition of new taxes is also likely to keep public spending under much tighter control than if it could be financed partly by a claim on future income. In short, requiring the government to run a balanced cash flow budget each year has much to recommend it.

But it's important to see that this "zero-borrowing" rule also has its drawbacks, which explains why it is almost never chosen by individuals, businesses, and even state and local governments. For example, while ostensibly preventing us from imposing a "burden on future generations," a balanced cash flow budget actually results in a transfer of purchasing power from the present to the future. It puts a net cost ("burden") on the present by forcing us to pay the full cost of current spending immediately even though the returns from the public investment part of that spending (g^i) will only be realized in the future. Put another way, when public capital formation is paid entirely from current taxes the result is essentially *pre*payment—pay now, enjoy later.

Although it's certainly a *nice* thing to provide net benefits to the future, scarcity ensures that it always has its price—more later, less now. Confronted with having to pay in advance for capital goods, the economic incentive would be for us to put a larger share of our spending into goods that yield current benefits rather than future benefits. If we can't spread the cost of a capital good over the years in which it yields its returns, we're likely to invest less and consume more. The imposition of a zero-borrowing (or balanced cash-flow budget) strategy on the government would tip the scales from public investment toward public consumption spending. Spending on large scale public capital (such as transportation, information networks, education, basic research, and so on) would be discouraged if we could not spread at least part of those costs over several years.[23] In other words, a balanced cash flow budget policy would tend to reinforce the alleged bias toward a "quick return" that is often said to afflict U.S. economic decision making, public and private.

Another important effect of this rigid "zero-borrowing" rule would be its impact on current economic performance. Not only would it mean that changes in fiscal policy could no longer be used to offset unwanted fluctuations in output and employment, but it even goes a step further and makes fiscal policy *pro*cyclical, reinforcing and magnifying the ups and downs of the business cycle. For example, when the economy slips into a recession (resulting say, from a drop in autonomous investment spending, $-\Delta i_0$), falling incomes reduce tax revenues ($\downarrow t = t_0 + t_1 y \downarrow$), pushing the cash flow budget into deficit ($\uparrow b = g - t \downarrow$). But if all deficits are prohibited this would require a prompt cut in public spending ($-\Delta g_0$) or increase in tax rates ($+\Delta t_0$) in response to the cyclical decline in tax revenues. As we've seen, this decreasing structural deficit is contractionary (shifting *IS* and *AD* to the left), and is exactly what we don't want in an economic downturn.[24]

To summarize briefly, the consequences of following a strict balanced cash-flow budget (zero-borrowing) strategy are not so beneficial as is popularly believed. Against the benefits of simplicity and safety, we must weigh the costs of (1) imposing a net cost on the present to pay for future benefits, as happens when we (pre)pay for public investment (g^i) out of current taxes; (2) a resulting bias away from public investment spending that comes when impatient taxpayers look for current benefits (g^c) to match their current taxes; (3) the loss of fiscal policy as a potentially effective tool in stabilization policy; and (4) the destabilizing impact when a cyclical decline (a $-\Delta y$, which causes $+\Delta b^{cyc}$) forces structural changes in fiscal policy ($-\Delta g_0$ or $+\Delta t_0$, which causes $-\Delta b^{str}$) in an inevitably contractionary attempt to maintain balance in the overall cash flow budget ($b = \uparrow b^{cyc} + \downarrow b^{str}$) during a recession.

Now these might be relatively small costs to pay if the *only* alternative to zero borrowing was irresponsible borrowing of the "consumption-draining" type. But we have seen that this is not the case. A major challenge for U.S. fiscal policy in the coming years will be to find a goal for the responsible conduct of fiscal policy that avoids the disadvantages of a strict balanced cash-flow budget ($b = 0$), yet also maintains effective control over public spending and keeps us well away from the possibility of a capital account deficit ($b^k > 0$). The basic economics of the deficit issue are relatively straightforward. The real difficulty has been in finding a procedure that is both economically sensible and politically acceptable.

We will have more to say about this central policy issue in later chapters. But let's also note that fixation with the "deficit problem" may distract attention from more important dimensions of what most of us would regard as "fiscal responsibility." Remember that the deficit/tax choice is really just one of *when* to tax. This matter of timing is important in many ways, of course, but it's impact on our well-being is certainly overshadowed by at least three other fiscal choices.

---

[23] Applied to our private finances, a balanced cash flow budget would surely be regarded by most as simple and safe but quite ridiculous. It would eliminate the possibility of borrowing that is consumption-draining, but only at the sacrifice of mutually advantageous borrowing/lending in the consumption-smoothing and self-financing categories. For example, it would require cash in advance for a house rather than allowing us to pay off a mortgage over time as the housing services are received. We would become a nation of renters, quite the antithesis of the American dream of home ownership.

[24] As mentioned in Chapter 4, this scenario of attempting to balance the cash flow budget in a downturn helped deepen and prolong the Great Depression.

1. The *overall level of government spending,* the fraction of total output that we choose to allocate through the public sector. This is perhaps *the* most fundamental economic policy choice a society has to make. Currently about 35% of U.S. output is channeled through the public sector, up from 26% in 1965 and less than 15% in 1929.[25] It seems likely that much of the hostility directed at the deficit is simply misplaced frustration over what many believe to be a severely bloated public sector.

2. Underlying whatever compromise is reached over the *level* of public spending, there is the choice of the *specific kinds of government spending.* How much for education or national defense, for subsidies to farmers or homeowners, for transfers to the retired or the unemployed? These are the crucial decisions that affect us all and are far more fundamental than the "deficit issue" of whether we choose to pay for these particular goods and services now or later.

3. How do we *transfer resources from the private sector* to pay for our level of public sector output? This involves nothing less than the design of the tax structure — its breadth, efficiency, and perceived "fairness."

In comparison with our fiscal choices about the *size* of the public sector, the specific *composition* of public output, and the nature of the *tax system,* the choice about "*when* we tax" (implicit in the size of the deficit) looks almost trivial. There is no reason to think that a balanced cash flow budget leads automatically to wise and responsible decisions on the three issues above. Conversely, a nation that has made careful and farsighted decisions about these three fundamental issues might well choose to have a sizable cash-flow deficit, provided that its capital account deficit is balanced or in surplus. Put concisely, a balanced government cash-flow budget is neither a necessary nor a sufficient condition for prudent fiscal choices. It is important to understand that any meaningful notion of "fiscal responsibility" lies well beyond simple slogans like "balance the budget."

ᏂᏂ *5.8 OVERVIEW*

1. The experience of the Great Depression, the development of demand-oriented models of the macroeconomy (following the lead of John Maynard Keynes), and the dramatic return to full employment during World War II all contributed to a new attitude toward macroeconomic policy. This was embodied in the **Employment Act of 1946** and subsequent legislation that acknowledged *public responsibility for economy-wide economic performance,* a dramatic change from the classical tradition's emphasis on automatic market mechanisms that ensured full-employment equilibrium.

2. During the past fifty years the public has come to expect prompt and effective government responses to economic fluctuations. Unfortunately these expectations are not always matched by an understanding of the **capabilities and limitations of macroeconomic policy** to achieve these goals. This chapter begins a closer look at policy prospects that will continue throughout the book. Here we have exam-

---

[25] This is the figure for total government spending as a percentage of GDP and includes transfer payments (g^{tr}) and government interest payments (g^{int}). Just counting public spending on final goods and services (g), the current ratio is about 20%.

ined the basic workings of *fiscal policy*, particularly the "deficit issue." The next chapter docs the same thing for *monetary policy* and the following chapter extends these policy results from the domestic to the *international sector.*

3. In its most basic sense, **fiscal policy** is about how we choose and pay for the things our government buys. The *AD/AS* framework helps us see that the overall consequences of an increase in government spending depends not only on its size but also its financing. A tax-financed increase in government spending ($+\Delta g = +\Delta t$) has the smallest impact on aggregate demand, whereas a money-financed increase ($+\Delta g = +\Delta M$) has the largest. A bond or deficit-financed increase in government spending ($+\Delta g = +\Delta b$) lies between these two. Because U.S. monetary policy is controlled by the separate Federal Reserve system, the financing options open to the fiscal authority (the U.S. Treasury) are limited to current taxes or current deficits (hence, future taxes).

4. Deficit financing has become the liveliest of fiscal topics in recent years following a significant increase in the size of the U.S. government's **cash flow deficit** ($b = g - t$) and the more rapid growth of the resulting accumulated **national debt.** There is much fear that our deficits have been shortsighted and irresponsible and that we will be paying the price for many years to come. To understand whether these fears are warranted requires us to examine the *size of the deficit*, it's *impact on current economic activity*, and the *conditions determining its sustainability.* Making sense of the "deficit issue" takes some effort and, for most of us, requires that we set aside some common but misleading preconceptions.

5. Even such a basic topic as the **measurement of government deficits** is more involved than is commonly understood. The conventional numbers—seized on by both the media and politicians—count both too much and too little. By including intragovernmental holdings of debt, failing to include state and local surpluses, and failing to adjust for the "inflation tax" on the real value of outstanding debt, the deficit measure that appears in the headlines is hugely inflated. But in failing to include governmental promises to make future payments beyond those that show up as U.S. Treasury bonds, the so-called stealth budget, it vastly understates the total outstanding claims on our future tax dollars.

6. The **impact of the deficit on current economic activity** is also more complicated than is usually thought. It first requires a clear separation between the cyclical and structural components of the *cash-flow deficit* ($b = b^{cyc} + b^{str}$). We must then focus on *changes* in the structural deficit and, finally, consider the extent to which *tax-discounting behavior* weakens the strength of a changing structural deficit.

7. The ability to **sustain continued borrowing (deficits)**—private or public—depends essentially on how the borrowed funds are used. If our deficits are matched by investment activities they can be **self-financing,** adding as much or more to future returns as to future liabilities. Similarly, deficits that rise during recessions and fall with recovery are a way of moving part of the cost of bad times to more prosperous years. Such borrowing for **consumption-smoothing** is an entirely legitimate and sustainable practice for private and public sector alike. Borrowing that is either self-financing or consumption-smoothing is considered "sustainable" in the sense that it falls within the limits of our future income levels.

8. But borrowing that exceeds these two categories will simply postpone costs without providing future returns to match. Such borrowing is clearly not sustainable and is said to be **consumption-draining.** It is widely presumed, often without un-

derstanding these distinctions, that *public* borrowing—deficit financing—is *always* of the "consumption-draining" variety. The fact that the United States is now into its second decade of running large structural deficits is tangible evidence that continued borrowing is sustainable without a major economic collapse. It does not necessarily follow that continued borrowing is, therefore, "desirable." This judgment depends on issues to be developed in later chapters.

9. Underneath all the debate about the government deficit lies the one *big* question: "How long can this continue before . . . (pick your favorite metaphor)". . . "the bottom falls out," "we self-destruct," "we have to pay the piper," and so on. What we want is some yardstick to tell us whether our government deficits are of the self-financing, consumption-smoothing, or consumption-draining type. In standard business accounting terminology, what we desire is a measure of the **capital account deficit** rather than just the **cash-flow deficit** that currently grabs all the headlines. A measure of the capital account deficit requires that we start with the *cash-flow measure* and subtract the level of current **public investment** ($b^k = b - g^i$). Unfortunately, there are no official or generally agreed-on measures for government investment spending, leaving us unable to make a reliable estimate of the government's capital account deficit and, therefore, unable to provide a definitive answer to the crucial "Can this continue?" question.

10. Fortunately, there is another way to see if government deficits are remaining within the sustainable range or not. Three key numbers—**the ratios of interest payments, cash-flow deficits, and the national debt to total output**—would be rising at increasing rates if we had been running government deficits on capital account. The data show no evidence of such acceleration and we conclude that the fear that government borrowing has exceeded the bounds of our ability to repay is groundless. This does not tell us that we "should" continue to run such historically large cash flow deficits but only that we "can" sustain them if we so choose.

11. Continuing with our assumed sustainable deficit, we can then consider its **impact on economic growth** and, hence, on future consumption. In this respect we see an important difference between the self-financing and the consumption-smoothing categories. Although both are sustainable, deficits that are self-financed involve borrowing now for public investment activities that yield returns later. But consumption-smoothing deficits represent a decision to move some future public consumption to the present ($+\Delta g^c$). The absence of public investment to accompany the borrowing means a lower rate of capital formation and a reduction in the rate of economic growth. This will be explored more fully in later chapters.

12. "Fiscal responsibility" is an important phrase that is typically used in a variety of careless and inconsistent ways. Clearing away the many confusions about government deficits allows us to see that although the deficit issue—*when* should the tax be paid?—is obviously important, it has a much smaller impact on our economic well-being than three other fiscal choices: the level of government spending, the composition of that spending, and the level and kinds of taxes by which we pay, now or later, for our public sector. A meaningful concept of **fiscal responsibility** must go beyond whether or not the government is running a cash flow deficit. It must consider these three fiscal fundamentals: *How much* to spend? *What* to spend it on? *Who will pay* for it?

ᏬᏬ *5.9 REVIEW QUESTIONS*

1. Define the following basic concepts or terms:

Employment Act of 1946	Cash-flow deficit	Sustainability
Council of Economic Advisers	National debt	Public investment
	Gross and net deficit	Public consumption
Fine-tuning	Inflation tax	Self-financing
Fiscal policy	Stealth budget	Consumption-smoothing
Tax financing	Cyclical deficit	
Deficit financing	Structural deficit	Consumption-draining
Treasury bonds	Tax discounting	Capital account deficit

2. Evaluate the following statement fully, considering both the measurement issues underlying the government deficit and the short- and long-term consequences of this deficit for the economy: "The federal deficit for next year is expected to be in excess of $200 billion and that doesn't include the additional promises incurred through the various entitlement programs. What clearer evidence could there be of continued fiscal irresponsibility on the part of our political leaders?"

3.
   a. Explain, in your own words, why current inflation reduces the nation's net indebtedness.
   b. Under current accounting procedures, Social Security payments are counted in the budget only as they are made. Explain the logic for including a change in *future* obligations to make Social Security payments as part of the government's *current* deficit.

4. Evaluate the following statements:
   a. "Deficits cause recessions."
   b. "Recessions cause deficits."

5. Explain in commonsense terms why the ratio of national debt to total output is a better indicator of whether we're borrowing too much than is the actual level of national debt.

6. Evaluate the following statement, incorporating the notion of "tax discounting" into your answer: "The issue of a burden to the debt is in good part an issue of how farsighted we are in our consumption decisions."

7. Evaluate the economic content of each of the following statements. Be sure to read each statement carefully and explain your reasoning.
   a. "Deficits are a means for living high now at the expense of those who have to pay them off later."
   b. "A large national debt is sufficient evidence to conclude that past generations have left a net burden on the current generation through their expenditure and tax policies."
   c. "You can't spend your way to prosperity. When a recession comes, we must tighten our belts, spend less, and pray more."
   d. "A continued unbalanced budget, by an individual, business, or government, is not sustainable and must eventually have adverse consequences."

8. Suppose a balanced-budget law is politically inevitable, but the debate centers on *which* budget to balance—cash flow ($b = 0$), structural cash flow ($b^{str} = 0$, so $b = t_1(y^* - y)$), government capital account ($b^k = 0$, so $b = g^i$), or a combined structural-capital account ($b^{str/k} = 0$, so $b = t_1(y^* - y) + g^i$). Discuss the costs and benefits associated with each.

9. It's 2006, and the aftermath of the failed Balanced-Budget Amendment has brought a gradual but real end to decades of agonizing over the government deficit. For better and worse, the federal government has finally reached a balanced, cyclically adjusted, cash-flow budget. But the president decides that she wants to do something about the accumulated deficits of the past—namely, eliminate the $8 trillion national debt.

   a. She asks you for an economic evaluation of the basic macroeconomic consequences (short- and long-run impacts on y, P, and r), and related costs and benefits of the following three proposals for ending the national debt. For each proposal, explain your reasoning.

      i. Pay it off by a combination of higher taxes and lower public spending, gradually, over the next thirty years.

      ii. Require the Federal Reserve to use its monetary powers to buy up outstanding U.S. Treasury obligations, gradually, over the next thirty years.

      iii. Simply declare a one-time national moratorium on government debt in which all existing U.S. Treasury obligations, for the economic good of our great nation, are declared null and void.

   b. Suppose one of these is chosen and implemented, and the national debt is entirely eliminated. In terms of macroeconomic performance, present and future, in what ways do you think this economy is better or worse off now that this huge public debt has been repaid? Be specific and explain your reasoning.

10. Perhaps the most confusing thing about all the discussion of the government deficit is that people mean different things by the word "deficit."

   a. "Some kinds of deficit are clearly more dangerous than others. Forbidding all government borrowing may, contrary to most people's expectations, impose more costs than benefits on the economy." Describe circumstances in which the preceding sentence would be true, explaining the costs and benefits carefully.

   b. "Although a law that requires surplus or balance in the government's capital account budget ($b^k \le 0$) may have some immediate appeal, the problem is that it leaves the cash-flow deficit (b) in deficit, which just means continued and unending growth in our total national debt. We might get away with this for a while, but it obviously can't go on forever." Do you agree or disagree? Explain.

   c. "Deficit spending can have some real benefits in certain circumstances. But, even so, we must be aware of the costs, particularly the drain on the economy from the resulting huge interest payments. This wouldn't be so bad if our national debt were all internally held. But with 12% of it held by foreign investors this continued leakage of purchasing power can only result in a lower standard of living for us." Evaluate and explain.

11. "A look through history will show that there is no basic relationship between government deficits and macroeconomic performance. Sometimes the economy

prospers despite large deficits. Other times, the deficit seems to grab onto the economy and strangle it into a recession. The only thing we can say for certain is that the relationship between deficits and economic prosperity is not the simple one that most people think. In fact there's no clear relationship at all." Evaluate this statement and explain your reasoning.

12. Virtually everyone has a strong opinion about the government debt and deficit situation. Two such views are captured in the following quotes, which are identical except for the first word. Do you agree with either, both, or neither? Explain.

   a. "*Unless* we do something about this huge government debt, the economy will be devastated."

   b. "*If* we do something about this huge government debt, the economy will be devastated."

5.10 FURTHER READING

MARIO I. BLEJER AND ADRIENNE CHEASTY, "The Measurement of Fiscal Deficits: Analytical and Methodological Issues," *Journal of Economic Literature*, XXXIX (December 1991): 1644–1678.

ROBERT EISNER, *How Real Is the Federal Deficit?* (New York: The Free Press, 1986).

ROBERT HEILBRONER AND PETER BERNSTEIN, *The Debt and the Deficit: False Alarms/Real Possibilities* (New York: W. W. Norton & Co., 1989).

LAWRENCE J. KOTLIKOFF, *Generational Accounting: Knowing Who Pays—And When—for What We Spend* (New York: The Free Press, 1992).

HERBERT STEIN, *The Fiscal Revolution in America*, rev. ed. (Washington D.C.: The AEI Press, 1990).

HERBERT STEIN, *Washington Bedtime Stories: The Politics of Money and Jobs* (New York: The Free Press, 1986).

CHAPTER 6

MONETARY POLICY

🕮 6.1 INTRODUCTION

Continuing our analysis of the strengths and limitations of macroeconomic policy, we now turn from fiscal to monetary policy. We have been using the term "money" throughout the book as if we knew exactly what it is and why it matters. **Money,** in some important ways, is a much more elusive concept than our day-to-day experience suggests. We need to look at what "money" means and how it functions—as a way to *store purchasing power* as well as to *make transactions*—before we can begin to understand the difficulties and temptations faced by those who control the nation's money supply.

Money can assume a multitude of shapes and forms. At various times and places it has been many things—stones, shells, tobacco, vodka, salt, furs, dried fish, copper, silver, gold, and even pieces of paper, to name only a few. Some of these (gold, silver, and furs) have a relatively high *intrinsic value*—that is, value in uses other than as money. Others (stones, shells, and paper) have a very low non-monetary value. Since 1971, all the monies of the world have been fashioned solely out of paper, with no "backing" from gold or silver or any other commodity.[1] Paper currencies are called **fiat money**—money by "declaration" (*fiat* in Latin).

We commonly think of "money" as the same thing as "income" or "wealth," reasoning that if we just had more money we would also have a higher standard of living. But this is a partial truth and does not hold for the economy as a whole. An increase in the nominal supply of money, as we saw in both the classical model of Chapter 2 and the expanded *AD/AS* model of Chapter 4, doesn't increase real output or income in the long run. The addi-

---

[1] Coins also accompany a paper currency but account for only a small fraction of the value of the money supply. Like paper, they have very little intrinsic value.

tional dollars $(+\Delta M)$ just bid up the average price level $(+\Delta P)$, pointing up the fact that money is a *claim* to output, not the output itself. The vertical long run aggregate supply curve tells us that while nominal or "money income" will rise with the price level $(Py^* = Y^*$, so $+\Delta P \Rightarrow +\Delta Y^*)$, our "real income" will not. The useful slogan "You can't print your way to prosperity." is an invaluable reminder that "money" is not the same thing as "real output" or "wealth."[2] It is a distinct commodity, used to trade for (and measure) the goods and services that comprise our real output and wealth.

A world without money requires either **economic self-sufficiency,** consuming only what we individually produce, or, more likely, **barter.** Those wanting to trade A for B would not only have to find someone willing to trade B for A but also have to bargain until a mutually agreeable terms of trade, say 2A for 5B, is reached. Barter works well enough in rudimentary economies with little specialization. It also exists as an appendage to a monetized economy, usually as a way to evade the tax collector. Compared to self-sufficiency, barter is far more efficient because it brings the substantial productivity gains that flow from specialization. For a given amount of labor or capital, a barter economy would have a much higher standard of living than one composed of self-sufficient, nontrading individual units.[3]

But bartering one good for another is a time-consuming, laborious, and sometimes impossible way to conduct trades. With barter, buying one good or service requires the simultaneous sale of another and this can be difficult to arrange, particularly if one happens to be something like "theoretical physics" or "poetry" and the other is "milk" or "plumbing services." The great usefulness of money lies in its ability to separate buying from selling—geographically and temporally. For example, you can sell your labor services here and now and be paid in money which can be spent across town or across the ocean, later in the day or later in the decade. By freeing resources (especially "time") previously consumed by the process of barter, **monetization** creates a more efficient institutional structure $(+\Delta i^{nst})$. It means an outward shift in both the aggregate supply curve and the production possibility frontier, making the degree of monetization a vital part of the institutional fabric of any economy. When this fabric weakens (for example, because of rapid inflation which "taxes" the purchasing power of money holdings), the resulting demonetization means a negative supply shock as the economy loses some of the gains provided by a sound, efficient money.

While the form and substance of monies can differ dramatically—from precious metal or addictive plant to intoxicating liquid or fancy paper—all must share one common characteristic: **acceptability.** To function as "money" requires an object to be widely accepted in exchange for virtually all goods and services.[4] Assets that are not *quickly and easily* converted into commodities—like a house or a sailboat, a continental dollar in 1780, a Confederate dollar in 1865, or a Ukranian karbovanet in 1994—can't satisfy this most basic and important function of money. "Money," whatever its form, must have our collective economic vote of confidence. We accept

---

[2] We saw this in another way in Chapter 1 when we talked about investment and capital formation as the mechanism for moving goods and services from the present to the future. Saving money, by itself, won't do the trick. It moves *claims* to output from now to later, but not the output itself.

[3] In terms of our underlying model, "self-sufficiency" and "barter" can be treated as alternative *institutional structures.* Moving from a world of self-sufficiency to barter is an improvement in institutional efficiency $(+\Delta i^{nst})$ through the creation of an array of mutual gains from specialization and trade. It shows up as an outward shift of both the *PPF* and *AS** curves.

[4] This includes its acceptability by the government as payment for public goods and services—namely, as taxes. The official designation of a money as "legal tender" in payment of taxes and fulfillment of contracts, as enforced by the Courts, is an important part of what makes something function as "money." But such a declaration, by itself, cannot ensure that other important functions of money, described later, will be satisfied.

it only when we believe others will also. Once that confidence is lost, the object can no longer separate buying from selling and therefore can no longer keep us from the inefficiencies of barter or self-sufficiency. Unless an alternative money is soon found, economic decline must follow.

Put more carefully, for an object to accomplish all the things we expect of money it must function not only as a **medium of exchange,** but also as a **store of value** and a **unit of account.** The "store of value" characteristic refers to its ability to hold its exchange value over time. For example, if you decide to keep some of your income each month in the form of "money," this reflects your confidence that it will keep its purchasing power until you're ready to spend it later. Rapid inflation, however, erodes this purchasing power and encourages us to convert the official currency, at a cost, into something with more lasting value—like land, gold, diamonds, baseball cards, or a stable foreign currency. If a single object can be effective as both a medium of exchange and a store of value, we gain the advantage of not having to undertake additional transactions when we decide to "store" rather than to "exchange."

If a particular money is serving well as both a medium of exchange and a store of value, then it is also likely to be an effective "unit of account," a particularly dull-sounding but important concept. It refers to sellers setting prices in terms of the official money rather than in other units (ounces of gold, pairs of Levi's, bottles of vodka, and so on). In countries with a healthy monetary system, not only is currently produced output priced in terms of that money, but so are claims to future output—the stocks and bonds and other capital market assets and liabilities that embody the net worth of that economy. In other words, a strong currency also becomes a convenient and reliable economic measuring rod across space and time for that economy.[5]

This "unit of account" role is integral to the process called **national income accounting,** which lumps the production of so many tons, gallons, hours, and so on of final goods and services into a single unit (such as American dollars, Canadian dollars, Japanese yen, or Polish złotys) order to measure gross domestic product, net investment, government spending, and all the other economic aggregates so familiar in macroeconomics. When a money fails to hold its value and hence its acceptability, we have difficulty in assessing economic performance simply because there is no longer a reliable common unit of measure to act as a reference point across time. This is just as much a problem for households and businesses as it is for national income accountants. An unreliable currency makes it difficult to assess where we're at and where we're headed, creating obvious problems for economic decision making, both private and public.

In short, if an official currency loses its ability to act jointly as a medium of exchange, store of value, and economic "yardstick," the economy experiences a negative supply shock as it struggles to find alternative objects to fulfill these three key roles. Such monetary disarray can place a heavy burden on a nation. Uncertainty, anxiety, and suspicion spread as the art of coping with a decaying currency comes to dominate the thoughts, conversations, and actions of the populace. Leisure time vanishes as buyers and sellers turn their energies to the economics of making trades in a world of uncertainty, waiting lines, and mistrust that accompanies a failing monetary system.

---

[5] This "unit of account" role for money probably seems so obvious to you that it's hard to imagine how anything but the official currency could be the standard economic unit of measure. But a look at the experience of countries with very high rates of inflation (such as Germany in the early 1920s, Bolivia in the mid-1980s, and Russia in the early 1990s) reveals a reluctance to trade in terms of the national money. As a result, many prices are listed only in terms of other assets, such as dollars or other *foreign* currencies.

✆ 6.2 *WHAT GIVES MONEY ITS VALUE?*

A healthy monetary system is the indispensable lubricant in a high-performance economic engine. An unstable currency serves to drain this lubricant from the engine and can result in serious structural damage. So the obvious question is what determines the ability of a particular money to maintain a stable value over time. Until well into the twentieth century it was widely believed that the true value of a nation's money was its nonmonetary value or intrinsic worth. While paper currency has been in general use for many centuries, until quite recently it was usually just a *representation* of the gold or silver or other commodity "backing" each bill.[6] Without that backing, it seemed clear that a currency would be quite worthless. However sensible you may find this presumption, it is simply wrong.

Gold, to take the perennial favorite "true" money, has many non-monetary uses (industrial, artistic, and decorative among others) that ensure a strong, continuing demand. The difficulty in finding and recovering gold insures a limited supply. Together these circumstances of strong demand and restricted supply have meant that the real price of gold, adjusted for inflation, has been remarkably stable over the years, decades, and even centuries. This relative stability ("as good as gold") is a major factor underlying the fascination and temptation that gold has long held for mankind. As both a symbol and an actual claim to wealth and power, it has spurred many of the great and tragic and foolish adventures in history. The quest of medieval alchemists to turn base metals to gold; the discovery and exploration of the New World (accompanied by the eviction or slaughter of the native peoples) inspired in good part by tales of great riches and Cities of Gold; the gold rush to California and then to the Klondike that turned from dream to disappointment and sometimes nightmare—all illustrate the influence that the quest for gold has exerted on our cultures and our lives.

Because of its relatively stable value—stemming from entirely accidental circumstances of supply and demand—gold has long been an obvious choice to serve the three major functions of a money (medium of exchange, store of value, and economic yardstick). The United States, along with other major industrial nations, was part of an "international gold standard" that dominated international finance and trade during the last part of the nineteenth and early twentieth century. Even after the system's demise during the Great Depression, gold continued to "back" most of the world's major currencies. Why, then, have the linkages between all currencies and gold now been severed? Like many big questions in economics, this one has no simple answer. There are political factors and accidents of history, as well as economic considerations that guide the evolution of monetary systems.[7] But the most compelling *economic* reason for leaving a gold-backed system is surprisingly straightforward—there are much less expensive monetary arrangements that can work as well or better. Tying a currency to gold is a tremendously expensive undertaking because of the cost of the gold itself. Substantial resources must first be expended to locate and recover gold deposits. Then the metal must be separated, purified, and poured into the carefully measured ingots of pure gold bullion that back the circulating paper

---

[6] The use of unbacked paper money was confined to national emergencies, namely wartime or its aftermath. The unbacked continental dollars issued by the newly formed government during the Revolutionary War and the greenbacks issued by the federal government during the Civil War both failed to hold purchasing power, confirming the view that a currency's value depends on the "real" commodity backing it.

[7] See Steven Russell, "The U.S. Currency System: A Historical Perspective," *Review*, Federal Reserve Bank of St. Louis (September/October 1991): 34–61, for an excellent discussion of the evolution of our currency system.

currency. Even then we must use substantial amounts of labor and capital just to store and defend this immensely valuable stock of mineral from fortune hunters.

The whole process—from discovery to recovery, processing, refining, and the final entombment in guarded vaults—diverts a sizable amount of labor and capital from the production of the goods and services that comprise our standard of living. The fact that such a costly arrangement as a gold-backed currency survived for so long tells us just how expensive a system of barter is and how much a well-functioning monetary system contributes to economic efficiency. But it would be better still if we could devise a workable system with *un*backed paper currency (that is, "fiat money"), gaining the benefits of monetization while freeing all those scarce resources that would otherwise go into producing and defending gold reserves. Such an improved institutional structure ($+\Delta i^{nst}$) promises a very real economic gain, as illustrated in Figure 6.1. As with any other technological innovation, public or private, it generates an outward shift in both aggregate supply and the production possibility frontier.

The big question, of course, is whether the arrangements underlying a system of fiat currency can possibly do the job of a full-fledged, gold-backed monetary structure. One way to begin to answer this is with the help of the *AD/AS* model. Figure 6.2 shows the now-familiar picture of our model macroeconomy in equilibrium at point *A*. Remember that the *LM* curve is a relationship that equates the real money supply (M_0/P_0) with money demand ($L/P = j_0 + j_1 y - j_2 r$). In using this curve, nothing whatsoever was said about whether the nominal money supply (M_0) had any intrinsic value or not. What we found was that as long as its quantity was kept constant

■ FIGURE 6.1

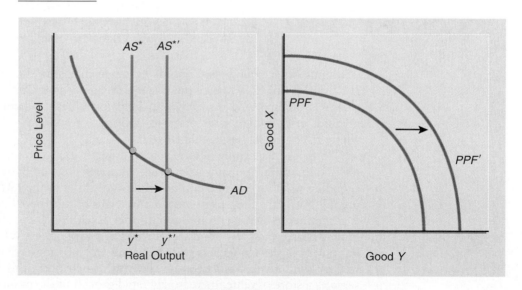

Whether Moving from Barter
to a Commodity-Backed Money or from a Backed to
a Fiat (Unbacked) Money, the Promise of a More
Efficient Monetary System Lies in Its Ability
to Expand Aggregate Supply
and Production Possibilities

■ FIGURE 6.2

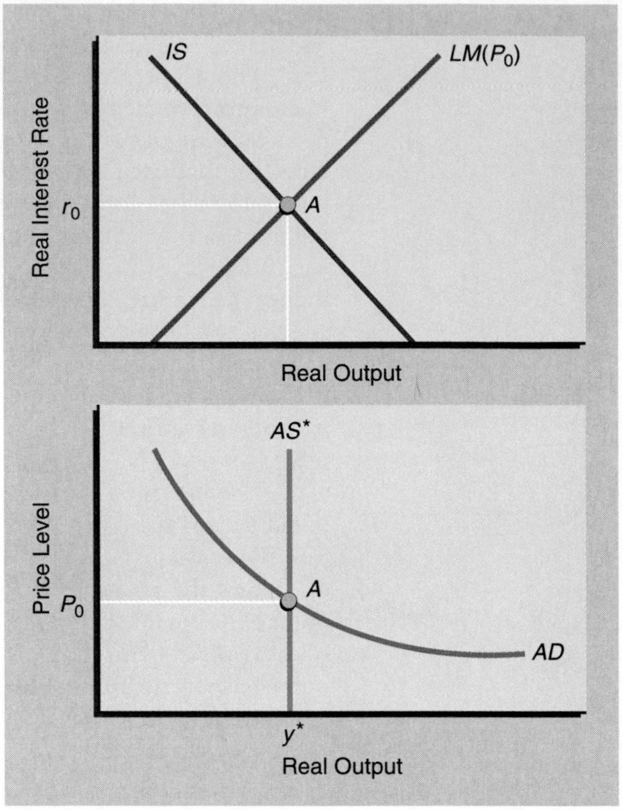

Stable Price Level with Long-Run Equilibrium
at Points *A*; Given Money Supply Holds Its
Value Because It Is Limited in Supply, Not
Because of Its Intrinsic Value

(assuming other policies and outside events unchanged), the price level remained at P_0. In other words, whether the money is made of gold or silver or any other substance is unimportant. Its ability to hold its value—and function as an efficient medium of exchange, store of value, and unit of account—depends solely on our ability to control its supply relative to its demand.

Suppose the supply of money is continually increased while the aggregate supply of output (AS^*) remains fixed. This continued creation of money in a zero growth economy would result in continued rightward shifts in the LM and AD curves. Figure 6.3 shows the long-term outcome in terms of just the AD/AS graph. The result is a continuing increase in the overall price level, the classic situation of "too much money chasing too few goods." Because the rising price level reduces the purchasing power of the money, essentially levying an "inflation tax" on money holders (as well as bond holders as we saw in the previous chapter), this weakens its ability to serve as a store of value. Increasingly rapid growth of the money supply can result in an accelerating inflation that attacks the heart of the monetary system—undermining confidence in the exchange value of the money for both present and future transactions.

Don't conclude, however, that price stability is ensured if we just keep the nominal supply of money constant. That depends on what else is happening in the

■ FIGURE 6.3

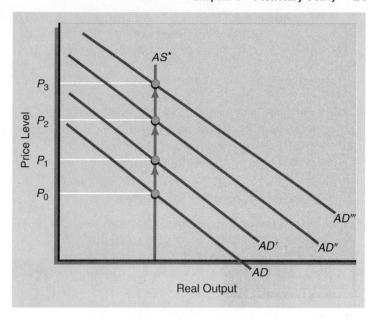

Continued Increases in the Supply of Money in a
Zero-Growth Economy at Full Employment Means
Continued Increases in *AD* and, Hence, in the Price
Level in the Long Run

■ FIGURE 6.4

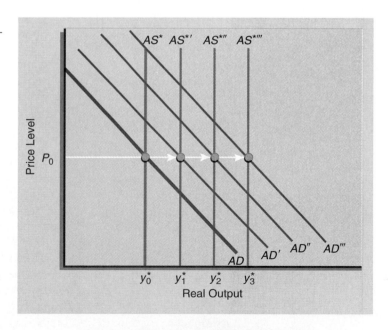

Continued Increases in the Supply of
Money Can Be Consistent with Price Stability
in a Growing Economy

economy and is part of what makes the job of the Central Bank so difficult. In a growing economy, as shown by the rightward shift of AS^* in Figure 6.4, simultaneous growth of aggregate demand is needed for price level stability. So whether or not a "money" functions well has nothing to do with the mystique of "intrinsic value." It has everything to do with how effectively the monetary authority controls the money supply relative to its demand. One way to limit the growth of money is to tie it to a commodity that is relatively fixed in supply. But another is to limit it by law or by the legal authority of a Central Bank, avoiding all the acquisition and preservation costs of a commodity-backed currency. A paper money, "backed" only by the commitment of the monetary authority to limit its supply, can be entirely consistent with price stability and hence serve as an effective money.

ECONOMIC "WARFARE" AND THE MONETARY SYSTEM

When national interests collide and diplomacy fails, the consequence can be warfare—a process in which we seek to inflict crushingly high costs on our enemy. But instead of scenes of death and destruction, let's picture it in terms of a production function, $y^* = f(n^*, k, i^{nst})$. Military warfare seeks to destroy productive capacity through the loss of lives ($-\Delta n^*$) and capital ($-\Delta k$), forcing an inward shift of the enemy's aggregate supply curve and production possibility frontier.

Economic warfare works toward the same ends by less violent means. The most common economic weapon is the **embargo,** which inevitably accompanies and often precedes the outbreak of fighting. The goal is to cut off supplies of war-related goods to the other country and to reduce the general gains in efficiency that come from *national* specialization combined with *inter*national trade. A successful embargo imposes a negative supply shock on the enemy just like the military destruction of capital or lives.

Another strategy is to **attack the opposing monetary system,** creating a negative supply shock by forcing the enemy into the inefficiencies of barter and self-sufficiency that impair its institutional efficiency, $-\Delta i^{nst}$ in our notation. Though these activities are typically shrouded in great secrecy, even after the fact, it is generally believed that attacks on the value of the enemy's currency are a standard weapon in most wartime situations. John Maynard Keynes, as a consultant to the British Exchequer (Treasury) during World War II, was said to have devised speculative actions on international currency markets to destabilize and weaken the international value of the German mark. The more direct route is to introduce large amounts of **counterfeit** currency into the enemy economy in hopes of creating a hyperinflation that weakens if not destroys its monetary system. Political terrorists have allegedly used large scale counterfeiting activities to attack currencies as a complement to their highly visible strikes against individuals and structures.

✿ 6.3 MONETARY FLEXIBILITY—
BENEFITS AND COSTS

In contrast to a system backed by gold, a currency backed by the commitment of the monetary authority to limit its supply has two notable advantages: (1) It is *less expensive* to operate, as we've seen; and (2) it is *more flexible*, allowing us to choose a monetary policy appropriate to specific macroeconomic goals. For example, with a fiat money the Central Bank could follow a policy of steady but gradual monetary expansion, matching the growth of money to the long run growth of the macroeconomy. Such an approach could provide a signficantly more stable long run price level than if the growth of the money supply were tied to the availability of gold and therefore depended on such factors as the luck of discovery, the pace of technological innovation in recovering and processing gold, and international political events affecting gold production and trade.

This monetary flexibility can also be carried a step further, with the Central Bank attempting to respond to short run macroeconomic disturbances by adjusting the nominal money supply appropriately. So a drop in aggregate demand that resulted in an economic downturn ($-\Delta y$) would be countered with a monetary stimulus ($+\Delta M$), whereas an inflationary boom (continuing $+\Delta P$) would call for restrictive monetary actions ($-\Delta M$). In combination with fiscal policy, such monetary manipulation could be used to pursue at least some of the ambitious economic goals of the Employment Act of 1946 and later legislation. Under a rigid gold-backed monetary system such a strategy would not be feasible.

But this flexibility of an unbacked currency presents both promise and peril. We noted in Chapter 4 that the possibility of unpredictable time lags in the policy process could mean that a monetary stimulus designed to speed recovery from recession might have its impact on aggregate demand only after the economy had already returned to full employment, resulting in an unwanted surge in the price level. In such circumstances the flexibility of a fiat money allows Central Banks to engage in policies that, however well intended, could end up being *de*stabilizing rather than stabilizing. The larger concern is the pressure on the monetary authority to use its monopoly power over the supply of money to pursue goals other than price stability. Its every action will inevitably hurt some groups and help others. So a necessary condition for the economic success of a system of fiat money is the ability to resist the ever-present political and economic pressure to increase the rate of money creation.[8] The flexibility of a fiat money opens the door to a world of difficult policy issues. It creates the potential for significant gains in efficiency and control at the same time as it increases the potential for abuse and instability.

✿ 6.4 FEDERAL RESERVE CONTROL
OF THE U.S. MONEY SUPPLY

How is this double-edged sword of monetary flexibility handled in the U.S. economy? Although a detailed look at Federal Reserve operations is not our goal, a brief sketch of how the "Fed" (its nickname) controls the basic money supply will provide

---

[8] A considerable degree of independence from immediate political events helps a Central Bank resist the many political pressures to increase the growth of the money supply. Members of the Federal Reserve's Board of Governors, for example, are not elected through the political process but are appointed by the president, with the consent of Congress, to 14-year terms.

the necessary background for understanding the central issue addressed in the remaining sections of this chapter—the link between monetary policy choices and macroeconomic consequences.

The basic U.S. money supply has two major components. The first and most familiar part includes *currency* ("Federal Reserve Notes") and *coins,* both of which are issued and controlled by the government. But this category comes to only about 25% of the total. The biggest part of our money supply is not issued by the government at all. It consists instead of the liabilities (IOUs) of private, profit-seeking businesses. More specifically, about three-fourths of the nation's basic money supply consists of **demand deposits,** popularly called "checking accounts," issued by financial institutions.[9] Because these deposits are "payable on demand," they are easily and quickly converted into currency. This convertibility, along with government insurance against loss of these funds, makes them widely acceptable and essentially interchangeable with currency.

It is through this process of extending loans to its customers that the banking system, regulated by the Federal Reserve, plays a major role in determining the nation's money supply. For example, suppose you want to borrow $5000 and your bank agrees. You give the bank your IOU for $5000 and, in return, they give you theirs—a checking account with $5000 in it. Though your liabilities have also increased, the nation's money supply has just risen by $5000! Now it's obvious that banks don't just extend credit and thereby expand the money supply without limit. If they did, the monetary system would quickly collapse in a frenzy of bankruptcy or hyperinflation. In fact, commercial banks are required by law to hold a fraction (currently about 10%) of their total demand deposit liabilities either as cash in their vault or on deposit with the Federal Reserve. These **reserve requirements** are established and enforced by the Federal Reserve. So a bank can create new demand deposits through loans only if it currently has **excess reserves** sufficient to support the new loans. Once these excess reserves disappear, the bank is said to be "loaned up" and can no longer create new demand deposits by extending credit. Only by attracting new deposits will it be able to increase its outstanding loans.

The Federal Reserve's influence over this demand deposit component of the money supply is much less direct than its control over the amount of currency. It comes from its power to alter the reserves of commercial banks. Actions that diminish those reserves push banks into an "insufficient reserves" position, forcing them to cut back on their volume of loans, thereby reducing the amount of demand deposits. Actions that increase those reserves create excess reserves that allow these private, profit-seeking businesses to expand their loans by creating new demand deposits and, in the aggregate, to increase the nation's stock of money.

There are three ways in which the Federal Reserve can change the reserves of commercial banks and thereby alter the money supply—changing the **reserve requirement** itself, changing the **discount rate,** and engaging in **open market operations.** The ability to alter reserve requirements is the most direct and powerful way for the Fed to alter the amount of demand deposits. Raising the reserve requirement (say, from 10% to 12%) would force banks to cut back on their outstanding loans, reducing their demand deposits until the higher reserve requirement was

---

[9] For now we'll use a general definition of money as "currency plus demand deposits," a concept that has come to be known as the *M*1 definition of money. Later in the chapter we'll expand this to incorporate additional money-like assets, such as certain savings accounts and certificates of deposits. The existence of broader definitions of money (*M*2 and *M*3, as they're known) will, of course, complicate issues of Federal Reserve control over "the" money supply.

met. Similarly, by lowering reserve requirements the Fed creates excess reserves that banks can put to work by extending credit, hence increasing demand deposits and expanding the money supply. Though the Federal Reserve has rarely chosen to use this especially powerful tool to influence the nation's money supply, it remains available.

Another way that the Federal Reserve can influence the quantity of demand deposits—changes in the **discount rate**—is used often. A bank that falls temporarily below its required reserves can borrow needed reserves from the Fed and the charge for this short-term loan is called the "discount rate." By changing this rate the Fed can make it more or less expensive for banks to borrow reserves, inducing them to change their borrowings and adjust their reserves accordingly. For example, raising the discount rate makes it more costly for banks to continue in a situation of insufficient reserves and thereby encourages them (through the bottom line, profits) to be less aggressive in making loans. But because most banks are not below the required reserve level very often, the discount rate plays a relatively small direct role.[10] However, the Federal Reserve has often chosen to enhance the influence of the discount rate by using it as an advance signal of monetary changes to come. A rise in the discount rate, for example, typically means that the Federal Reserve will be pursuing contractionary (or at least less expansionary) policies in the coming months, alerting banks to be more cautious in creating new demand deposits through loans. Similarly, a drop in the discount rate is generally used to signal a period of increased monetary expansion.

But if changes in reserve requirements are not used and if changes in the discount rate are only a signal, how is it that the Fed actually changes bank reserves? The key monetary tool of the Federal Reserve is **open market operations.** The Fed holds a substantial inventory of U.S. Treasury securities (government bonds) for the specific purpose of making sales or purchases of these bonds to alter reserves of the banking system. Suppose it wants to encourage monetary expansion by increasing bank reserves. It will proceed to buy additional government bonds, placing an order through a broker who looks for a willing seller at the quoted price. In buying on the "open market," the Fed doesn't known who the seller is and doesn't care. The important thing is that it has bought something from someone and in return has simply created, under authority granted by Congress, a checking account balance to pay for it.[11] Because no existing account is being reduced to pay for these bonds, there is a net increase in the reserves of the banking system as the former holder of the bond deposits the check. This then permits an expansion of loans through the creation of new demand deposits and the ultimate result is an increase in the overall money supply.

Similarly, if the Fed sells some of its stock of government bonds on the open market it gives up bonds in return for payment by check. However, this check is not deposited in the banking system and the Fed essentially destroys the funds. Bank reserves will fall because the check, though cashed, is not redeposited. This, in turn, forces banks to reduce their lending activities, which ultimately lowers the total money supply.

---

[10] Be careful not to confuse the Fed's discount rate with the real rate of interest in our *IS-LM* analysis. The discount rate is a very tiny part of the conglomerate of interest rates that are essentially averaged together and represented by the real interest rate. Changes in the discount rate, by itself, would have no significant impact on the economy-wide interest rate in our model.

[11] This open market purchase could actually be for a car, a house, or anything else, and accomplish the same result—inject new reserves into the system. But as a practical matter it's simpler to stick with something more neutral (and easy to store) like government securities.

■ FIGURE 6.5

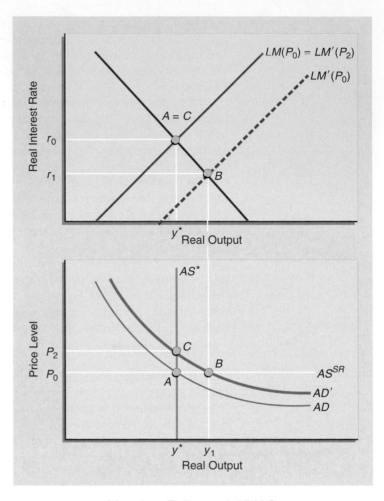

Monetary Policy and *AD/AS*:
Short-Run Impact, *A* → *B*;
Long-Run Impact, *A* → *C*

⚙ *6.5 MONETARY POLICY—*
   IMPACTS ON THE "REAL" ECONOMY

It is through open market operations, sometimes preceded by a changing discount rate, that the Fed alters commercial bank reserves. In this indirect way the Federal Reserve can change the nominal amount of money in circulation, setting off a sequence of events that define the influence of monetary policy on the macroeconomy. What is this influence? Using the basic *AD/AS* model, let's follow an increase in the **nominal money supply** through the economy, focusing on its impact on the so-called real variables like output, the real interest rate, investment, and net exports.

As shown in Figure 6.5, the growth in *M* shifts *LM*(P_0) and, hence, aggregate demand to the right, causing a short run adjustment from points *A* to *B*. The monetary stimulus lowers the real rate of interest ($-\Delta r$) and increases real output ($+\Delta y$) and can be broadly characterized by the following sequence:

Short-Run Impact of an Increased Money Supply

$$+\Delta M \Rightarrow +\Delta M/P \Rightarrow -\Delta r \Rightarrow +\Delta i \text{ and } +\Delta x \Rightarrow +\Delta y \Leftrightarrow +\Delta c$$

In words, an increase in the nominal money supply initially increases the real value of the money stock (shifting LM to the right), thereby lowering the price of credit—the real rate of interest. This lower real interest rate then stimulates investment and net export spending, setting off a multiplier process (as LM slides along the IS curve). This is shown as the movement from points A to B in Figure 6.5. The result is that a change in the nominal money supply has triggered a sequence of events that shifts aggregate demand to the right along the horizontal aggregate supply curve and, in the short run, decreases the real rate of interest while increasing investment, net exports, consumption, and real output.

It is clear that the classical **monetary "neutrality"** result—changes in the money supply have *no* impact on real variables like output, the real interest rate, consumption, investment, and net exports—is not to be found in our short run *AD/AS* model. Changes in the nominal money supply are anything but "neutral" and the popular view that the Federal Reserve has the power to set and control economy-wide interest rates seems to be confirmed by these results. Expansionary monetary policy (accomplished through open market purchases by the Fed) reduces the real rate of interest, just as a contractionary policy (open market sales) would raise it. This change in the interest rate is then transmitted via the multiplier process to investment, net exports, income, consumption, and, ultimately, total output.

However, remember that the presumed short run price rigidity must soon yield to market clearing as the economy adjusts to a long run outcome at point *C* in Figure 6.5. We can see that the final legacy of the increase in the nominal money supply is the higher price level. Output, the real rate of interest, and all the other "real" variables have returned to their initial levels. By this point it won't surprise you that simply increasing the amount of money in a fully employed economy won't increase the nation's standard of living. "Monetary neutrality" is just another way to say that "A nation can't *print* its way to prosperity."

But what may seem surprising is the corollary to this result—*the Federal Reserve's power to alter bank reserves and the nominal money supply does not translate into an ability to change the long run real rate of interest.* If our *AD/AS* framework is a reliable guide to the real world, then the process of market clearing following a change in the nominal supply of money will shift the *LM* curve back to its original position. The end result of an increase in the nominal money supply in a fully employed economy is equiproportionately higher levels of both *M and P*, leaving the real money supply (*M/P*) and the real interest rate at their original levels. That is,

Long Run Impact of $+\Delta M$ in a Fully Employed Economy

$$+\Delta M \Rightarrow +\Delta P, \text{ such that } \Delta(M/P) = 0$$

All other variables—real interest rates, consumption, investment, net exports, and real output—remain unchanged as the economy adjusts from points A to C in Figure 6.5. Money is said to be "neutral" in the long run because it alters the price level only, leaving the real variables unchanged.

How can we reconcile this conclusion with the widespread belief that the Federal Reserve "controls" interest rates? According to our analysis, the monetary authority (e.g., the Federal Reserve, the Bank of England, the German Bundesbank, and all the rest) can have no lasting impact on real interest rates. Can we have confidence that this implication from our simplified abstract model of the macro-economy is valid when we consider the complexities of the "real world"? To link model and reality we begin with two important points about the real interest rate concept.

1. The real interest rate (r) is essentially an *average of many different interest rates*. Just as the price level (P) is a single number measuring the average of many prices, the real rate of interest in our model reflects many different kinds of interest rates that characterize our financial and capital markets—prime rates, mortgage rates, bond rates, consumer loan rates, bank card rates, home equity loan rates, car loan rates, and on and on. These very different rates tend to rise and fall together and, to this extent, an average can capture the overall changes in the economy that are the focus of our *AD/AS* framework.

2. It is a "real" rate of interest in the standard economic sense that it embodies the notion of *constant purchasing power*. For example, suppose you lend $1000 for a year at a rate of 10% and it turns out that there is 5% inflation ($\%\Delta P$) over that 12-month period. When the loan is repaid and you receive the $1100, it is in dollars that have 5% less purchasing power than the dollars you loaned. Put another way, if there is 5% inflation in year 1, it will take $1050 in year 2 to buy what $1000 bought 12 months earlier. Hence, 5% of the 10% return has gone merely to keep the purchasing power of your loan constant. In general, we can say that the real rate of interest is the nominal rate of interest (10% in this example) *minus* the loss of purchasing power due to inflation during the period of the loan. More concisely, $r = R - \Pi$, where r is the real (or net-of-inflation) rate of interest, R the nominal (or market) rate of interest, and Π the inflation rate (that is, the percentage change in the price level, $\%\Delta P$).

The preceding example presumed that we knew that the actual rate of inflation during year 1 was 5%. Obviously we couldn't make this calculation until after the fact *(ex post)*. History is important, but economic decision making typically involves anticipating the future rather than accounting for the past. So we'd really like a before-the-fact *(ex ante)* estimate of what the real rate of return is likely to be if we take a specific action now. Will a 10% nominal return end up, after inflation, giving us an attractive *real* rate of return? Or should we do something else with our $1000, perhaps put it into the stock market or buy a new refrigerator? We're now making an *estimate* of what the real return will be, based on our best guess as to **expected inflation,** which we represent by Π^e. Reflecting our interest in where we're headed rather than where we've been, we amend the equation to $r = R - \Pi^e$, which we finally rewrite in a form that has come to be called the **Fisher equation**[12]:

$$R = r + \Pi^e$$

As you'll see in later chapters, it's often helpful to think of the nominal or market interest rate (R) as reflecting not only the **time value of money** (based on our

[12] This hypothesis about interest rates and expected inflation was developed and applied by American economist Irving Fisher (1867–1947).

collective "rate of time preference" and built into r), but also the various **risks** involved with lending money *now* in return for a promise to repay *later*. One obvious danger is that the borrower will fail to make the agreed upon repayment. This **default risk** is a component of the real rate of interest (r) and explains why unsecured loans (such as credit cards) typically involve much higher interest rates (both nominal and real, R and r) than less risky secured loans (like a home mortgage). The other major threat is that the purchasing power of the currency will drop over the life of the loan. To protect the real return against this **inflation risk,** the expected inflation term (Π^e) is added to the nominal rate.[13]

The relationship given in the Fisher equation, $R = r + \Pi^e$, allows us to bridge the gap between the *unobserved* real rate of interest (r) in our *AD/AS* analytics and the *observed* nominal or market rate (R). Only in a world of zero expected inflation ($\Pi^e = 0$) would the nominal rates quoted by banks, mortgage lenders, and brokers be the same as the real rate that has been our focus throughout the book. Put another way, anticipated **inflation risk**—captured in Π^e—acts as a "wedge" between observed nominal interest rates and the (unobserved) real rates of our analysis. This real/nominal distinction is central to understanding how and why monetary changes alter interest rates in both the short and long run, the issue to which we now turn.

◊◊ 6.6 MONETARY POLICY AND INTEREST RATES

If this prediction from the *AD/AS* model is accurate—that the Fed has no lasting impact on either real interest rates or real output—how do we account for the popular view that the Federal Reserve wields its considerable influence over the macroeconomy primarily through its ability to alter interest rates? The chairman of the Federal Reserve is often referred to as the second most powerful person in the country, after the president, and bond markets often react sharply to even the slightest hint of a change in monetary policy. What, then, is the relationship between Central Bank actions and interest rate responses—short and long run, nominal and real?

Let's return to the earlier case of an expansionary monetary policy in an economy with full employment. Starting at point A in Figure 6.6, we see that the *initial* impact is to reduce the real rate of interest ($-\Delta r$). Assuming there is no short-run impact on prices, there will be no change in actual inflation. Let's assume for the moment that this results in no change in expected inflation as well ($\Delta \Pi^e = 0$). The short-run result will be a decline in both the real and nominal interest rates. As seen through the Fisher equation, $\downarrow R = \downarrow r + \Pi^e$. This short-run effect of expansionary monetary policy is shown as the movement from points A to B in Figure 6.6. Temporarily, at least, it looks like an excellent policy choice since not only have interest rates (nominal and real) dropped, but output (and, with it, employment) has also risen. But as we saw in the previous section, the story cannot end here because the output market in the bottom graph is not cleared. As the excess demand at point B forces the price level from P_0 to P_1, the real value of the given money supply falls

---

[13] Of course this estimate of future inflation may well turn out to be too high or too low, causing the actual (or *ex post*) real rate to diverge from its anticipated *(ex ante)* value. We'll have much more to say about the consequences of such misperceptions as we examine economic fluctuations in Chapters 8 and 9.

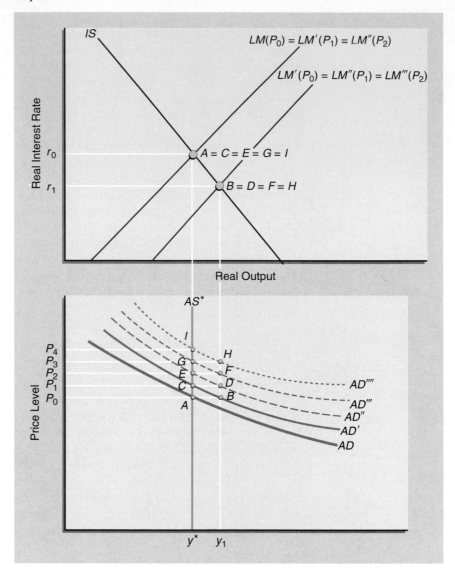

Continued Monetary Expansion
in a Fully Employed Economy

■ FIGURE 6.6

and the economy moves to point C in the graphs. Note that the LM curve has now shifted back to its original position *but* with the higher money supply accompanied by a proportionately higher price level so that the new LM curve, $LM'(P_1)$, is identical to the original one, $LM(P_0)$.[14]

_____

[14] Recall that the equation for the LM curve is $y = [(M_0/P_0) - j_0]/j_1 + (j_2/j_1)r$. The reason that the curve shifts back to its original position is that the $+\Delta M$ has led to a proportionate change in the price level ($+\Delta P$). So with a 10%, say, increase in the money supply matched by a 10% rise in prices, the real value of the money supply is unaffected. That is $M_0/P_0 = M'/P_1$ and the intercept of the LM curve is not changed.

But now suppose that as the initial expansion of real output begins to evaporate into rising prices, the Federal Reserve calls up a second monetary stimulus to restore those short run output gains. Starting this time at point C on IS and AD', the monetary expansion again shifts LM to the right, from $LM'(P_1)$ to $LM''(P_1)$, moving the economy to the point D in the two graphs. Again the increased demand will eventually spill entirely into higher prices, returning the economy to full employment at a still higher price level (P_2) at point E. The rising price level again reduces the real value of the money supply, shifting LM back to its initial position, this time at $LM''(P_2)$. You can see that if the Federal Reserve continues the monetary expansion, the progression would continue from F to G, then H to Π. Although the real interest rate fluctuates back and forth between r_0 and r_1, the price level continues its steady climb from P_0 to P_1, P_2, and so on.

The important result here is that the Federal Reserve cannot use monetary expansion to hold the interest rate at r_1 or output at y_1 in Figure 6.6. The attempt to do so will only result in a continued increase in the price level. With the best of intentions and with the short-run lure of success, the Federal Reserve will merely end up increasing inflation ($+\Delta \Pi$) rather than lowering interest rates or increasing output. The rising inflation will soon be incorporated into expectations ($+\Delta \Pi^e$). This rising inflation premium means that the perverse consequence of this attempt to reduce interest rates has been to *increase* the nominal rate while the real rate ultimately returns to its initial level ($\uparrow R = r + \uparrow \Pi^e$).

One possible popular response to these rising nominal interest rates is increased pressure on the Federal Reserve to expand the money supply even faster, disregarding the fact that this is what *caused* the rising rates in the first place. If so, the economy is caught in a policy trap until it understands the fallacy in thinking that the monetary authority can have a lasting impact on the *real* rate of interest—the one crucial to our investment, net export, and money demand decisions. While it is relatively easy to accept the notion that "We can't print our way to prosperity," it's harder to see precisely the same point when it comes to the real rate of interest. If the monetary authority could permanently alter the real rate of interest (shift LM in the long run) it could also permanently alter our real income (move the intersection of IS and LM). *Attention to the distinction between real and nominal rates and between short and long run outcomes is essential to understanding how monetary policy influences output, interest rates, and the other components of macroeconomic performance.*

A note of caution should be added. You may be tempted to conclude that the previous discussion proves the futility of activist attempts to manipulate the macroeconomy through monetary policy. But remember that the situation we analyzed was one in which the monetary authority attempted to lower interest rates and increase economic growth in a *fully employed economy*. The activist/nonactivist controversy is not about this. It is about the government's ability to use its control over aggregate demand (through both monetary and fiscal policy) to hold the economy closer to its full employment level of output. Let's turn to Figure 6.7 which portrays an economy initially in short run equilibrium *below* full employment. What impact would expansionary monetary policy have on real output and interest rates when the economy is initially in recession?

Starting at point A in Figure 6.7, suppose the Federal Reserve expanded the money supply to shift $LM(P_0)$ to $LM'(P_0)$ and AD to AD'. As the economy returns to full employment at point B, the real rate of interest falls from r_0 to r_1. Because this new position is sustainable in the long run, we reach quite different conclusions about the consequences of monetary expansion than in the previous example. In an

MONETARY SLOWDOWN IN THE EARLY 1980s

In the 1970s the United States experienced the highest average inflation rate in its peacetime history, with the price level doubling between 1970 and 1980. Price controls and guidelines during the decade had proven ineffective and it was not until Federal Reserve Chairman Paul Volcker led an aggressive slowdown in the growth rate of the money supply that inflation was finally reduced.

The most dramatic result of this monetary contraction was a quick rise in unemployment to its highest level since the Great Depression followed by a steady decline through the rest of the decade. What was the impact on interest rates? As we'd expect from the *AD/AS* model, the immediate result was a rise in interest rates. The leftward shift in *LM* meant a short-run increase in the real interest rate. This was reflected in the nominal rate ($\uparrow R = r \uparrow + \Pi^e$), which quickly shot up to record levels. The prime rate (the nominal rate charged by banks to their most credit-worthy corporate customers) topped 20% at one point and averaged nearly 19% in 1981. (For comparison, the average prime rate in the 1960s was about 5.3% and in the 1970s, 8.1%.)

But as the monetary slowdown began to reduce inflation (also pushing the economy into recession), nominal interest rates also declined to under 15% in 1982 and less than 10% by 1985. (This fall in nominal rates was entirely a reflection of declining inflation expectations, $-\Delta \Pi^e$, because the fiscal expansion of the Reagan tax cuts was simultaneously raising the real rate of interest.) The U.S. experience in the early 1980s shows the *importance of distinguishing between **real and nominal interest rates** as well as between **short and long run impacts.*** The contractionary monetary policy initially pushed interest rates, both real and nominal, higher. But as the short-run effect on the real rate disappeared and the inflation rate began to fall, the nominal rate soon followed.

economy initially below full employment, expansionary monetary policy can lead to a lasting decline in the real rate of interest and an increase in real output without inducing any rise in the price level. Hence, both real and nominal interest rates, r and R, may decline in both the short and long run. This scenario portrays the activist vision of the appropriate role for monetary policy as a countercyclical instrument.

If you now find yourself thinking that this is proof in favor of the activist view, remember that this analysis excludes a key ingredient in the activist/nonactivist controversy—the issue of policy lags and the timing of policy changes. Though monetary policy is not subject to many of the political and administrative delays of fiscal policy, its impact on aggregate demand (from open market operations to falling real

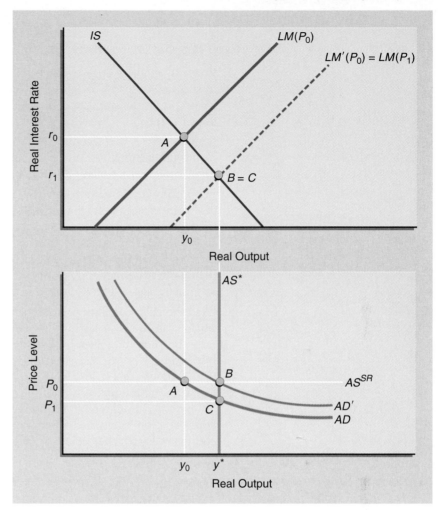

Monetary Expansion ($A \rightarrow B$) versus Market
Clearing ($A \rightarrow C$) in an Economy Initially
Below Full Employment

■ FIGURE 6.7

interest rates to increased spending on investment and net exports) may take many months and our ability to predict these lags is far from perfect. While expansionary monetary policy begins to spread its effects through the economy, the market-clearing process may already have pushed us back to full employment. This is shown as the movement from points A to C in Figure 6.7. If the monetary expansion takes hold only after we're at point C, the result would be just as we saw in Figure 6.6—monetary expansion in a fully employed economy. Its lasting impact would be on inflation and nominal interest rates, not on real output or real interest rates.

IN SUMMARY . . .

Monetary Policy and Interest Rates

1. In a fully employed, zero-growth (i.e., fixed AS^*) economy, a change in the money supply will have no lasting impact on real output, employment, or the real rate of interest. Its impact will be felt entirely in higher prices.

2. Because $R = r + \Pi^e$, continued monetary expansion at full employment will eventually result in higher expected inflation ($+\Delta \Pi^e$) and higher nominal (or market) interest rates ($+\Delta R$).

3. In an economy initially below full employment, monetary expansion may or may not speed the return to full employment. It depends on timing. If the impact of the monetary expansion (shifting AD to AD' and moving from points A to B in Figure 6.7) is faster than market clearing (a falling price level and a movement from points A to C), then an activist monetary policy will be successful. Issues of timing and policy lags will be addressed in Chapters 8 and 9.

4. Expansionary monetary policy when the economy is initially in a recession can mean a lasting drop in both real and nominal interest rates. But note that even *without* a change in the money supply—relying entirely on market clearing—the real rate of interest will drop to the same level, r_1 in Figure 6.7. So the important conclusion remains: monetary policy cannot have a lasting impact on the real rate of interest, although in an economy below full employment it may—depending on the speed of monetary policy compared to market clearing—hasten the decline.

6.7 TODAY'S REFLECTIONS OF TOMORROW'S OUTCOMES

Let's take this analysis of interest rates one step further and identify the role that expectations of inflation can play in causing long run outcomes to alter *current* rates of interest. Returning to the case of monetary expansion in a fully employed economy, we've seen that the real interest rate falls in the short run but returns to its initial level in the long run. We also found that if the monetary expansion is continued it means continued outward shifts in aggregate demand. This, in turn, brings increased inflation and thereby higher long-run nominal interest rates to reflect the higher inflation risk. The question we now ask is whether the higher expected inflation will affect nominal interest rates in the short as well as the long run.

Here we need to modify our practice of thinking only in terms of a *single* nominal interest rate or a *single* real interest rate. Let's consider *two* nominal interest rates—**short term** and **long term.** The Fisher equation ($R = r + \Pi^e$) tells us that the nominal rate is the real rate plus a premium for expected inflation (Π^e). An anticipated increase in future inflation will obviously have much more impact on a long-term agreement, say a 10-, 20-, or 30-year bond or mortgage, than on a short-term financial instrument like a 90-day U.S. Treasury bond. Current short-term contracts will have come and gone long before the expected inflation surge reaches the economy. So the expectation of higher inflation ($+\Delta \Pi^e$) will have little or no impact on short-term rates, but is likely to become quickly incorporated into the interest rates of newly issued long-term bonds. Without this premium for increased inflation risk, savers will turn to other instruments (like stocks) forcing issuers of new bonds to increase interest rates to find purchasers.[15]

The result, then, is that current monetary expansion in a fully employed economy can cause current nominal interest rates to *both* fall and rise. That is, nominal rates on short-term commitments ($R^S = r + \Pi^e$) would fall because the $+\Delta \Pi^e$ is too remote to matter and the initial $-\Delta r$ will dominate. Nominal rates on long-term commitments ($R^L = r + \Pi^e$) would rise because the $-\Delta r$ is too short-lived to matter much while the threat of higher inflation ($+\Delta \Pi^e$) is very real. Though it may seem peculiar that the same increase in the money supply can cause some interest rates to rise and some to fall, it's really just common sense. If the monetary expansion means a temporary drop in interest rates but a continuing rise in inflation, then today's short-term rates (immune from long run consequences) will fall, whereas today's long-term rates (fully exposed to the risk of future inflation) will rise. Long-run consequences, then, cannot be dismissed as remote and unimportant to what happens today. Despite the popularity of Keynes' quip that "In the long run we're all dead," long run events won't stay obediently in the future as long as there are capital markets that link current events to future outcomes and thereby "discount" or import anticipated future events back to the present.

6.8   DIFFICULTIES IN MONETARY POLICY MAKING

Criticism of monetary policy, like fiscal policy, is inevitable. No matter what choice is made, someone would benefit if it had been made differently. Borrowers want low interest rates, lenders high, and both sometimes mistake the Federal Reserve's short run influence over real interest rates for lasting control. Industries where financing plays an important role (such as construction) urge the Federal Reserve to take steps to minimize the volatility of interest rates in order to avoid the inefficiency of feast-or-famine episodes in which overtime in booms alternates with layoffs in busts. But other groups want the Federal Reserve to worry less about interest rates and more about inflation, or unemployment, or the international value of the dollar, or the balance of trade.

Each nation entrusts its Central Bank with a *single* great power—exclusive control of the nominal money supply. But it then puts pressure on it to use this power to accomplish a *multitude* of economic (or political) goals, some of which may turn out to be conflicting or simply unattainable.[16] As we expand our understanding of economic stabilization and growth in coming chapters, additional obstacles to attaining and even defining "appropriate" goals for monetary policy are discussed. At this point, we can use the basic *AD/AS* framework to get a quick preview of why monetary policy making is so difficult and controversial.

The most obvious component of "monetary responsibility" is the Central Bank's ability to maintain a currency that serves as the primary medium of exchange,

---

[15] Although newly issued bonds will have to suit their interest payments to the altered conditions, the huge amount of *existing bonds* retain the fixed interest payment specified at their original issue. For bonds with lower specified interest payments to remain competitive their prices must fall on the bond market. This underlies the observed inverse relationship between nominal interest rates and bond prices—rising nominal interest rates, or even the expectation of their future rise, mean falling prices in the bond market, whereas falling interest rates cause existing bond prices to rise.

[16] For example, we saw that monetary policy cannot bring about a lasting reduction in the real rate of interest. Continued attempts to use it in this way only result in rising inflation and higher nominal rates of interest.

store of value, and unit of account. This means that the money supply must not grow so rapidly or so erratically that high or variable inflation rates undermine acceptability and lead to demonetization. Conversely, it is also important for the supply of money to expand fast enough to facilitate full employment and economic growth. Failure to take expansionary actions in a deep recession or depression can be as damaging as continually overexpansionary policies. The final section of this chapter— "Monetary Policy and the Great Depression"—details the Federal Reserve's perverse responses and puzzling nonresponses at critical junctures of that troubled decade.

But what confronts most monetary policy makers most of the time is the wide interval between the obvious extremes of "too much" and "too little." This is the territory where *different goals* and *different views of the workings of the macroeconomy* come into play. To appreciate some of these difficulties, let's examine a situation in which monetary policy is being used to bring about general price stability, i.e., zero inflation. Although this might seem to be an appropriate target for the Central Bank, a closer look reveals some complications. Suppose the price level begins to rise above its target level. What should the monetary authority do? The answer may at first seem obvious—offset the upward pressure on prices with a prompt, carefully measured contraction of the money supply through open market sales of bond holdings. Our model tells us that this will shift the *LM* and *AD* curves to the left, thereby eliminating the excess demand that was causing prices to rise.

However, this answer ignores some complicating factors. One is that the impact of policy changes is never immediate and the **time lag** between the unwanted price rise and the impact of our policy response may be significantly longer (or shorter) than expected. For example, suppose an increase in autonomous investment spending $(+\Delta i_0 \Rightarrow +\Delta z_0 \Rightarrow +\Delta IS \Rightarrow +\Delta AD)$ begins to push up the equilibrium price level. A prompt monetary contraction $(-\Delta M_0 \Rightarrow -\Delta LM \Rightarrow -\Delta AD)$ *might* offset this outward shift in aggregate demand, quickly halting then reversing the price rise. But if the time lag is long, and aggregate demand doesn't respond until after the price level has already stabilized at the higher level, the result could be a costly contraction that causes output to fall below the full employment level as it forces the price level back to its original level.

Because the length of these time lags appears to vary in unpredictable ways, it is widely agreed that we should not try to react to each and every blip in the price level. This is particularly apparent when we realize that such price level disturbances don't just occur once in a while or come from one place. They come often and from many directions, singly or in bunches, sometimes offsetting but other times reinforcing one another.[17] So in our example above $(-\Delta M_0$ in response to $+\Delta i_0)$, it might happen that soon after the money supply is contracted there is also a drop in autonomous consumption. This would then combine with the reduced money supply to shift aggregate demand to the left of its original level. Our intended anti-inflation response could actually end up pulling output below its full employment level in the short run, and (other things unchanged) causing *de*flation in the long run.

But if we aren't to respond to *every* change in the price level, how do we decide when a given change is large or persistent enough to justify a policy change? There is no single "correct" answer to this crucial question. Those who consider zero inflation a major goal, for example, may choose to react quickly and frequently, even if it

---

[17] In addition to changes in autonomous investment, there may be changes in any of the other "autonomous" terms in our model, including consumption $(\pm \Delta c_0)$, net exports $(\pm \Delta x_0)$, money demand $(\pm \Delta j_0)$, and even aggregate supply $(\pm \Delta k \Rightarrow \pm \Delta AS^*)$.

sometimes *de*stabilizes output or other variables. Others may also favor such an activist "fast-and-often" strategy but with a target set on full employment (or interest rates or some other goal), even if it sometimes destabilizes the price level. Still others advocate only gradual and infrequent policy changes in the belief that policy lags are so variable and unpredictable that repeated changes in monetary (or fiscal) variables are likely to become a major source of instability rather than stability.

Think of the controversy over monetary actions as reflecting two kinds of disagreement—(1) what policy *can* do and (2) what policy *should* do. Debate over the first issue reflects our incomplete knowledge of the workings of the macroeconomy. More specifically it reflects current disagreement over such questions as: "What is the primary source of economic fluctuations?"; "How rapidly do markets clear?"; "How precise is the Federal Reserve's control over the relevant supply of money?"; and "How accurately can we forecast policy time lags?" Each question is the focus of active research as you will see in coming chapters, and disagreement on these issues largely defines the modern macroeconomic "schools of thought"—monetarist, new classical, real business cycle, and new Keynesian views.

The second area of dispute—over what policy *should* do—is not about cause-and-effect relationships among economic variables. It's about the *desirability* of alternative economic goals. This lies in the domain of individual preferences and value judgments and is not a topic that can be resolved by additional data or further analysis. For example, those with a preference for a small, relatively passive economic role for government will oppose active manipulation of monetary policy whether or not it is effective in reducing fluctuations in prices, output, or any other variable. Such differing preferences also play a part in distinguishing the various schools of thought. For now, just be aware that reliable assessment of monetary policy is far more difficult than it might seem given the easy confidence with which so-called experts cheer or jeer the actions or inactions of the Federal Reserve. Even the most responsible and efficient Central Bank imaginable will receive constant criticism from those with *differing economic goals* or *differing theories on the best means to particular goals*.

Many of the vexing issues of monetary policy require further understanding of short-run economic fluctuations, the subject of Chapters 8 and 9. But this is a good point to introduce another fundamental difficulty facing the monetary authority—*which* concept of money should it use in guiding its policy decisions.

☯ *6.9 MONETARY CONTROL OVER WHICH MONEY?*

Up to now we have presumed that "money" is easy to identify ("currency plus demand deposits"), an asset readily distinguished from the rest. It's time to drop this simplification and view **money** as the more liquid end of the spectrum of asset holdings ("liquid" in the sense of being readily convertible to cash). Money's primary attribute, that it is generally accepted in exchange, applies not only to the traditional "cash and checks" category (henceforth denoted as $M1$). It also fits assets that can be quickly and cheaply converted to $M1$, such as savings deposits or other low-risk, short-term holdings like certificates of deposit or money market funds.

The existence of close substitutes for money is nothing new, but their quantity has mushroomed in recent years. This is partly a consequence of faster information networks, but mostly it reflects heightened competition among financial institutions following an extensive deregulation of the U.S. banking system in the 1980s. Savings and other time deposits are, in practice, often payable on demand and can usually be transferred to a checking account by automatic teller machine, a phone call, or from your home computer. Such balances are popular because they yield a higher return than checking accounts. And even though they are not as liquid as cash, their ready convertibility means that they often function very much like cash in our decision making. These are included in the $M2$ concept of money, which begins with currency and demand deposits ($M1$), then adds savings deposits, "small" time deposits (under $100,000), money market funds, and some other relatively liquid deposits. The still more inclusive $M3$ starts with $M2$ but adds large time deposits, holdings of money market mutual funds, and other assets.[18]

If you find this loss of a single, clear-cut definition of "money" annoying, you're not alone. The resulting potential for confusion is apparent from a look at the annual growth rates of these measures since 1960 (Figure 6.8). Although their long-run profiles have broadly similar peaks and valleys, the year-to-year changes often vary widely. (Month-to-month growth rates, not shown, are more erratic still.) Not only can we no longer say how rapidly "the" money supply is growing, it is some-

■ FIGURE 6.8

From "Economic Report of the President 1994"; and Federal Reserve Bulletin.

Growth Rates of
$M1$, $M2$, and $M3$

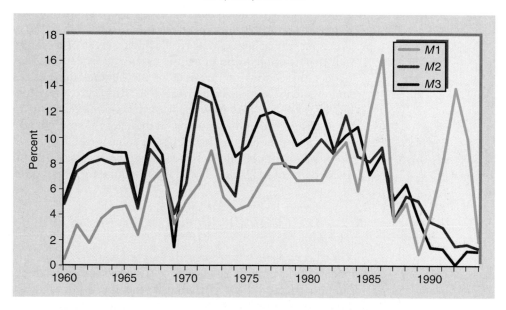

[18] By way of magnitude, $M1$, $M2$, and $M3$ in the United States stood at about $1160 billion, $3660 billion, and $4390 billion as of May 1995. There are still broader definitions of money that go further along the spectrum of assets. Even holdings of stock or bond mutual funds, although certainly not acceptable payment at the shopping mall, can often be converted into checking account balances by telephone. Data on the money supply and other financial statistics are available in the monthly *Federal Reserve Bulletin* from the Board of Governor's of the Federal Reserve System. For non-technical presentation of alternative measures of money see Norman Frumkin, *Tracking America's Economy*, 2nd ed. (Armonk, N.Y.: M. E. Sharpe, Inc., 1992), chap. 7; or David B. Johnson, *Finding and Using Economic Information: A Guide to Sources and Interpretation* (Mountain View, Calif.: Mayfield Publishing Company, 1993), chap. 6.

times unclear whether money growth is rising or falling. For example, the U.S. economy was officially in a recession through much of 1990 to 1991. President Bush decided against a fiscal stimulus, not expecting the sluggishness to linger into the 1992 election season. Was Mr. Bush pinning his hopes entirely on a nonactivist scenario of rapid "market clearing"? Or did he believe that the needed stimulus was coming from the monetary side? If he looked at the traditional measure of money, he might have been encouraged. The growth of $M1$, which had fallen precipitously after 1986, rose from just 1% in 1989 to 4% the next year and almost 9% in 1991, suggesting a sizable stimulus from the Federal Reserve. But if Mr. Bush looked beyond $M1$ to the broader monetary aggregates, $M2$ and $M3$, he might have reason for concern. As Figure 6.8 reveals, the growth rates of the broader measures continued along a downward trend that had begun in the mid-1980s.

So the obvious question now becomes "*Which* measure of money is most closely linked to macroeconomic activity?" If it's $M1$, then monetary policy in the early 1990s was appropriately expansionary for a recession (though don't forget the possibility of the "long and variable lag" problem). But if either $M2$ or $M3$ are better measures of money's impact on the macroeconomy, then the downturn was being reinforced by the effects of monetary contraction. So which one of these Ms is the "true" one, the one that will give us a reliable gauge as to whether monetary policy is becoming more expansionary, more contractionary, or holding steady?

You probably realize that if there were a clear answer to this important question, we surely wouldn't be having this tedious "alternative monetary aggregates" discussion. The bottom line is that the use of a multiplicity of monies reflects the fact that no single measure consistently bears a close and reliable relationship to short-run changes in the macroeconomy. A look at the past shows some periods in which changes in "narrow money" ($M1$) are strongly connected to changes in output and prices. But then the relationship will vanish without warning. It may then be that a broader measure of money, say $M2$, seems to have the close link to economic activity that we seek as a guide to short-run policy making. But soon this, too, disappears. The regrettable conclusion is that *no* concept of money bears a steady and predictable short-run relationship to macroeconomic performance.[19]

This is not really news, but it's an economic fact of life easily forgotten even in high places. In our understandable eagerness to use policy to "improve" the economy, we may presume a closer, more stable relationship than is really there. An easy way to summarize and remember this short-run unpredictability of the effects of monetary changes is to return to the notion of the *velocity of money*—the rate at which an average dollar flows through the economy (or "changes hands") during a given time period.[20] Since total spending or nominal income ($P \cdot y = Y$) must equal the number of dollars times their rate of turnover (velocity), we have the Quantity Theory relationship that $M \cdot V = Y$.

So the velocity of money is just the ratio of total spending (or nominal GDP) to the size of the money supply, $V = Y/M$. *In other words, velocity (V) is an index of how*

---

[19] Note that the concern here is with a predictable short-run correspondence between money and the macroeconomy. Since all three growth rates have a similar long-run pattern (see Figure 6.8), any of them can be used to reveal the important long-run relationship between money growth and inflation.

[20] Remember that the classical model relied on the long-run constancy of velocity to reach its "money is a veil," "only money matters," and "inflation is a monetary phenomenon" conclusions. It was the short-run variability of velocity that sent us to the Keynesian *IS-LM* analysis of aggregate demand for a relevant short-run model.

closely current economic performance (measured by Y) is connected to the money supply (M). A constant velocity would be consistent with a tight, predictable link between M and Y. At the other extreme, totally random movements of velocity over time would indicate no relationship between monetary policy and total spending. Combining this with the existence of alternative concepts of money, we can view the relationship between each of the Ms and total spending by its associated velocity: $V1 = Y/M1$, $V2 = Y/M2$, and $V3 = Y/M3$.

The velocity of these three measures of money in the United States is plotted in Figures 6.9 and 6.10. There is much that could be said about these results—the individual trends and their changes, the correlations among the different Vs, and so on. But the main point is the obvious lack of year-to-year constancy and the presence, particularly since 1980, of large and frequent changes in all three measures. To be more specific, the more or less steady upward trend in $V1$ was shattered by events of the 1980s and now offers no apparent clue as to what to expect for the $M1,Y$ relationship in the coming years. This is particularly important because it is $M1$ (currency plus demand deposits) that is most directly influenced by Federal Reserve actions. The broader monetary aggregates, dominated by components not controlled by the monetary authority, are considerably more unwieldy.

Of the three measures of velocity, $V2$ comes closest to long run constancy. For this reason, it is $M2$ that receives most attention when we look at long-run relationships between money growth and inflation. But year-to-year variations around its long-run average (1.60 for the 1960–1994 period) are still substantial and don't follow a predictable pattern of peaks and troughs. This means that even $M2$ offers little hope as a reliable policy instrument for control of the short-run ups and downs of the macroeconomy.

■ FIGURE 6.9

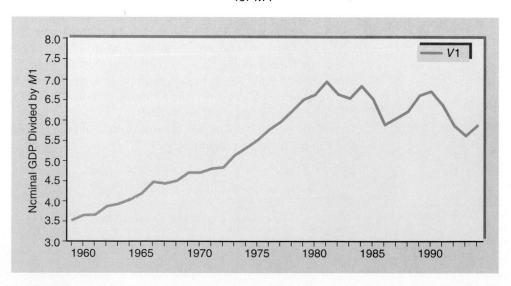

Velocity of Money
for *M*1

Velocity of Money
for *M*2 and *M*3

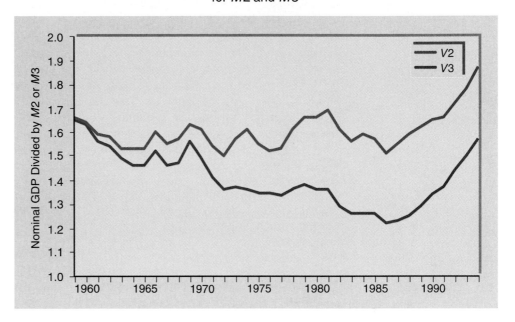

■ FIGURE 6.10

IN SUMMARY . . .

Monies, Velocities, and Policies

This discussion of the *M*s and *V*s (short for, "alternative monetary aggregates and their associated velocities") arose because of the existence of a *range* of "money-like" assets. Neither common sense nor economic theory provides a clear place to draw the line between "money" and "nonmoney" financial instruments.

One consequence is that even a simple question like "Is the money supply growing as rapidly this year as last?" can throw an economist into a flurry of hemming and hawing about "this measure is growing faster, that one slower, but a third held steady." No one likes such indecision and it's tempting to just draw a line somewhere, anywhere, along the spectrum of assets and say that everything below is "money" and everything above "not money." Then we could at least give *clear* answers to simple money supply questions. And in terms of our analytical framework, we could say *exactly* which asset changes shift *LM* and *AD*, and which don't.

"Clear" and "exact," perhaps, but very likely *wrong!* Albert Einstein is credited with saying "We should make things as simple as possible, but not simpler." The difficult fact is that the availability of many very close substitutes for narrowly defined money means that any specific measure draws a line where

(Continued)

there's only a "fuzzy band." Pretending otherwise helps in learning the basics but distorts our understanding of the real world. It's reasonable to turn to the data to see which M ($M1$, $M2$, $M3$, or some exotic blend of the three) is most closely linked to actual year-to-year movements in the macroeconomy. But we continue to find no reliable connection between any measure of money and short run macroeconomic performance. This is indicated in Figures 6.9 and 6.10, which show the erratic movements of the individual velocities ($V1$, $V2$, and $V3$). It tells us that none of these definitions of money bear the steady year-to-year relationship with nominal income ($V = Y/M$) that would help us decide which measure of M is most useful as a short-run policy instrument.

Does all this mean that we must abandon the word "money" altogether in favor of some hazy "money-like substance"? Fortunately not. We can still use the term money in both general discussion and in the specific context of our models. All of the basic definitions move similarly over longer periods, and the crucial long-run relationship between money and inflation is present for any of the Ms. But the unpredictable yearly changes in the Vs mean that we should not pretend that we can predict the short-run impact of changes in any of the Ms with any degree of reliability.

◈ 6.10 MONETARY POLICY AND THE GREAT DEPRESSION

The events of the Great Depression, which afflicted so many hundreds of millions throughout the world, have long attracted the attention of economists, financial analysts, historians, and many others. Investigators continue to sift the past for clues, applying the most recent theories and statistical techniques to this calamitous epoch. It's been appropriately said that "The Great Depression is to economics what the Big Bang is to physics. As an event, the Depression is largely synonymous with the birth of modern macroeconomics, and it continues to haunt successive generations of economists."[21] Although the major events of that decade, sketched briefly in Chapter 4, are well known, our understanding of just why this particular downturn was so deep and so prolonged continues to grow.[22]

Although some important disagreements persist, it is generally accepted that Federal Reserve policies played an unintended yet major role in both initiating and sustaining the huge collapse in aggregate demand that underlay the Great Depression. The monetary chapter of the story begins at least as early as 1928 with Fed worries about the consequences of wild and undisciplined speculation in stock and

[21] Robert A. Margo, "Employment and Unemployment in the 1930s," *Journal of Economic Perspectives* 7 (spring 1993): 41.

[22] Major contributions to this understanding include Milton Friedman and Anna J. Schwartz, *A Monetary History of the United States, 1867–1960* (Princeton: Princeton University Press, National Bureau of Economic Research, 1963); Charles Kindleberger, *The World in Depression, 1929–1939* (Berkeley: University of California Press, 1973, revised and enlarged 1986); Frederic S. Mishkin, "The Household Balance Sheet and the Great Depression," *Journal of Economic History* 38 (December 1978): 918–937; Ben Bernanke, "Nonmonetary Effects of the Financial Crises in the Propagation of the Great Depression," *American Economic Review* 73 (June 1983): 257–276; Peter Temin, *Lessons From the Great Depression* (Cambridge: The Massachusetts Institute of Technology Press, 1989); and a Symposium on the Great Depression in the *Journal of Economic Perspectives* 7 (spring 1993): 19–102, including articles by Christina Romer, Robert A. Margo, Charles W. Calomiris, and Peter Temin.

bond markets. The Fed's reaction was to undertake a substantial monetary contraction, pushing market interest rates from just over 5% to nearly 10% within a year. The goal was to discourage speculation by making it more expensive to gamble on borrowed funds, restoring a measure of sanity to capital markets. The result was further pressure on already fragile markets, hastening and perhaps deepening the stock market crash of October 1929.

The resulting loss of wealth and liquidity combined with ensuing financial market volatility to cause a dramatic drop in spending (particularly on consumer durables) and a corresponding contraction in aggregate demand. This was soon followed by a series of banking panics between 1930 and 1933. Thousands of banks, unable to return the funds demanded by worried depositors, simply closed their doors, causing massive losses to depositors and stockholders. The Federal Reserve failed to take the major expansionary actions so clearly needed to offset the contractionary impacts.[23]

But the damage from this 33% drop in the nominal money supply over less than 4 years wasn't the only monetary problem. Disarray in the banking system also interrupted the process of financial intermediation—the flow from consumer saving through financial institutions to business borrowers. The resulting loss of institutional efficiency $(-\Delta i^{nst})$ showed up as a negative supply shock for the economy. The net result was an unemployment rate that soared to 25% by 1933.

The period from 1934 to 1937 turned out to be one of rapid recovery, but the Federal Reserve still refrained from any major expansion. As the economy and the banking industry recovered, the Fed became concerned with the large amount of excess reserves held by banks. Fearing that these might result in a spurt of lending and resulting monetary expansion that could interfere with continued recovery, it initiated a contractionary policy to soak up the excess reserves, thinking that this would have little impact on lending behavior. Unfortunately, they had again miscalculated and the resulting contraction of the money supply pushed a partially recovered economy into a sharp recession in 1938.

There may be many reasons that the Federal Reserve failed to respond to the events of the early 1930s, including attachment to policy rules of thumb not suited to extreme circumstances and an ill-fated attempt to observe the rules of the collapsing gold standard when gold was leaving the country.[24] But the fact is that the Great Depression finally ended with no serious attempt at expansion by the Federal Reserve at any time during more than a decade of economic crisis. Its contribution had been the sharp contractions in 1928 and 1937 and inaction during the bank panics and monetary contraction of 1930 to 1933. A number of factors finally brought the Great Depression to a close—including the process of market clearing, the stimulus of increased military expenditures, and significant changes in the structure of the banking system including Federal insurance of bank deposits. There's also evidence of monetary expansion from substantial inflows of gold to the United States.[25] But at no time did the Fed use its major weapons—reserve requirements, discount rates, and open market operations—in an aggressive manner to expand the money supply.

---

[23] The reasons for Fed inaction are not clear. Some attribute it to weak leadership, others to timidity about aggressive actions for fear that it would result in massive gold outflows and further undermine the shaky international gold standard.

[24] For a readable introduction to this issue see David C. Wheelock, "Monetary Policy in the Great Depression: What the Fed Did, and Why," *Review*, Federal Reserve Bank of St. Louis 74 (March/April 1992): 3–28.

[25] See Christina Romer, "What Ended the Great Depression?" 52 *Journal of Economic History* (1992): 757–784.

☯ *6.11 OVERVIEW*

1. We often equate "money" with the things it can be exchanged for. This simplification, harmless in some ways, can be most damaging at the public policy level. Since the publication of Adam Smith's masterpiece, it has been known that the "wealth of nations" lies in the value of its goods and services, not in the quantity of the commodity used to measure this value. Money makes an important contribution in permitting us to escape the high costs of self-sufficiency and barter. But money cannot substitute for the goods and services it trades for and symbolizes.

2. A sound monetary system—in which the currency is **generally accepted** in exchange, **holds its value** relatively well across time, and serves as the **basic economic measure** throughout the economy—makes a major contribution to economic efficiency. The strength of the currency and the economy's degree of monetization (fraction of trade conducted through money rather than barter) both have important impacts on production and exchange and are captured in the "institutional efficiency" term (i^{nst}) of the production function. An effective money lowers the economic costs of making trades, thereby freeing resources to produce the final goods and services that underlie our standard of living.

3. The belief that a money has value only to the extent that it has **intrinsic (nonmonetary) worth** has a long and proud tradition. But it's wrong. With the help of the *AD/AS* framework, we can see that a money's value depends on the Central Bank's ability and willingness to limit its supply.

4. A **fiat money,** "backed" only by the commitment of the monetary authority to keep close control over its supply, uses many fewer resources than, say, a system in which the currency is backed by gold. So fiat money has great potential for efficient monetization. But if the Central Bank is unable or unwilling to limit its supply, this potential will be lost. Controversy over how to limit the issuance of fiat money in the U.S. has reflected the inevitable tension between the promise and the dangers of centralized decision making.

5. The **Federal Reserve System,** a structure that balances private and public control, was established in 1913 to regulate money creation in the United States. It has direct control over the currency and coin which makes up about 25% of the money in circulation. But its primary means of influencing the money supply stems from its ability to alter the monetary reserves of commercial banks and, thereby, to influence the amount of the major component of money—demand deposits.

6. **Open market operations**—sales and purchases of government bonds—are the Fed's mainstay for changing monetary reserves. Through its power to create demand deposits to pay for its purchases (and to destroy them when it makes a sale), the Federal Reserve can act quickly and powerfully to make desired changes in bank reserves and, thereby, the nation's money supply.

7. Central Banks are responsible for setting their nation's monetary sails in the face of changing economic winds and dangerous currents as well as seeing the economy through occasional storms and high seas. In fact how important is monetary policy in not only guiding the macroeconomy but also in propelling it forward? Our expanded *AD/AS* model provides a good starting point. In a fully employed economy, an increase in the nominal money supply expands aggregate demand and, in the short run, decreases the real rate of interest while increasing investment, net exports, consumption, and real output. In the long run, the price level rises, but all the real variables return to their initial levels. *Monetary policy, so powerful in altering*

economic activity in the short run, is said to be "neutral" in the long run, when its only power is to alter the price level.

8. The result that monetary changes, at full employment, can have no lasting impact on real output is hardly surprising. But the result that monetary policy, again at full employment, has no lasting effect on the real rate of interest seems counterintuitive to many. To clarify the relationships between monetary policy and interest rates requires a distinction, often ignored by politicians and the media, between real (r) and nominal (R) rates of interest. The relationship between them is given by the Fisher equation, $R = r + \Pi^e$, which is a concise way to say that the nominal (or market) rate of interest that we observe is the real rate plus a premium for expected inflation. Even though the Federal Reserve can have no lasting impact on the real rate, it certainly can alter the rate of inflation and, thereby, change the nominal rate of interest.

9. Two points need particular emphasis. (a) It is the *real* interest rate that matters for aggregate demand (specifically the investment and net export decisions in our model) and (b) the long run impact of an expansionary monetary policy at full employment is to *increase*, not decrease, the nominal interest rate while leaving the real rate unchanged.

10. In an economy initially below full employment, the impact of monetary expansion comes down to the issue of **timing**—the speed of market clearing compared to that of policy manipulation. If expansionary policy can shift aggregate demand more quickly than the market clearing process moves the economy down the aggregate demand curve, then an activist monetary policy can be successful in speeding the return to full employment. But the presence of long policy lags could mean that the expansion comes too late and only adds to excess demand and hence rising prices.

11. Criticisms of Central Bank policies are inevitable, in part because we often have unrealistic and even conflicting expectations about what monetary policy can achieve. Because monetary actions are sometimes subject to both unpredictable policy lags and unwanted side effects on other variables, the choices facing the Federal Reserve are difficult. Beyond the obvious importance of controlling the growth of the money supply so as to avoid high and variable inflation, achieving monetary goals is complicated by limits in our understanding of time lags as well as subjective differences in our rankings of alternative economic goals and our willingness to accept trade-offs among them.

12. The presence of an **array of different assets,** with different degrees of riskiness and liquidity, poses a serious challenge to our desire to think of "money" as something simple and clear-cut. Deregulation and technological change have led to the creation of new money-like assets by financial institutions. Some have characteristics very close to the traditional "currency plus demand deposits" definition of money ($M1$). Others include assets that are readily converted to $M1$. The result is that we have several plausible monetary aggregates ($M1$, $M2$, and $M3$, being the best known) to complicate our model-building and policy-making activities.

13. Over long periods, the growth rates of alternative monies have been similar. But over shorter intervals these different concepts often move quite differently, as do their associated rates of turnover (velocity). The result is that in the context of short-run stabilization issues—like "What should the Federal Reserve do over the next three months to help pull the economy out of recession?"—we can say very little with a high degree of confidence.

ᏰᏴ *6.12 REVIEW QUESTIONS*

1. Define the following basic concepts or terms:

Fiat money	Counterfeiting	Fisher effect
Self-sufficiency	Reserve requirements	Time value of money
Barter	Discount rate	Inflation risk
Monetization	Open market operations	Default risk
Acceptability	Excess reserves	Activist view
Medium of exchange	Nominal money supply	Nonactivist view
Store of value	Real money supply	Time lags
Unit of account	Monetary neutrality	Conflicting goals
National income accounting	Real interest rate	$M1$, $M2$, and $M3$
Demand deposits	Nominal interest rate	$V1$, $V2$, and $V3$

2. Suppose a critic of monetary policy argues that the Federal Reserve should reverse recent policy and expand the money supply at a faster rate. In so doing, he contends, they will be able to lower interest rates, stimulate investment and net exports, and increase output, all at the same time. These benefits would more than outweigh, in his opinion, the relatively small cost of a little inflation. Evaluate this argument and explain your reasoning in terms of the basic macro model.

3. "Money is the root of all evil." Evaluate this adage in light of the material in this chapter. Do you think the elimination of money from the economy would eliminate the alleged "evil"?

4. Suppose a careful statistical study shows that the real rate of interest does *not* influence money demand at all.

   a. How would this change the *LM* equation, the *LM* curve, and the *AD* curve? Explain.

   b. Would this new information alter our conclusions about the impact of fiscal and monetary policy on aggregate demand? Explain.

5. A potential presidential candidate believes that a neglected and important long-run economic goal should be lower interest rates. As her expert economic adviser, you must answer the following questions and explain your reasoning.

   a. "Do you agree with me that lower interest rates are an important ingredient in bringing about a more prosperous and secure economic future?"

   b. "I heard some economist say that high interest rates were the result of too *much* money supply, not too little. Does that make any sense?"

   c. "Suppose I had total control over both monetary and fiscal policy. What combination of policies should I run to get mortgage rates down from 9% to 5% where they belong?"

   d. "Would there be any unpleasant side effects from these policies?"

6. Though the use of money goes back many millennia, David Hume, the eighteenth-century Scottish philosopher, was among the first persons to give careful thought to its implications for the overall economy. His conclusion was that "It is of no manner of consequence, with regard to the domestic happiness of a state, whether money be in a greater or less quantity" (1742). Put this into modern

terms and explain what it implies for the use of monetary policy. Do you agree with it? Explain.

7. When asked whether she expects a monetary expansion to result in lower or higher interest rates, an economist replies "Yes." Explain why this cryptic remark, implying that *both* may happen, is not just an idle witticism.

8. "The conclusion that monetary policy can have no lasting impact on the real rate of interest is true under certain conditions, but these conditions are so restrictive that the conclusion is of little real significance. If the economy is initially below full employment, an increase in the money supply will cause a lasting drop in the real rate of interest and therefore provide a real and lasting stimulus to the macroeconomy through investment and net exports." Evaluate this statement.

9. Evaluate both statements below and explain your reasoning.
    a. "Expansionary monetary policy is ultimately inflationary, so when an aggregate demand stimulus is needed, it's preferable to use fiscal policy."
    b. "Expansionary fiscal policy raises the real rate of interest, whereas expansionary monetary policy lowers it. This needs to be considered in choosing between them."

10. Evaluate both statements below and explain your reasoning.
    a. "To illustrate how irrational capital markets can be, when the Federal Reserve chairman announced a goal of immediately lower interest rates for the economy, there was an immediate *increase* in interest rates on bonds, mortgages, and other long-term obligations."
    b. "To further illustrate how irrational capital markets can be, when the Federal Reserve chairman announced a *long-term goal* of lowering interest rates in the economy, the immediate impact was rising interest rates. It just doesn't make sense."

11. When diplomacy fails and warfare begins, we most often think of it in military terms. Destruction of capital and lives imposes obvious costs on society that show up in our model as negative supply shocks. They are typically accompanied by sizable demand increases to finance the war effort, and the result is both falling output and rising prices. These ends can also be accomplished by *economic* warfare, most commonly through embargoes and boycotts, but sometimes through massive counterfeiting of the enemy's currency. Using the *AD/AS* framework, evaluate and explain the destructive power of these economic weapons.

12. The reunification process in Germany has created a huge and growing cash flow deficit for the nation. At the same time, the German Central Bank has been running a relatively contractionary policy through open market operations and through its control of the German discount rate. Predict the short- and long-run impacts of this policy package on y, P, r, R, i, and x in Germany.

13. The Federal Reserve has great power over the nominal value of money, but it has no long-run control over the real value of the money supply. Do you agree or disagree? Explain.

14. The analysis in this chapter has assumed a zero-growth economy. But suppose there is steady growth in the full employment level of output, showing up as a continued rightward shift in AS^*. What are the relationships among monetary policy, real interest rates, and real output under these circumstances? How do they differ from those of a zero-growth economy?

⊗⊙ *6.13 FURTHER READING*

NIGEL W. DUCK, "Some International Evidence on the Quantity Theory of Money," *Journal of Money, Credit, and Banking* 25 (February 1993): 1–12.

MILTON FRIEDMAN, *Money Mischief: Episodes in Monetary History* (New York: Harcourt, Brace, & Jovanovich, 1992).

MILTON FRIEDMAN AND ANNA J. SCHWARTZ, *A Monetary History of the United States, 1867–1960* (Princeton: Princeton University Press, 1963).

DAVID LAIDLER, "The Legacy of the Monetarist Controversy," *Review*, The Federal Reserve Bank of St. Louis 72 (March/April 1990).

DAVID LAIDLER, *The Demand for Money: Theories, Evidence, and Problems*, 4th ed. (New York: HarperCollins, 1993).

ANN-MARIE MEULENDYKE, *U.S. Monetary Policy and Financial Markets* (New York: Federal Reserve Bank of New York, 1989).

STEVEN RUSSELL, "The U.S. Currency System: A Historical Perspective," *Review*, Federal Reserve Bank of St. Louis (September/October 1991): 34–61.

STEVEN SOLOMON, *The Confidence Game* (New York: Simon & Schuster, 1995).

CHAPTER 7

INTERNATIONAL TRADE

🔮 7.1 INTRODUCTION

The influence of international trade on the U.S. economy, traditionally quite small, has grown dramatically in recent decades. Increasingly, global events are helping to shape our individual and collective decisions and our economic lives. This chapter presents an analytic framework for understanding the major threats, challenges, and opportunities posed by trade across nations.

When goods and services cross national borders it generally involves two different currencies as well as special balance of payments accounting procedures to keep track of who owes what to whom. This makes international trade look far more complicated than its domestic counterpart. But it's really not so different. There's still a buyer and a seller brought together by the possibility of mutual gain. They trade a good or service in exchange either for payment now or for a promise to pay later (evidenced by a promissory note or other "security"). The buyer's primary concern is to get a good product at a "good" price. Of course, the seller also wants a "good" price and it's through the give and take of the market that a compromise is reached. Whether the buyer and seller happen to live within the same political boundaries is unimportant to the underlying forces that inspire economic transactions. Both parties are simply trying to do the best they can with their available resources.

In recent years, international trade has become increasingly important to virtually all nations. The data confirm what we all sense—that more and more high-quality, low-price imported goods have become available to consumers throughout much of the world. Overall economic growth, declining costs of transportation, the global spread of technology, and diminished political restrictions on trade are among the major factors underlying the growing appeal of foreign goods and foreign markets. In the U.S., imports and exports have nearly tripled as a fraction of our total output over the past 30 years [(Figures

U.S. Imports
(1959–1994 as % of GDP)

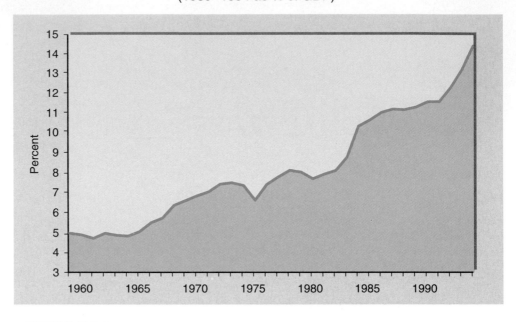

■ FIGURE 7.1(a)

From "Economic Report of the President, 1994."

■ FIGURE 7.1(b)

U.S. Exports
(1959–1994 as % of GDP)

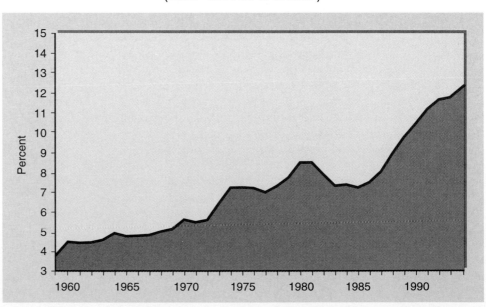

7.1(a, b)]. Even so, we remain far more self-sufficient than other industrial nations (Figure 7.2).

But import growth in the U.S. has tended to outpace export growth. The result is a balance of trade deficit (Figure 7.3) that widened spectacularly in the mid-1980s, then diminished but recently reappeared. The consequence of buying more goods and services from other countries than they buy from us is that we must make up the difference by giving them claims to our *future* output. If we spend $100 billion on their goods and services but they buy only $80 billion of ours, they have $20 billion in yet-to-be-used claims on our output. They could choose to just hold onto this, perhaps speculating on a rise in the international value of the dollar. In reality they mostly convert these dollars into stocks and bonds of corporations, U.S. government bonds, real estate, and other earning assets. But whatever the form in which these claims against future output are stored, by not using them to purchase current goods and services foreigners are essentially providing us with a loan. Put another way, their willingness to hold these claims represents a net inflow of capital to the U.S. from abroad. They're sending us more output than we're sending them, choosing to take the difference in the form of a "piece of the action," a claim on expected future returns. The importance of this dual relationship—that every *balance of trade deficit* is necessarily a *capital account surplus*—will be emphasized later in the chapter.

With large balance of trade surpluses over a number of years, the United States had once been a substantial net investor in other countries. But the trade deficits of recent decades have continued to erode its net investor (lender) status. Official (though rough) estimates of the market value of U.S. asset holdings abroad compared to foreign assets here show that by 1987 the United States had become a **net debtor nation** with respect to the rest of the world. In other words, our yearly trade deficits

■ FIGURE 7.2

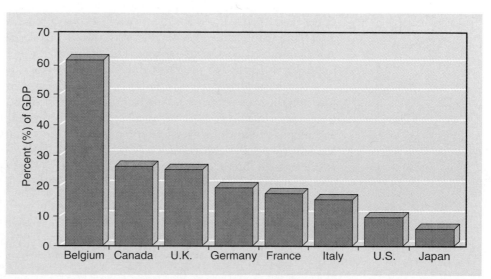

Imports as % of GDP
(Selected Countries, 1993)

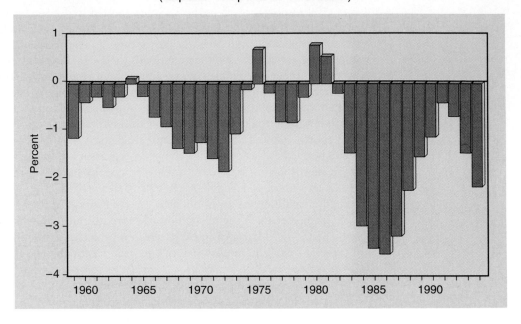

FIGURE 7.3

Positive levels of net exports mean a *trade surplus;* negative, a *trade deficit.* The prominent U.S. trade deficits since the mid-80s reflect the accumulation by foreigners of claims to *future* U.S. goods and services.

finally overtook the accumulated surpluses of previous years.[1] Figure 7.4 reveals that this gap has continued to widen.

Another highly visible dimension of world trade is the value of the dollar in terms of the currencies of our trading partners. Figure 7.5 shows the *real international value of the dollar*—relative to an average of foreign currencies, weighted according to their importance in U.S. trade and adjusted for inflation. The **real exchange rate,** as it's also called, has ridden the proverbial roller coaster over the past twenty years. The rapid climb from 1979 to 1985 was followed by an even steeper descent and has since continued on its bumpy way. The causes of these fluctuations as well as their implications for us as consumers and producers will also be examined in this chapter.

It's clear that these are important and rather complicated events. They are made all the more difficult by the fact that, for most of us, the primary source of economic information is the news media. The need to simplify and compress a "story" and emphasize its "newsworthy" components—the sensational, the menacing, and the controversial—can leave issues oversimplified and, sometimes, badly distorted. In the case of international trade, the daily benefits that flow from world trade may go unremarked by the media while accounts of "chronic trade deficits," "unprece-

---

[1] In addition to borrowing to cover the gap between imports and exports each year, the U.S. as a nation sends additional dollars abroad in the form of *net transfer payments.* These are gifts, private or public, to persons or institutions or governments outside the United States and represent a claim to our output, present or future, just like any other dollar outflow. In 1989, for example, U.S. imports exceeded exports by about $83 billion, and, in addition, our net transfers to the rest of the world were more than $15 billion. Altogether, then, we borrowed about $98 billion more from other countries in 1989 than they did from us. This amount is added to whatever net debt existed as of the beginning of the year (more than $260 billion), bringing the end of 1989 net U.S. debt to about $360 billion.

U.S. Assets Abroad and
Foreign Assets in the United States

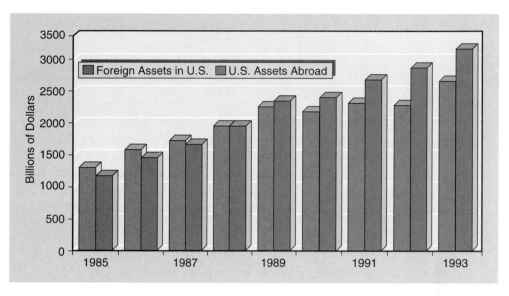

■ FIGURE 7.4

■ FIGURE 7.5

International Value of the Dollar
(Real Exchange Rate)

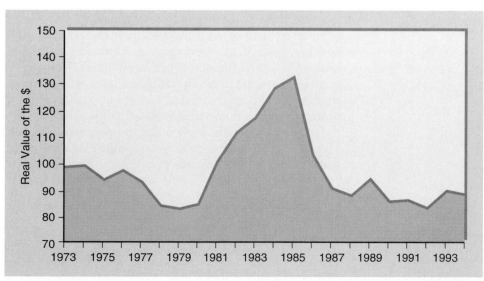

dented indebtedness to other nations," "plummeting exchange rates," and the "destruction of American jobs" proliferate. With this litany of problems it can sometimes seem like trade with other nations is a curse and that we would be better off literally going about our own business. In fact, just the opposite is the case as you will understand by chapter's end.

✆ 7.2 FREE TRADE, TARIFFS, AND THE MACROECONOMY

Two powerful words—**free trade**—define a concept that lies at the heart of economic exchange. Unfortunately it's a concept with so many different connotations and usages that it often means very different things to different people. Most commonly we encounter "free trade" as a political slogan, invoked to justify such a wide array of policies that it seems to have little specific meaning. Beyond the sloganeering, however, "free trade" represents a well-defined and very practical approach to the use of economic resources in a market economy. Although economists often celebrate its inherent efficiency, most beneficiaries of free trade are quite unaware of how much it contributes to their standard of living. But "victims" of free trade, actual and potential, tend to be quick to seek trade restrictions in order to protect their individual economic security from threats of foreign competition.

Let's begin our analysis of this controversial topic with the help of the familiar *AD/AS* model of the macroeconomy. Our development and use of this model in previous chapters quietly assumed a world without tariffs, quotas, or other barriers to trade across nations. Like anything that we customarily take for granted (food, shelter, good health, hopes for the future), a striking way to see its importance is to take some of it away. Accordingly, suppose a **tariff** on imported goods is signed into law, leading consumers to switch to the now relatively cheaper domestic goods protected by the tariff. The reduction in import demand means a rise in autonomous net exports $(+\Delta x_0)$, which leads to an outward shift in *IS* and *AD* as shown in Figure 7.6.[2] The immediate impact is to move the economy from points *A* to *B*, with both real output and the real interest rate rising in the short run. The tariff has caused us to switch consumption from foreign to domestic goods, stimulating output and employment. Along with economic expansion, the tariff has also brought increased tax revenues, helping to reduce our government deficit.

All these benefits without costs should arouse your suspicion. We have ignored a crucial element of the story—*because of the tariff, we are now using our scarce resources to produce goods that we cannot provide as efficiently as someone else.* Only by "artificially" raising the price of imported goods with a tariff have we stimulated demand for domestic production. The switch to domestic goods and services gives a short-term stimulus to aggregate demand and output (points *A* to *B*). But as market clearing proceeds, the economy adjusts initially to point *C* and finally to point *D*, reflecting the reduced productive efficiency of this **protectionist policy.**

In sum, a tariff diminishes our production possibilities by forcing us to use our scarce resources less efficiently.[3] The aggregate supply curve has shifted to the left

---

[2] Remember that net exports are defined as exports minus imports. We have stressed their inverse relationship to both real output and the real rate of interest, as described in the equation $x = x_0 - x_1 y - x_2 r$. Other events that alter net exports, such as tariffs or changes in consumer preferences, are captured in the autonomous net export term (x_0).

[3] For a look at the empirical evidence on the cost of trade restrictions, see Cletus C. Coughlin, K. Alec Chrystal, and Geoffrey E. Wood, "Protectionist Trade Policies: A Survey of Theory, Evidence and Rationale," *Review*, Federal Reserve Bank of St. Louis 70 (January/February 1988): 12–26; and Robert C. Feenstra, "How Costly is Protectionism?" *Journal of Economic Perspectives* 6 (Summer 1992): 159–178.

■ FIGURE 7.6

The imposition of a tariff initially expands *IS* and *AD* by reducing imports and, thereby, increasing autonomous net exports $(+\Delta x_0)$. So the short run impact is expansionary, as shown in the movement from point *A* to *B*.

But the tariff also reduces our economic efficiency on the supply side, shifting *AS** to the left. This eventually contracts real output and pushes the price level still higher as the economy moves to point *D* in the long run.

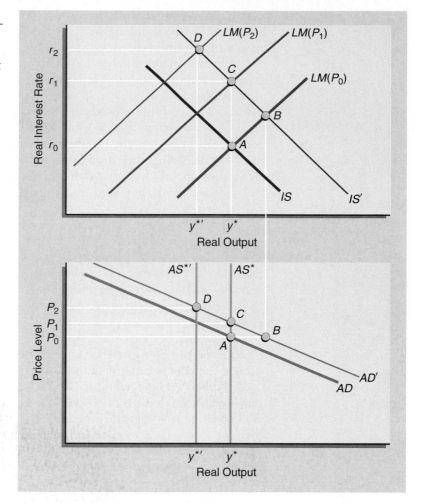

Impact of a Tariff:
Short Run: $A \rightarrow B$;
Long Run: $A \rightarrow D$

because we have eliminated some economic transactions that would have been mutually beneficial to buyer and seller. Since "taxing the efficient" is just the flip side of "subsidizing the inefficient," free trade in its most basic and powerful sense has thereby been diminished. While domestic producers protected from foreign competition clearly gain, the rest of us lose. The end result is a decline in full employment output and a drop in our overall standard of living via a drop in institutional efficiency $(-\Delta i^{nst})$. Put the opposite way, eliminating the tariff would increase output by ending the monopoly power that the tariff bestows upon inefficient industries.

But suppose we fail to see that this loss in our standard of living is due to our own decision to restrict world trade. Perhaps it's small enough to be obscured by other major events of the times. Or, scapegoats being always abundant in aggregate economic issues, we might put the blame elsewhere. We may even deceive ourselves into thinking that the tariff has been a boost to our economic health instead of a self-inflicted wound. This tension between "free trade" and "protectionism" is a central and enduring economic issue. It has been a battleground for many centuries and will surely continue to be contested for many more. It involves a very basic struggle for resources and economic power and is heightened by nationalistic sentiments that draw a strong line between "us" and "them."

There is nothing inherently harmful in such a struggle over self-interest, so long as it leads to competition to produce a better, cheaper product than your competitors, domestic or foreign. This is precisely what drives a market economy, providing incentives for improved efficiency, continuing product development, and technological innovation. Firms who don't do these things are left behind as the consumer searches for the best bargains and, in the process, rewards the most efficient suppliers. But when producers turn from the economic to the *political* arena to secure a competitive advantage, the results are likely to be very different. The resulting trade restrictions typically create a negative supply shock that reduces that entire nation's standard of living.

Let's extend this discussion to cover the impact of our trade restrictions on other economies. Although the tariff increases our net exports $(+\Delta x_0)$ and shifts our *IS* and *AD* curves outward, it has just the opposite effect abroad. The reduced exports of the other country—let's say Japan, so $-\Delta x_0^J$—means contraction of IS^J and AD^J in Japan. The immediate effect, of course, is a decline in output in Japan. Suppose the Japanese then decide to retaliate by increasing their tariffs on American goods coming into Japan. This will result in fewer Japanese purchases of our exports, this drop in net exports shifting our *IS* and *AD* back to the left and theirs to the right. If the two protectionist policies are of similar magnitude, the result is a standoff that leaves both countries at preprotectionist levels in terms of aggregate demand.

Why all the concern about "trade wars," you might ask, when they just offset one another and leave aggregate demand basically unchanged? The problem is that while demand-side shifts may be offsetting, the retaliation results in an even more inefficient worldwide allocation of resources and, hence, in further declines in aggregate supply and production possibilities in both nations. This is shown in Figure 7.7, in which it is assumed that the impact of the initial tariff on aggregate demand is ex-

■ FIGURE 7.7

If we suppose that one country's tariff meets with immediate and equal retaliation, the demand-side stimulus of the initial tariff $(+\Delta x_0 \Rightarrow +\Delta IS$ and $+\Delta AD)$ will be entirely neutralized leaving $\Delta x_0 = \Delta IS = \Delta AD = 0$. But as first one economy and then the other puts up trade restrictions protecting relatively inefficient producers, scarce resources are increasingly diverted into less efficient uses, creating negative supply shocks shown as the shift to $AS^{*\prime}$ and $AS^{*\prime\prime}$. The end result is a lower standard of living for both economies.

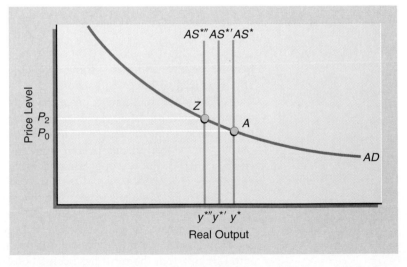

Trade War

actly offset by the retaliatory tariff, leaving us with only the "supply shocks" (AS^* to $AS^{*\prime}$ to $AS^{*\prime\prime}$) from the trade war. The standard of living of both countries continues to shrink as they become more and more insulated from foreign competition. Put another way, the only thing consumers are "protected" from by tariffs is the benefits of an efficient use of scarce resources.

IN PRAISE OF FREE TRADE

The advantages of free trade have been extolled by economists since the profession began to claim a separate identity following Adam Smith's *Wealth of Nations* (1776). But celebration of trade with distant nations dates back at least to the beginnings of written language. Whether expressed in words, graphs, or equations, the message is the same—*all* parties can gain from expanded trade. Since there are always powerful forces working (or lurking) to restrict trade in the interest of particular groups, it is important to have a strong image of the potential gains from expanded trade. Perhaps the observations of the essayist Joseph Addison (writing, in 1711, as the fictional Sir Roger de Coverly) will freshen your view of the power of international trade, even if his examples may seem a bit quaint today.

> *Nature seems to have taken a peculiar care to disseminate the blessings among the different regions of the world, with an eye to this mutual intercourse and traffic among mankind, that the natives of the several parts of the globe might have a kind of dependence upon one another, and be united together by this common interest. The food often grows in one country, and the sauce in another. The fruits of Portugal are corrected by the products of Barbadoes; the infusion of a China plant sweetened with the pith of an Indian cane. The Philippine Islands give a glamour to our European bowls.*

> *If we consider our own country [England] in its natural prospect, without any of the benefits and advantages of commerce, what a barren, uncomfortable spot of earth falls to our share! . . . [Yet] our ships are laden with the harvest of every climate: our tables are stored with spices, and oils, and wines; our rooms are filled with pyramids of China, and adorned with the workmanship of Japan. . . . My friend Sir Andrew calls the vineyards of France our gardens; the spice-islands our hot-beds; the Persians our silk-weavers, and the Chinese our potters. Nature indeed furnishes us with the bare necessaries of life, but traffic gives us a great variety of what is useful, and at the same time supplies us with everything that is convenient and ornamental. Nor is it the least part of this our happiness, that while we enjoy the remotest products of the north and south, we are free from those extremities of weather which give them birth; that our eyes are refreshed with the green fields of Britain, at the same time that our palates are feasted with fruits that rise between the tropics.*

> *Trade, without enlarging the British territories, has given us a kind of additional empire: it has multiplied the number of the rich, made our landed estates infinitely more valuable than they were formerly, and added to them an accession of other estates as valuable as the lands themselves.*

✎ 7.3 *BEHIND THE GAINS FROM TRADE: COMPARATIVE ADVANTAGE*

The argument for "free trade" may seem eminently logical and straightforward in terms of the mechanics of the *AD/AS* model. But you should be warned that the preceding analysis asserted rather than demonstrated that expanded trade yields net economic gains to the economy. It simply presumed that more trade expands aggregate supply while trade restrictions contract it. In some ways this seems to make sense, but how can we be sure that this is always or even usually the case? After all, when foreign competition means reduced demand for our textiles or our steel, the impact is to reduce employment and output in those industries and impose very real hardships not only on these groups but on related industries and surrounding communities. With these declining industries generating less employment and less income, this also means reduced buying power that spreads far and wide through the multiplier process. Anyone in the path of these falling dominos becomes a victim rather than a beneficiary of free trade.

What makes economists so sure that the net result of increased foreign trade is to expand rather than contract the economy? Why do we think the benefits will outweigh the costs? Don't we first have to measure the precise effects on employment and output of any particular change in international trade patterns before we can reach a conclusion about its net impact? Thanks to a remarkable relationship first formulated by British economist David Ricardo in his path-breaking *Principles of Political Economy and Taxation* (1817), the answer is a clear "no." The **theorem of comparative advantage** reveals that even if one nation is more productive in all things than another, both will benefit by specializing where they are *relatively* most efficient, trading for the goods in which other nations are *relatively* more efficient.

The rationale behind this "specialize and trade" conclusion is no different for a nation than it is for an individual. Because "time" is one of our scarce resources, a useful measure of the cost of producing one thing is how much we could have produced of something else had we used our time (and other resources) differently. Although a star executive may have risen to the top by demonstrating competence in every aspect of the business—production, sales, marketing and so on—it is her managerial abilities that are most valuable to the company. Even if she could do everything from typing to selling to cost accounting better than anyone else in the company, she is constrained by the 24-hour day and can't do everything. The most efficient choice is for her to specialize in what she does *relatively* better than anyone else as measured in terms of her contributions to the firm's profitability. The other tasks will be left for those who may be less skillful in all things than their chief executive officer but who will find areas in which their *relative* productivity is highest.

Poor nations are in much the same situation as low-skilled individuals. Though their production possibilities are limited, they will always have a *comparative* advantage in some area. Specialization in the production of those goods and services where their comparative advantage lies, trading with other nations for the rest, will provide them with a higher standard of living than will national self-sufficiency. Restricting such trade diminishes the gains to all parties precisely because it reduces the degree of specialization and thereby lowers world economic efficiency.

Although the economic consequences of restricting free trade have been well established for more than two centuries, political battles continue. Specific groups assert, as they have throughout recorded history, that protection from foreign competition is also in the *national* interest. Although it is obviously in *their* economic interest to be granted monopoly power by the government, this will be paid for entirely by higher prices to consumers or, in the case of subsidies, by taxpayers. The adverse consequences of elevating the interests of producers above those of consumers seems to resist incorporation into the conventional wisdom, despite the fact that it has been perhaps the single issue upon which economists have shown both constancy and virtual unanimity across the centuries.[4] The satires of Frederic Bastiat on this topic (see the following text box) will continue to be as pertinent to the twenty-first century as they have been to the nineteenth and twentieth.

The most notorious example of protectionist legislation in U.S. history was the **Smoot-Hawley Tariff** of 1930. In the twilight of 1920s prosperity, President Hoover made a campaign promise to raise tariffs on agricultural products in order to increase U.S. farm output and income. But what began as a snowball quickly became an avalanche. In congressional hearings on the proposal (chaired by Senator Reed Smoot and Congressman Willis Hawley), manufacturers and other producer groups testified that they, too, should be given protection from foreign competition in order to strengthen their industries and thereby, they claimed, the entire U.S. economy. Rising unemployment and falling output at the beginning of 1930 only strengthened support for this plan to "protect" American jobs. These tariffs, it was asserted, would stimulate American industry and essentially "export our unemployment" to other nations whose exports were said to be destroying our jobs.

Despite objections (and threats of retaliation) from scores of nations as well as a petition of protest from over 1000 economists, Congress enacted this legislation and President Hoover signed the tariff into law in 1930. The Smoot-Hawley Act raised tariffs on more than 12,000 products, as tariffs came to account for about 60% of total import values. The volume of world trade plummeted as nation after nation retaliated with tariffs against our exports. Rather than "shipping" our unemployment overseas, we only succeeded in moving it out of inefficient protected industries to the efficient export industries. Combined with falling aggregate demand from the massive monetary contraction of the early 1930s, the negative supply shock from Smoot-Hawley pushed the economy still further toward the quicksand of the Great Depression.

By 1933 foreign trade was less than one-third its 1929 level and unemployment in the United States was up to 25% of the labor force. The supposed economic stimulus from these huge tariffs had obviously not materialized—just what the principle of comparative advantage had told us all along. Smoot-Hawley was soon overridden by the Reciprocal Trade Agreements Act of 1934. Since then tariffs in the United States have continued to decline, amounting to only about 5% of the value of imports at present.

But "free versus restricted" trade remains an active battleground, with constant pressure from special interest groups for protection from foreign competition. Most commonly we hear that tariffs "protect" or even "create" American jobs. The principle of comparative advantage makes it clear that although some jobs might be "saved," the overall effect is reduced efficiency and a lower standard of living. Tariffs

---

[4] Adam Smith stated the issue clearly in 1776. "Consumption is the sole end and purpose of all production; and the interest of the producer ought to be attended to, only so far as it may be necessary for promoting that of the consumer. The maxim is so perfectly self-evident, that it would be absurd to attempt to prove it. But in the mercantile system [of tariffs designed to create a balance of trade surplus], the interest of the consumer is almost constantly sacrificed to that of the producer; and it seems to consider production, and not consumption, as the ultimate end and object of all industry and commerce" (*The Wealth of Nations*, p. 625).

FREDERIC BASTIAT AND FREE TRADE

Frederic Bastiat (1801–1850) combined his reading of Adam Smith and Jean-Baptiste Say with firsthand observations of the economic crises occasioned by the Napoleonic Wars and their aftermath to become a lifelong disciple of free trade. His parodies of protectionist arguments remain both relevant and readable. Hearing of a proposal for a break in the tracks of the Paris to Bayonne railway to "stimulate employment of porters, boatmen, and owners of hotels," Bastiat proposes a break at every city in order to stimulate the entire economy. "By this means, we shall end by having a railroad composed of a whole series of breaks in the tracks, i.e., a *negative railroad*."

His most enduring essay is "A Petition" to the Chamber of Deputies from the fictional Candlemakers of France: "We are suffering from the ruinous competition of a foreign rival who apparently works under conditions so far superior to our own for the production of light that he is flooding the domestic market with it at an incredibly low price; for the moment he appears, our sales cease, all the consumers turn to him, and a branch of French industry whose ramifications are innumerable is all at once reduced to complete stagnation. This rival . . . is none other than the Sun."

Bastiat then describes the numerous benefits that would flow to the French economy from a law requiring "the closing of all windows, dormers, skylights, inside and outside shutters, curtains, casements . . . , in short, all openings, holes, chinks, and fissures through which the light of the Sun is wont to enter. . . . What industry in France will not ultimately be encouraged? If France consumes more tallow, there will have to be more cattle and sheep, and, consequently, we shall see an increase in cleared fields, meat, wool, leather, and especially manure, the basis of all agricultural wealth. If France consumes more oil, we shall see an expansion in the cultivation of the poppy, the olive, and rapeseed. These rich yet soil-exhausting plants will come at just the right time to enable us to put to profitable use the increased fertility that the breeding of cattle will impart to the land."

Anticipating the response of the Chamber of Deputies, he then drives home his criticism of their protectionist policies. "Will you tell us that, though we may gain by this protection, France will not gain at all, because the consumer will bear the expense? We have our answer ready: You no longer have the right to invoke the interests of the consumer. You have sacrificed him whenever you have found his interests opposed to those of the producer. You have done so in order to encourage industry and to increase employment. For the same reason you ought to do so this time too."

create incentives for workers and capital to stay in areas where they are relatively inefficient. In fact, trade restrictions actively discourage inputs from moving toward their comparative advantage.

When the economy is at full employment, tariffs and other trade restrictions are more easily seen as the elevation of the interests of producer and worker groups over the interests of consumers. But during a recession, when emotion sometimes dominates our reason, arguments to "protect our jobs" from foreign competitors seem to make both economic and patriotic sense. In those times it's important to remember that while an increase in tariffs may provide a popular short run stimulus (at least until retaliation erupts into a "trade war"), the same impact could come from expansionary monetary or fiscal policy or from the market clearing process, *neither of which would be accompanied by a negative supply shock.*

Not all arguments for tariffs are as narrowly focused and shortsighted as the contention that they stimulate total employment and output. Another rationale is in **retaliation** for tariffs imposed by other nations. If this threat has the desired effect of causing repeal of the other country's tariff, then it will actually restore the gains of free trade. But if it does not succeed in forcing tariff reductions abroad, it will only deepen the losses to both countries by further limiting the gains from specialization and trade. The same reasoning applies to *economic boycotts,* an extreme case of trade restriction which uses "economic warfare" instead of (or in addition to) military action. If the boycott accomplishes the desired political goal, the restrictions are dropped and free trade restored. If it fails, as is typically the case, all parties to the boycott share in the costs of lost trade.

There are other reasons that we might knowingly and responsibly support some restrictions on free trade. But these involve very specific situations relating to **national defense, "infant" industries,** and decreasing cost industries known as **natural monopolies.** The important thing about each is that they lead to *very limited* amounts of trade restriction. Protecting industries that produce materials crucial to our ability to defend our nation is obviously sensible and legitimate. The advantages surely outweigh the costs. Similarly, protecting fledgling industries that promise to soon stand on their own—without tariffs—is easily justified. In fact, it is entirely consistent with the notion of comparative advantage.

In practice, however, these arguments are repeatedly used by special interest groups trying, knowingly or not, to further their own interests at consumer expense while invoking specious arguments of "national defense," "infant industry," or "natural monopoly." We would all like to have our chosen career protected from competition—all competition if possible, but at least from those who seem so "foreign." Having a guaranteed demand for our services at a good income would certainly benefit each of us. But what's attractive to each would spell disaster if given to all. It would freeze resources in current uses and make them impervious to *competition* and to changes in *preferences* and *technology*—the three driving forces behind economic growth. In short, the law of comparative advantage tells us that trade restrictions are more costly to all than they are beneficial to some. They betray the growth of opportunities promised by the market system.

Arguments for restricting trade may take a variety of other forms. For example, all nations define categories of illicit goods or services that are not permitted legal entry into the country. We may also put restrictions on goods that, while acceptable themselves, are produced under conditions that are regarded as unacceptable. So we may try to exclude the importation of commodities produced with the use of child labor or in ways that cause serious environmental damage. Economics, of course, can't say whether we should or should not impose such moral restrictions on trade. But it does tell us something very important—that the extent to which we choose to make such restrictions will be reflected in reductions in our standard of living.

IN SUMMARY . . .

Tariffs and Trade

When the mutual gains from trade (to buyer and low-cost seller) are reduced by a tariff on imports, the following events are set in motion.

1. The tariff reduces demand for foreign imports, increasing our demand for domestic products and thereby expanding our *IS* and *AD* curves and causing a short-run stimulus to real output.

2. By reducing the exports of other nations, our tariff contracts their *IS* and *AD* curves causing a short run drop in their real output.

3. As resources within both nations flow from efficient to less efficient protected industries, the productive potential of both nations shrinks $(-\Delta PPF$ and $-\Delta AS^*)$.

4. If retaliation ensues, shifts in aggregate demand across countries will tend to offset one another. But each new round of trade restrictions means yet another negative supply shock. The principal casualty of such trade wars is the mutual benefits of free trade, i.e., the standard of living in all nations.

5. While ending these barriers will increase the overall standard of living in both countries, it will also hurt the industries that have been protected from more efficient competitors. As this monopoly power is lost, sales and employment in these industries will diminish.

6. But we can't have it both ways! When we isolate parts of the economy from competition (by tariffs or any other means), we *all* pay the bill as consumers. As more so-called economic security is thus legislated, the only *real* guarantee of economic health—vigorous, relatively unrestricted trade—is increasingly hindered from doing its job of creating the "wealth of nations." An extreme example of trade restrictions—both domestic and international—is the so-called "planned economy" (characteristic of the former Soviet Union and its Eastern European satellites for much of the twentieth century), now a generally acknowledged failure in its attempt to achieve economic security and economic equality.

7.4 IS "FREE TRADE" ALSO "FAIR TRADE"?

Suppose a nation, newly converted to the logic of free trade, takes steps to dismantle its existing tariffs, quotas, and subsidies (with appropriate but limited exceptions for illicit goods, national defense, infant industry, and natural monopoly cases). The transition must inevitably be painful for those losing government protection from competition. But we have seen that the overall gain from reallocating our resources to areas in which they have a comparative advantage will be larger than the losses to particular groups. To what extent a portion of the overall gains should be transferred to compensate those harmed by the change is a contentious political issue. However that is decided, the principle of comparative advantage tells us that the movement toward free trade is a clear net economic gain to the economy.

But sometimes this fundamental insight about the gains from trade is pushed aside by the argument that what we really want is *"fair* trade" not just "free trade." The reasoning is that if we move toward free trade but our trading partners don't, this puts us at a competitive disadvantage. Specifically, if other countries keep tariff barriers against our exports while subsidizing their own exports to us, this is said to constitute "unfair" competition to our domestic producers who have to survive without public help. The implication is that we should match the trade restrictions of other nations in order to ensure a "level playing field" for our producers.

Economic analysis sheds little light on the issue of "fairness," because our subjective views of what is fair often depend on where we're standing. If you're a widget producer facing competition from foreign widget makers who receive government subsidies, you will naturally see this as unfair and you may ask the government to tax widget imports by at least enough to offset those subsidies. But if the government agrees and imposes a widget tariff in the name of "fair" trade, domestic widget consumers will now have to pay a higher price in the name of "fair" trade. What is "fair" for you has come from the pay checks of your customers and has lowered their overall purchasing power and hence standard of living. Whether this should be labeled "fair" or "unfair," then, is debatable.

However, economic analysis *can* demonstrate that the tariff must result in a net loss in our overall standard of living since it cuts off some of the gains from trade. When a foreign government decides to forgo the gains from free trade, it imposes a cost on its consumers and taxpayers in order to confer benefits on the protected industry. If a foreign government actually subsidizes that industry then, ironically, it is also subsidizing the American consumer through lower prices. By retaliating in the name of "fairness" we just deepen our losses (and theirs) by losing more gains from trade. Only if our retaliation convinces them to drop their restrictions could this "fair trade" strategy improve matters for us. Otherwise, it will further diminish our overall standard of living by keeping resources in an area which cannot meet the prices of its foreign competitors.

☞ 7.5 TRADING CURRENCIES: THE FOREIGN EXCHANGE MARKET

Perhaps the single most useful lesson to learn about international trade is that the underlying economics is fundamentally no different than for any other economic exchange. Buyers and sellers seek to make a deal that is mutually beneficial, just as they would if we existed in a "closed" economy where trade must stay within economically arbitrary geographic borders. Opening up these boundaries doesn't change the motives or mechanics of economic exchange; it merely expands the range of specialization and competition, further increasing the potential gains from trade.

But although the fundamentals remain the same, there are some obvious differences. Our *nationalistic orientation* leads us to think in terms of "us" and "them," something that is present but much less pronounced in trades within countries even where distinct geographic and cultural differences exist. Nationalism is a political not an economic trait, but when it erupts into tariffs, trade wars, boycotts, or military conflict it affects economic policy and the country's material well-being.[5]

A second difference between domestic and international trade stems from the

---

[5] The continuing upheaval in the former Soviet Union and the former Yugoslavia is a vivid example of the power of nationalistic yearnings. The unresolved tensions in the Middle East, in Ireland, and many other parts of the world remind us that millions are prepared to pay a huge economic price—even their lives—to restore or retain a national identity.

first: most nations want control over their own money supply. So the international trade of goods and services necessitates trade across *different currencies*. Put another way, wc "speak" different economic languages. Here it's dollars, in Japan yen, lira in Italy, and pesos in Mexico. So before the gains from trade can be realized, there must be a translation across currencies: 100 yen "means" one dollar, as does 1600 lira, 5 francs, 1.36 Canadian dollars, though these ratios change continually in an institutional setting of **flexible exchange rates.** This is where the **foreign exchange market,** a ubiquitous collection of buyers and sellers of the worlds' currencies, comes into play. In a world of many different monies, an effective international currency market is a precondition to realizing the full gains from international trade.

The integral role played by the foreign exchange market is illustrated in Figure 7.8. For simplicity we look at trade between just two nations—Japan and the United States. But the same principles extend to trade among any number of nations and we could just as well encompass all U.S. foreign transactions by replacing Japan with a "Rest of the World" in the diagram. The flow of goods and services and securities (bonds, stocks, and other assets) are represented by the large outside arrows. These are paid for with domestic currency which is then transformed into "foreign exchange" as shown by the arrows to the foreign exchange market. For example, U.S. purchases of Japanese goods and services or securities necessitate a conversion of dollars into yen. That is, the transactions in the top arrow are paid for by the currency flows represented by the interior arrows connecting the U.S. to Japan via the foreign exchange market. Our demand for their goods, services, and securities is revealed in the supply of dollars ($S^\$$) offered in exchange. In other words, our dollar supply is essentially a demand for yen ($D^\yen$) to pay Japanese producers, in their own currency, for our imports.

The reasoning is identical for U.S. goods, services, and securities purchased by Japan. The bottom arrow shows the flow of output and securities from the U.S. to

■ FIGURE 7.8

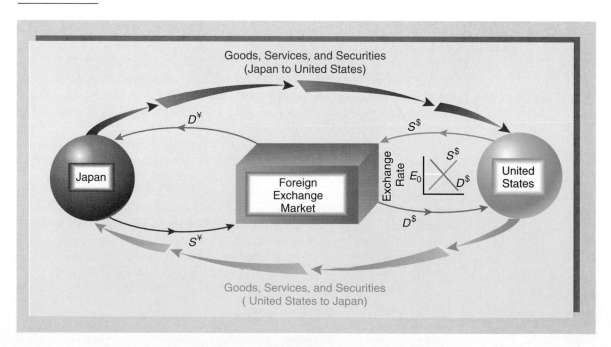

Trade Flows and the Foreign Exchange Market

Japan. It is matched by the return arrows that transform Japanese payments ($S^{¥}$) into a demand for dollars ($D^{\$}$) via the foreign exchange market. The foreign exchange market is an intermediary that converts one currency into another. It functions much like the translators at the United Nations. Both provide services, for a fee, that wouldn't be necessary if we all used a common currency and a common language.

Out of these cross-country transactions comes the international value of the dollar, illustrated here in relation to the Japanese yen. Specifically, the **nominal exchange rate** between the yen and the dollar (defined as $E = ¥/\$$) depends on the supply of dollars ($S^{\$}$) and the demand for dollars ($D^{\$}$), shown in the interior graph of Figure 7.8 and then expanded in Figure 7.9.[6] Because the supply and demand for dollars reflect the demands for goods, services, and securities between the two countries, the exchange rate (E) between the dollar and the yen is influenced by anything that affects our demand for their exports or their demand for ours. Beginning on the $S^{\$}$ curve (Figure 7.9) with a yen per dollar rate of E_0, suppose the exchange rate doubles to $2E_0$. With twice as many yen for a dollar (say, 200 rather than 100), Japanese merchandise then becomes half as expensive to us. This leads us to buy more of their products, supplying more dollars as the exchange rate rises. The result is an upward sloping supply of dollars curve.

From Japan's perspective this rise in the U.S. exchange rate means a drop in the value of their currency. They must now give up twice as many yen to buy the same amount of U.S. merchandise. Accordingly their demand for our goods drops as will the number of dollars they demand. Hence, the demand for dollars curve is downward sloping.

The familiar mechanics of supply and demand operate here to determine an

■ FIGURE 7.9

The nominal exchange rate ($E = ¥/\$$) depends on (1) U.S. supply of dollars ($S^{\$}$) to pay for imports from Japan and (2) Japanese demand for dollars ($D^{\$}$) to pay for their imports from the U.S.

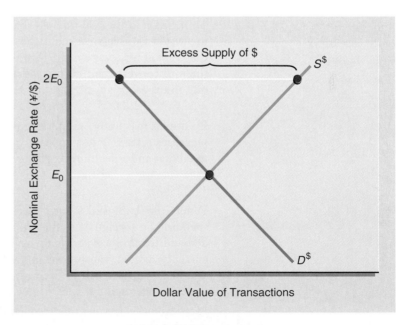

Foreign Exchange Market
for Dollars and Yen

[6] This discussion is about the supply and demand for dollars *on the foreign exchange market*, to be used to purchase imports from other countries. Be careful not to confuse it with the domestic supply of money (M_0) by the Central Bank or the demand for money to hold as an asset (described by $L/P = j_0 + j_1 y - j_2 r$).

equilibrium exchange rate at which the quantity demanded is equated with the quantity supplied. For example, the excess supply at $2E_0$ leads to a fall in the yen/dollar rate until equilibrium is established at the intersection of supply and demand, shown at E_0 in Figure 7.9. The nominal exchange rate is simply the terms of trade between two currencies. Like any other market price, it is determined by the underlying conditions affecting buyers and sellers. Though it's not drawn in the graph, you can see from Figure 7.9 that anything that increased the international demand for dollars (causing the $D^\$$ curve to shift to the right) would also raise the equilibrium exchange rate $(+\Delta E)$, an outcome known as **appreciation** of the dollar. Events that decreased the international demand for dollars (shifting the $D^\$$ curve to the left) would lower the equilibrium exchange rate $(-\Delta E)$, a **depreciation** of the dollar. In the same way, an increase in the supply of dollars on the foreign exchange market would mean an outward shift in the $S^\$$ curve, causing the exchange rate to depreciate. Similarly, anything that caused a $-\Delta S^\$$ would cause the equilibrium exchange rate to appreciate.

There are many different events that could result in such shifts of the $D^\$$ and $S^\$$ curves. Anything that alters *our demand for foreign goods*, services, or securities will change the supply of dollars. Any change in *foreign demand for U.S. goods, services, or securities* will change the demand for dollars. But rather than trying to itemize a long list of specific events, let's look at four broad categories that commonly shift the $D^\$$ or the $S^\$$ and thereby alter international exchange rates: (1) changing real interest rates; (2) changing real incomes; (3) changing consumer preferences, producer technologies and trade restrictions; and (4) changing price levels. The impact of these events on the nominal exchange rate is straightforward, so a few examples should suffice.

1. *Real Interest Rates*

   - An increase in the real interest rate in the U.S. will attract funds from around the world as savers seek out the highest returns (for whatever level of risk they're willing to assume). To buy U.S. bonds and other securities requires them to convert their currencies into dollars, shifting the demand for dollars out and causing an increase in the international value of the dollar $(+\Delta r \Rightarrow +\Delta D^\$ \Rightarrow +\Delta E)$.

   - By similar reasoning, an increase in real interest rates in Japan will make U.S. securities relatively less appealing and lead to a reduction in the demand for the dollar and a declining exchange rate.

2. *Real Incomes*

   - When the U.S. slides into recession, declining real income reduces our spending on foreign as well as domestic goods and services. This drop in the demand for imports shows up as a reduction in the supply of dollars on the currency market, causing the international value of the dollar to rise $(-\Delta y \Rightarrow -\Delta S^\$ \Rightarrow +\Delta E)$. In the same way, real income growth would mean a drop in the exchange rate.

   - A recession in Japan would reduce their demand for U.S. exports and hence contract the demand for dollars, leading to a fall in the international value of the dollar.

3. *Consumer Preferences, Producer Technologies, and Trade Restrictions*

   - This is a catch-all category, encompassing an array of events. Changing consumer tastes lead to increases in the exports of some nations and decreases of others. This will obviously show up in the demand for their currencies and hence in their exchange rates.

- Technical innovations that increase productive efficiency will increase the demand for that nation's currency, pushing up its rate of exchange.
- A tariff or other trade restriction that results in fewer imports means a reduced supply of currency on the exchange market and, other things the same, causes that nation's currency to appreciate. Retaliation by the trading partner would push the exchange rate in the opposite direction.

4. Level of Prices

- A final important influence on the international exchange rate is the purchasing power of the currency as reflected in the domestic price level. A rising price level, other things the same, reduces the real value of the currency and this will not go unnoticed by foreign purchasers of our goods and services. Hence rising inflation in the United States will make our goods less competitive internationally and this will show up in currency markets as a decreasing demand for the dollar. In other words, there will be a depreciation of the dollar internationally to match its declining value domestically ($+\Delta P \Rightarrow -\Delta D^\$ \Rightarrow -\Delta E$).
- Similarly, an increase in the price level in Japan would cause us to supply fewer dollars as we reduce our demand both for their goods and their currency. The result would be an increase in the value of the dollar relative to the yen ($+\Delta P^J \Rightarrow -\Delta S^\$ \Rightarrow +\Delta E$).

This discussion of the influence of relative price levels (or inflation rates) on international currency levels brings us to an important distinction between *nominal* and *real* values. The market rate of exchange between two currencies (E) is known as the "nominal" exchange rate because it compares currencies at their face value rather than their purchasing power over goods and services. Common sense and an abundance of empirical evidence tell us that currency traders are primarily concerned not with how many units of currency they get but with how much foreign purchasing power those units represent. In other words, we presume that it is the goods and services themselves that are of interest, not the currencies that are used to trade for them. So what we seek is a concept of the **real exchange rate** that captures the relative purchasing powers of two currencies. This requires us to deflate the dollar by the U.S. price level (P) and the yen by the price level in Japan (P^J), yielding the "real" yen/dollar exchange rate as

$$e = \frac{¥/P^J}{\$/P}$$

Because the nominal exchange rate is $E = ¥/\$$, we can simplify by substitution and write the real exchange rate as [$e = E(P/P^J)$].

Thus, the real exchange rate [$e = E(P/P^J)$] between the dollar and the yen equals the nominal exchange rate (E) adjusted for the U.S. price level (P) relative to the price level in Japan (P^J). Although the nominal exchange rate (E) tells us the *relative value of two currencies*—that is, how many of their "pieces of paper" can be purchased with one of ours, the real exchange rate (e) tells us the *relative value of traded goods* between the two countries. When the nominal exchange rate rises we only know that we get more yen for a dollar. An increase in the real exchange rate, on the other hand, tells us that a dollar buys more Japanese goods and services than it did before.

A final point will complete our basic understanding of exchange rates. We've seen that changes in any of the four categories listed above (real interest rates, real incomes, consumer preferences, and price levels) can alter the demand or supply of dollars and change the nominal exchange rate (E). Is every change in the nominal rate also a change in the real rate? A little thought should lead you to the conclusion that the first three categories affect not only the nominal but also the real value of the dollar internationally. A rise in the exchange rate from any of those sources will make foreign *goods*, not just currencies, cheaper in terms of dollars.

But the fourth category—changes in the price level—is different. Suppose the U.S. price level doubled while prices in Japan stayed constant. We saw above that Japanese demanders of dollars will reduce their demand for dollars as the dollar loses purchasing power and the nominal exchange rate will fall. Because traders' goals are in terms of purchasing power and real values, it's reasonable to suppose that this doubling of our price level ($P \Rightarrow 2P$) will be fully incorporated into the nominal exchange rate so that it will fall to just half its previous level ($E \Rightarrow \frac{1}{2}E$), leaving the real value of the dollar relative to the yen ($e = \frac{1}{2}E \cdot 2P/P^J$) unchanged.[7]

We conclude that all changes in the nominal exchange rate are also changes in the real exchange rate *except* for changes in the relative price levels between the two nations. Changes in price levels and hence the domestic purchasing power of currencies are quickly reflected in offsetting changes of the nominal exchange rate, leaving international currency values unchanged in real value. In terms of the equation $e = E(P/P^J)$, $\Delta(P/P^J)$ creates an equal and opposite ΔE restoring e to its initial level.

7.6 INTEREST RATES, EXCHANGE RATES, AND "TWIN DEFICITS"

In earlier chapters we saw that it was *real* output and the *real* interest rate, not their nominal values, that concerned decision makers. And for similar reasons, as we've just seen, it's the real rather than the nominal exchange rate that is of primary interest. A glance back at Figure 7.5 shows that the real exchange rate in the U.S. has changed often and sometimes dramatically in recent years. Of the three broad influences on real exchange rates (categories 1–3 in the previous section), one has been particularly prominent—the linkage between the real interest rate in the United States (r) and the real value of the dollar on foreign exchange markets (e). The graph in Figure 7.10 shows annual averages of both variables since 1973 and it's apparent that their paths have been similar.

This relationship between the real exchange rate and the real interest rate is actually something that we have been using in our analytics for many chapters. It was quietly incorporated in the *AD/AS* model way back in Chapter 3 through the net export relationship: $x = x_0 - x_1y - x_2r$. Remember that the last term of this equation captured the hypothesis that a rise in the real interest rate diminishes ("crowds out")

[7] To the extent that the nominal exchange rate (E) fell less than half, the United States would end up with increased international purchasing power and the Japanese with less ($+\Delta e$). Because information on national inflation rates is easily available and international currency markets are notably quick to process relevant new data, it's unlikely that such a partial adjustment would remain for long.

Real Exchange Rate and Real Interest Rate

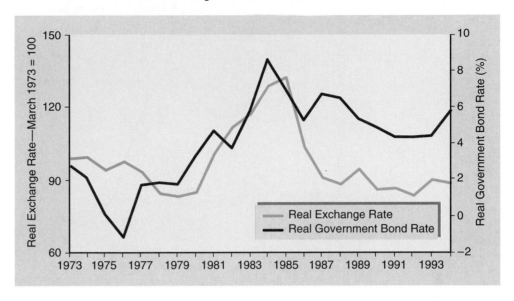

■ FIGURE 7.10

net exports. We have now added what was noted only in passing then—the real exchange rate is the "missing link" between rising real interest rates and falling net exports, ie., $+\Delta r \Rightarrow +\Delta D^\$ \Rightarrow +\Delta e \Rightarrow -\Delta x$. Figure 7.10 looks at the first links in this chain, showing that the real interest rate (r) and the real exchange rate (e) have tended to move together in recent years.

Some evidence on the final link—the inverse relationship between e and x—is presented in the graph of Figure 7.11. Though the statistical correspondence is not as strong here, it is still apparent that low real interest rates occurred in years with relatively high net exports and that as the real interest rate climbed in the first half of the 1980s, net exports plummeted.[8] This is just what common sense tells us once we get a grasp on how international transactions come into play. Remember that the outside arrows in our trade flows (Figure 7.8) represented imports of goods and services as well as *securities*—purchases of financial instruments or physical capital, including corporate and government bonds, stocks, and real estate. For example, although foreign purchasers may not choose to buy as many of our goods and services

<hr/>

[8] Although it's nice to be able to look at the movement of two variables over time and have the graph confirm our hypothesis about how they're related, it's important to understand that such a picture really *proves* nothing. Moreover, even if the graph showed values that were not predicted—say we discovered the real interest rate and the real exchange rate went in opposite directions or just moved about in apparently unrelated, random ways—this would not be sufficient reason to reject the hypothesis that they were positively related. This may sound baffling at first, but it's really quite simple. Macroeconomics is about interactions among *many* different variables. Although it may be true that, *other things the same*, a rise in the real interest rate causes a rise in the real exchange rate, it is a rare circumstance in the life of any macroeconomy when "other things" have in fact stayed conveniently the same. At best, it might happen that other things have moved in such a way as to more or less cancel each other's impacts, exposing, essentially by accident, the particular relationship we were looking for. This issue will be taken up in Chapter 15 as we discuss some statistical techniques for unraveling the many interactions within a simultaneous system.

Real Exchange Rate and Net Exports, 1973–1994

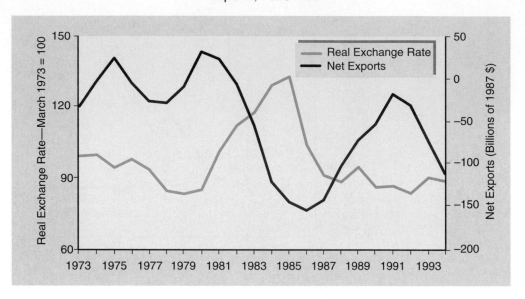

■ FIGURE 7.11

as we buy from them, they could decide to use those "excess dollars"—represented by the balance of trade deficit—to purchase our bonds. In so doing, they are essentially making a loan to the U.S. economy by converting those dollars from immediate claims to our goods and services into securities that represent claims on *future* goods and services.

Many different forces come to bear on this issue of a balance of trade deficit and they will be carefully developed in the following sections. Our immediate interest is in the connection between government deficits and trade deficits, a relationship that has come to be called the "twin deficits" and is commonly applied to U.S. experience in recent years. The story begins with a rise in the government deficit in the 1980s. We've seen that such a rising structural deficit (i.e., the result of expansionary fiscal actions rather than cyclical decline) shows up in an increased real rate of interest (outward shifts in *IS* and *AD* in our model).[9] By making it more expensive to borrow, higher real interest rates crowd out some private investment spending ($+\Delta r \Rightarrow -\Delta i$) at the same time that they attract savings from other countries. In the 1980s, foreigners (individuals, financial institutions, and even governments) bought our bonds and other securities in record amounts.

Because this required them to first convert their currencies into dollars, the surge in the demand for dollars caused a similar surge in the nominal and real value

---

[9] Advocates of the "tax discounting" hypothesis, it should be noted, do not accept this characterization. They argue that the rising deficit had little impact on the *IS* curve and real interest rates because individuals offset the dissaving of the government with higher private saving. Any observed change in the real interest rate, this view says, could not have come from the rising structural deficit.

of the dollar on international exchange markets. With the international purchasing power of the dollar rising, foreign goods became increasingly cheaper to U.S. consumers, leading to the steep rise in imports in the Eighties [see Figure 7.1(a)]. At the same time, the dollar became more expensive in terms of other currencies, making U.S. exports increasingly less attractive and leading to a decline in exports. Together, falling exports and rising imports meant a plunge in net exports for the U.S. (Figure 7.3). Foreigners were holding a record fraction of the dollars we spent on imports as claims against our future production rather than exercising those claims to buy our current output.

This story began with a rise in one deficit ($+\Delta b$) and ended with the rise of another ($-\Delta x$). Our almost irresistible reaction to these rising "twin deficits" is one of concern as we picture a nation embarked on a private and public consumption binge that leads us deeper and deeper into debt, an increasing portion of it owed not to ourselves but to other nations. Such a view may or may not be appropriate, the point to which we now turn.

IN SUMMARY . . .

The "Twin Deficits"

Let's summarize the relationships between interest rates, exchange rates, net exports, and trade deficits using U.S. experience since 1980 as an example.

1. The substantial increase in the government's structural cash flow deficit in the early 1980s ($+\Delta b$) increased the real rate of interest.

2. With interest rates climbing relative to those of other countries, the United States became a magnet for saving from all over the world.

3. To buy into these high yields, foreigners had to first buy dollars on the foreign exchange market ($+\Delta D^{\$}$), thereby forcing up the real value of the dollar ($+\Delta e$).

4. This, in turn, raised the price of our exports to foreign buyers since a dollar now traded for more units of their currencies. At the same time, a stronger dollar lowered the cost of imports to U.S. consumers because their money now commanded more yen and francs and pesos. The resulting plunge in net exports ($-\Delta x$) was essentially just the international overflow of our rising federal deficit. We were allowing the rest of the world to participate in our increased willingness to borrow, privately and publicly.

It is this rather extended linkage—from rising government deficit to rising real interest rate to rising real exchange rate to falling net exports—that underlies the phrase "twin deficits," which is often applied to the U.S. situation in the 1980s and early 1990s. More concisely, we can restate this as $+\Delta b \Rightarrow +\Delta r \Rightarrow +\Delta D^{\$} \Rightarrow +\Delta e \Rightarrow -\Delta x$, where $+\Delta b$ and $-\Delta x$ signify the rising "twin" deficits.

ᏩᏋ 7.7 *BALANCE AND*
IMBALANCE IN FOREIGN TRADE

In an important definitional sense, trade flows *always* "balance" since goods and services exchange for an equivalent payment.[10] This is as true for international as for domestic trade. But the presence of national political boundaries creates an interest in "who sold what to whom?" that is reflected in the considerable detail of the **balance of payments accounts.** We want to know the country and amount involved; whether the trade was with an individual, business, or government agency; and, especially, whether payment was made now—on **current account**—or whether it involved a promise to pay later—making it a **capital account** transaction.

Fortunately, a general understanding of the macroeconomics of international trade does not require us to learn all the details of balance of payments accounting. We need only establish a connection between the key balance of payments categories—*current* and *capital account*—and the *net export term* that we have been using all along in the *AD/AS* model. While this is a somewhat tedious process, it yields some useful insights into issues of both world trade and economic growth.

Let's start with the familiar division of output among expenditures on consumption, investment, net exports, and government: $y = c + i + x + g$. Because every dollar spent on output is received by someone as income, we can also express income/output in terms of how it's used by its recipients. A significant part of our income goes to pay *taxes* (t), of course. Most of the rest is spent on *consumption* (c), and whatever's left is defined as *private saving* (s). In short, $y = c + s + t$. Setting these two different ways of accounting for the same thing equal:

$$c + i + x + g \equiv c + s + t$$

and subtracting c from both sides,

$$i + x + g \equiv s + t$$

Rearranging terms in a way that will prove to be useful,

$$i + (g - t) - s + x \equiv 0 \text{ or, because } b = g - t, \text{ then}$$
$$i - (s - b) + x \equiv 0$$

You might find it tempting to solve this equation for one of the variables, say x or i, expressing it in terms of the others. The best advice is *don't!* Provided it's done correctly there's obviously nothing wrong with the algebra of such a rearrangement. But it can easily lead to confusion concerning economic cause and effect. Remember that we *already* have theories of net exports and investment in the equations underlying the *AD/AS* model ($x = x_0 - x_1 y - x_2 r$ and $i = i_0 - i_2 r$). An essential message of macroeconomic analysis is that these and all other dependent (endogenous) variables are jointly determined, hence interdependent. Events or policies that change any one of them will generally change several others. Hence it's erroneous to think of the above equation as a theory of investment $i \equiv s - b + x$, using it to conclude, for ex-

---

[10] When no payment is received the transaction is called a *transfer* as when a gift or donation is made. The transfer payment doesn't change the two-way nature of trade, it just assigns the income from a trade to another party. When you make a charitable contribution, for example, you will trade your labor services for income, but you allow someone else to spend part of your earnings. As we saw in the discussion of government transfer payments, transfers do not add to total output or income, they merely redistribute them.

ample, that an increase in the government deficit $(+\Delta b)$ must mean an equal decline in private investment $(-\Delta i)$. All four of the variables in the equation are potentially interrelated and we need to use the full *AD/AS* model to predict how an increase in the public deficit will be spread over the other three.[11]

If the "balance of payments" equation above is not the simple substitute for the complete model that it at first appears to be, why use it at all? The reason is that it gives a clear picture of otherwise hard to spot links among an economy's balance of payments, net exports, investment, and public and private saving. Let's begin by noting that the term $(s - b)$ is actually a measure of **national saving**. Because the government cash flow deficit (b) is just the dissaving of the public sector, we can represent total saving—private plus public—for the macroeconomy as $(s - b)$.[12] Representing national saving by *ns*, we can rewrite this relationship as

$$(i - ns) + x \equiv 0, \text{ where } ns \equiv s - b$$

This accounting identity tells us that net investment minus national saving plus net exports *must always* equal zero, for every economy at any time. Put another way, it describes a balance across the **capital account** $(i - ns)$ and the **current account** (x).[13] It tells us that

1. A capital account surplus always requires an offsetting current account deficit, $i - ns > 0 \Rightarrow x < 0$.

2. A capital account deficit always requires a matching current account surplus, $i - ns < 0 \Rightarrow x > 0$.

3. Balance in one is necessarily balance in the other, $i - ns = 0 \Rightarrow x = 0$.

It's important to see how these results come from manipulating the equations, but even more important to understand what they mean in economic terms. Looking at U.S. data for 1987, the peak of our balance of trade deficit, imports of $507.1 billion far exceeded the $364 billion in exports, leaving a net export balance for the year of $$-143.1$ billion. That is, we paid for $364 billion of our imports with exports of goods and services. The remaining $143.1 billion was essentially paid with IOUs (securities)—promises to pay future goods and services (plus interest). This willingness of foreigners (individuals, businesses, and governments) to hold "claims" rather than to demand current goods and services gave us the *capital inflow* that allowed our domestic investment spending to exceed our national saving $(i - ns > 0)$ by $143.1 billion.

In contrast, Japanese exports exceeded imports by $87.0 billion in 1987. That is, the Japanese paid for all their imports (with exports) and then sold an additional

---

[11] For example, we know that an increasing structural deficit will generally cause a rise in the real rate of interest, reducing both investment and net exports. Moreover, to the extent that there is tax discounting behavior it might also reduce consumption and increase saving. In a world of full tax discounting, a tax reduction would cause private saving to rise to match the higher deficit (future taxes), leaving both investment and net exports unaffected.

[12] If the government were running a budget *surplus*, this negative deficit would, of course, be *added* to private saving instead of subtracted.

[13] Actually the balance of payments accounts also includes a third category—Official Reserve Transactions—that reflects sales and purchases of foreign currency by the government itself. This is relatively insignificant when the exchange rate is "floating" as it has been for the dollar for two decades. In addition, while equating "net exports" with the "current account," as we do here, is generally correct it is not literally accurate. The current account of the balance of payments treats a few items differently than does the national income accounting for exports and imports. Fortunately, we can ignore these details and still understand the important ways in which foreign trade influences macroeconomic activity. Two relatively painless and useful treatments of these issues are Norman Frumkin, *Tracking America's Economy*, 2nd ed. (Armonk, N.Y.: M. E. Sharpe, Inc., 1992) and *The Economist Guide to Global Economic Indicators* (New York: The Economist Books/John Wiley & Sons, 1994).

$87 billion in goods and services abroad in return for other countries' securities. Japan's current account surplus was the mirror image of its capital account deficit. As a net lender to the rest of the world, it had a net *capital outflow*.

The important result in all of this is that the level of net exports is the same thing as the "current account" surplus or deficit which, in turn, is the mirror image of the "capital account" deficit or surplus. So a country's *current account deficit* is not only the same as its "balance of trade deficit" ($x < 0$) but necessarily means that it has a *capital account surplus*. As in our earlier discussion of the government budget deficit, we've again discovered that our instinctive aversion to a trade deficit (capital account surplus) represents an incomplete understanding of the issues involved.

✆ 7.8 HOW LONG CAN A TRADE DEFICIT BE SUSTAINED?

Since this isn't the first time we've looked at a "consequences of continued borrowing" issue, we'll build on the intuitive answer given back in Chapter 1 when we discussed a foreign trade deficit under the name of "external borrowing." We saw that borrowing from outside the economy allows an initial movement beyond our national PPF curve, but then requires the payback of both principal and interest as the loan comes due. Whether we wind up better or worse off than before the loan depends not on *who* we borrow from, *how much* we borrow, or *how long* this borrowing persists. The key determinant is simply how the return on the use of these funds compares with the rate of interest paid for them.

We extended this intuition in Chapter 5 by characterizing borrowing (public and private) as either "self-financing," "consumption smoothing," or "consumption draining." In the first two categories, repayment will come from higher expected future income levels either as the result of investment of the borrowed funds themselves ("self-financing") or as a result of other events or choices that result in economic growth ("consumption smoothing"). But if these future payments are *not* matched by higher future incomes, borrowing will then become "consumption draining." Repayment of principal and interest will be drawn from a stagnant income stream, thereby leaving less for future consumption. The very same considerations apply to the case of a trade deficit. A nation cannot continue to borrow externally to support increased spending on current consumption. By accumulating future liabilities without future returns to match, an economy (or individual, business, or government) will eventually find itself in a situation in which its key ratios (debt, deficit, and interest rates relative to income) soar as its future economic outlook dwindles.

In the case of external borrowing there is an important automatic mechanism that often works to limit "excessive" trade deficits. We've seen that a strong economy acts like a magnet in attracting foreign savings to purchase our securities. But an economy pursuing consumption draining activities will experience just the opposite. As more and more of its future output is pledged to creditors, investors will be undertaking increased levels of risk by committing their resources to this future. As a result there is likely to be a drop in foreign demand for that nation's securities and so a corresponding drop in the demand for its currency. As we saw earlier, this will lower its real exchange rate. By raising the cost of imports and lowering the cost of exports, this decline in the real exchange rate will thereby work to reduce the trade deficit/capital inflow of a nation that has pushed its borrowing (internal and external) too far.

Another way to express this result is to say that whether a nation is able to sustain ongoing trade deficits is, in good measure, under the control of decision makers *outside* the country. A politically stable nation with strong economic prospects will inevitably attract savings from abroad. To the extent that this demand for its securities increases the demand for its currency, its real exchange rate must rise. As it does, imports become cheaper and exports more expensive, forcing the economy into larger and larger trade deficits. Remember that the balance of payments identity showed that the *only* way that an economy can have a net capital inflow is through a trade deficit (because $i - ns > 0 \Rightarrow x < 0$). The negative connotations of the word "deficit" are particularly misleading under such circumstances.

7.9 DOES THE FORM OF THE CAPITAL INFLOW MATTER?

We've now established that a balance of trade deficit ($x < 0$) means a net capital inflow (to create $i - ns > 0$) and that such a situation may or may not be sustainable depending on how the borrowed funds are used. Suppose we have a sustainable ("self-financing") foreign trade deficit, driven in good part by foreign demand for our securities that makes imports so inexpensive. Does it matter whether this capital account surplus reflects foreigners purchasing our corporate or government bonds, buying our real estate, acquiring equity in our corporations through the stock market, or actually setting up foreign-owned businesses in our country?

The popular view, and an almost instinctive reaction for most of us, answers, "Of course, it makes a difference!" In particular, **foreign direct investment** in the United States—purchases of U.S.-owned businesses or real estate or the creation of foreign firms in the U.S.—is usually regarded as more threatening than the sale of our bonds to foreign savers. The difference between *foreign lenders* and *foreign owners* seems large and obvious. In one case, it seems, *we* get to decide how the funds are used; in the other, *they* do. As so often in economics, the reality is considerably different than the popular view. In this case it also happens to be more comforting.

First, and most importantly, the focus belongs on how the incoming funds are used by *us*. It's much less important whether we're selling bonds, shares of stock, land for a manufacturing plant, or even Rockefeller Center. In each case, if the receipts are spent on capital goods then the result is an increase in total capital in the United States and no reduction in the amount of domestically owned capital. And even if we borrow to spend on current consumption, the *form* of the inflow has little impact on the outcome—by trading future obligations for current returns, we're digging ourselves into a hole regardless of the type of shovel offered us. The blame, in such a situation, properly lies with our own decision (private or public) to support our consumption on a borrow now/pay later basis. This can be responsibly done within limits ("consumption smoothing") but, like borrowing from any source and in any form, can certainly be misused. Again, the key is not the "source" but the "use" of the funds, and this is under nobody's control but ours.

But even if foreign capital inflows are not "consumption draining," many worry that direct foreign ownership of assets can be harmful to our economic health. In various ways—such as discriminating against our workers, using imported rather than local inputs, or "pirating" our technology—it is feared that rising foreign ownership will leave the U.S. economy vulnerable to outside influence.[14] There are many

---

[14] For discussion of these issues see Cletus C. Coughlin, "Foreign-Owned Companies in the United States: Malign or Benign?" *Review*, The Federal Reserve Bank of St. Louis 74 (May/June 1992) and Edward M. Graham and Paul R. Krugman, *Foreign Direct Investment in the United States* (Institute for International Economics, 1991).

dimensions to this controversy, but the best general response to such concerns is to assume that the overwhelming majority of foreign direct investment in the U.S. occurs for the same reasons that the United States has long invested in other economies—resources flow to take advantage of economic opportunities.

Foreigners invest here because our economy offers a combination of features not available elsewhere. A skilled work force, excellent transportation facilities, many abundant (hence relatively inexpensive) resources, low inflation rates, high real interest rates, and a highly stable political system among others. In short, if we make the reasonable assumption that foreign investors have the same economic goals as us, then the various "conspiracy theories" quickly evaporate. Instead of a flood of economic threats and dangers, we begin to see an outline of the forces of free trade guiding scarce resources to where they are most productive, thus generating the mutually beneficial "gains from trade" that are the main goal and allure of a market system.

✆✆ 7.10 NATIONAL EVENTS— INTERNATIONAL CONSEQUENCES

We've emphasized that the heart of all trade—domestic or international—is mutually beneficial exchange across buyers and sellers. The incentive is the gains from trade that arise when all parties are free to specialize in their areas of comparative advantage. We pursue what we do best and trade with others for what they do best. When this pattern is interrupted and these gains are lost, we become aware of the "down side" of **economic interdependence**—others' actions can hurt us, just as ours can hurt them. In Section 7.2 (Free Trade, Tariffs, and the Macroeconomy) we saw the details of how protectionist policies spread to other nations. Tariffs raise the costs of imports and thereby encourage demand for domestically-produced products, reducing aggregate demand in other nations as their export markets shrink. So the flip side of our short run gain from protectionist action is their loss. This sets the stage for possible retaliatory actions, eliminating our initial gains and leaving a legacy of inefficiency that hurts all nations.

Of course, trade barriers aren't the only way that economic events spread across nations. In fact the fewer the trade restrictions, the more interdependent we become and, like in a family, all members tend to share in the good times as well as the bad. Let's return to the *AD/AS* framework to see how an economic downturn in one nation can affect the well-being of its trading partners. Suppose a major recession, brought on by declining investment and falling consumption demand, starts in economy A as shown in Figure 7.12. With an initial drop in autonomous investment and consumption spending ($-\Delta i_0^A$ and $-\Delta c_0^A$) contracting IS^A and AD^A, both real output and the real interest rate decline as the economy moves initially from points A to A'.

This short run story is familiar to you by now. But let's push it a step further to consider how economy A's decline affects other nations. Remembering that net exports are inversely related to both real output and the real rate of interest, we know that the movement from A to A' means rising net exports for economy A ($\uparrow x^A = x_0 - x_1 y \downarrow - x_2 r \downarrow$). For its trading partner, economy Z, the impact will be just the opposite. Z will see its exports decline due to the drop in A's real income. It will also experience an influx of imports from A as declining interest rates in A cause an appreciation of Z's currency relative to A's. The graphs on the right side of Figure 7.12 picture the events in A—a decline in i_0^A and c_0^A—from the perspective of

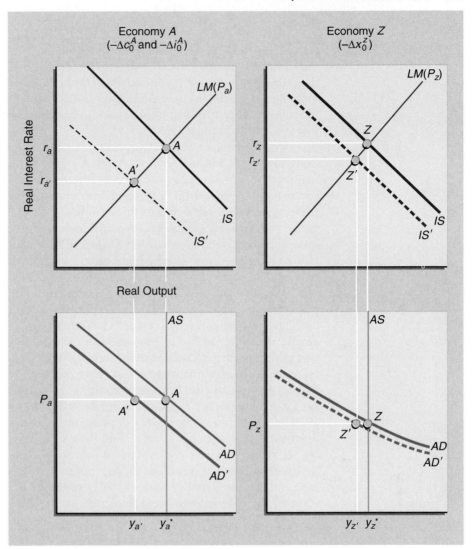

Real Interest Rate

Real Output

Recession Begins in Economy A with $-\Delta c_0^A$ and
$-\Delta i_0^A$ and Finds Its Way to Economy Z through Net
Exports $(-\Delta x_0^Z)$

■ FIGURE 7.12

economy Z. The drop in autonomous net exports $(-\Delta x_0{}^Z)$ means a "sympathetic" inward shift of IS^Z and AD^Z as Z catches a mild case of A's recession through its foreign sector.

If there had been no trade between the two countries, the recession would have stayed entirely in A. In a world of **closed economies,** with neither imports nor exports, the net export term $(x = x_0 - x_1 y - x_2 r)$ simply vanishes, taking with it the primary mechanism linking the fates of different economies. If you're thinking that this suggests turning trade flows off and on, depending on our trading partners' economic health, you're forgetting the nature of the underlying "gains from trade." The reason that a recession in the United States hurts Canada is because some of these *gains* are lost when one economy experiences a downturn. Curtailing or ending economic relationships because they mean sharing in the "downs" as well as the "ups" only insures the loss of all the potential gains from trade. It makes no more sense than ending a mutually beneficial friendship because sometimes its benefits are higher than others. In other contexts, we may characterize such action as "cutting off the nose to spite the face," "throwing the baby out with the bath water," or "a cure that is worse than the disease."

From a happier perspective, remember that if a recession can spread across nations so can an *economic recovery*. As economy *A* returns to full employment, rising real income will cause its purchases of foreign as well as domestic goods to expand, reversing the earlier drop in autonomous net exports in economy *Z*. The "spillovers" from recovery are just as real as those from recession. Most important, the long-term gains from *economic growth* also spread across trading partners. Even economies not experiencing the initial expansion of their PPF and *AS** curves can share in others' rising prosperity through expanding export markets as well as the spread of technology through capital flows.

We have just seen how economic fluctuations and growth spread across trading partners, primarily through the net export term. In the same way, domestic policy changes can sometimes have unintended effects on seemingly distant shores. For example, the combination of expansionary fiscal and contractionary monetary policy that yielded such high real interest rates in the U.S. in the Eighties also caused interest rates to rise in other countries. As higher interest rates here attracted savings from around the world, firms and governments in other nations were forced to compete by paying higher real rates to attract funds for their domestic capital projects.[15] Particularly hard hit were many developing nations with large amounts of external borrowing. As older loans came due, they were forced to refinance at higher and higher rates. This increase in interest payments combined with the devaluations of their currencies relative to the dollar, represented a "ripple effect" from our highly expansionary fiscal policy that was little noted in the United States. Nevertheless, some of the repercussions were felt here as more and more of our loans to developing nations ended in at least partial default.

In a world increasingly linked by international trade, it's hardly news that economic events and policies spread easily across political boundaries. So it's important to be aware that this does not necessarily hold for one major economic event—*inflation*. We've seen (Section 7.5 "Trading Currencies") that in a world of flexible exchange rates, relative changes in inflation rates alter the demand and supply of international exchange but have at most a temporary impact on the *real* exchange rate. For example, rising inflation in the U.S. relative to Japan is likely to mean a drop in the demand for dollars by Japanese and a proportional fall in the nominal value of the dollar relative to the yen, leaving the real exchange rate unchanged $[e = \downarrow E \cdot \uparrow (P/P^J)]$.

If this were not the case and a rise in our price level were not "neutralized" by a falling nominal exchange rate, then the real exchange rate would also rise. With foreign goods cheaper to us and our goods more expensive abroad, our net exports would fall as those of our trading partners' rose. The resulting increase in their ag-

---

[15] In other words, the U.S. economy is sufficiently large that its policies can significantly alter worldwide real interest rates. For smaller nations, the real interest rate is basically a given and is unaffected, except perhaps fleetingly, by even major changes in their economic policies.

gregate demand would eventually push up prices in those countries and the rising U.S. price level would have spread to Japan through the net export term. Both the underlying logic of markets (it's in traders' self-interest to reduce their demands for currencies that are losing domestic purchasing power) and statistical evidence suggest that nominal exchange rates will react to changing relative inflation rates fairly quickly and that we do not have to fear catching inflation through trade.

INTERNATIONAL INTEREST RATE DIFFERENTIALS

Savers, looking for the best yields in an increasingly interconnected and changing world economy, can and do respond quickly to interest rate changes. The resulting potential for large and rapid capital flows across national boundaries leads to a tendency for real interest rate differentials across countries to diminish. This process of convergence—termed **interest rate parity**—is yet another dimension of the interplay between self-interest and free markets, Adam Smith's ubiquitous "invisible hand." As savings flow away from low returns, real interest rates in those nations will begin to rise. In the same way, the influx of savings in areas of high return pushes downward on those rates. This process works across nations no differently than it does across cities or states.

Don't confuse the *convergence of expected real interest rates* with the *equalization of market rates.* Extremely high market (nominal) interest rates, at home or abroad, generally reflect a large premium needed to attract savings to risky ventures. Buying foreign securities involves a risk of **default** and of **unexpected inflation** just as with a domestic security. The greater these two risks, the higher will be the nominal interest rate needed to keep the expected real return competitive with less risky securities. But international capital flows add a third element of uncertainty through potential **changes in the real exchange rate.** Savers lending abroad must first translate into the foreign currency and eventually convert back to their home currency. In a world of flexible exchange rates, this exposes them to **exchange rate risk.** If the purchasing power of the foreign currency falls relative to the home currency, international lenders suffer a capital loss when they reconvert. (If it rises, of course, they welcome the resulting capital gain.) Many Japanese savers who bought U.S. bonds in the late 1980s were unpleasantly surprised by the subsequent drop in the value of the dollar relative to the yen. To illustrate, suppose the nominal exchange rate (E) was 120 yen per dollar when a Japanese investor bought dollars to purchase a government bond yielding 10%. But if the dollar then fell 25% to 90 yen per dollar, the net real return on that investment will be -15%.

Because these three risk factors—default, inflation, and fluctuating real exchange rates—vary over countries and over time, there's no reason to expect the underlying tendency for risk-adjusted real rates to converge (interest rate parity) to also show up as a reduction in disparities between observed market interest rates around the world.

⊙⊙ 7.11 *OVERVIEW*

1. The U.S. economy, with its vast size and rich endowment of resources, has traditionally been far more self-sufficient and much less affected by world economic events than other economies. But in recent decades our interdependence with other economies has grown steadily. The availability of foreign goods and the lure of foreign markets affects our economic lives in many important ways. This chapter explores the nature of this economic interdependence across nations—its sources, its benefits, its costs.

2. International trade continues to grow despite the ever-present resistance of specific groups that stand to lose from foreign competition. And the reason is a simple one—by extending the size of markets and allowing increased specialization, expanded trade promises **gains from trade** that mean a higher overall standard of living to all trading partners. In an important sense, the United States was founded upon the "gains from trade." Among the many freedoms sought by colonists was the economic freedom to trade with minimal interference from the government. In fact it was attempts by Great Britain to limit such trade, through the Townsend Acts and Stamp Acts, that finally ignited a volatile political situation.

3. Although **trade restrictions,** domestic and international, are now at historically low levels in many parts of the world, the struggle between narrow group interests and overall consumer interest is always present. It is a constant source of tension and an ongoing political compromise. Restrictions on foreign imports, usually under the guise of protecting U.S. jobs, can yield a short-run stimulus to aggregate demand. But the lasting legacy is nearly always a contraction of aggregate supply—a negative supply shock. Tariffs, quotas, and other devices for limiting foreign competition work to freeze our domestic resources in relatively inefficient uses. In so doing they prevent our scarce resources from flowing to the areas in which they have a **comparative advantage.**

4. It must be noted that not *all* arguments for trade restrictions reflect the narrow self-interests of certain groups lobbying for protection from more efficient competitors. Retaliation that causes other governments to lower their tariffs or subsidies, protection of national defense interests, incubation for "infant industries" and "natural monopolies" all represent circumstances in which trade restrictions would not automatically mean a net loss to the overall economy. Yet what's most important about these exceptions is how rarely they actually apply in comparison with how often they're invoked. Lobbyists inevitably use them to try to convince politicians that *these* restrictions on trade are really for the good of that dangerous abstraction "the American people." Seldom is this actually the case. Frederic Bastiat's satirical "Petition of the Candlemakers" for protection from the unfair competition of the Sun is a classic exposé of protectionist arguments.

5. All nations have at least some restrictions on trade that extend beyond the categories above and result in a net loss of efficiency and a resulting decline in the overall standard of living. Economics should not be thought of as saying that we *shouldn't* make such restrictions. It only tells us that to the extent we do add these trade barriers, they will be purchased at a cost. Every nation attempts to restrict the importation of what it views as "illicit goods," such as drugs or weapons of mass destruction. Some nations extend this to include legal goods that have been produced in some unacceptable way. The use of child labor, prison labor, or production tech-

niques that cause serious environmental damage have been used to justify restrictions on certain imports into the United States. Economic analysis can't tell us whether we should or should not take such actions. It can help us see the true costs of such moral restrictions.

6. Economic efficiency demands flexibility of resources and this, of course, is a threat to labor or capital that happen to be in the wrong place at the wrong time. Again, economics yields no insights about whether it's "fair" or not for certain groups to be exposed to outside competition from low-wage workers. But it does reveal the underlying issue more clearly and less emotionally. If we decide on political grounds that a particular industry should receive protection from foreign competition, it is the responsibility of economists to remind us not only that this "protection" of one group is paid for by another (consumers or taxpayers), but that on top of it, there is a net output loss as scarce resources are kept in uses in which they do not have a comparative advantage. Put another way, economics can help us see that what may seem "fair" to producers and workers in a particular industry may be quite "unfair" to the less visible consumers and taxpayers who have to pay for any "free lunch" that trade restrictions give special interest groups. Economics also makes us aware of the potential returns to building flexibility into our economic system so that it can adjust to changing preferences and technologies by reallocating its resources as called for by market forces. This has important implications for the design of educational and re-training programs, both public and private.

7. Since most nations choose to issue and control their own currencies, international trade requires someone to make a stop at the foreign exchange market in order to obtain the foreign currency needed to pay for our imports. The rates at which these currencies trade for one another, called **exchange rates,** are determined largely by the forces of supply and demand in the current system of flexible exchange rates. Governments may choose to intervene in this market in order to stabilize the price of their currency (e.g., the United States buying up dollars and selling yen to keep the yen/dollar ratio from sinking too rapidly). But in the current international setting such interventions are relatively limited in both time and magnitude. They are designed to smooth fluctuations rather than alter the equilibrium exchange rates.

8. The **nominal exchange rate** (E) is defined as the number of units of a foreign currency that the domestic currency can buy, e.g. yen per dollar. This rate varies with anything that influences either the demand for dollars by foreigners (to buy our commodities and securities) and our supply of dollars (to buy foreign commodities and securities). The main determinants include (1) relative real interest rates, (2) relative real incomes, (3) consumer preferences, producer technologies, and trade restrictions and (4) relative price levels across countries.

9. Both common sense and factual evidence tell us that our focus here, as elsewhere, should be on "real" rather than "nominal" magnitudes. Hence we define the **real exchange rate** (e) between the yen and dollar as the ratio of the real value of yen ($¥/P^J$) to the real value of the dollar ($\$/P$). The relationship between real and nominal exchange rates is given by $e = E(P/P^J)$.

10. The real exchange rate has fluctuated widely over the years and a primary (but not the only) reason has been fluctuations in relative real interest rates. Higher real interest rates ($+\Delta r$) in the United States in the 1980s increased the demand for the dollar, pushing up both the nominal ($+\Delta E$) and real ($+\Delta e$) exchange rate. The stronger dollar provided a stimulus to U.S. imports while discouraging our exports,

resulting in a sharp decline in net exports $(-\Delta x)$ that further increased the U.S. balance of trade deficit.

11. The **twin deficits** refers to a possible linkage that runs from growing (structural) government deficits $(+\Delta b^{str})$ to rising real interest rates $(+\Delta r)$ and then to increased demand for dollars $(+\Delta D^{\$})$ that causes a rising real exchange rate $(+\Delta e)$ and finally an increased trade deficit (via $-\Delta x$). To the extent that individuals act as *tax discounters*, we've seen that a rising structural deficit due to a tax cut will simply be viewed as a tax postponement. There will be no increase in consumption, no expansionary impact on *IS* and *AD* and so no upward pressure on real interest rates. In these conditions the connection between budget and trade deficits would not exist. To the extent that we act myopically as taxpayers, as seems to be the case, the twin deficit relationship is real.

12. The existence of "twin deficits" is typically interpreted by the media as "double trouble." This is an incomplete and generally distorted picture. Increased twin deficits only tells us that some of the current federal borrowing has been provided by investors who are not citizens of the U.S. They have bought the bonds for the same reason as U.S. consumers, businesses, pension funds and other domestic purchasers—it's a relatively low risk investment offering a competitive rate of return. By drawing on savings in other countries, this will generally mean that we can borrow at lower interest rates than if we had to rely only on the supply of funds from U.S. savers. As we've seen in several contexts, whether borrowing is sustainable or not depends on the rate of return to the use of those funds relative to the interest rate paid for them. The nationality of the lenders is quite unimportant.

13. Balance and imbalance in foreign trade is measured in terms of the international **current** and **capital accounts.** Because it is true by definition that net investment minus national saving plus net exports sum to zero $(i - ns + x \equiv 0)$, a current account deficit $(x < 0)$ necessitates a capital account surplus $(i - ns > 0)$. Whether this is sustainable or not depends, again, on how the borrowed funds are used rather than who they are borrowed from.

14. It is often thought that foreign purchases of our bonds are somehow less threatening than direct foreign ownership of capital in the United States. These worries are largely misplaced and, again, the issue comes down to how the capital inflow is being used, not what particular form it happens to take.

15. It is through imports and exports, hence the net export term $(x = x_0 - x_1 y - x_2 r)$, that national events and policies spread their effects to other economies. For example, a recession in the United States lowers our demand for imports, raising our net exports. But this means a reduction in exports for our trading partners, contracting their aggregate demand and spreading unemployment into their export industries. Economic interdependence, like a marriage, works in good times and in bad.

16. Inflation, unlike other macroeconomic events, does not generally spread through trade. With flexible exchange rates the nominal exchange rate acts as a cushion, keeping changing rates of inflation from having lasting impacts on the crucial *real* exchange rate. As a nation's inflation rate rises, the purchasing power of its currency is reduced, leading to a drop in its demand internationally. The resulting decline in the nominal exchange rate will continue until the higher inflation has been compensated for, leaving the real exchange rate little changed from its preinflation level [i.e., $e = \downarrow E \uparrow (P/P^f)$].

☯ *7.12 REVIEW QUESTIONS*

1. Define the following basic concepts or terms:

Gains from trade	Natural monopoly	Capital account
Trade restrictions	Flexible exchange rates	National saving
Balance of trade deficit	Foreign exchange market	Economic interdependence
Self-sufficiency	Appreciation/depreciation	Arbitrage
Free trade	Nominal exchange rate	Exchange rate risk
Tariff	Real exchange rate	Interest rate parity
Smoot-Hawley Tariff	Balance of payments	
Comparative advantage	Current account	
National defense		
Infant industry		

2. With all the problems associated with international trade (plummeting exchange rates, balance of trade deficits, contagious recessions, and so on) it's almost a wonder that we permit the menace of "free trade" to stalk the economies of the world. Why is it that economists not only accept the existence of free trade, but actually *celebrate* it?

3. Suppose the "Buy American" lobby becomes so powerful that Congress is persuaded to add tariffs and quotas to a large number of imported commodities. Use the *AD/AS* framework to forecast the short and long run impact of this action on our real output, real interest rates, the price level, both the nominal and the real values of the dollar internationally, the balance of trade, and the government deficit.

4. Suppose it is decided that economic policy should be directed toward a significant long run reduction in our balance of trade deficit. The following policies have been suggested; evaluate each one and explain which one is most likely to achieve the goal most efficiently.

   a. A reduction in the federal deficit.

   b. An expansionary monetary policy.

   c. Higher tariffs on foreign goods.

5. Suppose it is a policy goal to increase the real value of the dollar internationally. Evaluate each of the following in terms of their ability to achieve that goal in the long run.

   a. A significant and lasting reduction in the federal deficit.

   b. A rapid increase in the money supply and consequent inflation.

   c. A significant tax subsidy for those who save rather than consume.

6. "We ought to pass a law that would make it illegal for foreigners to hold U.S. government bonds. This would mean that our debt would be held entirely internally and, since we would just owe it to ourselves, there could be no net burden." Evaluate.

7. "The president is in a dilemma. His desire to significantly improve the balance of trade (i.e., increase net exports) over the next few years is in direct opposition to his stated goals of balancing the federal budget, increasing the growth of the capital stock, and strengthening the international value of the dollar." Do you agree with this statement?

8. Suppose the large balance of trade deficit in the United States ($x < 0$) becomes an issue in the election of 2000. All the Presidential candidates are proposing ways to get rid of the "World's Largest Debtor Nation" label.

   a. Candidate A argues that the only sensible way to improve the balance of trade is through monetary policy. He argues that we should make a balanced current account ($x = 0$) a goal for the Federal Reserve to pursue. Would this work?

   b. Candidate B argues that this should be accomplished by fiscal policy instead. Would her strategy work?

   c. Candidate Z shocks everyone by arguing that there's no good economic reason for trying to eliminate a balance of trade deficit. Is he just joking or is there any economic rationale behind this view?

9. "It is as natural that the U.S. should import savings from countries that are good at saving as that we should import coffee from countries that are good at producing coffee. Even if this means that our balance of trade deficit gets worse and worse, any attempt to interfere with it would be improper and unwise." Evaluate.

10. "The great thing about specialization and trade is that it expands our potential standard of living. But the still greater problem is that free trade, while wonderful for the winners, leaves the losers not only economically weak but subservient to the winners. In reality, we need to include some economic protection for the losers if we want to reap the *net* gains promised by international trade." Do you agree or disagree? Give a full evaluation of this statement and explain your reasoning.

11. Your rich uncle is convinced that the trend toward less restrictions on international trade is about to end and that the rest of the Nineties will see round after round of tariffs and subsidies designed to increase one nation's advantage at the expense of the others. Knowing of your interest and training in economics, he has set up a fund of $1,000,000 for you to manage in a way that would take advantage of his virtual certainty of a coming round of trade wars and a reduction in the volume of world trade. Use your understanding of the macroeconomy to devise a strategy for maximizing his return by appropriate investments—both stocks and bonds—in the U.S. economy. Assume his forecast, which differs completely from current conventional predictions, nevertheless comes true. Explain your reasoning.

✆ 7.13 FURTHER READING

FREDERIC BASTIAT, *Economic Sophisms* (Princeton: Van Nostrand Company, 1964).
The Economist Guide to Global Economic Indicators (New York: The Economist Books/John Wiley, 1994).
PAUL KRUGMAN, *The Age of Diminished Expectations* rev. and updated ed. (Cambridge: The MIT Press, 1994).
ROBERT Z. LAWRENCE AND CHARLES L. SCHULTZE, ed., *An American Trade Strategy: Options for the 1990s* (Washington, D.C.: The Brookings Institution, 1990).
RUSSELL D. ROBERTS, *The Choice: A Fable of Free Trade and Protectionism* (Englewood Cliffs, N.J.: Prentice Hall, 1994).
PAUL VOLCKER AND TOYOO GYOHTEN, *Changing Fortunes* (New York: Times Books, 1992).

PART III

Smoothing Business Cycles and Controlling Inflation

Each of us, every day of our life, swims in an ocean of choices and constraints, economic threats and opportunities. Like it or not, the fact of *scarcity* keeps forcing us to compromise between "this or that?" and "now or later?" These choices fall primarily in the domain of microeconomic decision making and its many applied areas in economics and management. But the options facing individuals and businesses are influenced by national and global economic events that are the concern of *macro*economics. Although they may lie beyond our individual control, the better we understand these economy-wide forces the better we can respond to them in our multiple roles as consumers, savers, investors, workers, taxpayers, and voters.

For most of us, the two most worrisome macroeconomic events are the threat of **unemployment** from the recurrent ups and downs of the *business cycle* and the cost and uncertainties posed by **inflation,** particularly when it is highly variable. The *AD/AS* framework that we have been using gives a useful first look at these two problems, but much remains unexamined. For example, our present model explains unemployment as the result of reduced aggregate demand in the presence of short-run price rigidity. But we've said almost nothing about *why* this price rigidity exists or *how* it comes to be transformed into price flexibility, market clearing, and full employment in some magical "long run." We need to examine the *nature and timing of this transition from short to long run* if we are to answer some very basic and practical questions, such as: (1) Is there a primary source of macroeconomic fluctuations or do they come from different directions at different times? (2) Why are economic downturns sometimes brief and mild, but other times prolonged and deep? (3) What role can monetary and fiscal policy play in moderating this volatility?

Similarly, inflation can be depicted in our current model as the long run outcome of a situation in which aggregate demand grows more rapidly than aggregate supply, keeping upward pressure on the equilibrium price level. Useful as this approach will turn out to be, it erroneously presumes that unemployment and inflation are unrelated events. It says that unemployment occurs only in a short run with fixed prices and, therefore, no inflation. Inflation, however, means price flexibility and so exists only in a long run in which the economy is, by definition, fully employed. Such an "either/or" restriction prevents us from explaining situations in which we observe high rates of inflation and unemployment simultaneously, a phenomenon known as "inflationary recession" or "stagflation." It also fails to explain the frequently observed inverse relationship between inflation and unemployment in the short run, known as the "Phillips curve trade-off." Without an analytical framework that captures these short-run connections between inflation and unemployment, we cannot address important policy questions, such as: (1) How much unemployment will be created if we take steps to reduce the current inflation rate? (2) Why do governments knowingly choose policies that result in continued or even increased inflation? (3) Are there policy options that can reduce *both* unemployment and inflation together?

The next four chapters will take a careful look at the causes and consequences of unemployment and inflation. Particular emphasis will be put on **stabilization policy**—what can be done to smooth the business cycle and dampen inflation, and what are the costs and benefits of alternative choices? These chapters attempt to capture the essence of much highly technical theoretical and statistical work in an accessible but careful way. They seek to provide a practical overview of the present state of agreement and disagreement about unemployment and inflation, and the ability of government to undertake effective stabilization policies.

You'll discover that these issues are analytically demanding as well as controversial and the lack of definitive, smoking-gun evidence in favor of one particular theory can be frustrating. A common reaction is: Why go to so much trouble just to end up in disagreement about what policies can best deal with unemployment and inflation? One answer is that although the disagreement is very visible and highly publicized, there is a far wider area of agreement. By understanding the noncontroversial aspects of this issue, you are more likely to make economic and political choices that you will not regret later.

Another reason for putting some effort into untangling these controversial issues is that decisions have to be made every day. They can't be postponed until we learn the "truth." We want these decisions—private and public—to be based on the best and most current knowledge available, not on slogans, ideology, hunches, or random guesses. Where there is honest disagreement about interactions and outcomes, we should not proceed as if things were clear and simple. Otherwise we enter the realm of "pop economics," a blend of wishful thinking and careless analysis that shows up in the economic fads that sweep through the political process. The result of such a simplistic approach to difficult issues is all too often just a rerun of past mistakes.

CHAPTER 8

MACROECONOMIC FLUCTUATIONS

✆✆ 8.1 INTRODUCTION

The previous five chapters have developed and applied a basic aggregate model of macroeconomic activity. Though associated with the work of John Maynard Keynes, this analytical framework can also be thought of as a modification of the simpler classical model of Chapter 2. It drops the demand-side assumption of constant velocity of money and adds a supply-side assumption of fixed prices and variable output in the short run. Much of our time was spent learning and applying the somewhat intricate demand-side interactions (such as the "multiplier" and "crowding out") embodied in the *IS-LM* model of aggregate demand. Little attention was paid to aggregate supply as we simply asserted the existence of a horizontal "short-run" supply curve that becomes vertical as markets clear in the "long run." We made no attempt to be specific about the duration of these short and long runs.

But even with such a rudimentary treatment of supply, the resulting *AD/AS* model has proved to be a very useful tool for understanding many macroeconomic essentials such as fiscal policy, government deficits, and the national debt; monetary policy, interest rates, and inflation; international trade, exchange rates, and trade deficits (major topics of Chapters 5 through 7, respectively).[1] Where the basic *AD/AS* model is least helpful is, ironically, on

---

[1] There are some issues, like economic growth, for which the *AD/AS* framework is not particularly useful. It's also true that most current macroeconomic research is done outside the confines of this model with more complex dynamic models. This has led some economists to argue that this approach has outlived its usefulness and should be abandoned. But what will we replace it with? Advanced theoretical models are accessible only to specialists and are often far removed from practical applications. They have little to offer the household, business, or government decision maker looking for guidance on the likely outcomes of alternative choices. We've seen that the basic classical model, although relatively simple, is of limited help because its preoccupation with the long run excludes important short-run events and issues. Many alternative models have been devised but usually turn out to be just minor variations on *AD/AS*—old wine in new bottles. The *IS/LM-AD/AS* framework endures because it's a useful way to present basic macroeconomic interactions within a consistent, manageable framework. It is also extremely flexible, and can usually encompass the latest events and newest research findings. As you'll see in this chapter, the *AD/AS* model is not a single theory representing a particular policy viewpoint. It's more like a bazaar or a town meeting where theories from all over can come together to display their wares and interact with one another.

the very issues that inspired its development—unemployment and recession. We have portrayed changing levels of real output (and, implicitly, unemployment) as an initial shift of aggregate demand along a horizontal short-run aggregate supply curve. This was then followed by a long-run movement along aggregate demand as the price level adjusted to restore full employment. This model shows how a drop in aggregate demand, private or public, might trigger a recession or even a depression. That's a good start, but it falls short by *failing to explore the nature of the path that leads from short to long run.* Put another way, our current framework leaves the process of market clearing—how much? how fast?—unexplained. Therefore it offers no insights into the crucial issue of "timing" that lies at the heart of **macroeconomic fluctuations.** Lacking such knowledge we are unable to understand the circumstances under which countercyclical stabilization policies may be effective, ineffective, or even harmful to the macroeconomy.

Before we remedy this analytical shortcoming, let's take a brief look at the actual fluctuations in economic activity in the U.S., shown in Figures 8.1 to 8.3. The first graph shows real output over the past century. Its most obvious feature is not the year-to-year fluctuations in production but the tremendous long-term growth in annual output. This is an important fact to keep in mind. Although periodic recessions have certainly imposed real hardships on many people, the upward trend shows that they came in a world that was steadily, if not smoothly, becoming increasingly prosperous. The turbulence on the surface is dwarfed by the rising tide of prosperity upon which it rides.

Even though growth may be the most significant economic story in the U.S. over the past two centuries, the most *dramatic* story is the year-to-year variability of this growth. Figure 8.2 plots the annual rates of output growth since 1890 and essentially zooms in on the "noise" along the surface of the first picture. Instead of the

■ FIGURE 8.1

A Century of U.S. Real Output
(Billions of 1958 $)

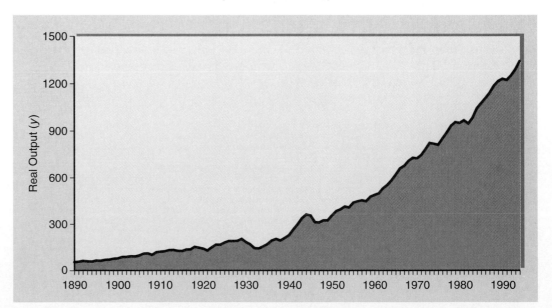

Annual Growth of Real Output
(United States, 1891–1994)

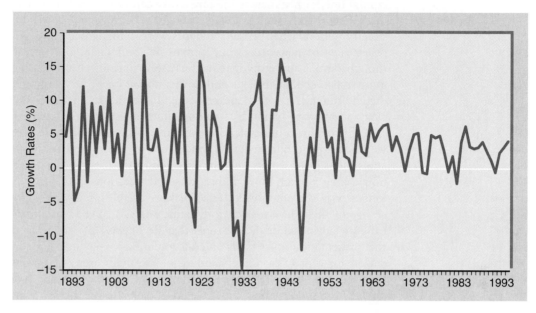

■ FIGURE 8.2

■ FIGURE 8.3

A Century of U.S. Unemployment
(% of Civilian Labor Force Unemployed)

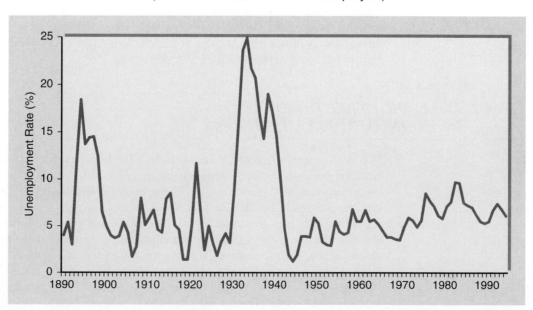

level of real output, we now see the annual percentage changes in that level (%Δy). The 3.4% average growth rate of real output over this period now shows up as a horizontal line, rather than as the upward sweep of Figure 8.1. Fluctuations around this line reveal the variability of economic growth. Negative growth rates show the recessionary periods when living standards were actually declining. Figure 8.3 offers another view of macroeconomic activity by looking at the unemployment rate. Although output and employment fluctuations are often called "business cycles," it is quite apparent that the ups and downs do *not* occur at evenly measured, easily predicted intervals. It is this unevenness and irregularity that presents the biggest obstacle to attempts to "smooth" economic fluctuations with *counter*cyclical policies.

To begin to understand the nature and causes of these economic fluctuations we must expand our analytical framework to accommodate the main features of the adjustment process that links short to long run. It should be understood that we are now asking a much more ambitious set of questions than before. Our concern is no longer with the equilibrium *levels* of key variables, but with the equilibrium *rates of change* of those levels. Such a dynamic analysis quickly becomes very complex and calls for advanced analytical tools that lie beyond the scope of this course. Hence, this presentation must focus on conceptual basics, laying a broad and intuitive foundation for a practical understanding of the main areas of agreement and disagreement in this area of "short-run dynamics." References are given throughout the chapter for those willing and able to pursue these issues at a more technically advanced level.

A brief preview should prove helpful. The goal of this chapter is to help you gain a practical understanding of (1) the main causes of **fluctuations in output and employment;** (2) the nature of the **market-clearing forces** pulling the economy back toward full employment; (3) the various **frictions that act as sources of resistance;** and (4) the circumstances under which **monetary or fiscal responses** can be expected to quicken the return to full employment. The notion that "frictions" can account for the economy's failure to return quickly to full employment is certainly plausible and hardly new. But until we put some precision and substance into this metaphor, it can offer us a vocabulary but little insight. So this chapter begins the analysis of "frictions" in three key areas—the *perceptions and expectations* of decision makers, the *wage and price-setting* choices of firms, and the *formulation and implementation of policy.* This is a highly controversial area and the "gray area" of honest disagreement is substantial. So part of the challenge lies in not being too quick to surrender to simple explanations of complex events.

✆ 8.2 *ROLE OF EXPECTATIONS IN ECONOMIC FLUCTUATIONS*

We begin with an ingredient common to all modern explanations of economic fluctuations—the influence of **expectations** on individual decision making and, thereby, on macroeconomic performance. The premise is the obvious one that our current choices are made on the basis of some expectation of their future consequences. These expectations incorporate our perceptions of cause-and-effect connections in the macroeconomy as well as our anticipations of coming events and policies. Such a potential role for expectations was certainly not excluded from our previous analysis. But it was left implicit, treated as an outside and occasional factor. We now incorporate these important but elusive ingredients—uncertainty, expectations, and misperceptions—as systematic and integral parts of our analysis.

Of the many different avenues through which expectations can and do affect our economic choices, we will focus on just one—the **expected price level** (P^e). This simplifies things immensely yet still yields results similar to those of more elaborate expectations-oriented models. Instead of beginning with a particular theory or hypothesis, let's start from an empirical observation. Statistical studies seem to find a significant relationship between *unexpected* changes in the price level and the level of real output. Specifically, real output is observed to increase when the price level rises above its expected level and to fall when the price level is unexpectedly low. Without speculating just yet on what this might reflect, let's explore its implications by expressing it in equation and graph form. This relationship is known as the **expectations-augmented aggregate supply curve,** denoted by AS^e, and written as

$$y = y^* + \beta(P - P^e) \qquad\qquad AS^e \text{ equation}$$

where $y^* = F(n^*, k, i^{nst})$ defines full employment as before, the parameter β is a positive constant, and the "expectations gap" $(P - P^e)$ is a measure of the accuracy of our price-level information.

Suppose, to begin, that the actual and expected price level are the same, i.e., $P = P^e$. This makes the last term in the AS^e equation equal to zero, so that actual real output will equal its full employment, market-clearing level, i.e., $y = y^*$. Although this is basically the same long-run vertical aggregate supply relationship we've been using all along, there is an important difference. In saying that it holds only for the case of "perfect information" $(P = P^e)$ we've finally put some substance into the meaning of "long run." In a long run in which price expectations are up-to-date and accurate, the graph of the AS^e equation becomes the familiar vertical AS^* curve in Figure 8.4.

■ FIGURE 8.4

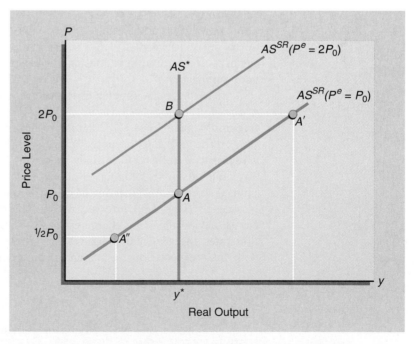

Expectations-Augmented Aggregate Supply Curve:
Vertical at AS^* in the Long Run ($P^e = P$);
Upward Sloping in the Short Run (e.g., $P^e = P_0$, $P^e = 2P_0$, etc.)

But the real importance of the AS^e model lies in what it tells us about short run situations in which expected and actual price levels can differ. To see the role that these **misperceptions** (i.e., $P \neq P^e$) can play, suppose the economy is initially in long-run equilibrium at point A in Figure 8.4 when an unexpected event causes the actual price level to rise suddenly to $2P_0$, leaving expectations temporarily stranded at $P^e = P_0$.[2] It takes time, perhaps several months, before our experience with changing individual prices combined with the government's collection and gradual release of preliminary and then revised data on prices provides the necessary information to reformulate perceptions and anticipations. In terms of this new supply equation— $y = y^* + \beta(P - P^e)$—the lag in the adjustment of expectations to changes in the price level creates a positive short run gap so that $(P - P^e) > 0$. Because y^* is fixed, this increase in the right-hand side of the equation must be a $+\Delta y$ on the left-hand side as real output rises above its long run full employment level. So this unanticipated increase in the price level $(+\Delta P)$ has meant a rise in real output $(+\Delta y)$, shown as the movement from point A to A' in Figure 8.4.[3] By the same reasoning, should the price level unexpectedly decline to $\frac{1}{2}P_0$ then $(P - P^e)$ would be negative and output would fall below its full employment level as shown by the movement from point A to A''.

The three points A, A', and A'' show three different combinations of the actual price level (P) and the supply of output (y). But they have an important common characteristic—by assumption, the *expected price level* is the same $(P^e = P_0)$ at each point. We represent this by connecting the points with a **short-run aggregate supply curve,** defined for the given expected price level of P_0 and denoted by $AS^{SR}(P^e = P_0)$. If we think of the long run AS^* curve as defined by *perfect information* $(P^e = P$ for all values of $P)$, then the short-run $AS^{SR}(P^e = P_0)$ curve is defined by the presence of *fixed expectations* (at P_0). If these expectations are correct then the economy is on both the short and long run curve at point A. But if expectations are too low $(P > P^e = P_0)$ we'll be on the short-run curve to the northeast of point A with $y > y^*$. Similarly, when expectations are too high $(P < P^e = P_0)$ we'll be to the southwest of A. To summarize, changes in the actual price level, when the expected price level is constant, show up as a movement along a short run aggregate supply curve.

What happens as price expectations adjust to the new circumstances? In terms of the AS^e equation, the value of $(P - P^e)$ goes to zero and the economy returns to full employment $(y = y^*)$. That is, we return to a point of long run perfect information on the vertical AS^* curve. As shown in Figure 8.4, an unexpected increase in the actual price level $(+\Delta P)$ initially moved us from point A to A'. Assuming the price level remains at this higher level, as expectations adjust $(P^e \rightarrow 2P_0)$ we move from point A' back to AS^* at point B. We will now be on a new short run aggregate supply curve, $AS^{SR}(P^e = 2P_0)$, intersecting the long run curve at a higher price level but otherwise having the same characteristics as the initial short run curve. Figure 8.4 thus illustrates the two main features of the expectations-augmented supply curve: (1) with fixed expectations, a change in the price level results in a *movement along* the

---

[2] The implicit downward-sloping aggregate demand curve intersecting AS^* at this point has been left out simply to keep this first graph as clean and clear as possible. The relationships underlying aggregate demand (embodied in the *IS-LM* model) are, of course, essential to any complete explanation of output and the price level.

[3] The size of the increase in y in response to the given $+\Delta(P - P^e)$ depends on the size of the coefficient β. The larger is β the further to the right A' will be and the shallower the slope of the line connecting points A and A' will be. We assume that β is a constant whose value can be determined statistically.

given short-run aggregate supply curve; however, (2) as price expectations adjust to the actual price level, the entire short-run relationship *shifts*.[4]

Combining these supply-side expectations with the familiar *IS-LM* model of aggregate demand alters the implications of our previous *AD/AS* model in two important ways. The first can be seen in Figure 8.5, which traces the impact of a given increase in aggregate demand with and without the influence of price expectations.[5] The short-run impact of an increase in *AD* now shows up partly in real output and partly in the price level (point *A* to *A′* in Figure 8.5). This is in contrast to the movement from point *A* to *H* when we previously assumed a fixed short-run price level. This **partial price adjustment,** resulting from the upward tilt of the new short-run supply curve, offers a more realistic portrayal of observed short-run adjustments in the macroeconomy.

The second major difference is that although both models end up at exactly the same long run position (point *Z* in the graph), the expectations-augmented approach offers an explanation for the adjustment from short to long run that is completely absent in the original model. Turning to Figure 8.6, we find that the given increase in aggregate demand moves us from *A* to *A′*, the price level rising to P_1 while price expectations lag behind at P_0. The subsequent path linking short to long run (*A′* to *B′* to *C′* and on to *Z*) can now be explained as a process in which expectations respond to the changes in the actual price level.

■ FIGURE 8.5

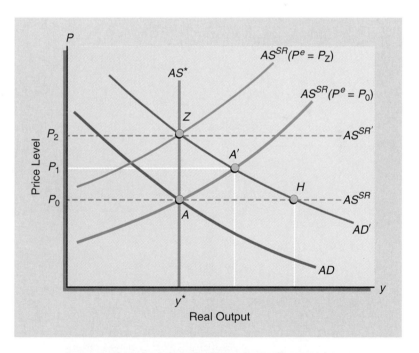

Impact of an Increase in Aggregate Demand on:
Previous Model (*AD/AS*): $A \rightarrow H \rightarrow Z$;
Expectations Augmented (*AD/AS^e*): $A \rightarrow A′ \rightarrow Z$

[4] The single equation underlying our expectations-augmented aggregate supply curve—$y = y^* + \beta(P - P^e)$—actually becomes a whole "family" of different curves when graphed. This is because it has three unknowns (y, P, and P^e) and when we graph it in two dimensions (y and P), the third variable—price level expectations—ends up in the intercept term, serving as a "shifter."

[5] This increase in aggregate demand must, of course, have originated in an outward shift in either *IS* or *LM*. To keep the focus on the supply side for now, the *IS-LM* graph underlying the *AD* curve has not been drawn.

To take a simple example, suppose there is a one month lag between changes in P and changes in P^e. (Perhaps it takes this long to collect and analyze the official price data, so that today's expectations are always equal to last month's actual prices.) Following the initial short-run movement to A' in response to the increased aggregate demand (Figure 8.6), the economy will then move to B' in the following month as price expectations adjust and $AS^{SR}(P^e = P_0)$ shifts upward to $AS^{SR}(P^e = P_1)$. This brings about a subsequent increase in the price level to P_2 which, when perceived a month later, will shift $AS^{SR}(P^e = P_1)$ to $AS^{SR}(P^e = P_2)$ causing the actual price level to rise to P_3 at point C'. This ongoing upward shift of short run supply along AD' continues until expected and actual price levels are again equal at point Z with the economy back on its long run aggregate supply curve.

■ FIGURE 8.6

Response to an increase in AD when price expectations *lag behind* the actual price level. The adjustment path is $A \rightarrow A' \rightarrow B' \rightarrow C' \rightarrow D' \rightarrow \ldots \rightarrow Z$ as the rising P^e shifts AS^{SR} upward.

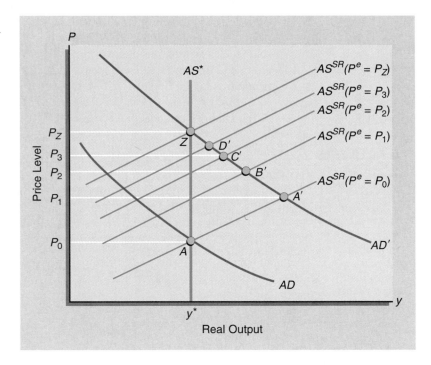

Real Output

IN SUMMARY . . .

Adding Expectations to the Model

Expectations can be incorporated into our analysis with just one new variable, the expected price level (P^e), added to one relationship, aggregate supply. The resulting expectations-augmented aggregate supply curve (AS^e)—$y = y^* + \beta(P - P^e)$—tells a story of how an *unexpected* change in the price level initially causes real output to move along an upward-sloping short run aggregate supply curve (A to A' in Figure 8.6). Then, as the initial misperception is corrected over time, short-run supply shifts along the aggregate demand curve (point A' to B' and so on) until equilibrium real output reaches its long run, full employment level.

(Continued)

Inherent in this AD/AS^e model is a redefinition of short and long run. "Short run" is now characterized by a fixed level of *price expectations* rather than by the fixed price level of the earlier model. "Long run" is the condition of equality of actual and expected price levels, in contrast to the undefined "market clearing" of the earlier model.

The AD/AS^e model offers both a more realistic description of the short run (in which *both P* and *y* adjust) and a mechanism to explain the adjustment from short- to long-run equilibrium. In the process, it provides a theory of economic fluctuations in which deviations of output from full employment arise when unanticipated shifts in aggregate demand create misinformation about prices. This misinformation leads us to decisions that ultimately cause real output to depart from its full-employment level. Our misperceptions essentially act as a friction that keeps us away from full employment. Whether this friction is short-lived or prolonged depends, in this view, on the speed at which expectations adapt to changing conditions.

8.3 EXPECTATIONS—WHY THEY MATTER

Combining this new model of supply with our *IS-LM* model of demand yields the full expectations-augmented model, AD/AS^e. It connects output fluctuations to price level misperceptions resulting from unexpected changes in aggregate demand. Recovery from recession is entirely a process of correcting our expectations—the more quickly they adjust, the shorter the downturn. In attributing so much power to expectations and misperceptions, this is clearly a strong and ambitious hypothesis. To assess how reliable and useful it is as a theory of the business cycle, we must address two key questions: What is the **underlying logic** that leads us to believe that expectations are so strongly linked to real output? Can we find **hard evidence** to support such a view?

We begin with the issue of *why* expectations matter. So far we have justified adding them to the model only with an assertion that this seems to be consistent with empirical observations and statistical tests. But statistical regularities in economics, as elsewhere, have sometimes turned out to be short-lived or even illusory. (We'll see a classic example of this in next chapter's discussion of the Phillips curve.) So before we put too much weight on the apparent facts, let's ask whether there are some good commonsense, cause-and-effect reasons to support the hypothesis that price level misperceptions, reflecting frictions in the adjustment of price level expectations, keep us from full employment. Could something as intangible and changeable as expectations really be responsible for something as big and real and persistent as a recession?

Much attention has been devoted to this question over many years. Modern views stem largely from the independent studies done by Milton Friedman and Edmund Phelps in the late 1960s, soon followed by a series of important theoretical and statistical contributions by many economists, most notably Robert Lucas.[6] From this sizable literature has emerged a number of plausible linkages between price level

---

[6] Edmund S. Phelps, "Phillips Curves, Expectations of Inflation, and Optimal Unemployment over Time," *Economica* 34 (August 1967): 254–281; Milton Friedman, "The Role of Monetary Policy," *American Economic Review* 58 (March 1968): 1–17; and Robert E. Lucas, Jr., "Some International Evidence on Output-Inflation Tradeoffs," *American Economic Review* 63 (June 1973).

misperceptions and economic fluctuations. All require us to go behind the expectations-augmented aggregate supply curve (AS^e) to look at its underlying "microfoundations."[7]

To establish a connection between expectations and economic fluctuations, we begin with **uncertainty**—a fact of life largely ignored in previous chapters. No one, of course, can know the future. Even the most astute and careful predictions will almost always be a little off and will sometimes be far from the mark. And sometimes even our most casual hunches or wildest guesses will come to pass. It turns out that the inevitable uncertainty of everyday life, combined with delays in obtaining and reacting to new information, can lead us to individual choices that collectively mean systematic fluctuations in macroeconomic performance. Do you take the first job offer that comes along after graduation or keep searching for something better? Should a company raise the price of its product in the wake of an unexpected increase in sales? In the midst of a downturn, should you take advantage of bargain prices to buy a new car or reduce your spending until the clouds of recession have receded a bit further? Such choices—involving uncertainty and affecting many decision makers—have the cumulative potential to create an economy-wide surge or lull in economic activity.

We'll examine two specific ways in which this can happen. Both involve choices based on a temporary misperception of the level of prices—one by workers, distorting their labor supply decision; the other by businesses, distorting their output decision. Let's start with the *worker misperception hypothesis* that focuses on decisions in the labor market. Figure 8.7 pictures the labor market of an economy initially at full employment equilibrium at point A. Suppose a sudden increase in aggregate demand (not pictured) causes the price level to double, thereby reducing the real wage from W_0/P_0 to $W_0/2P_0$.

If we presume (as we did in deriving the classical model back in Chapter 2) that both labor suppliers and demanders are fully aware of this price change, they will respond by moving down their labor market curves to points S and D, respectively. The result is a labor shortage shown by the gap between labor demand and supply curves at $W_0/2P_0$. Basic market mechanics tell us that this shortage will put upward pressure on the nominal wage until the labor market has returned to equilibrium at point A with both prices and wages doubled. The equilibrium levels of the real wage, employment, and real output are unaffected by the outward shift in aggregate demand. This familiar result underlies the vertical AS^* curve that we saw first in the classical model and then again as the long-run result of the Keynesian AD/AS model. But we now stress the point that this is a "perfect information" outcome ($P = P^e$), based on the presumption that both suppliers and demanders of labor are fully aware of the price level change.

Let's change this slightly by supposing that the sudden increase in aggregate demand and resulting doubling of the price level is initially perceived by labor demanders but not by labor suppliers. According to the "worker misperception" hypothesis, such asymmetrical information is likely because firms have more resources and more incentive to keep in touch with economic events than do individual work-

---

[7] The term *microfoundations* is used in a general sense here to denote the process of constructing a richer, more detailed analysis than is provided by the highly aggregative *AD/AS* framework. Sometimes "microfoundations" is given a narrower meaning that refers to the use of microeconomic models of consumer and firm behavior to build an aggregate model that *presumes* constant market clearing. This book does not impose such a strong assumption. For a careful development of that approach see Robert J. Barro, *Macroeconomics*, 4th ed. (New York: John Wiley & Sons, 1993) or George T. McCandless, Jr., with Neil Wallace, *Introduction to Dynamic Macroeconomic Theory: An Overlapping Generations Approach* (Cambridge, Mass.: Harvard University Press, 1991).

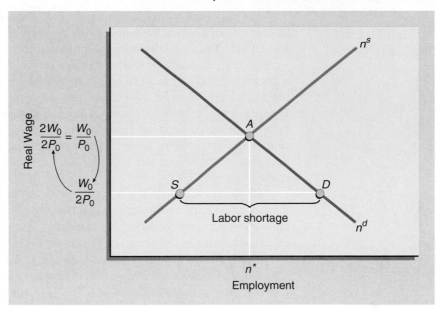

Perfect Information Model of
the Labor Market

■ FIGURE 8.7

A doubling of the price level initially creates a labor shortage, forcing a proportional rise in the nominal wage and returning the economy to full-employment equilibrium at point A.

ers. Although workers will see individual price increases at the stores, it takes time—perhaps many months—to determine whether this is an economy-wide trend in the price level rather than just the ever-present ups and downs of various individual prices as markets adjust to constantly changing economic conditions.

If workers had spotted this increase in the price level, they would have realized that it meant a reduction in their real wage and would have moved down their labor supply curve as shown in Figure 8.7 (points A to S). But failing to recognize the rising price level and falling real wage, they now base their labor supply decision on a misperceived higher real wage. They think the real wage is at W_0/P_0 so they continue to supply n^* hours of labor, believing they're at point A on n^s in Figure 8.8. In reality, the doubled price level means that they are actually at point M in the graph. If they knew their real wage was lower they would have moved down n^s as in Figure 8.7. Lacking that knowledge, they continue to supply the same amount of labor at the lower real wage, *effectively causing the labor supply curve in Figure 8.8 to shift out to* $n^{s\prime}$.

Putting the pieces together, the "worker misperception" hypothesis argues that a sudden increase in the price level is likely to be seen more quickly by firms than by workers. So although the rising price level and falling real wage will cause firms to *move along* their (perfect information) n^d curve, the misperceptions of workers cause their labor supply curve to *shift* to the right. The net result will be a new equilibrium in the labor market at the intersection of $n^{s\prime}$ and n^d shown at point A' in Figure 8.8. Instead of the equilibrium real wage and employment remaining constant as in the perfect information case, the new equilibrium now brings a lower real wage (W_0/P_0 to W_1/P_1) and increased employment.

As long as this price misperception lasts, the economy will find itself producing at point A' in Figures 8.6 and 8.8, well beyond its perfect information, full employment level. Then as workers' expectations adjust to the changed situation, the labor supply curve moves back toward the perfect information n^s curve, and the short-run aggregate supply curve shifts up, returning the economy to full employment at the higher price level. The adjustment process from short to long run that we saw in Figure 8.6 as the movement from A' to B' and so on back to Z is a reflection of initial price level misperceptions being corrected over time.[8] So the "worker misperception" hypothesis tells a more or less plausible story of why expectations matter and one that is fully consistent with the expectations-augmented aggregate supply curve—$y = y^* + \beta(P - P^e)$.

A second rationale for AS^e stays with the output market rather than the labor market and avoids the strong assumption that businesses always have perfect information, whereas workers do not. According to the *firm misperception hypothesis* an unexpected change in the price level causes confusion as to the meaning of the individual price increases that make up the change in the overall price level. This approach suggests that when a particular firm observes a sudden change in market conditions, it won't know at first whether this reflects a change in the demand for its product relative to others or whether it merely means an increased demand for output throughout the whole economy, leaving the real demand for its product unchanged.[9] If the

■ FIGURE 8.8

The rise in the price level now *shifts* labor supply to the right. The result is equilibrium at point A', with a lower real wage and higher level of employment because of the misperception.

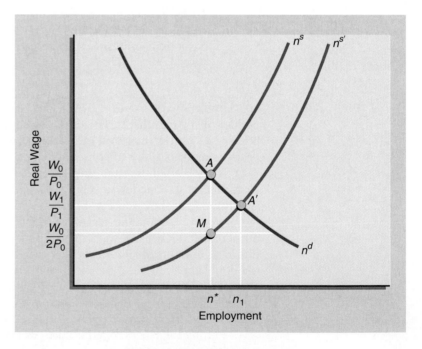

Worker Misperception Model

---

[8] By similar reasoning, an unexpected $-\Delta P$ would lead to a decrease in the supply of labor, causing equilibrium employment and real output to fall below their full employment (perfect information) levels.

[9] The model underlying this hypothesis was first developed by Robert Lucas in a series of influential articles collected in his *Studies in Business-Cycle Theory* (Cambridge, Mass.: The Massachusetts Institute of Technology Press, 1981).

increased demand is thought to be firm-specific, a profit-maximizing firm will increase its production through requiring overtime work, hiring new workers, or even expanding its facilities. But if it is perceived as an economy-wide increase in nominal demand rather than a switch in favor of their particular product, the firm would not want to increase production levels because the relative price of its product hasn't changed.

Returning to our example of an unexpected increase in aggregate demand, it is likely that some firms will initially misread the rising price level as an increase in their particular product price relative to others. They will respond by increasing their production levels. So the increased aggregate demand will not merely push up prices but, because of firms' misperceptions, also lead to increased output. This shows up as a movement along the short-run expectations-augmented aggregate supply curve (points A to A' in Figure 8.6). As firms discover that the rising prices do not reflect increased demand specific to their product, production will be returned to its original level. In the aggregate, these diminishing misperceptions will show up as a series of shifts of the short-run aggregate supply (points A' to B' etc. to Z) as the economy moves back to its long run, perfect information aggregate supply curve (AS^*) at the new higher price level.

Combining the potential for worker misperceptions of *real* wages and firm misperceptions of *relative* prices, we have an underlying rationale (based on the microfoundations of individual and firm behavior under uncertainty) that is consistent with the implications of the aggregate expectations-augmented supply model—$y = y^* + \beta(P - P^e)$. Deviations from full employment reflect a combination of change and uncertainty. An unexpected shift in AD creates short run misperceptions on the part of decision makers that lead to employment and output choices that are not market clearing. The subsequent adjustment to the vertical long-run aggregate supply curve mirrors the adjustment of worker and firm expectations (and the labor and output decisions based on them) to the new conditions.

Having found some plausible explanations for why expectations and misperceptions might be systematically related to departures from full employment, we must now address the question of whether the factual evidence supports the strong contention of the "misperceptions" model (embodied in AD/AS^e) that fluctuations in real output and employment are due primarily to unexpected shifts in aggregate demand followed by the gradual correction of initial misperceptions.

8.4 EXPECTATIONS—HOW THEY CHANGE

Let's change metaphors for the moment, trading the useful but drab equations and graphs of an "equilibrium system" for the more vivid setting of a "criminal case." Our investigation has turned up a pattern of behavior (misperceptions) and two suspects (workers and firms) accused of being the perpetrators of the business cycle. But the evidence to this point is largely anecdotal. It's obvious that the existence of uncertainty and change ensures that our expectations will sometimes be wrong, leading us to make some choices that we would otherwise not have made. It's also apparent that after the initial surprise of an unexpected event, we collect and evaluate the new information and sometimes reverse past choices. But can this, even when magnified over millions of decision makers, really account for the ups and downs of the business cycle? Is the *timing* as well as the *magnitude* of these misperceptions consistent with the observed fluctuations of output and employment?

Can we find the hard evidence to back up our suspicion that changing misperceptions of decision makers ($\pm \Delta(P - P^e)$) are guilty of causing ongoing fluctuations in real output ($\pm \Delta y$)? Thanks to the efforts of national income statisticians, it's quite easy to account for past movements of real output (y) and the price level (P).[10] We can turn to official statistics, readily available from many private and public sources in a variety of formats, including disk, CD ROM, on-line via the Internet, and the traditional hard copy. But, unfortunately, one vital piece of information—the *expected* price level (P^e)—is not to be found in the official measures. Without this data we're unable to reconstruct the past movements of price level misperceptions ($P - P^e$). If we can't tell whether or not they were at the scene of the crime, then we can't reach a verdict on the AD/AS^e theory of the business cycle.

Rather than abandon every hypothesis incorporating expectations as untestable, we must look elsewhere for the missing empirical evidence on price expectations. The most obvious approach might be to simply ask decision makers for their expectations through *sample surveys*. Useful as this can be in profiling individuals' attitudes and preferences, it has not turned out to be very helpful in providing reliable information on economic expectations. Experience has shown that answers to survey questions about expectations are extremely sensitive to how the question is worded. The same question put in slightly different contexts, for example, can lead to very different responses. In other words, the witnesses aren't giving the consistent and reliable testimony needed to test our business cycle theory.

Strange as it may sound at first, the solution to this problem of *measuring* expectations has been to turn to a *theory* of expectations. By creating a model of how price expectations are formed and what causes them to change, we are able to generate the data that we're not able to measure directly. Put another way, we can get an indirect measure of our unobservable variable if we can establish a cause-and-effect linkage between it and related but observable variables. This may seem like a highly contrived and artificial attempt to avoid having to give up on our expectations-oriented theories. But it's actually a quite common procedure and one that most of us use in a variety of different situations. Consciously or not, we often make projections from observables to unobservables. Sometimes this is done in a simple, almost instinctive way. Other times we apply more complex means. For example, we make inferences from observables to unobservables in virtually every forecast we make. Whether it's about future interest rates, end of semester grades, or the best choice of a career or spouse, we use what we can learn from the past and present to imagine the future. When we make a decision in the present, it is frequently based, at least in part, on a projection to the future. It seems safe to presume that the individuals and firms making labor supply and production decisions in our AS^e model are not just plucking their price (and other) expectations out of thin air. Knowing that poor choices will lower their standard of living, they will base their perceptions and forecasts on what they see and hear.

So our strategy for obtaining the necessary evidence to evaluate the misperceptions theory of the business cycle is to *add a theory of the formation of price expectations to our AD/AS^e framework*. In so doing we essentially generate the missing information (P^e) needed to create a measure of price-level misperceptions ($P - P^e$). This in turn will allow us to put the expectations-augmented aggregate supply hypothesis— $y = y^* + \beta(P - P^e)$—to the test. Do the facts support this view that price level mis-

---

[10] This is not to imply that measures of these variables are without their shortcomings, as will be discussed in Chapter 15. But for many purposes, including studies of the business cycle, the standard measures are accurate enough to discriminate among major hypotheses.

perceptions are the primary cause of macroeconomic fluctuations? If not, how can we supplement the model to get a better explanation of the business cycle?

Let's begin with a very basic and easily implemented model of expectations, one that extrapolates future values of a variable from its own past and present values. This general procedure, within which there could be many variations, falls under the broad heading of the **adaptive expectations hypothesis** (AEH). Applied to price level expectations, it says that as updated information on the actual price level becomes available, our expectations—inferences from observed to unobserved—adjust accordingly. To take the simplest example, suppose we forecast next month's price level with the assumption that it will equal this month's. We can write this as

$$P^e_{t+1} = P_t$$

where t represents the current time period (a month, in this case) and $t + 1$ is the next period. If this simple model (or "rule of thumb") captures the way we formulate our expectations, then forecasts of next month's price level will always adapt to the latest information as t moves from January to February to March and $t + 1$ from February to March to April.

A more elaborate forecast would incorporate more information than just this month's price level. It might go further back in time, perhaps giving diminishing importance to earlier observations. For example, in forecasting next month's price level suppose we suspect that people look back over the last three months. But instead of using a mean value (unweighted average) they might give the current month most importance, with diminishing weights attached to older information. If they gave half the weight to the current month, 30% to last month, and 20% to the prior month, this could be expressed as

$$P^e_{t+1} = .5P_t + .3P_{t-1} + .2P_{t-2}$$

Obviously this is just one of many ways by which we might use past observations on a variable to forecast its future. But instead of exploring variations on the adaptive expectations hypothesis (AEH), let's look at it with a more critical eye and note that it represents a process that is inherently *backward looking*. Expectations, in this approach, adjust only after the fact, reacting to the past rather than anticipating the future. Put another way, the AEH imposes a substantial amount of "friction" in the adjustment of P^e to changes in P. Therefore, using this hypothesis to calculate expectations produces relatively large values for misperceptions $(P - P^e)$ and a gap that closes relatively slowly because expectations respond only to past events.

If we're confident that this is a good approximation to the actual, but unobservable, price expectations, then it's a simple and useful way to gather the necessary evidence to take the AD/AS^e model to court. However, there are some good economic reasons to suspect that the simple extrapolations underlying AEH make misperceptions appear more sluggish than they actually are. If so, then it will generate biased evidence that could lead us to the wrong verdict on whether misperceptions are the primary cause of business cycle fluctuations. By making misperceptions look more important than they really are, we may convict the wrong party and let the actual perpetrator get away scot free.

Is the AEH a reasonable approximation to the way in which we actually go about forming our expectations? It is sometimes compared to driving a car down the highway while looking only through the rearview mirror. We try to anticipate what lies ahead by looking only at where we've been. Depending on the road, this may occasionally work well, but it could also turn out very badly. In refusing to consider the possible impact that other variables and events and policies are likely to have on the price level, the AEH ignores readily available and potentially useful information. This implication that decision makers knowingly waste a scarce resource makes most economists uncomfortable with the use of the AEH. By forbidding the driver from looking out the side or front window of the car, it essentially ignores all that we have done in previous chapters toward devising an explanation of how real output, interest rates, the price level, the trade deficit, and so on are determined. We have emphasized *interconnections* among the many current variables, events, and policies that underlie macroeconomic change. But in the world of adaptive expectations this information is, in effect, treated as if it provides no better view of what lies ahead than a simple extrapolation from past to future. So the issue we now address is whether there is a way to overcome the shortcomings of the AEH by formulating a more sophisticated model of expectations that allows decision makers to use all available information in forming their expectations.

The **rational expectations hypothesis** (REH) starts from the assumption that decision makers base their choices on a wide array of information about economic events and macroeconomic connections. In forming price level expectations, for example, the REH assumes that decision makers will consider the rate at which the Federal Reserve has been increasing the money supply in recent months, as well as any major changes in fiscal policy, supply shocks, or other events that may be on the horizon. In short, the REH is based on the presumption that people "optimize"—do the best they can with what they've got. So they base important decisions not only on a variable's own past (as presumed by the AEH), but also on current and expected future events. And because these events don't "speak for themselves," the rational expectations hypothesis further assumes that decision makers combine this information within a cause-and-effect framework (e.g., the AD/AS^e macroeconomic model) to generate price and other important expectations that will help them make better choices in a changing and uncertain world.

The REH is obviously a much more sophisticated and ambitious way to generate expectations data than is the AEH. Although this makes it more appealing in some ways—namely, that it doesn't imply that we ignore useful information—it also makes it far more difficult to use. The result has been the creation, over the past 25 years, of virtually a new industry within the field of macroeconomics, devoted to exploring the theoretical and statistical characteristics of alternative ways of incorporating expectations into macroeconomic models.

This "expectations revolution" in macroeconomics has brought forth a great deal of ingenuity, hard work, and sharp disagreement among a good number of the best and brightest economists. Connecting the AD/AS^e framework of Edmund Phelps and Milton Friedman (cited earlier) with the pioneering work on expectations by Philip Cagan (1956) and, especially, John Muth (1961), a group of young economists in the 1970s began a serious exploration of how price-level expectations can be incorporated into macroeconomic models. Robert Lucas, Thomas Sargent, Neil Wallace, Christopher Sims, Robert Barro, Bennett McCallum, Finn Kydland, and Edward Prescott, among others, were particularly important in formulating what was initially known as the "rational expectations school."

This intense exploration of expectations seemed to uncover some very *un*expected policy implications, quite different from those of standard macroeconomic models. The result was a bitter clash among macroeconomists over the very foundations of the field: What should a theory provide and by what logical criteria should it be judged? What kinds of empirical and statistical evidence represent a legitimate test of that theory? As you'll see by chapter's end, the rational expectations school (like the Keynesian School it was reacting to) now appears much less radical than it once did. This is partly because it has adapted somewhat to its critics but even more because its influence (again like that of the Keynesians) has been incorporated into the mainstream. Rational expectations has had an important impact on the way that most economists view economic fluctuations and stabilization policy. It is a topic that seems destined to become a permanent part of macroeconomic analysis. A recent survey of the field concludes that

> *Rational expectations has undoubtedly become the standard way of modelling expectations in macroeconomics. Whatever the reason for this dominance, whether it is due to its own theoretical appeal or the absence of any theoretically attractive alternative, it is certainly true that there is hardly a branch of macroeconomic theory in which rational expectations has not been introduced and its implications explored; that its introduction has radically influenced the conduct of applied research in macroeconomics; and that for the moment it appears to have no serious rival.*[11]

The remainder of the chapter presents a nontechnical and practical assessment of current thinking of the implications of expectations for economic fluctuations and stabilization policy.

8.5 CAN "RATIONAL MISPERCEPTIONS" EXPLAIN THE BUSINESS CYCLE?

We began this chapter with the confession that our previous *AD/AS* framework is of limited help in understanding the short-run fluctuations in output that constitute the business cycle. We sought to remedy this by introducing "expectations" into the analysis through the *expectations-augmented supply curve* (AS^e)—$y = y^* + \beta(P - P^e)$. Adding this "price misperception" component to real output (the $\beta(P - P^e)$ term) gives a descriptively more realistic upward-sloping aggregate supply curve in the short run that shifts over time with changing expectations. Output fluctuations, in this view, are the short-run result of unexpected changes in the price level, i.e., $\pm \Delta(P - P^e) \Rightarrow \pm \Delta y$. How quickly the economy returns to full employment depends entirely on the speed at which these misperceptions disappear.

To make this approach operational requires information on how price expectations adjust to new information. We saw that the initial appeal of the simple and intuitive AEH diminished as the implications of its backward-looking orientation were explored. This led to the so-called REH, which starts from the commonsense presumption that in a world of scarcity important economic decisions will not be made carelessly. With so much available information (and a framework in which to analyze it—the AD/AS^e model), it would be surprising if the actual manner in which we form our price expectations isn't more "rational" than "adaptive."[12] Although this

[11] C. L. F. Attfield, D. Demery, and N. W. Duck, *Rational Expectations in Macroeconomics: An Introduction to Theory and Evidence*, 2nd ed. (Oxford: Basil Blackwell, Inc., 1991), p. 225. Those who would like to pursue this technically demanding topic further will find no better place to begin than this superb expository treatment. Another excellent treatment, at a more advanced level, is William M. Scarth, *Macroeconomics: An Introduction to Advanced Methods* (Toronto: Harcourt Brace Jovanovich, 1988).

[12] Of course, even economists don't believe that anyone *literally* uses these models to calculate precise optimal choices at each moment in time. The actual choice process is clearly a far different and richer blend of calculation, rule-of-thumb, tradition, superstition, and much else. Economics is *not* trying to provide realistic explanations of *why* people act the way they do. Instead, we try to get some relatively simple, hence manageable, hypotheses that yield testable implications of the "if _____ , then _____ " sort. The fact that a particular theory may provide a good description of past behavior and have good predictive power provides us with a crucial stepping stone in our exploration of economic interactions. It does *not* tell us that people, even economists, literally follow the intentionally simplified hypotheses of our models.

may seem obvious for large corporations and financial organizations that can afford to employ economists or economic consultants, it is also likely to apply to ordinary consumers trying to be careful with their money. When the economic stakes are large—a house and mortgage, a career change, a second job, a retirement plan— many of us use professional advice without even being aware of it. Through newspapers, magazines, books, radio and television and, increasingly, money management software programs, we have ready access to the latest information, state-of-the-art forecasts, and expert advice at very little cost.

It's important to remember that the REH does *not* mean "perfect information" regarding the consequences of our choices. Omniscience is not the issue here. The REH explicitly acknowledges that as economic conditions change in unforeseen ways, our expectations and perceptions will initially be caught unawares. Unanticipated events create a gap between actual and expected prices and, thereby, between actual and full employment output as described by $y = y^* + \beta(P - P^e)$. So even the most rational of expectations can certainly be wrong and, when they are, the economy moves away from full employment. But rational expectations (looking out all the windows of the car) respond with relatively little delay to end these misperceptions and restore full employment. For convenience, let's nickname this combination of "misperceptions" and "rational expectations" ($AD/AS^e + REH$) the **rational misperceptions** model.[13]

How useful is this framework as a theory of fluctuations and a guide to countercyclical policy? Certainly its foundations seem plausible. It is widely accepted that misperceptions can play an important part in overall economic instability and the premise that expectations are formed in a "rational" rather than a more restrictive "adaptive" manner is difficult to oppose. But these seemingly plausible assumptions have a strong implication that initially shocked many economists. According to the rational misperceptions model, *countercyclical policies are powerless to stabilize the economy.* If this model is a reliable guide to the workings of the macroeconomy, then the attempt to use monetary or fiscal policy to speed the return to full employment or smooth the business cycle is simply futile.

Within the logic of the model, this result is straightforward. Because countercyclical policy by its very nature is *predictable*—expansionary actions in a recessionary downturn, contractionary in an inflationary boom—it will be foreseen and built into expectations. Because any predictable events or policies can have no effect on misperceptions, they will have no impact on real output. The whole notion of countercyclical policy, so ingrained in our thinking since the Great Depression, Keynes, and the Employment Act of 1946 is, according to this model, simply wrong. This implication has come to be known as the **policy ineffectiveness proposition**.[14]

Reaction to this unexpected result was predictable. Those in the nonactivist, small-role-for-government camp, could only be pleased that scientific research seemed to corroborate their views. Many saw this as a long overdue correction to

---

[13] This is often referred to by economists as the "*new*" classical" model. As the name implies, it is characterized by relatively rapid market clearing, making it more akin to the classical tradition than to a Keynesian world of sticky prices. But on the topic of what's "new" and what's "classical," the ambitious reader is referred to an excellent presentation by Kevin D. Hoover, *The New Classical Macroeconomics: A Sceptical Inquiry* (Cambridge: Basil Blackwell, 1988), particularly Part V, "The New Classical Methodology." To keep from getting too caught up in the knee-jerk responses that most of us have to words like "classical" and "Keynesian," we've used the more neutral and more descriptive "rational misperceptions" name.

[14] This name can be confusing. It certainly does not say that monetary and fiscal policies have no impact whatsoever. They can still alter the price level and interest rates and all the nominal and real variables that respond to these. "Policy ineffectiveness" only means that predictable aggregate demand policies will not alter total real output or employment. They may well alter the *composition* of these variables as well as the levels of others.

what they believed was an ideological bias that had entered the profession with the advent of activist-oriented "Keynesianism." To this group, "policy ineffectiveness" appeared to be just a modern manifestation of the classical market-clearing process that keeps the economy at or near full employment without government intervention.

The initial response of most economists to this result, however, was one of disbelief. Those who had long accepted the need for monetary and fiscal changes to offset unwanted fluctuations in economic activity had seen many challenges to this view drop by the wayside over the years. The only one that had endured was Milton Friedman's contention that "long and variable policy lags" could mean that countercyclical policy changes took effect too late to be of help and might sometimes mean added instability in aggregate demand and, hence, output and employment. Friedman and his "monetarist" followers accused the government itself of being the main source of fluctuations in economic activity, ironically through its well-intended but shortsighted countercyclical policies. The mainstream regarded this as a possibility and potential threat, but one that could be minimized by prompt, measured policy responses. They pointed to the relative stability of output and unemployment in the post–World War II period (see Figures 8.2 and 8.3) as tangible evidence that the activist approach had been effective in smoothing the business cycle.

But because the "rational misperceptions" view had been carefully constructed on widely accepted microfoundations and was also consistent with initial statistical results, it was not so easily dismissed. Those unwilling to abandon long-standing activist views initially focused their criticism on the assumption of rational expectations. They argued that while people may be forward-looking to some extent, the extreme degree of calculation and economic farsightedness implied by the REH was highly unrealistic. Though many conceded that the AEH was too restrictive and shortsighted, its implication of a high degree of friction in the adjustment of expectations could account for what seemed so obvious to so many—countercyclical policies have been an important factor in bringing about the relative stability of most macroeconomies in the postwar period. Without them the ups and downs of the business cycle would have been larger and longer.

But further statistical and theoretical research continued to weaken the case for adaptive expectations. As more and more studies revealed the logical and empirical superiority of the rational expectations approach, it looked as though the pendulum had swung from models consistent with activist stabilization policies (AD/AS, at first, then AD/AS^e + AEH) to those with nonactivist implications (AD/AS^e + REH). The ensuing controversy was strong and sometimes bitter. At the same time, the analytics were highly technical, prompting an increasingly mathematical framework that sometimes seemed to lose sight of the immensely practical underlying issue—the causes and cures for the costly ups and downs in output and employment that afflict all market economies.

The result was a period of considerable disagreement and confusion. Nonactivists maintained that the incorporation of expectations and the use of more powerful statistical tools had discredited the biased activist analysis associated with Keynesian economics. Those whose instincts and policy preferences kept them from embracing these new nonactivist conclusions found themselves increasingly on the defensive. They were accused of letting their value judgements cloud their science— clinging to the defunct adaptive expectations hypothesis only because it supported their preconceived conclusions.

It took a while for the dust to settle, but it eventually became apparent that the key issue in the activist/nonactivist debate is *not* how expectations are formed. Instead it is whether changing misperceptions $[\pm \Delta(P - P^e)]$ are really the only important source of output fluctuations $(\pm \Delta y)$ as assumed in the AS^e model.[15] A series of statistical studies confirmed that while the rational misperceptions model can account for some of the fluctuations in output and employment that have characterized the business cycle since World War II, a large part remains unexplained.[16] Put another way, the rational misperceptions model describes an economy in which economic fluctuations are smaller and shorter-lived than is observed in actual economies. Without denying its importance as a partial explanation of the dynamics of the macroeconomy, we must add some more ingredients before drawing any major conclusions about what government can or cannot do to reduce economic fluctuations. As you'll see in the next two sections, the fate of the controversial "policy ineffectiveness" proposition depends on whether the as-yet-unexplained fluctuations come from the *supply side of the economy* or whether they reflect *frictions in the price and wage-setting process* following demand-side shocks.

8.6 ADDING FLUCTUATIONS FROM THE SUPPLY SIDE

One expansion of the rational misperceptions framework—called the **real business cycle model**—turns to the supply side of the economy and argues that the "missing fluctuations" in real output can be found in fluctuations in the full employment level of output itself.[17] In terms of the expectations-augmented aggregate supply equation, $y = y^* + \beta(P - P^e)$, it hypothesizes that observed fluctuations in real output $(\pm \Delta y)$ are coming not only from misperceptions $(\pm \Delta(P - P^e))$ but also from fluctuations in the natural rate of output $(\pm \Delta y^*)$. Because demand-side stabilization policies are known to have little impact on the supply side, the real business cycle hypothesis retains the non-activist flavor of the rational misperceptions model.

The real business cycle model is a radical break from the standard approach to the business cycle. At least since Keynes's *General Theory*, aggregate supply has been regarded as relatively unimportant for short run issues, exerting its undeniably important influence through the slower and steadier forces of long run growth (see Figure 8.1). For example, activists and nonactivists alike have treated negative supply shocks as unusual and infrequent events, outside the regular workings of the macroeconomy. Hence the supply side of the model, so crucial to long-term economic growth in both classical and Keynesian views, has always taken a back seat in explanations of the short run ups and downs of the business cycle.

But the real business cycle hypothesis puts the supply side in the driver's seat. Stressing random shocks to the capital stock $(\pm \Delta k)$ through uneven and unpredictable changes in technology, this approach sees economic fluctuations as largely a reflection of instability in the long run aggregate supply curve itself $(\pm \Delta AS^*)$. In

---

[15] The testing of the "rational misperceptions" model has been particularly difficult because it requires quantification of the elusive "expectations" variable in order to determine whether: (1) "misperceptions" are primarily responsible for fluctuations in output and employment, and (2) expectations respond quickly to predictable events and policies (the "rational expectations" hypothesis). Any error in estimating the rate at which expectations adjust means a mismeasurement of the expectations gap and a corresponding bias in the testing of the misperceptions hypothesis.

[16] For a clear exposition and assessment of these issues, see Bennett T. McCallum, *Monetary Macroeconomics: Theory and Policy* (New York: Macmillan, 1989), chaps. 9 and 10.

[17] This approach stems largely from the work of Finn E. Kydland and Edward C. Prescott, "Time to Build and Aggregate Fluctuations," *Econometrica* 50 (November 1982): 1345–1370. For discussions of the Real Business Cycle theory see Bennett T. McCallum, "Real Business Cycle Models," in Robert Barro, ed., *Modern Business Cycle Theory* (Cambridge: Harvard University Press, 1989), pp. 16–50; Charles I. Plosser, "Understanding Real Business Cycles," *Journal of Economic Perspectives* 3 (Summer 1989): 51–77; and N. Gregory Mankiw, "Real Business Cycles: A New Keynesian Perspective," *Journal of Economic Perspectives* 3 (Summer 1989): 79–90.

keeping with the rational misperceptions model, unexpected fluctuations in aggregate demand have only a small and brief impact on real output while expected demand changes have none at all. Whatever your personal view on whether the government *should* follow an active stabilization policy, acceptance of the real business cycle model carries the implication that the government *cannot* succeed in smoothing the business cycle. It provides no support for an activist approach to the business cycle.[18]

How convincing is this? Does the real business cycle model—a combination of *rational misperceptions* with *supply-side instability* ($AD/AS^e + REH \pm \Delta AS^*$, for short)—provide a convincing explanation of actual business cycles? A few very good economists think so. But these kinds of aggregate models are extremely difficult to test and evaluate. Several quite different hypotheses are broadly consistent with the observed facts of business cycles, and no one has yet found a crucial test that can reject all but one. To a considerable majority of macroeconomists, the evidence offered by real business cycle theorists has not been persuasive. Though it has served as an important reminder that supply shocks are sometimes large enough to cause substantial changes in output and employment, the real business cycle hypothesis has yet to demonstrate, in the opinion of most economists, the ability to account for the actual patterns of cyclical fluctuations observed in the U.S. economy.

IN SUMMARY . . .

Economic Fluctuations—Two Nonactivist Views

1. The **expectations-augmented aggregate supply curve** (AS^e), in conjunction with the *IS-LM* model of aggregate demand (*AD*), provides a useful framework for analyzing macroeconomic fluctuations. It predicts that *unanticipated shifts in aggregate demand* in a fully-employed, no growth economy change both price and output at first, but over time the impact on output disappears while the price level change grows larger. (This is illustrated by the movement from points *A* to *A'*, *B'*, *C'* and so on to *Z* in Figure 8.6.) *Anticipated changes in aggregate demand*, conversely, are predicted to have no output effect, with the adjustment entirely absorbed by price level changes (points *A* to *Z*, directly, in Figure 8.6). These predictions are partially confirmed by statistical studies showing that anticipated demand shifts have smaller output and employment effects on the economy than do unanticipated shifts.

2. This adjustment process appears to reflect, at least in part, the impact of **temporary misperceptions** of the price level on decisions taken by workers and businesses. In a changing and uncertain world we cannot know the future and we will sometimes make choices, based on the best available information, that can cause employment and output to deviate from their full employment levels.

(Continued)

---

[18] But one could certainly be an "activist" on issues other than economic stabilization and still accept the real business cycle theory as the best explanation of economic fluctuations.

3. Since these misperceptions have costly individual consequences (such as unemployment or loss of profits), there is every reason to believe that rational decision makers will adjust their expectations quickly as new information becomes available. This means that price misperceptions might certainly last for a matter of weeks or even months, but are unlikely to account for a drop in output that continues for a number of quarters or even years. This is the basic premise of the **rational expectations hypothesis.**

4. One implication of combining misperceptions with rational expectations is a prediction of **policy ineffectiveness.** This result argues against the use of countercyclical policy on the grounds that it is predictable and hence unable to create misperceptions that cause output to change. But a second implication is that with rapidly adjusting expectations, misperceptions cannot be large enough to explain fluctuations of the size routinely experienced by the U.S. economy. The suggestion that the Great Depression was a consequence of a decade of massive misperceptions about the price level is ludicrous at best. It points out the need to go beyond the misperceptions model in forging a complete explanation of the business cycle.

5. It is possible that the unexplained portion of the output and employment fluctuations could originate on the supply side through fluctuations in technology and the capital stock. The **real business cycle theory** argues that supply side instabilities account for whatever fluctuations the "rational misperceptions" model does not explain. Since supply side changes cannot be offset by ordinary, demand-side monetary and fiscal responses, the real business cycle view is also nonactivist in its policy implications. To date, the statistical evidence to support this hypothesis is relatively weak and has failed to convince most macroeconomists and policy makers.

⚭ 8.7 *ADDING FRICTIONS TO THE ADJUSTMENT PROCESS*

If supply-side instability comes up short as an explanation of the missing economic fluctuations, we must find another way to supplement the promising but incomplete "rational misperceptions" theory of economic fluctuations. To fit the facts, our solution must explain why the adjustment process following a demand shock is considerably slower than predicted by the rational misperceptions model (AD/AS^e + REH). Put another way, we must find a substantial source of *friction* in the market-clearing process. The slight resistance created by the adjustment of rational expectations simply can't explain the observed sluggishness of actual economies. Although adaptive expectations can supply this missing friction, it's a solution that conflicts with both the logic and the facts of what we've learned about expectation formation.

So we turn to the possibility that these additional frictions reflect a "stickiness" in the way in which wages and prices are set in labor and output markets. Even after price misperceptions have disappeared, according to the **market frictions** view, the economy may not have reached full employment if some prices and wages are slow to adjust. There's an obvious Keynesian flavor here. It is essentially a *milder version of the price rigidity of our original horizontal short run aggregate supply curve.*

But remember that we abandoned that earlier assumption not only because it was too strong but also because it left the adjustment from short to long run unexplained. Moreover, our subsequent discussion of "microfoundations" made it seem quite improbable that workers and firms would blindly cling to wages and prices that lead to unemployment, falling profits, and a declining overall standard of living. So the "market frictions" view of economic fluctuations must face some difficult and basic questions: How could it happen that some workers can't or won't lower their wage demands even in the face of unemployment? Why is it that some firms can't or won't lower their prices even though sales are falling, inventories rising, and production levels dropping?

We begin our look at these "*new* Keynesian" models, as they are often called, with unemployment and the labor market.[19] Given the obvious costs of unemployment, why don't recessionary periods lead to market clearing through nominal wage cuts? Why don't unemployed workers, seeing a real wage that is too high for full employment, initiate or at least accept a nominal wage cut that will restore full employment? We've seen that misperceptions are a partial factor but not enough to explain the observed persistence of high unemployment. The **sticky nominal wage hypothesis** points to additional factors that can delay the adjustment of nominal wages to changing labor market conditions. These include the presence of *labor contracts*, legal restrictions such as *minimum wage laws*, and even *unwritten agreements* that when business is slow, employers will reduce hours worked or lay off employees rather than engage in wage-cutting. The existence of varying degrees of *monopoly power* can also add frictions to both wage and price adjustments.

There are a number of plausible explanations for such sources of sticky nominal wages. One that fits comfortably under the umbrella of the "rational misperceptions" model is to suppose that workers and employers are bargaining over a three year wage contract and that both parties are trying to hit a "target real wage" at which labor demand and supply are equal and the market is cleared.[20] Since future price levels are unknown, they will substitute current expectations of the price level (P^e) and then bargain for a nominal wage (W) that gives the target real wage that is their goal. If expectations prove correct, the nominal wage set in the contract will be consistent with labor market clearing.

But suppose that using their best estimates and most rational expectations, the bargainers fail to foresee a major monetary contraction that results in unexpectedly lower price levels over these three years. The result is that the real wage will be kept above its target level. Profit-maximizing firms will reduce the amount of labor hired, thereby keeping the labor market at a point like B in Figure 8.9. While this involves a "misperception"—a deviation of actual real wage from target real wage because of a price level misperception—if differs from our previous analysis because even after the error in predicting the price level becomes apparent, the existence of the contract

[19] The pioneers of this approach include Stanley Fischer, Olivier Blanchard, Alan Blinder, Robert Gordon, Lawrence Summers, John Taylor, Gregory Mankiw, Robert Hall, Joseph Stiglitz, Laurence Ball, David Romer, George Akerlof, and Janet Yellen, among others. Major technical contributions to this research have been usefully collected into two volumes by N. Gregory Mankiw and David Romer, eds., *New Keynesian Economics* (Cambridge: The Massachusetts Institute of Technology Press, 1991).

[20] An early model of this type was presented by Stanley Fischer in his "Long-Term Contracts, Rational Expectations, and the Optimal Money Supply Rule," *Journal of Political Economy* 85 (February 1977): 191–205. For a concise review of related work see Lee E. Ohanian and Alan C. Stockman, "Short-Run Effects of Money When Some Prices Are Sticky," *Economic Quarterly*, Federal Reserve Bank of Richmond (summer 1994): 1–23.

freezes the incorrect expectation into subsequent outcomes. So the impact of the misperception persists even after expectations have been corrected.[21]

This additional source of market friction added to the rational misperceptions model restores the possibility that a timely countercyclical policy response can be effective. By shifting aggregate demand to the right, raising the price level, and thereby lowering the real wage and moving the labor market from point B to A in Figure 8.9, it could override the sluggishness built in by contracts. This, of course, puts this "rational misperceptions" plus "market frictions" combination very much in the Keynesian/activist tradition.

There are other reasons why the nominal wage could remain too high for labor market clearing even in a world of rational expectations. But it should be noted that these hypotheses, like the "sticky nominal wage" approach, all imply the existence of something that may not be present in most actual business cycles. If the sticky wage view were correct, then we would expect to see falling employment and output when the real wage was *rising*. (Remember, it's the higher real wage that leads firms to reduce the quantity of labor hired as we move from point A to B in Figure 8.9.) Similarly, when employment and output are rising (moving us from point B to A), the sticky wage model predicts a *decline* in the real wage, encouraging firms to hire more

■ FIGURE 8.9

If a labor contract freezes the real wage above its target level (at W_1/P_0 rather than W_0/P_0), firms will demand less labor and the economy will come to rest at a point below full employment (with $n_1 < n^*$) because the initial price misperception is locked into the contract. Expansionary AD policy could move the economy toward full employment by raising P and lowering W/P.

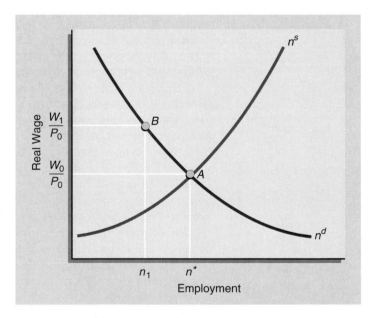

Sticky Nominal Wage Hypothesis

[21] You might wonder why the bargainers don't avoid price level uncertainty altogether by simply negotiating for a real wage in terms of current prices and then dealing with price changes through "escalator clauses," often termed "cost of living allowances" (COLAs), that would automatically adjust this year's money wage for last year's actual price level change. Many such contracts exist, of course, most notably in payments to Social Security recipients. But the actual implementation of escalator clauses can be quite difficult and there can be good economic reasons for either party to avoid them and to instead bargain for its best guess as to future inflation over the life of the contract.

workers. But the data seem to show that increases in output and employment are typically associated with modest *increases* in the real wage rather than decreases as predicted by this hypothesis. The inverse relationship between the real wage and employment predicted by this model is not found.[22] It's possible that there are other unrelated factors that might account for the rise in the real wages when output rises, but even so it seems apparent that the "sticky nominal wage" view, by itself, cannot provide the additional explanatory power we seek.

Another and better option is to turn our attention to the price-setting process in an attempt to put together a substantive and testable **sticky price hypothesis** that can explain why the return to full employment is slower than can be accounted for by the rational misperceptions model.[23] There are many factors that come to mind when we search for reasons why a firm might be hesitant to adjust its product price in the face of substantial changes in demand. An obvious one is **sales contracts** that obligate the firm to sell a specific number of goods at a particular price. Manufacturers of electronics or automotive components, for example, will often make such arrangements with firms that assemble final products from components supplied by many different manufacturers.

Apart from such explicit contractual agreements, firms may be reluctant to raise their prices in response to a sudden increase in demand for fear of losing the loyalty of long-standing customers. Instead they may meet the higher demand at the existing price until they are convinced that the increased demand is a lasting change and not just a transitory spurt. A related consideration is that frequent price changes are costly to a firm. Depending on the industry, a price change can mean informing a large sales force, printing new catalogs or new menus, changing coin-operated machines, or incurring other such **menu costs** as they have come to be called. It will generally not pay to respond to every fluctuation in market conditions by changing prices. Only with solid evidence that the changed circumstances are lasting and sizable would it be sensible to finally change the price.

Yet another potentially significant source of price rigidity comes from firms that have some degree of **monopoly power** in their markets. For several reasons, their pricing policies are likely to result in less frequent price changes than for comparable firms in more competitive industries.[24] The bottom line is that there are several factors, generally consistent with the microfoundations of rational firm and consumer behavior, that could result in a certain amount of "stickiness"—prices and wages failing to adjust rapidly to changing market conditions. These added frictions in the market-clearing process can potentially explain that part of output fluctuations missing from the rational misperceptions model.

---

[22] It should be noted that this evidence also works against the "worker misperception" hypothesis discussed earlier, since it argues that unexpected changes in the price level alter the real wage, thereby causing firms to hire more or less labor as they move along the labor demand curve. A sudden increase in the price level, unperceived by workers but quickly detected by employers, would lead them to hire more workers. It is precisely this implication of "rising employment but falling real output" that is not observed in the data.

[23] But remember that what we're after here is not just a *plausible* case that some prices don't adjust smoothly and quickly to changes in economic conditions. That would be easy. We can always concoct any number of stories that seem to explain the direction of observed changes. To know enough about business cycles to make wise policy choices, we need a model with enough detail about price changes to enable us to make quantitative predictions about just how quickly or slowly prices will adjust in various situations.

[24] See, for example, Olivier Jean Blanchard and Nobuhiro Kiyotaki, "Monopolistic Competition and the Effects of Aggregate Demand," *American Economic Review* 77 (September 1987): 647–666, and other articles in Section III, Imperfect Competition of N. Gregory Mankiw and David Romer, eds., *New Keynesian Economics* (Cambridge: The Massachusetts Institute of Technology Press, 1991).

To take this a step further, let's integrate these additional market frictions into our basic analytical framework. Remember that we were able to incorporate the effect of *misperceptions* into the model in a relatively simple way by adding a term— $\beta(P - P^e)$ —to the aggregate supply equation. In a similar way we can add another term to aggregate supply— $\lambda(y - y^*)_{-1}$ and explained below—that mimics the effect of *market frictions* by slowing down the return to full employment. To see how this works, let's begin with the rational misperceptions model and take the case of an unexpected decline in aggregate demand that pushes the economy into recession as shown in Figure 8.10.

The initial short run movement from point A to A' reflects misperceptions as the actual price level falls below the expected. In the model we've been using, when P^e catches up to the lower P the economy returns to long run, perfect information equilibrium at point Z. But if we now add wage/price stickiness, the economy will remain below full employment longer and even *after* all misperceptions have been dispelled (i.e., $y < y^*$ even when $(P - P^e) = 0$). Put another way, we're now going a step beyond the rational misperceptions model by saying that perfect information is not enough to guarantee that the economy has fully adjusted to long run equilibrium at y^*. In terms of the economy in Figure 8.10, the addition of wage/price stickiness would result in a slower rate of adjustment from short to long run (point A' to Z) than with rational misperceptions alone.

This more sluggish return to full employment is exactly the outcome we've

■ FIGURE 8.10

The addition of frictions in the setting of wages and prices slows the adjustment of the economy to fluctuations in aggregate demand. This added stickiness will retard the market-clearing process linking points A' to Z.

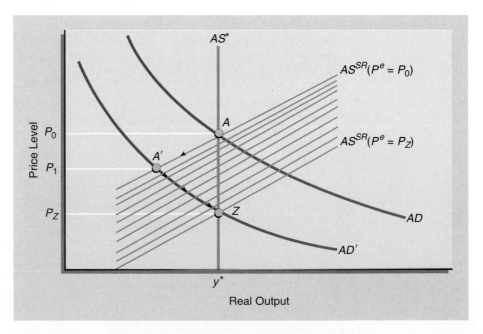

Adding "Frictions" to the Adjustment Process

been seeking. We can incorporate this added friction into the aggregate supply equation in an indirect but simple way by linking it to the gap between actual output (y) and its full employment level (y^*) from the *previous* period (denoted by a -1 subscript). When an economy is pushed below full employment by a negative demand shock, the stickiness of the return to full employment can be captured by adding the previous period's *negative* output gap—$(y - y^*)_{-1} < 0$—to current output.[25] The aggregate supply equation can now be written as

$$y = y^* + \beta(P - P^e) + \lambda(y - y^*)_{-1}$$

where λ is assumed to be a constant that, in combination with the output gap $(y - y^*)_{-1}$ reflects the degree of market friction. So the larger is $\lambda(y - y^*)_{-1}$, the greater the market friction and the slower the return to full employment.

8.8 A GENERAL MODEL OF ECONOMIC FLUCTUATIONS

How much do we really know about the causes and mechanics of the business cycle? Does it start on the demand or the supply side or, perhaps, both? To what extent is the recovery prolonged by price misperceptions and to what extent by frictions in the adjustment of prices and wages? Are there other important factors to consider? Do we have enough solid evidence to build a strong case for—or against—the use of monetary and fiscal policies to reduce cyclical fluctuations in real output and employment?

The answer, of course, is implicit in the fact that a number of quite different views coexist among economists. The combination of *ambiguous statistical results, inability to conduct carefully controlled experiments,* and *differing personal views on the economic role of government* can lead one economist to an activist conclusion on stabilization policy while another takes the nonactivist path. It would simplify policy making greatly if we could assert, beyond a reasonable doubt, that countercyclical policy is always effective or always ineffective in smoothing the business cycle. Unfortunately we cannot. Research on this topic continues at a rapid pace and it is possible that the next decade will see the development of dynamic macroeconometric models that substantially increase our detailed knowledge of the market-clearing process. For now, however, we must make do with the incomplete and mixed evidence at hand.

This may well make you wonder whether all the work on the microfoundations of expectations, real business cycles, and market frictions over the past 25 years has made much practical difference. In fact, it has. Even though we don't have a single, simple model of fluctuations that is accepted by all, the range of disagreement has been narrowed substantially. This will be discussed carefully in the next chapter when we combine the inflation issue with stabilization of output and employment.

Before leaving the discussion of macroeconomic fluctuations, let's fit these various pieces into a larger picture. Major advances in the modeling of expectations and market frictions in the 1970s and 80s have stirred much controversy. But instead of thinking in terms of competing "schools of thought"—classical, Keynesian, new classical, monetarist, new Keynesian, activist, nonactivist, rational expectations,

---

[25] Whenever there is a continuing, persistent effect (or friction), we can get a simple measure of its *current* influence by including its *past* values. This should look familiar from our earlier discussion of the backward-looking AEH.

real business cycle, and so on—suppose we acknowledge the possibility that the observed fluctuations in real output ($\pm \Delta y$) can sometimes come from the *supply side* ($\pm \Delta y^*$) and sometimes from the *demand side* ($\pm \Delta AD$); that departures from full employment can reflect *rational misperceptions* ($\beta(P - P^e) \neq 0$) or *market frictions* ($\lambda(y - y^*)_{-1} \neq 0$) or both; and that the relative importance of these different ingredients is likely to differ under different circumstances.

From this more general perspective, the economy can be in full, long run equilibrium (on its AS^* curve) only when misperceptions and market frictions have disappeared. In terms of the expanded aggregate supply equation

$$y = y^* + \beta(P - P^e) + \lambda(y - y^*)_{-1}$$

this requires that the last two terms on the right hand side of the equation must be equal to zero (i.e., $P - P^e = 0$ and $(y - y^*)_{-1} = 0$). Unexpected changes in aggregate demand will cause initial short run departures from full employment via misperceptions ($P \neq P^e$), the severity of which depends on the size of the resulting misperceptions and the magnitude of the coefficient β. How quickly output returns to full employment following this demand shock then depends on how rapidly expectations adjust to end the misperceptions and also on the degree of market friction or stickiness as reflected in the size of the lagged output gap $(y - y^*)_{-1}$ and its coefficient λ. If the two crucial coefficients β and λ differ across time or nations, then looking for a simple answer and a correct "school of thought" is inappropriate.

Combining the competing hypotheses into a more general model obviously doesn't get us to a simple answer. But it can keep us aware that there may be a different mix of factors for different cyclical episodes. This means that the appropriate policy response to one downturn might not fit another. For example, if we suspect that the main source of a particular fluctuation in real output comes from the supply side (as with supply shocks induced by "oil crises" or natural disasters), ordinary demand-side stabilization policy will be of little help. When the shock is more clearly from the demand side, then we need to make some judgement on the magnitude of the size of β and λ and the relative importance of "misperceptions" and "market frictions."

Currently the dominant view among macroeconomists is that while misperceptions disappear fairly quickly (through rational expectations), market frictions are significant enough to result in a substantial slowdown in the return to full employment. Therefore, when fluctuations originate on the demand side, a prompt monetary or fiscal counterresponse has the *potential* to speed up the return to full employment. But it should be noted that the presence of demand-side fluctuations in a world with significant market frictions doesn't automatically mean that an activist response is appropriate. To the extent that there are additional frictions in the policy-making process itself, for example, our response carries the risk of coming too late to be of much help. In some cases it may actually destabilize the economy by taking effect *after* market-clearing is complete. This is the "policy lag" issue stressed by Milton Friedman and other monetarists for so many years.[26]

---

[26] Another very important outcome of the debate over macroeconomic policy analysis has been the discovery of some underlying flaws in the policy-making process. The issue of an *inflationary bias* stemming from activist policies is a concern regardless of one's theory of economic fluctuations. It leads to a discussion of whether policy "rules" could usefully replace policy "makers" in certain areas of macroeconomic policy. This is covered in Chapter 9.

Policy makers can't avoid making a judgement, perhaps informally, about which of these several factors are most important in a given cyclical fluctuation and which can be safely disregarded. Thinking in terms of this more general model instead of slogans from one of the schools of thought can keep us from being too dogmatic on an issue in which we are all very fallible. In recent years the extremes of the early positions—one said "markets clear quickly," the other said "it's obvious they don't"—have been reduced dramatically as our theoretical and empirical knowledge has advanced. Few applied economists would now argue that a well-executed and timely countercyclical policy could never succeed in reducing fluctuations in output and employment. But it surely does not follow that everyone embraces an activist position on stabilization policy. Many economists continue to be persuaded by the classical tradition, arguing on philosophical grounds that even if the government "can," it "shouldn't." Others, many favoring a broader and more active economic role for government in *some* areas, oppose activist countercyclical policies as both (1) too uncertain in their benefits because of the possibility of unforeseen time lags in the policy making process, and (2) too risky in the political arena because of the possibility that the political process itself will hinder the implementation of a "well-executed and timely" countercyclical policy.

On the surface, it might appear that although all the evidence isn't in, the verdict is going in favor of a Keynesian **market friction** view. But if we look more closely, we also see that those who adopt the activist position on economic stabilization today, unlike the "old" Keynesians of earlier decades, set quite narrow limits for the scope of these policies. The most important new ingredient is the limitation that **rational expectations** puts on the extent to which policy can deal with issues involving misperceptions. In addition, concerns with potential destabilization from **policy lags** and with the possibility of political compromises that handicap such policies have resulted in a modern activist position that is quite cautious in its recommendations and much more modest in its expectations for smoothing the business cycle.

It is a considerable irony that in some important ways the modern Keynesian position is closer to the modern classical view than to the original policy activism associated with Keynesian economics.[27] This tempering of views on stabilization policy seems to be a very healthy development in macroeconomics. Not only does it reflect progress in using careful theoretical and statistical analysis to narrow the range of disagreement but also allows us to more easily disentangle our views on what the government *can* do from what we think it *should* do.

---

[27] See N. Gregory Mankiw, "The Reincarnation of Keynesian Economics," *European Economic Review* 36 (1992): 559–565, for a nontechnical discussion of the difference between old and new Keynesian economics. Mankiw argues that the contrast is sufficient to suggest the possibility "that the term "Keynesian" may have outlived its usefulness."

IN SUMMARY . . .

A Guide to Business Cycle Theories

Underneath the broad umbrella of the expectations-augmented aggregate supply model, we find some related but distinct theories of economic fluctuations. They all begin from the AD/AS^e framework but differ on some other basic assumptions, including their answers to the following questions:

1. What is the *primary source of disturbances* to the macroeconomy?
2. *How fast do expectations adjust* to changing circumstances?
3. Are *other frictions* in the market clearing process important?
4. Are *policy lags* highly variable and unpredictable?

Because they have quite different policy implications, these variations define what are often thought of as different "schools of thought" on the issue of stabilization policy. Even though there's no reason to declare allegiance to one and reject all others, it is useful to know the major characteristics of these views because of their widespread use among politicians and the media.

Keynesian Model $(AD/AS^e \pm \Delta AD +$ AEH$)$

1. The main source of disturbances is thought to be from fluctuations in aggregate demand ($\pm \Delta AD$), primarily from the private sector [such as autonomous consumption ($\pm \Delta c_0$), investment ($\pm i_0$), and money demand ($\pm \Delta j_0$)].
2. Expectations adjust relatively slowly to changing circumstances in a manner that is best captured by the adaptive expectations hypothesis (AEH).
3. Policy lags can usually be anticipated and taken into account in advance in our policy responses.
4. No other frictions are explicitly added, though it is presumed that additional sources of nonmarket clearing are present but their effects are captured in the lag in expectations assumed by the AEH.

Monetarist Model $(AD/AS^e \pm \Delta M +$ AEH $+$ LAGS$)$

1. The main source of disturbances is from the demand side, specifically from erratic stop-and-go policies of the monetary authority ($\pm \Delta M$).
2. Expectations adjust relatively slowly, as described by the AEH.
3. Policy lags are thought to be "long and variable" and, most importantly, unpredictable. As a result, policies intended to be countercyclical can end up being procyclical.
4. No other frictions are thought to be important.

(Continued)

New Classical Model $(AD/AS^e \pm \Delta M^u + \text{REH})$

1. Fluctuations in the macroeconomy are primarily from unexpected changes in the money supply $(\pm \Delta M^u)$.

2. Expectations adjust very quickly, as described by the rational expectations hypothesis (REH).

3. Policy lags are not thought to be of much importance.

4. No other frictions are important.

Real Business Cycle Model $(AD/AS^e \pm \Delta AS^* + \text{REH})$

1. Fluctuations from the demand side are relatively unimportant in their impact on output and unemployment. The main source of business cycles comes from the "real" side of the economy—the supply side $(\pm \Delta AS^*)$. Random fluctuations in capital, primarily from uneven technological change, cause business cycles.

2. Expectations adjust rapidly and are best described by the REH.

3. Policy lags are not significant.

4. No other frictions are important.

New Keynesian Model $(AD/AS^e \pm \Delta AD + \text{REH} + Z)$

1. The main source of disturbances is thought to be from fluctuations in aggregate demand $(\pm \Delta AD)$, primarily from the private sector [such as autonomous consumption $(\pm \Delta c_0)$, investment $(\pm \Delta i_0)$, and money demand $(\pm \Delta j_0)$].

2. Expectations adjust rapidly and are best described by the REH.

3. Policy lags are not a major problem.

4. The market-clearing process is characterized by a number of frictions that result in an observed "stickiness" in wages and prices. Collectively symbolized as Z, they slow down the economy's return to full employment even though expectations may have adjusted rapidly.

8.9 OVERVIEW

1. This chapter starts by questioning the simple *AD/AS* assumption of a price level that is absolutely *rigid* in the short run but completely *flexible* in the long run. Useful as that model is in many contexts, it tells us little about the nature of economic fluctuations and the prospects for smoothing them through *countercyclical* stabilization policies. Understanding these issues requires that we develop a *theory of the adjustment process that links short-run with long-run outcomes.*

2. An important ingredient in any explanation of fluctuations in real output and employment (often termed the "business cycle") is the influence of *uncertainty, expectations,* and *misperceptions* on economic decision making. A relatively simple way

to incorporate these elements is through the **expectations-augmented aggregate supply equation** (AS^e): $y = y^* + \beta(P - P^e)$. The graph of this equation in the long run is the familiar vertical AS^* curve, where "long run" is defined as a situation of perfect information, $P = P^e$, so that the last term of the equation disappears, leaving just $y = y^*$. The "short run" is now defined as an interval during which price *expectations* (P^e) are fixed. Geometrically the short run shows up as a family of upward-sloping supply curves rather than the horizontal short run curves of the earlier model.

3. Combining this new theory of supply with the standard *IS-LM* model of aggregate demand yields a more realistic AD/AS^e framework. According to this approach, unexpected shifts in aggregate demand initially cause the economy to move away from full employment by creating price level misperceptions ($P \neq P^e$). This happens because of the way in which these misperceptions distort the labor supply choices of workers and the production decisions of businesses. As expectations adjust to the new circumstances, these distortions disappear and the economy returns to its full employment level of output and employment.

4. The duration of these short-run fluctuations depends entirely on the speed at which price expectations adjust to the actual level of prices. To evaluate how well the AD/AS^e model can explain real world business cycles, we must add a *theory of price expectations*—that is, an explanation of how rapidly they adjust to new information. The **adaptive expectations hypothesis** (AEH) portrays a process in which we learn from our past forecasting errors and essentially extrapolate current price level expectations from observed price levels of the past. The main appeal of the AEH is that it is a very easy way to infer the value of something that is not directly measurable. But the adaptive expectations hypothesis implies that decision makers ignore all other information in formulating their price expectations, focusing only on the actual price levels of the past. This backward-looking implication makes it much too narrow to be a plausible explanation of much actual behavior. Despite its operational convenience, the AEH has gradually been abandoned by most macroeconomists.

5. It has been replaced by the **rational expectations hypothesis** (REH), which supposes that decision makers use a wide array of information in forming their price (and other) expectations. The development of this more sophisticated model of expectations ignited a major controversy among macroeconomists in the 1960s and 1970s. The reason was that when the REH is combined with the misperceptions theory (AD/AS^e), the resulting *rational misperceptions* model yields an implication of **policy ineffectiveness** that directly challenges the mainstream view that active fiscal and monetary policies are needed to moderate the inherent instability and fluctuations of a market economy.

6. The subsequent flood of research on expectations increasingly supported the rapid expectations adjustment implied by the REH over the sluggish adjustment of the AEH. This appeared to imply that misperceptions would disappear so quickly that there was no time for countercyclical policies to be implemented. Long-standing advocates of an activist role for government seemed to be put in the position of clinging to the primitive and erroneous adaptive expectations hypothesis in order to justify their belief that the use of policy manipulation was necessary to moderate the instability of the macroeconomy.

7. It eventually became clear that the "rational misperceptions" model ($AD/AS^e + REH$) of the business cycle yields a useful but incomplete picture of actual economic fluctuations. Its implication of a quick return to full employment, which seemed to reinforce the nonactivist view, does not account for the observed

slower responses of real world economies. But rather than return to the more sluggish "adaptive misperceptions" model (AD/AS^e + AEH), most economists have chosen to stick with the rational expectations hypothesis and look elsewhere for the "missing" fluctuations.

8. The most radical attempt to supplement the rational misperceptions approach is the **real business cycle** theory. Departing from nearly all previous models, activist and nonactivist alike, the real business cycle approach argues that the origin of the missing fluctuations is on the supply side rather than the demand side of the economy. Instability in the full employment level of real output itself (i.e., $\pm \Delta y^*$ and $\pm \Delta AS^*$) is said to be a major source of the business cycle. Since there is little evidence that monetary and fiscal changes can offset supply-side instabilities, the real business cycle model (AD/AS^e + REH $\pm \Delta AS^*$) supports the nonactivist implications of the "policy ineffectiveness" view. While the "real business cycle theory" is a serious contender, it has not been accepted by the vast majority of macroeconomists as a convincing explanation of macroeconomic fluctuations.

9. If the missing components of the business cycle aren't to be found on the supply side, we must return to our basic framework and search for other explanations as to why economic fluctuations aren't as shallow as predicted by the rational misperceptions framework. We must find additional frictions, beyond the adjustment of price expectations, that can explain why deviations of real output from its full employment level last as long as they do. Two simple explanations— *rigid short run prices* and *sluggish (adaptive) expectations*—can provide the additional friction but in ways that are theoretically and empirically unconvincing. The alternative has been the development of a theory of *price and wage stickiness*, carefully grounded in the microfoundations of rational choice. This **new Keynesian** approach goes inside the price and wage-setting process in search of underlying sources of friction (Z) in the market-clearing process. It considers the influence of contracts, menu costs of price change, and monopoly power in attempting to paint a richer and more convincing picture of market adjustments. In supplementing the rational misperceptions model with market frictions (AD/AS^e + REH + Z), it retains the *possibility* that activist stabilization policies can smooth macroeconomic fluctuations.

10. But this new Keynesian framework is much more highly evolved than its primitive Keynesian/activist ancestors. In grounding its conclusions in microfoundations rather than assertions of rigidities, it resembles new classical and real business cycle models more than it does the early Keynesian models. By focusing on frictions within the market-clearing process, it portrays an economy in which timely counter-cyclical actions can potentially hasten the return to full employment and thereby smooth the business cycle. But the success of activist policy is far from guaranteed. This will depend on the specifics of the case for a particular economy at a particular time. We will need to know not only the degree of stickiness that is keeping the economy from full employment, but also the extent of any lags that may afflict the policy-response process.

11. Research in this area of market frictions is still in its infancy. At least for the foreseeable future, policy makers will need to continue to use the combination of science, value judgement, hunch, slogan, and whatever else has guided them in the past. Although the argument over whether the government can smooth the business cycle still goes on, the distance separating activists and nonactivists has diminished notably. In particular, strong views in favor of aggressive activist "fine tuning" have little support today. Activists who view the world through a new Keynesian lens are

quite different than the activists of earlier decades. They are likely not only to put more faith in the automatic forces of market clearing but also to be less optimistic about the ability of a large centralized political decision maker to respond in a consistent and timely fashion.

✆ 8.10 REVIEW QUESTIONS

1. Define the following basic concepts or terms:

Macroeconomic fluctuations	Market frictions
Stabilization policy	Sticky nominal wage hypothesis
Expectations-augmented aggregate supply	Sticky price hypothesis
Worker misperception hypothesis	Menu costs
Firm misperception hypothesis	Policy lags
Adaptive expectations hypothesis	Keynesian model
Rational expectations hypothesis	Monetarist model
Rational misperceptions	New classical model
Policy ineffectiveness proposition	Real business cycle model
	New Keynesian model

2. It is widely believed that private saving in the U.S. has diminished over recent decades and that this is responsible for a number of our economic problems. But suppose there is a sudden and substantial increase in saving as it returns to earlier levels, with a resulting decline in autonomous consumption $(-\Delta c_0)$. In terms of our new expectations-augmented model (AD/AS^e) trace the impact of this event from short run *through* long run, explaining the process linking short- and long-run outcomes. Specifically, use the model to explain how this drop in autonomous consumption will affect y, P, r, i, x, b, and e.

3. According to the AD/AS^e framework, price level *expectations* can play a significant role in determining real output, real interest rates, and so on.

   a. Use this model to show the likely impact of a sudden doubling of the *expected* price level, assuming no other changes in events or policies. In particular, explain whether there is good reason to fear that such an economy would be highly susceptible to the problem of "self-fulfilling prophecies."

   b. How does the extent to which changing price expectations affect real output depend on whether expectations adjust "adaptively" or "rationally"? Explain.

4. According to the AD/AS^e model, *why* do price level misperceptions have such a potentially powerful impact on the overall economy? Explain fully.

5. Evaluate the statements below, noting how they depend on the presence of certain specific conditions.

   a. "The "policy ineffectiveness proposition" is nonactivist propaganda masquerading as scientific analysis. It has no logical foundation and it obviously doesn't apply to the world in which we live."

   b. "Fine tuning is likely to do more harm than good because it treats the symptoms of instability rather than their underlying cause."

6. The call for an end to continuing government budget deficits is not only politically bipartisan but has advocates from all the schools of thought on macroeco-

nomic fluctuations. Suppose a substantial cut in government spending is made to try to end the large cash flow deficits. How would the predictions of its macroeconomic consequences differ across the following groups: Keynesian, new Keynesian, new classical, real business cycle, and monetarist? Explain.

7. Recent studies have shown that for every $100 loss of income/output in the economy $(-\Delta y)$ the government absorbs approximately $33 of it. About $25 of the $100 drop in before-tax income comes out of taxes. Another $8 comes from increased transfer payments (e.g., unemployment compensation and welfare payments) and increased interest payments (on the rising federal deficit). The net result is that household income falls only about $67 instead of the full $100. Many believe that this "automatic stabilizer" mechanism has been responsible for much of the apparent reduction in output and employment fluctuations in the U.S. in the post–World War II period.

   a. Explain how the declining tax payments and increasing transfer payments work as an "automatic stabilizer."

   b. In what ways is that preferable to using discretionary policy changes to deal with the problem? In what ways is it inferior? Explain.

   c. Suppose we extend the scope of this program by increasing transfer payments so that the *entire loss* in income is cushioned. Evaluate the likely costs and benefits of such an aggressive automatic stabilization program. Explain.

8. To which explanation of cyclical fluctuations—classical (C), Keynesian (K), monetarist (M), new classical/real business cycle (NC/RBC), or new Keynesian (NK)—do you think each of the following statements applies? (*Note:* they may fit more than one or they may fit none.) Briefly defend your answer.

   a. "Economic fluctuations associated with the ups and downs of the business cycle are not a major economic problem. In fact, they're the inevitable side effects of the workings of a market system."

   b. "The primary justification for having policy rules is the presence of long and variable lags in the policy-making process."

   c. "The major reason that unemployment persists so long is the failure of price expectations to adjust rapidly enough."

   d. "The credibility of the government (our confidence that it will carry through on its announced policies) determines, in part, the size of the business cycle."

   e. "As sincere as policy makers' intentions may be, the unfortunate result is that their attempts to smooth the business cycle actually make it worse."

   f. "As sincere as policy makers' intentions may be, their attempts to smooth the business cycle are futile. They have no impact whatsoever on output and employment and they only end up diverting our attention away from those areas in which government policy can make a difference."

   g. "Changes in government spending cause equal and opposite changes in private spending, leaving total demand unchanged."

9. The new Keynesian view of macroeconomic fluctuations is obviously a descendent of earlier views in the Keynesian, activist tradition. Compare these two views in terms of both their basic assumptions and their implications. Evaluate the statement that "the new Keynesian view is closer to the new classical approach than to the old Keynesian model."

10. "It is the responsibility of the government to take such steps as are necessary to minimize the recessionary phase of the business cycle. The cost in terms of lost output and jobs is simply one that cannot and need not be tolerated." It seems almost impossible to disagree with such a noble statement, the kind that any successful politician can unleash at a moment's notice. Yet a careful economic analysis would reveal a number of substantive issues that would put this into the "easier said than done" category. Evaluate this statement from the perspective of the following views of economic fluctuations: monetarist, classical, real business cycle, Keynesian, and new Keynesian. Explain your reasoning carefully.

8.11 FURTHER READING

C. Attfield, D. Demery, and N. Duck, *Rational Expectations in Macroeconomics*, 2nd ed. (Cambridge, England: Basil Blackwell, 1990).

Kevin D. Hoover, *The New Classical Macroeconomics: A Sceptical Inquiry* (Cambridge, England: Basil Blackwell, 1988).

N. Gregory Mankiw and David Romer, eds., *New Keynesian Economics*, 2 vols. (Cambridge, Mass: The MIT Press, 1991).

Bennett T. McCallum, *Monetary Macroeconomics: Theory and Policy* (New York: Macmillan, 1989).

CHAPTER 9

STABILIZATION POLICY AND THE PHILLIPS CURVE

🔖 9.1 INTRODUCTION

The missing link between short and long run was provided by the "short-run dynamics" of the expectations-augmented model (AD/AS^e) of Chapter 8. Our focus was on the forces underlying fluctuations in output and employment. Modern explanations begin by combining (1) **unstable aggregate demand** with (2) **price misperceptions.** They then add (3) **a theory of price expectations,** with "rational expectations" increasingly preferred to "adaptive." The model is completed by incorporating one or more of the following factors: (4) **market frictions** in the adjustment of prices and wages, (5) **fluctuations in aggregate supply** from an unstable full employment level of output, and (6) **long and variable lags** in the policy-making process.

Which of these specific elements are chosen determines whether the model yields nonactivist implications of "policy ineffectiveness" (e.g., the new classical "rational misperceptions" and real business cycle views) or "policy perversity" (the procyclical threat from unpredictable lags feared by monetarists) or whether it supports the activist use of policy to stabilize real output and employment (associated with new Keynesian models). Difficulties in measuring and testing these alternative models leave us unable to make a choice based on hard and unambiguous statistical evidence. But there is enough evidence to rule out extreme positions that, even a decade ago, had many supporters. For example, few would now maintain that "macroeconomic stabilization policy can *never* speed up economic recovery and will usually make things worse." Similarly, the widely held view in the 1960s that "the government can virtually eliminate the business cycle altogether by the aggressive and responsible use of countercyclical fiscal and monetary changes" has few advocates today. But we *cannot* dismiss positions, such as the following:

> While the government certainly can't "fine tune" the economy and iron out all the
> wrinkles in economic activity, it can generally diminish the variations in output

and employment that inevitably arise in market systems. Our experience since World War II makes it apparent that the benefits from counter-cyclical policy are no mirage. Since the individual and social payoffs from even very modest reductions in the depth or length of a recession are enormous, it would be irresponsible were the government not to exercise these powers in a careful and timely fashion.

Nor can we disregard views such as the following:

The government's ability to smooth the business cycle is much over-rated by politicians, the media, and the public. We give too much credit to the President or Congress when the economy is booming and too much blame when it stagnates. While countercyclical policy may sometimes accelerate economic recovery, it can also increase fluctuations in output and employment because of the presence of unpredictable policy lags. And even when they are successful, aggressive full employment policies often leave behind a costly legacy of higher inflation.

How do we handle such a large but legitimate "gray area" over prospects for stabilization policies? Decision makers can't stop making choices while economic researchers try to diminish the range of disagreement. Based on *current* knowledge, what should we understand in trying to decide upon the appropriate degree of public-sector involvement in macroeconomic stabilization? *Underneath all the slogans and partisan quarrels, how much can economic analysis tell us about prospects for a meaningful reduction of economic fluctuations in output, employment, and inflation?*

This sets the agenda for the next three chapters. The last chapter provided the analytical foundation with a general model of short-run fluctuations in real output and, implicitly, the price level. But by focusing on output it side-stepped unemployment and completely ignored inflation. The current chapter simply uses the previous analysis to look a bit further—to the relationship between *inflation and unemployment*, a connection called the **Phillips curve.** This, in turn, will provide the framework for a more detailed examination of the causes and consequences of inflation (Chapter 10) and unemployment (Chapter 11).

ᖍᖆ *9.2 "MODERN TIMES"— FROM PRICE LEVEL TO INFLATION RATE*

The misperceptions framework *(AD/AS^e)* is an extremely useful way to examine how expectations and market frictions are involved in the adjustment from short- to long-run outcomes. But it is set in a static world that is decidedly old-fashioned and unrealistic. For example, a recession is said to come from a decline in aggregate demand that causes not only a drop in real output but also a decline in the price level. Is this really what recessions look like? When was the last time that the price level actually *fell?*[1]

In fact, we live in a world in which the price level is always climbing—slowly, moderately, or rapidly, but always headed up. In periods of contraction and recession, aggregate demand doesn't actually fall; it only increases more slowly. So prices, instead of falling, just rise more slowly. In other words, in real life our attention is not on the price *level* but on the *rate of change* of the price level—the **inflation rate** (de-

---

[1] The U.S. price level, as measured by the GDP deflator, has declined in only one year since 1940—by less than half a percent in 1949. As data in the next chapter show, the U.S. price level has sometimes surged and sometimes plummeted, leaving the average level of prices virtually the same in 1940 as it was in 1776. Since World War II, however, yearly inflation has averaged over 4%.

noted by $\%\Delta P = \Pi$). If our analysis is to have any direct bearing on current economic issues, we must present it in terms of the ups and downs of the inflation rate ($\pm\Delta\Pi$) rather than of the price level ($\pm\Delta P$). *We must essentially put the AD/AS^e model in motion by converting its vertical axis from P to Π.* Fortunately, this transformation to a more realistic setting of ongoing price change is relatively straightforward. It takes a little attention and patience, but the underlying analysis is entirely consistent with what you've been doing in both the *AD/AS* and *AD/AS^e* models of previous chapters.

The first two graphs in Figure 9.1 show the transition from "level" to "rate of change" of prices. Assume, to keep things simple at the start, that the economy is always in long run equilibrium (perfect information and market-clearing). Now suppose the initial 5% rate of inflation rises to 10%. On the left is the familiar *AD/AS^e* graph (but without the upward-sloping short-run supply curves). The 5% rate of increase of the price level shows up as a *sequence* of points [$a \rightarrow b \rightarrow c \rightarrow d$] each assumed to be 5% higher than the previous one. Then, as aggregate demand shifts out more rapidly, the increase in the price level rises to a 10% rate [$e \rightarrow f \rightarrow g \rightarrow h$].

You can see that depicting this more realistic situation of *ongoing* price change threatens one of the main advantages of the *AD/AS* framework—its relative clarity and simplicity. Even without including the underlying *IS-LM* graph and all the short run aggregate supply curves, continuing shifts of aggregate demand create a cluttered picture. If we tried to add short-run misperceptions that cause deviations from *AS** along upward-sloping and (as expectations adjust) *shifting* short-run supply curves, it would quickly become a confusing tangle. Yet if we don't get these ongoing changes into the analysis, we'll be stuck with a model that describes a world that hasn't existed for more than half a century and is not likely to return.

■ FIGURE 9.1

The ongoing price level changes in (1) are initially at 5% ($a \rightarrow b \rightarrow c \rightarrow d$) and then rise to 10% ($e \rightarrow f \rightarrow g \rightarrow h$). The 5% inflation is captured in the points *A* of each graph; 10% in points *E*. In all cases we're looking only at a long run, market-clearing, full-employment outcome, with $y = y^*$ and $U = U^*$.

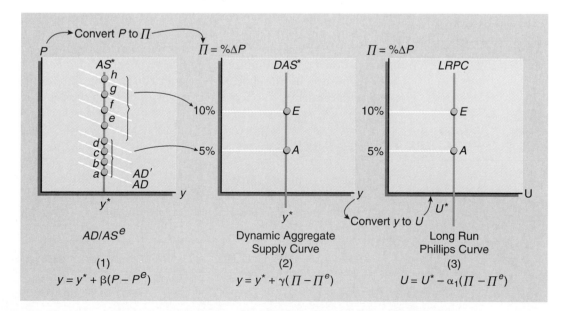

Three Portraits of the Long Run, with Inflation

The middle graph presents a simple solution to this problem. The vertical axis now measures the rate of change of the price level ($\%\Delta P = \Pi$) rather than just its level (P). It's like we've hopped on a train going the same speed as the price level. Viewed from the train, the constant rate of inflation now becomes a stable point that moves right alongside us. So in this graph, the *sequence* of points ($a \rightarrow b \rightarrow c \rightarrow d$) in the static AD/AS^e model becomes the *single* point A, showing a fully-employed economy ($y = y^*$) with a stable inflation rate (ongoing price level increase) of 5%. When the more rapid growth of aggregate demand causes the price level to rise at a 10% rate ($e \rightarrow f \rightarrow g \rightarrow h$, at left), this becomes a movement from points A to E in the middle graph. Since our example only considers the long run market-clearing situation, output remains at full employment as the acceleration in aggregate demand at left pushes us from points A to E on this new long-run curve (sometimes called the "dynamic aggregate supply curve"—DAS^*).

This transformation of the vertical axis from P to Π is a simple way to convert our static analysis to a real world setting of ongoing price level change. But let's take this a step further and, for reasons explained below, also adjust the horizontal axis as shown in the third graph. This picture keeps inflation on the vertical axis, but puts *unemployment* rather than real output on the horizontal axis. Both real output and unemployment are common aggregate measures of economic performance that are closely (albeit inversely) related. When real output is at its full employment level ($y = y^*$), employment is at its full employment level ($n = n^*$) and unemployment at its "natural" rate ($U = U^*$). So points A and E, representing the sequence of points [$a \rightarrow b \rightarrow c \rightarrow d$ and $e \rightarrow f \rightarrow g \rightarrow h$] in the first graph, now show up at U^* in the third graph and define what is known as the **long-run Phillips curve** ($LRPC$).

The differences among the three graphs in Figure 9.1 are purely cosmetic. They only paint a different face on precisely the same thing—an economy at full employment (denoted by y^* or, equivalently, U^*) with an initial rate of price increase of 5% that then rises to 10%. The first graph is the basic analysis used throughout the course. Because it becomes so cumbersome when dealing with *ongoing* changes, the translation from price level to inflation rate in the second graph reduces much of the visual clutter and simplifies the analysis of inflation. The third graph then alters the horizontal axis from real output to the unemployment rate. This last change doesn't make things particularly easier or harder, but serves the important function of linking the analysis to a well-known topic in macroeconomic research and policy analysis known as the **Phillips curve.**[2] It is in terms of *inflation* and *unemployment* that we now explore the short run dynamics underlying stabilization policy and connect it with the activist/nonactivist issues introduced in the previous chapter.

9.3 PHILLIPS CURVE BASICS

The connections among the three graphs in Figure 9.1 also extend to short run situations in which price misperceptions ($P \neq P^e$) move the economy away from full employment. In the AD/AS^e model, misperceptions were incorporated through the un-

---

[2] The curve is named for the British economist A. W. Phillips (1914–1975), originally from New Zealand, who discovered an inverse relationship in long run data between the rate of change of money wages (called "wage inflation") and the unemployment rate ("The Relation between Unemployment and the Rate of Change of Money Wage Rates in the United Kingdom, 1861–1957," *Economica* 25 (August 1958): 283–300). Subsequent investigation has greatly refined the analysis and testing procedures and linked them to mainstream macroeconomic analysis. Though its name has not changed, Phillips's original curve has been transformed into a study of short- and long-run relationships between inflation (Π) and unemployment (U) that yields very different conclusions from his original work.

derlying $y = y^* + \beta(P - P^e)$ relationship. To convert this into a relationship between inflation and real output, as in the middle graph, we substitute $\Pi - \Pi^e$ for $P - P^e$ and rewrite it as $y = y^* + \gamma(\Pi - \Pi^e)$. Here the parameter γ is analogous to the β of the static formulation. This dynamic version of the expectations-augmented supply curve says that real output will be at its full employment level so long as expected and actual inflation are equal, that is, $\Pi = \Pi^e$. Fluctuations of output around full employment are the result of fluctuations in *inflation misperceptions*, that is, $\pm\Delta(y - y^*)$ comes from $\pm\Delta(\Pi - \Pi^e)$.

To then convert this into a Phillips curve requires only the addition of the inverse relationship between unemployment and output $(+\Delta U \Rightarrow -\Delta y)$.[3] For a given institutional structure and fixed capital stock, a decline in employment (hence, a rise in unemployment) means a drop in output, hence $+\Delta U \Rightarrow -\Delta n \Rightarrow y\downarrow = F(n\downarrow,k,i^{nst})$. This gives a basic Phillips curve equation as follows:

$$U = U^* - \alpha_1(\Pi - \Pi^e),$$

where α_1 is a positive constant, analogous to the γ above but preceded by a negative sign since we're using a mirror image of real output (y) when we switch to unemployment (U).

The Phillips curve (so famous in the 1960s and 1970s that it even made the cover of *Time Magazine*) is a simple and appealing way to summarize the relatively complicated and forbidding analytics of the AD/AS^e model in a world of continuing change. In viewing the economy in terms of *inflation* (Π) and *unemployment* (U) rather than the price level (P) and real output (y), it focuses on the two most familiar indicators of current economic performance. To see how it works we turn to Figure 9.2. Starting with price stability ($\Pi = 0$) and full employment ($U = U^*$) as shown at point A, suppose a sudden increase in the rate of growth of the money supply causes both LM and AD to shift out resulting in an unexpected surge in the inflation rate to 5%. (Remember that the basic IS-LM and AD-AS curves, though now hidden, are still essential to the underlying analysis.) According to the Phillips curve equation this change in inflation misperceptions ($\Pi - \Pi^e = 5\% - 0\% = 5\%$) causes unemployment to decline as the economy moves to a situation of "over-full" employment like point B in the graph.[4] For as long as this misperception lasts, unemployment will remain below its "natural" rate at U_1.

But assuming this higher rate of inflation continues, working its way into our perceptions and decisions, unemployment will return to its full employment level and the economy will adjust to point C in Figure 9.2. Not surprisingly, we find that the end result of faster money growth in a fully employed economy is only a temporary reduction in unemployment (U^* to U_1) but an ongoing increase in inflation (0% to 5%). If policy makers decided to try for another short-run drop in unemployment, they would again have to create inflation misperceptions of 5%. But because decision makers are now starting with inflation expectations of 5%, actual inflation would have to rise to 10% as shown in the movement from points C to D. And, again, as inflation expectations catch up, unemployment will return to its natural rate but this time at point E with 10% inflation.

---

[3] This relationship has come to be called Okun's Law following the work of Arthur Okun in "Potential GNP: Its Measurement and Significance," *Proceedings*, Business and Economic Statistics Section of the American Statistical Association (1961). We will discuss it more fully in Chapter 11 when we seek to determine the economic costs of unemployment in terms of lost output.

[4] This is the dynamic counterpart to the short-run rise in real output in AD/AS^e when the price level rises above its expected value as AD shifts out along a short-run aggregate supply curve.

■ FIGURE 9.2

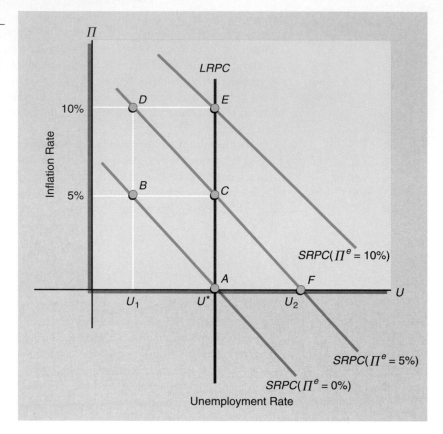

Short- and Long-Run Phillips Curves
$$U = U^* - \alpha_1(\Pi - \Pi^e)$$

Put another way, there is a "family" of downward-sloping **short-run Phillips curves** *(SRPC)*, one for each level of expected inflation.[5] For a given expected rate of inflation, a change in the actual rate of inflation moves the economy *along* one of these curves and defines a short-run "trade-off" between inflation and unemployment. But when inflation expectations adjust in the long run, the entire short run curve *shifts* to reflect the new level of expected inflation. So the short-run impact of a change in inflation on unemployment (and output) is soon lost. In Figure 9.2, as inflation expectations change from 0% to 5% and then to 10%, the economy moves from $SRPC(\Pi^e = 0\%)$ to $SRPC(\Pi^e = 5\%)$ and finally to $SRPC(\Pi^e = 10\%)$. Each short-run attempt to "exploit the trade-off"—that is, move up along the short-run curve—ends in a return to U^* at a higher and higher rate of inflation. Finally, we're left with points *A*, *C*, and *E* along successively higher short-run curves, tracing out the long-run Phillips curve *(LRPC)*.

After the first round of inflation has left the economy at point *C*, suppose we decide that the wisest choice is to *dis*inflate and move back to point *A*. As monetary contraction (actually a *slowing* of the monetary expansion now that we're in a dy-

---

[5] This should look familiar since these are just the dynamic counterparts of the short run aggregate supply curves that we derived back in Figure 8.1. Each of those curves was defined for a given expected price level, whereas these are for a given expected inflation rate. Those curves had output on the horizontal axis and sloped upward; these have unemployment on the horizontal axis and slope downward.

USING THE PHILLIPS CURVE

The Phillips curve (Figure 9.2) is a graphical view of the equation $U = U^* - \alpha_1(\Pi - \Pi^e)$. It forces us to make a clear distinction between short and long run (fixed vs. flexible Π^e) and, hence, between a movement along and a shift ($\Delta\Pi$ vs. $\Delta\Pi^e$) in the Phillips curve. The following rules, combined with a little practice, will help you to learn its mechanics quickly:

1. The initial level of inflation expectations (Π^e) tells us *which SRPC* the economy is on.
2. The initial level of actual inflation (Π) determines our *specific location* on that short-run curve.
3. We must turn to the underlying AD/AS^e framework to determine how a given event or policy change will alter the actual inflation rate. Once we've determined this $\Delta\Pi$ we can see how far the resulting misperceptions move the economy *along* its initial short run Phillips curve.
4. How long it takes the economy to return to its *LRPC* depends on how quickly inflation expectations adjust ($\Delta\Pi^e$) to end the inflation misperceptions and shift the *SRPC*.

namic setting) squeezes out inflation, the initial misperceptions ($\Pi - \Pi^e < 0$) move us along the $SRPC(\Pi^e = 5\%)$ from points C to F as the economy slips into a recession. Only when inflation expectations have readjusted and $\Pi^e = \Pi = 0\%$ can the economy regain its initial point A.

9.4 EXTENDING THE PHILLIPS CURVE

This first look at the relationship between inflation and unemployment has used a Phillips curve derived directly from the "rational misperceptions" model (AD/AS^e + REH). Just as that earlier model led to the nonactivist "policy ineffectiveness" implication, so does the Phillips curve that comes from it—$U = U^* - \alpha_1(\Pi - \Pi^e)$. In this approach (1) deviations from the *LRPC* are *entirely* due to inflation misperceptions ($\Pi \neq \Pi^e$), (2) rational expectations ensure a quick end to these deviations, and (3) anticipated events (like stabilization policy) do not create misperceptions and can therefore have no impact on unemployment.

But because the "rational misperceptions" approach explained only part of the observed fluctuations in output, we had to supplement the analysis with additional sources of instability. One way is to follow real business cycle proponents and add *supply-side fluctuations* ($\pm\Delta y^*$) to the model. They argue that the missing fluctuations in real output come from an unstable aggregate supply curve ($\pm\Delta y^* \Rightarrow \pm\Delta AS^*$). In a Phillips curve setting, the real business cycle view says that the missing fluctuations in unemployment are accounted for by an unstable long-run Phillips curve

($\pm \Delta U^* \Rightarrow \pm \Delta LRPC$). Adding such supply-side instability to the basic misperceptions approach maintains the nonactivist tone of the model since it is generally acknowledged that monetary and fiscal manipulation can do little to offset fluctuations in the natural rate of unemployment itself.

But since most macroeconomists find the real business cycle story incomplete if not totally unconvincing, the path most often taken is to include *frictions in the market-clearing process.* As we saw in the previous chapter, this can reflect a diverse group of factors (contracts, monopoly power, menu costs, and so on) with one thing in common—all represent plausible situations in which some markets adjust slowly even in a world where expectations adjust rapidly. These market frictions—whose impact was captured by adding a lagged deviation term, $\lambda(y - y^*)_{-1}$, to the model—prolong and deepen the effect of demand-side instabilities and, thereby, account for the missing fluctuations. Their impact can be captured in the **expanded Phillips curve equation** in a similar way by adding the effect of last period's gap between the actual and natural rates of unemployment, $(U - U^*)_{-1}$, as follows:

$$U = U^* - \alpha_1(\Pi - \Pi^e) + \alpha_2(U - U^*)_{-1}$$

In this equation, the impact of market frictions is reflected in the $\alpha_2(U - U^*)_{-1}$ term, where α_2 is a positive constant representing the degree of stickiness as λ did in our earlier formulation. So instead of putting the "stickiness" directly in the model, which is very complicated, we are using a "proxy" or "surrogate" variable that yields a similar outcome in a simpler way. This should not be interpreted as saying that yesterday's unemployment *causes* today's. Instead, it says that the effect of price/wage stickiness on unemployment can be *described* by a model in which high unemployment from the recent past $[(U - U^*)_{-1} > 0]$ is partially carried over to the present $(U - U^* > 0)$ even when there are no misperceptions $(\Pi - \Pi^e = 0)$.

While the graph of this expanded Phillips curve looks the same as before, the short run curves now shift more slowly and there is a more sluggish return to the long run Phillips curve because of the added market frictions. The importance of these frictions for a given economy is represented by the size of its α_2 parameter. If this is zero or very small, then the frictions are relatively insignificant and the model will yield nonactivist implications for stabilization policy. Larger values of α_2 mean stronger market frictions and a slower return to full employment, thereby restoring the potential for stabilization policy to smooth the business cycle.[6]

The Phillips curve in Figure 9.3 includes this "lagged" unemployment gap as specified in $U = U^* - \alpha_1(\Pi - \Pi^e) + \alpha_2(U - U^*)_{-1}$. Starting at full employment with 10% inflation (point $\mathcal{J}$), suppose policy makers contract the growth of aggregate demand, reducing the inflation rate to 5% and moving the economy along its *SRPC* to point K. This is exactly the same as in our earlier analysis with no market frictions (implicitly, $\alpha_2 = 0$). The difference comes in the subsequent adjustment back to full employment. The presence of market frictions slows down the adjustment from points K to L. Even if the misperceptions disappear quickly (so $-\alpha_1(\Pi - \Pi^e)$ goes to zero), the influence of the lagged unemployment gap (the distance $U_1 - U^*$ in the graph) will disappear gradually each period (inversely to the size of α_2). The result will be like a local train that stops at K', K'', K''', and so on, in contrast to the previous express train that goes directly from points K to L.

---

[6] For example, if $\alpha_2 = .5$ then an economy that has unemployment 2% higher than its natural rate this year will be 1% above its natural rate next year even after inflation expectations have adjusted to actual inflation. The unemployment gap will continue to decline by half each year, simulating the presumed sluggishness of the market-clearing process.

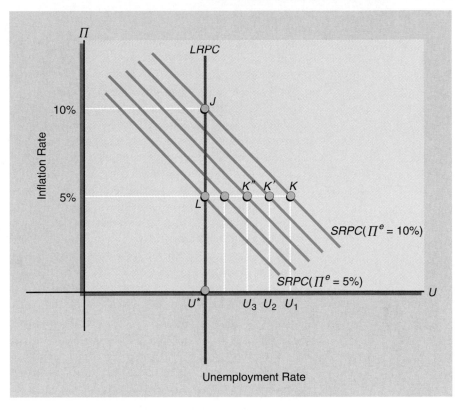

Phillips Curve Dynamics with Market Frictions
$$U = U^* - \alpha_1(\Pi - \Pi^e) + \alpha_2(U - U^*)_{-1}$$

■ FIGURE 9.3

IN SUMMARY . . .

Inflation, Unemployment, and the Phillips Curve

This is a good point to consolidate what we know and don't know about economic fluctuations as they pertain to the issues of inflation, unemployment, and stabilization policy. The Phillips curve offers a particularly clear look at these short-run dynamics. It is not an alternative to aggregate demand and supply analysis, but a specific way to package that underlying model. What does the Phillips curve perspective tell us about the relationship between inflation and unemployment?

1. **There is no lasting tradeoff between inflation and unemployment.** The trade-off— $+\Delta\Pi \Rightarrow -\Delta U$ —that originally made the Phillips curve so famous, vanishes with the misperceptions that caused it. Macroeconomic policy discussions that complain about the "cruel dilemma" of having to choose between higher unemployment and lower inflation, are focusing only on a short run relationship. There is *no* lasting trade-off, so more inflation *cannot* buy a sustainable reduction in unemployment. This important and now widely-accepted result is unaffected by the presence or absence of market frictions.

(Continued)

While departures from full employment last longer when there's wage/price stickiness, they eventually disappear. Whether this is a matter of a few months or a few years is disputed, but there is no evidence that the trade-off can persist into a long-run "when we're all dead" as activist views of earlier decades often implied. The *long run Phillips curve* is vertical!

2. ***Disinflation causes unemployment.*** An unexpected reduction in the inflation rate initially moves the economy down a given short run Phillips curve, pushing it into recession. The *misperceptions hypothesis* tells us that the length of this downturn depends on how quickly inflation expectations respond. The presumption of "rational expectations" is that the resulting recession will be short-lived provided the disinflation policy is a "credible" one. To the extent that previous pledges by the government to reduce inflation have gone unfulfilled, expectations may not adjust and the result could then be a more prolonged downturn. The duration of the downturn is further extended by the presence of *market frictions*. Even with a credible policy and a quick end to misperceptions, wage/price stickiness will cause high unemployment rates to linger a bit longer. The larger these frictions (the larger the value of α_2), the greater will be the loss of output and jobs when inflation is reduced.

3. ***If policy makers persist in the attempt to keep unemployment below its natural rate ($U < U^*$), the inevitable result will be accelerating inflation.*** We saw in Figure 9.2 that reducing unemployment to U_1 required inflation misperceptions of 5%. To maintain this level of unemployment in a world in which expectations keep catching up with reality requires increasingly expansionary policy to maintain the gap between actual and expected inflation. Eventually such policies will be foreseen, expectations will incorporate a continually *increasing* rate of inflation, and the economy will return to its long run Phillips curve at U^*. The presence of a high degree of market friction (large α_2) slows the return to U^* and might give the illusion that expansionary policy has a lasting impact on unemployment and real output. But the final outcome of any policy that tries to keep unemployment below its natural rate will be spiraling inflation with no lasting reduction in unemployment. Tempting as it may be, the short-run inflation-unemployment trade-off is not a path to a lasting reduction in unemployment. *Failure to heed this message is an expressway to accelerating inflation.*

4. ***Stabilization policy must operate within a relatively short "window of time" if it is to be successful.*** Our basic Phillips curve, mirroring the "rational misperceptions" model ($AD/AS^e + REH$), presumes that inflation misperceptions are the *only* factor causing unemployment. The increasing acceptance of the rational expectations hypothesis over more sluggish alternatives leads to a dynamic version of the "policy ineffectiveness" proposition that rejects the usefulness and even the need for stabilization policy because of the rapidity of market-clearing. But this conclusion is based on a model that leaves an important part of observed economic fluctuations unexplained. If we follow the mainstream and complete the model by adding "market frictions" (rather than "supply side instability"), these frictions extend the time interval during which countercyclical policies can prove effective. However, the case in favor of activist stabilization policy depends not just on the existence of such frictions or even their magnitude; it depends on the size of these market frictions relative to the size of the *frictions in the policy process* known as "policy lags."

⊙⊙ 9.5 THE VANISHING TRADE-OFF

The Phillips curve, though relatively young as economic theories go, has experienced a series of theoretical and statistical attacks that have dramatically transformed its features since its birth in 1958. A. W. Phillips's original contribution was rapidly extended and incorporated into macroeconomic policy making on the basis of its claim to have revealed a *long-run stable trade-off* between inflation and unemployment. The early statistical analysis and the model created to explain those findings proclaimed the discovery of a simple, lasting trade-off between inflation and unemployment. For example, the 1960s Phillips curve (shown in Figure 9.4) shows that years of high inflation were times of low unemployment and when inflation fell, unemployment rose.

Initial observations like this led to the widespread belief that the Phillips curve was a downward-sloping curve that did *not* shift over time. In our basic formulation—$U = U^* - \alpha_1(\Pi - \Pi^e)$—this stability implies fixed expectations ($\Delta \Pi^e = 0$), so that the given short-run curve was the *only* relevant curve. In this setting, macroeconomic policy making became a simple choice of which point to select along the given curve. The Phillips curve seemed to present policy makers with a fixed menu of inflation-unemployment combinations. Though we would like to reduce *both* unemployment and inflation, the regrettable fact seemed to be that we could reduce one only by increasing the other. The particular point on the tradeoff was chosen through the political process and then economists simply maneuvered the economy into the desired position.

It all seemed simple (much too simple, we now see) and this was certainly one of its most inviting characteristics. Moreover, although the existence of an (apparent) inflation-unemployment tradeoff was unwelcome news for the economy, it provided an explanation and excuse for policymakers who had failed to achieve simultaneous full employment and stable prices mandated by the Employment Act of 1946. This "Phillips curve menu" view dominated economic policymaking for more than a decade. But eventually it became apparent that the supposed stable tradeoff, if it had ever existed, was not present in the industrial economies of the 1970s and 1980s.

The graphs in Figure 9.5 show the reality that finally undermined the original Phillips Curve and led to the analytical innovations that added the "natural rate" of unemployment, expectations, and market frictions to the analysis. A plot of the annual observations of inflation and unemployment since 1960 is shown in Figure 9.5(a). These data are widely scattered and fail to reveal a tradeoff or any other apparent pattern to the inflation-unemployment relationship. But if we connect the observations sequentially, as in Figure 9.5(b) we see some hints of a *pattern that has been shifting systematically over time*. As Figure 9.5(c) shows, this is roughly consistent with the modern view of a temporary trade-off that shifts upward as inflation and expected inflation increase.

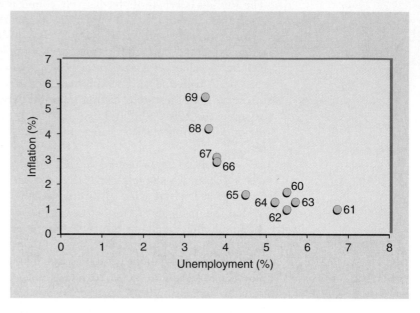

■ FIGURE 9.4

■ FIGURE 9.5a

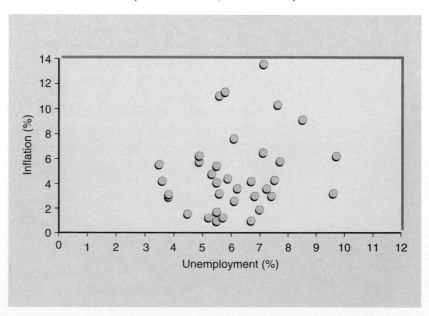

Inflation and Unemployment
(United States, 1960–1994)

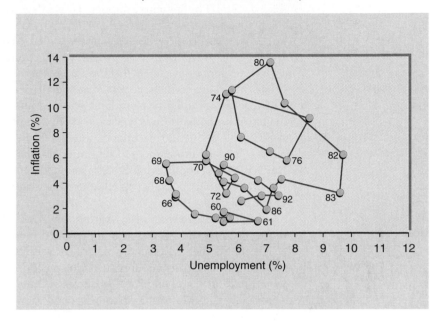

■ FIGURE 9.5b

■ FIGURE 9.5c

Inflation and Unemployment
(United States, 1960–1994)

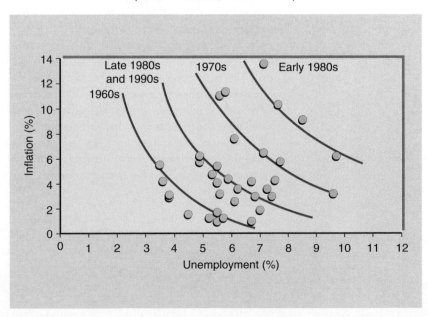

☯ 9.6 *POLICY LAGS AND ACTIVIST STABILIZATION*

The general Phillips curve model, $U = U^* - \alpha_1(\Pi - \Pi^e) + \alpha_2(U - U^*)_{-1}$, shows fluctuations in the actual rate of unemployment ($\pm \Delta U$) that can be decomposed into three sources: *supply-side instabilities* ($\pm \Delta U^*$), *changing inflation misperceptions* ($\pm \Delta(\Pi - \Pi^e)$) from unstable growth of aggregate demand, and *changing market frictions* (represented by $\pm \Delta(U - U^*)_{-1}$). Except for a handful of real business cycle theorists, macroeconomists generally agree that some combination of misperceptions and market frictions best explains the ups and downs of actual economic performance. This conclusion is consistent with popular views that the government has the ability (and obligation) to take countercyclical policy actions when the economy departs from full employment. The Employment Act of 1946, the Humphrey-Hawkins Bill (1978) and countless political pronouncements and campaign platforms, obligate the government to use its fiscal and monetary powers to achieve and maintain full employment.

But, as noted in the last chapter, the conduct of stabilization policy has become more restrained and less activist than in previous decades.[7] For the public this reflects a perception that government responses are less reliable and have more costly side effects than previously thought. Among economists this moderation stems largely from theoretical and empirical advances in the microfoundations of macroeconomics, specifically the role of misperceptions and market frictions. There has also been renewed awareness of frictions in the policy process itself—policy lags that complicate our ability to make an "appropriate and timely policy response" to rising unemployment or rising inflation.

Serious concern with the problems posed by **policy lags** was, until recently, associated largely with the monetarist school of thought. Unlike other nonactivists (most notably the new classical and real business cycle views), monetarists generally do not dispute the existence of wage/price stickiness and other frictions in the market-clearing process. They base their nonactivist view of economic stabilization, instead, on the premise that countercyclical monetary and fiscal policies are plagued, in Milton Friedman's oft-quoted phrase, by "long and variable lags," which can delay the impact of policy until it is no longer needed. They believe the "window of time," propped open by market frictions, is still too small for countercyclical actions to be effective because of the inevitable time lags in the policy process. This leads monetarists to focus their concerns on longer-term issues like economic growth and inflation, arguing that short run fluctuations in output and employment are largely beyond the influence of policy manipulation. They characterize the mainstream as having succumbed to a siren song of "fine tuning." They even contend that because of these unpredictable policy lags the government has often become a cause rather than a cure for macroeconomic fluctuations.[8]

What is the nature of these lags that act as frictions in the policy-response process? The following diagram categorizes several crucial stages in policy making. Starting at point *E*—the moment the destabilizing *event* (say a negative demand

---

[7] Remember that this discussion is not about the general role of government in the economy but about the specific topic of using government policy to reduce short-run fluctuations in economic activity. It is possible to be a nonactivist on this issue yet support an active role for government in other areas, such as economic growth or redistribution. Similarly, one may be an activist on stabilization policy but favor a smaller role for centralized decision making in other areas.

[8] For an excellent assessment of the strengths and weaknesses of the monetarist view see David Laidler, "The Legacy of the Monetarist Controversy," *Review*, The Federal Reserve Bank of St. Louis (March/April 1990): 49–64.

shock) occurs—a series of events must follow before we reach point *I* when the full *impact* of the policy response has been felt.

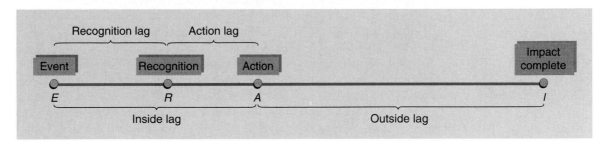

Time Lags in the Policy-Making Process

The "recognition lag" refers to the time before we realize the event has occurred (the drop in investment or consumption that precipitates a recession, for example). Because it takes a while to get reliable data on macroeconomic events, several months may elapse before we have a clear picture of the problem and are ready to make a policy response. The recognition lag is then followed by an "action lag"— the time between the decision to change policy and the policy change itself. Together, the information and action lags are often called the *inside lag*, which is shown as the interval between event and actions (points *E* and *A*). This is followed by an *outside lag* that describes the interval (points *A* to *I*) between the policy action and the time when all its effects are complete.

Many factors influence the length of these lags and can cause them to change unexpectedly. Although there is a great deal that we simply do not understand in this area, some generalizations are possible. Fiscal policy, having to wend its way through Congress and the White House, typically has a relatively long inside lag. But once a fiscal policy action has been taken, its impact on economic activity is likely to be felt quite rapidly. Monetary policy, which can be changed by the Federal Reserve without political consent of other groups, has a very small inside lag. But the work of Milton Friedman and others have shown that it can have a long and unpredictable outside lag (6 to 18 months is the standard estimate) as its initial impact on interest rates spreads through investment decisions to aggregate output and employment.

To what extent are countercyclical policies afflicted by "long and variable," hence, unpredictable, lags? Monetarist pessimism on this point distinguishes it from the view of the more activist mainstream. Is this pessimism about the timeliness of stabilization policies warranted by the facts? Or is it largely a reflection of the nonactivist political preferences of those who are drawn to the monetarist view?

This is an inherently difficult question to answer because of our inability to perform controlled experiments on the macroeconomy. What we would like, of course, is to have a careful other-things-held-constant comparison of alternative policies. For example, what would have happened following the 1990 to 1991 U.S. recession if an activist fiscal or monetary response had been chosen instead of the relatively nonactivist response taken by President Bush and Federal Reserve Chairman Alan Greenspan? History tells us that the ensuing recession was considerably more prolonged than expected by policy makers and most economic forecasters. This can make it tempting to dismiss the nonactivist view on the grounds that it was "obviously" a poor choice. Unfortunately, an understanding of short run dynamics doesn't come that easily. Can we be sure that an activist response in late 1990 or early 1991 would have taken hold in time to significantly hasten the recovery? If the policy delays turned out to be unusually long, an activist policy could have ended up with the same recession followed by a postrecessionary inflationary surge.

Because we can't turn the clock back and try other policies under identical conditions, we can only search for indirect clues in the "uncontrolled experiments" that constitute our past experience. Sometimes such econometric analyses come up with convincing results. More often, particularly on issues of "timing," enough fuzziness remains that several quite different theories may be consistent with the facts. It's at such barriers that economic research keeps chipping away—searching for additional data, better tools for extracting clues from existing data, and more ingenious ways to restate theories to make them easier to test. In the meantime, though, choices must be made. From among several more or less plausible explanations of short run fluctuations, policymakers must decide—with assistance from their subjective political preferences—which strategy to follow.

⌘ 9.7 DOES STABILIZATION POLICY CAUSE INFLATION?

An important by-product of all the controversy over expectations, stabilization policy, and Phillips curves has been the discovery that policies designed to reduce fluctuations in output and employment might actually end up causing permanently higher rates of inflation. The debate has uncovered a problem of **inflationary bias** inherent in the proces of *discretionary policy making*. "Discretionary" policy making is the policy process we've been talking about throughout the book. It is characterized by the fact that a particular policy change is at the "discretion" of some individual or group who must look at current economic performance and make a decision about when to change policy and by how much.

It turns out that when stabilization policy is done on such a discretionary basis, it may lead to a permanently higher rate of inflation than if policy changes were made according to a set formula or rule. To see this, suppose there are two identical economies except that economy I has chosen a nonactivist stabilization strategy, whereas economy II takes an activist approach through discretionary policy adjustments. Regardless of which economy ends up with the smallest fluctuations in output and employment, economy II is likely to have a higher average rate of inflation because of its use of discretionary policy. This "inflationary bias" result is illustrated in Figure 9.6 where we start at point A with full employment ($U = U^*$) and price stability ($\Pi = 0\%$). This would seem to be a highly desirable situation, with markets cleared and inflation expectations at zero. Hence, it's a bit surprising to find that policy makers are unlikely to choose to keep the economy at point A unless they are subject to restrictions that limit their range of discretion.

To understand the forces pushing the economy away from this optimal full employment-stable price position, we begin by noting that "unemployment" is a singularly decisive issue in U.S. elections. It arouses far more concern than other issues like the "budget deficit," the "trade deficit," high "inflation" (at least when it stays away from double digit levels), or sluggish "economic growth." The importance of a low unemployment rate to so many voters is a fact that cannot be ignored by any politician, incumbent or aspiring. Because of this attention to unemployment and because of our ability to temporarily reduce it through expansionary policies that cause a bit more inflation, there can be substantial political gains from the pursuit of an expansionary policy even when the economy starts at a situation of full employment

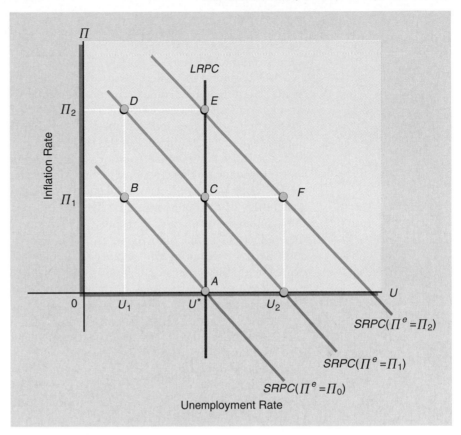

Inflationary Bias in Discretionary Stabilization Policy

■ FIGURE 9.6

and stable prices (such as point A in Figure 9.6). A monetary or fiscal stimulus would move us to point B and bring about a popular reduction in unemployment and a corresponding increase in real output.

But as expectations are revised and frictions overcome, we know what the political discussion is likely to obscure—that this economy will move back to the original unemployment level at the higher rate of inflation shown at point C. With the next election, policy makers may again succumb to the payoffs from a further expansion of the growth of aggregate demand, leading initially to point D but ending up at point E. Eventually inflation rather than unemployment will be perceived as the primary economic problem and the expansionary process will end. But because the immediate cost of disinflation is a rise in unemployment (such as from points E to F in Figure 9.6), there will be less incentive to undertake aggressive contractionary policies—particularly if voters are willing to believe the assertions of those who say that a rise in unemployment is *not* a necessary short run cost of disinflation.

We are left with a situation in which there are real incentives for policy makers to take actions that increase inflation and disincentives to decrease it. If the adjustment process is fairly sluggish, as the dominant "misperceptions plus frictions" view suggests, this bias will be all the more pronounced because the short term incentives and disincentives last longer before the economy returns to its *LRPC*. Finding ourselves at point E in a world of substantial market frictions, the rational choice may be to continue inflation at this level rather than incur the lost output and higher unemployment from disinflation.[9] In this setting, once policy makers have bitten into the apple of discretionary stabilization policy, the likelihood of regaining price stability seems remote.

It's tempting to view this scenario as one in which the desirable full employment, zero inflation outcome (at point A) is undermined by the shortsighted and self-serving decisions of irresponsible policy makers. You may be thinking that honorable politicians who understand that the long run Phillips curve is vertical would never pursue such myopic policies. But the fascinating and important thing about this issue is that it is *not* just a simple issue of good or bad economics or responsible or irresponsible policy making. In fact, this "inflationary bias" is built into the situation precisely *because* political decision makers are willing and able to be responsive to the preferences of their constituencies. To see this, look back at Figure 9.6 and suppose the economy is at point C with full employment and moderate inflation. Realizing that reductions in unemployment, even if temporary and unsustainable, are popular and, therefore, tempting to "responsive" policy makers, voters have good reason to expect that policy expansion lies ahead and that the inflation rate will rise. Anticipating that policy makers will act in their own political interest, then, decision makers will revise their inflation expectations accordingly.

As we've seen in these last two chapters, expectations of what lies ahead influence current decisions. In this example the increased inflation expectations will shift the $SRPC$ out, say to $SRPC(\Pi^e = \Pi_2)$ in Figure 9.6. Policy makers now face a difficult choice. They can keep inflation at its current rate and watch unemployment rise to U_2 as the economy moves from points C to F and suffers high unemployment for as long as these misperceptions and accompanying frictions continue. Or they can implement the anticipated expansionary policy so as to match the expected increase in inflation ($+\Delta\Pi = +\Delta\Pi^e$). By doing what people expect them to do they prevent misperceptions and thereby keep unemployment from rising. The good news is that this can keep the economy at full employment; the bad news is that it does so only by increasing inflation and moving the economy from points C to E in Figure 9.6.

How can this inflationary bias be removed? One obvious way is to create **policy rules** that simply take away the ability of policy makers to change current policy at their discretion.[10] A rule or law (or constitutional amendment) prohibiting **discretionary stabilization policy** would seem, at first glance, to lead directly to the nonactivist position and an admission that the goals of the Employment Act of 1946 and its successors are unattainable. But a little more thought tells us that the inflationary bias problem arises because of the expectation that stabilization policy will be used in shortsighted ways that would favor points like B and D (but ending in points C and E) over point A (in Figure 9.6). Replacing policy makers with policy rules doesn't have to mean *fixed* rules, unresponsive to current economic conditions. A *feedback* rule could be specified that would incorporate some measure of the current state of the economy into the policy formula.

To see this, let's start with a traditional nonactivist policy rule for determining the money supply. We can set monetary policy in advance by specifying that the nominal money supply grow at a certain rate each year regardless of economic per-

---

[9] This, of course, depends on how the ongoing costs of higher inflation compare with the temporary costs of the "planned recession" induced by disinflation. This will be discussed in the next chapter.

[10] For some early and enduring statements of the case for policy rules, predating the "inflationary bias" issue, see Henry C. Simons, *Economic Policy for a Free Society* (Chicago: University of Chicago Press, 1948) and Milton Friedman, "A Monetary and Fiscal Framework for Economic Stability," in *Essays in Positive Economics* (Chicago: University of Chicago Press, 1953), pp. 133–156.

formance at the time. This could be a specific number that roughly reflects the long term growth of real output in the economy or it could be a formula that sets money growth equal to the average growth of output over a certain number of years.[11] Either way, it ensures that policy is unable to respond to current economic conditions and so eliminates expectations that monetary policy will be used in a shortsighted pursuit of over-full employment, eradicating the tendency toward an inflationary bias. For nonactivists this rule kills two birds with one stone by also eliminating the threat that stabilization policy itself will become a source of the fluctuations in output and unemployment that it's supposed to cure.

But we could also have a less rigid policy rule that allows us to incorporate current economic performance into the formula. For example, a monetary rule could tell us to set the growth of the money supply equal to 2.5% (an estimate of expected long term growth in AS^*) plus an amount equal to the size of the current "excess" unemployment $U - U^*$,

$$\%\Delta M = 2.5\% + (U - U^*)$$

For an economy in recession, the last term will be positive so that money growth will vary directly with the magnitude of unemployment. When the economy has temporarily low unemployment rates ($U < U^*$), this rule would reduce money growth below 2.5%, restraining inflationary pressures. For an economy at full employment, the last term would simply disappear. The inflationary bias problem is eliminated while still allowing policy changes to be responsive to current economic conditions. Such a strategy appeals to activists troubled by the inflationary bias of discretionary stabilization policies. But nonactivists generally criticize rules with feedback because they are either futile ("rational misperceptions" or the real business cycle model) or still face the problem of unpredictable policy lags (monetarist view). While rules can reduce the "action lag" in getting monetary or, especially, fiscal policies changed, the other sources of delay are still present.

Policy rules currently exist on a relatively small scale and are typically called "automatic stabilizers." For example, unemployment benefits rise during recessions without any need for explicit policy changes. They could obviously be extended to monetary policy as discussed earlier. Recent years have seen a major struggle over fiscal policy rules in the form of the ineffective Gramm-Rudman-Hollings Law to eliminate the federal deficit and the oft-proposed Balanced Budget Amendment to the U.S. Constitution. It seems safe to conclude that the political environment does not now welcome such changes and that no major dismantling of discretionary monetary and fiscal policies appears likely.

Inflationary bias, however, is not inevitable if the government has a sufficiently strong commitment to low inflation that it will firmly resist temptations to indulge in temporary expansions at the cost of lasting increases in inflation. In particular, if Federal Reserve promises are viewed as credible, inflation expectations will not be raised and the inflationary bias scenario can be avoided. But if the government also makes employment and output promises that are regarded as too ambitious, this could rekindle inflation fears, shift the short run Phillips curves up, and create the conditions under which a change in expectations *forces* an expansionary policy that just accommodates those expectations.

---

[11] This rule has long been associated with the monetarist school, which, in addition to its fear of long and variable policy lags, is characterized by a belief in the long run stability of the velocity of money. This is a modern version of the classical Quantity Theory view discussed back in Chapter 2. But the instability of money demand (essentially the mirror image of velocity) since the 1980s has weakened the appeal of such a fixed monetary rule.

IN SUMMARY . . .

The Debate Over Activist Stabilization Policy

Where does this winding trail through expectations, misperceptions, and stabilization policy finally leave us? Obviously not with the clear view of "who's right?" and "who's wrong?" that we'd like. A high degree of confidence about "what the government must do to stabilize the macroeconomy" is a characteristic of someone substituting slogans or wishful thinking for analysis. This particular issue is complex and the actual facts of past experience can support several very different interpretations.

The fact that we can't get the "smoking-gun" evidence to resolve the dispute over what the government *can* do about economic fluctuations should make us all the more careful about proclaiming what it *should* do. We can at least try to be clear on the basic economic issues that distinguish activists from nonactivists, namely the answers to the following questions:

1. How fast do our *expectations* adjust to unanticipated events?
2. How widespread and long-lived are the various *frictions* in the market-clearing process?
3. How predictable are the *time lags* for monetary and fiscal policies?
4. What part of economic fluctuations comes from *supply-side instabilities* that lie beyond policy control?

Although serious conceptual and measurement problems result in different answers to these four questions, the range of disagreement has narrowed in recent years. The most notable change has come from those who hold an activist view of stabilization. Most have moderated their expectations about the extent to which policy manipulation can diminish the business cycle. Concern about problems of inflationary bias have also created significant interest among economists in the use of policy rules rather than discretionary changes.

⚙️ 9.8 DOES RISING INFLATION TODAY BRING UNEMPLOYMENT TOMORROW?

After our careful discussion of a short-run *inverse* relationship ($+\Delta\Pi \Rightarrow -\Delta U$ in *SR*) and *no* long run relationship ($\Delta\Pi \nRightarrow \Delta U$ in *LR*) between inflation and unemployment, the suggestion of a *positive* relationship between today's inflation and tomorrow's unemployment (i.e., $+\Delta\Pi_{\text{now}} \Rightarrow +\Delta U_{\text{later}}$) must seem confusing. But this possibility is fully consistent with our preceding analysis and differs only in that it adds one new factor—a disinflationary policy response triggered by increasing inflation. For example, if there is a long-term acceptable inflation range (say between 3% and 5% for the U.S. in recent decades), periods in which inflation is allowed to rise above this range will then be followed by a disinflationary episode until inflation has diminished to an acceptable level.

So to the extent that rising inflation is followed by a contractionary policy response, we would expect to see a sequence of events something like that shown in Figure 9.7. An inflationary surge from, say, 4% to 8% would initially reduce unem-

■ FIGURE 9.7

Clockwise loops in the Phillips curve graph (such as $A \rightarrow B \rightarrow C \rightarrow D$) reveal the sense in which increased inflation today (4% → 8%) can mean a recession ($U_D > U^*$) tomorrow.

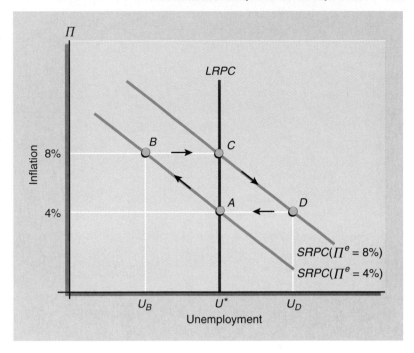

ployment, moving the economy from points A to B and then back to point C as expectations adjust and market frictions are overcome. If ongoing inflation at 8% is beyond the economy's tolerance level, a switch to disinflationary policy will then push unemployment temporarily above U^*, as shown in the movement from points C to D and finally back to point A. This "clockwise loop" in the inflation-unemployment path ($A \Rightarrow B \Rightarrow C \Rightarrow D \Rightarrow A$) is the outcome of basic Phillips curve dynamics (bringing the economy back to U^*) combined with a policy response that alternates between periods of rising and falling rates of inflation.

A look at the Phillips curve observations for the U.S. economy since 1960 (Figure 9.8) shows a pattern of rising inflation followed by periods of disinflation and higher unemployment. For example, the rising inflation of the 1970s was followed by the disinflationary monetary policy of the early 1980s when unemployment rose to its highest level since the Great Depression. This phenomenon helps us understand the contention of those in the mid-1990s, like Fed Chairman Alan Greenspan, who contend that having gone through the costly recession of the early 1980s to get inflation down to relatively low levels in the 1990s, it is important that the monetary authority respond quickly to any signs of gathering inflation so that it will not become necessary to later "slam on the brakes" and suffer a costly recession in the future.

In this sense, then, they argue that a tight monetary policy is not, as is often charged, an antijobs/antigrowth program. Instead, it is a recognition that a prompt response to threats of rising inflation is protection against a period of high unemployment in the future should inflation's rise go unchecked until too late. Their more careful critics don't dispute the possibility that this could happen. Instead, they are likely to question their tendency to react too quickly and thereby slow down the economy prematurely. They accuse the "inflation hawks" of being more concerned with the *threat* of future inflation than with the impact of their precautionary actions on current output and unemployment.

Inflation and Unemployment
(United States, 1960–1994)

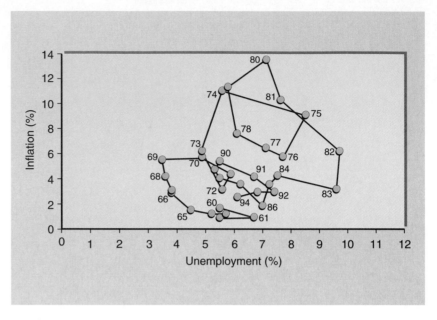

■ FIGURE 9.8

⚭ *9.9 OVERVIEW*

1. This chapter extends the analysis of *short-run dynamics* that started with the development of the **expectations-augmented *AD/AS^e* model** in the previous chapter. The focus of this analysis is on fluctuations of output and employment over a time period measured from a few months to, perhaps, a few years. The main concern is with the causes of deviations from full employment and the potential for policy to shorten these deviations. It assumes zero growth on the supply side and analyzes variations around a fixed long-run supply curve. In later chapters we will add the dynamics of economic growth that underlie long-term shifts in aggregate supply.

2. The *AD/AS^e* model provides a useful framework for incorporating expectations and misperceptions into our standard macroeconomic model. But it does this in a setting that portrays a world of fluctuating price levels ($\pm\Delta P$). For example, recessions are seen to be the result of a drop in aggregate demand that also leads to a falling price level, a scenario that no longer fits the world in which we live. In reality we see a price level that is *always rising* and our attention is on changes in its rate of increase—in other words, on the ups and downs of the *inflation rate* ($\pm\Delta\Pi$) rather than the level of prices. Incorporating these ongoing changes within the *AD/AS^e* framework itself is awkward, but a transformation of the analysis—equation and graph—from output and price level to *unemployment* and *inflation rate* allows us to get at the dynamics of inflation and economic fluctuations in a direct and manageable way.

3. This way of looking at the results of the *AD/AS^e* model in a context of continuing change is called the **Phillips curve.** The Phillips curve model is not a new and different macroeconomic theory. It is based on exactly the same analysis as

the AD/AS^e model, but simply redirects our attention from real output, interest rates, and price levels to **inflation** (Π) and **unemployment** (U). From the perspective of economic fluctuations, the Phillips curve can be viewed as a theory of changes in the unemployment rate. The equation of the expanded Phillips curve—$U = U^* - \alpha_1(\Pi - \Pi^e) + \alpha_2(U - U^*)_{-1}$—reveals three sources of fluctuating levels of unemployment ($\pm\Delta U$): (1) supply side instabilities, $\pm\Delta U^*$; (2) changing inflation misperceptions, $\pm\Delta(\Pi - \Pi^e)$, caused by unstable aggregate demand, $\pm\Delta AD$; and (3) market frictions, represented by $\pm\Delta(U - U^*)_{-1}$.

4. Statistical analysis of the Phillips curve model has not yielded a definitive picture of the relative importance of these three sources of unemployment change. The existence of different views about the underlying sources of fluctuations is significant because of its implications for stabilization policy. Underneath the **activist/nonactivist** debate over the usefulness of countercyclical policy is a disagreement over the sizes of these different sources of economic fluctuations.

5. The **real business cycle** view contends that actual fluctuations in unemployment are partly the result of short-lived inflationary misperceptions and partly the result of instabilities in aggregate supply that show up as changes in the natural rate of unemployment itself. It argues that market frictions are unimportant and concludes that policies designed to stabilize unemployment and output are futile. When the source of the fluctuations is from the demand side, they are so short-lived that policy can't react quickly enough. When the fluctuations come from the supply side, they are simply beyond the reach of traditional demand-side stabilization policies.

6. Though the statistical evidence is mixed and inconclusive, most economists are unpersuaded by the real business cycle hypothesis. The broad **mainstream view** is that the combination of *misperceptions* and *market frictions* offers the best description of the short run dynamics of real world economies. But this view of the workings of the economy can lead to either activist or nonactivist policy recommendations. Those who think market frictions play an especially large role, tend to see a greater opportunity for countercyclical policy to reduce deviations from full employment. But even with a relatively large "window of opportunity," there is still the possibility that frictions on the policy side—*policy lags*—can delay the policy impact often enough to make activist stabilization policy unreliable.

7. Disagreements about the effectiveness of countercyclical stabilization policy continue to get much attention. But beneath this there is an important and wide range of agreement about the relationship between inflation and unemployment. Specifically, it is generally agreed (1) that there is *no lasting trade-off* between inflation and unemployment, (2) that *sustained reductions in the inflation rate typically result in a short-run economic recession*, (3) that policy *attempts to keep unemployment below its natural rate will lead to accelerating rates of inflation*, and (4) that the *use of discretionary stabilization policies imparts an additional "inflationary bias"* to the policy process. Consensus on these basic points, which has solidified over the past twenty years, is surely one of the brighter spots in macroeconomic analysis. These implications directly refute a number of popular policy strategies, telling us to beware of those who promise recession-free disinflation, and cautioning us against the belief that expansionary policy can bring a lasting reduction in unemployment in an economy that is at or near its natural rate of unemployment.

8. These points of agreement are the outgrowth of several decades of theoretical and statistical work on expectations, misperceptions, and microfoundations. Though much of this work has been quite technical, it has had practical implications that have significantly altered the mainstream view of day-to-day policy making.

Policy making in most nations today still reflects, in varying degrees, the activist belief that the government has the ability to act in a timely and responsible way to shorten episodes of recession and to reverse inflationary surges. But in contrast to the height of activist optimism in the 1960s, the current practice is far more cautious. The earlier depiction was of a rigid and unresponsive macroeconomy requiring the quick responses of alert policy makers to reduce large and prolonged deviations of output and unemployment from their full employment levels. This has been discarded by most macroeconomists. Activist stabilization today has dropped the pretence of "fine-tuning" and is willing to put considerable reliance on the automatic market-clearing process for relatively minor ups and downs in economic activity. Deeper and more prolonged fluctuations still bring the standard prescription for a prompt monetary or fiscal response, but in more moderate doses than in the past.

☙ 9.10 REVIEW QUESTIONS

1. Define the following basic concepts or terms:

Phillips curve	Inflation-unemployment trade-off
Inflation	Stabilization and the Phillips curve
One-shot price level change	"Inside" and "outside" policy lags
Disinflation	Inflationary bias
Long-run Phillips curve *(LRPC)*	Political business cycle
Short-run Phillips curve *(SRPC)*	Discretionary stabilization policy
Inflationary recession	Policy rules

2. With the coming of national elections, particularly presidential, comes renewed awareness of the so-called political business cycle—that is, fluctuations in real output and employment attributable to political incentives and electoral politics. In addition to the possibility of four-year cycles in output, there is the related issue of a long term trend in inflation which also seems to have its roots in policy choices rather than in the private sector of the economy. Which, if any, of the modern theories of economic fluctuations—new classical, new Keynesian, monetarist, and real business cycle—are consistent with the existence of "political business cycles" and "inflationary bias"? Explain your reasoning.

3. Suppose that the trend toward a rising natural rate of unemployment finally turns around and that we experience $-\Delta U^*$ for the remainder of the 1990s. Assuming that there are no other major events or policy changes, what impact would you predict this would have on Π, y, r, R, c, i, x, b, e, and E? Explain.

4. In terms of the basic equation and graph of the Phillips curve—$U = U^* - \alpha_1(\Pi - \Pi^e) + \alpha_2(U - U^*)_{-1}$—suppose that $\Delta\Pi^e = 0$ always. Graph the Phillips curve and discuss its policy implications.

   a. Why does constant expectations make such a difference?

   b. How might this relate to the observed long-run trade-off originally identified by A. W. Phillips? Explain.

5. Suppose an empirical study finds that the Phillips curve for the United States can be represented by the following relationship: $U = .06 - .5(\Pi - \Pi^e)$.

   a. Graph it and discuss the specifics of the trade-off.

   b. Now suppose that a second study identifies a significant omission and finds that the United States is best described by $U = .06 - .5(\Pi - \Pi^e) +$

$.5(U - .06)_{-1}$. Graph it and discuss the trade-off. How would the implications of this relationship differ from those of the first? Explain.

6. Occasionally the economy finds itself in a situation of "inflationary recession," which means high inflation but output below the full employment level. In terms of the Phillips curve it shows up as $\Pi > 0$ *and* $U > U^*$ simultaneously.

    a. How would this situation show up in the Phillips curve graph and, according to the modern view of the Phillips curve, how could misinformation contribute to the situation? Be specific.

    b. "The solution to inflationary recession requires a combination of contractionary monetary policy (to reduce inflation) and expansionary fiscal policy (to stimulate output)." Evaluate.

7. Evaluate the statements below in terms of the *AD/AS^e* model and modern views of the Phillips curve.

    a. "Long-run equilibrium means full employment, but it can occur at *any* rate of inflation. Only by accident would inflation happen to be zero." Do you agree?

    b. "Reducing inflation without causing a rise in unemployment can be achieved only with a careful and intelligent blend of monetary and fiscal policies." Do you agree?

8. Evaluate the following statements:

    a. "The basic message of the modern Phillips curve is that once high inflation is built into an economy, reducing it is very difficult and costly. The strong implication is that it is not worth the recession it would take to reduce it."

    b. "The Employment Act of 1946 and subsequent acts commit the government to policies that will bring about full employment and price stability. Not only is this beyond the government's power but it is dangerous in failing to recognize that the costs of unemployment are far greater than the costs of inflation. We need to strike a realistic balance between these two evils that reflects their importance in our lives."

9. Suppose there are three very similar economies, initially at full employment with no inflation. All three suddenly increase money supply growth by 10%. In country *A* the unemployment rate declines, in country *B* it doesn't change at all, and in country *C* it actually rises. How could such different outcomes be explained in terms of the Phillips curve model?

10. Assuming that both the data and the statistical testing are reliable, how would you explain the apparent fact that there *was* a long-run trade-off between inflation and unemployment in the United States until sometime in the 1970s, at which time it seems to have simply vanished?

9.11 FURTHER READING

Milton Friedman, "A Monetary and Fiscal Framework for Economic Stability," in *Essays in Positive Economics* (Chicago: University of Chicago Press, 1953), pp. 133–156.

Albert O. Hirschman, *The Rhetoric of Reaction: Perversity, Futility, Jeopardy* (Cambridge: Harvard University Press, 1991).

FINN E. KYDLAND AND EDWARD C. PRESCOTT, "Rules Rather Than Discretion: The Inconsistency of Optimal Plans," *Journal of Political Economy* 85 (June 1977): 473–492.

ROBERT E. LUCAS, JR., "Econometric Policy Evaluation: A Critique," in *Studies in Business-Cycle Theory* (Cambridge: The Massachusetts Institute of Technology Press, 1981).

BENNETT T. MCCALLUM, *Monetary Economics: Theory and Policy* (New York: Macmillan, 1989), chaps. 9–12.

WILLIAM NORDHAUS, "The Political Business Cycle," *Review of Economic Studies* 42 (1975): 169–190.

THOMAS SARGENT, "The Ends of Four Big Inflations" in Robert E. Hall, ed., *Inflation: Causes and Effects* (Chicago: University of Chicago Press, 1982).

CHARLES L. SCHULTZE, *Memos to the President: A Guide through Macroeconomics for the Busy Policymaker* (Washington: The Brookings Institution, 1992).

HENRY C. SIMONS, *Economic Policy for a Free Society* (Chicago: University of Chicago Press, 1948).

JAMES TOBIN AND MURRAY WEIDENBAUM, EDS., *Two Revolutions in Economic Policy: The First Economic Reports of Presidents Kennedy and Reagan* (Cambridge: The Massachusetts Institute of Technology Press, 1988).

INFLATION

✆ 10.1 INTRODUCTION

Inflation is a well-established fact of life in virtually every economy throughout the world. Whether slow, moderate, or rapid, an ongoing rise in the average level of prices ($+\Delta P$ in our model) has been a prominent feature on the economic landscape of most nations for at least the past 50 years. You may be surprised to learn that until World War II this was not the case. As Figure 10.1 shows, the U.S. price level prior to the 1940s would sometimes rise but later fall so that, on average, it exhibited almost no upward trend for nearly a century and a half.

Today, however, the continued rise in the price level is the backdrop against which all our decisions are made. As a result, capital market transactions that involve agreements extending years or even decades into an unknown future become especially vulnerable to unexpected changes in the inflation rate. As our earlier discussion of monetary policy and the Fisher equation ($R = r + \Pi^e$) revealed, unexpectedly rapid inflation ($\Pi > \Pi^e$) can turn a fixed *nominal* return (R) on a long-term commitment into a very low or even negative *real* return (r). For example, home buyers who took out a 25-year mortgage in 1965 at that year's average mortgage rate of 5.8% ended up paying a real rate of virtually zero. With an average inflation rate of 5.7% between 1965 and 1990, the real rate of interest turned out to be just 0.1% ($r = R - \Pi^e = 5.8\% - 5.7\%$). In other words, the total purchasing power paid out over the life of the mortgage was scarcely higher than the amount borrowed a quarter century earlier.[1]

The windfall gain that an unanticipated rise in inflation bestows on borrowers is, of course, a windfall loss to lenders. In the example above, those who

---

[1] But because nominal interest payments are deductible for income tax purposes, borrowers in 1965 ended up actually paying back *less* purchasing power than they borrowed, with the taxpayer providing the additional subsidy.

U.S. Consumer Price Index Since 1800

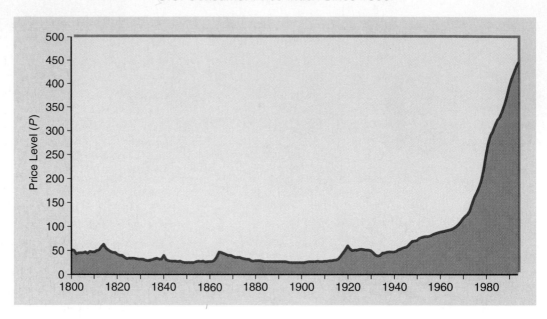

■ FIGURE 10.1

provided mortgage money received a mere 0.1% annual real rate of return for giving up the use of their money for a quarter century. None of these lenders would likely have agreed to a 5.8% market rate if their inflation expectations had been more accurate. Such meager real returns because of the unexpectedly high inflation of the 1970s and early 1980s was an important factor in the subsequent wave of insolvencies among savings and loan institutions. Because deposit insurance was provided by the federal government, the losers from this unexpectedly high inflation were primarily the taxpayers rather than depositors or owners of the savings and loans. So the net result was a transfer of purchasing power from taxpayers to those who had been far-sighted or lucky enough to take out mortgages at what turned out to be a real rate of interest of almost zero.

This unexpected spurt of inflation in the United States had consequences that were felt throughout the economy. But in comparison with most nations, our infla-tion has been exceptionally mild. The experience of some high-inflation countries is shown in Figure 10.2. Average annual inflation rates in Argentina, Bolivia, Brazil, and Peru in the 1980s were well into the "triple-digit" range, far above their 1970 to 1980 levels). The remarkable *dis*inflation in Chile—from a yearly average of 188% in the 1970s to just above 20% in the 1980s—made it unique among its Latin Amer-ican neighbors. Even more spectacularly, after 1990 the stratospheric inflation rates in both Argentina and Bolivia were quickly brought under control, dropping into the moderate 20% to 30% range by 1993 and below 10% by 1994.

In contrast to these high and variable rates of inflation, Figure 10.3 shows the markedly different experience of the major industrial economies. For this group the 1980s was a period of "single-digit" inflation with annual rates ranging from 9.5% in Italy, to 4.2% in the U.S., 2.8% in Germany, and just 1.5% in Japan. Compared to

Some High-Inflation Countries
(1970–1980 and 1980–1991)

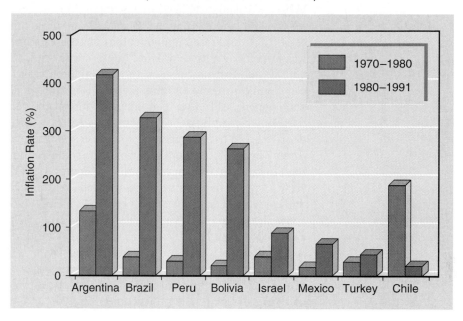

■ FIGURE 10.2

■ FIGURE 10.3

Moderate-Inflation Countries
(1970–1980 and 1980–1991)

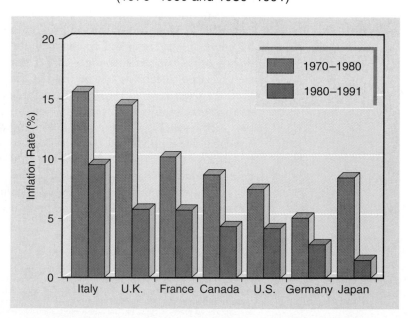

the high-inflation economies, these price increases seem almost trivial. Yet when U.S. inflation rises even to 5% our attention quickly turns to the "inflation problem": Who's to blame? What's to be done? When inflation reached "double digits" in 1979, 1980, and 1981, it provoked a strong monetary contraction by the Federal Reserve that raised unemployment to almost 10% in 1982 and 1983 as the economy was forced down its short run Phillips curve.

It's clear from these charts that inflation varies widely across nations and that it can change abruptly and dramatically. This potential volatility is cause for both hope and concern. Although seemingly uncontrollable galloping inflations have sometimes been quickly extinguished, apparent victories over high inflation have also been suddenly lost. What can account for these sudden reversals? What can explain the extreme variability across countries? Are some economies simply more susceptible to high inflation or are they just more tolerant of it? Why was inflation in the 1970s and early 1980s so high in the United States? Was this largely the result of events beyond our control, such as the energy crisis engineered by OPEC, or was it the predictable consequence of our own policies? This chapter will address such questions and, for once, you should be pleasantly surprised to find some answers that are reasonably straightforward and relatively uncontroversial.

Before going further, however, some basic definitions and clarifications will prove helpful. Continued increases in the U.S. price level have meant that the **cost of living** has more than quadrupled since the 1960s.[2] But it doesn't follow that this higher cost of living necessarily means a lower **standard of living.** In fact, aggregate real output has increased by about two-and-a-half times since 1960. In other words, it has been an era of both real economic growth (averaging almost 3% per year) *and* inflation (averaging almost 5%). Figure 10.4 portrays this experience in terms of our *AD/AS* framework. We see continued outward shifts in long run aggregate supply but an even more rapid growth in aggregate demand. The supply-side forces underlying the long-term growth of real output (the rightward movement along the horizontal axis) will be examined in Part IV (Chapters 12–14). Our attention in this chapter is on the vertical dimension—that is, on the *causes and consequences of inflation.*

The inflation issue is easier to understand if we make a distinction between **one-shot changes** in the price level and **ongoing price level changes.** Countless numbers of events can and do change individual prices. While the individual ups and downs of *relative* price changes cancel out in the aggregate, a few events are sufficiently large to cause a net increase in the overall price level. These are shown in Figure 10.5(a) as a rightward shift in aggregate demand and 10.5(b) as a leftward shift in aggregate supply. Either way the result is a situation of "excess demand" at the initial price level (P_0) that then leads to a higher equilibrium price level (P_1). So a sizable negative supply shock (such as the loss of capital from a hurricane, drought, war, or embargo) can cause a one-shot rise in the price level. Similarly, a surge in aggregate demand (such as an increase in public spending, a rise in private investment expenditures in response to an improved profit outlook, or an injection of new money by the central bank) can cause a jump in the equilibrium price level.

---

[2] There is no single "correct" measure of the price level, in part because there are many different but reasonable choices about how much weight to give which particular prices in the average. The consumer price index (CPI), for example, uses prices of those goods and services that a "representative consumer" buys. The more comprehensive GDP deflator incorporates not only consumption prices but also prices of the other categories of GDP, such as investment and net exports. In practice, these two measures move similarly across most years and essentially paint the same portrait of the ups and downs of inflation over time.

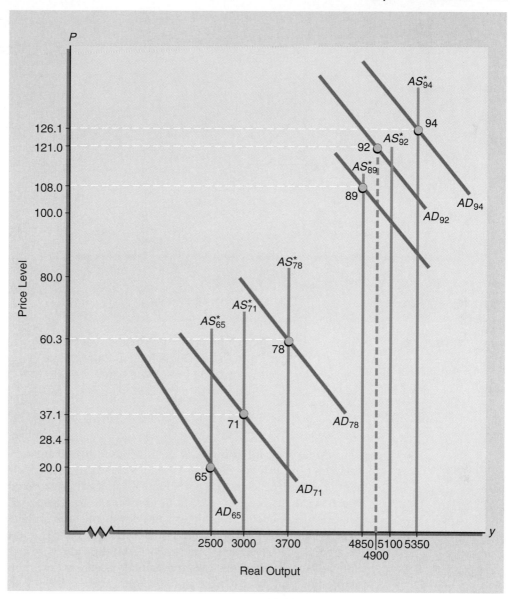

Economic Growth and Inflation in United States
Selected Years Since 1965
(GDP Deflator; Real GDP in 1987 $)

■ FIGURE 10.4

But, as the name reveals, a *one-shot* change in the price level does not continue. The rising price level chokes off the underlying excess demand created by the shift in either aggregate demand or supply and the price level stabilizes at the higher level. So a one-shot change in the price level describes an *event* rather than a *process* and it is the latter that constitutes what we will term "inflation." Although a one-shot change might sometimes *trigger* an inflationary episode, as we'll see in the next section, it cannot properly be called a "cause" because it doesn't contain the fuel needed to keep the inflation process burning.

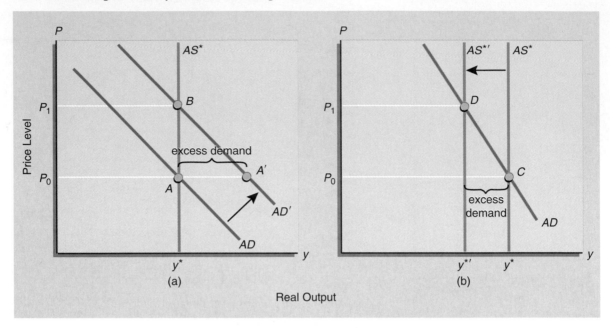

One-Shot Changes in the Price Level Can
Come From Either Demand or Supply Shifts
(a) $+\Delta AD \Longrightarrow A$ to A' to B
(b) $-\Delta AS^* \Longrightarrow C$ to D

■ FIGURE 10.5

Measured inflation—for example, monthly or annual increases in the CPI—includes both *transitory* (one-shot) and *persistent* (inflationary) events. It is the persistent changes, the ones that put continued upward pressure on prices, that are at the heart of the ongoing or "core" *rate of inflation*. To estimate this underlying inflation rate we filter out the monthly ups and downs of some highly variable prices (such as energy and food) from measured inflation. For example, the CPI since 1960 has increased anywhere from 1% to nearly 14% annually in response to changing events and policies that included the large military build-up during the Vietnam War as well as the huge oil price shocks and some unusually cold and dry periods that affected growing conditions in agriculture. The average yearly rise in the CPI during this period was 5%. If we eliminate the highly volatile energy and food prices from our measure of inflation, the year-to-year variation diminishes considerably but the average for the whole period still remains at 5%. In formulating policy responses to current inflation it's important not to react to the sudden ups and downs of volatile one-shot changes. The result could be erratic stop-and-go policy changes that only add further instability to the economy.

A final warning may prove useful: Rising prices are an obvious *symptom* of inflation, but they are not its *cause*. Causes must be sought in the underlying events that result in ongoing shifts in aggregate demand or supply and generate the *continued excess demand* that exerts steady upward pressure on prices. Those who neglect this seemingly obvious distinction between symptom and cause can be seduced by simplistic and ineffective remedies. For example, if we accuse rising prices of causing inflation the obvious remedy would appear to be some form of **price controls.** While making it illegal to raise prices might, depending on the penalties and enforcement, reduce or even end *measured* inflation, its primary impact is likely to be to convert an **open inflation** of rising prices into a **suppressed inflation** of increasing shortages. By preventing the continued excess demand that lies at the heart of inflation from pushing in the vertical direction (ongoing $+\Delta P$), price controls lock the excess demand into the horizontal direction as *continuing shortages* ($AD > AS$). The result is waiting lines, blackmarkets, and a raft of other economic misallocations and inefficiencies. In leaving underlying supply and demand conditions unchanged, price controls do nothing to address the basic causes of the excess demand. When controls are lifted, suppressed inflation comes back into the open.

🕮 10.2 COSTS OF INFLATION

Most of us take it for granted that inflation does a great deal of economic damage and should be avoided even at the cost of a contractionary policy that pushes the economy down the short run Phillips curve and into recession. We don't like the resulting loss of jobs and output but we accept it as the price of avoiding the *still higher costs* that continued inflation would bring. But a closer look at how inflation affects the overall economy reveals that its true costs are considerably smaller and much less obvious than is commonly thought. In fact, as explained in this section, the primary damage done by inflation comes from its *variability* rather than its level.

The most common way in which we overestimate the cost of inflation is to think of it as a direct attack on our economic well-being—a theft of part of our hard-earned purchasing power. When we see that last year's 4% salary increase was largely gobbled up by a 3% rise in the price level, our first reaction is understandable but probably wrong. We are likely to think that if only inflation were brought under control, our *real* income would have risen by 4% rather than just 1%. But this, of course, presumes that our money income would still have increased by the full 4% even without inflation. A little thought should convince you that such a presumption could not hold for the overall economy. Earlier in the book we introduced the basic identity that "every dollar spent on goods and services is also a dollar received as income." This tells us, among other things, that the higher prices we pay because of inflation must also be part of the higher nominal incomes we receive. Take away last year's 3% inflation and the average nominal increase in incomes would also have fallen by 3%. Although each of us likes to think that any increase in *our* money income reflects our increasing skill and productivity, the truth is that the inflation component in our raises comes from outside forces that have nothing to do with how hard or how well we work.

To make the same point in a different way, Figure 10.4 showed that the continued rise in the *cost of living* since World War II did not mean a continued fall in our *standard* of living. The independence of our standard of living (measured by real output) from changes in the price level is built into our analytical framework through the assumption of a vertical long run aggregate supply curve or, in a dynamic setting, a vertical long run Phillips curve. Suppose aggregate demand had shifted at exactly the same rate as aggregate supply since 1960. There would have been no inflation but the growth in our standard of living would still have remained the same. In other words, our analytical framework incorporates the empirical finding that—barring the extremes of hyperinflation and monetary breakdown—a higher price level or a higher inflation rate doesn't increase *or* decrease the long run level of real output. Economic growth is a supply-side phenomenon, largely independent of what happens to the money supply, aggregate demand, and the price level.

The previous discussion pertains to the overall economy. Obviously some groups suffer a loss of purchasing power from inflation because their nominal income doesn't grow as rapidly as the price level. But since every dollar spent is a dollar received, this means that someone else's income is growing more rapidly than inflation. For every loser, there's a gainer. Although this redistributional impact of inflation may be judged (especially by the losers) as highly undesirable, it's important to understand that it is a *transfer* rather than a *loss* of real income. The redistributional effects of inflation can be greatly limited through a policy of **indexation**—linking incomes and other nominal values to a measure of the overall price level. This strategy, common in high inflation countries but also used in the United States for Social Security payments, some labor union contracts, and adjustable rate mortgages or loans (e.g., "prime plus x%" loans), is a way to lower the distributional consequences of inflation. Indexation is sometimes characterized as a capitulation to rising prices, a way to "live with inflation" while reducing some of its costlier side effects. In some perennially high inflation countries it has functioned this way. But in the context of U.S. experience, indexation is typically seen as a way to ease the redistributional effects of inflation while monetary and fiscal efforts are made to return it to acceptable levels.

The presumption of our models that the level of inflation has no impact on total real output or unemployment—that the long run Phillips curve and the aggregate supply curve are both vertical—implies that the macroeconomic costs of inflation, though not zero, are below the threshold of what can be detected at such an aggregate level.[3] This certainly doesn't mean that inflation has no net costs, but simply that they are smaller and less obvious than is usually thought. To help us locate the real costs of inflation, let's start with the simplifying assumption that inflation is moderate, steady, and fully anticipated and therefore built into all transactions and contracts. Everyone is aware of the ongoing price level change—buyers and sellers, borrowers and lenders, employers and employees, taxpayers and tax collectors, and so on. Capital markets, domestic and foreign, will have built the expected inflation rate into nominal interest rates (R) and nominal exchange rates (E) and, because $P = P^e$ and $\Pi = \Pi^e$, there will be no "inflation misperceptions" to push the economy away from its full employment level of output.

Although such conditions are obviously not descriptively realistic of most inflations, this gives us a convenient starting point to investigate the economic costs of *perfectly anticipated inflation*. Let's now go back to our analytical model to amend an earlier assumption that was legitimate for one-shot price level changes but does not fit a world of continuing inflation. Specifically, we assumed that the real demand for money holdings (L/P) depended on, among other things, the *real* rate of interest (r).[4] The inverse relationship between money demand and the real interest rate ($+ \Delta r \Rightarrow - \Delta L/P$) came from the fact that the interest rate is the opportunity cost of holding purchasing power in the form of money balances instead of as an earning asset such as a bond or stock. The logic is that a higher real rate of interest means a higher opportunity cost of money, leading individuals and firms to reduce their money holdings in order to purchase the relatively higher-yielding nonmoney assets. It's just the familiar notion that we demand less of something as its price rises. The

---

[3] Extreme inflationary situations, triple digits and up, are not usefully described by a vertical aggregate supply and vertical long run Phillips curve. Such huge rates of inflation are generally a companion to an array of other problems and inefficiencies that affect supply as well as demand.

[4] Remember that this was expressed in the money demand equation ($L/P = j_0 + j_1 y - j_2 r$) that is incorporated in the *LM* equation.

small but important qualification that we now make is to note that the opportunity cost of holding money in a world of inflation is the foregone *nominal* interest rate, $R = r + \Pi^e$, not just the real rate.[5]

Reformulating the analysis of money demand to allow for nonzero inflation yields the relationship $L/P = j_0 + j_1 y - j_2 R = j_0 + j_1 y - j_2 (r + \Pi^e)$. With this addition we see that there will be a difference in the money holdings of otherwise identical economies that are experiencing different rates of anticipated inflation. The real demand for money in an economy with 400% inflation will be much smaller (the magnitude depending on the size of the j_2 coefficient) than one with 40% inflation, which, in turn, will have lower real money holdings than a country with 4% inflation. It is this shrinking of money holdings that is the primary social cost of anticipated inflation. Admittedly, it's a rather elusive phenomenon but it's a potentially important cost of inflation that must be considered. We can think of it as a source of "demonetization" because it means that the nation's money supply no longer provides as efficient a "store of value" when money's purchasing power is dropping at the rate of inflation, be it 4% or 40% or 400%. As the inflation rate climbs, we move to protect our purchasing power by holding less and less of our assets in the form of money. As a result we lose the convenience that larger money holdings would provide and also incur additional costs through inefficiencies known as **"shoe leather" costs** and **"menu" costs.**

"Shoe leather" cost is an old-fashioned term for the costs of having to make more frequent trips to the bank when inflation leads us to reduce our cash and checking account holdings. More specifically, high nominal interest rates (created by high inflation rates) lead us to hold higher-earning nonmoney assets right up to the time when we need the liquidity of money to make a payment. The costs associated with making these frequent switches include more trips to the bank and, always, the opportunity cost of our time and attention. Statistical studies have shown that an expected inflation of 10% could impose annual shoe leather costs as high as 0.3% of GDP, which would come to $15 billion in our roughly $5 trillion economy.[6] In a country with 4% inflation this cost would be relatively small, but with 400% it would certainly become large enough to show up as a significant inward shift in the long run aggregate supply curve.[7] In a growing economy this would appear as a reduction in the rate of growth of aggregate supply.

A second cost of high inflation is the so-called *menu cost*. This refers to the fact that frequent price change is an activity that involves real economic costs as time and materials are diverted into recalculating, resetting, reprinting, and relabeling prices. As the rate of inflation rises, the costs of changing price lists, catalogs, and menus (not to mention altering vending machines, and parking meters) will surely increase. Menu costs, though quite visible, are generally believed to be considerably smaller than shoe leather costs. For one thing, the widespread use of computerized spreadsheets now makes recalculation of costs and prices relatively easy. In addition, businesses in high inflation countries typically substitute price codes for prices. The code for each item can stay the same (e.g., *A*, *B*, *C*, or red, white, green tags etc.) while only the pricing key for each coded label is adjusted.

---

[5] Our earlier use of the real interest rate in the money demand equation was correct, but only for a setting of zero inflation, in which case $\Pi = \Pi^e = 0\%$ means $R = r$.

[6] See Stanley Fischer, "Towards an Understanding of the Costs of Inflation: II," in K. Brunner and A. Meltzer, eds., *Carnegie-Rochester Conference Series on Public Policy* 15 (Autumn 1981).

[7] As discussed in Chapter 6, the demonetization that would result from high rates of inflation would be a loss in institutional efficiency $(-\Delta i^{inst})$ that would shift the *PPF* and *AS** curves inward.

To summarize, as long as the inflation is quite steady and anticipated, the costs of inflation are not the obvious "theft of purchasing power" that most of us expect. They show up instead as a diversion of scarce resources from the production of final goods and services to the basically defensive activities described as "shoe leather" and "menu" costs.[8] If we were to incorporate them into our AD/AS^e framework they would show up as a leftward shift of the long run aggregate supply curve as expected inflation rises. In other words, this negative supply shock would be the reverse of the efficiency gains from increased "monetization" (Chapter 6) or the "gains from expanded trade" (Chapter 7). Because these costs are *relatively* small, especially at single-digit rates of inflation that characterize the U.S. economy, it seems preferable not to add a new variable to our AD/AS structure to encompass them. But remember that rising inflation is working behind the scenes to lower the efficiency of our money and divert scarce resources into the process of changing prices.[9]

The magnitude of these shoe leather and menu costs depends on the level of inflation, regardless of whether it has been anticipated or not. But what is far more disruptive is the damage that comes when the inflation rate is erratic and unpredictable. By adding additional elements of uncertainty and risk to our economic decisions, a volatile inflation rate can result in very substantial misallocations and inefficiencies. In countries where inflation is traditionally high and unstable, many people refuse to enter any long term economic contracts. They often put a great deal of effort into finding ways to protect their individual income and wealth holdings through speculative activities that can actually reduce the nation's standard of living.

Those of us living with a relatively stable inflation rate are largely unaware of how often we place bets on future inflation by making arrangements that involve payments or receipts at future dates. It takes a sudden spurt in inflation, such as the movement into double digits in the U.S. in the late Seventies, to remind us of the potential risk embodied in our economic contracts. For example, savings accounts and bond holdings include a wager that inflation will not dilute the purchasing power of our interest receipts below a certain anticipated level. But those who bought long term government bonds in the 1940s and 1950s were surely not expecting that their nominal interest receipts would be so eroded by inflation that their real return would actually be negative.

Unexpected changes in inflation create risks not only for the borrowing/lending process but also for *wage and salary contracts*. For example, a three year money wage agreement between a labor union and employer is inevitably a bet on inflation. If inflation during that interval turns out to be lower than anticipated in the negotiated wage, workers gain purchasing power at the expense of the employer. Similarly, a higher-than-anticipated inflation reverses the pluses and minuses, with the workers

---

[8] There are additional economic costs even when an inflation is perfectly anticipated, but most of these are either relatively small or represent transfers from one sector to another rather than a net loss to the macroeconomy. For example, a tax system that is not indexed for inflation suffers from "bracket creep" and means that purely inflationary gains in our income can increase our real tax payments. This loss to taxpayers is primarily a redistribution from private to public sector. Although it may have some negative incentive effects that adversely effect economic growth, as we saw in our discussion of fiscal policy (Chapter 5), the net result also depends on whether these funds are used for public consumption or investment activities.

[9] In extreme cases, of course, this cost can be substantial. As Paul Krugman has said, "The most concrete cost of inflation is that it discourages the use of money. In economies experiencing "hyperinflation" (i.e., inflation at an annual rate in the thousands of percent), people may stop using money altogether, resorting to barter or to the use of black market foreign currency to avoid holding cash that loses value by the hour. This obviously cripples a modern economy. For an economy with inflation of 10 percent or less a year, however, the demonetizing effect of inflation is trivial" *The Age of Diminished Expectations: U.S. Economic Policy in the 1990s*, Rev. and updated ed.; Cambridge, Mass. MIT Press, 1994.

receiving (and employers paying) a lower than anticipated *real* wage. These kinds of agreements represent a gamble by parties on both sides of the contract that inflation will be at or near a particular level at a particular time. Unless there is an arrangement to explicitly "index" the nominal payment/receipts for changes in the price level, their real value will vary inversely with the inflation rate.

You may be thinking that all this redistribution, while a misfortune to the losers at least has the virtue of having an equal amount of winnings on the other side of the contract. This is an important point but needs some qualification. As inflation becomes increasingly variable and arbitrarily transfers larger and larger chunks of purchasing power from one group to another, it changes our behavior in ways that result in a *net loss* in total output. This occurs because most of us are **risk averse** and would prefer not to face uncertainty even with an equal chance of winning or losing. Put another way, given the choice between living in an economy with steady inflation at 5% and an otherwise identical economy where inflation averages 5% over the very long run, but jumps frequently and unpredictably between 0% and 10%, most of us would choose the steady inflation. In a world of highly variable inflation we try to reduce our risk in a variety of ways, including the development of more sophisticated forecasts, the use of "hedging" activities (where we straddle both sides of the market), and the avoidance of transactions that expose us to inflation risk. This requires us to sacrifice some of our resources to purely defensive activities that would not occur if inflation were stable and predictable. The result is a net loss of output and economic well-being compared to a situation in which inflation, whatever its level, was predictable.

IN SUMMARY . . .

The Costs of Inflation

What would seem to be the largest cost of inflation—a loss of purchasing power equal to the rate of inflation—is in fact illusory in the aggregate. The higher prices we pay become the higher income received by someone. So although disinflation would reduce the price rise, it would reduce the growth in nominal income as well.

The real macroeconomic costs of inflation are less obvious, considerably smaller, but nonetheless very real. They are largest when the inflation rate is erratic and unpredictable. This adds an additional element of risk and uncertainty to every long term transaction. Because most of us are risk averse, we will avoid some otherwise mutually beneficial transactions even though we have an equal chance of winning or losing from unexpected inflation. Foregoing such opportunities means a less efficient use of resources and a corresponding drop in real output.

However, when inflation is relatively stable and predictable, its impact is smaller but still important. While the redistributional effects can either be foreseen and avoided or handled with contracts that are "indexed" to changes in the cost of living, there is still a reduction in the real value of our money holdings that is inefficient and costly. Adding the additional shoe leather and menu costs generated by inflation completes the picture.

ᛒᛒ 10.3 *WHAT CAUSES INFLATION?*

We said earlier that while rising prices are the symptom of inflation, its source lies in an underlying condition of **continuing excess demand.** So to get to the cause of inflation, we must find what's at the root of this continued excess demand—the origin of the ongoing rightward shift in aggregate demand or leftward shift in aggregate supply that sustains the excess demand. There are literally scores of possibilities. On the supply side this could include anything from adverse weather conditions or embargoes to regulatory restrictions or increased monopoly power of corporations or labor unions. Such events create excess demand by contracting aggregate supply ($-\Delta AS^*$). On the demand side, excess demand could be the result of increased spending in any of the autonomous components—consumption ($+\Delta c_0$), investment ($+\Delta i_0$), or net exports ($+\Delta x_0$)—or increased government spending ($+\Delta g_0$) or decreased tax rates ($-\Delta t_0$). Each of these events would shift both *IS* and *AD* outward. Excess demand could also stem from events that begin with a rightward shift in the *LM* curve—reduced autonomous money demand ($-\Delta j_0$) or increased money supply ($+\Delta M_0$).

Although the *potential* causes of excess demand are many, once we make the distinction between one-shot price level change and the ongoing change that constitutes ("core") inflation, the possibilities dwindle dramatically. For example, while negative supply shocks have sometimes had large impacts on the price level (e.g., the oil crises of the 1970s), it would require a *continued* contraction of aggregate supply—*negative* economic growth—to account for the ongoing price level increases in which we're interested. Because most inflations have been accompanied by positive output growth, we must turn to aggregate demand to find the causes.

On the demand side, continued excess demand might come from actions by consumers, businesses, or the public sector. But remember that any spending is constrained by available income. Households and businesses, for example, can't just arbitrarily push their portion of aggregate demand further and further to the right by spending more and more. Once they reach the limit imposed by available resources, they no longer have the capacity to expand their demand and put further upward pressure on the price level. Even if they decide to push beyond their current income and into expected future income through borrowing, it doesn't follow that aggregate demand will necessarily grow. Remember that for each borrower there must be a lender, so the increased demand of borrowers is offset by the decreased demand of lenders.[10]

So while events on the supply side and in the private components of aggregate demand may frequently cause one-shot price level changes, they are not a probable source of the *ongoing* excess demand that underlies inflation. This leaves only the public portion of aggregate demand—namely, fiscal policy or monetary policy. In some ways this is unsurprising since, rightly or wrongly, we're used to blaming the public sector for all manner of economic ills. But to say that the government is the main source of inflation is actually quite an extraordinary accusation. If true, it says that half a century of chronic inflation in virtually every nation has been caused by economic policy itself! We usually think of policy as a potential remedy for our eco-

---

[10] Increased *external* borrowing would allow domestic borrowers to increase their demand, but it also shows up as a growing trade deficit (or diminishing trade surplus) causing autonomous net exports to decline ($-\Delta x_0$) and aggregate demand to fall.

nomic woes, not the cause. Why would any government choose to run continued inflationary policies? Would it be out of ignorance, political expediency, or conspiracy? Or is it possible that we're simply mistaken and the source of inflation lies elsewhere?

Although every important issue in macroeconomics supports some differences in opinion, there is remarkably little disagreement on this one. Abundant analytical and statistical evidence support the hypothesis that the monetary authority—sometimes with and sometimes without the participation of fiscal policy—is the underlying source of inflation.[11] You're probably wondering why, if this were really true, all nations don't just reduce their money supply growth until inflation is extinguished. This takes us to the heart of the issue. While the *symptom* is a continuing rise in the overall price level, and the *immediate cause* is a too-rapid growth of the money supply, we must dig still deeper to find the *underlying causes*—the reasons why governments routinely choose to keep the money supply growing in excess of the growth of real output.

10.4 WHY WOULD A GOVERNMENT CHOOSE INFLATION?

While all national governments have the power and the responsibility to control their money supply, this doesn't mean that these powers are without limits. In most countries there are a number of restrictions that work to limit the government's ability to increase the money supply in excess of the growth of real output. For example, unless it's an authoritarian regime, policy makers are **answerable to an electorate** or, as in the case of the Federal Reserve, an oversight group such as Congress. If the **money supply is backed by a commodity** (such as under the international gold standard of the 19th and early 20th century), then the monetary authority's discretionary power over the money supply is obviously limited. The supply of money can rise or fall only with the amount of the base commodity or if revaluation alters the amount of money backed by each unit of the base. Similarly, if the country is operating under a **fixed international exchange rate system,** control of the money supply will be limited to such actions as are necessary to offset unwanted changes in the nominal exchange rate. When the nominal value of its currency is falling relative to others, this will generally require a contraction of the money supply in order to reduce its inflation rate, increasing the demand for its currency and thereby raising its nominal exchange rate. There could also be **policy rules** that automatically trigger specific policy responses under certain economic conditions, further limiting the discretionary power of the monetary authority.

However, the current policy environment in most economies offers relatively few impediments to discretionary control of the money supply. Fiat (unbacked) monies, flexible exchange rates, and an absence of explicit policy rules give policy

---

[11] The classic study of the link between inflation and the money supply is Milton Friedman and Anna J. Schwartz, *A Monetary History of the United States, 1867–1960* (Princeton: Princeton University Press, National Bureau of Economic Research, 1963). Also see Thomas J. Sargent "The Ends of Four Big Inflations" in his *Rational Expectations and Inflation* (New York: Harper and Row, 1986). For more recent evidence see Bennett T. McCallum, *Monetary Economics: Theory and Policy* (New York: Macmillan Publishing Company, 1989), chap. 15, "Episodes in U.S. Monetary History"; Gerald Dwyer and R. W. Hafer, "Is Money Irrelevant?" *Review*, St. Louis Federal Reserve Bank (May/June 1988); and Nigel W. Duck, "Some International Evidence on the Quantity Theory of Money," *Journal of Money, Credit, and Banking* 25 (February 1993): 1–12.

makers considerable latitude to act in accordance with their economic goals, their perception of the current direction of the economy, and their understanding of how policy actions are linked to macroeconomic outcomes (i.e., their economic model). But the question remains as to why the very group charged with protecting the value of the money supply should take steps that undermine this goal? It's like charging the fire department with setting fires or hospitals with spreading diseases. Such anomalies occur, but so seldom that they're newsworthy. Why would Central Banks the world over consistently take actions that continue rather than end inflation? What possible motive could they have?

■ MOTIVE 1: INFLATION CAN HELP PAY FOR PUBLIC SPENDING

Although the separation of the Treasury and the Federal Reserve in the U.S. means that monetary policy is largely independent of fiscal policy, in many nations the Treasury and the Central Bank are a single entity. In some of these countries, the government rarely or never borrows when its spending exceeds its tax revenues. Instead, it simply prints new money to cover the gap—an act of counterfeiting if done by anyone else.

The macroeconomic impact of such a *monetized deficit* is easily seen in our *AD/AS* framework. Even if the government is running a constant cyclically adjusted deficit (a neutral *fiscal* policy, as we've seen), the expansion of the money supply each year to cover the gap between spending and taxes ($\Delta M = g - t$) means a steady outward shift of the *LM* and *AD* curves. Now if this continually monetized cash flow deficit is used to finance public investment (self-financing) or if it is small enough to fall within the bounds of normal economic growth (consumption smoothing), then the growth of real output (%ΔAS^* and %Δy^*) would match the growth of aggregate demand and there would be no inflation. The government would essentially have used its monopoly power over the money supply to transfer resources from private to public use—an ages old way of taxing known as **seigniorage.**

But if the cash flow deficit is beyond what can be supported by economic growth (thereby spilling into the consumption-draining category) *and* it's monetized, then aggregate demand will be growing more rapidly than aggregate supply. Continued monetization of consumption-draining deficits will then create seigniorage in the form of an **inflation tax,** perhaps the historically most common reason for high inflations. More specifically:

1. The inflation tax is a common wartime means for helping to transfer resources from civilian to military uses.

2. Large monetized deficits and high inflations also accompany economic and political crises, such as the massive institutional reorganizations by the former communist bloc countries. As the move from a planned to market economy transfers property rights from the public to the private sector, governments with little experience in collecting taxes are struggling to provide public services. Unless government spending is drastically curbed (very difficult politically during such crises), monetized deficits and an inflation tax are inevitable until an effective system of taxation is in place. Loans from foreign governments, of course, can prevent the entire deficit from being monetized and can slow down inflation but only at the cost of loan repayments later.

3. Monetized deficits that result in an inflation tax aren't only a product of extreme conditions like war or institutional transformation. They can and do emerge through regular peacetime political channels. A notable example has been the chronic monetized deficits that characterized such nations as Argentina, Brazil, Peru, and Bolivia in the 1980s and that continue into the Nineties in Italy, Greece, and Turkey among others. In the face of political opposition to spending cuts and tax hikes, these nations either had to find lenders or resort to the monetary printing press. A long history of high and unstable inflation in many of these countries scares away most potential lenders, leaving a monetized deficit and the inflation tax as the only alternative. Not until the government's deficit was virtually eliminated were Argentina and Bolivia able to bring their money supply growth under control and escape from self-inflicted inflations in the hundreds and even thousands of percent each year.

So one reason that a government would choose policies that cause inflation is to help it transfer resources from private to public use. Although this can work during brief periods of economic or political crisis, growing monetized deficits cannot increase their "tax power" once inflation begins to accelerate. The reason is that inflation transfers resources from private to public use primarily by eroding the purchasing power of the currency. It means a capital loss to all holders of money and a capital gain to the issuer of the money. As inflation soars, however, people begin to switch to alternative means of payment, including more stable foreign currencies and certain commodities (such as jewelry or other personal possessions). They may even return to barter, foregoing the efficiency gains from monetization because the inflation tax on money is prohibitively high. So the higher the inflation, the less the currency is used and therefore the lower the amount of revenue that can be raised by further "debasing" the currency. Sustainable seigniorage has been as much as 10% of the government's total revenue in some countries. But attempts to increase the revenues raised by the inflation tax through spurts of hyperinflation are soon frustrated by demonetization.

■ MOTIVE 2: MORE INFLATION IS A SHORT-RUN BOOST TO OUTPUT AND EMPLOYMENT

Another incentive for governments to undertake inflation-causing policies is the existence of the short run Phillips curve tradeoff between inflation and unemployment. Because this *inflation bias* in discretionary policy-making was discussed carefully in the previous chapter, we just summarize the results here. Disinflation typically means a temporary rise in unemployment as the economy slides down its short run Phillips curve. Given the political unpopularity of higher unemployment, policy makers may be inclined to continue with the current inflation, even if it's quite high, rather than face the costs and criticisms that accompany recession. Under certain circumstances (like an approaching election), they may even be tempted to increase inflation to reap the short-term political gains of lower unemployment.[12] In fact, we even saw that just

---

[12] This, of course, presumes that the voters typically hold them more accountable for recession than for inflation. This seems to be a reasonable general assumption but there are certainly situations when the pendulum swings from concern with unemployment to concern with inflation. The highest U.S. unemployment rates since the Great Depression were the result of the commitment to disinflation in the early 1980s.

the expectation of higher inflation can cause an upward shift in the short run Phillips curve (*SRPC*) and force the government to "ratify" these inflation expectations with expansionary monetary policies in order to avoid rising unemployment.

There are also several variations on this inflationary bias theme. If monetary policy is regularly used to insure high levels of employment and real output, the stage is set for the government to fuel inflation by "accommodating" supply-side events. For example, suppose a significant negative supply shock leads to rising unemployment and falling real income. A quick monetary expansion may be used as a "shock absorber" to soften its impact. In such a situation, monetary policy is said to have "accommodated" the supply shock. But because it has treated a symptom (falling output and rising unemployment) rather than its cause (whatever triggered the supply shock), the end result is additional excess demand ($+ \Delta AD$ added to the $- \Delta AS^*$) and an increase in the underlying rate of inflation.

■ MOTIVE 3: INFLATION CAN BE A SIDE EFFECT OF PURSUING OTHER GOALS

If the only responsibility of the monetary authority was to provide price stability, it is very likely that over the long run there would be virtually no inflation. But we've seen that Central Banks are sometimes forced to monetize chronic fiscal deficits (motive 1) or to play an active role in stabilizing output and employment (motive 2) even at the cost of compromising their inflation-fighting duties. There are still other demands put on monetary policy that further threaten price stability. The most common are interest rate and exchange rate goals but they may also include balance of trade and other targets as well.

For example, Figure 10.6 uses the basic *AD/AS* model to illustrate how a goal of real interest rate stability can turn what would have been a one-shot price level increase into ongoing inflation. Starting at point *A* in a fully-employed/zero-inflation economy, suppose an increase in autonomous investment (or consumption or net exports) shifts *IS* and *AD* to the right, causing an immediate rise in both real and nominal interest rates. A Central Bank committed to this policy of "leaning against the wind" in credit markets must respond to the rising rates by increasing the nominal money supply. This will, of course, shift *LM* out and result in a *further* increase in aggregate demand, moving the economy to point *C* in the short run.[13] It has temporarily succeeded in holding interest rates down, but only at the cost of further enhancing excess aggregate demand. As this upward pressure pushes up prices (reducing the real money supply, hence contracting *LM*), the real interest rate will rise toward its equilibrium value at point *D*. Should this inevitable rise be met with further expansion of the money supply, in the mistaken belief that monetary policy can set interest rates, the result will be the classic "too much money chasing too few goods" scenario created by an interest rate goal that, in this situation, was incompatible with the goal of stable prices. Including the impact on inflationary expectations, the end result will be an even greater rise in market interest rates ($R = r + \Pi^e$) because we now add the higher expected inflation ($+ \Delta \Pi^e$) to the inevitable rise in the real rate ($+ \Delta r$). The paradoxical outcome of such misguided attempts to stabilize interest rates is to inflate market rates and leave real rates unaffected.

---

[13] We could make this more realistic by using the expectations-augmented aggregate supply equation of the *AD/AS^e* model so that there would be an upward-sloping short run aggregate supply. But because this more primitive model is so much simpler to use and has the same result in this context, there's no need to go further.

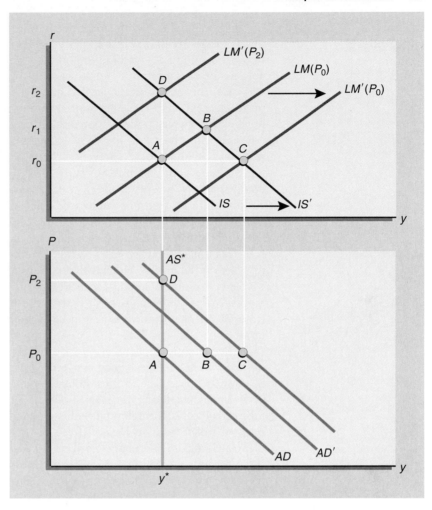

■ FIGURE 10.6

An initial outward shift in *IS* (*A* → *B*), if followed by expansionary monetary policy to reduce the real interest rate (*B* → *C*), will end up increasing the price level *further* (*C* → *D*). If continued, such an attempt to "stabilize" the interest rate would mean *ongoing inflation* and higher nominal interest rates, with real rates unchanged ($R\!\uparrow\, = r + \Pi^e\!\uparrow$).

IN SUMMARY . . .

Why Would Policy Makers Choose to Inflate?

Unlikely as it may at first seem, the monetary authority in all nations has a number of strong motives to "commit" inflation. However much central bankers may protest their innocence, the relationship between money growth and inflation cannot be satisfactorily explained by an "innocent bystander" plea. Of all the economic actors in the macroeconomy, only the monetary authority

(Continued)

has both the ability and the incentive to pursue policies that result in continued upward pressure on the overall price level. Motive and opportunity, in the eyes of most economists, combine to find the Central Bank guilty, beyond a reasonable doubt, of perpetrating inflation.

But this guilt reflects neither ignorance nor conspiracy, making an appropriate sentence elusive. The source of the problem is that the demand-side power of monetary policy is potentially so vast that Central Banks must always contend with enormous pressures to pursue a wide array of policy goals. "Financing the war effort," "preventing fiscal collapse of the government," "ending the recession," "stimulating job growth," and "stabilizing interest rates and credit markets" are just some of the goals that we thrust on our Central Bank and that interfere with its pursuit of "price stability." It would be nothing short of miraculous if we could achieve all these wonderful outcomes simultaneously by simply altering the rate at which fiat money is created.

It's not ignorance, malevolence, or conspiracy that explains why governments so often choose policies that end up feeding inflation. Their choices reflect a compromise among conflicting goals and pressures. In some times and places "price stability" is pushed to the bottom of the list. The unfortunate irony of this predicament is that most of their other targets are ones over which monetary policy has little or no lasting impact.

Persistently high inflations are nearly always the result of persistently high *monetized* deficits. They occur in situations where the Central Bank has become an appendage to fiscal policy. Not surprisingly, the more the monetary authority is shielded from such political and economic pressure groups, the more likely it is to undertake policies that result in relatively low and stable rates of inflation. The Federal Reserve System of the United States and the Central Banks of Germany, Switzerland, and Japan are generally regarded as the most independent in the world and these four nations typically have among the lowest rates of inflation. But even in these countries, zero inflation has yet to be achieved, indicating that they are also pursuing multiple economic objectives and that only when inflation begins to rise above acceptable levels—4% or 5% in the U.S., a percent or two lower in the other three countries—does monetary policy focus primarily on reducing inflation.

ᛒᛒ *10.5 REDUCING INFLATION: COSTS AND BENEFITS*

We have seen that high and variable inflation rates arise when the Central Bank's control of the money supply is loose and erratic. In countries with extremely high continued rates of inflation, the money supply is usually at the mercy of fiscal authorities bent upon monetizing large budget deficits. The result is continued rapid growth of aggregate demand and huge inflation rates. There can be little doubt that very high and unstable inflation is a serious economic handicap to these nations. Fortunately, economics can offer a solution that is both simple and effective—*reduce and stabilize the growth of the money supply.* Countries that ignore this remedy choose to pursue other goals (as discussed in the previous section) instead of lowering inflation. Their economic difficulties are predictable consequences of underlying political choices.

But let's turn from extreme cases of galloping inflation to the more common situation where the government has exercised sufficient monetary control to keep inflation relatively stable and at low to moderate levels (say, under 20% yearly). What economic factors should policy makers in these countries consider in deciding whether or not to take steps to lower the core inflation rate? Suppose an economy is initially at full employment with 10% inflation, as shown at point A in Figure 10.7. What are the expected costs and benefits of contracting money supply growth until inflation is reduced to 5%?

Because we're beginning at full employment on the long run Phillips curve (LRPC), we know that the initial 10% inflation is built into expectations, decisions, and contracts. As we saw earlier in the chapter, the costs of anticipated inflation are considerably smaller than is usually believed. Therefore the benefits from reducing this steady, widely expected inflation will also be relatively small. The tangible gains will be reductions in "shoe leather" and "menu" costs and the increased convenience brought by increased real money holdings as inflation diminishes.

What about the cost side of disinflation? We see an immediate rise in unemployment as shown in the movement along the *SRPC* from point A to B in Figure 10.7. There is no doubt that the *initial* costs of reducing inflation exceed its benefits. But what makes this a challenging issue is that the unemployment costs of reduced inflation are temporary as the economy overcomes misperceptions and market frictions to return to its *LRPC* but the gains continue for as long as the lower inflation

■ FIGURE 10.7

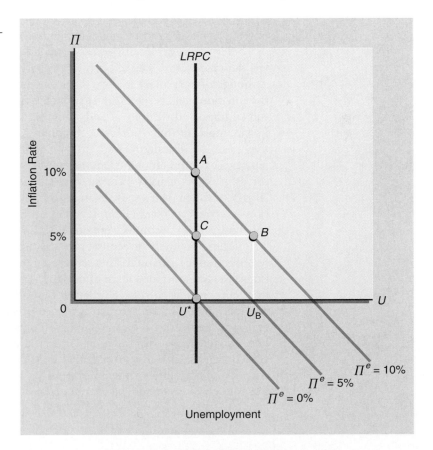

The Short-Run Cost of Disinflation $(-\Delta\Pi)$
is Higher Unemployment $(+\Delta U)$

rate is maintained. Is the sharp, short pain of unemployment from disinflation justified by the milder but longer-lasting benefits of reduced inflation? To make an informed choice, we need further information on both the magnitude and duration of these costs and benefits.

Starting on the cost side, the amount of unemployment caused by reduced inflation will depend on underlying characteristics of the economy that determine the *slope of the SRPC* as well as the *length of time until the market-clearing process brings an end to the recession.*[14] As we saw in the preceding two chapters, there is considerable disagreement over how quickly this adjustment (from point B to C in Figure 10.7) occurs. In the absence of carefully controlled experiments, it has been impossible to get general agreement as to the timing of these short-run dynamics.

So it's not surprising that differences of opinion on the cost of disinflating follow the same pattern as that of the activist/nonactivist controversy over fluctuations in real output and employment. For example, those who see deviations from full employment output caused largely by inflation misperceptions in a world of rational expectations (the "rational misperceptions" of the new classical and real business cycle views), predict a short, shallow recession and relatively small costs to reducing inflation. So although they tend toward nonactivist views on stabilizing output and employment, they are inclined to be more aggressive in using contractionary policy to reduce inflation. They are sometimes characterized as "inflation hawks" by the media. In contrast, those who believe that market frictions play an important part in prolonging periods of unemployment (new Keynesians) are more concerned that disinflation policy can end up being a proverbial "cure worse than the disease." Their fear of relatively large costs of reducing inflation earns them the "inflation doves" label.

But our eagerness to resort to such labels to help simplify an important issue has the unfortunate side effect of emphasizing and even magnifying the controversy. Although disagreement is always more newsworthy than consensus, the real story on the inflation issue is the extent to which past disagreements have diminished as a result of improved theoretical and statistical knowledge over the past several decades. For example, the once popular belief that wage-price controls can bring about a relatively painless disinflation with little or no loss of output or increased unemployment has few advocates among economists today. Similarly, early Keynesian views of rigid prices, sluggish market clearing, and stable long run Phillips curve trade-offs have largely vanished. With these changes we find few economists advocating higher inflation as a route to lower unemployment or flatly opposing any disinflation as unthinkably costly. Both positions were quite commonly held as recently as the 1970s.

There is broad agreement that **credibility** is the crucial ingredient in any attempt to reduce inflation. This reflects a general acceptance that inflation misperceptions are an important source of deviations from full employment. Governments that frequently pledge to reduce inflation but fail to follow with the necessary monetary contraction will find it hard to convince private decision makers that "this time we really *will* be firm with our anti-inflation program." As a result, when they finally reduce monetary growth, inflation expectations may stay at past levels for a considerable time. This means an extended episode of inflation misperceptions ($\Pi < \Pi^e$), correspondingly higher unemployment ($U > U^*$), and the increased likelihood that the policy will eventually be abandoned as too costly. Governments that have earned

---

[14] The cost of higher unemployment in terms of the value of lost income and output can be quite staggering, both individually and in the aggregate. To anticipate the discussion of the next chapter, a 1% rise in unemployment in the current U.S. economy would mean a loss of goods and services of approximately $140 billion annually.

THE DISINFLATION OF THE EIGHTIES

U.S. inflation fell dramatically in the 1980s—from a peak of 13% (measured by the CPI) in 1980 to just 4% by 1986. Eliminating the influence of one-shot changes in energy and food prices still reveals a significant decline in the core rate of inflation from about 10% to 4% over a seven year period. Although this is widely regarded as a major triumph for economic policymaking, it was a costly victory. This may, in part, explain why little subsequent progress toward reduced inflation has been made even though many are convinced that "zero inflation" should be our ultimate target.

As an estimate of the unemployment cost of the "Volcker disinflation" (named after the Federal Reserve chairman who showed a resolve not demonstrated by his several predecessors in the 1970s), suppose we take the value of lost output from the induced recession. The average gap between real output and full employment ($y - y^*$) over those seven years (1980–1986) was about 3%. If we assume that the economy would have stayed close to full employment had it not been for the disinflationary monetary policy, then the accumulated cost of reducing inflation by 6% was an output loss of 21% of GDP. This would come to an astounding $1.25 trillion in our current $6 trillion economy!

The fact that the cost of disinflation is not directly out of our pockets no doubt explains why we would undertake such a huge sacrifice to achieve such relatively modest (though, of course, continuing) gains. But it's important that you understand that from an economic standpoint, opportunity costs are a "real" cost in every sense of the word. Some economists look back on the disinflation of the 1980s as an unwise and irrational choice and believe the huge costs can never be balanced by the relatively modest benefits of a 6% reduction in inflation. But many economists and the general populace seem to believe that this disinflation was a good choice and that its admittedly high initial costs are justified by the ongoing benefits of continued lower inflation. Nearly everyone agrees that having paid the unemployment costs of disinflation, it would be most unfortunate if we were to sacrifice that investment by allowing the inflation rate to creep back up to earlier levels.

the confidence of private decision makers by matching their words with their deeds will find disinflation much less painful.[15]

Turning to the benefit side of lower inflation, the magnitude of reduced "menu" and "shoe leather" costs are much more difficult to assess than the unemployment costs of disinflation. It seems likely, however, that the benefits of reduced inflation decline with the level of inflation. Therefore, although *further* disinfla-

---

[15] Countries with a history of extremely high inflation will obviously have more difficulty convincing the public to lower its inflationary expectations. One technique sometimes used in these situations is to replace the deteriorating currency with a new one. Following World War II, the deteriorating French franc was replaced with the "new franc" and the inflation rate plummeted. While a new currency can help to gain credibility, it obviously must be combined with tight control over the supply of that currency. So when Brazil introduced its new currency, (the "real") in 1994 skeptics were quick to point out that this was its fifth new currency in eight years and that unless the monetary authorities did the unexpected and reduced money growth, it would suffer the same fate as the cruzado, the cruzeiro, and the other predecessors.

tion—say, from 5% to 0% in Figure 10.7—would be equally expensive for each percentage reduction in inflation, its benefits (lower shoe leather and menu costs) would be smaller with the lower initial rates of inflation. This suggests that a balance between the costs and benefits of disinflation is likely to be found at some inflation rate above zero. Combining this result with last chapter's discussion of an inherent inflationary bias to discretionary policy making gives us some insight into why virtually all governments continue to choose policies that result in positive rather than zero (or negative) rates of inflation.

10.6 MONETARY POLICY AND INFLATION RATE STABILITY

A final aspect of inflation and monetary policy should be noted. Suppose we've agreed on a long run target rate of inflation for the economy (whether 15%, 5%, 3%, or 0%). Let's also assume that this has been accepted as the *primary* goal for the Federal Reserve—a big assumption, particularly if the economy is below full employment. Given this commitment, how close can we expect the economy to stay to this chosen mark? Will frequent policy changes be needed to keep us from straying too far on either side of the target? Or will we do better to just set and maintain a long run monetary policy consistent with our target inflation, resisting the urge to respond to periodic ups and downs in measured inflation?

This question will have a familiar ring since it's almost the same as asking whether activist policy manipulation can reduce cyclical changes in real output and unemployment. If we follow the dominant view that fluctuations around either side of the long run Phillips curve $[\pm \Delta(U - U^*)]$ typically originate in demand-side shifts that create inflation misperceptions $[\pm \Delta(\Pi - \Pi^e)]$, then the goal of stabilizing the inflation rate is coincident with that of minimizing employment and output fluctuations.

As we saw in the last chapter, "timing" lies at the heart of the matter. Can policy respond quickly enough to overcome the problems posed by the assorted time lags that run between "Need for Policy Change" through "Perception of that Need" to "Policy Action" and the final "Policy Impact"? The difficulty this poses for policy makers is that they need to act promptly because of the sometimes long lags. But the more quickly they act the more likely they are to respond to what turn out to be merely transitory (one-shot) events. This can mean erratic and unpredictable policies that create the very instability they're designed to cure.

Deciding when to act and how strongly is the trick here and there is as much "art" as science to it. It's a problem that every Central Bank faces each day. The differences of opinion here mirror those that we've identified in the activist/nonactivist controversy. They're a combination of economics (what "can" policy do?) and ideology (what "should" policy do?). Those who believe policy lags to be generally unpredictable or who are especially fearful of active government involvement in the economy will be disposed toward a steady money supply policy that does not react until it is abundantly clear that the long run target will not be reached with current policy. From their perspective the considerable attention of the media and many politicians to every blip in the monthly CPI is unfortunate. It puts additional public pressure on the monetary authority to pursue superficial or unattainable goals. Those who think that policy lags do not typically interfere with our ability to respond soon enough to improve economic performance and who are not ideologically opposed to responsible government actions to stabilize the macroeconomy will favor a more active role for monetary policy.

IN SUMMARY . . .

Inflation, Unemployment, and Monetary Policy

These last three chapters have explored a number of practical issues in the very fertile area of *short-run dynamics*. In terms of our basic model (AD/AS^e and its dynamic counterpart, the Phillips curve) this has been about **what happens during the market-clearing process** as the economy adjusts from short to long run equilibrium. In terms of policy applications, it has been about (1) the underlying causes of fluctuations in output and employment called the **business cycle,** (2) the conditions under which **countercyclical policy** can smooth these unwanted changes, (3) the nature of short and long run **linkages between inflation and unemployment,** (4) the costs and benefits of a **disinflation policy,** and (5) the prospects for **using monetary policy to stabilize inflation near its long-run target rate.**

The Federal Reserve, like all Central Banks, is steadily bombarded with criticism. No matter what action it takes or fails to take, it will be charged with ignorance, incompetence, or partisanship by the media, politicians, or special interest groups, here and abroad. The reason is simple: Its decisions have a tangible impact on the economic lives of virtually everyone in the economy and even those in other countries. The result is immense and conflicting pressures on the Central Bank from a dizzying array of "constituencies." Much of this criticism (and praise) reflects reactions of specific "micro" interests whose goals are incompatible with a stable inflation rate or other "macro" targets of the Federal Reserve.

Is there some objective standard by which we can say that the monetary authority is doing an excellent, good, mediocre, or terrible job? Although the broad answer is "yes," the problem is that there are a number of "objective" standards on which such judgments can be made. Your evaluation of the Federal Reserve may depend on which of the many variables affected by monetary actions you think are most important to your individual well-being. But most of us would agree that an erratic inflation rate or one that reaches double-digits is evidence that the Central Bank is not meeting its most basic responsibility of providing a currency that is an effective medium of exchange, unit of account, and, especially, store of value. Whatever else it may be doing, there is good reason to criticize a monetary authority for not accomplishing what it alone can do—maintain a growth rate of the money supply that keeps inflation at reasonably low and predictable levels.

🕸 *10.7 OVERVIEW*

1. Inflation is a *continuing* increase in the overall level of prices and is distinguished from occasional one-shot changes that quickly disappear. It has become a permanent characteristic of virtually all economies since World War II. Whether low, moderate, or high, inflation is something that we have come to expect and to factor into our long-term decisions.

2. Most of us have also come to think of inflation as a process that lowers our standard of living every bit as much as unemployment. However, a closer look at the actual costs of inflation reveal it to be much less damaging than commonly thought.

Because higher prices also become higher money incomes, it is wrong to think that 5% inflation has somehow "stolen" 5% of our nation's purchasing power or output. In fact, excluding huge triple-digit inflations that lead to demonetization and other inefficiencies, the main costs of inflation itself come from frequent price changes (menu costs) and the fact that inflation erodes the real value of money holdings leading us to hold smaller money balances and thereby creates inefficiencies called "shoe leather" costs. Although these costs can't be neglected, they are small in comparison to popular views of the cost of inflation. A greater cost is associated with the *variability* of inflation as distinct from its level. By adding uncertainty and risk to so many of our decisions, it encourages choices that use scarce resources and that would not be needed in a world with a more stable, predictable inflation rate.

3. Although we customarily think of inflation in terms of rising prices, this is really just the *symptom* of a situation of continuing excess demand. To get at the *cause* of inflation requires us to find the source of the ongoing excess demand—the source of continuing leftward shifts in aggregate supply or rightward shifts in aggregate demand. Many factors can and do cause one-shot shifts in demand or supply. But a search for the source of the ongoing upward pressure on prices that describes the "core" rate of inflation inevitably leads us to the steps of the Central Bank.

4. Inflation is a consequence of our own policy choices. This is not because the government is ignorant or acting irrationally. It reflects the fact that there are many pressures to use the power of monetary policy to pursue a variety of different goals. To the extent that other goals—financing government spending, reducing unemployment, lowering interest rates or exchange rates, to name a few—are substituted for a target of low inflation, the end result is that policy makers have *chosen* to inflate.

5. Because ongoing inflation is a consequence of policy choices, the option of reducing the core inflation rate is always open to us. But the decision to *dis*inflate is far more difficult than it might seem to someone whose primary macroeconomic goal is zero inflation. Because of the high degree of interconnectedness among macroeconomic events, a reduction in the growth of the money supply will have an array of short- and long-run impacts that affect virtually everyone in the economy and even spill over to our trading partners. As the Federal Reserve disinflates, the economy initially moves down its short run Phillips curve and into recession. Whatever the long-term gains from lower inflation, the initial cost of unemployment is the primary barrier to disinflation.

6. How much output is lost during the disinflation process depends on the *slope of the short run Phillips curve*, the *speed at which inflation misperceptions are ended*, and the *extent of market frictions*. Differences of opinion over the relative magnitudes of these three factors define different policy views on the desirability of reducing inflation. But there is general agreement that the more *credible* the monetary authority, the more quickly expectations will adjust and the economy return to full employment.

7. As the inflation rate gets low—say, 2% or 3%—we are more inclined to live with its relatively small costs rather than incur the unemployment costs of further disinflation. Combined with the inflationary bias accompanying discretionary policy making (discussed in the last chapter), this seems to account for the presence of positive inflation rates in all nations today.

8. Although control of the growth of the money supply is an effective tool in achieving a given inflation rate target, it does not follow that inflation can be simply

fixed at a steady rate. The combination of numerous one-shot disturbances and significant policy lags means that we cannot "fine tune" the inflation rate or any other macroeconomic variable. This suggests that the monetary authority needs to set its sights on the long term performance of the core rate of inflation rather than reacting to each monthly surge or lull in the CPI.

10.8 REVIEW QUESTIONS

1. Define the following basic concepts or terms:

Nominal vs. real measures	Wage-price controls	Costs of inflation
Cost of living	Open inflation	Costs of disinflation
Standard of living	Suppressed inflation	Monetized deficits
One-shot price change	Indexing	Incentives to inflate
Continuing price change	Shoe-leather costs	Policy credibility
	Menu costs	

2. "Increased government spending, unless it's tax financed, will be inflationary. It might have some short-run benefits in terms of lower unemployment, but in the long run it will simply increase inflation." Evaluate using the *AD/AS^e* and Phillips curve models.

3. "Those who believe that the government itself is the primary cause of inflation are substituting ideology for logic. Certainly governments have the power to cause inflation and there are examples where that power has been abused. But to suggest that inflation "everywhere and always" has its roots in government actions reflects either ignorance or paranoia. Governments that continue to pursue inflationary policies would soon lose the support of the electorate unless they mended their ways. Politics is a competitive activity and if current decision makers refuse to act responsibly then they will be replaced by those who act in the public interest." Evaluate carefully.

4. There is no longer much dispute about what causes inflation. The evidence strongly supports the view that inflation is nearly always generated by a too-rapid increase in aggregate demand, fueled by a too-rapid increase in the nation's money supply. The real puzzle in this case is not "what?" but "why?" Does it really seem plausible that the government itself would consciously take steps to maintain or even increase inflation? Carefully evaluate this issue of *why* the government apparently chooses inflation when it has the power to eliminate it. Explain fully.

5. Suppose the Central Bank was forced to follow a *monetary policy rule* rather than use their judgment in deciding on monetary policy. Evaluate the three rules below, in terms of their likely impact on the economy's inflation rate. Assume there's a sudden increase in autonomous investment and that fiscal policy is unchanged.

   Rule 1. Adjust the money supply so as to keep the real interest rate constant.

   Rule 2. Adjust the money supply so as to keep the international value of the dollar constant.

   Rule 3. Keep the money supply fixed over time.

6. Which if any of the events below will lead to sustained increases in the overall rate of inflation. Explain your reasoning. If the answer depends on unspecified factors, explain what they are.

   a. An attempt by the Federal Reserve to reduce the real rate of interest.

   b. An attempt by the Federal Reserve to reduce the market rate of interest.

   c. A decision to raise the government's structural deficit and keep it at that higher level for the next decade.

   d. The use of discretionary monetary policy as a stabilization tool.

   e. Adoption of a monetary rule that instructs the Federal Reserve to adjust the money supply as needed to keep the domestic real value of the nation's money supply constant over time.

7. "The reason we need to be concerned with inflation is simple and obvious—a rising cost of living means a declining standard of living." Evaluate.

8. "The inflation history of Latin America in recent decades tells us that once high inflation gets a firm foothold in an economy, it is virtually impossible to eradicate." Evaluate.

9. "Though wage-price controls by themselves can't do much to reduce the ongoing excess demand that lies at the heart of inflation, they can give a boost to the government's credibility and thereby bring about a quicker, less painful disinflation." Evaluate this statement in terms of the Phillips curve model.

10. Discuss the advantages and disadvantages of using inflation as a primary source of taxation.

11. Do you think there is any connection between a particular hypothesis of the business cycle (e.g., Keynesian, new classical, real business cycle, monetarist, new Keynesian) and a person's willingness or unwillingness to accept a disinflationary policy? Explain carefully.

10.9 FURTHER READING

ALBERTO ALESINA, "Politics and Business Cycles in the Industrial Democracies," *Economic Policy* (April 1989).

BEN BERNANKE AND FREDERIC MISHKIN, "Central Bank Behavior and the Strategy of Monetary Policy: Observations from Six Industrialized Countries," in Olivier Jean Blanchard and Stanley Fischer, eds., *Macroeconomics Annual, 1992,* National Bureau of Economic Research (Cambridge, Mass.: The MIT Press, 1992), 183–228.

PHILLIP CAGAN, *Persistent Inflation: Historical and Policy Essays* (New York: Columbia University Press, 1979).

RICHARD COOPER, "The Gold Standard: Historical Facts and Future Prospects," *Brookings Papers on Economic Activity* 1 (1982).

NIGEL W. DUCK, "Some International Evidence on the Quantity Theory of Money," *Journal of Money, Credit, and Banking* 25 (February 1993): 1–12.

STANLEY FISCHER, "Seigniorage and the Case for a National Money," *Journal of Political Economy* (April 1982): 295–313.

STANLEY FISCHER AND LAWRENCE SUMMERS, "Should Governments Learn to Live with Inflation?" *American Economic Review* (May 1989): 382–387.

MILTON FRIEDMAN, "The Optimum Quantity of Money," in *The Optimum Quantity of Money and Other Essays* (Chicago: Aldine, 1969).

Milton Friedman, *Money Mischief: Episodes in Monetary Theory* (New York: Harcourt, Brace, Jovanovich, 1992).

Milton Friedman and Anna J. Schwartz, *A Monetary History of the United States, 1867–1960* (Princeton: Princeton University Press, National Bureau of Economic Research, 1963).

Milton Friedman and Anna J. Schwartz, *Monetary Trends in the United States and the United Kingdom: Their Relation to Income, Prices, and Interest Rates, 1867–1975* (Chicago: University of Chicago Press, National Bureau of Economic Research, 1982).

William T. Gain, ed., *Price Stability: A Conference Sponsored by the Federal Reserve Bank of Cleveland*, published as a supplement to the *Journal of Money, Credit, and Banking* 23 (August 1991).

Manfred J. M. Neumann, "Seigniorage in the United States: How Much Does the U.S. Government Make from Money Production?" *Review*, Federal Reserve Bank of St. Louis (March/April 1992): 29–40.

CHAPTER 11

UNEMPLOYMENT

⊚⊚ 11.1 INTRODUCTION

Unemployment has been a primary issue, directly or indirectly, throughout all the previous chapters. In fact the dominant theme of macroeconomics from its beginnings in the 1930s has been the ability of automatic market forces to keep the economy at or near full employment and, taking it a step further, the conditions under which monetary and fiscal policies can improve this outcome. These are common threads that run through all our analytic models—from the simple classical framework to the Keynesian elaborations and on to their modern counterparts embodied in the AD/AS^e and Phillips curve models.

Macroeconomics was created at a time when unemployment was either a reality or a tangible threat for a large segment of the population in the industrial nations of the West. The average unemployment rate in the U.S. for the entire decade of the 1930s was more than 18%. Other economic ills were forgotten as attention turned to what had happened to the jobs and what could be done about it. The orthodoxy of the classical tradition emphasized the ability of the market-clearing process to automatically generate jobs that would keep the economy from coming to rest anywhere except full employment. Unemployment can occur in a classical setting but it is the role of flexible wages, prices, and interest rates to bring it to an end without help from fiscal or monetary changes. Government's proper role, according to this view, should be limited to rule maker and enforcer, preventing the formation of monopoly power so that the forces of competition and self-interest can do their work.

We've seen how the Great Depression shook the nation's confidence in this automatic correction mechanism and prompted John Maynard Keynes to develop a model of the short run characteristics and workings of the economy. Following the path blazed by Keynes and his followers, much has been learned about unemployment and its causes and cures. Most economists (real business cycle school excepted) now agree that changes in aggregate demand can cause significant short-run changes in real output and unemployment. There is also general agreement that the economic events of the Great Depression were not just the result of a "market failure" signalling the end of laissez faire capitalism. The stagnation of the 1930s came from many sources feeding the large and continuing contraction of aggregate demand. The downturn originated with (1) a drop in private consumption and investment spending, but was then magnified by (2) contractionary monetary and fiscal policies, (3) a self-inflicted negative supply shock from the imposition of the protectionist Smoot-Hawley tariff, (4) the breakdown of the international gold standard, and (5) the near collapse of the U.S. banking system. Though there is disagreement over the relative importance of these specific elements, this general portrayal is widely-accepted among economists. It has also become tightly woven into the fabric of our macroeconomic models and our political consciousness. To this extent, it is appropriately said that "We are all Keynesians now."

But agreement over basic causes and cures for an *economic depression* induced by a collapse in aggregate demand is not the same as agreement over the causes and cures for the ups and downs of the *business cycle*. Although we have not experienced anything close to a recurrence of the Great Depression, periodic and persistent episodes of high unemployment have continued. The hope that activist demand management would bring an end to **cyclical unemployment** has not been realized. So although we may all view unemployment in terms of a framework inspired by Keynes, it is certainly *not* correct to say that "We are all activists now." We've seen

■ FIGURE 11.1(a)

From *Historical Statistics of the United States: Colonial Times to 1970* (Washington, D.C.: U.S. Department of Commerce, Bureau of the Census, 1975); and *Economic Report of the President 1995.* Estimates of the natural rate of unemployment from Stuart E. Weiner, *Economic Review,* Kansas City Federal Reserve, 4th quarter, 1993, "New Estimates of the Natural Rate of Unemployment," pp. 53–69.

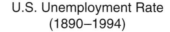

U.S. Unemployment Rate
(1890–1994)

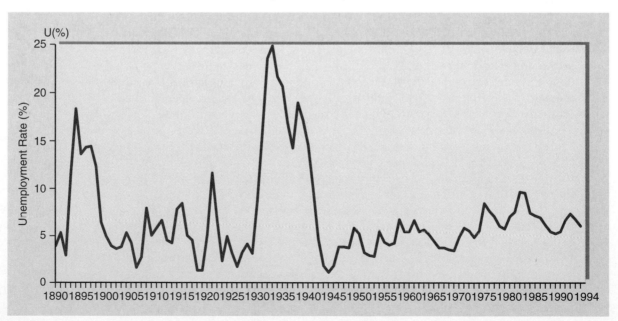

that the classical/nonactivist tradition is very much alive and, most important, that the gap between activists and nonactivists on the issue of economic fluctuations has narrowed appreciably. Advocates of an activist full employment policy today are generally far more moderate in their recommendations and expectations than their counterparts of earlier decades.

A century-long look at the U.S. unemployment rate is shown in Figure 11.1(a). There have been just two extended periods of extremely high unemployment—the depression of the 1890s and the Great Depression. Otherwise the story is one of cyclical ups and downs in unemployment. Figure 11.1(b) focuses on the period since 1961 and shows both the *actual unemployment rate* (U) and the estimated *natural rate of unemployment* (U*). The gap between the actual and natural rates of unemployment—the deviation from the long run Phillips curve—is called **cyclical unemployment.** Having talked about it over many chapters, we finally give it a formal notation $U^{cyc} = U - U^*$. Years of positive cyclical unemployment lie above the U^* line, whereas the observations below U^* show periods of "over-full" employment during boom years.

While the basic facts of unemployment are relatively clear, disagreement persists over the cause of cyclical unemployment and what, if anything, can be done to reduce it. Areas of agreement and disagreement on the unemployment issue were explored in Chapters 8 and 9. Cyclical unemployment is obviously a major economic issue and continues to receive much attention from academics and policy advocates. What is often overlooked, however, is that only a small fraction of U.S. unemployment since World War II fits into the cyclical category. This chapter will investigate the nature and causes of the far larger component—the **natural rate of unemployment**—as we work toward an answer to the question, "Why is the natural rate of unemployment so high and what, if anything, can be done to reduce it?"

■ FIGURE II.I(b)

Actual (U) and Natural Rates (U*) of Unemployment (United States, 1961–1994)

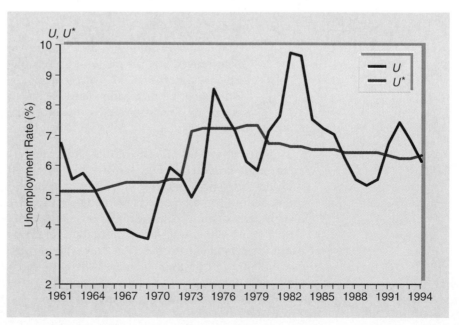

☜ *11.2 OVERVIEW OF THE LABOR MARKET*

To begin to appreciate why there's substantial unemployment even when we're at "full employment" let's start with a look at the *labor market*, in actuality an intricate and extensive network of supply and demand decisions by individuals, firms, and governmental organizations. Most of us think of full employment as the "normal" state of affairs, the "default setting" for the macroeconomy. *Unemployment* is what makes the news; full employment, we like to think, is just business as usual. But this might be compared to taking our personal health for granted. Even when it's justified, it puts a lot of faith in the continued favorable outcome of an incredibly complex process. Taking our economic health for granted can keep us from inquiring into *why* things work so well most of the time, leaving us puzzled and anxious when they don't.

Maintaining high employment in a world of continuous economic change is a formidable challenge for any economic system. It requires the economy in general and the labor market in particular to adjust constantly to a stream of economic assaults, such as the following:

1. *Continued labor force growth*, punctuated by occasional spurts and lulls in the form of baby booms and busts, population migration, and even political unification and disintegration. A responsive labor market must find room not only for a continued flow of new entrants of differing skills and attitudes, but also for re-entrants who had temporarily withdrawn from the work force.

2. *Constantly changing consumer preferences and increased international competition* both require the continual transfer of workers at all skill levels from job to job and industry to industry to channel resources to where they are most productive, as the economy struggles to identify and follow the sometimes surprising twists and turns of its comparative advantage.

3. *Discoveries of new resources and new technologies*, here and abroad, that often arrive in unforeseen bursts and ultimately spread their effects to all but the most remote corners of the economy. The obvious challenge for the labor market is to adapt to the need for new skills and the obsolescence of old ones.

4. *Political change*, both big and little, that closes off some opportunities, opens others, and often adds a further element of uncertainty to our decision-making process. This category is vast—ranging anywhere from major institutional reorganization (such as the switch from a planned to a market system) to demilitarization, regulatory changes, or revisions in minimum wage legislation.

Since World War II each of these four categories has changed in ways and to an extent unprecedented in U.S. history. To maintain full employment in such a setting is like trying to hit a rapidly and erratically moving target. Yet, as Figure 11.1 reveals, the economy has stayed remarkably close to full employment during this period. This is certainly not to suggest that this is the best of all possible worlds or that we should stop seeking ways to further reduce cyclical unemployment. But let's at least pause for a moment to marvel at how well our economic system handles the truly monumental task of keeping an ever-changing economy reasonably close to full employment. Awareness of the complexity of the workings of the labor market can help us appreciate why reductions in unemployment don't usually happen as quickly and

THERE'S NOTHING "NATURAL" ABOUT U*

It's important not to read too much into the word "natural" in the *natural rate of unemployment*. All it really means is that U^* is an "equilibrium" level to which the actual (or measured) rate of unemployment (U) keeps returning. This long run equilibrium must not be taken to denote a normal, correct, or inevitable rate of unemployment. Nor should it be understood as any sort of unchanging "constant of nature." The "natural" rate of unemployment can and does respond to a variety of demographic and policy changes as we'll discuss shortly.

Some economists find the "natural rate" terminology sufficiently open to misunderstanding that they have adopted the more descriptively accurate but far clumsier *nonaccelerating inflation rate of unemployment* (NAIRU). This name captures an important characteristic that emerged in our look at short and long run Phillips curves—U^* is the lowest level to which actual unemployment (U) can fall without an acceleration in the inflation rate.

We'll continue with the earlier and simpler "natural rate," originally coined by Milton Friedman. Feel free to substitute NAIRU if you prefer new Keynesian connotations to the monetarist and new classical affinities of Friedman's work. By either name, U^* remains the same.

easily as promised by the latest fads in "pop economics." It can keep us from being so quick to propose simplistic solutions that "put the country back to work." Most such schemes will have little impact one way or the other on overall unemployment. Some may actually make things worse. A very few have a reasonable chance, always at a cost, to reduce unemployment.

11.3 INSIDE THE "NATURAL" RATE OF UNEMPLOYMENT

We have been using the concept of a *natural rate of unemployment* without saying much about what this cryptic "rate of unemployment when we're at 'full employment'" really means. But even this skimpy treatment was sufficient to make the point that full employment isn't zero unemployment and, especially, to embody the notion of an underlying limit (U^* or y^* or AS^* or PPF or "scarcity," depending on the setting) that yields slightly to changes in aggregate demand in the short run, but finally remains unchanged by purely demand-side events.[1] For a full understand-

---

[1] To expand on this point, you may be surprised to learn that an explicit concept of "full employment" did not exist prior to the Great Depression. Its development is associated with the Keynesian belief that appropriate aggregate demand stimulus from the public sector is a desirable supplement to reliance on market forces. The practice of demand management (which can range from aggressive "fine tuning" to the infrequent, hence, relatively nonactivist use of a fiscal or monetary boost) obviously requires a reliable measure of the target so we can know when to use this stimulus and when to turn it off. Specifically, we must know whether the current level of unemployment is a candidate for policy stimulus (namely, if $U > U^*$) or the result of more lasting factors that do not yield to increases in aggregate demand (if $U \leq U^*$). In other words, we need a reliable measure of the natural rate of unemployment (U^*) before we can distinguish a situation in which expansionary demand policy can potentially speed the return to full employment from a situation in which the stimulus will merely feed inflation and leave no lasting reduction in unemployment.

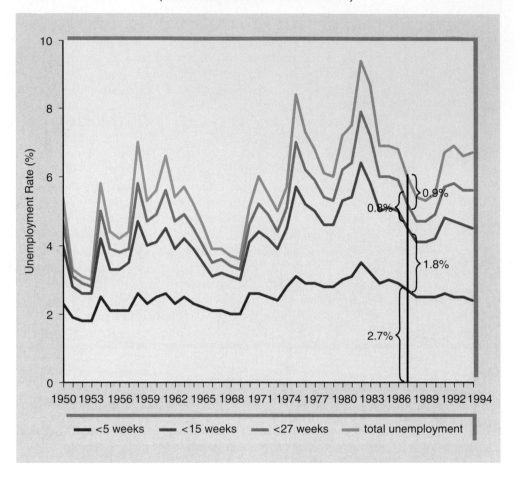

Unemployment by Duration
(1950–1994 in the United States)

■ FIGURE 11.2

ing of just what government policy can and cannot do about unemployment, however, we need to look at what's hidden inside U^*. Though we have treated it as a
monolithic constant, in reality the natural rate of unemployment is a changeable
conglomeration of numerous types of unemployment that come from many different causes and that last for varying lengths of time. Let's begin with a look at
its *duration*.

Even though the natural rate may vary little from year to year (Figure 11.1),
its "members" are in constant flux. That is, although the size of the crowd usually changes very little and very slowly, most of the *faces* in that crowd change
frequently. The graph in Figure 11.2 breaks down yearly unemployment rates by
the number of weeks the unemployment lasted. The lowest line (above the cross-

hatched area) gives observations on what percent of the labor force was unemployed for less than five weeks in each year. The next series adds in those who were unemployed between 5 and 14 weeks, then 15 to 26 weeks, and finally over 26 weeks. They sum to the actual unemployment rate, shown in the top series. Note that as the duration of unemployment increases in a given year (as we move "north" on the graph), the fraction in each interval typically diminishes. Thus, the long-term or "hard core" unemployment in the upper (dotted) area—unemployment lasting more than 26 weeks—is a relatively small portion of total unemployment.

To get a closer look, let's pick a year of virtually full employment like 1987 when the actual unemployment rate of 6.2% was close to its natural rate.[2] The data underlying Figure 11.2 tell us that 2.7% of the labor force experienced unemployment for less than five weeks, 1.8% between 5 and 14 weeks, 0.8% between 15 and 26, and 0.9% for more than 26 weeks.[3] So about three-quarters of the unemployed (4.5% of the 6.2% unemployed) were jobless for under 15 weeks while less than 15% of the unemployed (0.9% of 6.2%) were out of work more than six months.

This tells us that the lion's share of the natural rate of unemployment comes from workers who enter and exit the jobless ranks relatively quickly. We can think of this short-term or **frictional unemployment** (U^{fr}) as a reflection of ongoing labor market change and mobility. Shifting consumer tastes and the rush of new technologies combine with the dictates of comparative advantage to force resources out of declining industries and into expanding sectors. While one sector is eliminating jobs, another will be hiring. But it takes information, effort, and time to accomplish this unending transformation. The result is "unemployment here" matched by "job vacancies there," the essence of "frictional" unemployment. Note that the continued turnover of the frictionally unemployed means that its economic cost, though sizable, is spread quite widely across the population.

The remaining component of the natural rate of unemployment is the long-term joblessness of "hard core" or **structural unemployment** (U^{str}).[4] In this case, the resulting lost income affects relatively few, but hits them very hard. In 1987 1.7% of the U.S. labor force (about two million workers) experienced unemployment of 15 weeks or longer. Structural unemployment is caused by a diverse mixture of economic, social, and psychological factors and most com-

---

[2] This figure is for the "total unemployed (16 years and older) as a percentage of the civilian labor force." Another commonly used measure of unemployment is the "total unemployed (16 years and older) as a percentage of the labor force, including the resident armed forces." Either one is suitable for our purposes. In 1987 the latter measure was 0.1% lower.

[3] These figures are calculated from information in *The Economic Report of the President* (1995), Table B-42, p. 322.

[4] Because these are not official classifications in the national economic statistics, we can define "frictional" and "structural" unemployment to suit the problem we're addressing. In some contexts we might set the boundary between them at 15 weeks; in others, 26 weeks may be more appropriate. In making such distinctions, it's often helpful to take the perspective of a dispassionate outside observer of the macroeconomy rather than that of a participant. Although a three-month spell of unemployment may feel "long term" to those afflicted, especially at the time, from outside it looks "frictional" compared to those who remain jobless for more than six months at a stretch. The quip that "it's a *recession* when your neighbor is unemployed but a *depression* when you are" raises the same issue. But a certain amount of inherent relativity and subjectivity need not keep us from using our common sense to come up with concepts that fit the purpose at hand.

monly afflicts workers whose job skills don't match those required in the job openings. This *skill mismatch* problem obviously raises very different policy issues than the "transitional" problems of the frictionally unemployed, telling us why it's important to look at the duration of U^* in formulating unemployment policy.[5]

Let's now turn from *duration* of unemployment to some specific *causes* of "unemployment when we're at full employment."

1. *Sectoral changes.* The process of economic growth and change inevitably means that some segments of the economy expand while others contract, necessitating a transfer of resources across sectors. As mentioned above, this process takes time (creating "frictional" unemployment) and can result in a mismatch of skills (creating "structural" unemployment). As the pace of change quickens, other things the same, we would expect U^* to rise.[6]

2. *Demographics.* Changes in the age distribution of the population or in the labor force participation rates of particular groups can be important factors in altering both the frictional and the structural components of the natural rate of unemployment. For example, the surge of "baby boomers" into the labor market from the late 1960s into the Seventies increased U^* by accelerating the flow of new entrants. Similarly, the increased labor force participation rates of women at about the same time also worked to increase the "natural rate" because women, on average, have tended to enter and exit the labor force more often than men.[7]

3. *Union power.* The remarkable postwar growth of union power that continued into the 1960s had effects on both the distribution of income and its overall level. To the extent that unionization succeeds in raising the real wages of its members by restricting labor supply, the overall result is a lower level of employment and hence output than if there were no such labor market restrictions. It essentially acts as a negative supply shock in the aggregate. Because increased aggregate demand can't reach this particular source of unemployment, it falls into the "natural rate" category.[8] The dramatic decline in union membership and power over the last 25 years, by itself, has therefore worked to reduce the natural rate of unemployment.

---

[5] Not only is the frictional/structural distinction important, but there are many other characteristics of those who become U^* statistics that are relevant for targeting and implementing policy. These include gender, marital status, race, and age. For a breakdown of the unemployed by these characteristics see Tables B-37 and 38 in the "Economic Report of the President, 1993."

[6] See David Lillien, "Sectoral Shifts and Cyclical Unemployment," *Journal of Political Economy* (August 1982) and, for a skeptical view of the importance of sectoral change, Katherine Abraham and Lawrence Katz, "Cyclical Unemployment: Sectoral Shifts or Aggregate Disturbances?" *Journal of Political Economy* (June 1986): pt. 1.

[7] See Robert Gordon, "Inflation, Flexible Exchange Rates, and the Natural Rate of Unemployment," in Martin Baily, ed., *Workers, Jobs, and Inflation* (Washington, D.C.: The Brookings Institution, 1982) and Daniel Mitchell, "Wage Pressures and Labor Shortages: The 1960s and the 1980s," *Brookings Papers on Economic Activity* 2 (1989).

[8] See Assar Lindbeck and Dennis Snower, *The Insider-Outsider Theory of Employment and Unemployment* (Cambridge, Mass.: The Massachusetts Institute of Technology Press, 1988).

4. *Minimum wage.* A legal minimum wage set above the market-clearing level is a market restriction that works to reduce the demand for unskilled workers, thereby increasing unemployment in this category. Though politically popular because it seems to ensure a "livable wage" to those at the bottom of the income distribution, the minimum wage is regarded with suspicion by most economists. Most disturbing is its tendency to increase unemployment among teenagers, making it more difficult for them to gain experience and training needed to escape from the ranks of the unskilled.[9]

5. *Unemployment compensation.* "Unemployment insurance" has been provided by the Federal government since 1936. Its goal is to create a cushion for our income should we become unemployed, providing us with a certain fraction of previous earnings for a specified maximum period of time. Ironically, but inevitably, softening the blow of unemployment (by spreading the costs across all taxpayers) creates incentives to stay unemployed longer than otherwise. Often this extended time for job search will allow workers to find a better match for their skills and hence a higher wage. In such cases the incentive to use unemployment insurance to search longer turns out to be an individually and socially productive investment. But there's no doubt that some will use these benefits as a paid vacation and only begin a serious job search when their jobless benefits are about to expire. In this case, the existence of unemployment insurance works to raise the natural rate of unemployment without a corresponding improvement in job placement. This is a difficult and quite common situation in which two or more policy goals conflict, making compromise inevitable. The extent to which unemployment compensation increases U^* will depend on the size of the payments and how long they continue.[10]

There are many other underlying sources of unemployment that are unrelated to cyclical fluctuations and, hence, fall under the natural rate of unemployment. But the list above should give you a sense of why the natural rate of unemployment lies beyond the reach of standard monetary and fiscal policies. These sources of unemployment simply have little to do with how quickly or slowly aggregate demand is growing. Instead they reflect such things as *changes in the composition of demand* (point 1 on the previous page); long-term *social, institutional, and demographic trends* that lie well beyond the network of cause and effect captured in our *AD/AS^e* framework (2 and 3); and *side effects of government programs* that may achieve some goals but only at the expense of hindering others (4 and 5). Before we discuss the kinds of long term, structural (and often very costly) changes needed to diminish frictional and structural unemployment, let's examine the macroeconomic costs of unemployment.

---

[9] However, recent evidence suggests that the size of its negative employment effects may be a bit smaller than previously assumed. See Charles Brown, "Minimum Wage Laws: Are They Overrated?" *Journal of Economic Perspectives* 2 (summer 1988): 133–145.

[10] See Lawrence F. Katz and Bruce D. Meyer, "Unemployment Insurance, Recall Expectations, and Unemployment Outcomes," *Quarterly Journal of Economics* 105 (November 1990): 973–1002.

11.4 COSTS OF UNEMPLOYMENT

Unlike the costs of inflation, the losses from unemployment are far from subtle. Individuals, businesses, and governments all feel the pinch when unemployment rises and production falls. But putting a specific dollar value on these costs is complicated by the fact that certain types of unemployment are much costlier than others. Let's begin with the cyclical component ($U^{cyc} = U - U^*$) and take a situation with a 7% actual unemployment rate and a natural rate of 6%. How much does this cyclical unemployment of 1% represent in terms of lost output and income? Put another way, what is the dollar value of goods and services that *could* have been produced this year, but were not? A convenient starting point is **Okun's law,** a modest but very useful little formula devised by Arthur Okun.[11] This empirical relationship, derived from a simple statistical analysis of the two variables, finds that each 1% change of cyclical unemployment translates into a change of about 2.3% in real output. With GDP in the U.S. economy at about $6 trillion, 1% cyclical unemployment represents a staggering $138 billion in lost output and income each year.

It is tempting to think that while this is a large number, the actual cost isn't really that big since we're only losing "potential" output, something we never actually had. By now you should be well aware that such an "opportunity cost" is every bit as real as losing something you already have. Let's take a brief digression to establish this widely applicable point once and for all. Suppose two $6 trillion identical-in-every-way economies suddenly diverge, with economy F continuing at full employment while economy U slides into a three-year recession with average cyclical unemployment of 2%. How will this affect the well-being of its citizens? The unmistakable difference is that economy U's recession deprives its people of real goods and services that according to Okun's law are worth $828 billion ($2 \times 2.3\% \times \$6$ trillion $\times$ 3 years).

This decline in economic activity must show up as a loss of consumption, now or later, in economy U. It can pay the full price of the recession with an $828 billion reduction in consumption (private or public) during those three years. Or it can maintain its consumption during this time by sacrificing its investment spending (again, private or public) by $828 billion. In the second case, the cost of the recession has merely been deferred, not avoided, and will show up as diverging rates of economic growth between economies U and F.[12] In terms of the production possibility curve in Figure 11.3 the recession in economy U would initially show up as a movement from points F to U_c if it decides to pay the full price by sacrificing *current* levels of consumption in each of the three recession years. If it chooses the other extreme and gives up investment goods in order to maintain its current consumption level, the movement will be from F to U_i. This is an example of "consumption smoothing" behavior by economy U, spreading the cost over many years instead of absorbing it

---

[11] Arthur Okun, "Potential GNP: Its Measurement and Significance," *Proceedings*, Business and Economic Statistics Section of the American Statistical Association (1961). We have modified Okun's formula slightly to allow for the fact that unemployment has some benefits (in the form of leisure) as well as costs. This adjustment, following Robert J. Gordon, "The Welfare Cost of Higher Unemployment," *Brookings Papers on Economic Activity* 4 (1973): 133–195, is relatively small but ensures that our estimates of the dollar cost of cyclical unemployment are, if anything, on the low side. We implicitly used Okun's law in deriving the Phillips curve in Chapter 9 when we transformed the horizontal axis from real output (y) to unemployment (U) as we went from $y = y^* + \gamma(\Pi - \Pi^e)$ to $U = U^* - \alpha_1(\Pi - \Pi^e)$.

[12] Note that by cutting investment in order to postpone the decline in consumption, economy U will eventually sacrifice *more* consumption than if it accepted the decline during the recession. This is because investment yields a positive rate of return, which is now being foregone. In other words, if the entire drop in output during this recession came out of investment, the cost in future consumption would be $828 billion *plus* the interest return that would otherwise have come from the investment.

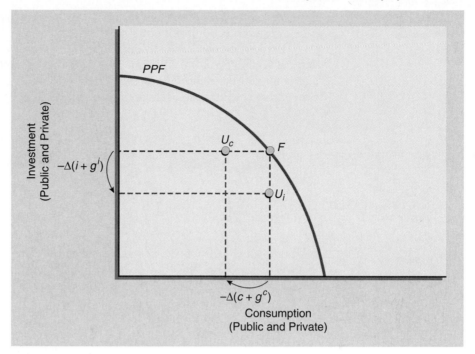

■ FIGURE 11.3

Two initially identical economies are at point *F*. Economy *U* is hit by a recession, forcing it inside its PPF. It must sacrifice either current consumption ($F \rightarrow U_c$) or current investment ($F \rightarrow U_i$), or some combination between U_c and U_i. To the extent that economy *U* chooses to maintain current consumption, sacrificing investment, the cost of the recession will be felt in *future* consumption. The growth rate of its PPF (not shown in this graph) will fall behind that of economy *F*.

all at once. We'll have much to say about such "intertemporal" decision making in the next chapter. But the important point here is that with either choice it's the familiar situation of "pay now" or "pay *more* later." Watching the faster growth and higher consumption of economy *F* (which escaped the recession), citizens of *U* should have no difficulty understanding that opportunity costs are indeed very real.

Throughout this book we've presumed that the special contribution of macroeconomic analysis lies in its ability to see the "big picture," the net outcome in a system where connections are important and interactions sometimes lead to the unexpected. But the cost of taking such a bird's eye view is that we may neglect the *distribution* of these outcomes across the population. So while Okun's law can tell us that each percentage point of cyclical unemployment in a $6 trillion economy means a sacrifice of about $140 billion in goods and services each year, it doesn't tell us *who* pays the cost. If it were spread equally among all 260 million residents, the $540 per person loss would certainly be noticeable, but hardly debilitating to very many.

In fact, a key characteristic of cyclical unemployment is that its costs fall predominantly on a relatively small part of the population. The economic, social, psychological, and emotional costs to the individuals and families hit directly by cyclical unemployment can be enormous and leave scars that last long after the recession has ended. And in a society in which joblessness often feels like worthlessness, the safety net provided by unemployment insurance, as effective as it is in easing economic loss, offers little protection from other costs.

Perhaps it's now easier to understand the intensity of the debate over the causes and cures of cyclical unemployment—reducing unemployment by a single percentage point translates into almost $140 billion more in goods and services for the nation each year. But even at the depths of a recession, cyclical unemployment (U^{cyc}) is

SHARING THE COSTS OF CYCLICAL UNEMPLOYMENT

Without losing sight of the fact that the cyclically unemployed are the primary victims of recession, let's look at how the costs of unemployment radiate outward from this epicenter of job losers to affect other people, places, and times.

Other People

As the unemployment rate rises, government spending on unemployment compensation, food stamps, and other social services all rise. At the same time, the drop in incomes means that the nation's tax base has diminished. The result— additional public spending and a reduced roll of taxpayers—is inevitably a reduction in the after-tax incomes of the employed.

Other Places

International trade, integrated into our AD/AS^e framework through the net export term, offers another direction for cyclical unemployment to spread. A recession means a drop in spending on both domestic and imported goods. So its effects are felt in other nations as a decline in exports (hence, a leftward shift in their IS and AD curves) with the usual adverse short run impacts on output and employment.

Other Times

Although the output loss from cyclical unemployment can't be dodged, we always have the "now or later?" choice about *when* this loss will show up in consumption. For example, one option is for the government to respond to its higher spending and lower tax base by accepting a "cyclical" rise in the deficit (a consumption-smoothing strategy) that postpones taxes until, it is hoped, income has returned to its full employment level. Alternatively, taxes could be raised or other public spending cut *during* the recession if we chose to "bite the bullet" right then and there. Unfortunately, as we've seen, these contractionary responses can deepen and prolong the cyclical downturn. (To the extent that individuals are tax discounters, it should be noted, their individual consumption/saving choices would override the "tax now or deficit now/tax later" decision by the government. We'll take a close look at this in the next chapter.)

seldom more than about one-quarter of total unemployment and usually much less. So it might appear that we've only scratched the surface of the total costs of unemployment. What about the social and individual costs of the remaining portion, the *natural rate of unemployment* (currently about 5½%) that we've divided into frictional and structural components ($U^* = U - U^{cyc} = U^{fr} + U^{str}$)?

The economic costs of frictional and structural unemployment are quite different than those imposed by cyclical fluctuations. Remember that we have assumed that neither of these components of the natural rate yield to changes in aggregate demand. Pumping up aggregate demand in an economy at U^* is a route to higher inflation not lower frictional or structural unemployment. We've also seen that frictional unemployment, by definition, is relatively short-term and that it is primarily a reflection of labor market mobility. In other words, frictional unemployment is an integral part of the ongoing flow of scarce resources toward their most productive use in a changing world. So any plan to reduce the frictional component of U^* that inhibits such mobility could create inefficiencies that might leave us *worse off* than before. Only if frictional unemployment can be lowered through increased efficiency in the job search process (such as computerization that speeds communications between job seeker and job vacancies) will it yield benefits of the magnitude predicted by Okun's law. Otherwise, efforts to lower frictional unemployment are of dubious value, as evidenced by the sometimes astounding inefficiencies and inequities that characterized the self-proclaimed "zero unemployment" planned economies of the old Soviet type.

The final component of unemployment—structural or "hard-core" unemployment—is also resistant to the ordinary workings of monetary and fiscal policies and hence considered part of the natural rate of unemployment. But whereas frictional unemployment reflects something beneficial (labor market mobility), structural unemployment reflects the opposite—a "skill mismatch" predicament that benefits no one. Although a reduction in structural unemployment offers significant potential gains, it presupposes a solution to the underlying skill mismatch problem. Such solutions, through various kinds of job retraining programs, are typically expensive and often ineffective. The result is that structural unemployment continues to frustrate the best attempts of both private and public sector institutions to provide usable training and skills for this most unfortunate segment of the population.

∞ 11.5 CHALLENGING THE "NATURAL RATE HYPOTHESIS"

Though we haven't given it a formal name, the notion that the long run Phillips curve is vertical at the natural rate of unemployment is sometimes called the **natural rate hypothesis.**[13] We've seen that this is just the dynamic counterpart to the vertical long-run aggregate supply curve from the *AD/AS* and *AD/AS^e* models. It is a representation of a sustainable lower-bound for unemployment within a given institutional and demographic structure.

While the natural rate of unemployment can certainly vary over time (and nations) as these underlying factors change, most economists believe that it moves quite slowly and, of course, is unresponsive to fiscal and monetary manipulation. In this view, most of the observed fluctuation in actual unemployment is the result of cyclical events related to the misperceptions, market frictions, and policy lags discussed in

---

[13] This term was coined by Milton Friedman in his presidential address to the American Economic Association published as "The Role of Monetary Policy," *American Economic Review* 58 (March 1968): 1–17.

earlier chapters. But there are those who disagree with the approach embodied in the "natural rate hypothesis." Depending on the nature of their disagreement, these economists reach policy conclusions quite different from what we've seen. While these are minority views, they draw our attention to the need to keep an open mind on these issues and to keep looking for new ways to refine and test our models.

We've already discussed the real business cycle hypothesis that the major source of fluctuation in output and employment comes from the supply side. In the context of the Phillips curve this says that most fluctuations in actual unemployment are really fluctuations in the natural rate of unemployment and hence the long run Phillips curve itself. In other words, they would not accept the standard estimates of U^* shown in Figure 11.1. They conclude that very little of the actual changes in measured unemployment are due to cyclical fluctuations and therefore favor a non-activist role for government on the employment issue.

Another challenge to the mainstream "natural rate" point of view derives from an apparent puzzle in recent European experience. A continuing rise in unemployment for nearly two decades has brought the average unemployment rate from levels of 2% to 3% up to 10% to 12% in several nations, including Great Britain, France, and Germany. The persistence of such high levels of unemployment is not consistent with cyclical unemployment as embodied in our natural rate approach. It would therefore seem that there must have been a continuing increase in the natural rate that has shifted the long run Phillips curve steadily outwards in these nations. But studies of the underlying factors that might have caused such increases in the frictional and structural components of unemployment in these nations have generally failed to find events or policies that could account for the enormity of this change.

So either economists have failed to identify some important factor that is responsible for the rising natural rate in these countries or, it has been suggested, the natural rate hypothesis itself is seriously incomplete.[14] Several alternatives have been proposed that fall into the general category of **hysteresis models of unemployment.** The exotic term "hysteresis" refers to a system in which current values of a variable are strongly influenced by their past values. It is something like our earlier look at market frictions, which we incorporated through the inclusion of a lagged value of past cyclical unemployment, $U = U^* - \alpha_1(\Pi - \Pi^e) + \alpha_2(U - U^*)_{-1}$. But the important difference in these models is that the natural rate itself (U^*) is hypothesized to depend on past levels of cyclical unemployment, $U^* = f(U^{cyc})_{-1} = f(U - U^*)_{-1}$. There are a number of plausible reasons to think that such a relationship might exist. For example, when unemployment is unsustainably low ($U < U^*$) there may be a general improvement in worker skills and experience that will work to reduce frictional or structural components of unemployment and thereby shift the long run Phillips curve to the left. Similarly, when the economy is stuck in a recession there may be a loss of skills and changes in attitudes that end up increasing underlying components of the natural rate and shifting the long run Phillips curve to the right.

Those who believe that this relationship between the current natural rate and past values of actual unemployment is important urge policy makers to be aggressive in trying to avoid recessions since today's downturn raises tomorrow's natural rate. Even if policy overshoots and ends up pushing unemployment below its natural rate, they argue, the long run result could be a decline in the natural rate of unemployment rather than just the accelerating inflation predicted by the mainstream natural rate hypothesis view. However there seems to be no evidence of such hysteresis at work in the U.S. economy and even for Europe the empirical evidence is rather incomplete. At present this remains a minority view and one with quite different policy implications than the standard natural rate hypothesis.

✿ 11.6 PROSPECTS FOR REDUCING UNEMPLOYMENT

Nearly all of us believe that it is the government's responsibility to see that the macroeconomy stays "reasonably close to full employment." Sixty years ago it was much the opposite and many feared that a larger economic role for government would hamper the ability of the market system to operate flexibly, efficiently, and automatically. This dramatic change reflects the influence of the Great Depression, the *General Theory* of Keynes, the economic boom accompanying World War II, and half a century of analytical macroeconomics and policy experiments. A great deal has been learned about the nature of unemployment and it is generally accepted by economists that future generations need never experience anything like the Great Depression.

But apart from the extremes of depression or deep recession, the extent to which the government can lower unemployment, as we've seen over several chapters, remains controversial. In this chapter we have looked at the unemployment issue in more detail, dividing total unemployment into three groups: frictional, structural, and cyclical ($U = U^{fr} + U^{str} + U^{cyc}$). Let's pull this together by examining its implications for unemployment policy.

Cyclical Unemployment

In spite of being the most extensively analyzed topic in macroeconomics, the causes and cures of cyclical unemployment remain controversial. Disagreement over expectation formation, tax discounting, policy lags, supply shocks, and market frictions lie beneath this controversy and these tough issues will continue to divide activists and nonactivists for some time. But the lure of this topic is powerful. Not only is it a major intellectual challenge (hence a potential path to the Nobel Prize in Economics), but the practical consequences are immense. A discovery that reduces cyclical unemployment by a mere 0.1% per year, on average, would boost real output by .23% — approximately $14 billion in goods and services each year in today's economy!

Frictional Unemployment

Because frictional unemployment is so closely tied to labor mobility, we need to be careful in tinkering with this category. Standard monetary and fiscal policies leave it untouched. But specific programs to speed the flow of information and workers to new jobs can potentially yield the substantial benefits described by Okun's law. In the same way that companies have found big savings in various programs that cut their inventory holdings, streamlining the linkages between job searchers and job vacancies can have substantial payoffs. Computerization of the services of the United States Employment Service and relocation loans or subsidies are among the programs that have been used with some success to reduce frictional unemployment without impeding labor market mobility. Proposals to reduce the amount or duration of unemployment compensation in order to speed job search would also fall in this category. As discussed earlier, though, this could lead some workers to accept jobs too quickly and end up being less productive than if they had searched a bit more. Given the diversity of individual responses to unemployment benefits, finding a balance point must be a matter of judgement and compromise. It seems likely that although a major cutback in unemployment benefits would reduce frictional unemployment, there would be little net benefit from such a policy. It would also result in the unemployed bearing an even larger fraction of the costs of joblessness than they currently do.

Structural Unemployment

> *Those who are chronically unemployed are usually so for powerful reasons. Somehow the extensive educational network that works to provide most of us with skills and employment opportunities has failed for these people. This category is a repository of economic, social, and psychological problems that are disheartening. Various job retraining programs, targeted at specific segments of this population, have met with some successes and many failures. Those who fall in this "skill mismatch" category are such a diverse group that progress is likely to be slow and expensive. It seems that the main policy response here will continue to be one that treats the primary symptom—low income—through various transfer programs, leaving its many causes unattended.*

It is hard not to be frustrated by our inability to achieve sustainable reductions in measured unemployment. The issues are difficult and there seem to be no easy answers. But this is surely not the view that emerges when political attention periodically turns to the "unemployment problem." We begin to hear of "jobs programs," "public works programs," "job tax credits," or, still more comprehensively, "employer of the last resort" programs that promise substantial cuts in the huge individual and social costs of unemployment.

Do such proposals somehow circumvent the problems that we've been struggling with on this issue? Do they provide a direct, reliable reduction in total unemployment through various public programs or through subsidies to private employers? Unfortunately the answer is "no." If we think of such programs in terms of the three categories of unemployment discussed in this chapter, how do they fare? Hiring workers in new government programs surely does nothing to reduce the number of frictionally unemployed. Although it may be that such programs will provide skills that reduce structural unemployment, the benefits are likely to be small and the costs high. To make any real impact on this "hard core" unemployment, as noted above, will take carefully targeted programs rather than the large scale, one-size-fits-all approaches that typically come out of the shallow economic waters of election campaigns.

Suppose a sizable "jobs program" is instituted and doesn't reduce frictional and structural unemployment. Can't it still provide jobs to people who currently are jobless and thereby justify its existence? Perhaps, but the important thing to see is that we are now back to a discussion of *cyclical unemployment* and *stabilization policy*. What seems like a simple, direct, common sense plan to reduce total unemployment must be viewed in the context of a temporary stimulus to speed the return to full employment. It can help under certain conditions, but it can also backfire. Moreover, to the extent that such expanded "jobs programs" live on even after the return to full employment, they have ceased to serve the function of stabilization policies. Instead they will only alter the composition of employment from the private to the public sector. There may be some good reasons to make such a change, but they should originate from a decision about the relative sizes of private versus public outputs, not from a well-intended but ill-considered plan to lower the overall rate of unemployment in the economy.

11.7 OVERVIEW

1. This chapter combines some of our earlier findings about **cyclical unemployment** ($U^{cyc} = U - U^*$) with an analysis of the underlying determinants of the **natural rate of unemployment** (U^*) itself. The goal is to reach some basic conclu-

sions as to what policy can and cannot do in achieving a sustainable reduction in unemployment.

2. While there is general agreement about the causes and cures for extreme situations (such as the Great Depression) there is a diversity of views on how to deal with unemployment in the context of the periodic ups and downs, shocks, and trends of recent decades. The task of keeping an economy near full employment—whether accomplished through a system of free markets, a massive planning organization, or some combination of private and public action—is enormously complex.

3. The "labor market" is a shorthand expression for an extremely complex set of decisions and interactions involving suppliers and demanders of labor. On the supply side, a varied and changing composite of workers is constantly entering, exiting, and re-entering the labor force. On the demand side, firms are continually shifting the numbers and types of workers they hire as well as training and retraining existing workers in response to changes in consumer preferences, technological innovations, increased competition, and changing government regulations. *Full employment is a moving target that involves huge and continuing flows of information and movements of workers to where they are most productive.*

4. Our concern is with whether macroeconomic stimulus from the public sector can combine with market forces to improve the workings of the labor market and thereby lower the overall rate of unemployment. The reason this question is so important is that the total costs of unemployment are extremely large. For the individual, unemployment can represent anything from a temporary setback to virtual economic devastation. To the overall economy, cyclical unemployment represents a waste of resources that could be used in the ongoing battle with scarcity. Okun's law tells us that 1% unemployment translates into about $140 billion in lost goods and services each year.

5. A useful way to address this issue is to break unemployment down into three categories. **Cyclical unemployment** (U^{cyc}) corresponds to the gap between the actual and natural rates of unemployment ($U - U^*$). It has been a main concern of this text—and of macroeconomics—from the start. It is also the primary fuel for the activist/nonactivist dispute over stabilization policy. The extent to which macroeconomic stimulus can reduce cyclical unemployment depends on the immediate circumstances and these, in turn, depend on answers to a familiar array of difficult questions about expectation formation, policy lags, supply shocks, and barriers to market clearing.

6. We can then divide the *natural rate of unemployment* into two segments—the short-term "frictional" component (U^{fr}) and the more persistent "structural" component (U^{str}). **Frictional unemployment** is largely a reflection of labor market mobility. As such, it is an important ingredient in economic efficiency. In a changing economy there are always many workers "between" jobs for relatively short periods of time. Standard macroeconomic tools, namely monetary and fiscal expansion, have no lasting impact on this component of unemployment. More specific policies that quicken information flows and decrease relocation time between job vacancies and job seekers can potentially reduce frictional unemployment without hindering labor market mobility. They can thereby bring lasting benefits in real output and income, showing up as an outward shift of the long-run aggregate supply curve ($+ \Delta AS^*$) and a leftward shift of the long run Phillips curve ($- \Delta U^*$). But these programs are expensive and need to be designed and implemented carefully in order to keep their costs from far outrunning their benefits.

7. **Structural unemployment** is a much smaller but longer-lasting part of U^* and also lies beyond the reach of monetary and fiscal stimulus. Its population, for many and varied reasons, lacks the skills needed to qualify for job openings. Job retraining programs to deal with this "skill mismatch" problem have a mixed record. It seems clear that there are no easy or inexpensive answers to the hard core unemployment represented by this component of the natural rate.

8. Much has been learned about the nature and causes of unemployment since the Great Depression provided the impetus for a separate branch of economics to deal with aggregate issues like unemployment and inflation. The disastrous contractionary policies of the Thirties that only deepened the Great Depression would not be tolerated today. But there is still much to be learned about how to achieve sustainable reductions in the unemployment rate and thereby increase the overall standard of living. It seems clear that *conventional monetary and fiscal policy is quite limited in its ability to deal with the bulk of unemployment, which is structural and frictional rather than cyclical.* The search for policies to reduce the natural rate of unemployment requires attention to long term, structural issues that have been relatively neglected until recently. Both the real business cycle hypothesis and the "hysteresis" theory of unemployment have made an attempt to uncover more about the nature of the natural rate of unemployment (U^*) itself. But both have serious shortcomings as complete theories of unemployment.

9. Because the costs of unemployment are so obvious, even the slightest hint of a coming recession can unleash a flood of "pop economics" filled with well-intended but usually primitive and ineffective remedies for unemployment. Those who turn to slogans or so-called common sense for easy answers to hard questions are likely to repeat the errors of the past. In the oft-quoted final paragraph of *The General Theory*, Keynes warned that "Practical men, who believe themselves to be quite exempt from any intellectual influences, are usually the slaves of some defunct economist."

⌘ 11.8 REVIEW QUESTIONS

1. Define the following basic concepts and terms:

Natural rate of unemployment	Frictional unemployment
Cyclical unemployment	Okun's law
NAIRU	Natural rate hypothesis
Structural unemployment	Hysteresis model of unemployment

2. "One of the reasons that the Great Depression was so deep and prolonged and so devastating to so many was that there were simply no "floors" to protect against the continued downward spiral of spending and output and income and spending and output and income and so on. One important attempt to put a floor on incomes and hence purchasing power and spending was the Minimum Wage Law passed in the mid-1930s. By interrupting the wage-cutting and price-cutting hysteria, it finally gave workers an assured floor on their income that they could count on in their spending plans. In the aggregate, it finally stabilized aggregate demand." Evaluate fully.

3. A major concern about organizing an economy around a so-called market system has been whether decentralized decision making is sufficiently responsive to economy-wide performance and issues such as unemployment. One plan to help

out the "invisible hand" has been termed the "Employer of Last Resort" policy. When events and circumstances find the economy in recession, this strategy obligates the government to automatically hire workers for public service jobs until the unemployment rate has returned to the full employment level. Conversely, as unemployment goes below its natural rate, these public programs would be scaled back and workers released back into the private sector. Advocates of this fiscal policy rule stress its automatic stabilization properties on both real output and the price level. *Analyze the likely consequences of such a policy, using what you have learned about the workings of the macroeconomy in this and previous chapters. Explain your reasoning.*

4. Suppose your research on the unemployment problem convinces you that the NAIRU is systematically related to the *actual* rate of unemployment. Specifically, you find that when measured unemployment (U) remains high for an extended time, there is a resulting increase in the natural rate of unemployment ($+ \Delta U^*$). Similarly, the longer U stays at very low levels the more likely it is that U^* itself will decline.

   a. What reasons can you give that might support the existence of such a relationship?

   b. If such a relationship exists and is significant, how would it alter the basic policy implications that we derive from the Phillips curve analysis? Explain.

5. A bipartisan *Commission on Economic Prosperity* is created to make recommendations to deal with chronic problems of unemployment in modern industrial economies. As chief economic advisor to the Commission your responsibility is to provide careful and intelligible explanations of the three areas listed below. You should address your analysis to the nation's "opinion leaders"—that is, thoughtful and responsible men and women in both the public and private sectors who are not trained in economics and are concerned with practical results rather than abstract theories.

   a. Give a complete, accurate, and balanced explanation of what the economics profession believes is the best way to ensure that the economy stays as close as possible to full employment.

   b. Provide an effective long term plan, including likely costs and benefits, for a gradual drop in the rate of unemployment when the economy is at full employment.

   c. Write an appendix to the Commission's report that addresses the connection between the problem of maintaining full employment and the related problem of achieving a low and stable rate of inflation.

11.9 FURTHER READING

ANTHONY B. ATKINSON AND JOHN MICKLEWRIGHT, "Unemployment Compensation and Labor Market Transitions: A Critical Review," *Journal of Economic Literature* XXXIX (December 1991): 1679–1727.

C. BEAN, R. LAYARD, AND S. NICKELL, *The Rise in Unemployment* (Oxford: Basil Blackwell, 1987).

NATHAN BALKE AND ROBERT GORDON, "The Estimation of Prewar Gross National Product: Methodology and New Evidence," *Journal of Political Economy* (February 1989): 38–92.

RALPH BRYANT, PETER HOOPER, AND CATHERINE MANN, EDS., *Evaluating Policy Regimes: New Research in Empirical Macroeconomics* (Washington D.C.: Brookings Institution, 1993).

MILTON FRIEDMAN, "The Role of Monetary Policy," *American Economic Review* 58 (March 1968): 1–17.

BRUCE GREENWALD AND JOSEPH STIGLITZ, "New and Old Keynesians," *Journal of Economic Perspectives* 7 (winter 1993): 23–44.

G. JOHNSON AND R. LAYARD, "The Natural Rate of Unemployment: Explanation and Policy," in O. Ashenfelter and R. Layard, eds., *Handbook of Labor Economics* (Amsterdam: Elsevier Science Publishers, 1986).

LAWRENCE F. KATZ AND BRUCE D. MEYER, "Unemployment Insurance, Recall Expectations, and Unemployment Outcomes," *Quarterly Journal of Economics* 105 (November 1990): 973–1002.

RICHARD LAYARD, STEPHEN NICKELL, AND RICHARD JACKMAN, *The Unemployment Crisis* (Oxford: Oxford University Press, 1994).

N. GREGORY MANKIW AND DAVID ROMER, EDS., *New Keynesian Economics*, 2 vols. (Cambridge, Mass.: The Massachusetts Institute of Technology Press, 1991).

KEVIN M. MURPHY AND ROBERT H. TOPEL, "The Evolution of Unemployment in the United States, 1968–1985," *NBER Macroeconomics Annual* (Cambridge, Mass.: The MIT Press, 1987), 11–58.

EDMUND S. PHELPS, ED., *Recent Developments in Macroeconomics*, 3 vols. (Brookfield, Vt.: Edward Elgar Publishing Company, 1991).

CHRISTINA D. ROMER, "The Prewar Business Cycle Reconsidered: New Estimates of Gross National Product, 1869–1908," *Journal of Political Economy* (February 1989): 1–37.

JOHN B. TAYLOR, *Macroeconomic Policy in a World Economy: From Econometric Design to Practical Operation* (New York: Norton, 1993).

PART IV

Long-Run Dynamics: Saving, Investment, and Growth

Our analysis so far has taken the full employment level of output as predetermined—a known limit defined, depending on the context, by a production possibility frontier (PPF), a long-run aggregate supply curve (AS^* at y^*), or a vertical long-run Phillips curve (LRPC at U^*). This simplification allowed us to focus attention on the issue of *reaching and maintaining full employment* without also having to worry about the target itself moving. The discussion in Chapter 1 of the choice between "now or later?" was largely neglected in the subsequent chapters in order to develop an understanding of basic macroeconomic interactions and policy issues in a relatively simple world of "zero growth." [1]

This analytical convenience was purchased at the price of ignoring the most important aspects of our economic well-being over time—the ingredients underlying **economic growth**. Figure IV.1 is a reminder that the big story across decades and generations has been the *trend* in real output rather than the *cycles* around that trend. Our collective hope for a ris-

---

[1] One exception was the treatment of fiscal policy in Chapter 5. A full understanding of the implications of deficits required a look at long term consequences of the "pay now" or "pay more later" choice. By combining this with the "now or later?" implications of the spending side of fiscal policy (public consumption or public investment) we could then determine whether deficit financing would later prove to be consumption-draining, consumption-smoothing, or self-financing. This was essentially a preview of some of the issues covered in the next three chapters.

A Century of U.S. Real Output
(Billions of 1958 $)

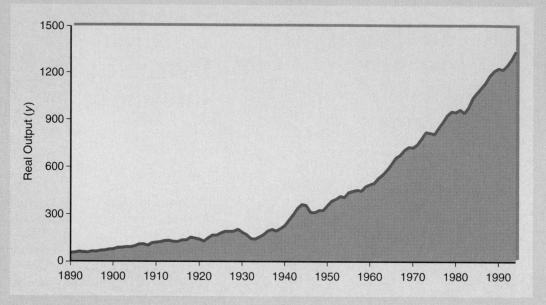

■ FIGURE IV.1

ing standard of living depends on the long term rate of economic growth, not on the ups and downs of the business cycle. Previous chapters have dealt with variations around the aggregate supply curve—the *cycles* of $\pm \Delta(y - y^*)$. We now turn to the long-term movements in aggregate supply itself—the *trend* of $\pm \Delta y^*$.[2]

Specifically, the next three chapters look at the elements determining the growth of potential output in the macroeconomy. They examine the process of *transforming inputs into both private and public output* as described by the production function $y^* = F(n^*,k,i^{nst})$. One kind of output—**investment**—is of particular importance because it feeds the capital stock ($i = \Delta k$) by "recycling" as an input. Chapter 12 examines investment in the context of the *consumption-saving* choice of households and the *investment* decision of businesses. This is done explicitly in terms of the "now or later?" decision, a setting formally known as **intertemporal choice.**

Chapter 13 sketches the main features of **capital markets,** the general term for a multitude of paths through which borrowers and lenders, savers and investors—public and private, domestic and international—make the important decisions that determine not only the rate at which funds flow through saving to investment and capital but also the kinds of capital formation that occur. Together, Chapters 12 and 13 examine the dynamics and linkages in the saving/investment process underlying capital formation (Δk). This is combined with other elements in Chapter 14 to build a broad foundation for understanding **economic growth.**

---

[2] Finding a name for this new undertaking is a bit of a problem because macroeconomists have persisted in using "long run" to denote market clearing *without* growth. Even though it was a long run in which, according to Keynes, "we're all dead," it was still not long enough to change the capital stock or the population or the institutional structure in order to get economic growth. So we might term our present analysis "long run *plus* growth" or just "long-run dynamics."

CHAPTER 12

CONSUMPTION, SAVING, AND INVESTMENT

✆ 12.1 INTRODUCTION

With the economic news so strongly focused on government policies—how spending, taxes, deficits, and the money supply are causing or curing various economic problems—it is easy to forget that what provides the real power to the U.S. economy is the multitude of "this or that?" and "now or later?" choices by individuals and businesses. While the media focuses our attention on public-sector actions, Figure 12.1 shows that four-fifths of total output comes from **private consumption spending** by households and **private investment spending** by firms.[1] Private investment, though only about 15% of total spending, is particularly volatile and is a key factor in the cyclical swings of the economy. Its jagged time series profile, shown in Figure 12.2, contrasts sharply with the much smoother stream of consumption.

We've seen that an understanding of changes in private consumption and investment spending is central to an explanation of the trends and cycles in overall economic activity. Our model macroeconomy (AD/AS and its "expectations-augmented" variation, AD/AS^e) is built around theories of these components. Consumption—represented by the "consumption function" $c = c_0 + c_1(y - t)$—was assumed to vary directly with after-tax income $(y - t)$. The strength of this relationship is represented by the size of the coefficient c_1. The multitude of other factors that can and do affect total consumption

---

[1] How do we find the percentage of total spending ($y = c + i + x + g$) accounted for by each category when one, net exports, is negative? Negative net exports tells us that the totals for consumption, investment, and government spending include some expenditures on foreign goods in addition to the spending on U.S. output. To adjust for this, we've made the simple assumption that each category of domestic spending (consumption, investment, and government) is overstated by the same amount; in other words, that our negative net exports occur uniformly by type of spending. This approximation is sufficient for present purposes, which is to get a general picture of the relative importance that consumption and investment play in U.S. economic activity.

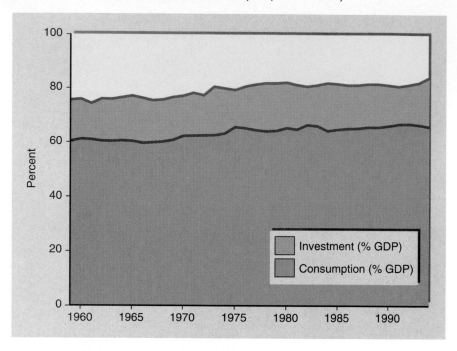

■ FIGURE 12.1

■ FIGURE 12.2

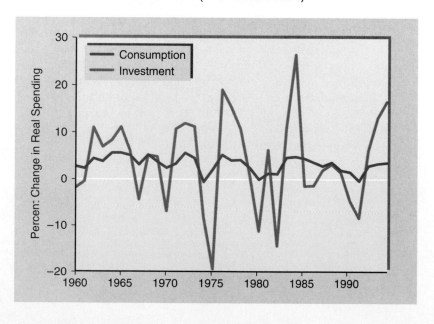

spending—from gradual demographic change to stock market gyrations or altered expectations of future events or policies—are lumped together in the "autonomous consumption" term c_0.

Investment spending—captured in the "investment function" $i = i_0 - i_2r$—was assumed to move inversely to changes in the real rate of interest (r). The magnitude of this relationship is given by the size of the estimated coefficient i_2. Anything else that causes firms to alter their investment expenditures—from changes in product lines due to changing consumer tastes to technologically induced changes in production processes or expected changes in the tax system—goes into the "autonomous investment" term (i_0). Autonomous investment is presumed to be independent of other variables within this model, at least for the relatively short time period for which the "no growth" AD/AS analysis is designed.

Consumption and investment spending, then, have played the same crucial roles in our model that we think they play in the "real world" the model seeks to mimic. Consumption, in particular, forms a symbiotic relationship with income through the two-way causality described by $y = c + i + x + g$ and $c = c_0 + c_1(y - t)$. A change in one is transmitted to the other, starting a continuing but diminishing sequence of events ($\Delta y \Leftrightarrow \Delta c$). This interaction—the heart of the demand-side *multiplier*—plays a key part in the process by which the impact of a change in one variable spreads throughout the macroeconomy. Investment plays a less obvious but still important role, because both the volatility of its autonomous component ($\pm \Delta i_0$) and its sensitivity to changes in the real interest rate lead to changes in total income ($y = c + i + x + g$), which are then magnified through the multiplier process. All this has been built into the workings of our model, allowing it to capture quite complicated economy-wide interactions and repercussions from many different events and policies.[2]

But so far we have viewed consumption and investment as largely independent entities, done by different decision makers responding to different influences. This is a reasonable and useful simplification for understanding short-run issues. But it leaves out a deeper relationship between consumption and investment—a connection through **saving** and **capital markets**—that lies at the heart of the process of economic growth. To see this, let's start with a simple closed economy ($x = 0$) with no government sector ($g = t = 0$) and assume it is always at full employment. In this setting all income goes either to consumption or saving ($y^* = c + s$, because $t = 0$) and all output is divided between private consumption and private investment ($y^* = c + i$, because x and g are both zero). At full employment, investment will always be limited by saving because $c + i = y^* = c + s$, hence, $i = s$. Though obviously much simplified, this structure helps us see the vital *consumption-saving-investment linkage to economic growth*, while avoiding details that complicate but don't alter the story.

---

[2] There is much, much more that can be said about the specific determinants of consumption and investment spending in the context of stabilization policy and the AD/AS^e model—issues of definition, measurement, and forecasting. For example, the high level of aggregation that we have used obscures features of different kinds of consumption (consumer durable goods, nondurable goods, and services) and investment (plant and equipment, inventories, residential housing, research and development, education) that can be important for particular questions. Such detail is not needed for the general understanding of macroeconomic interactions that is the goal of this book. For a more detailed look at consumption and investment spending as determinants of economic fluctuations, see Robert J. Gordon, *Macroeconomics*, 5th ed. (New York: HarperCollins, 1990), chap. 18, "Instability in the Private Economy: Consumption Behavior" and chap. 19, "Instability in the Private Economy: Investment." A more complete and advanced presentation of the intertemporal approach of this chapter is available in Jeffrey D. Sachs and Felipe Larrain, *Macroeconomics in the Global Economy* (Englewood Cliffs, N.J.: Prentice Hall, 1993).

Within this setting, each of us must decide how much of our current income to consume (c) and how much to leave for future consumption via saving (s). What we consume now cannot be used to feed the investment ($s = i$), capital formation ($i = \Delta k$), economic growth ($\Delta k \Rightarrow \Delta PPF$ and ΔAS^*) process. These connections are illustrated in Figure 12.3, which shows the long-run implications of a consumption-investment choice at point Q. This sends enough resources through saving ($s_Q = y^*_0 - c_Q$) to support current net investment of i_Q which, in turn, increases the total capital stock ($+ \Delta k$) and shifts out both the production possibilities and aggregate supply curves.

Incorporating this connection between our consumption-saving choice and the investment-capital formation outcome finally brings economic growth *inside* our analysis. Figure 12.3 shows that we can have faster growth but only at the cost of cutting current consumption and moving up the PPF. It requires a cut in current consumption (and increased saving) which moves more resources into current investment. This, in turn, accelerates the growth of the capital stock and causes PPF and AS^* to shift out at faster rates. This is a simple but essential point, first made back in Chapter 1—*economic growth is determined, in part, by how we choose between consumption and saving*. It involves the inescapable tension between "consume now" or "consume more later" that, whether we are conscious of it or not, underlies each and every economic choice we make. Chapters 12 to 14 will develop an analytical structure that incorporates the "now or later?" choice into the connection between consumption and saving, through capital markets, to investment and economic growth.

■ FIGURE 12.3

From a given initial real income ($y_0^* = c_0 + i_0$) the choice between consumption and saving ($y_0^* = c_Q + s_Q$), reflected at ①, determines how many resources are available for investment ②. Because $i_Q > 0$ means an increase in the capital stock ($+ \Delta k$), this is also an outward shift in PPF ③ and in AS^* ④. Movements up the PPF from Q would quicken the rate of growth at the cost of less current consumption, i.e., $- \Delta c \Rightarrow + \Delta i \Rightarrow +\%\Delta k \Rightarrow +\%\Delta PPF$ and $+\%\Delta AS^*$.

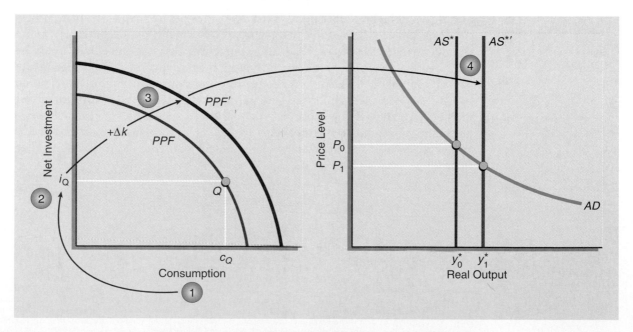

"Consumption/Saving/Investment/Growth" Connection

✆ 12.2 CHOOSING THE BEST CONSUMPTION PATH

We have seen that "scarcity," so obvious yet so often surprising in the breadth of its reach, means that decisions made today have consequences for our well-being 1 year and 10 years from now. By the same reasoning, the options we face today reflect choices that we (or others) made 1 year or 10 years ago. In other words, our basic condition is one in which every choice exists in a "web of time" that hampers our desires to change the economic present or future. We need to understand these **intertemporal linkages** before we can know whether we're making promises that we can't or won't keep—privately through our college loans or home mortgages, publicly through continued government deficits or off-budget commitments to pay for future retirement and medical care programs.

This connection between our current decisions and our future options was illustrated in Figure 12.3. It showed, rather clumsily, that the level of current consumption influences the rate at which AS^* and PPF shift over time. The two key determinants of the size of these shifts are

1. How much of our current income we *don't* consume now ($s = y - c$), allowing us to put additional resources into *capital formation* through the saving-investment channel ($s = i = \Delta k$).
2. The *real rate of return on additional capital* ($r = \Delta y^*/\Delta k$, hence, $\Delta y^* = r\Delta k$) that tells us how much additional output the new capital produces.

This way of posing the "now or later" issue comes from the ingenious "two period diagram" introduced and developed decades before Keynes' *General Theory* by American economist Irving Fisher.[3] Although Fisher's framework is a marvelous simplification, it requires some patience to get accustomed to the notation now that each variable has a "time period" attached to it.

Using a single graph and temporarily continuing our earlier assumptions (full employment and no government or foreign sectors), we can portray an individual's *intertemporal consumption options* in a revealing way. Suppose we know that our income in two periods—0 and 1—will be some specific values given by y_0^E and y_1^E. This particular income path over periods 0 and 1 is usually called the **initial endowment** (E). Suppose also that there is a given real interest rate (the "rate of return" on capital) at which we can either borrow or lend. Given our initial endowment and the real interest rate and recognizing that consuming more now means less later, how much *should* we consume now? To get a handle on this *intertemporal optimization problem*, let's examine the constraints on what we can and cannot do. This requires us to identify which consumption paths are attainable.

We begin with the arithmetic of "compounding" and "discounting." If we have $100 now and the interest rate is 10%, this can be transformed into $110 in the next period if we save/invest it all. We can express this intertemporal relationship by saying that $100 now is equivalent to $100 + r \cdot $100 or $100(1 + r)$ next year.[4] So if we could go without consuming any of our current income (y_0^E), we could transform it into the amount $y_0^E(1 + r)$ by saving for one year. That means that if we starve ourselves now, next year's total consumption will be $y_0^E(1 + r)$ *plus* next year's income y_1^E.

---

[3] Irving Fisher, *The Nature of Capital and Income* (New York: Macmillan, 1906); *The Rate of Interest* (New York: Macmillan, 1907); and *The Theory of Interest* (New York: Macmillan, 1930).

[4] This return grows exponentially over time (compounds) as we get interest on previous interest as well as on the principal. Its value in period n is given by $100(1 + r)^n$

This accumulated value of both periods' incomes (plus interest on the first period) is a measure of total potential "wealth" as of next period—$W_1 = y_0^E(1 + r) + y_1^E$. This value, plotted along the vertical axis of Figure 12.4, represents the maximum value we could consume next period out of our given endowment (y_0^E, y_1^E) if we took the miserly "always tomorrow, never today" approach and consumed nothing this period. Thus point F represents a consumption *path* in which current consumption is zero, whereas consumption next period is the amount W_1.

Another possible consumption path is simply to consume at point E, the initial endowment of income. This choice forgoes any manipulation of the consumption stream through saving or dissaving (borrowing). It's a sort of "easy come, easy go" strategy in which we spend all our income on consumption each period. So a consumption path at point E is identical to the income path, hence, $c_0 = y_0^E$ and $c_1 = y_1^E$.

The final step in mapping available consumption paths (for our given income endowment and given interest rate) is to "discount" future income back to the present. Suppose we entirely ignore the future and decide to maximize our consumption now. In this "life's short, grab for all the gusto" approach we consume all our current income (y_0^E) plus all we can borrow on next period's income as well. What is the **present value** of y_1^E? We saw above that $100 now is worth $100(1 + r)$ next period so, turning it around, the present value of next year's $100(1 + r)$ must be $100 or $100(1 + r)/(1 + r)$. Just as we *compound* (multiply by $(1 + r)$) to get from this period

■ FIGURE 12.4

For a consumer with a given endowment (income path) of (y_0^E, y_1^E) facing a given rate of interest (r), any point on (or inside) the wealth constraint (line FEG) is an attainable consumption path.

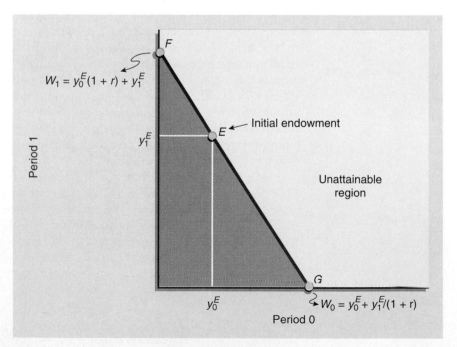

Wealth Constraint

to next, we *discount* (divide by $(1 + r)$) to get back to the present.[5] So the present value of next year's y_1^E is $y_1^E/(1 + r)$ and the maximum we can consume now (leaving nothing for next period) is given by $y_0^E + y_1^E/(1 + r_0) = W_0$.

Thus W_0 is simply our current wealth or, more precisely, the *present value of our endowed income path at interest rate* r. This value, plotted on the horizontal axis at point G in Figure 12.4, represents another possible consumption path. The line FEG connecting these three points shows all the attainable consumption time paths ("now/later" combinations) for someone with the given income endowment (y_0^E, y_1^E) facing a constant real interest rate of r. It's called the *intertemporal budget constraint* or, more simply, the **wealth constraint.**

The slope of the wealth constraint, $\Delta c_1/\Delta c_0 = - W_1/W_0 = - (1 + r)$, is of particular importance because it is an intertemporal exchange rate, representing the terms on which we can trade "consumption now" for "consumption later" and vice versa. It's a "minus" because more later means less now. It's greater than one since giving up $1 in consumption now returns principal plus interest later. For example, if the interest rate is 10% the slope $(- 1.10)$ tells us that every $1 that we don't consume now will be worth $1.10 next period. Equivalently, every $1 that we consume this year lowers next year's potential consumption by $1.10. Hence the haunting implication that every dollar we've *ever* spent has reduced our attainable consumption this year by that dollar plus accumulated interest. This is the previously noted "web of time" with which scarcity binds our every choice.

The wealth constraint defines the boundary between attainable and unattainable consumption paths. But which point on (or inside) this constraint should we pick? Which balance between "now" and "later" should we strike?[6] Should we consume all our income in each period, staying at the endowment E? Or should we save and move toward point F or borrow and move toward G? In Chapter 1's brief discussion of the "rate of time preference" we saw that any such choice is inevitably a matter of preference that will differ across individuals. Suppose that person A, with initial endowment E, selects the consumption pattern (c_0^{A*},c_1^{A*}) at point A^* in Figure 12.5. Her optimal consumption path is for consumption now to exceed her current income, requiring her to borrow against future income. In other words, her preference is to consume beyond her current income even though it will cost her that amount plus interest—$(1 + r)(c_0^{A*} - y_0^E)$—in reduced "consumption later."[7]

Another person with exactly the same wealth constraint (initial endowment and interest rate) might make a very different choice. For example, suppose individual Z selects the consumption path (c_0^{Z*},c_1^{Z*}), shown at point Z^* in Figure 12.6. His choice, compared to A's, reveals a stronger preference for future over present consumption. Z is said to have a lower "rate of time preference" than A, because he's more patient with respect to *when* he consumes. Though both have the same income path (and

---

[5] Discounting $100 *n* periods from now back to the present gives a *present discounted value* of $100/(1 + r_0)^n$.

[6] Presuming that more consumption is preferred to less in any period, any choice *inside* the budget line will be less desirable than another feasible combination on the line. This allows us to limit our attention to points along the wealth constraint, W_1W_0 in Figure 12.4.

[7] If you've had intermediate microeconomic theory, you're familiar with the notion of an *indifference map* as a way to describe our subjective preferences between "this" or "that." We could also use this device in our two-period model, as Irving Fisher originally did, to describe individual preferences between "now" and "later." Superimposing the family of indifference curves on the wealth constraint, we could then locate the "intertemporal optimum" (i.e., the best consumption path) by finding the (single) point at which an indifference curve is tangent to the given intertemporal budget (i.e., wealth) constraint. This joining of *preferences* (the indifference map) and *possibilities* (the budget constraint) portrays the solution to the "choice under scarcity" problem in a way that most economists find elegant and satisfying. The presentation here forsakes elegance and simply proclaims an optimum point (implicitly, the point of tangency) without actually drawing in the indifference map. The justification is an economic one—the time and effort to learn this technique adds little to our understanding of the basics of macroeconomic issues.

■ **FIGURE 12.5**

With endowment E, individual A chooses consumption path A^* with $c_0^{A^*}, c_1^{A^*}$. She chooses to *borrow now* $(c_0^{A^*} - y_0^e)$ and *repay later* $(y_1^E - c_1^{A^*}) = (c_0^{A^*} - y_0^E)(1 + r)$.

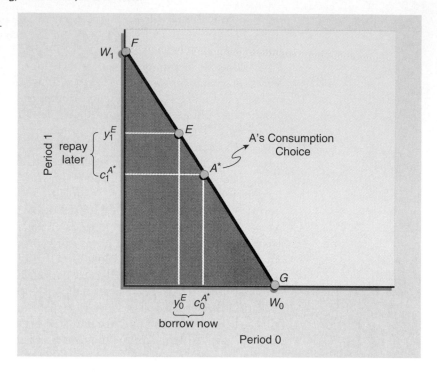

■ **FIGURE 12.6**

A *very* patient consumer, with a low rate of time preference, might choose a consumption path like Z^*. He would "save now" and "enjoy later," moving consumption from present to future at the rate $(1 + r)$. Relative to consumer A's choice (A^*), he puts a higher value on his *future* consumption.

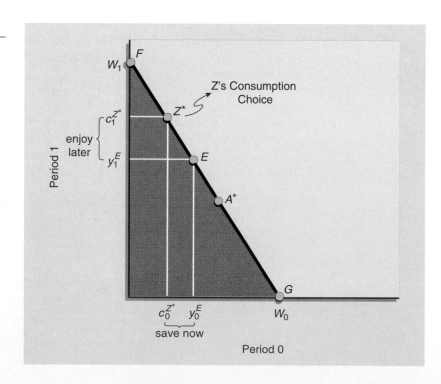

wealth constraint), Z's intertemporal preferences have induced him to "save now, consume (more) later," whereas A chooses to "borrow now, repay (more) later."

Neither choice can be said to be "better" than the other; they each reflect a balance between now and later that suits two different persons. The role of the *capital market* (next chapter's subject) is to link Z's saving with A's borrowing, making both better off by allowing them to move from their initial endowments (both at E, in our example) to their individually preferred consumption paths at A^* and Z^*, trading consumption across time at the rate $-(1 + r)$.

✆ 12.3 HOW FAR AHEAD DO WE PLAN?

This two-period framework offers a relatively easy way to portray the impact of current decisions on future well-being. We saw in Figure 12.5 that A's decision to borrow and consume beyond her first period's income, affected her consumption in the next period. Although the use of just two periods is very artificial, it is a simple way to portray a crucial point—*our current actions have future consequences.* You might think this so obvious that it hardly needs saying, much less the addition of another economic model. But it's one of those simple/subtle points that can get lost in the discussion of difficult issues such as the workings of the macroeconomy. For example, we saw in Chapter 5 that the belief that government borrowing ($b > 0$) *necessarily* means a falling standard of living in the future is a failure to examine how the borrowed funds were being used. Another example is that our assumption of zero growth in previous chapters means that even the elaborate ten-equation AD/AS^e analysis ignored the fact that more consumption now means less later.

Now that we have a workable framework to connect present with future, the obvious question is the degree to which consumers actually consider these future outcomes in making their consumption/saving choices.[8] How far ahead *do* we plan? Before discussing the empirical evidence on the length of our economic horizon, let's sharpen our view of the issue by returning to the two-period model. Although this intertemporal framework can be used to examine many different events and policies, for our purposes the analysis can be restricted to a very specific situation.[9] Suppose that A's initial endowment happens to change in a particular way—her current income drops while her future income rises and the relative sizes of these changes just happen to move her to a new point on the same wealth constraint as before.

This hypothetical and coincidental change is illustrated in the movement from E to E' in the two graphs in Figure 12.7. Though she's lost income now ($- \Delta y_0^E$), she's gained enough income later ($+ \Delta y_0^E$) to offset that loss plus interest and remain on the same intertemporal budget line.[10] The question is whether this change in the

---

[8] We ventured into this territory in our earlier discussion of rational expectations in the context of the AD/AS^e model. But we only looked at part of the issue—how misinformation in the "short run" could create an upward-sloping aggregate supply curve. The demand-side role of expectations was ignored. In addition, we lacked a multiperiod framework (like the two-period model) that could reveal the connection between current decisions and future outcomes. Instead we substituted categories (self-financing, consumption-smoothing, consumption-draining) that could describe but not analyze intertemporal relationships.

[9] For example, we could look at how an increase (or decrease) in the initial endowment (income path) *shifts the wealth constraint* out (or in), leading to a new optimal consumption path. Or, with the income path unchanged, we could see how a change in the interest rate alters the "intertemporal price ratio," thereby *rotating the wealth constraint* around point E and having differential effects on savers and borrowers.

[10] For this change in the timing of income to leave the wealth constraint unchanged, her future income must have increased by r% more than her current income fell. Algebraically, $\Delta y_1 = -\Delta y_0(1 + r)$ so that $\Delta y_1/\Delta y_0 = -(1 + r)$, which defines a movement along the curve, leaving its intercepts ($W_1 W_0$) unchanged.

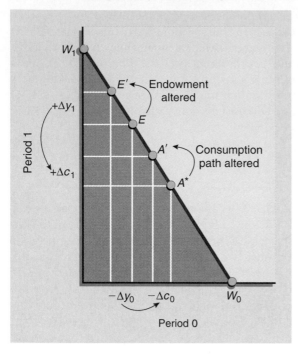

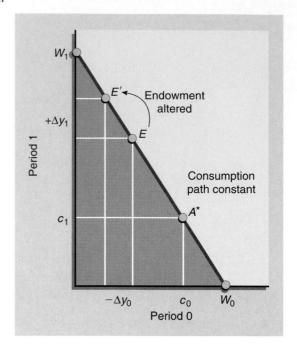

(a)
Myopic Response
$E \rightarrow E' \Longrightarrow A^* \rightarrow A'$

(b)
Forward-Looking Response
$E \rightarrow E' \Longrightarrow \Delta A^* = 0$

■ FIGURE 12.7

Two reactions to a change in the *timing* of income, leaving the wealth constraint unchanged.

timing of her income, leaving her "lifetime" wealth unchanged, will lead her to change the *timing of her consumption*. In other words, will the movement from E to E' cause her to move her preferred consumption path away from her earlier choice of A^*? The answer to this question reveals the extent to which her consumption/saving choices are forward looking.

Suppose her response is to adjust her consumption path to A' as shown in Figure 12.7(a). By cutting consumption in reaction to the decline in her current income, she is doing just what our basic consumption function described. But we now see this as **myopic behavior** because it ignores the fact that the drop in this period's income is exactly offset by next period's increase, leaving her wealth (present value) unchanged. The move from A^* to A' in response to a change in the *timing* but not the present value of her income path reveals a decision maker so trapped within the confines of the current period that she ignores anything that lies beyond it. Such extreme myopia is probably unusual. In varying degrees we look beyond the arbitrary boundaries defined by calendars (grounded in the motions of the solar system rather than the economy) and consider our longer-term prospects when making current choices.[11]

---

[11] Paul Samuelson has said that "Only primitive aborigines and accountants take the year to be sacred." It's useful for periodic reminders (birthdays and celebrations) and for setting definite deadlines (as for tax purposes) but there's no reason to think our decision making is similarly bounded.

What would A's response be if she was **forward-looking** and understood that this specific change in the timing of her income didn't change its present value (as defined by the intertemporal budget line W_1W_0)? Because she chose A^* as her preferred consumption path before, there's no reason for her to change now. Put another way, when her endowment was E she *could* have chosen the path A' but didn't. She decided that A^* was the most desirable consumption path along her budget line. Since this budget line hasn't changed, she can still reach A^* from her new income path (at E') by increasing her current borrowing. Hence, the forward-looking response to this altered income stream is to leave her consumption stream unchanged, as shown in Figure 12.7(b).

Which of these two options best describes the consumption behavior of the actual people living in the real economy, not the hypothetical decision makers of abstract models? Will a change in the income path that doesn't alter our total wealth (like E to E' in Figure 12.7) cause people to change the timing of their consumption? No doubt we could find some consumers whose behavior fits the nearsighted model and others who behave with all the foresight of the forward-looking model. But remember that macroeconomics works with bulky aggregates, combining all individual responses—the thoughtful and the thoughtless alike—into a single average. So the issue is one of determining an *average* **time horizon** that describes the degree to which consumers as a whole are forward looking.

Aggregate consumption behavior has been among the most thoroughly tested of all macroeconomic relationships over the past 50 years. Initial studies of the static Keynesian consumption function—$c = c_0 + c_1(y - t)$, where we're back to the notation in which c_0 and c_1 are the parameters defining the relationship between current income and consumption—confirmed that current after-tax income was an important explanatory variable. But they also uncovered a steady growth in autonomous consumption ($+\Delta c_0$) that was having a major influence on total consumption spending over time. Because this equation lumps everything but after-tax income into the c_0 term, it gives us no clues as to just what is causing it to grow systematically over time. Beginning in the 1950s, research turned to finding an expanded theory that could account for this "upward drift" in the standard consumption function. Which of the multitude of excluded determinants of consumption was responsible for this continuing change?

Many hypotheses were proposed and tested and it soon became clear that a key element missing from earlier studies was a measure of the income *path*. This was discovered independently in classic studies by Franco Modigliani and Milton Friedman, among others.[12] The explanations of these two Nobel Laureates-to-be—Modigliani's "Life Cycle Hypothesis" and Friedman's "Permanent Income Hypothesis"—were both grounded in an intertemporal framework. Both replaced current after-tax income as the independent variable with a measure that incorporated current *and* future elements of the income path. Modigliani added a measure of financial wealth while Friedman used a "permanent income" concept that represented lifetime average income discounted back to the present. And both hypotheses provided an explanation for the upward drift of the static consumption function that was broadly consistent with the statistical evidence.

---

[12] F. Modigliani and R. E. Brumberg, "Utility Analysis and the Consumption Function: An Interpretation of Cross-Section Data," in K. K. Kurihara, ed. *Post-Keynesian Economics* (New Brunswick, N.J.: Rutgers University Press, 1954), 383–436; A. Ando and F. Modigliani, "The Life-Cycle Hypothesis of Saving: Aggregate Implications and Tests," *American Economic Review* 53 (March 1963): 55–84; and Milton Friedman, *A Theory of the Consumption Function* (Princeton: Princeton University Press, 1957).

Decades of refinement in theory and econometric technique have largely reinforced the basic insights of these early models of Modigliani and Friedman, both inspired by Irving Fisher's work with the two-period model. But testing hypotheses at the aggregate level inevitably leaves many details in the dark and often raises new questions as it answers old ones. There's little doubt that aggregate consumption responds to changes in both current and expected future income, confirming the commonsense notion that consumers are forward looking in their consumption-saving decision. But the evidence also suggests that *current income has a larger influence on current consumption* than predicted by the life cycle hypothesis, the permanent income hypothesis, or their more recent extensions.[13]

This finding can have a variety of explanations and continues to draw much research attention. It may be that it reflects *measurement errors*. Measuring consumption is not as easy as it might seem, as will be discussed in Chapter 15. Another problem is that trying to estimate the influence of the *expected income path* leads us into the many difficulties associated with measuring expectations. So it's possible that consumers are more forward-looking than our studies reveal because problems of measurement are biasing our statistical tests. Another possibility is that consumers are **liquidity constrained** because of imperfections in capital markets. As explained in the next section, this condition can make it look like consumers are behaving myopically even if they're as supremely forward looking as presumed in the most abstract of models.

But the diversity of explanations for the apparent overly large influence of *current* income on consumption should not be allowed to obscure the main finding. The simple Keynesian consumption function of the *AD/AS* model offers only a partial explanation of aggregate consumption spending, and it's clear that, in some degree, people are forward looking in their consumption choices. Fisher's two-period model offers us a relatively uncomplicated avenue into the complex dynamics underlying the "consumption-saving-investment-economic growth" linkages in the macroeconomy. Any attempt to understand the strengths and limitations of fiscal policy, the workings of capital markets, and the dynamics of economic growth must incorporate these connections across time.

12.4 FISCAL POLICY WHEN CONSUMERS ARE FORWARD-LOOKING

So far our intertemporal analysis has looked only at the private sector. Still assuming a closed economy ($x = 0$), we move to a more realistic setting by adding government spending, financed by taxes or borrowing. This creates a relationship between current income and spending given by $c + i + g = y = c + s + t$. Let's start with the assumption that consumers are forward-looking (as described by the two-period model), so that in making their current consumption-saving choice they look beyond current after-tax income ($y - t$) to the anticipated after-tax income *path* that, along with the interest rate, defines their wealth constraint.

---

[13] Important studies include Robert E. Hall, "Stochastic Implications of the Life Cycle-Permanent Income Hypothesis: Theory and Evidence," *Journal of Political Economy* 86 (December 1978): 971–987; and Marjorie Flavin, "The Adjustment of Consumption to Changing Expectations about Future Income," *Journal of Political Economy* 89 (October 1981): 974–1009.

Does such an intertemporal setting with forward-looking consumers alter our understanding of the role of fiscal policy in the macroeconomy? In the most basic sense, our situation remains much the same. Bound by scarcity, we still have to contend with competing uses ($c + i + g$, private consumption, private investment, or public spending) for limited resources. Political rhetoric notwithstanding, we know that public goods and services use up resources just like their private counterparts and that every dollar of government spending will be paid—now or later, directly or indirectly—by taxes. Looking beyond these basics, however, we discover that the use of fiscal policy to stabilize output and employment ("smoothing the business cycle") loses some of its potency as consumers become more forward-looking. The reason is that if our consumption spending depends on our wealth rather than just our current income, policies that have only short-run effects on income (hence little impact on our lifetime wealth), will have relatively little impact on consumption.

For example, when a fiscal stimulus is used to speed the return to full employment (by shifting the *IS* and *AD* curves to the right), the impact is primarily on income over a few quarters or, at most, a year or two. However welcome this quicker recovery may be, consumers with long horizons will respond less vigorously than those who focus all their attention on the here and now. Since this reduced response diminishes the strength of the multiplier process that propels fiscal changes through the economy ($\Delta FP \Rightarrow \Delta y \Leftrightarrow \Delta c$), the result is a weakening of fiscal policy's ability to cause short run changes in output and employment. An economy populated by forward-looking decision-makers operates more like a large oil tanker than a small sailboat. Its greater stability tends to keep it closer to the desired course in the presence of adverse conditions. But when a correction is needed it takes considerably more time and effort to accomplish.

Is there evidence to support this hypothesis? For example, have fiscal changes that were expected to be temporary had less impact on current economic activity than those that were expected to be longer lasting? The answer is about as clear a "yes" as we ever get in a discipline that, in the absence of controlled experiments, must try to sift clues from highly aggregated data in which many things are changing simultaneously. The empirical results reinforce and overlap with those cited in the previous section, portraying an "average" consumer who looks beyond the present but not quite so far or so clearly as the hypothetical farsighted consumer of our two-period model.[14] Thus the actual impact of fiscal change on the macroeconomy is smaller than predicted in the basic, but shortsighted, AD/AS^e model. This is an important finding because it implies that our ability to manipulate aggregate demand through fiscal changes is more limited than is widely believed.

But we can't leave this area without re-examining what has been one of the most contentious topics in macroeconomics of recent decades—the "tax cut/tax postponement" issue first raised back in Chapter 5 (Fiscal Policy). Suppose there is a cut in taxes without any reduction in government spending, the difference being made up through deficit financing ($g = \downarrow t + b \uparrow$). Scarcity ordains that if we keep government spending unchanged, there *must* be higher taxes in the future. This is just the familiar "no free lunch" result and is uncontroversial among economists. But the **tax-discounting hypothesis** goes a step further and asserts that consumers are

[14] For evidence that the temporary tax surcharge imposed in 1968 (to restrain inflationary pressures from the Vietnam war spending) had almost no impact on consumption, see Alan Blinder and Angus Deaton, "The Time Series Consumption Function Revisited," *Brookings Papers on Economic Activity* 2 (1985): 465–511. Also see John Campbell and N. Gregory Mankiw, "Consumption, Income, and Interest Rates: Reinterpreting the Time Series Evidence," *NBER Macroeconomics Annual* (1989): 185–216.

aware of the time path of their tax liabilities and that they take this into account in making their current consumption-saving decision.[15]

In other words, "tax discounting" asserts that we are forward-looking in terms of our *after-tax* income path so that a transfer from tax to deficit financing ($-\Delta t$ but $+\Delta b$) will not make us feel richer. We'll perceive that deficit financing is essentially the government borrowing in our name, and we'll treat it as our future liability, just as if we'd borrowed privately. Therefore such a tax "cut" in a world of tax discounters is clearly seen as a postponement, not a lasting reduction, and will not lead to increased consumption. The bottom line is that tax discounting behavior implies that tax changes do not shift the *IS* and *AD* curves and therefore have no power to expand a stagnant economy or to subdue an inflationary one. This reinforces the ideological predispositions of nonactivists and presents a challenge to the activist case for the use of discretionary fiscal changes to keep the economy close to full employment.

Before turning to historical evidence, let's look at tax discounting in terms of the two-period model. In Figure 12.8 we return to individual A, whose initial income path is given at E, which she transforms into her preferred consumption path at A^* by borrowing now and repaying later. If A is a farsighted tax discounter then a cut in current taxes (assuming government spending unchanged) will have no impact on her consumption choice. She will realize that this tax postponement has only altered

■ FIGURE 12.8

A deficit-financed tax "cut" moves A's *after-tax* endowment from E to E' along her given wealth constraint. If she's a "tax discounter," her consumption path will stay at A^*.

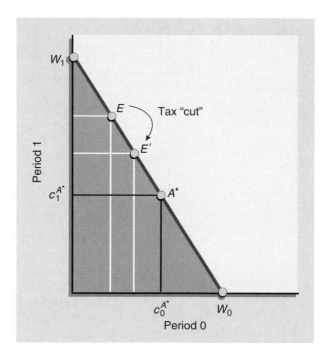

[15] Tax discounting is often called "Ricardian equivalence" in recognition of similar insights by British economist David Ricardo in the early nineteenth century. Its modern incarnation begins with the article by Robert Barro, "Are Government Bonds Net Wealth?" *Journal of Political Economy* 82 (November/December 1974): 1095–1118. Additional references include Martin Feldstein, "Government Deficits and Aggregate Demand," *Journal of Monetary Economics* (January 1982): 1–20; Douglas Bernheim, "Ricardian Equivalence: An Evaluation of Theory and Evidence," *NBER Macroeconomics Annual* (1987): 263–304; James Poterba, "Are Consumers Forward Looking? Evidence from Fiscal Experiments," *American Economic Review* 78 (May 1988): 413–418; and John J. Seater, "Ricardian Equivalence," *Journal of Economic Literature* 31 (March 1993): 142–190.

the *timing* of her after-tax income path (E to E'), not its present value (W_0), so she'll stay with her preferred balance between "now and later" at point A^*.[16] The increased deficit reduces her private borrowing, leaving her total borrowing unchanged. In other words, to a tax discounter public and private borrowing are equivalent and are therefore perfect substitutes. For individual A, changes in the current tax-deficit mix are offset by changes in her private saving, leaving consumption spending (hence, IS and AD) unaffected.

In contrast, Figure 12.9 shows the behavior of M, a well-known "tax myopic" we'll assume. When a tax cut increases M's current after-tax income (E to E'), he gives no thought to its implications for his future after-tax income. Instead, the (temporary) rise in his take-home pay leads him to increase his current consumption, moving from M^* to M'. As a tax myopic, he thinks his wealth constraint has shifted out. *We*, of course, know he's in for an unpleasant surprise in the next period when he discovers that his after-tax income and hence consumption will be less than he expects (by the amount of the current deficit plus interest).

Are most consumers tax discounters or tax myopics? A pure tax discounter would be such a meticulous and calculating person as to be boring beyond belief. They're probably a rare breed. But what about those who, however casually, do plan ahead and who consider current deficits as a potential drain on their future consumption? It is likely that their current saving will be higher than if the government were running a balanced cash flow budget. This sort of casual tax discounting is probably fairly common. In deciding how much to save or borrow now, most of us look be-

■ FIGURE 12.9

The same tax "cut" (postponement) will cause M to increase his consumption now (forcing him to reduce it later) if he is "tax myopic."

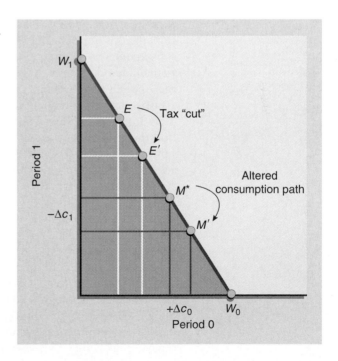

[16] As in our earlier analysis, because A^* was previously chosen over all other points on the budget line, then another point on the line must be regarded as less desirable.

yond our immediate circumstances and formulate some estimate, however rough, of our future *after-tax* income path. To that extent, we're displaying tax discounting behavior. Just because we're not as farsighted as eagles, doesn't mean we behave like ostriches. There are many possibilities between the two extremes.

The tax discounting issue is not about whether deficit-financed tax postponements (tax cuts without spending cuts) need to be repaid in the future. In a world of scarcity there's no doubt that they do. The real issue is the extent to which consumers, consciously or otherwise, take this future obligation into account in deciding how much to consume now. The more forward looking they are on taxes, the less impact changes in the tax/deficit balance will have on aggregate demand, limiting its use for macroeconomic stabilization. What does the historical evidence reveal? Where does the average consumer fall in the spectrum between pure tax discounting and total tax myopia? Are we eagles or ostriches when it comes to government deficits?

Statistical tests of tax discounting using aggregate data run into an array of measurement and conceptual difficulties leaving us in the undesirable but not uncommon situation in macroeconomics where several quite different hypotheses are consistent with available evidence. The result has been very sharp disagreement over the importance of "tax discounting" and a tendency for ideology to take over where empirical evidence is inconclusive. Not only has this slowed our progress in understanding the issue but has also used up an inordinately large amount of time of many of the best research economists.

After two decades, however, it appears that a middle ground has emerged that has drawn a majority of economists away from the extreme positions of "complete" versus "zero" tax discounting. This alternative offers an explanation that is consistent with statistical findings that tax cuts without spending cuts *do* have some impact on current consumption. But it doesn't require us to accept the hypothesis that the same consumers who we find to be somewhat farsighted with respect to future earnings are virtually blind when it comes to future taxes. This realignment comes from dropping the implicit assumption of *perfect capital markets* and introducing a **liquidity constraint** that prevents some consumers from borrowing as much as they would like.

Let's look at how a liquidity constraint can alter the predictions of the two-period model. One of the many simplifications we have made in this model was the assumption of a given interest rate at which individuals could borrow or lend to achieve a consumption path different from their endowment. This assumption of "perfect capital markets" is certainly not realistic, because for most of us the rate at which we can lend is less than the rate we have to pay to borrow.[17] Adding this "imperfection" to the analysis (which puts a kink in the wealth constraint at the endowment point) can change some of our previous conclusions, particularly when there are some consumers who can't borrow on their future earnings at all.

Before turning to the two-period diagram, let's work through this situation intuitively. Suppose that L is a forward-looking, tax-discounting, but liquidity-constrained consumer with a low income now but very good reasons to expect much higher earnings in the future. Rather than to also have low consumption now and high later, her preference is to smooth her consumption path by borrowing now and repaying later. But if we assume she is unable to borrow on her future income, then

---

[17] For example, those without equity in something tangible (like a home) or a track record of steady earnings generally pay much higher rates of interest for unsecured loans.

her current consumption can be no more than her current take-home pay. Now suppose that a deficit-financed tax cut is enacted that increases L's after-tax income. This tax postponement allows her to increase her consumption just as if she had borrowed privately. In essence the government has provided a loan to L, allowing her to pay part of her current tax bill later and enabling her to move toward her desired consumption path.

To an outside observer, L's increase in consumption in response to a tax postponement might look like myopic behavior. But what's at work here is the liquidity constraint, not tax myopia. Public borrowing has acted as a substitute for imperfect private capital markets. If there are a number of such liquidity-constrained consumers, the outcome of a pure tax postponement will still be to increase current consumption spending. The presumption that fiscal policy retains its ability to expand or contract the economy in an intertemporal setting is, therefore, not tantamount to assuming exceedingly shortsighted consumption behavior.

The impact of a tax cut on someone who is liquidity constrained is shown geometrically in Figure 12.10. Whether done in words or graphs, the importance of the liquidity constraint hypothesis is that it offers an alternative to tax myopia for explaining why a tax cut (without a spending cut) can stimulate current consumption (and thereby shift out IS and AD). In so doing, it is consistent with what most, but

■ FIGURE 12.10

Suppose L is "liquidity-constrained," unable to borrow to move to her preferred consumption path at L^*. The closest she can come to L^* is her initial endowment point E so her defacto wealth constraint is, therefore, W_1EW_0. A tax "cut" (postponement), shown in the right graph, moves her endowment to E', allowing her to move closer to L^* by spending the entire tax cut on current consumption. This tax postponement effectively expands the wealth constraint of someone who is liquidity constrained.

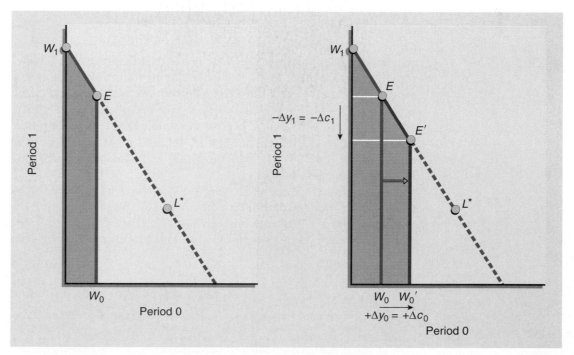

certainly not all, macroeconomists believe is revealed by the data.[18] Fiscal policy appears to have more influence on demand than predicted for a pure forward-looking, tax-discounting, two-period world. Some combination of "tax myopia" and "liquidity constraint" seems to be at work here. Additional analysis and further testing are needed before we will be able to bring this hazy picture into sharper focus. Those adopting extreme views (decision makers are all eagle or all ostrich) may turn out to be correct, but they're going beyond what current evidence can support.

12.5   WHAT DETERMINES THE RATE OF CAPITAL FORMATION?

To briefly review, out of current (after-tax) income we must make a joint consumption-saving decision—what we don't consume is, by definition, saved. Consuming beyond our current income means borrowing or dissaving. The intertemporal setting of our two-period model shows how *current saving* is connected to *future consumption*. It reveals the important fact that our current consumption-saving choice is really about the *timing* of consumption or the "consumption path." Saving (and dissaving) enables current consumption to escape the boundaries of current income by encroaching on the expected income of the future. Put another way, the act of saving frees our consumption decision from the tyranny of some arbitrary accounting period. The "terms of trade" between consumption now and consumption later are defined by the real rate of interest, which in this sense can be thought of as the "price of time."

But for the economy as a whole to move consumption from now to the future, it's not enough to just save. This saving must then find its way (via capital markets, the subject of the next chapter) into **investment activities** that increase the capital stock to produce the consumption goods of the future. "Plowing" current output back into the production process provides the compost for future crops. To be specific, we can increase our full employment level of output—$y^* = F(n^*,k,i^{nst})$—with investment activities that increase the *quality of the labor force* ($+\Delta n^*$ through education and training), increase the *quantity and quality of capital* ($+\Delta k$ by investment in plant and equipment or research and development), or improve the *efficiency of the institutional structure* ($+\Delta i^{nst}$ through political reforms and various public investment activities). This section presents a broad overview of the factors underlying such investment decisions. We move beyond the simple $i = i_0 - i_2 r$ relationship of the earlier model to get more detail on (1) what determines the level of investment spending that underlies $+\Delta n^*$, $+\Delta k$, and $+\Delta i^{nst}$; (2) why this spending is so volatile; and (3) how policy changes can alter it.

Suppose a corporation is trying to decide how much capital it needs to maximize profits.[19] For the overall economy we'll call this the **optimal capital stock** and represent it by k^*. The basic optimization rule tells us to keep expanding as long as this adds more to revenues than to costs. This process of equating costs and benefits

[18] Important studies of the role of liquidity constraints in aggregate consumption behavior include Marjorie Flavin, "Excess Sensitivity of Consumption to Current Income: Liquidity Constraints or Myopia?" *Canadian Journal of Economics* 18 (February 1985); Fumio Hayashi, "The Effect of Liquidity Constraints on Consumption: A Cross-Sectional Analysis," *Quarterly Journal of Economics* 100 (February 1985); and Stephen P. Zeldes, "Consumption and Liquidity Constraints: An Empirical Investigation," *Journal of Political Economy* 97 (April 1989).

[19] Though presented here in terms of business investment, this framework is equally applicable to households and governments, and to physical capital as well as financial capital decisions.

"at the margin" leads, under many conditions, to profit maximization. Without getting involved in the details, let's examine how this can be applied to a firm's capital spending decision.

On the benefit side, we know from the production function—$y^* = F(n^*,k,i^{nst})$—that adding another unit of capital $(+\Delta k)$ increases the maximum production level $(+\Delta y^*)$. This relationship, defined by the ratio of the change in output to the change in the input $(\Delta y^*/\Delta k)$, is called the **marginal product of capital** (mp_k). In most situations the marginal product of capital is *positive* (more capital means more output) and *diminishing* (as we add more capital, output grows but by smaller and smaller amounts). This relationship between the amount of capital and its marginal product is represented by the downward-sloping **mp_k curve** in Figure 12.11.

Knowing how much an increase in capital increases this year's output is half the story. The other half is how much it increases this year's costs. We can divide the relevant costs into three categories.

1. Because a capital good, by definition, lasts for many years we don't want to attribute its entire cost (p_k, for its "real price" or money price adjusted for the price level) to the year of purchase. So we have to *depreciate* this cost through "capital consumption allowances" that reflect its expected loss of value over time.[20] If the real purchase price is p_k and the yearly rate of depreciation is δ (where $0 < \delta < 1$ and assumed constant), then the **annual depreciation cost of an extra unit of capital is δp_k**.

■ FIGURE 12.11

The optimal capital stock (k^*) is defined by the equality of the marginal product of capital (mp_k) and the user cost of capital (uc_k).

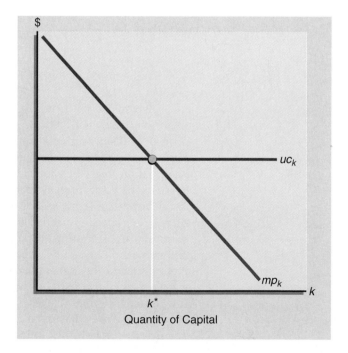

---

[20] So the cost of a $100 million plant that lasts 20 years will be spread over those years, in a particular pattern that depends on standard accounting procedures and tax laws.

2. Another important cost of purchasing this additional unit of capital is its *opportunity cost*—the return this firm *could* have gotten by spending the money on its next best alternative. Let's suppose this opportunity cost is what it could have earned by investing at the going real rate of interest, r. **The annual foregone interest cost of this extra unit of capital is rp_k.**

3. A final cost to be considered in the investment decision is taxes. A portion of the marginal product of this additional unit of capital will be taxed away by the corporate income tax, which we'll represent by a constant rate t_k. An increase in this tax can be thought of as lowering the after-tax marginal product of the additional capital or, equivalently, as raising the annual cost of this capital. Either way the **firm keeps only the fraction $(1 - t_k)$ of the returns to any new capital it puts into production.**

Combining these three ingredients gives us the amount an additional unit of capital would add to annual costs, known as the real **user cost of capital (uc_k).**

$$uc_k = p_k(r + \delta)/(1 - t_k).$$

The next step is to compare these additional costs of adding more capital with the additional benefits. If another unit of capital adds more to benefits than to costs ($mp_k > uc_k$), then profits will rise by undertaking this investment. If it adds more to costs than to benefits ($uc_k > mp_k$) then it will reduce profits and should not be carried out. The *optimal capital stock (k^*)* for this firm is, therefore, the level at which changing it would add the same amount to benefits as to costs ($mp_k = uc_k$). Thus the optimal level of capital is achieved when the firm accumulates capital up to the point at which

$$mp_k = p_k(r + \delta)/(1 - t_k)$$

This is illustrated in Figure 12.11 at the intersection of the user cost and marginal product curves.

As you can tell from the graph, anything that increases user cost ($+ \Delta p_k$, $+ \Delta r$, $+ \Delta \delta$, or $+ \Delta t_k$) will shift uc_k upward and lead to a lower optimal capital stock (a process of disinvestment). Similarly, decreases in any of these four components will raise the desired level of capital (through the investment process). Increases in the marginal product of capital (through technological change, for example) shift the mp_k curve to the right, thereby increasing k^* and stimulating increased investment.[21]

Now that we've seen what factors influence the firm's optimal capital stock, there's one last step needed to turn it into a *theory of investment*. Suppose this firm discovers that its optimal capital (k^*) is much larger than its existing capital stock (k_0) and moves to close the gap by undertaking net investment spending (that is, investment over and above that needed to replace depreciating capital). How *quickly* should it make this adjustment, i.e., at what *rate* should it invest in new capital? Should it do it all at once so that this year's net investment will be $i = k^* - k_0$? Or will it be better to spread the adjustment over several years? Closing the gap between the actual and desired capital stock quickly can be expensive. For example, getting a new plant

---

[21] Note that buried in here with these new relationships is a familiar one—a drop in the real rate of interest lowers user cost and leads to an increase in the desired capital stock and, hence, investment spending ($\uparrow i = i_0 - i_2 r \downarrow$).

built in a rush brings the higher costs of paying overtime to the contractors and sub-contractors. So the rate at which the actual capital is adjusted to the desired level may be quite gradual.

Thus the **rate of investment spending** depends on both (1) the **optimal capital stock** and the **existing capital stock** (specifically the gap between them, $k^* - k_0$, and all the underlying ingredients of user cost and marginal productivity of capital discussed earlier) and (2) a determination of the **optimal rate at which to close this gap** by equating the costs and benefits of adjustment at the margin.

We can express this very generally as

$$i^* = h(k^* - k_0) \text{ or}$$

where k^* is determined by $mp_k = p_k(r + \delta)/(1 - t_k)$, as shown in Figure 12.11, and the general functional relationship $h(\ )$ has the property that the firm will close this gap gradually over time. For example, a specific functional form might be

$$i^* = \lambda(k^* - k_0), \text{ where } \lambda \text{ is a constant between 0 and 1.}$$

With an adjustment coefficient λ of .7, the firm will close 70% of the remaining gap each period.

Statistical testing of this theory of investment spending (known as the "neoclassical model of investment spending") requires quantification of all these variables, a challenging undertaking.[22] While there is much we can't explain, the results generally confirm the broad picture that is our concern—aggregate investment spending varies inversely with the real interest rate (r), the real price of capital goods (p_k), the rate of depreciation (or obsolescence) of capital (δ), and the rate at which the resulting returns are taxed (t_k).

This treatment of investment has identified factors that were hidden in the autonomous investment term (i_0) of our previous formulation. From a policy perspective, an important instrument is the rate at which the returns to capital are taxed.[23] By lowering the tax on capital ($-\Delta t_k$) and raising the tax on income ($+\Delta t_1$), for example, the government would be taking a progrowth strategy. If the tax changes were balanced so that their expansionary/contractionary impacts on *IS* and *AD* canceled out, the long run (full employment) result would be a change in the consumption-investment *composition of output* that increases the capital stock and hence potential output. This is one way that fiscal policy can be used to alter the consumption-investment mix, but don't forget that the resulting increase in economic growth is no "free lunch." In a fully employed economy, the inevitable cost of this increased investment ($+\Delta i$) and the resulting economic growth ($+\Delta y^*$ through $+\Delta AS^*$ and $+\Delta PPF$) must be lower current consumption ($-\Delta c$).

Neither this nor any of the several other models of investment spending has

---

[22] There are a variety of approaches to the empirical estimation of an investment function. Among these are the accelerator model, the adjustment cost model, and "Tobin's *q*." See Jeffrey D. Sachs and Felipe Larrain, *Macroeconomics in the Global Economy* (Englewood Cliffs, N.J.: Prentice Hall, 1993), chap. 5, for an excellent presentation of the details of alternative investment models.

[23] While lowering the corporate income tax would serve to reduce t_k, a more common approach is to give a specific "investment tax credit" that lowers a company's tax liability depending on how much investment they undertake that year. "Accelerated depreciation allowances" are another way that essentially lowers the tax on capital and shows up in our analysis as $-\Delta t_k$.

been very successful at predicting the large and sudden jumps in real investment spending that constitute an important component of the business cycle. Hopes of significantly reducing the unpredictability of changes in investment spending have not been realized. However discouraging this may be, it should not be surprising. The optimal capital stock and optimal rate of investment are inherently intertemporal decisions—they involve current actions in anticipation of future consequences. Literally all of the variables involved in the investment decision require our best guess at expected future events. This is as true for the marginal productivity of capital and the interest rate as it is for taxes and even depreciation rates. Current events and policies can suddenly make our most careful calculations and past decisions look very foolish. Construction booms brushed by hints of recession, can quickly turn into the "overbuilding" that precedes a construction "bust." Because capital expenditures inevitably involve sticking our necks out with respect to future economic events, there will always be surprises (both pleasant and unpleasant) that can encourage us to pull back or extend even further.

This unpredictability as we move further into an intertemporal setting is frustrating, but should not necessarily be regarded as a failure of economic analysis. Much has been done in recent decades to systematize our understanding of the role and nature of expectations in macroeconomics. The development of theories of expectations, like the rational expectations hypothesis, has improved our predictive ability in some important ways. But it has also given us a clearer view of some limits to our predictive powers and, thereby, revealed important limitations to some old-fashioned kinds of stabilization policies.

✆ *12.6 OVERVIEW*

1. Private consumption spending makes up over 60% of total demand in the U.S. and private investment spending another 15%. An understanding of the determinants of consumption and investment is central to any useful theory of overall economic activity—both its long-term trend ($\pm \Delta y^*$) and its short run ups and downs around this trend ($\pm \Delta(y - y^*)$).

2. Starting from the basic consumption and investment functions of the *AD/AS* framework ($c = c_0 + c_1(y - t)$ and $i = i_0 - i_2 r$), we developed an **intertemporal framework** based on Irving Fisher's two-period model. This chapter begins to construct a bridge from the no-growth *AD/AS^e* model of previous chapters to a more complete framework incorporating economic growth. The first span of the bridge links consumption to **saving,** the second moves on to **investment.** The next two chapters will add **capital markets** and then combine investment with **other sources of input growth** to finally bring *economic growth* within our analysis.

3. The appeal of the two-period model is the relatively simple way in which it forces us to recognize that today's saving becomes tomorrow's consumption. It provides a framework, missing in the *AD/AS* approach, that links current decisions to a more meaningful concept of *long run*—one in which markets are cleared and expectations realized, as before, but also in which the process of saving, investment, and capital formation is considered. Hence, the consumption-saving choice is usefully seen as one between *consumption now* and *consumption later*; a choice of **consumption path.** It now becomes apparent that each decision we make involves both "this or that?" and "now or later?"

4. In dealing with intertemporal issues, the process of **compounding/discounting** is needed to compare values across periods in a meaningful way. A dollar now translates into $\$1(1 + r)$ in next year's real dollars and $\$1(1 + r)^n$ in n years. A dollar one year from now has a *present value* of $\$1/(1 + r)$, whereas a dollar that is n years away is worth $\$1/(1 + r)^n$ right now.

5. The real rate of interest can now be seen in its most basic and important role—as an **intertemporal price** or, intuitively, the "price of time." It is the rate at which we can move goods and services back and forth across present and future through the "borrowing and lending" and "saving and investing" activities that underlie capital markets.

6. The **wealth constraint** defines feasible consumption paths for a given expected income path (endowment) and given interest rate. Different individuals with the same wealth constraint typically choose a different "now/later" balance, reflecting their subjective **marginal rates of time preference.** Those eager to consume right away (high time preference) will choose a consumption path along their wealth constraint with relatively high current consumption but low future consumption. The more patient consumer (low time preference) will choose a consumption path that emphasizes current sacrifice in favor of more consumption later. Capital markets provide the borrowing and lending opportunities that allow us to move toward what we consider the "best" consumption path along our wealth constraint.

7. Do consumers really think in an intertemporal context, considering not only "this or that?" but its implications for "now or later?" One way to portray our degree of farsightedness is to ask whether a movement along a given wealth constraint (a change in the timing of income but not its present value) will lead us to alter our consumption/saving choice. If, for example, our current income drops but future income rises (by the same amount plus interest), the response of a **forward-looking consumer** would be to leave her consumption path unchanged. A **myopic consumer,** conversely, would reduce current consumption, unaware or uninterested in the fact that his increased future income offsets his lower income today. Even though his wealth (or "permanent income") hasn't changed, he feels poorer and cuts back current consumption.

8. How forward looking are we? This is a difficult question to answer at the macroeconomic level, but both common sense and statistical results confirm that we do look ahead to expected future income and other events in making today's consumption-saving decision. But it also appears that current income has a larger influence than predicted by the forward-looking hypotheses proposed by Franco Modigliani, Milton Friedman, and others. This could reflect many things and it is probably asking too much to expect aggregate, economy-wide data to give a very precise answer. One possibility is that fiscal policy doesn't have as much influence as we think but that **errors of measurement** have clouded our vision. Another is that the **aggregate statistics contain a blend of different perceptions** (ranging from eagles to ostriches) and there are enough myopic consumers (most families seem to have at least one) to give fiscal policy some traction. But even without myopic consumers, the presence of **liquidity constraints** in the capital market can result in current consumption responding "excessively" to current income even with very forward-looking consumers.

9. One important consequence of viewing consumption in an intertemporal setting is that to the extent that consumption responds to wealth as opposed to just current income, its time path will be much more stable because the ups and downs of

transitory income changes have little impact. Events and policies will therefore exercise less influence on consumption, an important correction to the impression in the AD/AS^e model that "fine tuning" can be done with some precision.

10. The **tax-discounting hypothesis** simply extends the forward-looking consumer's domain to include taxes as well as earnings. It implies that forward-looking individuals, making their consumption-saving choice with after-tax dollars, will not be fooled by public deficits. They'll see that part of their current taxes have been postponed and they'll save accordingly. Therefore, a tax cut without a spending cut will not cause them to increase consumption spending, a conclusion quite at odds with what we used in the AD/AS^e model and also at odds with most researchers' interpretations of the statistical evidence. While it seems apparent that we exhibit some forward-looking behavior with respect to future taxes, it may well be considerably less than for our before-tax earnings. In other words, while expected future earnings influence our current consumption-saving choice, it appears that we are somewhat less responsive to the expected future taxes from current deficits. However, statistical tests with aggregate data are often not very powerful and there is much disagreement over this. Aggregate data hide many clues and the relatively few clues we have could be consistent with a number of hypotheses.

11. The question is not whether we're pure tax discounters or pure tax myopics. Obviously we're somewhere in between, in the aggregate and probably for most individuals as well. A related issue is the extent to which we're **liquidity constrained.** Individuals who are unable to borrow on their future earnings will exhibit behavior that looks tax myopic—a tax postponement will lead them to increase their current consumption. But this actually reflects their economic relief at the government providing them with a low-interest loan (the deficit financing that allows them to postpone their taxes) that they couldn't get through the private sector.

12. Whatever unknown blend of myopia and tax constraint may exist, the result is that tax changes have a larger impact on spending and hence aggregate demand than is implied by the standard two-period model with forward-looking consumers. But this effect is still much smaller than predicted in our earlier, completely myopic, AD/AS^e framework. Even though much of our understanding of policy impacts remains imprecise, on many topics we have continued to reduce the range of disagreement over what the government *can* do.

13. The consumption-saving decision determines the maximum amount of resources that are being released from current consumption and are available for capital formation. But how or whether these available resources will actually be used requires an understanding of the determinants of **aggregate investment spending.** Using a cost/benefit framework we can spell out the conditions under which an additional unit of capital will add more to a firm's revenues than to its costs. From this we can define the **optimal capital stock (k^*)** as the level at which the **marginal product of capital equals its user cost.** In symbols, it requires that we pick that level of capital at which $mp_k = p_k(r + \delta)/(1 - t_k)$.

14. Investment occurs when the optimal capital stock diverges from the current one ($k^* - k_0 > 0$). But because the cost of closing this gap rises as we try to do it more quickly, the **optimal rate of investment** will generally be such as to close the gap gradually. Statistical analyses generally confirm that real investment spending varies inversely with the real rate of interest (r), the real price of capital goods (p_k), the rate of depreciation (δ), and the applicable tax rate (t_k). This gives us a considerably richer understanding of the investment process than the simple investment function ($i = i_0 - i_2 r$) of the AD/AS model.

15. Investment spending remains the most volatile category of aggregate demand and we still have little ability to predict these sudden changes that are crucial determinants of the business cycle. This volatility appears to be a reflection of the intertemporal nature of investment—it involves current actions in anticipation of distant outcomes. Any change in our expectations about future events can lead to quick and sizable alterations in our current investment decisions. Theories of expectation formation can give some important insights, but ultimately **it's the uncertainty of future events that creates the volatility in investment spending.**

16. Where does this venture into the dynamics of intertemporal decision-making leave us? A very important result for stabilization policy is the reduced leverage of fiscal policy as we acknowledge forward-looking, tax-discounting behavior by consumers. But the possibility of an important role for liquidity constraints and a degree of myopia that seems to characterize our aggregate behavior still gives fiscal actions an influence on aggregate demand and, in the short run, real output and employment. Though the myopic AD/AS^e model tends to overstate this influence, its short run analytics still provide a relatively complete and generally reliable analytical framework. The results of this chapter are intended to supplement and qualify the AD/AS^e analysis, not replace it. They also begin the analytical bridge that will take us to an analysis of economic growth.

⚭ 12.7 *REVIEW QUESTIONS*

1. Explain the following terms and concepts:

Consumption path	Discounting	Tax discounting
Initial endowment	Present value	Optimal capital stock
Income stream	Rate of time preference	Marginal product of capital
Intertemporal budget constraint	Two-period model	User cost of capital
Wealth constraint	Myopic behavior	Optimal rate of investment
Intertemporal "price"	Forward-looking response	
Compounding	Liquidity constraint	

2. Two nearly identical economies differ in one respect—in economy *A* households decide on their current consumption spending by looking only at their current after-tax income, whereas households in economy *B* have a longer horizon and look at their expected lifetime after-tax income in choosing a consumption path. Both economies are currently in recession and policy makers in both nations decide on a substantial one-time tax rebate (a 20% across-the-board tax reduction for one year) to give a quick stimulus and speed economic recovery. Predict the impact of this policy in each economy on

   a. The *IS* and *AD* curves. Explain.

   b. The optimal consumption path (use the two-period model). Explain.

   c. Short-run impact on *y*, *P*, *r*, *i*, *x*, *b*, and *e* using the AD/AS^e model. Explain.

3. How would adding "market frictions," "policy lags," and "liquidity constraints" to the analysis alter your answers to question 2? Explain.

4. Suppose these two economies (in question 2) decide to use a one-time monetary stimulus rather than a tax cut. Predict the impact of this policy in each economy on

  a. The *LM* and *AD* curves. Explain.

  b. Short-run impact on *y*, *P*, *r*, *i*, *x*, *b*, and *e* using the *AD/AS^e* model. Explain.

5. How would adding "market frictions," "policy lags," and "liquidity constraints" to the analysis alter your answers to question 4? Explain.

6. "It's ridiculous to think that a temporary tax cut will increase consumption spending. In fact, it will probably reduce it because the tax cut means an increased deficit and this means we'll have to pay the taxes *plus interest* back later, leaving us worse off." Carefully evaluate the logic of this statement using the analytical framework of the *AD/AS^e* model.

7. Use the *AD/AS^e* model to analyze the relationship between saving and investment in both the short and long run. Specifically, suppose there's an autonomous increase in saving (from an equivalent decrease in autonomous consumption). Will this result in an equal increase in investment spending? Explain carefully.

8. Suggest some ways in which we might get evidence on whether taxpayers in the United States behave as if they are tax discounters or not. Remember that we can't do controlled experiments and that there is much evidence to support the conclusion that sample surveys are a very unreliable way to find out how people actually behave. So you've got to dig for clues in the uncontrolled experiment of history. What sorts of things would you look for? Be specific and also cite reasons why your particular test might not be absolutely definitive.

9. "The longer the time horizon used by consumers the larger the impact that expectations can have on current spending and the more volatile consumption spending is likely to be. Therefore, we should expect cyclical unemployment to be less prevalent when decision makers have a relatively short horizon." Evaluate.

10. Thinking of investment spending as a process by which the economy adjusts its actual capital stock to its optimal stock, explain the impact of each of the following events on investment spending:

  a. A sudden drop in the marginal product of capital due to governmental limitations on its use.

  b. An "investment tax credit" that allows companies to decrease their taxes by a fraction of the amount spent on new capital equipment each year.

  c. Replacement of the income tax with a national sales tax on consumption spending but not on saving.

12.8 *FURTHER READING*

ALAN BLINDER, "Temporary Income Taxes and Consumer Spending," *Journal of Political Economy* 89 (February 1981): 26–53.

ROBERT E. HALL, "Intertemporal Substitution in Consumption," *Journal of Political Economy* 96 (April 1988): 971–987.

ROBERT E. HALL AND FREDRIC MISHKIN, "The Sensitivity of Consumption to Transitory Income: Estimates from Panel Data on Households," *Econometrica* 50 (March 1982): 461–481.

J. HIRSHLEIFER, *Investment, Interest and Capital* (Englewood Cliffs, N.J.: Prentice Hall, 1970).

FRANCO MODIGLIANI, "Life Cycle, Individual Thrift, and the Wealth of Nations," *American Economic Review* (June 1986).

CHAPTER 13

CAPITAL MARKETS

13.1 INTRODUCTION

The previous chapter looked at the implications of consumption, saving, and investment from an explicitly "now or later?" perspective. It was a formal acknowledgement of the central role that the "expected future" plays in our current decision making. It was also a first recognition of the inevitable uncertainty and risk that accompany these choices. When we *borrow or lend*, for example, we enter into a contract with an expected future outcome but always the chance that this could be altered by failure to make payments (default) or by the impact of unanticipated events on the real rate of return. When we *buy a capital good* we have an expected stream of future services in mind, but again there's always the risk that our expectations won't be realized. The purchase of *equity* in a corporation is done in the anticipation of a future stream of returns in the form of dividend payments or an increase in the price of the stock (a "capital gain"). Unforeseen events can enhance or diminish these returns.

Whether it's *borrowing* to spread the cost of a car, house, education, or highway system over several years or *saving/investing* to enhance our net worth, accumulate a retirement nest egg, or leave a legacy to our children, such exchanges across time occur through **capital markets.**[1] Capital markets connect *savers* with *users* of funds. Savers make resources available to users in exchange for either a *share of ownership* (the "equity market") or a promise of *future repayment* (the "credit market"). The distinctive characteristic of a capital market transaction is that it makes a current commitment to a future outcome. Because no one can know the future, capital markets always involve **uncertainty, expectations,** and **risk** and all the accompanying elements of hope, surprise, exhilaration, and disappointment that make up so much of our economic life.

---

[1] A more specific terminology is sometimes used to distinguish different types of capital markets—"real" capital markets, financial markets, credit markets, and so on. We'll use the broader definition of "capital market" to include all economic bets on future outcomes.

The presence of uncertainty creates further possibilities for mutual gain between those willing to accept risks associated with an unknown future and those willing to pay for a reduction in that risk. **Financial intermediaries**—such as commercial banks, savings and loans, insurance companies, investment companies, pension funds, and mutual funds—act as the go-between in such arrangements (see Figure 13.1). For a fee, they reduce the uncertainty facing individual households or businesses wishing to set aside funds now to have more later. Part of their ability to reduce risk is because their size allows them to *diversify* their asset holdings and avoid putting "all their eggs in one basket." Size may also enable them to support *research* departments that specialize in evaluating information about credit worthiness, the riskiness of specific loans, and the outlook for various sectors as well as overall macroeconomic activity. In addition, these companies may be owned by stockholders who have chosen to *assume more risk* in exchange for a higher expected return on their investment.

A well-developed capital market provides a wide variety of financial options to suit the particular characteristics and goals of a broad spectrum of savers and borrow-

■ FIGURE 13.1

In advanced economies most saving flows through financial intermediaries before reaching *users.* The uncertainty associated with capital market outcomes creates a demand for financial intermediaries to rechannel or reduce risk by *acquiring, analyzing,* and *acting* on information about the credit worthiness of particular users, the prospects for specific investments, and the general outlook for the macroeconomy.

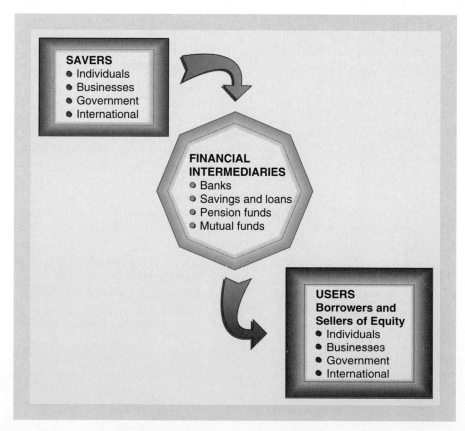

ers. Put another way, capital markets bring together suppliers and demanders with differing economic circumstances, time preferences, and attitudes toward risk, all hoping to make a favorable trade. The extent of *mutual gain* is an index of capital market efficiency, a measure of how successful financial intermediaries are at reducing and sharing the risks of an uncertain future. The growth of capital markets and the spread of financial intermediation creates "gains from trade" in precisely the same way as increased international trade or increased monetization of an economy. It's an increase in institutional efficiency ($+\Delta i^{nst}$) that expands productive capacity ($+\Delta y^*$, $+\Delta PPF$, and $+\Delta AS^*$ in our various models).

Think of the capital market as a rafting company trying to find just the right whitewater rafting trip for a wide variety of rafters, from beginner to advanced, from timid to foolhardy, from frugal to extravagant. Those companies that do the best job of matching rafter (saver) with the right stretch of river (investment) provide a useful service. They will thrive not only because they have equipment, facilities, and access to the rivers but because they provide useful information about the expected costs and benefits of specific journeys as well as accompanying guides (brokers). In regions where rafting is generally unfamiliar, the companies are likely to be inexperienced or even unscrupulous. Many rafters will find themselves in the wrong rafts on the wrong river and having an experience they will not wish to repeat. In such circumstances, the likelihood of mutual gain is small and many would-be rafters will find other places and uses for their time and money.

So when events or policies disturb or destroy capital markets—such as the near-collapse of the U.S. banking system in the 1930s; periodic credit controls and other well-intended but restrictive regulations; disruptions of international capital flows—the resulting *dis*intermediation means a "lose/lose" situation for the macro-economy. The losses from capital market disintegration spread throughout the system, much like we saw earlier for "restrictions on trade" and "demonetization" from escalating inflation. Events and policies that impede capital markets show up as a reduction in institutional efficiency ($-\Delta i^{nst}$) and inflict a negative supply shock on the macroeconomy. Nations without well-organized capital markets are at a great disadvantage in making the "now or later?" choice that lies at the heart of the growth process. Lacking well-developed and stable capital markets, they find it difficult and costly to channel resources from saving to investment and very expensive to attract resources from outside the economy. It could be one of the desperately poor nations of the world or the more advanced economies of the former Soviet bloc countries struggling to set up market structures. Without effective capital markets, the economic growth so fervently sought will remain beyond their reach.

13.2 ELEMENTS OF THE CAPITAL MARKET

Before we look further at the macroeconomic role of capital markets, it's important to have a clear view of their basic ingredients and some conclusions from the *micro*-economics of capital markets. Let's examine the capital market through your eyes, not too many years from now. You've completed your formal education (though it is likely to be resumed as changing opportunities and interests dictate), paid off your college loans and are a decade into your career. The endless stream of choices imposed by scarcity (formerly just the classroom abstractions of your economics courses) has become a daily reality at both work and home. The continual tension between "this or that?" and "now or later?" is more apparent and frustrating than you had expected and also occupies a larger portion of your time and energy than you'd figured on.

But suppose you've got a good income and an occupation that is challenging and (mostly) enjoyable. You're simultaneously a borrower, a saver, and an investor. You've accumulated the usual array of assets and liabilities that accompany economic success in a market economy. Your specific capital market choices concerning the level and composition of these *debts* (promises to repay) and *asset holdings* (hopes of coming returns) comprise your personal balance sheet, more fashionably known as an **investment portfolio.** On the **debt** side, things are straightforward. You understand that borrowing is sustainable if it is "consumption-smoothing" or "self-financing," so you use your common sense to steer clear of the "consumption-draining" scenario. Most of your borrowing is through *secured loans* (such as a mortgage on a house or an auto loan). If you fail to make your monthly payments, the lender has title to "your" house or car to assure repayment. *Unsecured loans* (such as bank or credit card loans) generally carry a much higher interest rate to compensate the lender for the possibility that you'll default. You are careful to do most of your borrowing through secured credit, leaving higher-cost loans for infrequent or temporary events like Christmas shopping or an occasional vacation splurge.

The lowest-cost loan in your portfolio is probably one that you never think about—the *postponed taxes* that are your share of the government's national debt. Whether or not you fit the "tax discounter" profile and actually think of current deficits as claims on your future income, they still represent taxes that must be repaid with interest. If current taxes are raised to eliminate the deficit, the resulting drop in your after-tax income will force you to either *cut your spending* or *substitute private borrowing* for the vanished public borrowing. Because the IOUs of the U.S. Treasury, unlike yours, are generally regarded as default-free, they carry a lower risk premium and hence a lower interest rate. In other words, the government—backed by the formidable power to tax ("legally steal" some would say)—can essentially borrow in your name more cheaply than you can.[2]

If you own a business you are likely to have some additional indebtedness to the banking system and if you're in the corporate world, your company will be a user of short-term loans from financial institutions and probably also an issuer of its own long term bonds. At home or work, your environment is permeated by a flow of borrowing and lending that allows you to alter your individual cost and return streams and represents an important dimension of the mutual gains from economic exchange. Your specific choice of loans involves not only a comparison of interest rates from different sources but also consideration of the loan's tax status.[3] You'll try to take into account whatever changes in interest rates or tax exemptions may be on the horizon, remembering also that any unforeseen change in inflation means an unexpected change in your *real* interest payments.[4]

On the **asset side** of your portfolio the choices are more numerous and, in varying degrees, more risky. To get a higher expected return you will generally have to assume a higher probability of taking a loss. Your specific choice of asset holdings will reflect many things, including your current income and wealth, your expecta-

---

[2] As a quick reminder, the macroeconomic impact of these public loans depends on (1) *how the borrowed funds are spent*—self-financing, consumption-smoothing, or consumption-draining; and (2) how taxpayer reaction, on average, is distributed across *tax-discounter, tax-myopic,* and *liquidity-constrained* consumers.

[3] Mortgage interest, for example, is a deductible expense for homeowners, lowering its net cost to the borrower by spreading part of the cost over the entire taxpayer population.

[4] Because the money rate of interest is the sum of the real rate and expected inflation ($R = r + \Pi^e$), agreement to a specific money rate (R) leaves both borrower and lender vulnerable (in opposite directions) to unexpected changes in inflation. New homeowners in the early 1980s, with mortgages in the 15% to 18% range, obviously did not expect the drop in inflation that soon pushed interest rates steadily downward through the 80s and 90s and left them paying huge real rates of interest. While refinancing at lower rates limits this risk, it still involves sizable closing costs.

tions of future income, your personal rate of time preference, and your willingness to assume risk. It may also involve the services of brokers and other investment advisors to help provide up-to-date information about current and expected future events that could affect the value and riskiness of your portfolio.

In addition, there is no shortage of self-annointed experts who will (for a fee, of course) share their "valuable" information on which are the best investment choices to make—specific stocks, for example, that they predict will yield above-average returns over the coming weeks, months, or years. Economists are virtually unanimous in their skepticism about the usefulness of such advice. Anyone who actually has significant and reliable information about where to find the "winners" could become immensely rich in a very short amount of time by acting on that information rather than passing it on to others. As with any promise of easy money, you should ask yourself why this person is willing to share such valuable information with you at such a relatively small cost.[5] In highly efficient markets with active trading among many buyers and sellers (like major stock, bond, and commodity exchanges), significant new information about future events or policies has its impact *very* quickly. In fact, the latest news is almost certain to be "built into" asset prices so rapidly—a matter of seconds or minutes, not weeks or months—that the average investor will be unable to act soon enough to take advantage of it.

In other words, it is very likely that "hot tips" from financial newsletters, TV or radio commentators, brokers, or prescient relatives have lost whatever special value they may have had by the time they get to you. They will bring you no higher return (for a given level of risk) than you can get by making your choices in any other way, even randomly.[6] Put another way, in efficient capital markets and without illegal inside information you cannot *systematically* find investments that will yield constantly above-average returns for a given risk level. In common sense terms, it's the familiar "no free lunch." This is certainly not to say that you can't make money by purchasing stocks or other financial instruments. It only says that your return will tend to be an average one for the amount of risk you're willing to assume. A higher expected return requires a riskier set of choices, not the advice of someone who claims the ability to consistently pick winners.

The world has always had an abundance of those who profess special powers to foresee the future. In the economic realm they may pretend to have some magic model, secret spreadsheet, or other system that gives them the ability to consistently pick winners. Those who make their living by selling these supposed "secrets of financial success" are, to put it bluntly, charlatans. If this was useful information, microeconomic principles and common sense suggest they'd simply use it themselves instead of going to the considerable trouble of marketing and then selling it. They make a living on our desire to get rich quick and our willingness to believe that there are cheap and easy ways to accomplish this. We allow our attention to be drawn to a few people making unusually large returns with apparently little effort and away from those making unusually large losses. We want to believe that there is a systematic method to acquire what is in fact just "good luck."

---

[5] Remember Adam Smith's oft-quoted remark that "It is not from the benevolence of the butcher, the brewer, or the baker that we expect our dinner, but from their regard to their own interest." (*The Wealth of Nations*, book 1, pp. 26–27 in the Liberty *Classics* edition).

[6] For more on the topic of forecasting asset prices, see Burton Malkiel's excellent presentation in *A Random Walk Down Wall Street: Including a Life-Cycle Guide to Personal Investing* (New York: Norton, 1990). For a fascinating look at the evolution of modern theories of stock market prices see Peter L. Bernstein's *Capital Ideas: The Improbable Origins of Modern Wall Street* (New York: The Free Press, 1992). For a more wide-ranging discussion of what economists can and cannot know, see Donald N. McCloskey's *If You're So Smart: The Narrative of Economic Expertise* (Chicago: University of Chicago Press, 1990).

In a world of scarcity, economic luck is a random variable and the only systematic way for us to increase our command over resources is the "old-fashioned way"—to *earn* it. A regimen for increasing your economic well-being has no secrets or surprises. It contains the willingness to work hard, make careful decisions, acquire new skills, postpone consumption, and assume risk. There is much useful advice that a broker or other investment professional can provide about the *riskiness of various alternatives*, about *prudent investment goals for your particular circumstances*, and about *ways you can diversify your portfolio to reduce risk*. Brokers can also make the actual financial transactions for you. It is when they go beyond this to offer you "special information" about specific stocks that you need to be suspicious. Even if this information is offered at "no charge," it is likely to require various adjustments to your portfolio, generating commissions for your broker and costs to you.

A fundamental relationship in asset selection is summarized in Figure 13.2, which shows the tradeoff between "expected return" and "safety" (the inverse of risk-

INTEREST RATES AND BOND PRICES

The relationship between interest rates and bond prices is a basic element of capital markets. Though it can seem puzzling and even counterintuitive at first, it is really very straightforward. Bonds, whether public or private, are an obligation to make periodic fixed money payments to the holder until the bond reaches maturity and is paid off at its face (par) value. So a newly issued 20-year bond may have a par value of $1000 and pay $100 a year for an effective nominal yield of 10%. At maturity the bond will pay $1000 to the holder.

But the fact that these bonds are contracts that extend across time make both borrower and lender vulnerable to unforeseen events. They also create opportunities for exchange so that a 20-year bond may have changed hands a number of times through "bond market" trades before it reaches maturity. Suppose that right after this 20-year $1000 bond is issued, economic conditions change and interest rates fall dramatically. To take an extreme case, suppose the day after you bought this bond, newly issued bonds of similar riskiness are only paying $50 a year for a 5% yield. Your good fortune at hitting interest rates at their peak is of course the bad luck of the borrower from whom you purchased your bond.

If you hold the bond until maturity you will receive annual dividends of $100 for twenty years and then be repaid the initial $1000 par value. But suppose you decide to sell it the day after you purchased it. Because new 20-year bonds are only offering half the return of yours, you will be able to sell it at a *premium*—well above the par value that you paid. In fact, a price of $2000 for this bond will make it competitive with the alternatives for lenders who weren't as fortunate as you to make their transaction yesterday. Hence, falling interest rates translate into rising bond prices in the capital market. Periods of monetary contraction, when interest rates are initially rising, cause much dismay among bond market participants because of the resulting capital losses on pre-existing bonds issued at lower rates of return.

■ FIGURE 13.2

For a carefully selected portfolio, a higher "expected return" requires increased risk and reduced "safety."

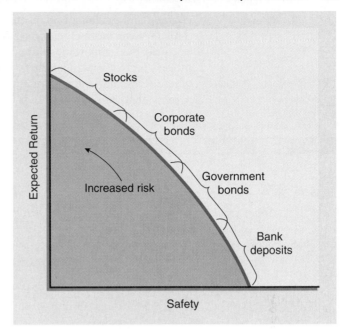

Portfolio Options

iness). The accompanying text box—"A Spectrum of Assets"—provides an overview of some specific asset options and their very approximate relative riskiness. The composition of your portfolio is always a bet on the future. The *degree* of uncertainty can be reduced at the cost of a lower return (by sliding down the hill in Figure 13.2 or moving down the list in the text box), but only up to a point. Neither individual nor collective (government) action can ever create a certain economic environment in an uncertain world. Consciously or not, you are continually striking a balance between risk and return that is revealed not only in the composition of your investment portfolio, but also in so many other commitments—like your choice of occupation or spouse, for example.

There is a wealth of fascinating information on portfolio choice and decision making under uncertainty. But it's time to end this excursion into the microeconomics of capital market events and examine their implications for macroeconomic activity. We have seen that information about expected future events is acted on by decision makers and thereby becomes embodied in current asset prices (stocks, bonds, real estate, and so on). As economic conditions and prospects change, this information alters supply and demand in capital markets, causing asset prices to adjust accordingly. These price "signals" affect decision makers throughout the economy, providing the latest information on where resources appear to be most productive. The inevitable presence of uncertainty means that an element of gambling enters all our capital market decisions. But don't conclude that capital markets are *just* a big casino. The crucial difference is that in gambling you gain only when someone else loses. To the extent that capital markets steer resources to more productive uses, our collective standard of living rises. The more sophisticated an economy's capital market structure in terms of the *range* of available financial instruments and the *speed* with which new information is embodied in asset prices, the more rapidly it can channel and rechannel its resources to match new conditions and new opportunities. This means a more efficient use of its available labor and capital.

So one important route to economic growth is through the development of more effective capital markets. But, of course, there's no "free lunch" here or elsewhere. Creating and maintaining an efficient network of capital markets is a costly activity that requires buildings, computers, telephone lines, traders, analysts and the

A SPECTRUM OF ASSETS
(In Approximate Order of Decreasing Risk)

High Risk, High Return

- Equity (stocks)
  From relatively safe "blue chips" to risky "high fliers"
- Stock market mutual funds
  Diversified combinations of stock holdings, oriented toward a specific goal, such as growth, security, specific types of holdings (high tech, international, etc.)
- Corporate bonds
  From long-term holdings of secure companies (Aaa-rated bonds) to "junk" bonds in high-risk companies
- Bond market mutual funds
  A diversification of bond holdings with specific goals in mind
- Pension funds
  Usually a diversified array of bond and stock holdings
- Government entitlements
  Food stamps, unemployment compensation, disaster relief, medicare, social security and other contingent events
- Equity in a home
- Government bonds
  Local school bonds, state highway bonds, to U.S. Treasury bonds, with varying maturities, yields, and tax status
- Money market funds
  Short-term government securities and bank certificates of deposit
- Savings deposits
  Time deposits in savings and loans, credit unions, and banks
- Checking accounts
  Deposits in various savings institutions that are payable on demand
- Cash
  Currency (Federal Reserve notes) and coin, declared to be "legal tender" in fulfillment of taxes, contracts, and so on

Low Risk, Low Return

usual array of inputs. Capital market efficiency also depends on the strength of other institutional arrangements. In particular, since the essence of capital markets is making current bets on future outcomes, there must be a well-defined and well-enforced legal framework governing contracts. Without a system of fair and impartial courts to enforce economic contracts and arbitrate disagreements, risk and uncertainty will greatly impair the effectiveness of a market framework.[7]

✆✆ 13.3 CAPITAL MARKETS AND MONETARY POLICY

The connections between capital markets and macroeconomic policy are numerous and important. They also run in both directions—*policy changes alter capital market prices, but capital market movements are also closely watched by and sometimes responded to by policy makers.* Let's begin with the obvious link from policy change to capital market response. Since capital markets are bets on our economic future, near and far, they necessarily embody a particular set of expectations about coming economic events and policies. To the extent that actual events and policies unfold more or less as anticipated, stock prices, bond prices, and interest rates will hold relatively steady. But when they change in unforeseen ways, capital market participants will re-evaluate their prospects and alternatives, adjusting their portfolios accordingly.

Suppose the Federal Reserve decides to alter the rate of growth of the money supply. We've seen that it typically does this through open market purchases (or sales) of existing federal government bonds. When it purchases bonds, for example, new reserves are injected into the banking system which are then loaned out in a process that expands the nation's total stock of money. Investment portfolios must be altered to absorb this increased supply of money and to reflect the reduced amount of government bond holdings available outside the banking system. If the Fed moves in the opposite direction and sells bonds on the open market, then portfolios will have to absorb the influx of bonds from the Federal Reserve's vaults and adapt to the reduced monetary growth.

If this monetary policy change comes as a surprise, it will create temporary misperceptions followed by a revision in expectations of future economic performance. The basic AD/AS^e framework shows us how an unexpected shift in aggregate demand can have short run impacts on real output (Δy), real interest rates (Δr) and real exchange rates (Δe). It can also have long run impacts on the price level (ΔP), the actual and expected rates of inflation ($\Delta \Pi$ and $\Delta \Pi^e$) and therefore on nominal interest and exchange rates (ΔR and ΔE). The current prices of stocks and long- and short-term bonds will respond to this constellation of changes as investors realign their portfolios in light of the new information. We've seen earlier how expectations of rising inflation are built into nominal interest rates (through the Fisher equation, $R = r + \Pi^e$). These rising nominal interest rates mean *falling* prices of existing bonds since their future interest payments, fixed in nominal dollar terms, will have lower purchasing power as inflation rises. Even rumors of monetary changes can trigger portfolio adjustments as investors scurry to avoid losses and accumulate gains.

So monetary policy affects capital markets directly by changing the relative availabilities of two key assets—money and government bonds—and indirectly through its economy-wide influence on output, prices, and interest rates. But the

---

[7] We tend to take such basic institutional arrangements for granted. But when they break down the consequences are staggering—not only a lack of capital markets to link savers, borrowers, and investors, but also the absence of courts, police protection, and even electrical and water supplies.

causality can also run in the other direction, with policy makers reacting to changing signals in the capital markets. This is because the capital market provides a continual assessment of how current events or policies are expected to affect coming economic performance. It is not an infallible crystal ball, of course, but it is a relatively sensitive instrument that reflects an overall market verdict, based on the latest information, as to what lies ahead for the economy. It reveals an outline of the future based on how the so-called smart money is placing its current bets.

For example, if expected events and policies are viewed as contractionary and likely to lead to recession, we would expect to see falling stock prices (reflecting reduced future earnings of corporations), but stable or even rising bond prices (reflecting steady or declining expected inflation that usually accompanies recession). Policy makers may use these signals (in combination with their own careful economic analysis of the economy) to move toward a more expansionary policy. As they implement the expansion they will surely keep an eye on market responses to see if capital market participants are convinced that sufficient stimulus has been applied. This two-way linkage between policy and capital markets has become increasingly evident in recent years and there is the general belief that it can operate as an important constraint on policy excesses.

■ FIGURE 13.3

An increase in the money supply shifts out *LM* and *AD* (point *A* to *A'*) and moves the economy from point *A* to *B* in the short run and on to *C* in the long run. To the extent this $+\Delta M$ is anticipated in advance, the path will be more like points *A* to *C*. Policy surprises, on the other hand, will follow the path from points *A* through *B* and on to *C*.

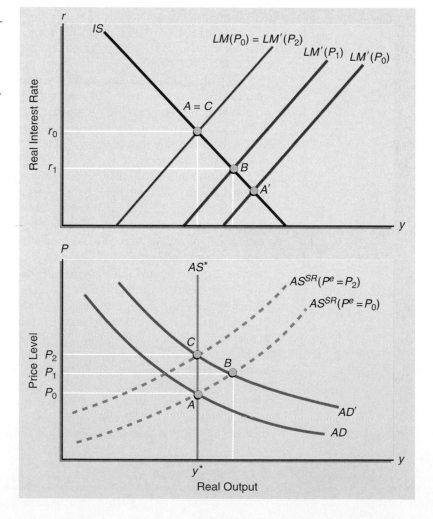

IN SUMMARY . . .

Monetary Actions and Capital Market Reactions

In earlier chapters we saw that *expected* **changes in monetary policy** have minimal impacts on the "real" economy (i.e., output and employment), their energy being dissipated largely in "nominal" changes of the price level, the inflation rate, the market exchange rate, the expected inflation rate, market interest rates, and bond prices. Moreover, as long as the actions of the monetary authority are correctly anticipated, they will already have been built into economic decisions and thereby into the relevant interest rates and asset prices on the capital markets.

This means that capital market volatility arises primarily when events and policies change in *unanticipated* ways, necessitating reassessments and portfolio realignments by decision makers. For example, suppose that what was expected to be continued moderate growth of the money supply actually becomes a rapid monetary spurt. As decision makers react to this new information they initiate a series of events that will reverberate throughout the real and financial sectors of the economy. Although "money is a veil" may be a useful rule of thumb for very long-term impacts, it gives us no insight into the short-run gyrations in real and nominal variables or capital market prices that follow *unexpected* **changes in monetary policy.**

To understand capital market reactions to Federal Reserve actions, let's go back to our AD/AS^e structure. As Figure 13.3 shows, an increase in the money supply through Federal Reserve open market purchases of government bonds will increase aggregate demand, shifting LM and AD curves to the right. This sets off a series of events, the short run impact of which depends upon (1) the extent to which this action had been foreseen, (2) the speed with which expectations respond to a "policy surprise," and (3) the degree of wage-price "stickiness" in the system. The short run impact on the real variables (as in the movement from points A to B in Figure 13.3) will be larger and persist longer to the extent that the *policy is unexpected, expectations are relatively sluggish*, and *wages and prices relatively sticky*. As long-run adjustment to point C is completed, capital markets will have responded by building the higher price level (P_0 to P_2) into market interest rates, exchange rates, and bond prices.

To put this in a more realistic setting of ongoing rates of change, we turn to the short run dynamics of the Phillips curve as shown in Figure 13.4. For an economy initially at full employment at point A (with inflation at 3%), suppose the unexpectedly rapid growth of the money supply increases the inflation rate to 6%. The economy will respond by moving toward point B in the short run and then to point C. The extent to which this policy surprise has real effects ($-\Delta U$ and $+\Delta y$) again depends on the speed at which expectations adjust and market rigidities are overcome. The *faster expectations respond* and the *less stickiness* there is, the *more quickly we move to point* C. As inflation expectations rise in response to this monetary surprise, the nominal exchange rate will decline, market interest rates rise, and long term bond prices fall.

■ FIGURE 13.4

In terms of the Phillips curve, anticipated monetary increases will cause relatively little change in "real" variables and result in a path like point A to C. To the extent the ΔM is unexpected, the adjustment process will be like point A to B to C as expectations adjust and market frictions are overcome. As expectations adjust ($+\Delta P^e$ in Figure 13.3; $+\Delta \Pi^e$ in Figure 13.4), market interest rates and market exchange rates respond ($+\Delta R$ and $+\Delta E$) and bond prices move in the opposite direction of market interest rates (here, $-\Delta P_{\text{BONDS}}$).

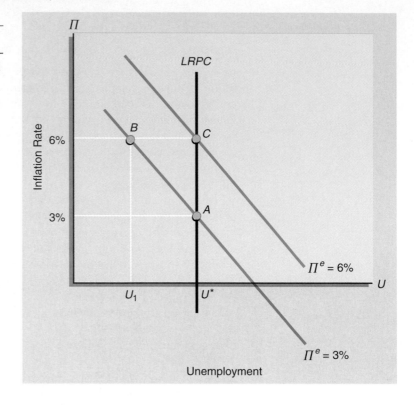

⚭ *13.4 CAPITAL MARKETS AND FISCAL POLICY*

Fiscal policy—the spending, taxing, and borrowing activities of the government—has been a main topic throughout much of the book.[8] But most of our discussion has been over its role in macroeconomic stabilization, an important but relatively small part of its total impact on our lives. Fiscal policy's primary task is the day-to-day job of keeping the government operating. When public spending outruns current tax revenues, as it does in most countries most of the time, the government must either print money (another way to tax) or borrow (postponing the tax). We have seen that tax postponement is sustainable under certain conditions, but can also end up in the unsustainable, consumption-draining category if the borrowing is not matched by expected future returns.

In either case, this year's borrowing joins with deficits of the past to make up the national debt. For the U.S. this now amounts to about $3.5 trillion (after netting out intragovernmental holdings, though ignoring promises made through "entitlement" programs). While this debt is obviously the taxpayers' liability, to the holders

---

[8] A brief summary might be useful. From the denial of its importance to macroeconomic stabilization in the classical tradition ("fiscal policy is powerless"), the pendulum swung to the early Keynesian emphasis on countercyclical policy—fiscal "fine tuning" to keep us close to full employment and price stability. Half a century of events, theories, and debate have diminished the extremes, but left us with an activist/nonactivist tug of war that involves different views of the source of fluctuations (demand or supply shocks), the speed of market clearing (reflecting the difficult-to-test roles of expectations and market frictions), the extent of lags in the policy process and, inevitably, different personal preferences about goals and the economic role of government. The debate over what fiscal stabilization *can* accomplish is now one of degree, not all or nothing. An increasing awareness that fiscal change is quite unwieldy, unable to respond quickly to changing events, has resulted in more reliance on monetary policy for short run adjustments to aggregate demand.

of these bonds it is very much an asset. So why don't we take the optimistic approach and call these outstanding government bonds our national asset?[9] Perhaps just a change in name would turn our agony over a rising debt into ecstasy over a rising asset. The truth, of course, is that both names are equally correct and every dollar of these Treasury IOUs is both asset and liability. Our insistence on emphasizing the debt side over the asset side leaves out the best part of the story, adding additional fear to an already emotional and complicated issue.

The reason for reviving this deficit/debt topic in a chapter on capital markets is that government bonds are a large and important part of our investment portfolios and hence in our choice between "now or later?" U.S. Treasury obligations not only offer a competitive rate of return, but are widely regarded as virtually default-free investments, giving them an important role in asset diversification.[10] Households, businesses and, financial intermediaries have made them a basic ingredient in their investment strategies. In addition, we've seen that the Federal Reserve buys and sells government securities via "open market operations" as its primary means of controlling bank reserves and, thereby, of changing the rate of growth of the money supply.

This adds up to a national debt/asset of sizable proportions and which serves a variety of functions in the capital market. To taxpayers it represents *tax postponement;* to the investor, a relatively low-risk option for *portfolio diversification;* and to the Federal Reserve, a conveniently neutral asset for conducting open market operations to *control money growth.* But to those seeking funds for capital expenditures, public borrowing can mean head-to-head *competition for the saver's dollar.* The process through which increased deficits bid up interest rates to attract funds that would otherwise go to private investment (through purchases of corporate bonds or stocks rather than government bonds) is called **crowding out.**[11]

Most economists see "crowding out" as the primary reason to be concerned with continued large public deficits.[12] They point out that greater reliance on tax rather than deficit financing would mean less competition for private saving and a lower real rate of interest. This, in turn, would lead to more private investment and ultimately a higher rate of economic growth. Continued large deficits, then, are seen as diverting private saving from private investment and thereby slowing the economy's rate of growth. So fiscal policy has an even broader impact on the economy than we have seen in our previous analysis. In carrying out its basic job of *transferring resources from private to public use,* fiscal policy also has the potential to influence both the *short-run stability of the macroeconomy* and, through capital markets, its *long-run rate of growth.* As you are aware by now, these three dimensions of fiscal policy will often be in conflict—with each other and with other desirable goals—setting the stage for some very difficult policy choices.

---

[9] While about 18% of our net national debt is held by foreigners, this still leaves nearly $2.9 trillion in the portfolios of U.S. individuals and firms.

[10] This does not, of course, make them risk free. Long-term bonds, in particular, are fully exposed to the chance of unexpectedly high inflation. Those who purchased long term government bonds in the 1940s and 50s learned about "inflation risk" the hard way. But since these bonds are both debt and asset, the buyer's loss was the seller's gain and the declining real value of the national debt was a benefit to taxpayers.

[11] We first encountered "crowding out" in Chapter 4 in comparing the effects of taxes versus deficits on real interest rates. Except in the case of perfect tax-discounting, a deficit-financed increase in spending ($+\Delta g = +\Delta b$) is more expansionary than for tax financing ($+\Delta g = +\Delta t$). This means that IS and AD are shifted further to the right, causing a larger increase in the real rate of interest ($+\Delta r$) and, thereby, more crowding out of investment and net exports ($+\Delta r \Rightarrow -\Delta i$ and $-\Delta x$).

[12] If an ongoing deficit is monetized ($b = \Delta M$), we saw in Chapter 10 that this can lead to continuing and accelerating inflation. In this discussion we presume that the deficit is not monetized.

IN SUMMARY . . .

Fiscal Actions and Capital Market Reactions

Fiscal policy actions, anticipated or not, affect the economy quite differently than monetary changes. For one thing, fiscal changes are certainly not a "veil" even in the long run. Like monetary actions, they have short run impacts on real as well as nominal variables. But unlike monetary policy, fiscal policy has "real" effects even in the long run. Though it doesn't affect the *level* of long-run real output, fiscal expansion or contraction changes the long-run real rate of interest (Δr) and thereby real investment spending (Δi), the real exchange rate (Δe), and net exports (Δx), hence, the *composition* of output in the long run.

Second, a fiscal change tends to have a one-shot impact on the price level, in contrast to monetary policy in which a change in the rate of money growth has a continuing impact that alters the rate of inflation, not just the price level. For example, suppose we run an expansionary fiscal policy with a deficit-financed increase in government spending that continues at its new higher level, year after year. The initial increase in public spending means the expansion of *IS* and *AD* curves as the structural deficit rises ($+\Delta b^{str}$). (These outward shifts would continue only if there were an *ever-increasing structural deficit each year*, something that is rarely observed except in economies that are monetizing their deficit ($+\Delta b = +\Delta M$) and are well along the path to hyperinflation and monetary breakdown.) As shown in Figure 13.5, the impact of this increased structural deficit is to move the economy from points *A* to *B* in the short run and on to *C* in the long run.

The implications of such a fiscal expansion ($+\Delta b^{str}$) for *capital markets* begin with the rising real interest rate ($+\Delta r$) and rising price level ($+\Delta P$). In both cases, the initial short run increase (points *A* to *B*) is followed by further increases in the long run (on to *C*). But these are *one-shot increases rather than ongoing changes*. This means that the underlying "core" rate of inflation (Π) is unaffected as is the expected rate of inflation (Π^e). Bond prices will still react, of course, as the higher real rate of interest raises the market interest rate ($\uparrow R = \uparrow r + \Pi^e$) and forces capital losses ($-\Delta p_{bonds}$) on holders of pre-existing bonds issued at lower market rates of interest. The extent to which this fiscal action alters *current* interest rates and bond prices will depend on whether this policy change had been anticipated and hence partially built into market rates and bond prices even before the policy change came about.

■ FIGURE 13.5

A fiscal expansion (+ ΔIS and + ΔAD) alters both real and nominal variables In the short run as it moves the economy from points A to B. As long-run equilibrium is restored, the economy moves to point C with a lasting increase in the real rate of interest, hence, lower investment and lower net exports. The speed of this adjustment from points A to C depends on the extent to which the fiscal change was anticipated, the speed at which expectations are revised, and the size of market frictions. The rising real and, hence, market rate of interest will cause bond prices to fall.

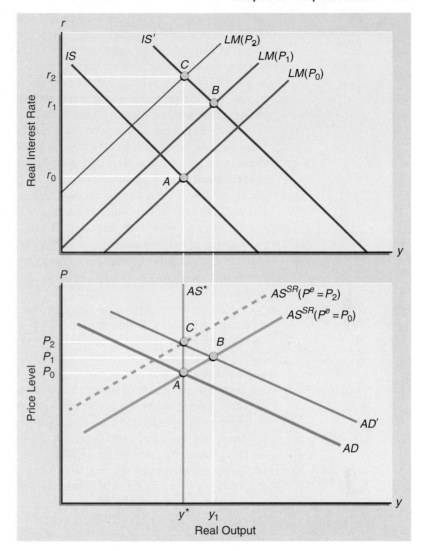

✆ 13.5 GLOBALIZATION OF CAPITAL MARKETS

The rapid expansion of world trade in recent years has dramatically altered the economic landscape in nearly every nation. Its impact is felt on literally the whole range of economic activities—our options as consumers, income earners, borrowers and lenders, savers and investors. Agricultural products, consumer goods, and manufacturing equipment flow across nations as never before. So do oil and minerals, knowledge, weapons, migrant labor, illicit drugs, pollution, insect pests and so much else. Multinational corporations increasingly blur the economic meaning of political boundaries. The "gains from trade" that incite all this are no less powerful in the capital markets where we make our "now or later?" choices. Stocks and bonds and other assets increasingly attract foreign buyers. Financial intermediaries alter global portfolios at the speed of electronic communication.

Although the increased volume of international transactions is of major significance, it is also important to see that expanding the playing field doesn't change the underlying rules of the game. In capital markets, funds still flow to the highest expected return and borrowers still search for the lowest rates of interest. The uncertainty of many foreign ventures means that fast and reliable information is more important than ever, adding increased cost and risk to these transactions. But the lure, as always, is the mutual gains from trade across individuals, businesses, or governments with differing economic circumstances and goals, as well as different rates of time preference and attitudes toward risk.

U.S. experience in recent years has been one of continuing *net capital inflows* from the rest of the world. We saw (in Chapter 7, "International Trade") that this is the mirror image of an ongoing *current account deficit*, popularly termed a **balance of trade deficit** ($x < 0$ in our model). In the international trade jargon, our capital account surplus is their capital account deficit, just as their balance of trade surplus is our trade deficit. Put another way, our demand for current foreign goods and services continues to outrun their demand for ours. But they're willing to cover the difference by using the "surplus" dollars to buy our securities—stocks and bonds and even physical capital that embody their claims to our future goods and services. It is these rising foreign claims to *future* U.S. output that make us net borrowers from the rest of the world.

Remember that increased borrowing, itself, is not evidence of economic decline or shortsightedness. In this as in other contexts, it depends on *how the borrowed funds are used* and the *cost of borrowing* relative to the return on the funds. For the United States, the expansion of international capital markets has meant a larger potential pool of lenders. And just as there are low-cost producers of sugar or sardines, there are low-cost producers of saving. For example, those with lower rates of time preference are willing to lend at lower rates of interest. Or those who are particularly risk averse may find it attractive to send their savings to the U.S. with its relatively stable political and economic environment. By attracting foreign lenders and increasing available saving, we are generally able to get lower rates on mortgages, student loans, consumer loans, and all the rest. The Treasury can finance the government's borrowing, 18% of which is held by foreigners, on more favorable terms than if it had to rely entirely on internal bond sales. Some might contend that global capital markets only give us cheaper rope to hang ourselves—publicly or privately or both, if we're really determined. But the point here is simply that if we decide to borrow, it's best to do so at the lowest possible rate. If someone is intent on pushing their borrowing into consumption-draining territory, at least they'll be able to do it more efficiently when the availability of foreign funds brings lower interest rates.

The main story here should be familiar to you by now. The globalization of capital markets creates mutual "gains from trade" through a more efficient allocation of the world's resources. The result is a favorable supply shock (expanding both the PPF and AS^* curves) for all participating nations. There will, of course, be costs imposed on certain domestic groups who have now lost their comparative advantage to foreign competition. Inevitably, those who stand to lose from global competition will seek protective legislation that limits foreign participation in capital markets. They will argue that it is in the interest of the U.S. economy that our capital markets be kept safe from the uncertainties and inefficiencies of foreign transactions. To the extent they succeed, there will be a net overall loss as scarce resources are kept in an area in which they are relatively inefficient.

One final dimension of expanded world trade (in goods and services *and* capital markets) is very important for macroeconomic issues—its consequences for *macro-*

economic policy making.[13] This has been implicit in our demand-side model since the introduction of *IS-LM* in Chapter 4, but this is an appropriate time to draw your attention to it. In our analysis of the macroeconomy the expansion of foreign trade shows up in two ways. On the supply side, the more efficient use of resources means a positive supply shock that shifts *AS** and PPF to the right. On the demand side, more world trade means a larger role for exports and imports, as represented by the net export equation $x = x_0 + x_1 y - x_2 r$. You may recall that this inverse relationship between real interest rates and net exports is a simplification of a chain of events that works by altering the real value of the dollar on foreign exchange markets. To be specific, *any* event that increases our real rate of interest will also increase the international demand for dollars. This in turn means a rise in the real exchange rate (e), discouraging exports and encouraging imports ($+\Delta r \Rightarrow +\Delta e \Rightarrow -\Delta$ exports and $+\Delta$ imports $\Rightarrow -\Delta x$).[14]

The final step is to see how this increased role of foreign trade (and this underlying exchange rate link to aggregate demand) affects the strength of fiscal and monetary policies. Expansionary fiscal policy (shifting *IS* to the right) increases the real interest rate. This not only crowds out investment spending but, for an open economy, reduces net export spending as described earlier. The result is that a given fiscal expansion will have a smaller impact on aggregate demand in an open economy than if there were no international transactions involved. In other words, the larger the foreign sector the smaller the impact of fiscal changes on aggregate demand.

For monetary policy, the affect is the opposite. Since monetary expansion causes a short run drop in the real interest rate (shifting *LM* to the right), this will lead to a decline in the international demand for the dollar and exchange rate depreciation. The lower value of the dollar will stimulate our exports and reduce imports, increasing net exports. Hence, in an open economy monetary policy affects aggregate demand through two channels—the lower real interest rate expands both investment spending and net export spending. The larger the foreign sector, then, the stronger the impact of monetary changes on aggregate demand.

⊗⊘ 13.6 OVERVIEW

1. The **capital market** is where we place our bets on the future, where we struggle with the unavoidable day-to-day choices between "now or later?" Borrowing and lending, saving and investing are current actions linked to future outcomes. Unavoidably they involve varying elements of risk and uncertainty.

---

[13] Like many issues in international economics, the question of how international transactions affect the strength of macroeconomic policies is both difficult and quite involved. There are a number of factors that influence the outcome. The most important is whether international exchange rates are fixed or flexible. Another is whether it is a "small" country, whose actions have no impact on world interest rates, or a "large" country which can send shockwaves throughout the world economy. Our brief discussion presumes the current U.S. situation of a "large" country operating with flexible exchange rates. For a more complete presentation of the international aspects of macroeconomic policies, see Jeffrey D. Sachs and Felipe Larrain, *Macroeconomics in the Global Economy* (Englewood Cliffs, N.J.: Prentice Hall, 1993), especially chaps. 13 and 14.

[14] These interactions are built into the multiplier process of our aggregate demand model. It's easiest to think of it in terms of its impact on the slope of the *IS* curve. The equation for the *IS* curve was $y = \mu(z_0 + g_0 - c_1 t_0) - \mu(i_2 + x_2)r$. The impact of the x_2 term is to "flatten" the *IS* curve because an increase in the real rate of interest now reduces aggregate demand in *two* ways—it crowds out private investment ($+\Delta r \Rightarrow -\Delta i$ via the i_2 term) and it also crowds out net exports ($+\Delta r \Rightarrow -\Delta x$ via the x_2 term).

2. The function of **financial intermediaries** is to provide services and expertise to improve the connections between savers and users of funds. A crucial part of the services of banks, savings and loans, mutual funds and other intermediaries is in gathering, analyzing, and distributing relevant information to their customers. Their economic contribution is to grapple with the uncertainty of the economic future in ways that either reduce risk or spread it in a more efficient way so that those who accept it are compensated by those willing to pay for reduced risk.

3. To the extent that capital markets reduce the barriers between savers and investors and borrowers and lenders, the result is an improved allocation of scarce resources. For the macroeconomy this means an outward shift in aggregate supply and a rising overall standard of living. More extensive capital markets provide the familiar **gains from trade** to the economy.

4. A basic understanding of the microeconomics of capital markets can help dispel some of the mystery that surrounds investment choices. Simply put, no one can know the future and those who claim to have information that is not already built into capital market prices are very likely to be either mistaken or mischievous. It's important to understand that the ups and downs of the stock and bond markets are not just an event to attract gamblers. These bets on the future serve the fundamental function of channeling the economy's resources one way or another. The crucial role of capital markets is to keep inputs flowing to where the most recent information and expectations tells us they're most productive. When capital markets sputter or collapse, it's more than a casino going bankrupt. It's a real loss of economic efficiency for the macroeconomy.

5. The **links between capital markets and macroeconomic policy run in both directions.** The most obvious is capital market reactions to policy changes that alter expectations of future economic performance. Bond markets are especially sensitive to changes in expected inflation and therefore to actions of the Federal Reserve. But it's also true that policy makers use feedback from the markets as a way to assess the results of their policy actions.

6. **Fiscal policy** is directly linked to capital markets through the United States Treasury bonds that finance our government deficits. This public borrowing creates a future tax liability, but also offers an asset that is useful for portfolio diversification and open-market operations. Hence a change in the current deficit sets off a series of portfolio adjustments that echo throughout financial and credit markets.

7. The legitimate concern about current U.S. deficits is not that they're consumption-draining, leading us to some sort of national bankruptcy. The real worry is the extent to which they raise interest rates and thereby **crowd out** private investment expenditures in a way that reduces the economy's rate of economic growth. This and related issues on growth are explored in the next chapter.

8. The **globalization of capital markets** is a companion to the expansion of world trade in goods and services. It represents the "now or later" dimension in international transactions and, again, is in response to the mutual gains from trade. As countries have lowered barriers to trade and as technological change has accelerated the flow of information, capital markets have become increasingly global. One consequence for countries operating under flexible exchange rates has been to weaken the impact of fiscal policy on aggregate demand. The rising real rate of interest from expansionary fiscal policy not only crowds out investment demand $(+\Delta r \Rightarrow -\Delta i)$ but also reduces net export demand via exchange rate appreciation

$(+\Delta r \Rightarrow +\Delta e \Rightarrow -\Delta x)$. Monetary policy, on the other hand, is enhanced by international linkages, since its *inverse* short run impact on real interest rates $(+\Delta M \Rightarrow -\Delta r \Rightarrow +\Delta i$ and $+\Delta x)$ increases its demand-side impact.

⊗⊗ 13.7 REVIEW QUESTIONS

1. Explain the following definitions and concepts:

Capital markets	Diversification
Savers and users of funds	Financial intermediaries
Equity	Disintermediation
Mutual gain	Portfolio
Risk	Crowding out

2. The basic mechanics of our AD/AS^e framework have incorporated connections between saving and investment in the overall economy. In reality, such a connection is much richer and more complex than can be captured in an aggregate model and involves the working of a system of domestic and international capital markets. In this context, discuss the elements through which saving and investment are related in a more realistic setting than can be encompassed in the AD/AS^e model.

3. Why is there a need for a highly specialized industry to link savers with investors? Address the charge that such "middlemen" only increase the costs to borrowers and thereby end up diminishing the amount of investment and capital formation in the overall economy. Explain.

4. In recent years, there has been a substantial flow of saving from the United States to developing nations in anticipation of large expected returns from new investments. This may reflect a number of factors, such as reduced political and economic instability and hence capital market uncertainty in many parts of the world. Whatever the reason behind it, the consequences can be fairly complicated. For example, one impact of this influx of dollars into these countries is increased demand for their currencies and upward pressure on their exchange rates. This rising exchange rate makes their exports more expensive in other nations and damages their export sector. To try to prevent this, governments may choose to buy these additional dollars before they have a chance to push up the price of the domestic currency.

   a. Suppose they do this by increasing the domestic money supply to buy up the dollars. What short and long run impacts would this inflow of U.S. savings have on these economies? Explain in terms of the AD/AS^e model.

   b. Suppose they buy up these dollars by issuing bonds rather than printing money. Would your answer in part *a* still apply? Explain.

5. Suppose foreign governments are buying up the influx of dollars and issuing new bonds to pay for it (as in part 4*b*). Further suppose that they now take these new dollar holdings and buy U.S. government bonds. If the value of the dollar continues to fall relative to their currency (as happened for many countries in the mid-1990s) what will be the consequence of this policy for these countries? Explain.

6. Money is just an asset, one among very many. In what ways does it differ from other assets? In what respects is it similar?

7. Those who can consistently predict an inflationary surge before others see it coming have a potentially valuable skill. If you had this ability, how could you put it to profitable use in the bond and foreign exchange markets? Explain.

8. Why are economists skeptical of those who claim to be able to see what lies ahead in capital markets?

9. The Federal Reserve is probably the most consistently criticized among policy-making groups. It's every action makes the headlines, especially when that action is a surprise. When an anticipated change in Federal Reserve policy fails to materialize, it is criticized for its inaction. Criticism comes from Wall Street and Main Street as well as from both the legislative and executive branches of the government. What are the underlying sources of all this criticism? Is the Federal Reserve incompetent or is it just misunderstood? Explain.

13.8 FURTHER READING

BEN S. BERNANKE, "Credit in the Macroeconomy," *Quarterly Review*, Federal Reserve Bank of New York (spring 1992–1993): 50–70.

PETER L. BERNSTEIN, *Capital Ideas: The Improbable Origins of Modern Wall Street* (New York: The Free Press, 1992).

BENJAMIN M. FRIEDMAN, "Capital, Credit and Money Markets," in *The New Palgrave: Money* ed. John Eatwell, M. Milgate, and P. Newman (New York: Norton & Co., 1989).

BURTON MALKIEL, *A Random Walk Down Wall Street*, 5th ed. (New York: W. W. Norton & Co., 1990).

DONALD N. MCCLOSKEY, *If You're So Smart: The Narrative of Economic Expertise* (Chicago: University of Chicago Press, 1990).

ANN-MARIE MEULENDYKE, *U.S. Monetary Policy and Financial Markets*, Federal Reserve Bank of New York (1989).

JEFFREY D. SACHS AND FELIPE LARRAIN, *Macroeconomics in the Global Economy* (Englewood Cliffs, N.J.: Prentice Hall, 1993).

CHAPTER 14

ECONOMIC GROWTH

◎ 14.1 INTRODUCTION

Capital markets bring savers, borrowers, and investors together to reach an economy-wide balance between consumption now and consumption later. The ability to use capital markets to alter both our consumption time path (by saving or borrowing) and our income time path (by investing in capital) is at the heart of **economic growth**.[1] We now complete the transition from the demand-oriented, zero-growth, AD/AS^e model to a framework that addresses the events and policies that lead to ongoing change in the economy's underlying production possibilities (ΔPPF) and long-run aggregate supply (ΔAS^*).

In switching the focus to the determinants of long term growth, we set aside *unemployment* and related market-clearing issues like the adjustment speed of *expectations*, the extent of *market frictions*, the erratic behavior of the *velocity* of money, and the sometimes *unpredictable lags* accompanying policy changes. Crucial as these are for understanding short-run cyclical events, they are overshadowed in the long term by other forces that change the economy's productive potential. At first glance it might seem that this switch to the long run would be a great simplification, because it side-steps the many ambiguities and controversies over market clearing, frictions and lags to focus on the basic connection between inputs and output described in the production function, $y^* = F(n^*, k, i^{nst})$. The long-run rate of growth of output is determined, in a seemingly straightforward way, by the growth of the inputs—$(+\%\Delta n^*, +\%\Delta k, +\%\Delta i^{nst}) \Rightarrow +\%\Delta y^*$.

---

[1] We are presuming a standard measure of economic growth—either the annual percentage change in real output ($\%\Delta y$) or, more revealingly, the growth of real output per capita ($\%\Delta y/n$). There are, in fact, many reasons why neither measure, by itself, can be considered a very accurate measure of economic well-being. We will examine this problem carefully in the next chapter.

But concluding that "output growth is determined by the growth of the inputs" only moves the puzzle back one step to "What causes the growth in the quantity and quality of inputs?" Part of the answer is already implicit in our analysis since net investment is a component of output that is "recycled" as an input. It changes the rate of growth of the capital stock ($i > 0 \Rightarrow + \%\Delta k$) and thereby the growth of output. So investment spending essentially migrates from the demand to the supply side of our model. We have justifiably neglected this link on the grounds that it is relatively unimportant for understanding the short run dynamics of the macroeconomy. But any explanation of *long-term growth* must not only include this fundamental saving-investment-growth sequence ($s > 0 \Rightarrow i > 0 \Rightarrow + \%\Delta k \Rightarrow + \%\Delta y^*$), but go still further to incorporate other sources of economic growth—like a growing population, a changing labor force participation rate, changes in education and training, and technological innovation. It must also allow for losses of capital from such things as natural disasters, wars, tariffs, embargoes, and regulatory restrictions.

Many of these events are primarily demographic, political or sociological and we must acknowledge them as important influences that lie outside the domain of economic analysis. But the more important these outside or **"exogenous"** variables are to growth, the less useful our purely economic models will be. Wherever possible, then, we want to expand our analytical framework to explain why and how the inputs change. The more variables we can legitimately make **"endogenous"** to the model, the greater its potential explanatory power. This is the reason for seeking economic explanations for such factors as population growth, the pace of technological advance, the rate of natural resource discovery, and regulatory change among others.

This process of enriching our understanding by digging deeper and wider for underlying causes should look very familiar by now. It's what we did in making the transition from the original classical model to the more inquisitive and ambitious Keynesian model (*AD/AS*) that allowed velocity to vary and markets to remain uncleared in the short run. It's also what we did in adding expectations and market frictions (*AD/AS^e*) to get at the short run dynamics that underlie the Phillips curve analysis. Of course, increased explanatory power comes at the cost of more complexity and less manageability. And as we add more and more detail, we eventually cross the boundary between microeconomics and macroeconomics. There's nothing wrong with crossing boundaries, particularly when they are as indistinct and, in some ways, artificial as this one. But remember that the point of macroeconomic analysis is not precision and completeness. Its usefulness lies in a deliberate sacrifice of realism in return for a manageable and practical framework that encompasses the "big picture." This chapter's presentation of the main issues and basic policy results of economic growth will stay well within the territory of macroeconomics.

Though the macroeconomics of growth ignores most of what's going on, it still paints a coherent broad-brush portrait of the major interactions and dominant patterns of the growth process. If this can help raise the growth rate even slightly, the long term consequences can be dramatic. For example, per capita real income in the United Kingdom in 1870 was about 15% higher than in the United States. Over the next 120 years, it grew 1.38% annually in the United Kingdom and 1.86% in the United States. This apparently slight difference—less than half a percent per year—was sufficient to raise current U.S. income per capita over 50% higher than in the United Kingdom.[2]

---

[2] This example comes from the "Economic Report of the President, 1993," p. 225.

VICTIMS OF GROWTH

Macroeconomics, in its eagerness to avoid complicating details, uses aggregates to get an overall "bottom line" on the big issues. Hence we characterize the growth process as a rightward shift of the PPF and AS^* curves. This makes it look simple, but hides much. For example, not everyone in the economy shares in the benefits of growth. Economic growth, like any economic change, creates winners and losers. Some inevitably find their standard of living reduced. They're the ones who ignore or misread the market signals or are simply innocent victims of unforeseeable events. For whatever reason, their resources are in the wrong place at the wrong time. This double-edged sword aspect of economic growth underlies its characterization as a process of **"creative destruction,"** a revealing term associated with the work of the economist Joseph Schumpeter in the first half of the twentieth century.

While compensation might be made to those most obviously damaged by growth, most victims of growth have to absorb the loss themselves. This may seem unnecessarily harsh, but note that the reason for these losses is that scarce resources were being used in ways or places that were relatively inefficient. The vitality of a market system is precisely because of its efficiency in rechanneling inputs in response to changing market signals reflecting altered consumer preferences, technological innovations, and policy changes. Just as it rewards those who are prescient, quick, or lucky, it punishes the shortsighted, lethargic, or ill fated. This may not be "fair" in any reasonable sense of the word, but several centuries of criticism of the market system have revealed no close substitutes in the quest for a higher standard of living. As long as we place so much importance on goods and services, the impersonal dynamics of the market will play a major role in our lives. Rightly or wrongly, those who fail the "market test" will lead economically difficult lives.

As we saw in earlier discussions of "free trade," potential losers from economic change have incentives to create barriers that protect their incomes. To the extent these protectionist groups succeed, they keep resources from moving to their most productive uses. The British weekly magazine *The Economist* (April 4, 1992) advocates a hard-nosed attitude toward those who resist the "creative destruction" of the market system:

> Every GM [General Motors] in its death throes releases talent and cash for an upstart like Microsoft, which can make better use of them. The decline and fall of a corporate empire disrupts the lives of thousands. But propping up ailing giants, as governments everywhere are constantly asked to do, only delays the final death-bed scene, as well as the birth of the new. Companies are not enduring institutions. Nor should they be.

You may or may not agree with the implication that government should ignore pleas for protection or relief. The important thing is that you understand the economy-wide costs of such programs. When the government protects a few potential losers in ways that keep resources in relatively inefficient uses, it reduces efficiency, inhibits growth and imposes net losses on the macroeconomy.

ᏬᏩ 14.2 ECONOMIC GROWTH: HOW IMPORTANT IS IT?

Before we launch into the formal analytics of growth, let's take a moment to put this goal in perspective. Economic growth is important to us for a very practical reason—short of turning to a more monastic way of life, it's the only way we can loosen the grip of scarcity on our lives! We can't escape the limits of the PPF, but economic growth allows us to expand those boundaries over time.

Life in an environment without reasonable prospects of growth is notably different than where steady economic growth is the rule, even when the growing economy is actually poorer than the stagnant one. For example, a climate of growth is often the key to making certain activities politically feasible. Whether it's a massive military build-up, the overhaul of an educational system, a "war" on poverty, or a broad-based attempt to establish an economic "safety net" for the disadvantaged, such fundamental redirection of resources may often be easier to sell in a growing economy than in a richer, but sluggish one. We are more willing to share a portion of new gains than we are to give up part of what we already have.[3] In recent years in the U.S. we have been increasingly "generous" in claiming *expected future gains* for the public sector, committing them by law to pay for the growing future costs of various "entitlement" programs. One obvious problem with this is that when gains from growth actually appear they are not available for new projects, public or private, having already been pledged to particular uses. A more serious problem is that overly-optimistic forecasts end up committing more future growth than will actually materialize, a fear that some think could come to pass with recent trends in government entitlements (the "stealth" budget discussed back in Chapter 5).

Economic growth is an outcome of the "web of time" that surrounds every economic choice we make. Our current actions bestow blessings or burdens on our future selves, our children, and even their children. Looking in the other direction, our ancestors' decisions touch our daily lives through their legacy of physical capital, knowledge, and institutions. Their choices set the stage that our actions are rearranging for those who come after us. What this tells us is that growth is an enormously complicated intergenerational issue in which we are constantly renegotiating—individually and collectively, consciously and unconsciously—a compromise between "now" or "later." The complexity of this process should make you suspicious of political slogans and economic fads that promise quick and easy paths to faster growth. At the very best, they'll be only a partial response to a far-reaching issue; at worst, they'll use scarce resources in unproductive ways.

At least since Adam Smith's *An Inquiry into the Nature and Causes of the Wealth of Nations* (1776), the promise of economic growth and its natural and man-made limits has been a central topic in economics. As the free enterprise system developed around the transformations wrought by the industrial revolution, economists and other "worldly philosophers" were understandably intrigued by the question of where all this hustle and bustle of economic activity was leading us.[4] Their predic-

---

[3] This point has been stressed by Moses Abramovitz who sees economic growth as soothing the social and political tensions of redistributive policies. See his *Thinking About Growth: And Other Essays on Economic Growth and Welfare* (New York: Cambridge University Press, 1989).

[4] Following Smith came Thomas Malthus, David Ricardo, John Stuart Mill, Karl Marx, Alfred Marshall, and Joseph Schumpeter (among many others) with more or less elaborate models of the long term dynamics of a market system. For recent discussions that link these earlier models to modern theories of growth, see Moses Abramovitz, *Thinking About Growth: And Other Essays on Economic Growth and Welfare* (New York: Cambridge University Press, 1989) and W. W. Rostow, *Theorists of Economic Growth from David Hume to the Present (With a Perspective on the Next Century)* (New York: Oxford University Press, 1990).

tions differed widely but were seldom optimistic—"population explosion dooming us to subsistence wages," "increasing 'immiserization' of workers and the collapse of capitalism and private property," "a stationary state," "long-term stagnation" and many others. In hindsight, their forecasts profoundly underestimated the power of scientific innovation to propel our standard of living (the same one we are so quick to complain about) to undreamt of heights.

Keynes stood almost alone among the great economists in the extent of his optimism about our economic potential. In a 1930 essay "Economic Possibilities for Our Grandchildren," he prophesied that in a century, if we could avoid major wars and uncontrolled population growth, we would be so far advanced that the condition of scarcity, though still present, would recede into the background.[5] He urged that we "[not] overestimate the importance of the economic problem, or sacrifice to its supposed necessities other matters of greater and more permanent significance. It should be a matter for specialists—like dentistry. If economists could manage to get themselves thought of as humble, competent people, on a level with dentists, that would be splendid!" Keynes acknowledged an ongoing role for those driven by the desire for higher and higher incomes and predicted that these

> *strenuous purposeful money-makers may carry all of us along with them into the lap of economic abundance. But it will be those peoples, who can keep alive, and cultivate into a fuller perfection, the art of life itself and do not sell themselves for the means of life, who will be able to enjoy the abundance when it comes. . . . Thus for the first time since his creation man will be faced with his real, his permanent problem—how to use his freedom from pressing economic cares, how to occupy the leisure, which science and compound interest will have won for him, to live wisely and agreeably and well.*

One wonders how Keynes, returned to the end of the twentieth century, might alter his forecast. Surely he would note that war and population growth have violated the assumed conditions of his forecast. Probably he would be puzzled by our inability or unwillingness to learn that after a certain point the consumption and display of goods and services cannot bring the kind of fulfillment that, Keynes believed, we really seek.

In any event, it's clear that the topic of growth will continue to concern us. We also know that economic growth doesn't happen by accident. It is a predictable consequence of our daily choice, private and public, between consumption now or later. The accumulation of these decisions, not our *words*, reveals our true attitude toward economic growth. This point deserves some emphasis. Opinion polls consistently reveal our worries about a sluggish growth rate. The "Economic Report of the President, 1993" (p. 225)—prepared by the outgoing Bush Administration—offers a good example of the usual (and bipartisan) political platitudes on the subject. "Strong and sustained economic growth is the key to providing Americans with rising real incomes and the resources to meet their needs, desires, and aspirations. Sustained economic growth will also provide employment opportunities and offer people the dignity and self-respect that come with full participation in the economy." The "Economic Report of the President, 1994" (p. 25)—from the Clinton Administration—sings the same refrain. "Productivity growth is the ultimate source of growing real wages and family incomes. Nothing is more important to the long-run well-being of the U.S. economy than accelerating productivity growth. Most of the Administration's economic strategy is therefore devoted to that end."

---

[5] "Economic Possibilities for Our Grandchildren" reprinted in John Maynard Keynes, *Essays in Persuasion* (New York: W. W. Norton & Co., 1963).

It *sounds* like we care a great deal about growth. But there is reason to think that this apparent concern often reveals little more than the truism that "if everything were free, we'd prefer more to less." *A meaningful gauge of the importance of growth must consider how much we're willing to sacrifice for it.* If growth is so important to us why hasn't private saving risen to bring about the additional investment that drives the growth? The reason, in large part, seems to be that we're unwilling to pay the price in reduced current consumption. We continue to talk about how we want more growth but we also pretend that it has nothing to do with the choices, private and public, that we make every day.

The worry that our private consumption-saving choices may be dangerously short-sighted is often used to support the case for government involvement in reducing consumption and increasing national saving and investment. Paul Krugman is representative of many economists who find our indifference, private and public, unfortunate. He maintains that "Productivity growth is the single most important factor affecting our economic well-being. But it is not a policy issue, because we are not going to do anything about it."[6] Others, such as economist Herbert Stein, see our decision not to increase saving and investment to offset the low growth rate of recent years as a conscious choice among alternative goals and one that the government should not necessarily try to overturn. Stein dismisses arguments that we're negligent or irresponsible on the growth issue by noting that

> individuals and families make decisions about [economic growth] . . . every day. They decide how much of their income to consume and how much to save, including saving in the form of investment in the education of their children. And what they invest is not only money but their time and attention in increasing their own earning power and that of their children. These individual decisions added together are the major factor determining the rate of national economic growth.[7]

In Stein's view there is no clear case for the government to mount a policy offensive to alter our private choice between "now or later?"

The pros and cons of government involvement in changing the economy's rate of growth are discussed later in the chapter and in the broader setting of Chapter 16, "The Macroeconomy: Choices, Policies, and Outcomes." Before we can begin to evaluate these arguments properly, we need a better understanding of our options and therefore of the basic dynamics underlying long-term growth.

✿✿ 14.3 THE NEOCLASSICAL MODEL OF ECONOMIC GROWTH

Throughout the book our emphasis has been on understanding cause-and-effect relationships—discovering how various economic events and policies are connected to macroeconomic performance. In extending this approach to long-term growth we quickly encounter the considerable complexities of a fully dynamic analysis. *To make much headway toward a manageable model of long-term growth requires some quite drastic simplifications of the underlying model.* To be specific, analyzing the basic "saving-investment-capital accumulation-output growth" process forces us to ignore nearly

---

[6] Paul Krugman, *The Age of Diminished Expectations: U.S. Economic Policy in the 1990s*, rev. ed. (Cambridge, Mass.: The Massachusetts Institute of Technology Press, 1994), p. 22.

[7] Herbert Stein, *"On the Other Hand . . . Essays on Economics, Economists, and Politics"* (Washington, D.C.: The AEI Press, Publisher for the American Enterprise Institute, 1995), p. 112.

everything else that's going on. And once we get a manageable model of the growth process, there's no simple way to connect it back to many of the important issues and relationships that had to be cut out in the first place. The development of more complete dynamic models is a subject for advanced theoretical analysis. Even learning the simplest kinds of growth models is a challenge, but crucial to a basic understanding of what our current decisions imply for our future well-being.

The dominant analytical model of long-term dynamics is called the **neoclassical growth model** and is derived in large part from the work of Robert Solow, who received the Nobel Prize in economics for his accomplishment.[8] As its name implies, this approach is an extension of the relatively simple long run classical model with its emphasis on the supply side of economic activity. It ignores nearly all the "Keynesian" details of aggregate demand in order to shed some light on long run dynamics. The main **simplifying assumptions** of the most basic version of the "Solow Model" (as it's often called) are

1. Constant market clearing, hence, full employment ($y = y^*$ and $n = n^*$).

2. No government sector ($g = t = 0$) and no foreign sector ($x = 0$).

3. Saving is a given fraction (β) of real income ($s = \beta y^*$).[9]

4. Net investment spending adjusts to the level of saving ($i = s = \beta y^*$).

5. The capital stock grows by the amount of net investment each year ($\Delta k = i = \beta y^*$), so its growth rate is $\%\Delta k = \Delta k/k = \beta y^*/k$.

6. Total output depends on the amount of capital and labor inputs. This relationship is given by the production function $y^* = F(n^*,k)$ and tells us *that the rate of growth of output ($\%\Delta y^*$) is determined entirely by the rate of growth of the inputs $\%\Delta k = \beta y^*/k$ and $\%\Delta n^*$.* The production function is assumed to exhibit

   a. *Diminishing marginal product to each input.* So an increase in labor (holding capital constant) increases output, but by smaller and smaller amounts with successive increments of labor. The same relationship applies to increases in capital (holding labor constant), which are met by diminishing marginal product of capital.

   b. *Constant returns to scale.* This means, to use an example, that a doubling of the amount of *both* inputs will double the amount of output.

7. The rate of growth of the labor supply is fixed and given as $\%\Delta n = \eta$.

8. Any combinations of growth of the two inputs are possible, but for reasons explained later, we'll focus only on situations where *labor and capital are growing at the same rate,* a condition given the imposing name "steady state." Specifically, we assume that $\%\Delta n^* = \%\Delta k$ and use this **steady-state solution** as a vantage point from which to view the impact of various events and policies on economic growth.

---

[8] His original article was "A Contribution to the Theory of Economic Growth," *Quarterly Journal of Economics* (February 1956): 65–94. Solow's subsequent work on growth models is summarized in his *Growth Theory: An Exposition,* 2nd ed. (New York: Oxford University Press, 1988).

[9] This is basically a simplified consumption function relationship, but expressed in terms of saving. Suppose consumption is a proportion of real income $c = \alpha y$, where $0 < \alpha < 1$ and is given. Because $y = c + s$, substitution yields $y = \alpha y + s$ and solving for saving, $s = y - \alpha y = y(1 - \alpha)$. For simplicity of notation we set $1 - \alpha = \beta$, yielding $s = (1 - \alpha)y = \beta y$. In words, because all our income goes to either consumption or saving, the fraction of income going to each must sum to one, $c/y + s/y = 1$. Our assumption is that $c/y = \alpha$ and $s/y = \beta$, so $\alpha + \beta = 1$ and $\beta = 1 - \alpha$.

The preceding list should convince you that we have indeed stripped the macro model down to its barest essentials. The government and foreign sectors are gone and there's hardly anything left of all the *IS-LM* mechanics on the demand side. We've added just a bit of detail to the input-output linkage on the supply side. We now examine the implications of these assumptions (if . . . , then . . .) for economic growth.

1. *The steady state rate of output growth is* η. Because the growth of labor is a given (assumption 7), the "steady state" requires that capital adjust to this same rate of growth (assumption 8) and "constant returns" (assumption 6b) tells us that when the inputs are both growing at a given rate, so must output. It also follows that the *capital-output ratio* is determined entirely by the fraction of income saved (β) and the growth rate of labor (η). That is, because $\%\Delta n^* = \%\Delta k$ in the steady state and because $\%\Delta n^* = \eta$ and $\%\Delta k = \beta y^*/k$, then $\eta = \beta y^*/k$ and $k/y^* = \beta/\eta$.

2. *The economy adjusts automatically toward a steady state growth path.* This is the reason that our attention to the "steady state" is more than just an analytical exercise. To see this, suppose we're initially in a situation where population is growing slower than the capital stock, so we have $\eta < \beta y^*/k$. With $\%\Delta n^* < \%\Delta k$ the capital-output ratio must be rising because the diminishing marginal product of capital means successive increments of $+\Delta k$ create smaller increments of $+\Delta y^*$—thereby diminishing y^*/k and increasing k/y^*.[10] This is portrayed in Figure 14.1 which shows a hypothetical steady state growth path of output across time for an economy with a population growth rate of η.

3. *Changes in the saving rate do not alter the steady state growth* rate. This is an unexpected and, at first glance, counterintuitive result. It says that we can't alter the long term equilibrium growth of output no matter how much or how little we save. Output growth depends only on the rate of population growth. To see why this happens, suppose we reduce our saving rate (to $\beta' < \beta$) causing, initially, $\eta > \beta' y^*/k$. The *immediate* impact of this lower saving (hence lower investment and slower growth of capital) is, of course, for output to grow more slowly as well. But we saw earlier that this slowdown in the growth of capital relative to labor will increase the marginal product of capital (as the marginal product of labor diminishes) and cause the ratio y^*/k to increase. The result is a rise in y^*/k until it offsets the decline in β, restoring the economy to its steady state growth. That is, the drop in the saving rate ($-\Delta\beta$) brings forth an increase in the marginal product of capital (increasing y^*/k) until we once again have $\eta = \beta'(y^*/k)'$. *Even though consumers in this economy have decided to save a smaller fraction of their income, steady state growth continues unchanged at* $\%\Delta y^* = \%\Delta k = \%\Delta n^* = \eta$.

4. *Changes in the saving rate alter the position of the steady state growth path.* This may seem to contradict the previous implication, but it doesn't because this

_____

[10] By similar reasoning if $\eta > \beta y^*/k$ and capital is growing more slowly than labor, diminishing marginal product of labor will mean increasing marginal product of capital (each machine works with more labor support). So k/y^* will diminish and y^*/k rise.

■ FIGURE 14.1

"Steady-state" growth with population growing at the rate η means that %$\Delta y^* = $ %$\Delta k = $ %$\Delta n^* = \eta$. (The vertical axis is a logarithmic scale, so that exponential growth shows up as a straight line.)

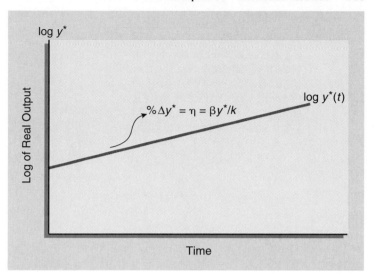

is about the *level* of output, not its *rate of growth*. Changing the amount we save definitely affects our standard of living—even in the abstract world of the Solow model. To appreciate how the saving rate makes a difference, let's turn to Figure 14.2. Along the first segment of the growth path (from 0 to t_0) we see an economy moving smoothly along a steady state path with %$\Delta y^* = $ %$\Delta k = $ %$\Delta n^* = \eta$. But suppose that at time t_0 the saving rate drops from β to β'. This reduction in saving means a lower level of net investment and reduced capital growth. With the capital input growing more slowly, output growth must also decline as shown by the flatter path between t_0 and t_1.

But this reduced growth of capital, as explained above, sets in motion a rise in y^*/k until the economy eventually resumes growth at the steady-state rate $\eta = \beta'(y^*/k)'$. *So even though the growth rate is ultimately unaffected by the drop in the amount we save, it's clear that reduced saving means a lower steady state growth path, shown as the segment after* t_1 *in Figure 14.2.* Comparing this new path with an extension of the original growth path (the dotted line), it is apparent that this drop in saving has resulted in a drop in the *level* of real output for this economy.

Taking this a step further, Figure 14.3 shows two initially identical economies growing along the same steady state growth path up to time t_0. At this point suppose Economy A decides to maximize its saving by increasing β to nearly 1, cutting consumption to a subsistence level. Economy Z goes to the other extreme by reducing β to virtually 0 and increasing consumption to get all it can today, with no thought of tomorrow. After the transition period the growth rates of both economies have returned to η, the steady-state rate of population growth. But the steady-state paths—the levels of real output—diverge noticeably as Figure 14.3 reveals.

5. *The highest steady state growth path of output will* not *yield the highest consumption path.* It might be tempting to conclude from the implication above that

■ **FIGURE 14.2**

A decline in the saving rate (from β to β') at time t_0 reduces the rate of growth of output during the transition period (t_0 to t_1) as $y*/k$ rises ($y*/k$ to $(y*/k)'$). Once the steady state is restored at t_1, growth resumes at the rate η but along a *lower* growth path.

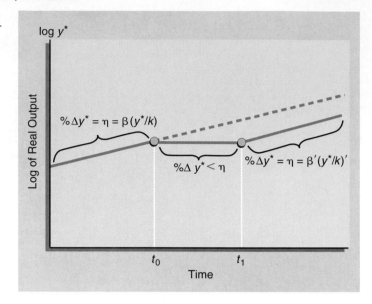

economy A would be the best place to live, since its steady state growth path is at the highest level of output. But remember that this economy has pared its current consumption down to subsistence and is devoting most of its output to producing future consumption. *It can sustain this high growth path only by continually sacrificing the present to the future.* It's the miser who remains in poverty in order to grow richer faster. For most of us this would be an inviting place to live only if it put more emphasis on *current* consumption by reducing the saving rate ($-\Delta\beta$). But we've seen that lowering β moves the economy to a lower income path. So in making current consumption a larger slice of our lifetime pie, we are causing that pie to shrink

■ **FIGURE 14.3**

Two economies begin on the same steady-state growth path with population growth η and saving rate β. At t_0 economy A decides to cut consumption to subsistence and maximize its saving ($\beta \rightarrow 1$). After a transition it reaches the higher steady-state growth path log $y*^A(t)$. In contrast, economy Z decides to maximize its consumption. Cutting saving to virtually zero at t_0 ($\beta \rightarrow 0$) it falls to the lower steady-state path, log $y*^Z(t)$. Both economies continue to grow at the same steady-state rate but with very different *levels* of income.

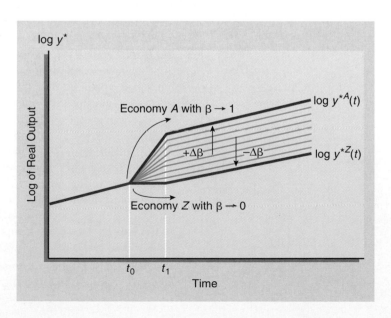

as well. If we go all the way to economy Z, common sense tells us that our large slice of a small pie won't provide much lifetime nourishment.

Somewhere between economy A (small slice of a large pie) and economy Z (large slice of a small pie), there's a steady state income path (not shown in Figure 14.3) that contains the highest consumption path. This economy G has a combined size of slice (β^G) and size of pie (growth path $\log y^{*G}(t)$) that yields the highest consumption path among alternative steady state growth paths. It is called the *Golden Rule growth path.*[11]

6. *Technological change is the* only *way that steady-state output per person can be increased in the Solow model.* In our analysis so far, output in the steady state has been growing at the same rate as the population, leaving output per person unchanged. But this is obviously not what most of us have in mind when we think of economic growth. We expect continuing increases in output per head. If this model can't explain such rising productivity over time, it's missing the single most important process in modern economic life.

The Solow model incorporates rising productivity by going outside the model and invoking an exogenous change in the **technology** with which we combine our labor and capital inputs. These increases in productivity can be incorporated into the analysis in several ways. Their common trait is that they increase the growth of output by making one or more of the existing inputs more efficient. For example, suppose that ongoing technological change increases the amount that each worker can produce by the rate γ. If we were initially on a steady state path with the quantity of all inputs and output growing at the rate η, this innovation tilts that path to a steady state growing at the rate $\eta + \gamma$. This is illustrated in Figure 14.4. *In this new steady state, output and capital are now growing at the rate $\eta + \gamma$ but population still at the rate η. Therefore, output per head is growing at the rate of productivity growth γ.*[12]

The six results above are logical implications (if . . . , then . . .) of the eight assumptions of the streamlined, stripped-down neoclassical (Solow) growth model. It's easy and tempting to criticize this exercise as pitifully incomplete and unrealistic. It ignores most of the interactions that we incorporated into the AD/AS^e framework and most of the economic events that we'd find in a statistical investigation of the patterns of economic growth in industrial nations over the past two centuries. Its main message seems to be "get as much technological improvement as you can." Of course we don't need a fancy steady state model to know the importance of productivity change. Moreover, because technological change is exogenous to the simple

---

[11] This notion was originally formulated in Edmund Phelps, "The Golden Rule of Accumulation: A Fable for Growthmen," *American Economic Review* (September 1961): 638–643. Its name comes from the fact that it's the only steady state path that meets an inter-generational "golden rule" criterion of "do unto future generations as you wish past generations had done unto you." If the economy is currently on a growth path below the Golden Rule path this requires it to raise β and, during the transition to the Golden Rule path, reduce its level of consumption. Depending on the adjustment speed, this could mean a substantial sacrifice of our current well-being in order to benefit all future generations. Accordingly the concept of a Golden Rule path is more of a lighthouse to give us our bearings than a destination. But something like a Golden Rule notion was presumably the rationale behind the infamous Five-Year Plans of the Soviet economy, when the production of consumer goods was severely limited to force more resources into capital accumulation via "forced saving."

[12] The steady-state situation is modified so that capital and the *effective* labor supply grow at the same rate. With labor productivity augmented by the amount γ, the effective labor supply is growing at $\eta + \gamma$. Following the same steps to determining the steady state rate as we did in implication 1, this leads to $k/y^* = \beta/(\eta + \gamma)$. The result will be $\%\Delta y^* = \eta + \gamma$ and $\%\Delta k = \eta + \gamma$. But because $\Delta n^* = \eta$, output per head will be growing at $\%\Delta y^* - \%\Delta n^* = (\eta + \gamma) - \eta = \gamma$.

■ **FIGURE 14.4**

An economy in steady-state growth $[\%\Delta y^* = \eta]$ experiences technological change at t_0 that increases worker productivity by the rate γ each year. This raises the steady-state growth path to that labeled $\%\Delta y^* = \eta + \gamma$.

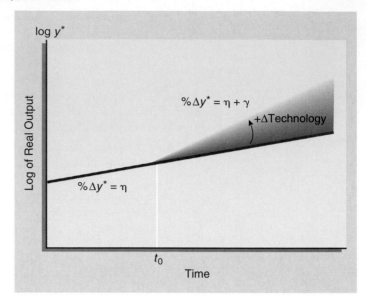

neoclassical model, it gives us no hints as to *how* to do this. Nor does it tell us anything at all about the role of the institutional structure in setting a favorable climate for growth.

What we'd obviously like is a richer framework that brings technological change inside the analysis, transforming it from an unexplained exogenous force into a well-understood endogenous variable. For example, we'd like our model to explain the link between *spending on research and development* and the resulting *technological change*. We'd also like it to address the connection between the *quality of labor (human capital)* and *spending on education and training*. As long as we're making a "wish list," we'd like our growth model to encompass the *economic determinants of population change and institutional change*. These and other topics are exactly what modern models of economic growth seek to address. They start from the basic Solow model but quickly reach quite advanced levels of theoretical analysis. Promising as they appear, they have not yet progressed to the point where they provide clear, practical conclusions for policymaking.[13]

Because an incomplete structure is more complete than none at all, we continue to rely on the neoclassical growth model for its careful insights into the nature of the long-term growth process. By adding the fundamental "saving-investment-capital accumulation and output growth" sequence $(s > 0 \Rightarrow i > 0 \Rightarrow +\%\Delta k \Rightarrow +\%\Delta y^*)$ to our analysis, it provides a technique for examining the long term sustainability of certain short run policies and events in a "steady state" setting.

Although it can be useful to know where long term steady state tendencies of current conditions are leading us, our actual growth experience is usually one in which underlying conditions and policies are constantly changing. The result is that most economies are in a continuing transition that cuts back and forth across the broad and meandering stream of steady state paths. In terms of Figure 14.5, chang-

---

[13] For a look at these advanced models see Olivier Jean Blanchard and Stanley Fischer, *Lectures on Macroeconomics* (Cambridge, Mass.: The Massachusetts Institute of Technology Press, 1989); and Costas Azariadis, *Intertemporal Macroeconomics* (Cambridge, Mass.: Blackwell Publishers, 1993).

■ FIGURE 14.5

A decline in technological change (productivity growth) from γ to γ' alters the steady-state growth rate. Changes in the saving rate ($\Delta\beta$) move us back and forth *within* a steady-state stream. A hypothetical economy experiencing periodic changes in β as well as the drop in γ at t_0 could have an *actual growth path* like log $y^{*H}(t)$.

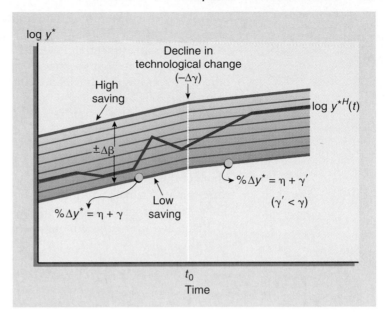

ing the saving rate will cause a transition to a higher or lower path within a given steady state stream. Changes in the pace of technological change (or labor force growth) will actually divert the stream itself, as shown in the graph.

So a hypothetical Economy H, experiencing several changes in the saving rate ($\pm \Delta\beta$) and a productivity drop ($-\Delta\gamma$) might, over several decades, trace out an *actual* growth path as shown in Figure 14.5. But because incorporating such changing conditions into the neoclassical analytics makes it too cumbersome, we clearly need another approach—one that will not do violence to the basic theoretical insights we've gained, but that will provide a practical framework for evaluating the impacts of various policies and events on the actual growth rates of actual economies. An obvious place to turn is to the actual experience of many nations over many years. Can history give us some helpful quantitative clues as to why some economies, at some times, grow rapidly while at other places and other times growth becomes so elusive?

14.4 EMPIRICAL MODELS OF ECONOMIC GROWTH

Searching for patterns in the existing data on economic growth sounds both sensible and easy in these days of cheap, fast personal computers, on-line data bases, and easy-to-use statistical software. Your common sense probably tells you that this is a more promising line of attack than manipulating highly abstract mathematical models of the macroeconomy. The **empirical approach** does have much to contribute, but perhaps not as much as you think. It has some real limitations and, by itself, can be extremely misleading.

To begin with, the difficulties involved in obtaining the underlying data are enormous. Even for countries with relatively sophisticated systems of national accounting, like the United States, we must often settle for rough approximations to the concepts we'd really like to measure. As we'll see in the next chapter, there is controversy over whether certain kinds of economic activity should be included in total output or not. There are similar disputes over exactly what should be counted in saving and investment and over how to incorporate *quality* changes in labor, capital, and output into our measures. Apart from these conceptual disagreements, the official data in some countries are simply unreliable. On top of all this are problems in making comparisons across economies with very different public/private structures, not to mention currencies.

In the face of such obstacles, empirical researchers have done a remarkably good job of weaving a large quantitative tapestry of national and international economic activity that has become increasingly useful and continues to be improved. Much of the pioneering empirical work on economic growth was done by Nobel laureate Simon Kuznets and many careful researchers have followed in his footsteps.[14] They have uncovered a number of patterns underlying the growth process across countries and over time. Among these **"stylized facts"** of economic growth are the following:

1. A consistent trait of growing economies is the relative *growth of both the manufacturing and service sectors* (as a percent of total output) and a dramatic *reduction of the agricultural sector* in terms of both employment and percent of total output. Resources flow steadily from farming to other sectors. This is accompanied by *increasing urbanization* as the population becomes more and more concentrated in economically efficient industrial centers.

2. The presence of *natural resources is not a necessary precondition for economic growth*. As long as a nation is able to trade for needed raw materials, the lack of its own natural resources has not been a barrier to growth. The rapid levels of growth in Japan, Korea, Hong Kong, Taiwan, and Singapore are recent examples of success through trading manufactured goods to obtain raw materials. In the 19th Century the tiny island of Great Britain was home to the industrial revolution and the world's highest overall standard of living.

3. *In recent decades virtually all nations have experienced economic growth*. Although the gap between richest and poorest remains wide—a factor of about 29 for the years 1960 to 1985—it has remained nearly unchanged.[15]

4. An important historical event is one we happen to be living through now— the marked *slowdown in productivity growth* that has continued for more than two decades. This is a worldwide phenomenon that can't be attributed to events or policies specific to the United States. We will discuss this separately in the next section of this chapter.

5. The data also indicate that economies with strong records of growth tend to be those with the most *stable macroeconomic performance*—the absence of

---

[14] See Simon Kuznets, *Modern Economic Growth: Rate, Structure and Spread* (New Haven: Yale University Press, 1966) and *Toward a Theory of Economic Growth* (New York: W. W. Norton & Co., 1968). For recent work in this area see Hollis B. Chenery and Moshe Syrquin, *Patterns of Development, 1950–1970* (Oxford: Oxford University Press, 1975); Angus Maddison, *Dynamic Forces in Capitalist Development: A Long-Run Comparative View* (Oxford: Oxford University Press, 1991); and Robert Summers and Alan Heston, "The Penn World Table (Mark 5): An Expanded Set of International Comparisons, 1950–88," *Quarterly Journal of Economics* (May 1991): 327–368.

[15] These findings are from a compilation of results for 102 countries by Stephen L. Parente and Edward C. Prescott, "Changes in the Wealth of Nations," *Quarterly Review*, Federal Reserve Bank of Minneapolis (spring 1993): 3–16. They also observe that "There have been development miracles and disasters. During the 1960–85 period, 10 countries increased their wealth relative to the wealth leaders by a factor of 2 or more. These miracles were matched by an equal number of development disasters: during the same period, the relative wealth of another 10 countries decreased by a factor of about 2."

extremes in terms of recession and inflation.[16] It is also apparent that economic growth is accompanied by an *increased role of government* as both a regulator of the private sector and as a direct economic participant.

6. Economic growth occurs at a faster pace in economies with higher educational and skill levels. We'd expect *output* to be higher in economies with higher levels of "human capital." And where the growth of human capital is higher, we'd expect this to increase output growth. But it's not obvious why the *rate of growth of output* should be higher in countries where skill levels are higher but not growing. Nevertheless, this relationship appears to hold across many nations.

Other patterns of growth have been uncovered, but these are enough to give you the spirit of the approach. By turning to the "facts" we hope to paint not only a broad brush picture of economic change, but one that reveals a common core of growth characteristics to guide policy makers. This approach can obviously be important in clarifying what has worked and not worked in the past. However, we must not forget that "facts don't speak for themselves." Without an analytical structure to drape these facts around, they are quite formless and can tell us very little if anything about cause and effect. For example, how should we interpret the finding that spending on education and training programs is positively related to economic growth? It could be that countries that experience higher rates of growth can simply afford to increase their investment in human capital, turning the causality in the other direction and not giving us the clear policy link we're seeking. Similarly, the growth of the relative size of government may be as much a result of economic growth as a cause. In fact we can easily think of ways in which government involvement is often quite harmful to growth.

What's missing is an analytical framework that can combine with the data to help us sort out issues of cause-and-effect that often run in two (or more) directions simultaneously. It should also be noted that a simple model can yield important insights long before they are uncovered in the data. For example, one implication of Ricardo's Theorem of Comparative Advantage and the gains from trade is that nations poor in natural resources can nevertheless prosper by specializing in other areas and trading for needed resources. While empirical evidence is always welcome, policy makers didn't need to wait for the development of national income accounts and the work of Simon Kuznets to act on this important relationship.

In short, reliance on "stylized facts" alone can provide little understanding of the underlying workings of the macroeconomy. A useful, practical approach must go further. Specifically, we need to stick our necks out and take a chance of being wrong by superimposing a cause-and-effect structure on the facts. In other words, we need to use a model that embodies a set of assumptions and hypotheses about key interactions. But we want to do this in a way that avoids the analytical complexities encountered in extensions of the neoclassical growth model.

This is just what the **growth accounting model** attempts to provide. It falls somewhere between the extremes of "stylized facts" and "steady-state models." It is strongly empirical but recognizes that facts can't "speak" without a causal framework and some assumptions about basic interactions. To retain manageability it uses only a

---

[16] As we saw in Chapter 10, a politically independent central bank seems to be an important factor in controlling inflation. But, as we also found (in Chapter 9), there is lack of agreement on the extent to which stabilization policies smooth fluctuations in output and employment.

rudimentary model, one that focuses on specific properties of the aggregate production function linking inputs to outputs. This alternative to the Solow steady state models was also developed by Robert Solow in a second major contribution to the growth literature.[17]

Following Solow, we begin with a production function that relates the level of real output at full employment (y^*) to the levels of three inputs—labor (n^*), capital (k), and technology (a). We make the standard assumptions of *diminishing marginal product for increases* in either capital or labor and *constant returns to scale* in capital and labor (discussed in section 14.3). The new wrinkle is in the third input. *Technology is assumed to augment both capital and labor equally, essentially magnifying their individual productivities.* We can represent these assumptions in the following relationship:

$$y^* = a \cdot F(n^*, k)$$

where the index of technology a is sometimes called a measure of **total factor productivity** since it amplifies changes in *both* labor and capital. Converting this relationship from *levels* to *rates of change* we can rewrite it (approximately) as:

$$\%\Delta y^* = \%\Delta a + \lambda_n \%\Delta n^* + \lambda_k \%\Delta k$$

where the λs represent the responsiveness (or elasticity) of output growth to the growth of the labor and capital inputs. A 1% increase in n^* causes a λ_n% increase in y^*; and a 1% increase in k causes output to grow by λ_k%. The assumption of constant returns allows a very important simplification since the λs can be interpreted as the *relative shares* ($\lambda_n + \lambda_k = 1$) of labor and capital in national income—numbers that can be readily calculated from available data.

Applying this framework to the U.S. for the years 1909–1949, Solow calculated the share of labor income in total income (λ_n) as 70%, leaving 30% as capital's share (λ_k), so that

$$\%\Delta y^* = \%\Delta a + (.7)\%\Delta n^* + (.3)\%\Delta k$$

Adding data for the growth of the quantities of inputs ($\%\Delta n$ and $\%\Delta k$) and the growth of the value of real output ($\%\Delta y$), he was then able to calculate the annual growth of technology ($\%\Delta a$) as whatever was left. That is, we can get an indirect measure of technological change from the following relationship because everything on the right hand side is measurable:

$$\%\Delta a = \%\Delta y - (.7)\%\Delta n^* - (.3)\%\Delta k$$

Solow's actual calculations were in per capita terms (instead of totals), but his startling finding was that a huge 88% of the actual growth in real output per capita could not be attributed to the growth of labor and capital inputs. This way of calculating $\%\Delta a$ as a residual obviously includes *anything* that affects output growth but was excluded from the measured values of the variables on the right hand side of the earlier equation. But Solow and others suggested that this primarily reflected the over-

---

[17] Robert M. Solow, "Technical Change and the Aggregate Production Function," *Review of Economics and Statistics* (August 1957): 312–320.

whelming quantitative importance of **technological change** to improvements in our standard of living—a theoretical implication we saw earlier in Solow's steady state model.

Explaining this "Solow residual" is a challenge that has attracted much research activity. What part of the 88% is truly due to technological change and what part to other unmeasured factors, including errors in the underlying concepts and measures of both output ($\%\Delta y$) and the inputs ($\%\Delta n$ and $\%\Delta k$)? Edward Denison's subsequent research was both thorough and careful.[18] In a series of studies over many years, Denison developed and refined the growth accounting approach. Using the same framework as above, Denison calculated that for the years 1929–82, the actual growth of real output in the United States averaged 2.92% per year. Having refined the concepts and measures of the capital and labor inputs substantially, he calculated that just 0.56% of this growth came from capital [the $(.3)\%\Delta k$ term], 1.34% came from growth of the labor input [the $(.7)\%\Delta n^*$ term], leaving 1.02% for the residual growth in technology term ($\%\Delta a$). That is,

$$\%\Delta y^* = \%\Delta a + (.7)\%\Delta n^* + (.3)\%\Delta k$$
$$2.92\% = 1.02\% + 1.34\% + 0.56\%$$

Many other researchers have worked on further improving the underlying data, with various adjustments for the quality of inputs and outputs and other alterations. But the basic picture that emerges from data on many countries over many years is much the same—the lion's share of the growth in output per person is *not* accounted for by more capital goods. It is the result of changes in technology and other difficult-to-measure variables. And the big economic news of the past twenty years is that this productivity growth has taken a worldwide plunge!

14.5 WHY HAS PRODUCTIVITY GROWTH SLOWED?

A look at Figure 14.6 confirms the experience of hundreds of millions of people, individually and collectively, over the last twenty years. We've suffered a significant and widespread slowdown in the growth of our standard of living. Accusations from the media and the politicians about "who or what's responsible for our anemic growth rates?" attract much attention, particularly when they're linked to other emotional issues like budget deficits, trade deficits, and inefficient government. Sometimes the allegations and the pessimism are so intense that it's hard to remember that real output hasn't fallen; it has only been growing less rapidly.

While the popular diagnoses and prescriptions are often superficial and sometimes quite preposterous, this mustn't blind us to the seriousness of the issue. This worldwide slowdown in the growth of output per head is a notable feature of the late twentieth century's economic landscape. And since even small annual differences are magnified into large absolute differences when compounded over a number of years, this means that our current standard of living is significantly lower, perhaps as much

---

[18] Edward F. Denison, *Trends in American Economic Growth, 1929–1982* (Washington, D.C.: The Brookings Institution, 1985). Also see Dale W. Jorgenson, Frank M. Gollop, and Barbara M. Fraumeni, *Productivity and U.S. Economic Growth* (Cambridge, Mass.: Harvard University Press, 1974).

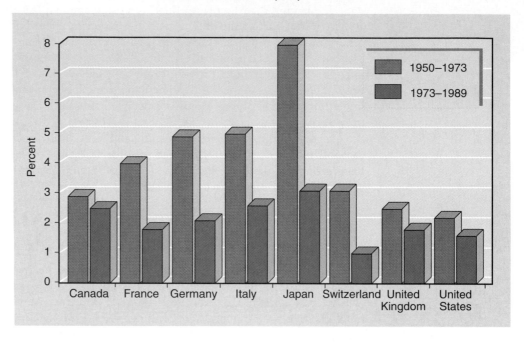

Growth Slowdown
(1950–1973 and 1973–1989)
Growth of Real Output per Person

■ FIGURE 14.6

From Angus Maddison, *Dynamic Forces in Capitalist Development* (Oxford: Oxford University Press, 1991), p. 49.

as 25%, than if output growth had continued along its previous path. Even if we return to a higher long term rate of growth soon, which does not appear likely, these effects will be noticeable well into the next century.

Not surprisingly, this issue has received much attention from economists as well as non-economists. Can "growth accounting," with its blend of theory and practicality, identify specific sources of declining growth and suggest some policy responses? Much research has focused on this problem. Denison, for example, separated his findings (noted earlier for the period 1929–1982) into subperiods as shown in Figure 14.7. The decisive event is clearly the *negative* productivity growth (%Δa = −0.26%) during the 1973 to 1982 period. Although this gives us the important information that dwindling growth rates have *not* come from a significant slowdown in the growth of labor or capital, it doesn't reveal why the "technology etc." residual (%Δa) has fallen so drastically.

There are scores of vaguely plausible reasons for the productivity decline and we hear them often—the "twin deficits"; changes in the composition of the workforce; the decline in SAT scores; the decline in the work ethic; the rise of greed and shortsightedness; a pessimistic and cynical media; unfair competition from abroad; oil price shocks; government—some say it's doing "too much," other's "not enough," and this then leads to the familiar accusations against particular presidents and politi-

Sources of U.S. Output Growth
(Percent per Year)

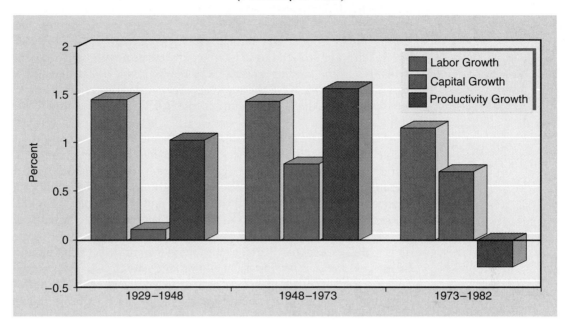

■ FIGURE 14.7

From Edward F. Denison, *Trends in American Economic Growth, 1929–1982* (Washington, D.C.: The Brookings Institution, 1985), p. 111.

cal parties. Some argue that the productivity decline is at least partly imaginary—an error in our national accounting system because of our inability to adequately measure improvements in the *quality* of output (especially high-technology goods and services).[19] Others suggest that we may simply have returned to a rate of "normal" sustainable long-term growth and that, for a variety of economic and political reasons, the post–World War II high-growth period was an historical aberration. Some, echoing the pessimism of nineteenth-century economists, think we are bumping up against some inevitable limits and that growth in per capita output will continue to diminish.[20]

This list of indictments could go on and on. But to make a long story very short, *we do not have a convincing explanation for this worldwide slowdown in the rate of growth of full employment output.* Some of the alleged causes may be correct, but

[19] See Michael Darby, in "Causes of Declining Growth," *Policies for Long-Run Economic Growth*, Federal Reserve Bank of Kansas City (1992): 5–13. Also see Martin N. Baily and Robert J. Gordon, "The Productivity Slowdown, Measurement Issues, and the Explosion of Computer Power," *Brookings Papers on Economic Activity* 2(1988): 347–420.

[20] John Stuart Mill, for example, said that "It must always have been seen, more or less distinctly by political economists, that the increase of wealth is not boundless: that at the end of what they term the progressive state lies the stationary state, that all progress in wealth is but a postponement of this, and that each step in advance is an approach to it." *Principles of Political Economy*, 1848, cited in Moses Abramovitz, *Thinking about Growth: And Other Essays on Economic Growth & Welfare* (New York: Cambridge University Press, 1989), p. 6.

studies find their quantitative impacts to be far too small to explain most of the slow-down. For others, the timing is not quite right. If the jump in oil prices was the cause, why didn't growth resume as the real price of oil returned to preshock levels during the 1980s? Many on this list have been specific to the U.S. and can't account for the global scope of the decline. The "government" is always a popular scapegoat, but this drop in growth rates has afflicted countries with very different governmental structures, some moving toward more public involvement during the period, some less. The closer we look, the more apparent it becomes that we have not found the "smoking gun" that would convict the party guilty of diminishing our rate of growth.[21]

Economist or noneconomist, it is difficult for us to admit ignorance on such a visible, vital issue. In the absence of strong evidence, we gravitate toward pet theories that are likely to fit our personal preconceptions far better than they fit the statistical evidence. There's nothing wrong with this as long as we remember that it's not good science and is not likely to lead to effective and responsible policy making. But until researchers come up with a convincing explanation, such casual theorizing will fill the vacuum and the productivity slowdown will remain a highly politicized issue. This makes it particularly important to understand that just because we haven't iden-tified a specific cause of the decline in productivity growth doesn't mean we can't use policy actions to offset its effects. Even if we don't know the cause of the illness we may still be able to find effective treatments for its symptoms. This leads us to the concluding section of this discussion of economic growth.

⚙⚙ 14.6 MACROECONOMIC POLICY AND ECONOMIC GROWTH

In popular discussions "growth policy" usually refers to any program designed to in-crease output and diminish unemployment—including short run fiscal and monetary expansion as well as long term policies designed to increase the productivity of labor and capital inputs. To minimize confusion we need to make a clear distinction be-tween **stabilization policy** (designed to deal with economic recovery and the main-tenance of full employment and stable inflation) and **growth policy** designed to in-crease the full employment level of output itself. Stabilization policy focuses on controlling the *level of aggregate demand (IS-LM* and *AD)* so as to minimize deviations from full employment, while growth policy sets its sights on *expanding the supply side* ($+\%\Delta AS^*$ and $\%\Delta$PPF).

Going one step further, let's also distinguish growth policy from *one-shot supply side policies*. For example, a permanent drop in trade barriers or a reduction in labor market frictions both mean a lasting outward shift in our productive potential. But they do not cause the continuing outward shifts associated with economic growth. In terms of the neoclassical growth model, they would act like an increase in saving— shift the steady state growth path upward but leave its slope (the rate of growth) un-changed (see Figure 14.3).

---

[21] See Federal Reserve Bank of Kansas City, *Policies for Long-Run Economic Growth* (Symposium 1992), and "Sym-posium: The Slowdown in Productivity Growth," *The Journal of Economic Perspectives* (fall 1988): 3–98, for the views of leading researchers in this area, including Charles Plosser, J. Bradford DeLong, Lawrence Summers, Zvi Griliches, Dale W. Jorgenson, Mancur Olson, and Michael Boskin.

Growth policy, then, is aimed at the very ambitious and important goal of creating ongoing increases in our full employment level of output. Good economics demands that we remind ourselves that any such policy—simple or elaborate, effective or worthless—has *costs* along with the hoped-for benefits. The primary cost of economic growth, as we've seen, is the sacrifice of consumption now (private or public) to move resources into activities that are expected to increase inputs and generate higher consumption later. Let's presume, then, that we're all aware that a higher growth rate requires us to reduce current consumption and that we're willing to make the sacrifice.[22] But we naturally want to be sure that these resources are used wisely. We want the best return for our money when we buy "economic growth," just as when we buy a car or an education. What insights can macroeconomic analysis provide about effective policies to increase growth?

The answer is a brief "*Very Little!*" The processes underlying the allocation of resources among different uses (this or that? now or later?) are at the heart of ***microeconomic analysis.*** Macroeconomics offers little help in understanding which *specific* policies can most effectively increase saving or which *specific* investment projects, public or private, yield the largest future payoffs from the use of these savings. This doesn't mean that it has *nothing* to contribute to growth policy making. Macroeconomics gives an overview of the growth process that highlights the main interactions and provides a coherent framework for identifying the key microeconomic issues. There's no law against combining micro and macro analysis and many researchers are doing just that. But we've had our hands full just doing *macro*economics for fourteen chapters. Since we've not taken time to develop the basic microeconomic tools, any foray into the microanalytics of growth would have to be superficial and could potentially be misleading.

So rather than going on a micro search for specific high-yield public and private investment projects, let's stick with our comparative advantage and use the macroeconomic perspective to sketch a rough map that we can then hand to microeconomists to fill in the details. The following text box characterizes the growth process as a set of connections that run from *reduced consumption* to *saving* to *investment* (broadly defined[23]) to *input growth* and finally to *output growth*. We'll use it to structure our discussion of the elements of growth policy.

---

[22] As we discussed earlier in the chapter, it is not inevitable that we will make such a choice. The lack of real steps in this direction over the last two decades might well mean that we are *not* willing to pay the price for higher growth. Alternatively, it may be that we're willing to pay the cost but are hesitating to implement policies because we're unable to agree on which steps are best.

[23] So think of "investment" as activities that improve the quality of labor (education and training), enhance technological change (research and development), increase the quantity and efficiency of public capital, as well as the traditional increase of plant and equipment.

INCREASING ECONOMIC GROWTH

Resources must be withdrawn from current consumption (private and public, $-\Delta c$ and $-\Delta g^c$) in order to increase national saving ($+\Delta ns = +\Delta(s-b)$). This increased saving, combined with any increased net capital inflows from abroad (trade deficits, $-\Delta x$), must then be channeled through capital markets to increased investment ($+\Delta i$), increased rate of input growth ($+\%\Delta n,k,a,i^{nst}$), and finally, faster output growth ($+\%\Delta y^*$).

$$
\begin{matrix}
-\Delta c & & & & +\%\Delta n^* \\
\text{and} \Rightarrow +\Delta(s-b) \Rightarrow +\Delta ns \Rightarrow +\Delta i \Rightarrow & \begin{matrix} +\%\Delta k \\ +\%\Delta a \end{matrix} & \Rightarrow +\%\Delta y^* \\
-\Delta g^c & & \text{and} & \text{and} & +\%\Delta i^{nst} \\
& & -\Delta x & +\Delta g^i &
\end{matrix}
$$

1. *Raise national saving.* An obvious place to stimulate growth is at the initial stage where national saving (ns) is determined by the amount of resources released from private and public consumption (c or g^c). National saving is the sum of private and public saving or $ns = s - b$.[24] A general **tax rate increase** with government spending unchanged, will reduce consumption and increase national saving, the extent depending on the degree of both tax-discounting and liquidity-constrained behavior. More specific policies designed to increase private saving involve various combinations of specific taxes or subsidies to make consumption less attractive and saving more.[25] Another path to higher national saving is to **cut public consumption expenditures** ($-\Delta g^c$) and **raise public investment** ($+\Delta g^i$). Although cutting public investment spending would also decrease the deficit and increase national saving, it would do so by reducing a source of capital formation which would lower the growth rate.

2. *Increase the trade deficit.* This may seem like a peculiar policy to use for growth. Most people think of the trade deficit as part of the growth "problem," not the solution. But remember that running a trade deficit ($x < 0$) makes a nation a net borrower from abroad. It is temporarily reaching beyond its PPF in exchange for a promise to consume inside the PPF later when the external loan is repaid. We saw that a current account deficit in

---

[24] Public saving is given by the difference between tax revenues and government spending or $t - g$. In reality, of course, this saving is a negative number equal to the size of the cash flow deficit. Because the deficit is $b = g - t$, then rearranging we get public saving $= t - g = -b$.

[25] Consumption or "value-added" taxes can be one way to do this while subsidies or tax breaks for saving are another. The specifics of such incentive/disincentive issues require a careful microeconomic analysis.

(Continued)

the balance of payments is essentially the mirror image of a **capital account surplus.** These external funds mix with our internal national saving in the capital market where, through financial intermediation, they are made available for various investment purposes.

For more than a decade, national saving in the United States has diminished because of a reduction in private saving and an increase in the public deficit. This increase in resources going into consumption would have meant a severe drop in investment in the U.S. and a huge decline in growth had it not been for the influx of foreign savings virtually offsetting our decline in national saving so that the level of investment spending could be maintained. For the poorest nations of the world, unable to generate any national saving, the *only hope* for higher growth is through external borrowing, i.e., a rising trade deficit.

The obvious difference between increased national saving and an increased trade deficit is that when we borrow from abroad we have to pay it back plus interest, whereas when we save internally we get to keep the whole return. But the less obvious flip-side is that when we borrow externally we don't have to sacrifice *current* consumption ($-\Delta c$ and $-\Delta g^c$) as we do when we increase our national saving. Instead, we sacrifice *future* consumption plus interest. Whether we end up with a net gain or loss depends, of course, on the return on the use of the borrowed funds relative to the cost of borrowing them.

External borrowing has not been an explicit U.S. policy. As we saw back in Chapter 7, it happened because high real interest rates in the U.S. attracted saving, in the process increasing the demand for dollars and pushing up the real exchange rate. This was the consequence of active international capital markets in a system of flexible exchange rates.

3. *Increase investment spending.* The amount of investment spending depends primarily on the level of our national saving and the amount of net foreign borrowing (points 1 and 2). But even with those funds fixed, investment spending can be increased by raising its net return to the user. This involves policies that offer tax breaks or subsidies for investment activities. Some examples include lowering the *capital gains tax*, increasing the *investment tax credit*, increasing *accelerated depreciation allowances* for tax purposes, and expanding the *deductibility of interest costs* for home mortgages to other loans. Such investment subsidies are highly visible and generally popular, in part because most people forget that a subsidy to one group is a tax to another. For a given level of government spending, the tax breaks given for

(Continued)

investment activities must become tax hikes for some other activity either now or (with deficit financing) later.

However, it must be noted that working to offset this loss of revenues is the possibility that the lower tax rate will increase the *tax base* by a larger absolute amount than it decreases the *tax rate*— $| -\%\Delta t_1 | < +\%\Delta y^*$—thereby generating *increased* tax revenues $(+\Delta(t_1 y^*) \rightarrow +\Delta t \rightarrow -\Delta b)$ and actually *reducing the budget deficit*. This is the hypothesis, most economists would say "wishful thinking," underlying the notion of **supply-side economics** that emerged in the late 1970s and came to have a decisive influence in the huge tax cut instituted by the Reagan administration and Congress in 1981. Much has been written about this subject but virtually everyone who has examined the issue carefully has found that it assumes an unrealistically large response of the tax base to the reduced tax rate.

This is not to say that cutting tax rates doesn't alter incentives and increase the tax base. They clearly do, some kinds of taxes more than others. And this needs to be carefully considered when devising tax hikes to reduce the budget deficit. But the evidence is that the *net* result of lower tax rates is lower tax revenues, hence a rising deficit. Selected tax cuts still may be a useful thing to do in terms of stimulating economic growth. But there is no evidence to justify pretending that lower tax rates will reduce the government's deficit.

4. *Increase the productivity of the inputs.* For a given amount of national saving (point 1) and foreign capital (point 2) flowing into investment activities (point 3) and thereby increasing input growth, we can boost the growth of output further if we can *increase the productivity of these inputs*. This raises the very controversial issue of whether government policy can channel these resources into more efficient directions than will the private capital market. The popular name for this plan to have the government "pick winners" in the capital markets is **industrial policy.** Because it involves the use of tax breaks, subsidies, and direct government investment toward certain areas and away from others, it obviously creates victims as well as beneficiaries. The key issue is whether it is likely to leave a net overall benefit by succeeding in redirecting resources to more productive uses.

The most naive advocates of industrial policy tend to ignore the existence of an elaborate capital market structure which exists precisely to guide resources to where their expected return is highest. These "growth activists" implicitly presume that some government decision maker has superior knowledge of where the high future returns will be and can act accordingly. With one exception, there is little evidence or logic to support

(Continued)

such an idea. And the experience of many countries who have used these policies reveals not only a list of successes but a list of failures, just as we see in the outcome of private capital market activities.

But the one exception is important and deserves serious consideration. There are certain activities that create **external benefits** (or costs) that extend beyond those actually paying for them. Because the total (social) return exceeds the (private) return to the demanders of those activities, the market alone will provide less of this output than would be optimal. You may know this from your introductory economics course as the "free rider problem." In cases where such "spillover" effects can be identified, we can improve overall efficiency by using government decision making to direct more resources to these areas and out of others. The government "infrastructure" (including transportation and communication systems) falls in this category as does public support for education.

In fact, this category has been clearly recognized as appropriate for public rather than private actions at least since Adam Smith.[26] This is a major topic in microeconomics and we won't delve into the details. But we do need to be aware that in practice these situations are very difficult to identify with any degree of precision and the result is an active controversy among economists as to the extent to which the government can and should take a more active role in rechanneling resources to supposedly high return areas.[27] Political decisions are subject to such a wide array of pressures and influences that resources may not always flow to only the high return areas. As we'll discuss in Chapter 16, just because the government *can* improve allocative efficiency in certain cases, doesn't mean that it *will*.

---

[26] In the *Wealth of Nations*, Smith argued that government should properly have "the duty of erecting and maintaining certain publick works and certain publick institutions, which it can never be for the interest of any individuals, to erect and maintain; because the profit could never repay the expense to any individual or small number of individuals, though it may frequently do much more than repay it to a great society" (book IV, p. ix).

[27] See the various articles and comments in the symposium papers collected in the Federal Reserve Bank of Kansas City, *Policies For Long-Run Economic Growth*, 1992.

After this extended discussion of policy impacts on economic growth, what general conclusions can we reach about the prospects of reversing the more than 20-year decline in the growth rate? We have reconfirmed what we saw back in the very first chapter—economic growth is primarily a matter of choice and, like any economic good, it has costs as well as benefits. We've also seen that once we accept the fact that faster growth requires moving resources out of consumption and into investment, there is still a complex array of issues involved in determining which specific investment activities will be most productive. There are clearly no easy answers here.

Economists J. Bradford DeLong and Lawrence H. Summers conclude that the growth slowdown

> *is a worldwide event that has occurred in countries with widely varying micro- and macroeconomic policies. This suggests that even with all the political courage in the world, there is no macroeconomic magic bullet that has the potential to reverse the productivity slowdown. . . . If public policy in the industrialized world does succeed in reversing any large part of the productivity slowdown, its success will have an important microeconomic component. Policy will succeed either by changing incentives in such a way that average returns on investment significantly increase, or by successfully raising the share of national output that is devoted to forms of investment that have large external benefits and therefore very high social returns. . . . Reducing budget deficits is good macroeconomic policy. But it is unrealistic to hold out the hope that reduced deficits alone will restore the magic of an earlier era, when standards of living in the industrialized world doubled in one generation rather than in two or more.*[28]

Macroeconomic policy makes its primary contribution to economic growth by providing a stable economic environment within which saving, investment, and capital markets can function. To the extent that monetary and fiscal policies can moderate unexpected changes in inflation rates and cyclical fluctuations in output and employment, they will have a noticeable impact on the nation's rate of economic growth. In this sense, successful short run stabilization and healthy long term growth go hand in hand. But there are also situations in which certain actions may achieve short run goals only by sacrificing some long term objectives. For example, an increase in the government's structural deficit can stimulate economic recovery, but will also lead to higher real interest rates and the crowding out of investment spending that diminishes prospects for growth. Balancing short and long run considerations from inside the arena of political decision making is a task guaranteed to generate controversy and frustration. Yet these decisions (this or that? now or later?) *must* be made. Macroeconomic analysis provides the broad framework that can help us see the likely consequences of our actions . . . *before* we act.

⚙ *14.7 OVERVIEW*

1. This completes the three chapters of Part IV, "Long-Run Dynamics: Saving, Investment, and Growth." It makes the final connection from consumption/saving and investment choices (Chapter 12) through capital markets (Chapter 13) to the consequences for overall economic growth (Chapter 14). It provides a long term framework to supplement the analytics of the zero-growth *AD/AS* framework.

2. Explaining output growth means understanding the determinants of input growth—labor, capital, technology, and the institutional structure in our framework. We'd like our economic analysis to explain as much of this input growth as it can, recognizing, however, that an important part of this involves demographic, social, and political factors that are beyond our domain. For these, we must be content to take them as given *exogenous* forces that influence economic growth from the outside.

3. The heart of the growth issue—the efficient use of scarce resources—resides in *micro*economics. While our aggregate perspective can't identify the specifics

---

[28] J. Bradford DeLong and Lawrence H. Summers, "Macroeconomic Policy and Long-Run Growth," in Federal Reserve Bank of Kansas City, *Policies for Long-Run Economic Growth*, 1992, pp. 122–123.

of the growth process, it does offer a useful panorama that captures the overall linkages and interactions of the growth process.

4. Economic growth is a universally supported goal. Everyone seems to think we need more of it, a sure indication of incomplete understanding. Growth is an economic good that has costs as well as benefits and when we are confronted with the actual "now or later?" choice, our decisions reveal less willingness to purchase economic growth than to complain or fantasize about it.

5. There are several general approaches to economic growth at the aggregate level—stripped-down *theoretical models of "steady-state" growth*, quantitatively focused *"stylized facts" distilled from past economic growth experience*, and a blend of theoretical and empirical analysis embodied in the *growth accounting model*.

6. The *neoclassical (Solow) growth model* is a framework that allows us to look at the very long term (steady state) consequences of the basic "saving, investment, capital, output" connection that was ignored in the no-growth *AD/AS* framework. It reveals that changes in the fraction of income saved will alter the *level* of the growth path but will have only a temporary impact on the steady state rate of economic growth. It also demonstrates that the primary source of growth in output per capita must come from increases in the *productivity* of the inputs, not just their quantities, and points to the crucial role of technological change in the growth process.

7. Letting the pendulum swing from the high level of abstraction of steady state models to the quantitative focus of *stylized facts* from past economic growth, opens up a wide array of events and issues that were assumed away in the neoclassical growth model. Looking at common patterns in the growth of different countries over many years gives us a framework for further analysis. But by itself it often raises more questions than answers. This is because the lack of an analytical framework will not allow us to pin down the direction of causality underlying these patterns, greatly limiting its use for practical policy making.

8. The *growth accounting model* begins with the concept of an aggregate production function—the process through which inputs are transformed into outputs. It tries to use what we know about the logic of production relationships to interpret what we observe in the data on economic growth. The findings continue to be that most of the actual growth in per capita output cannot be attributed to the growth of labor and capital inputs. This unmeasured "Solow residual" is primarily the result of technological change. It also appears that this is the crucial category that is mostly responsible for the worldwide decline in growth rates over the last two decades.

9. The attempt to unravel the specific causes underlying the decline in technological improvement and in economic growth has uncovered such a large number of suspects that it's impossible to fairly indict one or even a few. But while the underlying causes of the worldwide slowdown in economic growth remain hazy, we can still use economic policy to offset this decline—provided we're willing to pay the cost in terms of lower current consumption.

10. The growth process can be viewed as a sequence of events that run from *national saving* and *borrowing from abroad* to *investment spending*, the *productivity with which we use our growing inputs*, and, finally, to *output growth*. Devising policies that will efficiently tilt the balance from "now" to "later" is primarily a job for *micro*economics. What combinations of rewards and incentives will be most effective in increasing our levels of saving and investment and the productivity of our inputs is the heart of microeconomic analysis.

11. The main contribution that macroeconomic policy can make to the growth process is in providing a reasonably stable overall environment—particularly employment, output, inflation, and real interest rates—within which savers and investors can interact through capital markets. Direct government spending on public investment projects clearly plays an important role, but must be guided by microeconomic analysis if it is to do its job well.

✆ 14.8 *REVIEW QUESTIONS*

1. Explain the following terms and concepts.

Long-term growth	Constant returns to scale	Growth accounting model
Exogenous		
Endogenous	Steady-state growth path	Supply-side economics
"Creative destruction"		Industrial policy
Neoclassical growth model	Golden Rule growth path	Growth slowdown
Diminishing marginal product	Technological change	
	Total factor productivity	

2. Virtually all presidents in recent decades have put at least occasional pressure on the Federal Reserve to "ease up" on the money supply. The argument has been that we needed lower interest rates in order to achieve a strong recovery or restore a healthy rate of growth. Based on the *AD/AS^e* framework, what are the likely consequences of such a strategy?

3. "Those who profess to find the sluggish growth of recent decades such a puzzle are simply refusing to recognize the obvious. All we need is more public saving and less public consumption and the problem would be solved." Evaluate.

4. "An increase in private saving is necessary to speed up economic growth, reduce inflation, strengthen the value of the dollar, and end our balance of trade deficit." Evaluate.

5. Continued government deficits continue to cause irritation, much of it for the wrong reasons. We've seen that popular views of the budget deficit are quite primitive in a number of ways, particularly in the implicit assumption that a "cash-flow deficit" is identical to a "capital account deficit." A careful look at the issue of government deficits reveals no evidence (logical or statistical) to confirm widespread fears that continuation of the U.S. deficit at levels of the past decade is likely to lead to national bankruptcy. We've also seen that with the moderation of activist views of stabilization policy, there's little reason to believe that constant manipulation of government budget deficits are a vital tool in the attempt to keep the economy operating at or near its potential. But what about the impact of continued deficits on economic growth? Discuss the contention that "government deficits are a drain on our national saving and even if they're "sustainable" in a narrow sense, they eat away at our economic growth. They may not *lower* our standard of living but by keeping it from rising as fast as it otherwise would, they end up making us worse off." Explain.

6. Can we alter the rate of economic growth in the steady state? Explain what the neoclassical growth model has to say about this. Where do "policy irrelevance" and "tax discounting" fit into the picture of the ability of policy to influence economic growth?

7. A bipartisan Commission on Economic Growth is formed to unravel the mystery of the 20-year slowdown in the rate of growth of real output in the United States. You're in charge of the subcommittee on interest rates and are asked to recommend a policy package that would provide permanently lower interest rates in a way that would increase total U.S. investment and, hence, stimulate economic growth. Your recommendation and explanation is. . . .

8. Back in the very first chapter it was said that "economic growth" is an *economic good*, subject to all the laws of scarcity. Discuss this issue in the context of the debate over whether the government should take steps to increase the rate of growth in the United States.

9. The neoclassical growth model focuses on the linkage between investment spending and the growth in aggregate supply over time.

   a. What determines the steady-state rate of growth in this model? Explain.

   b. This model predicts that changes in the saving rate will have *no* impact on the rate of growth. Explain the logic behind this.

   c. Explain why the conclusion in part *b* does not contradict another implication of this model—that changes in the saving rate alter the steady state growth *path* and, with it, our standard of living.

10. Explain and contrast the empirical approach to understanding economic growth through *stylized facts* and through the *growth accounting model*. What are their specific strengths and weaknesses? Explain.

⊗⊙ 14.9 *FURTHER READING*

Moses Abramovitz, *Thinking about Growth: And Other Essays on Economic Growth and Welfare*, (New York: Cambridge University Press, 1989).

Council of Economic Advisers, "Economic Growth and Future Generations," in *"Economic Report of the President 1993"* (Washington, D.C.: Government Printing Office, 1993).

Hollis B. Chenery and Moshe Syrquin, *Patterns of Development, 1950–1970* (Oxford: Oxford University Press, 1975).

J. Bradford De Long, "Productivity growth, convergence, and welfare: Comment," *American Economic Review* (December 1988): 1138–1154.

J. Bradford De Long and Lawrence H. Summers, "Macroeconomic Policy and Long-Run Growth," *Economic Review*, Federal Reserve Bank of Kansas City, Fourth Quarter 1992, pp. 5–29 (and in Federal Reserve Bank of Kansas City, *Policies for Long-Run Economic Growth* [Symposium 1992]).

Edward F. Denison, *Trends in American Economic Growth, 1929–1982* (Washington, D.C.: The Brookings Institution, 1985).

Federal Reserve Bank of Kansas City, *Policies for Long-Run Economic Growth* (Symposium 1992).

Gene M. Grossman and Elhanan Helpman, "Trade, Innovation, and Growth," *American Economic Review* (May 1990): 86–91.

Paul Krugman, *The Age of Diminished Expectations* (Cambridge, Mass.: The Massachusetts Institute of Technology Press, 1990).

Simon Kuznets, *Modern Economic Growth: Rate, Structure and Spread* (New Haven: Yale University Press, 1966).

ROBERT LUCAS, "On the Mechanics of Economic Development," *Journal of Monetary Economics* (July 1988): 3–42.

ANGUS MADDISON, *Dynamic Forces in Capitalist Development: A Long-Run Comparative View* (Oxford: Oxford University Press, 1991).

JOEL MOKYR, *The Lever of Riches: Technological Creativity and Economic Progress* (New York: Oxford University Press, 1990).

STEPHEN L. PARENTE AND EDWARD C. PRESCOTT, "Changes in the Wealth of Nations," *Quarterly Review*, Federal Reserve Bank of Minneapolis (spring 1993): 3–16.

PAUL M. ROMER, "Increasing Returns and Long Run Growth," *Journal of Political Economy* (October 1986): 1002–1037.

W. W. ROSTOW, *Theorists of Economic Growth from David Hume to the Present (With a Perspective on the Next Century)* (New York: Oxford University Press, 1990).

JOSEPH A. SCHUMPETER, *The Theory of Economic Development*, trans. Redvers Opie (Cambridge: Harvard University Press, 1934). Paperback edition, New York: Oxford University Press, 1961. First German edition, 1911.

JOSEPH A. SCHUMPETER, *Capitalism, Socialism, and Democracy*, 3rd ed. (New York: Harper, 1950).

ROBERT M. SOLOW, "A Contribution to the Theory of Economic Growth," *Quarterly Journal of Economics* (February 1956): 65–94.

ROBERT M. SOLOW, "Technical Change and the Aggregate Production Function," *Review of Economics and Statistics* (August 1957): 312–320.

ROBERT M. SOLOW, *Growth Theory: An Exposition*, 2nd ed. (New York: Oxford University Press, 1988).

ROBERT SUMMERS AND ALAN HESTON, "The Penn World Table (Mark 5): An Expanded Set of International Comparisons, 1950–88," *Quarterly Journal of Economics* (May 1991): 327–368.

JOHN VICKERS AND GEORGE YARROW, "Economic Perspectives on Privatization," *Journal of Economic Perspectives* 5 (spring 1991): 111–132.

PART V

Models, Measurement, and Performance

The previous chapters have constructed a quite elaborate structure known as "modern macroeconomic analysis." This process has employed theoretical models of cause and effect to grapple with a variety of very practical economic issues like unemployment and recession, budget deficits and trade deficits, interest rates, inflation, and economic growth. Concern with aggregate economic performance has sent us searching for dominant patterns in the economy—stable relationships and interactions that define the workings of the macroeconomy.

The analysis has been built around connections—linkages between choices and outcomes, actions and consequences. These linkages in the "real world" constitute the macroeconomy itself, in all its rich and almost unfathomable complexity. The connections in our analysis constitute a *model* of the macroeconomy, a drastic simplification to help us separate the essential from the inessential for the issue at hand. Macroeconomics is actually composed of a series of models, each designed to deal with a particular aspect of overall economic performance—growth, business cycles, inflation, depression, and so on. *But it's important to see that these individual models—the comparative statics of AD/AS, the short-run dynamics of AD/AS^e and the "Phillips curve," and the long-term dynamics of growth models—are really just different "slices" of the same thing.* They are different ways to simplify the complexities of the real world so that we can get a practical understanding of the key issues. It is far easier to understand the basics of unemployment in a setting of zero economic growth, just as it's far easier to understand the basics of growth in a setting of full employment and price stability.

But when it comes to the bottom line—applying the results of these models to real world policy choices—we can no longer rely on simplifying assumptions that ignore one important thing to concentrate on another. We must fashion a policy package that encompasses different issues and goals and forces us to blend the results of different models. For example, what sort of policy mix is appropriate if our current goals include recovery from recession, stable inflation, and faster economic growth? There is no simple answer to such a question, but this is exactly the kind of question that policy makers face every day. The final chapter presents a concise summary of what we know and don't know about macroeconomic policy options.

But before any meaningful summing up is possible, we need to say something about why we have confidence in these analytical results. How have we chosen this small handful of models as "best" when there are untold numbers of possible alternative models of the macroeconomy, many of which seem at least as plausible as these? We've seen that different models can produce strikingly different pictures of the workings of the macroeconomy. What is the process by which a specific model is chosen over others? Most importantly, how will we know when it's time for our current models to give way to still "better" ones?

Choosing among models involves a series of activities that are generally unglamorous, highly technical or both. Though they receive little attention outside the boundaries of the economics profession, they are essential to any attempt to create a practical and reliable picture of macroeconomic events. The next chapter—"Models and Measurement"—provides an overview of some of the elements involved in choosing among alternative models. An awareness of this process can help us see when we're claiming too much for our results and thereby putting a heavier burden on a particular model than it can reasonably support. It can also help us distinguish the passing fads of "pop economics" from the reliable knowledge that can guide us to better economic choices.

CHAPTER 15

MODELS AND MEASUREMENT

ᏸᎶ *15.1 INTRODUCTION*

We have been so intent on using models to represent connections across variables that we have said little about the definitions and measurement of the variables themselves. On those occasions when we talked about actual events—such as the Great Depression, the post-WWII growth spurt, the swelling inflation of the late 1970s, the rise of the "twin deficits" during the Eighties, or the growth slowdown of recent decades—we avoided detail and stayed with the general facts only long enough to devise an analytical framework that seemed to account for them. The closest we came to a direct confrontation with these bare bones of macroeconomic "reality" was the discussion of the "stylized facts" of economic growth, which we quickly abandoned in favor of the growth accounting model.

By now, you're aware that this emphasis on models allows us to get beneath all the details and distractions on the turbulent surface of economic life so that we can identify the dominant underlying patterns that connect "choices" with "outcomes." We use simplified, but manageable models to approximate the primary cause-and-effect linkages and interactions that shape overall economic activity. *So the question isn't "whether" to use a model. We can't escape that. Even the simplest slogans of those who pretend to be "practical" instead of "theoretical" embody notions of cause and effect. The issue is always which model gives the best approximation to those parts of reality that concern us.*

Previous chapters offered a succession of models to address changing issues and increasingly ambitious questions. When the **classical model** was unable to focus on short run phenomena like *cyclical unemployment*, we turned to the **Keynesian model**. To learn more about the *timing* of short-run fluctuations and the gradual price level adjustment that connects short to long run, we developed the **expectations-augmented model** and its variations, forming the basis for the **Phillips curve model.** Although this gave us a broad framework for an-alyzing the pro's and con's of *stabilization policy*, it told us nothing about the long term consequences of such policies for *economic growth*. This required a quite different ap-proach that led to the highly abstract/simplified **neoclassical (Solow) growth model** and the more pedestrian **growth accounting model.**

Somehow we always seemed to know just *which* new model would be most use-ful for the issue at hand. But, of course, we only "knew" this with 20/20 hindsight. We have left out a crucial part of the story—the continuing "survival of the fittest" process through which a particular model or set of models must pass in order to be preferred over alternative models. To begin to remedy this omission, let's think about how we choose among competing explanations in everyday life. For most things we use a combination of facts and reason and intuition in an informal way that we call "common sense." But sometimes we allow other considerations to override facts and logic, such as whether a particular view leads to a conclusion that seems to be in our immediate *self-interest* (say a tariff that protects our incomes by raising prices to oth-ers) or is consistent with what we *want to believe* (the "party line" test) or has the most *persuasive advocates* (famous, attractive, or powerful).

To the extent that we use such subjective criteria, we won't achieve a practical understanding of how the mechanism in question actually works. It doesn't matter whether the topic is how to get a good grade in this course, choose a rewarding ca-reer, invest our time and money wisely, achieve a happy marriage, or use monetary and fiscal policy to reach specific economic goals. The world works in certain ways that have little to do with how we would like it to work or with how much we might gain if it worked differently. We diminish our chances of achieving our personal and political goals when we let careless or wishful thinking hide actual connections be-tween choices and outcomes.

Soviet Premier Nikita Khrushchev once made this point in a slightly different way by lamenting that "Economics is a subject that does not greatly respect one's wishes." Ironically, and tragically for many millions, the Soviet experiment in large scale economic planning turned out to be the definitive Twentieth Century example of how impractical it is to assume that an economy actually works in the way some think it *should* work, that people actually behave in the way some think they *should* behave. The crisis of the Soviet economic system stemmed from a continuing failure to use reasonable criteria to evaluate how well a particular model of the economy worked. The model was chosen to fit the rigid ideology of the Communist party. What began as a widely-shared hope that this bold experiment would bring great fu-ture rewards while avoiding much of the harshness of capitalism, soon became an in-tolerant dogma in which rival views were silenced. As prospects dimmed, its survival depended more and more upon distortion and indoctrination, followed by intimida-tion, coercion, and even deadly force.

At the root of this great historical tragedy was a mundane decision about how to choose an economic model, with dogma substituted for the scientific criteria that would have stressed logical consistency and consistency with observed facts. But because these objective criteria didn't yield the "correct" answer, they were labeled subversive and rejected as an at-tempt to betray the "people." The ultimate betrayal, of course, was the government's failure to make policy decisions on the basis of a realistic model of how the economy actually operated.

This chapter is about making careful, practical choices among alternative expla-nations (models) of reality. It is an enormous subject that spans the methodology of all disciplines and has its home in philosophy. The modest goal here is to offer an overview of the process through which macroeconomic models have been quantified, tested, and selected or rejected. We now turn to the main ingredients in this process: (1) **Measuring variables,** (2) **Measuring (estimating) relationships among variables,** and (3) **Using this knowledge to simulate and forecast economic consequences of particular events.**

ᏇᎶ *15.2 MEASURING MACROECONOMIC VARIABLES*

Throughout the preceding chapters it has been implicitly assumed that the variables in our models—real output and its rate of growth (y and $\%\Delta y$), consumption and investment (c and i), the price level and inflation (P and Π), real and nominal interest rates (r and R), unemployment (U), the money supply (M), the cash flow budget deficit ($b = g - t$), and all the rest—have readily-available, numerical counterparts. In truth, macroeconomic measurement is a difficult and laborious task that gets little attention and respect, even from most economists. It is taken for granted when it does its job well, but irritates us when we push the measures beyond their conceptual or operational limits, ending up with contradictions and inconsistencies. Because we're all users of economic information in some way or another, a general awareness of the limitations of macroeconomic data is important.

Quantitative information about the macroeconomy comes from a variety of public and private sources. In the United States the primary government providers are the Bureau of Census, the Bureau of Economic Analysis, the Bureau of Labor Statistics, the Treasury, and the Federal Reserve System. Much of the macroeconomic data is published in monthly issues of the *Survey of Current Business* and the *Federal Reserve Bulletin.* The yearly *Economic Report of the President* is particularly useful because it contains the "Annual Report of the Council of Economic Advisers" which includes a broad selection of statistical tables that paint a detailed portrait of the macroeconomy over several decades. Additional information comes from currency markets, commodity markets, stock exchanges, and bond markets. Most international economic data are from the statistical branches of the United Nations, the Organization for Economic Cooperation & Development (OECD), and the International Monetary Fund (IMF). On-line data bases and subscription data bases on CD-Rom put all this information literally at our fingertips.[1]

The backbone of U.S. macroeconomic data is the National Income and Product Accounts, prepared by the Bureau of Economic Analysis (BEA) in the Commerce Department. This framework can be viewed as an operational counterpart to the structure embodied in our *AD/AS* model ($y = c + i + x + g = c + s + t$) where total output is equivalent to total income (y) and can be divided into the various categories. In their entirety, the National Income and Product Accounts are extensive and intricate. Dropping most of the detail, the main components of the accounts are listed in Table 15.1. The right hand column measures output in terms of the *underlying expenditure categories*—consumption, investment, net exports, and government spending. Each of these can be subdivided into finer and finer groups as well as extended to connect with GNP, GDP, and other aggregate output measures. The *income generated by these expenditures* is divided among the various categories on the left hand side—employee compensation, proprietors income, rental income, corporate

---

[1] The most massive and comprehensive accumulation of economic information is on the Internet. See William L. Goffe, "Computer Network Resources for Economists," and Jeffrey K. MacKie-Mason and Hal Varian, "Economic FAQs About the Internet," in *The Journal of Economic Perspectives* 8 (summer 1994): 97–119 and 75–96.

■ **TABLE 15.1**

Gross Domestic Product

INCOME SIDE	PRODUCT OR EXPENDITURE SIDE
Compensation of employees	Gross domestic product
Wages and salaries	Personal consumption spending
Supplements to wages and salaries	Durables
Proprietors income with inventory valuation	Nondurables
adjustment and capital consumption	Services
allowance	Gross private domestic investment
Rental income of persons with capital	Nonresidential
consumption allowances	Residential
Corporate profits with inventory valuation and	Change in business inventories
capital consumption adjustment	Net exports of goods and services
Profits before tax	Exports
Profits tax liability	Imports
Profits after tax	Government purchases of goods and services
Dividends	Federal
Undistributed profits	State and local
Inventory valuation adjustment	
Capital consumption adjustment	
Net interest	
National income	
Business transfer payments	
Indirect business tax and nontax liability	
Less: subsidies less current surplus of govern-	
ment enterprises	
Plus: statistical discrepancy	
Charges against net national product	
Capital consumption allowances with capital	
consumption adjustments	
Gross national product	
Plus: payments of factor income to the rest of	
the world	
Minus: receipts of factor income from the rest	
of the world	
Charges against gross domestic product	

profits, and net interest income, each of which can be further broken down into numerous subcomponents as needed for specific uses.

Your first impression of these accounts is likely to be a negative one. After the relative simplicity of our analytical categories, the attention to detail and precise definition can come as a shock. Understanding the basics of the national income and product accounts well enough to use them properly takes some patience and more guidance than can be provided in one chapter of a text on macroeconomic analysis.[2] But since we're skipping over the intricacies of national income accounting, it is all

---

[2] Fortunately there is a very useful book that covers a broad spectrum of economic data: David B. Johnson's *Finding & Using Economic Information: A Guide to Sources and Interpretation* (Mountain View, California: Bristlecone Books, Mayfield Publishing Co., 1993). This book provides clear explanations of the main economic measures, where to obtain them, and warnings about their limitations. It is an excellent place to begin a search for macroeconomic data. Also see Norman Frumkin, *Tracking America's Economy*, 2nd ed. (Armonk, N.Y.: M. E. Sharpe Inc., 1992) and *The Economist Guide to Global Economic Indicators* (New York: John Wiley & Sons, 1994).

the more important that you acquire a general understanding of the ways in which these **measurements** of macroeconomic events can diverge from the **concepts** around which all our analysis has revolved. The following section compares some key macroeconomic concepts with their empirical counterparts.

15.3 CONCEPTS VERSUS MEASURES

1. Total output and economic growth. Our *concept* of total real output (y) represents the production of final goods and services (and the income it generates) during a particular interval of time. Its rate of change ($\%\Delta y$) is our concept of overall economic growth. Including only *final* goods and services means that we must exclude *intermediate* products (like wheat and steel) that become components of other output (like bread and autos) during the same period. Failure to make this adjustment is called "double counting" and would clearly overstate the amount of current economic activity. We use this concept of final output as a broad gauge of the nation's current standard of living and presume that growing levels of per capita real output, other things the same, reflect an overall improvement in economic well-being.[3]

GDP is the most widely used *measure* of overall economic activity (total output) and its rate of change is the standard measure of economic growth. Can we be confident that an increase in GDP signals a corresponding improvement in our standard of living? The answer is a definite "no!" There are many situations in which GDP can rise without a matching increase in economic well-being. To narrow this gap between concept and measure would require the following adjustments:

a. *Put GDP on a per capita basis.* Countries with rapid population growth can exhibit a simultaneous rise in total GDP and fall in GDP per person. The latter corresponds more closely to what's happening to economic well-being in the nation. This adjustment is easily done.

b. *Convert GDP from nominal to real dollars to eliminate purely inflationary changes.* Changes in measured GDP that reflect price rises rather than an increase in the amount of final goods and services produced should be "deflated out." This is readily accomplished but (as discussed below) is at best an approximation because of the "index number problem" and the "quality adjustment problem."

c. *Eliminate "double counting" from GDP by subtracting the amount of depreciation (capital consumption) each period.* As its name reveals, gross domestic product includes *gross* investment spending and makes no adjustment for depreciation of the capital stock. This leads GDP to overstate the true amount of final economic activity. Estimates of "capital consumption" are available to convert GDP to a net measure (Net Domestic Product [NDP]). But there are so many conceptual and measurement problems with these depreciation figures that most users think the GDP measure is a more reliable year-to-year indicator of what's happening to real output than NDP. So this is a gap between measure and concept that isn't easily removed and results in measured GDP *over*stating the true level of economic activity.

---

[3] It is sometimes suggested that economists believe these measures capture everything important to our general well-being. Even the narrowest of economists is surely aware that there can be no single, one-dimensional number that adequately captures anything as complex as the quality of life. What we do strive for is a reliable measure of that part of overall welfare that originates in all the economic hustle and bustle that, for most of us, is a dominant part of our daily lives.

d. *Include estimates of certain output that currently eludes the national accounting process.* GDP primarily measures those activities that go through markets and for which a monetary transaction is recorded. But there are many kinds of economic activity which cannot be picked up this way. For some of these, national income accountants make "imputations" that are added to GDP. For example, the rental costs of a home are payment for current housing services and are properly included as part of current income and output. But when the home is lived in by the owner, there is no comparable transaction (owners are essentially renting from themselves) and so an *imputation* must be made for the "rental value of owner occupied houses."

There are other areas where imputations should be made but are not. For example, housework, child care, and yard work done by hired workers shows up in GDP, but the part we do for ourselves does not. They represent productive use of scarce resources and should be reflected in a measure of real output whether there's a monetary transaction or not. Similarly, the national accounts fail to include the value of volunteer work and also ignore the potentially sizable amounts of unreported economic activity that takes place in the "underground economy." Legal or not, it's still activity that uses scarce resources to provide economic goods and services and generate incomes. Such exclusions from measured GDP lead it to understate the true level of current economic activity.

e. *Include estimates of certain costs and losses that are now ignored by the national accounts.* Measured GDP not only excludes some kinds of output, it also excludes some costs that should be subtracted from final output. An all too important example of excluded costs is environmental degradation. Current activities that cause damage to the environment through pollution, erosion, and so on, essentially reduce our capital stock and with it productive capacity. In terms of our model, they contract the PPF and AS^* curves. But since such "external" effects escape markets, their negative impact is not charged against output and does not show up in the national accounts until later, if at all. In fact, to the extent that they cause higher medical bills or expenditures on antipollution devices, current GDP can actually register an increase when it ought to be showing a decline.[4]

Taking this a step further, a little thought should convince you that many purchases that are now included as final output in GDP are actually "defensive expenditures," sometimes called "regrettable necessities," that only serve to counteract events that would otherwise make us worse off. They are means to an end, not the end itself. Medical bills and lawyers' fees are sometimes cited as expenditures that really shouldn't be included in final output. Some put spending on national defense and police protection as well as anti-pollution expenses in this category.

But as we think still further about what should and shouldn't be counted as productive economic activity, the issue becomes quite confusing. Although it's true that many medical expenses are just a cost of restoring us

---

[4] Although this problem afflicts all economic systems, it was particularly acute in the planned economies of the former Soviet bloc. Their measures of output, notoriously overstated for overt political reasons, ignored the huge levels of pollution and environmental degradation that resulted from the incentive structure associated with state ownership of most resources. As the economic costs of those practices now become increasingly apparent—in reduced productive capacity or clean-up costs to restore productive capacity—it's obvious that true *net* output in earlier years was far lower than what was advertised. The costs that are only now being registered should have been "charged" against output at the time they occurred.

to our normal level of physical well-being, it's also true that we are generally better off having made them. By easing our sore throat or mending our broken leg, such activities surely increase our well-being. Wouldn't it be a distortion *not* to include them? Isn't the same true of anti-pollution costs? And isn't crime reduction also the welfare-enhancing consequence of expenditures on police protection?

Some of the apparent ambiguity stems from the incompleteness of the accounts. If the economic costs associated with the onset of more pollution, crime, and illness had been properly deducted in the first place, then the expenses to offset some or all of this "depreciation" (broadly defined) would *not* result in a counter-intuitive net increase in measured output.[5] You may also sense that these questions lead us deeper and deeper toward what ultimately is, in the aggregate, an unresolvable subjective question—which of our expenditures provide goods and services that are ends in themselves, and which merely reflect costs that are only a means to an end? One person's "ends" (e.g., an expensive car that "makes a statement") may be another's means (transportation). So any means/end distinction made for accounting purposes inevitably involves some arbitrariness and compromise.

What does all this say about the reliability of this most commonly used measure of economic activity? For most purposes, our concern is not the accuracy of the GDP number for any specific year. Whether it is overstated by 15% or understated by 10% is not particularly important. What does matter is whether the various omissions and distortions are a relatively constant proportion of measured GDP from year to year. If they are more-or-less stable, so that the "concept/measure" gap is roughly constant, then year-to-year changes in measured GDP—measured economic growth—will be a relatively good estimate of corresponding changes in our economic well-being. But if the size of these excluded items varies substantially over time, our measures of growth will provide a warped picture of the actual cycles and trends of macroeconomic activity. Until official output measures are substantially improved, we must rely on our judgement and intuition to decide how far it's reasonable to use estimates that contain biases of unknown and probably changing amounts. That will depend not only on the particular question we're asking, but also how much is at stake if we act on a biased answer.

2. Nominal and real values. It was mentioned earlier that we must "deflate" measured GDP to make it correspond more closely to our concept of *real* output. In fact, we have relied heavily on the notion of a **price index** as the measure of the price level (P) and hence inflation $\%\Delta P = \Pi$) in all our models. How closely do existing price indexes approximate the concept we've been using? The two main difficulties in this case are the "index number problem" and the "product quality problem."

  a. The index number problem. The concept of a "price *level*," like all our aggregates, is an enormous simplification. In a single number, it attempts to embody underlying information about tens of thousands of individual prices. From hats to housing to heart by-pass surgery, from paper clips to computer chips, from plane tickets to pizzas—they're all included. All this detail

[5] For more on this issue of how to make our measures of output correspond more closely to true economic well-being, see William D. Nordhaus and James Tobin, "Is Growth Obsolete?" in *Economic Growth*, Fiftieth Anniversary Colloquium, vol. 5 (New York: National Bureau of Economic Research, 1972). Robert Eisner has taken this an ambitious step further in his patient work to revise aggregate concepts and measures for the U.S. See his "Extended Accounts for National Income and Product," *Journal of Economic Literature* (December 1988) and *The Total Incomes System of Accounts* (Chicago: University of Chicago Press, 1989).

becomes part of a weighted average of individual prices called a *price index*—a center of gravity for the constellation of individual price changes.

The individual prices inside a price index are each "weighted" in terms of their overall importance in our spending decisions. So the price of a Rolls Royce, though high, has relatively little influence on the index because it's weighted by such a small quantity. But the much lower price of a gallon of milk is far more important because its weight, the quantity sold, is so enormous. As with any average, such as a batting average or your GPA, the goal is to eliminate as much detail as possible while retaining something that is not only streamlined and manageable but maintains some resemblance to its underlying components. (In other contexts, the outcome of this process is called a caricature or a stereotype.)

There are several different uses for price indexes, but our main interest is in disentangling price and quantity changes in nominal GDP. If nominal GDP rises 10% from $7.0 trillion last year to $7.7 trillion this year, what part of this reflects a gain in our real standard of living $(+\Delta y)$ and what part reflects an increase in the price level $(+\Delta P)$? One way to answer this is to calculate *how much more the actual "bundle" of goods and services that we produced last year would cost to produce this year.* If it would now cost $7.35 trillion to produce exactly the same quantity of each item as last year, then with last year's quantities (bundle) as "weights," the price level has risen 5% and real output the remaining 5%. We say that the **base-year-weighted price index** increased by 5%.

But there's another reasonable way to calculate price change. We could use this year's actual quantities of each item as our reference and then compare *how much more this current-year bundle of goods and services costs now than it would have cost last year.* Only in the unlikely event that we're buying exactly the same proportions of everything, will this **current-year-weighted price index** yield the same answer as the base-year weighted index. This is unlikely not only because aggregate preferences tend to change over time, but also because basic microeconomic analysis (and common sense) tells us that when the price of a commodity rises we look after our own well-being by switching to lower-priced substitutes. This movement toward a more efficient consumption "bundle" when relative prices change is not captured by the *fixed* quantities of a base-year-weighted price index. For this reason, a base-year-weighted price index, other things the same, tends to *overstate the amount of price change* and therefore understate our implicit calculation of real output growth. But if we use a current-year-weighted price index we get just the opposite bias. Asking how much the current bundle would have cost in the prices of a previous year creates a hypothetical comparison that overstates the cost of living in the earlier year because it ignores the fact that consumers actually chose a different bundle, presumably more efficient, at the earlier prices. Hence a current-year-weighted price index, other things the same, tends to *understate the amount of price change* and, therefore, overstate the real output change.

There are several kinds of general price indexes available for the U.S. The Consumer Price Index is a base-year-weighted index. Hence it tends to overstate the amount of price change and, under certain conditions, can be thought of as an upper-bound on the true inflation rate. A second index, the implicit GDP deflator is not only more comprehensive (including prices of *all* final goods produced, not just consumer goods) but is also a current-year-weighted index. So it tends to understate the amount of price change and, under certain conditions, provide a lower-bound to the true inflation rate. The actual magnitude of the year-to-year differences between the %ΔCPI and the %ΔGDP deflator is usually small enough that the bias from the "index number problem" is not one of our major data problems.[6]

b. *The product quality problem.* A more serious distortion in our measure of price change comes from innovations in technology that create new products and improve the quality of existing ones. Technological improvements—so crucial to economic growth as we saw in the last chapter—typically come about through product innovations. But our indexes can't make direct comparisons to past prices when a new product is substantially different from its predecessors (e.g., personal computers and typewriters). Even when similar products existed (successive generations of personal computers, for example) it is difficult to quantify the quality improvement so that it can properly be counted as output change, not price change. For example, suppose the price of a car increases only because air bags have become standard equipment. If this quality change is missed by the national income accountants, the result is an upward bias in measured inflation.

In fact, price and quality adjustments for cars now get much attention and there is probably little distortion in this area. But quality change in computers, medical technology, and some services has been rapid and sizable and our overburdened and underfunded data collection systems have been slow to react.[7] Most observers think that U.S. price indexes currently overstate the inflation rate by perhaps a percent or more because of the failure to keep up with the pace of product innovation and quality change. This is important to keep in mind, because to the extent we overstate the general price rise, we also understate the change in real output and hence our measure of economic growth.

3. Consumption spending. How well does our ***measure** of consumption spending* in the national accounts match the **concept** *of consumption* used throughout the book? The two problems we've just discussed—"including too much/too little in output" and "improperly deflating from nominal to real"—apply to the *components* of real output as well as to the total. There are certain consumption activities that don't go through markets and so elude our measures. Similarly, changes in product quality can pose a problem in converting nominal consumption spending into a meaningful "real" measure. But, in general, measured real personal consumption spending does a good job of approximating the concept of *total real spending on final output by consumers.*

However, our previous analysis separated consumption from investment spending with a "benefits now" versus "benefits later" criterion. This important conceptual distinction is not consistently observed in the U.S. national accounts. The reason is a

---

[6] For more on the index number problem see Brian Motley, "Index Numbers and the Measurement of Real GDP," *Economic Review*, Federal Reserve Bank of San Francisco V1992(1): 3–13.

[7] A study by Manuel Trajtenberg ("Product Innovation, Price Indices and the (Mis)Measurement of Economic Performance," National Bureau of Economic Research Working Paper 3261, February 1990) found "that the rate of decline in the real price of CT scanners was a staggering 55% per year (on average) over the first decade of the technology. By contrast, an hedonic-based index captures just a small fraction of the decline, and a simple (unadjusted) price index shows a substantial price increase over the same period. Thus, conventional economic indicators might be missing indeed a great deal of the welfare consequences of technical advance, particularly during the initial stages of the product cycle of new products."

practical one—the national income accountant who has to turn our concepts into clear, operational definitions quickly discovers how imprecise we've been. While an ice cream cone or a haircut would obviously fall in the "benefits now" category, what about clothes, a stereo system, a book, or a car? We think of them as consumption-like activities, but they can yield a stream of benefits over time, moving them into the investment rather than consumption group.

In the national income accounts, the "consumer durables" category is used to convert this gray area into a black or white decision, albeit somewhat arbitrarily. Counting some of these investment-like expenditures as consumer *durables* allows us to make an approximation to the "benefits now" concept by subtracting consumer durables from total personal consumption expenditures. Whether to make this adjustment or not depends, of course, on whether our interest is only in an estimate of total expenditures by the household sector or whether the "now/later" distinction is crucial to the question we're trying to answer.

In the latter case, the logic of the analysis will usually require a similar "now/later" division between *government* consumption and investment. Unfortunately, as we saw in an earlier chapter, the United States does not have an official separation between current and capital accounts, so this cannot be done with any degree of reliability. Depending on the problem at hand, we may decide to use a rough estimate of the correct concept over a more precise measure of the wrong one. This is part of the judgement and trial-and-error that is an inevitable component of applied work in economics.

4. Saving and investment. Our earlier look at capital markets and growth revealed that *saving* and *investment* are partners in the process of moving goods from now to later. Investment can't happen without saving (though we can borrow external savings) and saving without investment won't lead to economic growth. In our models we defined private saving as what was left after both consumption and taxes were taken from income ($s = y - c - t$). We defined investment as new spending on capital goods, technology, education and other productive inputs. How well are these *concepts* approximated by available *measures?*

The answer has to be "quite poorly." The gap between what we'd like to measure and what's actually measured is so large that we can't even give a confident answer to a basic question like "What has been happening to private saving in the United States over the past decade?" Nevertheless, answers are given to this important question and the usual one is that both private and national saving in the United States have dwindled to all-time lows. This conclusion comes directly from our standard economic measures in the national income and product accounts. According to these measures, saving has been generally declining since the 1970s. Combining this with the *negative* saving of the public sector (the government deficit) reveals an apparently plummeting level of national saving.[8]

But if national saving has fallen so dramatically, why hasn't this shown up in a similar decline in private investment? Capital inflows from the rising trade deficit can explain only part of why private investment spending seemed to remain strong during this period.[9] Perhaps investment fell more than we realized. But many studies

---

[8] Because $ns = s - b$, then $-\Delta s$ and $+\Delta b$ both work to reduce national saving.

[9] Recall that in earlier chapters we found that $y = c + i + x + g = c + s + t$ could be rewritten as $i = s - b - x$, where $b = g - t$ is the cash flow government deficit. So the only way that investment can be sustained in a world of falling private saving ($-\Delta s$) and rising public deficits ($+\Delta b$) would be from capital inflows from abroad, i.e., an increasing trade deficit ($-\Delta x$).

have shown that when investment in human capital, research and development, and other traditionally excluded measures of investment are included, it has fallen little if at all in recent years. The explanation appears to be that a sizable amount of private saving is being ignored by the national income and product accounts.

This likelihood is confirmed by some alternate estimates of saving that are less restrictive than the national accounts. For example, the Federal Reserve's measure of private saving in its Flow of Funds Accounts, which counts such things as current un-realized capital gains on corporate equity as part of current saving, shows a highly volatile savings rate, but not one in steady decline. Other researchers have made esti-mates of U.S. saving that more closely correspond to our concepts and fail to find anything like the "saving crisis" implied by the standard accounts.[10]

Another source of the "collapse of saving" view comes from a comparison of the standard national accounts estimate of the U.S. saving rate with that of other countries. But again the issue seems to be partly one of mismeasurement rather than a drastic change in our saving behavior. Even the apparently polar extremes of saving between the U.S. and Japan are brought much closer once we put their saving rates in a comparable accounting framework. Japanese data on saving and investment are not only much more inclusive (adding spending on consumer durables and govern-ment investment) but they are inflated because depreciation is calculated on the basis of historical costs (rather than higher replacement costs) which therefore understates depreciation and overstates net investment. The official measured Japanese saving rate (as a percent of income) has been in the 20% to 25% range since the mid-1970s. But when economist Fumio Hayashi adjusted Japanese saving to the U.S. definition, he found that it varied within an 8% to 12% range for this period. It is still far higher than the 4% to 10% for the United States during this period. But the difference is not nearly so dramatic as shown in the official estimates.

In some ways it would be simpler if this story told by our biased measures of saving and investment were true. The popular belief that we've become a nation of spendthrifts would not only be consistent with the measured slowdown in economic growth, but would also offer a "happy ending" if only we would return to "normal" saving rates and not be so shortsighted in our now/later choice. But we saw in the previous chapter that dwindling growth is a worldwide event and its causes are not at all clear. There is little evidence to support the hypothesis (an ages-old morality tale) that we suddenly became greedy for current consumption and, with little thought for future consequences, reduced our saving and thereby lowered investment and our rate of growth. This fable is familiar and plausible, but our actual situation is not so simply diagnosed—or remedied.

5. Government budget. By this point you already know that the gap be-tween concept and measure of the Federal budget is quite enormous. There are many reasons for this, the two most important being the *failure to separate public con-sumption from investment spending* and *the exclusion of a huge amount of government lia-bilities from the budget.* Both issues were presented in Chapter 5, but a quick review of this very misunderstood topic is appropriate to a discussion of measurement prob-lems.

Without separate current and capital accounts for government consumption (g^c) and government investment (g^i), the budget figures can tell us little about what

---

[10] See William E. Cullison, "Saving Measures as Economic Growth Indicators," *Contemporary Policy Issues*, Vol. XI, January 1993, pp. 1–17, Robert Eisner, "Extended Accounts for National Income and Product," *Journal of Economic Literature*, December 1988, and Fumio Hayashi, "Is Japan's Saving Rate High?", Federal Reserve Bank of Minneapolis *Quarterly Review*, Spring 1989, pp. 3–9.

we most want to know: "Are government deficits pushing us into the danger zone of 'consumption draining' or are we generating future returns (through public investment) that will more than cover these growing future liabilities?" The simple cash flow measure of the deficit ($b = g - t$) says how much the government borrowed in a given period of time, but gives no clues as to how well or badly its funds were spent. As we saw earlier, to incorporate future consequences of current borrowing into a deficit measure we must turn to the **capital account deficit** ($b^k = b - g^i$).[11]

But for complicated and largely noneconomic reasons, the U.S. government continues to use only the misleadingly incomplete cash flow deficit measure. Disagreement over how and where to draw the line between public consumption and public investment have ended attempts to make a change. The result is a relatively precise measure of the wrong information. All corporations, most state and local governments, and most foreign governments have adopted rules to separate current from capital account items. However approximate and arbitrary the choice between public consumption and public investment, a capital account deficit figure would tell us far more about the economic consequences of public borrowing than the present cash flow number.

The second major distortion in the federal budget figures is the failure to include an estimate of the amount of the government's "unfunded liabilities." We saw earlier that not only has the government promised some of our future taxes to those who hold U.S. Treasury bonds, it has also committed what appears to be an even larger amount of our future taxes in a way that will not show up in the budget until the expenditures are actually made. If this were done in the private sector—an individual or corporation excluding a mortgage or a large bank loan from its financial statement—it would certainly be unscrupulous and probably illegal.

One estimate of the amount of unbudgeted Federal commitments puts this "stealth budget" at $4 trillion as of 1989.[12] In comparison, the total national debt (net outstanding government bonds) was about $2.2 trillion that year. As discussed back in Chapter 5, these unfunded liabilities reflect current commitments to make future payments through such programs as bank deposit insurance, social security, Federal employee retirement benefits, flood insurance, crop insurance, and insurance of private pensions. This $4 trillion figure also includes estimated future costs of dealing with nuclear waste from weapons production. The author of this study, Roy Webb, concludes that "The magnitude of unfunded liabilities suggests that many decisions by voters and by their elected representatives have been made without a full understanding of either the government's current fiscal position or of the full costs of programs under consideration."

Until the official budget figures eliminate these two major distortions, they will continue to provide potentially misleading information about future consequences of current economic actions by the federal government. Unofficial estimates suggest that government investment has become a smaller fraction of total public spending in recent decades and that the number of excluded "entitlement" programs has

[11] Even the 1992 report of the Council of Economic Advisers criticized this lack of information about government spending and concluded that "Separating the Federal budget into a current and capital account could dramatically alter the way the public views fiscal policy, as well as the way the public views particular components of government spending. The spending devoted to building the interstate highway system during the Eisenhower Administration, or the spending on infrastructure in the Intermodel Surface Transportation Efficiency Act signed by the President in 1991, would be considered investment and thus an addition to government assets" (p. 270).

[12] See Roy H. Webb, "The Stealth Budget: Unfunded Liabilities of the Federal Government," *Economic Review*, Federal Reserve Bank of Richmond (May/June 1991): 23–32.

mushroomed. If true, this means that the current measure of the federal deficit increasingly underestimates the net future liabilities generated by our current economic decisions.

6. Money supply. Another major problem area in aggregate measurement is the supply of money. In this case, however, it's not a gap between concept and measure but simply an inherent fuzziness in the concept of "money" itself. As discussed in the context of monetary policy in Chapter 6, there are a number of assets that are extremely close substitutes for the narrowly defined money that includes currency and checking accounts. This means they can also *function* like money in terms of our models—shifting the *LM* and *AD* curves when they change and setting off a constellation of short and long run economic interactions. With no clear theoretical line between "money" and "nonmoney assets," we must proceed pragmatically by looking to past data for guidance on which monetary measure (M_1, M_2, or M_3 are the official ones) bears the closest relationship to nominal GDP.

Put another way, this is a search for a concept/measure of money with the most stable and predictable velocity. Over long periods of time all the concepts exhibit relatively stable levels or stable trends in velocity. But none of these monetary aggregates are sufficient to guide monetary policy for *short-run* stabilization of the economy. This inability to predict which of several quite different measures of money will be the most reliable instrument to guide day-to-day monetary decisions is an important if unwelcome finding. Those who urge the Federal Reserve to avoid a strategy of short run "fine tuning" appear to be aware of this problem. But if they go on to insist on a policy of moderate and steady monetary growth, they need to tell us *which* monetary aggregate they mean. Policies that produce relatively steady growth in M_2 may create erratic changes in M_1. If it turns out that the short run velocity of M_1 is relatively stable at the time, the "steady M_2" policy could be highly destabilizing to aggregate demand and hence to short run real output and employment.

Which of these different money supply measures should we choose as a target for steady growth? There simply is no right answer in a world where short run velocities are unpredictable. Policy-makers who are concerned with both short and long run impacts of monetary change on the macroeconomy must be careful not to focus all their attention on one particular definition of money.

7. Unemployment. Employment and unemployment information in the U.S. comes from monthly surveys of a representative sample of about 60,000 households and almost 370,000 establishments (employers). The surveys ask questions about current employment, weekly hours worked, and for those who were not employed at the time, whether they sought work during this period. Measuring the "labor force" as the number of persons aged 16 or over who are either employed or currently looking for work, the *unemployment rate* is determined by dividing the number of job searchers by the size of the labor force.

In an earlier chapter we summarized the breakdown of the actual unemployment rate into *cyclical unemployment* and the *natural rate of unemployment*, which in turn is composed of "frictional" and "structural" components ($U = U^* + U^{cyc} = U^{fr} + U^{str} + U^{cyc}$). How well do available measures approximate these concepts? The only available official statistics are for the overall unemployment rate, with lots of additional detail about unemployment by age group, sex, race, and duration of unemployment. There are no official governmental measures of the frictional, structural, and cyclical concepts of unemployment.

How reliable are the available data on the overall unemployment rate (U) for the United States? Since we're extrapolating from a sample to the entire population, there's always the presence of sampling error. Because of this the Bureau of Labor Statistics only regards changes in the measured unemployment rate of 0.2% or more as reflecting significant changes in the true labor market picture. Monthly changes less than this amount, in either direction, could be due to sampling error and should not be used to infer a change in labor market conditions.

Another problem in the unemployment statistics concerns the "discouraged worker" effect. Studies show that perhaps as many as half of those who are presently counted as unemployed will never find jobs and eventually will just stop looking. This moves them out of the unemployed category and even out of the measured labor force and thereby lowers measured unemployment. To the extent that some of these persons still desire employment but are not actively looking, our standard measure of unemployment has a downward bias relative to the underlying concept of unemployment we're trying to approximate. As you'd expect, the degree of this downward bias in measured unemployment is highest during recessions and lowest during booms.

8. International statistics. As we are constantly reminded by the media as well as by the labels on the goods we purchase, we live in an increasingly *international* economic environment. This clearly has important implications for our decision-making at all levels—household, business, and government. And to avoid new threats and take advantage of new opportunities we need reliable data on worldwide economic events. Currently there are many agencies that work to provide internationally comparable economic data. The United Nations, the International Monetary Fund (IMF), and the Organization for Economic Cooperation and Development (OECD) prepare a wide array of comparative economic statistics while the World Bank compiles many additional international figures on literacy rates, life expectancy, pollution levels, and other vital indicators of our overall well-being.

After our discussion of some of the weaknesses in the U.S. statistics, you can imagine that such problems are only compounded when we turn to international data. The underlying national statistics are of varying quality, breadth, and detail and often reflect differing statistical methodologies and even slightly different definitions of basic concepts. The process of adjusting for these differences in order to put them on a comparable footing is laborious at best. It's no job for perfectionists. The goal is to create a body of world economic data that, however approximately, reflects major events and trends and allow us to make meaningful, if rough, comparisons of living standards, unemployment rates, growth rates and so on across different countries. These statistics provide important overall descriptive knowledge, as well as the more detailed information to help decision makers in world markets, and the raw material for testing and improving our economic models.

The most apparent problem in making national data comparable across countries is the existence of different currencies. A major job for the economic statistician is to try to convert all the different "economic tongues" into one "language," a single unit of measurement. The dollar continues to be the traditional common currency for such comparisons and the problem is how to make meaningful conversions of francs and yen and pesos and all the rest into dollars. The obvious place to look—currency markets where up-to-the-minute exchange rate data are readily available—does not provide the answer that we need for most purposes. These market exchange rates reflect the supply and demand for currencies needed to finance the current volume of imports, exports, and capital flows across nations. They could be used as a reliable indicator of purchasing power only if we spent *all* our income on imports.

A meaningful comparison of incomes across countries must be based on *the purchasing power of that currency within its own country*—how large a bundle of goods and services it can purchase at home. Then we must compare the size of these bundles across different countries. The standard approach is through "purchasing power parity" exchange rates. It is based on an underlying assumption called the "law of one price" which in its simplest formulation says that in an economy with active markets, a good will not sell for different prices at different places at the same time. If it did, alert buyers would move their demand to the low-price market, bidding up its price until the gap disappeared. Purchasing power parity says that what is true for one commodity is also true for the bundle of commodities underlying our calculations of the price level and hence our real income. We can use the price of this bundle like a single good and assume that it has the same dollar cost in each country. From this assumption, we can proceed to get an exchange rate for each currency based not on the current transactions in foreign exchange markets, but on the *assumption that the dollar price of a representative group of goods and services must be the same in each country*. If it were not, arbitragers would buy in the low-price markets and sell in the high price markets until parity was re-established.

Using purchasing power parity to make international comparisons has many drawbacks and should not be regarded as more than an approximation. For one thing, price indexes of different nations may reflect different bundles of goods and services and hence have different weightings. In addition, not all our purchases are traded internationally, so the "law of one price" may not apply to certain goods and services. Transport costs and tariff barriers also make it necessary to qualify and weaken the "one price" assumption. Despite these limitations, the use of purchasing power parity exchange rates at least moves us, however imprecisely, in the right direction if our interest is in making cross-country comparisons of economic well-being. The very first diagram in the book, Figure 1.1, compares world per capita incomes using purchasing power parity to translate across currencies.

Comparing interest rates, growth rates, and other currency-free numbers across nations avoids the difficulties of converting to a common unit of account. But other problems arise. For example, international comparisons of unemployment rates are all calculated as the fraction of the total labor force who are currently employed. But different countries have chosen to use slightly different definitions of just who is in the labor force and who is considered unemployed. In the U.S., for example, everyone 16 and older is counted as part of the labor force. But compulsory schooling ends at an earlier age in some countries, so Germany, Japan, and Canada count everyone age 15 and over while Italy uses 14 as its minimum labor force age. Workers who have been laid off but are awaiting recall are counted in U.S. unemployment figures but not in those of other countries. Some countries, like Japan, apply very stringent criteria in defining whether someone out of work is "actively seeking employment." Compared to the U.S., the Japanese measure is more likely to classify a person as not in the labor force and hence not unemployed. There is room for honest disagreement on the "correct" definition, but what it means is that we can't take cross-country comparisons of unemployment rates at face value.

IN SUMMARY . . .

Concepts Versus Measures

Macroeconomic data help us see where we've been and, used carefully, can provide clues as to where we're headed. Though we have been dwelling on their shortcomings, it should be stressed that the creation and development of macroeconomic statistics around a framework provided by economic theory has been one of the major accomplishments of the economics profession in the twentieth century. The volumes of statistics now available on the world's economies are extraordinarily useful in providing general descriptive knowledge, specific information for decision-makers in industry and government, and, for economists, a laboratory for testing new theories. As our economic goals become increasingly ambitious and our economic environment continues to change, continued improvements in these data will be essential.

As far as the quality of currently available statistics, there's no easy verdict as to the size of the gap between *real world measures* and *analytical concepts*. The gaps are wider in some places than others and if there were a simple way to take them into account, they obviously wouldn't exist in the first place. The only general conclusion we can draw is that users of economic data must be alert to the main limitations of key measures like the standard of living, economic growth, saving, deficits, inflation, and unemployment. Taking any of these data at face value, as is often done by the news media and by campaigning or crusading politicians, can create a warped view of economic reality and impair both private decision-making and public policy choices.

From a larger perspective, a reliable system of measurement plays an important role in keeping our perceptions and beliefs from straying too far from reality. Our propensity, increasingly confirmed by psychologists, to believe what we *want* to believe can lead to extraordinarily poor decisions that have no chance of accomplishing the goals for which they were intended. Hence it's particularly important for us to have credible quantitative information to help separate the true signals from the background noise of a complex, interdependent world.

15.4 "MEASURING" CONNECTIONS ACROSS VARIABLES

Now that we have easy access to a data base that is both extensive and generally reliable (subject to the limitations discussed earlier), just how do we go about using it? The simplest and most common use is for describing past economic performance in numbers, graphs, or charts either over time (time-series data) or across individuals, businesses, or countries at a particular time (cross-section data). Much of this descriptive information comes from the media and covers only the tiny fraction of the available data regarded as "newsworthy." It covers the latest releases on growth, unemployment, deficits, inflation, interest rates, but not much more. Most of the rich statistical information goes unnoticed except by a relatively few intensive users. These include financial analysts, industry specialists, and government policy analysts seeking clues to future developments in specific areas as well as economists trying to improve the explanatory power of their models. It's to this last use that we now turn.

The process of using *measurements* to quantify an *economic model* is called **econometrics.** Econometric theory combines economic and statistical theory to create procedures designed to squeeze every last drop of useful information out of the data. It's a separate and important field in economics that, like macroeconomics, requires its own courses and a certain amount of time and dedication to attain a working knowledge. But it's also a field that provides a set of tools used in every applied area of economics. The following discussion attempts to give you the flavor of this approach.

Once the national income accountants have quantified the *variables* for us, how can we use econometric techniques to extend the process of quantification to *connections across variables?* This extension can be thought of as a type of "measurement." But it is a much more ambitious and perilous undertaking than measuring observable variables. This is because it not only uses the **available data** but also depends on both an **underlying economic theory** (about *which* variables are connected and *how*) and a **statistical theory** of the probabilistic components of the relationship. This attempt to quantify the linkages across variables is usually called **estimation** to distinguish it from its more precise but less exciting cousin, "measurement."

To illustrate the estimation process in a simple setting, let's use a single component of our *AD/AS* framework—the relationship between real consumption spending (c) and real after-tax income ($y - t$). This is the familiar consumption function relationship, expressed as

$$c = c_0 + c_1(y - t)$$

where the two parameters (coefficients), c_0 and c_1, define an assumed linear relationship between after-tax income and consumption from our underlying theory. We saw that c_1 captures the sensitivity of consumption spending to a change in income-after-taxes [$\Delta(y - t) \Rightarrow \Delta c = c_1 \Delta(y - t)$ or $c_1 = \Delta c / \Delta(y - t)$]. We also saw that its size is an important determinant of the size of the demand-side multiplier process.[13] The c_0 term, called *autonomous consumption*, reflects all influences on consumption other than after-tax income. To combine data on consumption and after-tax income with econometric techniques to find clues as to the probable size of the parameters c_0 and c_1, we must make a slight but crucial transformation of the model.

The **economic model** ($c = c_0 + c_1(y - t)$) specifies an *exact* relationship between consumption and after-tax income. It says that once we know the values of the parameters c_0 and c_1, a given level of after-tax income *must* result in a single, precise value for consumption. But an **econometric model** (also called a "stochastic" model) recognizes that this *deterministic* hypothesis is unrealistic for a number of reasons, including (1) measurement error, (2) an underlying random component in our behavior, and (3) the fact that our simplified models omit important explanatory variables or assume a convenient functional form (in this example, linear) that distorts the estimated relationship in order to simplify the analytics. An econometric model presumes the existence of *underlying random elements* in economic relationships (and our measures) and tries to separate those sources of change from the systematic changes defined by the true (but unobservable) parameters of the relationship. Failure to make this separation leaves these random ups and downs as part of the basic relationship and wrongly incorporates them into the estimated parameters.

---

[13] Remember that the expenditure multiplier was given by $\mu = 1/(1 - c_1 + c_1 t_1 + x_1)$.

To be more specific, an econometric model of the consumption function says that even if we knew the true values of c_0 and c_1, our attempt to predict the actual levels of consumption for different values of after-tax income might come close to the mark, but would rarely if ever hit it. The actual values of consumption would form a more-or-less random scatter of misses around the predicted values associated with each level of after-tax income in our economic model. An econometric model accommodates this scatter through a *disturbance (or error) term.* In terms of our consumption function example, it adds a random component to the right hand side of the equation as one of the determinants of the actual level of consumption. It says that even when we've done our best to estimate the parameters defining the consumption/income connection, the actual value of consumption for 1995 (c_{95}) for a given level of after-tax income in 1995 ($(y - t)_{95}$) will end up being the predicted value $\hat{c}_{95}$ plus or minus a "roll of the dice" that we'll symbolize by ϵ. The econometric version of our consumption function is

$$c = c_0 + c_1(y - t) + \epsilon$$

where ϵ is the random disturbance term, introducing a measure of indeterminacy into the relationship between after-tax income and consumption.

This econometric model provides a framework that combines economic theory with the relevant data and also with some assumptions about the likelihood of various values of ϵ. The goal is to obtain the best possible estimates of the unknown parameters. That is, given the observed values of c and $(y - t)$ and some reasonable assumptions about ϵ (e.g., it's a random variable with a mean of zero and a constant variance), we want a procedure to estimate c_0 and c_1.[14] Whatever initial information we can bring to the investigation about (1) the details of the economic model, (2) the distribution of the error term, or (3) biases in the data will increase our ability to approximate the true values of the unknown parameters.

The danger is that to the extent that this initial information is at variance with reality, we weaken our ability to make good parameter estimates. It's a criminal investigation searching for the true parameters on the basis of a limited number of clues. Making some strong initial assumptions can narrow and thereby focus the investigation considerably. If these assumptions are correct they can lead to a quick arrest and conviction. But if they're wrong we'll be searching in the wrong places, turning up the wrong suspects, following false trails, and perhaps even convicting an innocent party.

In practice, the most frequently used estimation technique is the relatively simple **ordinary least squares** (OLS), a type of *regression analysis* ("regressing" back to the past to look for clues). When its relatively simple and strong assumptions about the disturbance term and other underlying conditions are met, it yields useful estimates of the unknown parameters. But in many applications these assumptions are not met and OLS regression can be quite misleading. We must then turn to one of the many other techniques for parameter estimation. An important part of becoming a good applied econometrician is learning which of many available estimation procedures is best suited to the problem at hand.

---

[14] Our ability to come up with good estimates of the parameters depends on many factors, but the nature of the disturbance term is perhaps the most crucial. Assumptions about the distribution of this disturbance term (its mean, variance, and other characteristics) are central to the estimation process. One of the tasks of econometric theory is to develop means for testing how well certain assumptions about the distribution of the error term fit certain kinds of data.

⚭ 15.5 FORECASTING

Estimating relationships among variables by combining data and theory into a **structural econometric model,** as it's called, is an elaborate and time-consuming undertaking. We obviously must expect that it will repay the effort by providing a useful quantitative bridge between choices and outcomes that can then be used to predict specific consequences of various events and policies. An econometric model of the consumption function, for example, could be used to generate a *forecast* of next year's actual consumption level. It could also be used to *simulate* the impact of alternative tax policies on future consumption spending. Or it could be used to "change" events of the past in order to inquire how those consumption choices might have been different had events or policies been different, a process of generating what are called "counterfactuals." [15]

But starting our discussion of economic forecasting with a structural econometric model is like learning to swim by being thrown into the deep end of the pool. If we begin at the shallow end instead, it is quickly apparent that this is something we've done many times before. In fact, forecasting the consequences of alternative actions and choices is something we do with virtually every decision we make. From the commonplace to the momentous, we typically have some expected outcome in mind when we decide how much to study for an exam, whether to cut class, change majors, buy a lottery ticket, change jobs and so on.

Since nearly every decision we make involves a forecast, we've all developed a variety of skills to help identify decision-to-outcome links. For the most part these methods are intuitive and informal, particularly when the consequences are relatively small. We rely on our common sense for quick, reliable guidance on most decisions. But as the stakes increase we tend to become more careful and systematic in our choices, particularly when the underlying issue is relatively complex. Economic forecasting, like that in any other area, can draw on a spectrum of approaches. These range from the *primitive and mystical* (omens or astrology, for example), the *knee-jerk reaction, slogan,* or *too-simple metaphor, common sense* (sometimes superb, other times overwhelmed by the complexity of the issue), and on to many kinds of *explicit and systematic forecasting techniques* of varying degrees of sophistication.

The existence of an uncertain future ensures that any prediction, however crude, has some chance of being correct. We've all discovered that playing a hunch sometimes "pays off." But if we look at how *well* it pays, with both successes and failures considered, it's apparent that in many situations we can do better. We've seen that one approach is to devise a representation of the underlying cause-and-effect mechanisms—an economic model—and then use statistical techniques to estimate actual values for the parameters of the structure. But an econometric model is quite costly in terms of time and know-how. Although such high-technology forecasting may be a good choice for large financial firms, government agencies, and economists testing their theories, less demanding forecasters often do quite well with techniques that are much simpler, faster, and cheaper. Two of the most popular of these simpler methods are **time series analysis** and **economic indicators.**

The goal of the "time series" approach is to predict the future value of a variable on the basis of its own past history. There's no attempt to determine how consumption varies

---

[15] For example, a text box in Chapter Four "A Policy Fantasy for the 1930s" used the *AD/AS* model to ask how things might have ended up if fiscal and monetary policy had not been contractionary for much of the early 1930s. This was only examined in qualitative terms since we didn't have specific values for the underlying parameters. An econometric simulation of the 1930s would yield actual magnitudes of change rather than just direction of change.

with after-tax income or how investment responds to changes in the real rate of interest as in an econometric model. Instead, we just look at past values of, say, consumption and search for patterns that can be extrapolated into the future. The simplest example is using an average of past values as an estimate of future values. Alternatively, we could use a moving average that puts more weight on the most recent observations. Or we might fit the past observations with a linear trend and simply extrapolate it to the future. More sophisticated techniques involve combinations of moving averages and linear extrapolations and look for patterns not only in past levels but in their rates of change. When a variable contains systematic intertemporal patterns—trends and cycles, time series techniques can be a very good and relatively simple forecasting tool.[16]

One of the virtues of time series analysis is its *flexibility*. It can be applied to population levels, church attendance, or highway congestion levels, as well as to gross domestic product, stock prices, or just about anything else that moves. But the flip side of such versatility is that *it employs no insights or information from the subject matter itself in making these forecasts*. It completely ignores all the systematic relationships and interactions that we have said are at the heart of macroeconomic activity. Because of this, most economists find the time series approach unappealing by itself although they often include it as part of their econometric models to search for residual cycles or trends after all the explanatory power of the economic variables has been taken into account. For noneconomists, time series forecasting often provides a practical middle ground between hunch or crude extrapolation and elaborate modeling.

The "indicators" approach is another common method of forecasting and is widely used in predicting business cycle turning points. Like time series analysis, it is based on an empirical search for past regularities that are then extrapolated to the future. The difference is that it uses past information on other variables, not the one being forecast, and in this sense can draw upon our understanding of economic connections. The best known example is the *index of leading indicators*, a weighted average of a number of variables that in the past have changed just before cyclical changes in output or unemployment.[17] It is prepared monthly by the Department of Commerce and is well-publicized by the news media.

The indicator method is a search for statistical associations and is unconcerned with whether this reflects causality or just correlation. It seeks to use these regularities, not explain them. The crucial thing for the success of indicator forecasting is that they continue to hold in the future. The obvious weakness of this approach is that changing events can and do cause such relationships to change. With no underlying theory of cause and effect to fall back on, the indicator method can't detect, much less reflect, these changes until well after they occur. When the old regularities lose their charm, new ones have to be found and the index must be redefined for the changed circumstances. Hence we never know just how much confidence to put in its predictions. It may work fine for many months or years and then suddenly give out a series of incorrect signals. This underlies the standing joke that the leading indicators have accurately predicted nine of the last five recessions. It is a method best used in combination with other sources of information.

While forecasting with time series or indicator methods is much simpler than with econometric techniques, don't forget the "no free lunch" principle. These tech-

---

[16] For an excellent treatment of a variety of forecasting techniques see Paul Newbold and Theodore Bos, *Introductory Business Forecasting* (Cincinnati: South-Western Publishing Co., 1990).

[17] The index includes such things as housing starts, the change in the level of inventories, an index of building permits, the average weekly claims for unemployment insurance, the Standard & Poor 500 stock index, the M_2 money supply, among others.

niques are easier only because they ignore so much potential information. An *econometric model* tries to encompass much more than those less ambitious methods. For example, unlike alternative methods it includes restrictions on individual relationships—which variables are most important, whether there's a linear or more complex relationship, and so on. It also makes assumptions about the characteristics of the "disturbance term" (ϵ). By separating the unexplainable random disturbances from the systematic changes we're after, we can get much more accurate parameter estimates and, ultimately, forecasts. As noted earlier, to the extent that this prior information is on the mark it adds predictive power, sometimes dramatically. But when it's off target, this extra information biases the analysis. We can end up with warped estimates of the parameters and resulting forecasts that can be far worse than those from much simpler methods.

Taking a closer look at the pros and cons of forecasting with an econometric model, let's start with the fantasy that all our economic and statistical assumptions turn out to be correct and that our estimates of the unknown parameters of the model also turn out to be exactly right. Should we expect this "perfect econometric model," as we'll call it, to give us perfect forecasts of the dependent variables? The answer, unfortunately, is a definite "no." One reason is that *random fluctuations* in behavior, measurement, or outside events create a certain amount of "noise" (i.e., unknowable variation) in the outcomes. This, of course, is a characteristic of the reality we're trying to explain and not a problem in our model. But in some cases these random fluctuations may be so large as to overwhelm the systematic part that our model is able to predict. Put another way, when the event in question is mostly in the grip of random forces, even the perfect econometric model can have little explanatory power.

But let's presume that in most cases this random element is small relative to the systematic components. Will our perfect macroeconometric model now be able to make forecasts that, except for random variations, are also perfect? Unfortunately the answer must again be "no"—unless we are also able to know the *future values of the exogenous variables.* That is, our perfect econometric model will give good forecasts of the endogenous (inside) variables only if it is "fed" accurate values for future levels of government spending, tax rates, the money supply, and any major supply shocks that might occur. When unexpected changes in the outside variables occur, even the most accurate econometric model may forecast badly.

This points up the obvious but sometimes-neglected fact that these models are not crystal balls for predicting the future. They are designed only to make **conditional forecasts**—predictions of the inside variables for assumed values of the outside variables. Careful forecasters sometimes deal with this problem of unexpected political events and policy changes by making many predictions, one for each of an array of plausible future values for the exogenous variables. This series of contingent forecasts, of course, does not appeal to those who just want a plain old (unconditional) forecast, such as "Is this a good time to get a mortgage? What's going to happen to interest rates?" But it's the best that the honest macro-econometrician can do when important and erratic exogenous factors are involved.[18]

---

[18] Even with a wide range of conditional policy scenarios we may often be way off in predicting actual events. For example, who would have imagined that the newly-elected Ronald Reagan, as persuasive and sincere a campaigner for balancing the Federal budget as we've ever had, would preside over eight years of deficit-financing at levels unprecedented in our peacetime history? Equally surprising, who would have predicted that Federal Reserve Chairman Paul Volcker would put on the monetary brakes hard enough and long enough to get the double-digit inflation rates of the 1970s down to 4% by the mid-1980s, in the process temporarily pushing nominal interest rates up toward the 20% range and unemployment to the highest levels since the Great Depression?

We have just seen two situations—large random fluctuations and unexpected changes in exogenous variables—in which even a perfect econometric model could give very poor forecasts of actual events. It's important to note that in such cases it's the circumstances not the model that's the problem. But in reality our econometric models are far from perfect and their estimated parameter values will sometimes be quite unreliable. In some cases we can improve the model by using more elaborate estimation techniques. For others there is little or nothing to do other than to use extreme caution in applying the model. To get a feeling for the kinds of problems that arise in creating an econometric model, let's look at three particular issues—*measurement error, specification error,* and what has come to be called *the Lucas critique.*

The data that we use to estimate the parameters of our model inevitably contain **errors in measurement.** These arise in the collection and processing of the information and also, as discussed earlier in the chapter, through gaps between our underlying economic concepts and their real world measures. To the extent that these cause systematic (i.e., nonrandom) distortions in the data base, the result is to bias our estimates of the parameters. In other words, *any initial mismeasurement in the variables must also infect our estimates of the relationships among those variables.* The distortion is then transmitted to our forecasts when the biased parameters are used to make conditional predictions of future outcomes with the model.

Another common and potentially serious shortcoming in our econometric models is the presence of **specification error.** This is a broad category that reflects the gap between the *structure assumed in the economic model*—which particular variables are included as explanatory variables and what functional form (linear, multiplicative, etc.) is assumed to capture the relationships—and the *unknown structure of the true relationship.* Since macroeconomics necessarily makes some drastic simplifications in order to achieve manageability, it's inevitable that our models will leave out many potential explanatory (independent or exogenous) variables. We consciously work to focus on what we think are the few dominant relationships, excluding what we hope to be the less important variables. In addition, unless we have solid evidence to the contrary, we typically make the analytically convenient assumption that all underlying relationships are linear.

But suppose we unwittingly exclude a variable that is in fact an important explanatory variable. Or suppose that our assumption of linearity is at odds with the true relationship which, unknown to us, is strongly nonlinear. When we then turn to the data for clues about the size of the unknown parameters, we will essentially be forcing those observations to fit a mold (our econometric model) that is different from the one ("reality") that generated it. This will mean parameter estimates that are, at very best, only approximations to the true parameters of the relationship we're examining.

For example, suppose that the current value of equity holdings in corporations are an important determinant of consumption spending but we leave them out of our model entirely. If the stock market has moved significantly during the period under study then it will be responsible for at least some of the movement in consumption spending. We'll obviously pick up the consumption changes in the data of our model. But this specification error means that the model simply ignores the changes in the stock market that caused it. The result is that our parameter estimation process will do its best to attribute these changes in consumption to whatever explanatory variables have been included in our model. In this sense, then, it forces the observations into the wrong mold and weakens our resulting image of reality.

Since we're assumed to be unaware of the importance of stock market prices, we'll also be unaware of just how this specification error is biasing our parameter estimates. To take just one possibility, suppose our model excludes stock prices but includes another explanatory variable, say the "trade deficit," that in reality has no impact whatsoever on consumption. But suppose that by sheer coincidence the trade deficit happens to have moved up and down in much the same pattern as the stock market during this period.[19] Our econometric estimation process will spot the correlation between these two variables and incorrectly attribute to the trade deficit what is actually the influence of the (excluded) stock market. This might be all right for predictive purposes if the trade deficit and stock prices typically moved much the same. But where their association is accidental and temporary, as assumed here, then our mis-specified model not only tells the wrong story about what causes consumption to change but also yields poor predictions whenever the trade deficit and stock prices don't happen to be moving in similar ways.

Unfortunately, the only cure for specification error is to try to avoid it in the first place. But in order to do this we would have to know the "true structure" of the model, which we surely do not. In practice we try to minimize specification errors by choosing our explanatory variables and functional forms as carefully as we can. This requires us to draw on whatever clues are available, particularly from microeconomic studies. In the end, it comes down to much trial-and-error and a healthy dose of "art" mixed in with the "science."

One other area of potential weakness in our econometric models deserves some attention. It is a type of specification error, but one that is specific to economic models in which expectations are thought to play an important role. It has come to be called the **Lucas critique,** after the economist who most effectively dramatized its potentially serious implications for policy applications of macroeconometric models.[20] Robert Lucas, noted in previous chapters as a major contributor to work on rational expectations and the new classical "rational misperceptions" model, maintains that many of the supposedly constant parameters that we estimate in creating our structural econometric models are, in fact, not constant at all. Therefore when we estimate a single value for them using available data, we are only finding an average of something that is actually moving around over time. We've seen that averaging our *variables* is a perfectly appropriate simplification in many circumstances. The price level, the real interest rate, and the unemployment rate are all calculated as averages. But the problem in this case is a bit different because (1) it takes an average value of a *parameter* (the quantitative link between changes in two variables), and (2) this value may well be *changing systematically with policy changes.*

If it is true that some of the underlying parameter values are changing systematically (that is, nonrandomly) over time, this tells us that we are mistakenly treating a *variable* as if it's a *constant.* If a particular parameter actually changes size as policies change, then estimating and using a fixed parameter value to predict policy impacts is obviously flawed. We must somehow incorporate this parameter change into our analysis before we can have any confidence in our policy conclusions.

---

[19] When two or more explanatory (right-hand side) variables tend to follow the same patterns of change they are said to exhibit *multicollinearity.* Even when there is no specification error involved, this situation creates obvious difficulties for our estimates of the parameters. If several explanatory variables follow the same pattern of change over time, how can we identify their individual impacts on the dependent variable? In some cases the underlying economic theory can provide hints on which of these variables is most plausibly linked to the dependent variable and we can drop the others from the model and remove the multicollinearity. Another alternative is to find another data set—for different years or a different country—in the hope of finding a setting in which these variables didn't follow the same pattern. Then our standard estimation techniques could identify the independent influence of each variable on the dependent variable.

[20] Robert E. Lucas, Jr. "Econometric Policy Evaluation: A Critique," in *The Phillips Curve and Labor Markets,* ed. Karl Brunner and Allan H. Meltzer (Amsterdam: North-Holland, 1976). Reprinted in Robert E. Lucas, Jr., *Studies in Business-Cycle Theory* (Cambridge, Mass.: The Massachusetts Institute of Technology Press, 1981).

To take a simple example, suppose an economy trying to end a lingering recession enacts a temporary, one-year, across-the-board tax cut. The rationale, of course, is that the increased after-tax income will lead to more consumption spending and thereby stimulate overall economic activity.[21] But, as we saw in Chapter 12, there is good reason to think that the impact of this *temporary* cut in taxes may be small and possibly even non-existent. Consumers tend to be forward-looking, so that their current consumption depends on an estimate of their longer term (permanent) income flow, not just their current take-home pay. Since a one-year tax cut is just a flicker in the stream of our expected lifetime income, it will add very little stimulus to current consumption spending.[22]

Will this relative ineffectiveness of a temporary tax cut be picked up in our econometric model? Not necessarily. It depends on how sophisticated the model is in treating the influence of expectations and also on how expectations actually changed during the time period for which we have data. Suppose we estimate the model's parameters using data from the past twenty years and that over this interval there were several tax rate changes but they were always perceived as permanent rather than temporary. Since lasting tax changes have a significant impact on our lifetime after-tax income, they will show a much stronger relationship to consumption than we'd expect from a temporary tax change. So this data will yield an estimated parameter linking tax changes with consumption spending that is too large for the issue at hand. The mis-specified model will predict a much stronger stimulus from this tax cut because it is unable to distinguish permanent from temporary tax changes.

The reason this type of specification error gets special attention is that expectations play an important role in our decisions and thereby in the level and especially timing of macroeconomic activity. *The importance of the Lucas critique is its underlying message that digging the relevant parameters out of our models in a reliable way is even harder than we'd like to think.* Expectations are very difficult to quantify and to incorporate into an econometric model. But without careful attention to the possibility of changing expectations, policy predictions from our models can often be very misleading. This is an especially important challenge to those who advocate the relatively frequent policy adjustments associated with an activist economic role for the government. In response to the Lucas critique, econometric practice in macroeconomics over the past two decades has become more technically sophisticated in identifying the impact of changing expectations on the underlying parameters.

15.6 ECONOMIC FORECASTS AND COMMON SENSE

Two obvious questions arise on the subject of economic forecasting. The first is whether it's any good or not. Do these formal and often expensive forecasting techniques—time series models, leading indicators, and large scale econometric models—provide information that can help individuals, businesses, and policy-makers make more informed decisions? The answer is contained in the simple fact that the

---

[21] In terms of our basic models, the tax cut would stimulate consumption $[c = c_0 + c_1(y - t)]$, shifting the *IS* and *AD* curves outward and speeding the return to y^*, AS^*, and the *PPF*. Policy lags, of course, must also be considered.

[22] If our consumer is not only forward-looking but also savvy about government deficits, she won't be taken in by this tax-postponement masquerading as a tax cut. As we saw in Chapter 12, a tax discounter will respond to a tax cut (postponement) only if she is also liquidity constrained.

demand for economic forecasts has continued to grow for many decades. We can't avoid making forecasts any more than we can avoid making choices. Techniques that narrow the range of likely future outcomes help us allocate our scarce resources more wisely. Even quite imperfect forecasts can lead to decisions that are far better than random guesses.

But this inevitably leads to a tantalizing second question. If economic forecasting is really able to provide useful information about the future, shouldn't this also bring great riches to its users, including the forecasters themselves? In other words, "If we're so smart, why aren't we rich?" There is much that could be said about the factors underlying this common misunderstanding of the art and science of forecasting.[23] But the bottom line is that the only time that an economic forecast can be counted on to bring great wealth is if the forecast is not only correct, but also secret. Whether it's a coming recession or an imminent drop in interest rates or a rise in the stock market, if you possess information that is both *unique* and *correct* you are well on your way to fame and fortune.

But before you bet all the money you can beg, borrow, or steal, remind yourself that the prediction needs to be *both* correct and unique. We've seen that unpredictable events will sometimes occur that invalidate even the best of forecasts. This is a chance that every investor and gambler must take. But the less obvious point is that even if your forecast turns out to be precisely correct, it will make you rich only if you act upon it before others do. A coming decline in interest rates, for example, means that the price of existing bonds will rise because their interest payments are fixed at a higher rate. Whoever owns these bonds while interest rates are falling will be the recipient of a capital gain. Had the previous holder kept the bond, he or she would have gotten the gain. So your strategy is to buy these existing bonds from the current holders at the current bargain price. Your informational advantage will bring you a capital gain on every bond you buy. The more you buy, the richer you'll get.

But let's return to the real world, a world of many people eager to make great riches and of many forecasters eager to sell them the latest and best forecasts possible. In this context it seems very unlikely that your forecast will be both correct and unique. Forecasting is a highly competitive industry and to the extent that others anticipate the change correctly, you lose your informational advantage. Current bond holders, hearing the same thing you do about the coming decline in interest rates, will sell to you only at the higher expected price. In other words, the current price will start to change as investor's expectations change.

So your dream of great riches will have to wait for a forecast that's both correct and unique or for a positive random fluctuation with you at the right place at the right time—in other words, "good luck." But remember that a correct and unique forecast doesn't have to be in the stock market or bond market. It can be a scientific discovery, a technological innovation, the anticipation of a new trend, or any of a myriad of ways in which true creators and innovators take the lead in reallocating resources to hitherto unsuspected areas of high return. Neither forecasters nor simple formulas for success can lead us to such results. The returns are high precisely because being correct and unique is such a rare combination.

---

[23] See the lively discussion of this and related issues in Donald N. McCloskey, *If You're So Smart: The Narrative of Economic Expertise* (Chicago: University of Chicago Press, 1990).

✿✿ 15.7 OVERVIEW

1. This chapter is essentially a reminder that understanding the workings of a "macroeconomic model" is not quite the same thing as understanding the workings of the "macroeconomy." With so much emphasis on the development and use of quite sophisticated models, we can forget that they are only simplified representations of a reality that is far too complex for mortal minds. Even the most rudimentary understanding of macroeconomic events must use a model to filter the essential from the unimportant.

2. How do we choose among the many competing models of the macroeconomy? The usefulness of a particular model depends on how well it can mimic the "real world." Establishing this correspondence between model and reality is, of course, the whole point of economic analysis. This is where the quantification of our models comes into play and where the roles of *measurement, parameter estimation*, and *forecasting* become essential activities in our attempt to choose among alternative models of an obscure and changing reality.

3. The diagram below sketches the process of combining an economic model with relevant data in order to estimate the unknown parameters and put some quantitative substance into our hypothesized relationships. The result is an *econometric model*. Its ability to give a convincing portrayal of "reality" can be tested through conditional forecasts and simulations. Our choice among competing models depends on how well they hold up to this process of measurement, estimation, and testing.

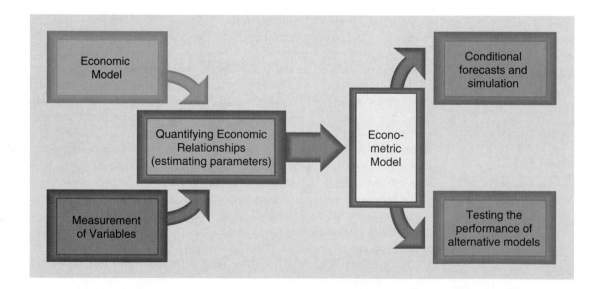

4. The *measurement of macroeconomic variables* is a crucial and difficult task that often goes unnoticed and unappreciated. The existing system of economic accounts in the U.S. and many other nations provides both an elaborate descriptive portrait of macroeconomic activity and a laboratory for evaluating the quality of our models. Despite its grand scope and rich detail, there are many shortcomings in the economic data. These inevitably warp our descriptive knowledge as well as our analytical understanding of the macroeconomy. An awareness of some of the main limitations

of the available statistics can help us to see situations in which we must use our models with particular caution.

5. Many of the shortcomings in the data could be remedied with more effort and resources. Most of the information is collected and processed by government agencies and many economists believe that political choices in recent decades have been notably short-sighted when it comes to investment in this key input. Improvements in our measures of gross domestic product, price indexes, and the government sector could substantially improve both our descriptive and analytical understanding of the macroeconomy. Other limitations in our measurements reflect conceptual puzzles that, though important, are unlikely to be easily resolved.

6. These data then become a basic ingredient in the transformation of our initial economic model into an econo*metric* model characterized by specific estimated values of the hypothesized parameters and assumed values of the policy and other exogenous variables. How faithfully this quantification of our theories will mirror reality can only be told by putting it through a variety of statistical tests of its explanatory power.

7. There are many factors that hinder and distort our econometric models. *Specification error* in the initial formulation of the economic model is always present in some degree. This can be particularly serious in situations where changing expectations affect decisions in ways that tend to obscure the underlying parameters. The *Lucas critique* tells us that extra precautions must be taken in trying to draw policy conclusions when the policies themselves can change our expectations of what's to come. *Measurement error*, particularly when it represents a systematic gap between the data and the concept, is another factor that can bias our estimated parameters.

8. One obvious use of an econometric model is to forecast the likely outcomes of current events and policies. If a particular model is unable to do this at least as well as alternative models it has not passed the most fundamental scientific test of usefulness. However it is crucial to understand that the appropriate test is *not* its ability to make unconditional predictions of future economic events. Instead, we must be concerned with the accuracy of its *conditional* forecasts. Even without the presence of biases from measurement and specification error, our unconditional forecasts of events will differ from the actual outcomes for at least two reasons—the *inherent randomness* captured in the disturbance term of our model and any error in our *guesses about future values of the key exogenous variables* of the model.

9. Economic forecasting, like any prediction of human behavior, is a perilous undertaking. Other than its inevitable imprecision, there are few valid generalizations we can make about economic forecasting. Forecast quality depends on what we're trying to forecast, how far ahead, and on the relative stability of outside factors during that particular period. Our poorest forecasts, unfortunately, tend to come when things are most in flux, when an accurate prediction would be particularly helpful to private and public decision making. It's at these times, understandably, that we can lose patience with the high-technology forecasters and search for something better.

10. What is a reasonable standard to expect from economic forecasts? How much error should we tolerate before looking for another supplier? There's no general answer to this, but the question we should ask is whether a specific predictive failure reflected poor forecasting skills—mistakes, *before* the fact, that could have been avoided by using more information or more powerful analytical tools in our econometric model—or whether it was simply the result of political events, sudden

policy shifts, or random twists of fate that could not have been anticipated by even the wisest observers?

11. Our fantasies of being able to foretell the future make us vulnerable to persuasive con-artists who claim to care so much about our welfare that they will sell us their "incredibly valuable secrets" for a modest sum. The extreme unlikelihood that their forecasts will be *both* correct and unique tells us that we've crossed the boundary between economic science and pure gambling.

⌘ *15.8 REVIEW QUESTIONS*

1. Define the following basic concepts or terms:

National income accounting	Econometrics	Economic indicators
Imputations	Estimation	Measurement error
Index number problem	Disturbance (error) term	Specification error
Product quality problem	Regression analysis	Lucas critique
Consumer durables	Structural model	Unconditional forecasts
Purchasing power parity	Time series analysis	Conditional forecasts

2. What are the main factors that need to be considered in a careful attempt to choose among competing models of the macroeconomy? Explain.

3. There are a number of reasons why the standard GDP measure is an incomplete measure of a nation's overall standard of living. Describe and discuss the major sources of discrepancy between "concept" and "measure."

4. It is often said that anemic levels of national saving are at the heart of the macroeconomic problems of the U.S. economy.

    a. What is the cause and effect connection, if any, between low national saving and poor economic performance? Explain in terms of an appropriate analytical structure.

    b. What are some of the reasons that make it difficult to measure the actual level of national saving with any high degree of accuracy? Explain.

5. The Japanese economy has been the envy of other nations on many counts. Its high rate of saving and low rates of inflation and unemployment have provided a stable, yet fertile environment for rapid economic growth. Moreover, when we convert its per capita GDP into dollars at exchange rates of the mid-90s, we find that its standard of living now exceeds that of the U.S. However, a look at some conceptual issues underlying these measurements suggest a number of reasons why these numbers could be misleading and should not be taken at face value. Discuss and explain.

6. "The whole point of a systematic, scientific approach to macroeconomics is to obtain a practical knowledge of the cause-and-effect linkages in the economy. Therefore the only meaningful test of a particular model is how well it can forecast the future. Models that provide poor forecasts won't survive the "predict or perish" standards of the scientific method." Evaluate.

7. Economic forecasts made with a structural econometric model can be incorrect for a number of specific reasons. What are they and what if anything can be done to reduce each of them? Discuss and explain.

✒ *15.9 FURTHER READING*

COLIN CLARK, *National Income and Outlay* (London: Macmillan, 1937).

ROBERT EISNER, *The Total Incomes System of Accounts* (Chicago: University of Chicago Press, 1989).

NORMAN FRUMKIN, *Tracking America's Economy*, 2nd ed. (Armonk, N.Y.: M. E. Sharpe, Inc., 1992).

SIMON KUZNETS, *National Income and its Composition*, 1919–1938, 2 vols. (New York: National Bureau of Economic Research, 1941).

THOMAS MAYER, *Truth versus Precision in Economics* (Brookfield, Vt.: Edward Elgar, 1993).

DONALD N. MCCLOSKEY, *The Rhetoric of Economics* (Madison: University of Wisconsin Press, 1985).

DONALD N. MCCLOSKEY, *If You're So Smart: The Narrative of Economic Expertise* (Chicago: University of Chicago Press, 1990).

JOHN B. TAYLOR, *Macroeconomic Policy in a World Environment: From Econometric Design to Practical Operation* (New York: W. W. Norton & Co., 1993).

CHAPTER 16

THE MACROECONOMY: CHOICES, POLICIES, AND OUTCOMES

ᏸᏫ 16.1 CHOICES TO OUTCOMES VIA MODELS

Scarcity and **choice** lie at the heart of every important and difficult issue in economics. The "dismal science" label will always fit because a central task of economics is to remind us of ever-present costs and constraints as we pursue material satisfactions. But economics is far more than a littany of limitations and frustrations. It's also a response to the challenges thrown up by a world of scarcity. An understanding of economic relationships helps us, individually and collectively, do the best we can with the resources at hand. So while economics is about tradeoffs and competition for limited resources, it is also about opportunities for cooperation and **mutual gain** among buyers and sellers, savers and investors, risk takers and risk avoiders. Good economic analysis helps us identify and create "win-win" situations through the efficient use of available inputs. It also helps us identify and avoid situations where ill-considered choices or policies hold down our standard of living.

The part of the economic spectrum allotted to *macro*economics came to prominence amid the crisis of the Great Depression and has retained a close connection to events, policies, and practical issues. Through six decades of rapid and sometimes turbulent developments in *theory, measurement,* and *statistical testing,* the study of macroeconomics has continued to focus on how policy can and cannot influence total output, unemployment, inflation, and economic growth. While much has been learned about the vast network of interconnections that comprise the macroeconomy, some important issues remain in dispute. But before making any assessment of the state of modern macroeconomics, we should emphasize a point on which virtually all economists agree but which is little appreciated by those without some economic training: *A practical understanding of the workings of the macroeconomy must be based on testable hypotheses of cause and effect—on theories and models rather than hunches and slogans.*

An economic model is the formal embodiment of the presumption that we can't avoid discussing connections if we want an understanding of where our individual and policy choices are taking us. The popular attitude that makes "theory" synonymous with "impractical" and dismisses careful analysis because it is sometimes complex is destructive to clear thinking and good decision making. It leads to the slogans and simplistic remedies of "pop economics" in which extravagant claims of huge benefits at little cost reveal wishful thinking covering a basic ignorance of well-established connections and interactions in the overall economy.

A working knowledge of the macroeconomy doesn't come easily or quickly, as you've learned from the preceding chapters. It also doesn't tell us everything we'd like to know. But when our analysis falls short, it is a non-solution to abandon the cause-and-effect framework of a model in favor of catchy slogans that feed our hopes or prejudices. Economists often say that "it takes a model to beat a model." We either need to find a way to improve our model or admit that we simply don't know what the consequences of a particular event or policy action might be in certain circumstances. Hence the underlying premise of this book: *There is nothing as practical as good theory!*

At the very beginning of the course we noted that a model is a metaphor—not the "thing itself" but a *representation* of it. We went on to develop algebraic and geometrical models as we searched for reliable and manageable representations of basic macroeconomic relationships. These models are essentially a language for converting the complexity of the "real world" into something simpler and more workable, yet still reliable. We have not tried for a grand all-purpose model that encompasses every important macroeconomic event. Instead, we've used an assortment of specialized models to suit the issue at hand. While having several different models can sometimes be confusing, its great benefit is to allow us to pick the simplest model for the question we're asking. The models that we have developed and used throughout the book fall into four broad categories.

1. The basic tradeoff between "this or that?" and "now or later?" that characterizes a world of scarcity is represented most simply by the PPF model. It offers a clear overview of the way in which the choices we make also mean alternatives foregone and an ever-present opportunity cost to all our decisions.

2. But the PPF model is largely descriptive and offers us little information about the underlying relationships that connect our choices with specific outcomes. For these linkages we turn to the comparative statics of the *IS-LM* and *AD/AS* models. This is an extremely useful and flexible analytical framework for uncovering a broad array of important implications of public and private choices for output, interest rates, the price level, investment, government deficits, exchange rates, trade deficits and other aspects of macroeconomic performance.

3. But the basic *AD/AS* model tells us little about issues of "timing" such as the persistence of economic fluctuations and the prospects for stabilization policies. Here we turn to the more elaborate short run dynamics of the AD/AS^e model and the *Phillips curve* model. Within this structure we can incorporate expectations, market frictions, policy lags, and supply side fluctuations in varying proportions and thereby capture the main alternative views of stabilization policy—Keynesian, monetarist, new classical, real business cycle, and new Keynesian.

4. But the cyclical fluctuations of "short run dynamics" take place in a "no growth" setting with aggregate supply (AS^e) assumed to be fixed. To get at the long

term dynamics of economic growth we turn to models that set aside the details of unemployment and business cycles in order to focus on the key features of the growth of inputs and output over time. These include the relatively simple *Fisher two-period model*, the elaborate *neoclassical (Solow) growth model*, and the more applied *growth accounting model*.

In this closing chapter we take a final inventory of what this collection of *models*, supplemented and qualified by the important issues of *measurement* and *statistical estimation* raised in the previous chapter, can tell us about the powers and limits of macroeconomic policy. What can we reasonably expect government to be able to accomplish and at what cost? What issues are sufficiently hazy and controversial that economic analysis alone can't tell us what we'd like to know? How do we proceed when our answers are incomplete?

16.2 ECONOMIC ROLE OF GOVERNMENT

Before we take stock of what's known, unknown, and disputed about the impact of public sector policy on the macroeconomy, let's take a brief look at government from a broader perspective. The fundamental economic power of government comes from its ability to set, enforce, and change the rules governing economic transactions. Constitutions, laws, and tradition all work to limit the tremendous potential for abuse. We have paid little direct attention to this larger role of government, relegating it to the "given institutional structure" category (the i^{nst} term) in the aggregate production function. But to understand the reasons behind the incredibly diverse performance of the world's economies at the end of the 20th Century we must be aware that underneath the so-called automatic market mechanism is a very elaborate and deliberate set of government regulations and procedures that define the *rules of the game* — the economic powers and limits of governments as well as individuals.

Where this underlying institutional structure is weak, a market system will not be able to deliver all the efficiencies that we associate with the "invisible hand." This is the present situation facing the postcommunist nations of the former Soviet bloc. Hundreds of millions of lives are directly affected by this unprecedented upheaval in basic economic organization. Those of us fortunate to be outside observers of these events can use them as a reminder of the importance and complexity of the governmental infrastructure needed to support a "free-enterprise" system. Though we sometimes alter our institutional framework in light of changing circumstances and goals, its strong foundation is a legacy that has been developed and passed down to us over many generations. This framework cannot be instantly erected on top of a very different institutional foundation. The unenviable situation of these countries might be characterized as an attempt to build an institutional "bridge" from a planned to a market system at the same time that great numbers of decision-makers are struggling to cross the unfinished bridge. The excesses, scandals, and inequities of this transitional process are sometimes referred to as *"frontier" capitalism*.

So free enterprise is not something "natural" that just springs to life when massive government ownership and control are abolished. The public sector must impose definite, well-understood limits on individual behavior (enforceable property rights and contracts, as well as mechanisms for settling disputes) if we are to succeed in channeling the so-called private vices of individual self-interest into something recognizable as the "public good." Samuel Butler, a 17th Century English poet, essayist, and clergyman, observed that "The world will always be governed by self-interest. We should not try to stop this, we should try to make the self-interest of cads a little more coincident with that of decent people." This is precisely what a market system attempts to do. Adam Smith, writing a century later, was the first to carefully map out the mechanisms by which it could do so. He was well aware of what we often take for granted—the need for an effective governmental infrastructure to allow the "invisible hand" a chance to do its work.

The policy focus of this book has been on what happens when the government goes beyond the roles of rule maker and referee to also become an active player in the macroeconomy. The authority to print money plus the power to command taxes to support public spending and borrowing gives a national government tremendous economy-wide influence. In an early chapter we dramatized this by likening it to "legalized counterfeiting" and "legalized theft." A great deal has been learned about the uses and abuses of monetary and fiscal policy since Keynes started things off with the publication of *The General Theory* (1936). But at the same time as we've been learning more about our policy tools, the policy environment itself has grown enormously large and complex. Herbert Stein observes that

> [Seventy] years ago when Calvin Coolidge was president, the federal government spent 3% of the gross national product. Almost all of that went for strictly federal functions, not performed by anyone else, such as national defense, postal service, care of veterans and interest on the war debt. Managing the federal budget could be left to bourgeois gentlemen who knew their multiplication tables up to 12 times 12 and a few maxims from Ben Franklin. The rest of the country could be left to the nation's business, which was, of course, business.

> Times have changed. It is not only that the federal government is spending more than 20% of the GNP. It is also profoundly affecting the part of the GNP it does not spend. It is borrowing about half of net private saving, and so greatly limiting private investment by Americans. Its taxes are affecting how much Americans spend for consumption, and who spends it and for what. Tax treatment of mortgage interest affects expenditures for housing. Tax treatment of fringe benefits affects expenditures for health. Regulations affect how much businesses spend for environmental protection and safety measures.

> We may not like this massive, pervasive influence of government, but it is not going to go away. Probably no other president in 200 years has been as determined to reduce the role of the federal government as Ronald Reagan. But his achievement in that direction [was] trivial.[1]

᙭ 16.3 WHAT CAN GOVERNMENT DO?

For better or worse, the existence of a large public sector means a powerful policy role for government. Policy successes can be dramatic and mistakes disastrous; running a "neutral" policy is difficult even to define, much less implement. How much do we actually know about what macroeconomic policy can and cannot do? Disagreements make the news and get so much attention that it's tempting to dismiss macroeconomics as an area in which every so-called expert has a different answer and little is actually known. In fact, the truth is much the reverse—there is a substantial range of agreement over how the macroeconomy works and over what we can and

---

[1] Herbert Stein, "Budgeting is Governing," *Wall Street Journal*, January 9, 1989.

cannot expect from government policy.[2] The following summary should help convince you that economic analysis has a great deal to say about responsible macroeconomic policy making.

POINTS OF GENERAL AGREEMENT

- There are no "free lunches" in a world of scarcity. All choices, public and private, have costs as well as benefits. Government spending always requires taxes—now or later, direct or indirect. Whether we pay in advance, pay now, or pay later, the price tag cannot be removed.

- There is a high degree of interaction and feedback within the macroeconomy which sometimes makes it very difficult to foresee the ultimate costs and benefits of our actions, private and public. Slogans and rules of thumb can be useful guides in some circumstances, but when underlying conditions change they may provide very bad advice. An analytical framework (model) that captures the main cause-and-effect linkages in the overall economy is essential to responsible policy making.

- The potential gains from "specialization and trade" are enormous but can only be realized to the extent that individuals are free to pursue their comparative advantages. Policies that protect certain individuals or industries from competition, domestic or international, will generally sacrifice these gains from trade. The legitimate exceptions to this rule of free trade—infant industries and natural monopolies—are seldom met with in actual practice. Most appeals for economic protection are thinly disguised attempts to use political means to transfer purchasing power from one group to another.

- International trade is economically no different than any other kind of exchange. Accordingly, restrictions on trade across nations (through tariffs or subsidies) typically reduce the nation's overall standard of living as they transfer resources to the protected industry. International trade makes for more efficient use of the world's resources. It results in net gains to all trading partners, accelerates technology and its diffusion, and keeps pressure on inefficient producers to improve or transfer their resources to more productive activities.

- The initial and primary impact of monetary and fiscal actions is on aggregate demand. The supply side impacts of macroeconomic policies are quite small. For issues of economic stabilization they can safely be ignored.

- Monetary and fiscal manipulation of aggregate demand typically has a strong initial impact on real output and employment and a weaker effect on prices.

---

[2] Bennett McCallum argues that "it is wrong to claim . . . that the present state of macroeconomic understanding is very bad. It is true that many wildly divergent modeling strategies appear in current research papers and that a wide variety of policy ideas are being put forth for consideration. . . . But mature and thoughtful members of the profession—even members whose articles feature very different models—will nevertheless take quite similar positions on most of the truly fundamental issues. One would get basically consistent answers from Friedman, Tobin, Lucas, and Solow to questions such as: Is sustained inflation likely without monetary accommodation? Would sustained inflation lead to faster growth over extended periods of time? Will an increase in government purchases increase aggregate demand? Will an open-market purchase of bonds increase or decrease demand? Can a nation's monetary authority simultaneously pursue both output and exchange rate targets?" (*Journal of Economic Education* [Summer 1994]: 219–234, as cited in Bernard Saffran, "Recommendations for Further Reading," *Journal of Economic Perspectives* 9 [winter 1995]: 195–196.)

- We can't "spend or print our way to prosperity," meaning that macroeconomic policy manipulation can have no lasting impact on the full employment level of output or its rate of growth.

- But there is a possibility that "spending" or "printing" (in other words, fiscal or monetary policy) can stimulate economic recovery by quickening the return to full employment. The degree to which such stabilization policy can be effective will vary with the source of the fluctuations, the speed at which expectations adjust to economic change, the extent of market frictions, and the magnitude of policy lags. The importance of each of these conditioning factors is subject to considerable controversy and defines the boundary between the activist and nonactivist views of stabilization policy, summarized later under "disagreements."

- The real rate of interest reflects the rate at which we can "move" goods and services back and forth across time—the price of future consumption in terms of foregone present consumption; alternatively, the price of present consumption in terms of foregone future consumption. In this role as "intertemporal price," the real interest rate has a decisive impact on borrowers and lenders, savers and investors, and every other choice involving "now or later?"

- Changes in government spending have a lasting impact on the real rate of interest and aggregate demand. Tax changes may or may not affect interest rates and demand, depending on the extent of "tax discounting" or "liquidity constrained" behavior.

- Money supply changes shift aggregate demand but have only a temporary effect on the real rate of interest. However, to the extent that monetary changes alter the rate of inflation they will have a lasting effect on the nominal (market) rate of interest.

- The "twin deficits"—the government budget deficit and balance of trade deficit—are linked through the real rate of interest in a system of flexible exchange rates. To the extent that a rising structural deficit increases the real interest rate, it will also increase the international demand for dollars, raise the real value of the dollar internationally and thereby result in a decline in net exports.

- But whether these deficits are sustainable or not depends on whether the borrowed funds are used for consumption or investment purposes. Like private borrowing, public deficits and trade deficits can be used well or they can lead to overcommitment and a proverbial "day of reckoning" scenario.

- Expectations about future events and policies are important determinants of current economic performance. Difficult as "expectations" are to conceptualize and quantify, any serious attempt to understand economic fluctuations must incorporate the role of misperceptions and the speed at which they respond to changing conditions.

- Political incentives for policymakers to exploit these misperceptions result in an "inflationary bias" from discretionary policy formulation. To the extent that we accept restrictions on policy maker's authority to respond to current conditions (tradition, rules, laws, constitutional amendments, automatic stabilizers), this bias toward inflation can be moderated or even eliminated. The inevitable cost is to reduce the flexibility and adaptability of macroeconomic policies.

- Predictable policies can reduce misperceptions, making real output and employment more stable than they would otherwise be.

- The underlying or "core" rate of inflation is a consequence of the rate of growth of the money supply. More bluntly, the rate of inflation is "chosen" by the monetary authority. While numerous events and policies can cause one-shot price level changes, they can only continue when accommodated by faster money supply growth.

- Reducing inflation brings rising unemployment and falling real output. The extent of the downturn depends on how rapidly expectations adjust and on the degree of "market frictions."

- Apart from extremely high and unstable rates of inflation, there is no important long run relationship between the level of inflation and either real output or unemployment. Faster inflation won't bring a lasting increase in the overall standard of living, nor will it bring a decrease.

- Wage-price controls convert open inflation into suppressed inflation, attacking the symptom but not the underlying excess demand that is the cause. To the extent that such controls are combined with monetary contraction, they may strengthen the policy's credibility and reduce the unemployment cost of disinflation. But monetary contraction, not controls, is the key to lower inflation.

- Economic growth is largely a supply-side event. Monetary and fiscal policies have little impact on the rate of economic growth and then only over very long periods of time.

- While economic growth is a consequence of many factors, productivity growth fed by technological innovation seems to be by far the most important.

- The specific determinants of technological change are not well understood. But an important underlying factor in the growth process is clearly our private and public choices between "consumption now" and "more consumption later."

- The government can "tilt" the playing field in a variety of ways if it is concerned that the rate of growth is too low (or high). But the case for using government policy to stimulate economic growth by discouraging consumption and encouraging saving and investment is not as obvious as it may seem. The fact that "everyone" seems to favor more economic growth should not blind us to the fact that it has a very real cost—less consumption now. As with any economic good, we can't conclude that more economic growth is better than less until we factor in its cost.

This list is far from comprehensive and you're encouraged to make your own additions. Its significance lies in the fact that these are not only important policy issues, but are also generally uncontroversial among economists today. They are not implications of particular, highly specialized models nor are they ideological pronouncements acceptable only to "true believers."

Let's now step into disputed territory to look at areas of substantial disagreement over what macroeconomic policy can and cannot do. While these controversies may be inflamed by ideological differences, they are not created by the subjective differences in preferences and goals that shape our ideological views. They involve issues of fact (what *can* the government do?) that remain unresolved because the historical record provides insufficient evidence to choose among two or more alternative explanations. In some cases there is a possibility that additional data, combined with better modeling and testing, could move the issue to the "agree" column in the foreseeable future. But for most of these disputes it is unlikely that there will be any resolution soon, if ever, given our inability to run careful controlled experiments on the macroeconomy.

POINTS OF DISAGREEMENT

- There is controversy over whether the primary source of economy-wide disturbances comes from the demand or the supply side. Keynes's presumption that economic fluctuations originated with fluctuations in aggregate demand went largely unchallenged for half a century. But the "real business cycle" view has shown that the evidence is not strong enough to simply dismiss the possibility that a substantial source of output and employment fluctuations come from technological changes and other supply side events. This is important to policy formulation since standard demand-side macroeconomic policies can do little to smooth a business cycle that originates on the supply side.

- Even among the substantial majority unconvinced by the real business cycle hypothesis, there is disagreement as to whether the demand fluctuations are inherently *private-sector volatility* in consumption, investment, and net exports or primarily *public-sector instability* resulting from misguided policy attempts to "fine-tune" the economy in a world of long and variable policy lags.

- A very basic dispute is over why departures from full employment persist from month to month and sometimes year to year. Is the market-clearing process generally rapid or sluggish? Different views reflect different judgments about several events, including

  - The speed at which *expectations of inflation* and other variables adjust to changing events and policies.

  - The importance of various inherent *market frictions* that slow the adjustment of prices and wages and delay the return to a market-clearing level of full employment.

- There is disagreement over how far-sighted individuals are with respect to the consequences of government budget deficits. To the extent that consumer behavior reflects "tax discounting" behavior, rising public deficits will be met by counterbalancing increases in private saving. Four policy implications specific to a world of *tax discounters* are:

  - Increased deficits mean reduced private consumption now so there is no threat of a future "day of reckoning" from consumption-draining deficits.

  - Since deficit-financed increases in government spending are met by a corresponding increase in saving and drop in consumption, the ability of government spending to alter aggregate demand is greatly reduced.

  - Tax changes not accompanied by spending changes will have no impact on aggregate demand at all, further reducing the government's ability to conduct countercyclical policies.

  - Since fiscal changes will have little if any impact on real interest rates, the connection between the "twin deficits" is severed.

These specific disagreements add up to active controversy over policies to stabilize output and alter inflation. Specifically, we find continuing disagreement over two big questions.

1. *Does the government have the ability to moderate cyclical fluctuations in output and employment?* This dispute pitches activists against nonactivists and pivots on the source of fluctuations as well as the various elements that determine the speed of market-clearing and the extent of policy lags.

2. *How costly is it to reduce the inflation rate?* Those who think that the market-clearing process is generally rapid (as in nonactivist views) predict a relatively small and brief loss of jobs and output when money growth is reduced. But the presence of significant market frictions that slow the return to full employment (as in activist views) could make the unemployment costs of disinflation prohibitively high.

It's not necessary to make an irrevocable commitment one way or the other on the stabilization issue. For one thing, the gap between activists and nonactivists has diminished greatly in recent years so their actual policy recommendations are no longer so dramatically different. Moreover, the statistical evidence is surely mixed as well as hard to read because of our inability to hold "other things constant" while the data are generated. There are past episodes where it seems quite obvious that fiscal and monetary changes have contributed to periods of exceptional overall stability. There are others where it appears that well-intended policies did not work as advertised and likely had procyclical consequences. This suggests the possibility of an agnostic stance in which stabilization policy is always cautious but is sometimes used more actively than others, depending on a careful reading of specific economic conditions and circumstances.

DOES "AGREEMENT" MEAN IT'S "TRUE"?

How much confidence can you place in this or any other categorization of "agreement/disagreement" in economics? After all, the economics profession has certainly championed theories and policies that turned out to be wrong. The original Phillips curve represented a supposed long-run trade-off between inflation and unemployment that was widely accepted by economists and policy makers alike. Only when subsequent events revealed the instability of the Phillips curve and led to the "expectations revolution" in macroeconomics did the errors of the model become apparent to more than a small minority. The contractionary fiscal policy of the early and mid-1930s met the approval of most economists, reinforcing the popular misconception that economic prosperity could not be regained until the government "put its house in order" and restored the supposed "fiscal responsibility" of a balanced cash flow budget. Again it was subsequent events—the persistence of the Depression, the subsequent recovery through the deficit spending of World War II, and

(Continued)

Keynes's analytical linking of changes in aggregate demand to short run changes in output—that led to an understanding of the macroeconomic consequences of fiscal changes.

So it is certain that some of our present areas of agreement will be exposed as partial truths or even untruths in the years to come. It would be foolish to think, or especially bet, otherwise. But until the new evidence, more powerful analytical tools, or altered conditions arrive, we can only go with our best understanding of the moment. In part that means not repeating the mistakes of the past, something that is not as easy as it might sound given the difficulties of transmitting hard-won experience across generations. It also means a careful assessment of the scientific merits of the many competing theories of the present. Of course it may turn out that what looks like a crack-pot theory today will grow into the scientific orthodoxy of tomorrow. But we won't know that until tomorrow. In this respect, as in others, economics is no different than any other science. Current agreement in medical science, for example, is in constant flux with the development of new diagnostic tools, new treatments, new hypotheses, new data, and even the arrival of new diseases. In some areas of medicine the conventional wisdom of even a decade ago now appears shockingly primitive.

While our understanding of economic behavior (and even the underlying behavior itself) will change in coming years, there is a hard core of economic fundamentals that will not. Scarcity, choice, opportunity cost, and the mutual gains from free trade would be prominent among these. Any responsible assessment of economic events or formulation of policy will always need to begin with an understanding of how these basics constrain both private- and public-sector actions.

16.4 WHAT SHOULD GOVERNMENT DO?

Macroeconomic policy making is a complex balancing of competing and conflicting goals. Virtually every fiscal or monetary choice draws criticism, not because it's necessarily "bad" but because in a world of scarcity there are always alternatives that would make some people better off (and others, of course, worse off). For most of us, taxes are always "too high" and whatever the level or type of government spending, each of us will have some objections—"too much of this, not enough of that." In democratic nations this discontent is typically open and, except perhaps during wartime or other national emergencies, widespread. Even policy makers themselves sometimes disavow responsibility for the outcome, finding real or imagined scapegoats for the unpopular parts.

Disagreement over what policy *should* be chosen is not necessarily a disagreement over how the macroeconomy works. It does not reflect, as we sometimes like to think, the eternal ignorance of people who don't agree with us. It signifies, instead, the eternal fact that economic choices, public and private, are inevitably a compromise—a choice between "this or that?" and "now or later?" And compromises, by their very nature, bring frustration—buyers want lower prices, sellers higher; borrowers seek lower interest rates, lenders higher; as taxpayers we want "no new taxes," but as beneficiaries of public goods and services we want new and better government programs; as consumers we may want lower inflation, but not the increased unemployment it brings in the short run. Disagreement—from mild and polite to harsh, bitter or even deadly—is the rule when it comes to economic policy.

What can an understanding of economics contribute to the policy-making process? Economic analysis is about feasibility and facts, about trying to determine which statements are true and which false. It works in the domain of science and attempts to quantify connections between choices and outcomes. Can we speed up an economic recovery and, if so, at what cost? Can we lower inflation and, if so, at what cost? Can we balance the budget and, if so, at what cost? True to its scientific objectivity, economic analysis passes no judgement on the desirability of one particular outcome over another.

As with any question in science—Can we build an atomic bomb? Can we put a man on the moon? Can we unravel the genetic code?—the missing ingredient is "should?". And this requires some valuation of the predicted benefits relative to the cost. This, in turn, moves us beyond the realm of science to one of subjective value judgements, preferences, and goals. No science worthy of the name can separate true from false when it comes to "correct" values or goals. Advocates of a particular policy view often try to convince us that their policy follows "scientifically" from their brilliant analysis. But somewhere along the way they have crossed the boundary between "can" and "should" without telling us or, perhaps, even realizing it themselves. They have melded their science with their value judgements, the means with the ends.

The endless controversy over macroeconomic policy is much easier to assess if we keep a clear distinction between "can" and "should." Much and probably most of the disagreement over economic policy is ultimately about what goals we should pursue, not about how the economy works. As a result it is a dispute that cannot be ended by any amount of analysis or research.[3] When two winners of the Nobel Prize in economics take exactly opposite views on a proposed policy it only seems to verify George Bernard Shaw's quip that "if all the world's economists were laid end-to-end they still couldn't reach a conclusion." Whatever this may mean, it obviously strikes a responsive chord with many. But there's no good reason why economists *should* agree about such important policy issues as the "proper" role of government or the "desired" rate of economic growth or the "optimal" level of the budget deficit. Even if they did, there's no reason why any non-economist should feel compelled to accept their views. Except for the factual issues of "speed of market clearing," "policy lags," and so on (discussed in the previous section), policy disagreements among economists are largely about issues of "should" rather than "can." They do not reflect a failure of science, but simply a recognition of the proper boundaries of science.

---

[3] One qualification of this partitioning of "means" and "ends" should be noted. When there is a basic misunderstanding of facts, it could well happen that goals change in response to improved economic analysis. For example, those who believe that we should move quickly to balance the government's cash flow budget may modify their goals if they discover that they were confusing the consequences of a "cash flow" deficit with those of a "capital account" deficit. Those who have been staunch advocates of zero inflation may change their position when they learn that not only do existing price indexes overstate the true rate of inflation but also that since every dollar spent on higher prices is a dollar received as higher income, the costs of inflation are not as sizable as often thought.

ᏬᏋ 16.5 WHAT WILL GOVERNMENT DO?

A final angle on economic policy takes us inside the decision process to consider the incentives acting on the policy makers themselves. Instead of thinking of policy choices just in terms of *can* and *should*, we add another dimension by asking what a rational policymaker *will* do. This view is a descendent of the ages-old cynicism that those in power—kings and queens, emperors, popes, premiers, prime ministers, and presidents, as well as parliaments, congresses, cabinets, and bureaucrats—are likely to act in their own self-interest even if it conflicts with some larger notion of the public interest. Outright fraud and corruption and other misuse of power come first to mind. But there are also more subtle, widespread, and fully legal factors that can be important.

Expressed in a different way, recognition of the forces acting on the choices of policy makers alerts us to the fact that we have left them entirely outside our model. We have overstated the range of what policy "can" do by assuming that there are no frictions or distortions in the policy-making process itself. In short, we've made things look considerably easier than they really are. According to public choice theory, some of our apparent policy options will not be feasible once we take into account the motivations and actions of the policy makers themselves. Todd Buchholz summarizes this approach as follows:

> *The Public Choice school thinks it can explain many economic and political problems: why we suffer from persistent budget deficits; why special interest groups proliferate; why bureaucracies continue to expand despite presidential promises to trim them; and why government regulators often protect businesses more than consumers. Most economists see politics as an irritating, incomprehensible, noneconomic obstacle to good policy. In contrast Public Choice economists insist that politics must be studied with the tools of economics. Politics is, they charge, an economic activity. Economists should not just throw up their arms and look disgusted. They should ask why bureaucrats and legislators frequently frustrate good policy.*[4]

It is not clear just how much the "public choice" perspective, intriguing as it may seem, changes our thinking about macroeconomic policy. Some of its concerns have already been addressed within our standard analysis—for example, the problem of a "political business cycle" and an "inflationary bias" inherent in discretionary policy formulation. But it can also remind us of the need for consistency and symmetry in comparing private with public decision-making. Economists have generally been quick to identify and react to situations of "market breakdown" by proposing government solutions. The public choice view alerts us to the flip-side of this coin—the policy-making process is not the seamless, frictionless abstraction that we so often append to our models. Policy formulation has its own dynamics and is also subject to "policy breakdown" and imperfections similar to the market flaws in the private sector.

This final reminder of the many layers of difficulty in finding solutions to economy-wide problems is perhaps a fitting note on which to end. Economics will always be difficult and controversial—it's too important to our individual and national well-being to be otherwise. There will always be a demand for (and resulting supply of) easy remedies to hard problems. Proponents of these quick cures inevitably turn to the government since it has the power to solve their problems or implement their vi-

---

[4] Todd G. Buchholz, *New Ideas from Dead Economists* (New York: Plume Books, 1990): 241–242.

sions by spending other people's money or restricting other people's actions. The potential for misuse of this power has grown apace with the enormous increase in the size and influence of the government over the past 50 years. Even if, as seems most improbable, it were to grow no further over the next 50 years, it represents a complex and powerful economic force that requires constant attention and guidance. A key ingredient in the responsible use of our individual, national, and world resources is a solid understanding of basic macroeconomic analysis.

⊗⊙ *16.6 FURTHER READING*

ALBERTO ALESINA, "Macroeconomics and Politics," *NBER Macroeconomics Annual, 1988* (Cambridge, Mass.: The Massachusetts Institute of Technology Press, 1988).

TODD G. BUCHHOLZ, *New Ideas From Dead Economists: An Introduction to Modern Economic Thought* (New York: Plume Books, 1990), especially Chapter 11, "The Public Choice School: Politics as a Business."

JOSEPH E. HARRINGTON, JR., "Economic Policy, Economic Performance, and Elections," *The American Economic Review* 83 (March 1993): 27–42.

DANIEL M. HAUSMAN AND MICHAEL S. MCPHERSON, "Taking Ethics Seriously: Economics and Contemporary Moral Philosophy," *Journal of Economic Literature* 31 (June 1993): 671–731.

DAVID B. JOHNSON, *Public Choice: An Introduction to the New Political Economy* (Mountain View, Calif.: Bristlecone Books, Mayfield Publishing, 1991).

HERBERT STEIN, *On the Other Hand . . . Essays on Economics, Economists, and Politics* (Washington, D.C.: AEI Press, 1995).

NATIONAL AND INTERNATIONAL MACROECONOMIC DATA

U. S. MACROECONOMIC PERFORMANCE

from Council of Economic Advisers, *Economic Report of the President*

YEAR	y	c	i	x	g	exp	imp	s/y	gdp deflator P	U	B/Y	3 mo. U.S. Rst	10 yr U.S. Rlt	Moody's Aaa R
				1987 $										
1929	821.8	554.5	152.8	1.9	112.6	36.0	34.1	3.0%	12.5	3.2	-1.0%			
1930	748.9	520.0	107.2	-0.3	122.0	29.8	30.1	2.5%	12.1	8.7	0.3%			
1931	691.3	501.0	67.2	-2.3	125.5	24.7	27.0	2.1%	11.0	15.9	3.8%			
1932	599.7	456.6	25.0	-2.4	120.5	19.6	22.0	-3.1%	9.7	23.6	3.1%			
1933	587.1	447.4	26.6	-3.0	116.1	19.9	22.9	-3.9%	9.5	24.9	2.3%			
1934	632.6	461.1	41.1	-1.0	131.4	22.3	23.4	-1.1%	10.3	21.7	3.4%			
1935	681.3	487.6	65.2	-7.2	135.7	23.9	31.1	2.3%	10.6	20.1	2.8%			
1936	777.9	534.4	89.9	-5.1	158.6	25.3	30.4	4.4%	10.6	16.9	3.9%			
1937	811.4	554.6	106.4	-1.9	152.2	31.9	33.8	4.0%	11.2	14.3	-0.6%			
1938	778.9	542.2	69.9	4.2	162.5	30.7	26.5	-0.3%	10.9	19.0	1.8%			
1939	840.7	568.7	93.4	4.6	174.0	32.7	28.1	2.4%	10.8	17.2	2.6%	0.02		3.01
1940	906.0	595.2	121.8	8.2	180.7	37.5	29.2	3.8%	11.0	14.6	0.5%	0.01		2.84
1941	1070.6	629.3	149.4	2.8	289.1	39.1	36.3	10.7%	11.7	9.9	3.0%	0.10		2.77
1942	1284.9	628.7	81.4	-11.1	586.0	26.3	37.4	23.1%	12.3	4.7	19.7%	0.33		2.83
1943	1540.5	647.3	53.5	-28.1	867.7	22.3	50.4	24.5%	12.5	1.9	23.0%	0.37		2.73
1944	1670.0	671.2	59.8	-29.0	968.0	24.6	53.5	25.0%	12.6	1.2	24.5%	0.38		2.72
1945	1602.6	714.6	82.6	-23.9	829.4	32.8	56.7	19.2%	13.3	1.9	18.7%	0.38		2.62
1946	1272.1	779.1	195.5	26.5	271.0	66.7	40.2	8.5%	16.7	3.9	-2.5%	0.38		2.53
1947	1252.8	793.3	198.8	41.9	218.8	79.7	37.1	3.0%	18.7	3.9	-6.1%	0.59		2.61
1948	1300.0	813.0	229.8	16.6	240.6	60.7	44.1	5.8%	20.0	3.8	-3.6%	1.04		2.82
1949	1305.5	831.4	187.4	17.3	269.3	59.9	42.5	3.7%	19.9	5.9	1.2%	1.10		2.66
1950	1418.5	874.3	256.4	3.2	284.5	53.0	49.7	5.9%	20.2	5.3	-2.4%	1.22		2.62
1951	1558.4	894.7	255.6	11.1	397.0	64.3	53.2	7.3%	21.3	3.3	-1.7%	1.55		2.86
1952	1624.9	923.4	231.7	2.3	467.6	62.3	59.9	7.2%	21.5	3.0	1.0%	1.77		2.96
1953	1685.5	962.5	240.3	-7.1	489.8	59.5	66.6	7.0%	22.0	2.9	1.5%	1.93	2.85	3.20
1954	1673.8	987.3	234.1	-2.3	454.7	62.2	64.4	6.2%	22.2	5.5	1.9%	0.95	2.40	2.90
1955	1768.3	1047.0	284.8	-5.2	441.7	67.7	72.9	5.7%	22.9	4.4	-0.7%	1.75	2.82	3.06
1956	1803.6	1078.7	282.2	-1.2	444.0	78.0	79.2	7.1%	23.6	4.1	-1.3%	2.66	3.18	3.36
1957	1838.2	1104.4	266.9	1.6	465.3	85.0	83.4	7.2%	24.4	4.3	-0.2%	3.27	3.65	3.89
1958	1829.1	1122.2	245.7	-14.9	476.0	73.7	88.5	7.4%	24.9	6.8	2.4%	1.84	3.32	3.79

U. S. MACROECONOMIC PERFORMANCE

YEAR	1987 $				g	exp	imp	s/y	gdp deflator	U	B/Y	3 mo. U.S.	10 yr U.S.	Moody's Aaa	E	e	M1	M2
	y	c	i	x	g	exp	imp	s/y	P	U	B/Y	Rst	Rlt	R	E	e	M1	M2
1959	1928.8	1178.9	296.4	-21.8	475.3	73.8	95.6	6.3%	25.6	5.5	0.6%	3.41	4.99	4.38			140.0	297.8
1960	1970.8	1210.8	290.8	-7.6	476.9	88.4	96.1	5.7%	26.0	5.5	-0.7%	2.93	4.12	4.41			140.7	312.3
1961	2023.8	1238.4	289.4	-5.5	501.5	89.9	95.3	6.6%	26.3	6.7	0.6%	2.38	3.88	4.35			145.2	335.5
1962	2128.1	1293.3	321.2	-10.5	524.2	95.0	105.5	6.5%	26.9	5.5	0.5%	2.78	3.95	4.33			147.8	362.7
1963	2215.6	1341.9	343.3	-5.8	536.3	101.8	107.7	5.9%	27.2	5.7	-0.3%	3.16	4.00	4.26			153.3	393.2
1964	2340.6	1417.2	371.8	2.5	549.1	115.4	112.9	6.9%	27.7	5.2	0.2%	3.55	4.19	4.40			160.3	424.8
1965	2470.5	1497.0	413.0	-6.4	566.9	118.1	124.5	7.0%	28.4	4.5	-0.2%	3.95	4.28	4.49			167.9	459.3
1966	2616.2	1573.8	438.0	-18.0	822.4	125.7	143.7	6.8%	29.4	3.8	0.1%	4.88	4.92	5.13			172.0	480.0
1967	2685.2	1622.4	418.6	-23.7	667.9	130.0	153.7	8.1%	30.3	3.8	1.7%	4.32	5.07	5.51			183.3	524.3
1968	2796.9	1707.5	440.1	-37.5	686.8	140.2	177.7	7.1%	31.8	3.6	0.5%	5.34	5.65	6.18			197.4	566.3
1969	2873.0	1771.2	461.3	-41.5	682.0	147.8	189.2	6.5%	33.4	3.5	-1.0%	6.68	6.67	7.03	122.4		203.9	589.5
1970	2873.9	1813.5	429.7	-35.2	665.8	161.3	196.4	8.0%	35.2	4.9	1.1%	6.46	7.35	8.04	121.1		214.4	628.1
1971	2955.9	1873.7	475.7	-45.9	652.4	161.9	207.8	8.3%	37.1	5.9	1.7%	4.35	6.16	7.39	117.8		228.3	712.7
1972	3107.1	1978.4	532.2	-56.5	653.0	173.7	230.2	7.0%	38.8	5.6	0.3%	4.07	6.21	7.21	109.1		249.2	805.2
1973	3268.6	2066.7	591.7	-34.1	644.2	210.3	244.4	9.0%	41.3	4.9	-0.5%	7.04	6.84	7.44	99.1	98.9	262.8	861.0
1974	3248.1	2053.8	543.0	-4.1	655.4	234.4	238.4	8.9%	44.9	5.6	0.3%	7.89	7.56	8.57	101.4	99.4	274.3	908.5
1975	3221.7	2097.5	437.6	23.1	663.5	232.9	209.8	8.7%	49.2	8.5	4.1%	5.84	7.99	8.83	98.5	94.0	287.5	1023.2
1976	3380.8	2207.3	520.6	-6.4	659.2	243.4	249.7	7.4%	52.3	7.7	2.2%	4.99	7.61	8.43	105.7	97.6	306.3	1163.6
1977	3533.3	2296.6	600.4	-27.8	664.1	246.9	274.7	6.3%	55.9	7.1	0.9%	5.27	7.42	8.02	103.4	93.4	331.1	1286.5
1978	3703.5	2391.8	664.6	-29.9	677.0	270.2	300.1	6.9%	60.3	6.1	-0.1%	7.22	8.41	8.73	92.4	84.4	358.2	1388.6
1979	3796.8	2448.4	669.7	-10.6	689.3	293.5	304.1	7.0%	65.5	5.8	-0.4%	10.04	9.44	9.63	88.1	83.2	382.5	1497.0
1980	3776.3	2447.1	594.4	30.7	704.2	320.5	289.9	7.9%	71.7	7.1	1.3%	11.51	11.46	11.94	87.4	84.9	408.5	1629.3
1981	3843.1	2476.9	631.1	22.0	713.2	326.1	304.1	8.8%	78.9	7.6	1.0%	14.03	13.91	14.17	103.4	101.0	436.3	1793.3
1982	3760.3	2503.7	540.5	-7.4	723.6	296.7	304.1	8.6%	83.8	9.7	3.4%	10.69	13.00	13.79	116.6	111.8	474.3	1953.2
1983	3906.6	2619.4	599.5	-56.1	743.8	285.9	342.1	6.8%	87.2	9.6	4.1%	8.63	11.10	12.04	125.3	117.4	521.0	2187.6
1984	4148.5	2746.1	757.5	-122.0	766.9	305.7	427.7	8.0%	91.0	7.5	2.9%	9.58	12.44	12.71	138.2	128.9	552.1	2377.9
1985	4279.8	2865.8	745.9	-145.3	813.4	309.2	454.6	6.4%	94.4	7.2	3.1%	7.48	10.62	11.37	143.0	132.5	619.9	2575.0
1986	4404.5	2969.1	735.1	-155.1	855.4	329.6	484.7	6.0%	96.9	7.0	3.4%	5.98	7.68	9.02	112.2	103.7	724.5	2818.2
1987	4539.9	3052.2	749.3	-143.1	881.5	364.0	507.1	4.3%	100.0	6.2	2.5%	5.82	8.39	9.38	96.9	90.9	750.1	2920.1
1988	4718.6	3162.4	773.4	-104.0	886.8	421.6	525.7	4.4%	103.9	5.5	2.0%	6.69	8.85	9.71	92.7	88.2	787.4	3081.4
1989	4838.0	3223.3	784.0	-73.7	904.4	471.8	545.4	4.0%	108.5	5.3	1.5%	8.12	8.49	9.26	98.6	94.4	794.7	3239.8
1990	4897.3	3272.6	746.8	-54.7	932.6	510.5	565.1	4.2%	113.3	5.5	2.5%	7.51	8.55	9.32	89.1	86.0	826.4	3353.0
1991	4867.6	3259.4	683.8	-19.5	944.0	542.6	562.1	5.0%	117.6	6.7	3.2%	5.42	7.86	8.77	89.8	86.5	897.7	3455.2
1992	4979.3	3349.5	725.3	-32.3	936.9	578.8	611.2	5.5%	120.9	7.4	4.3%	3.45	7.01	8.14	86.6	83.5	1024.8	3509.0
1993	5134.5	3458.7	819.9	-73.9	929.8	602.5	676.3	4.1%	123.5	6.8	4.1%	3.02	5.87	7.22	93.2	90.0	1128.4	3567.9
1994	5342.3	3578.5	955.5	-114.2	922.5	654.8	769.0	4.1%	126.1	6.1		4.29	7.09		91.3	88.6	1147.6	3600.0

MACROECONOMIC PERFORMANCE OF THE G-7 INDUSTRIAL NATIONS

Source:
IMF, *International Financial Statistics Yearbook*, 1994;
updated with revised figures from Council of Economic Advisers, *Economic Report of the President 1995*

Year	U.S.			CANADA			JAPAN			FRANCE			GERMANY			ITALY			U.K.		
	%U	%P	%y	%U	%P	%y	%U	%P	%y	%U	%P	%y	%U	%P	%y	%U	%P	%y	%U	%P	%y
1970	4.9	5.7	0.0	5.7	3.2	2.6	1.2	7.5	10.2	2.5	4.7	5.7	0.6	3.7	5.0	3.2	1.2	5.3	3.1	6.9	2.3
1971	5.9	4.4	3.1	6.2	2.8	5.8	1.3	6.2	4.3	2.8	5.6	4.8	0.5	-0.6	3.0	3.3	4.8	0.0	3.9	9.2	2.0
1972	5.6	3.2	4.8	6.2	5.0	5.7	1.4	4.9	8.2	2.9	6.3	4.4	0.6	11.6	4.3	3.8	6.2	4.3	4.2	7.1	3.5
1973	4.9	6.2	5.2	5.5	7.4	7.7	1.3	11.7	7.6	2.8	7.1	5.4	0.7	7.0	4.8	3.7	10.2	7.1	3.2	9.4	7.4
1974	5.6	11.0	-0.6	5.3	11.1	4.4	1.4	23.2	-0.6	2.9	13.9	3.1	0.7	7.0	0.1	3.1	19.4	5.4	3.1	15.8	-1.7
1975	8.5	9.1	-0.8	6.9	10.8	2.6	1.9	11.7	2.9	4.2	11.7	-0.3	1.6	6.0	-1.3	3.4	17.1	-2.7	4.6	24.5	-0.7
1976	7.7	5.8	4.9	7.1	7.4	6.2	2.0	9.6	4.2	4.6	9.6	4.2	3.4	4.2	5.5	3.9	16.7	6.3	5.9	16.4	2.8
1977	7.1	6.5	4.5	8.1	8.0	3.6	2.0	8.2	4.7	5.2	9.6	3.2	3.4	3.6	2.6	4.1	19.3	3.7	6.4	15.8	2.4
1978	6.1	7.6	4.8	8.3	9.0	4.6	2.3	4.2	4.9	5.4	9.1	3.3	3.4	2.7	3.4	4.1	12.5	3.7	6.3	8.3	3.5
1979	5.8	11.3	2.5	7.4	9.2	3.9	2.1	3.7	5.5	6.1	10.6	3.2	3.3	4.2	4.0	4.4	15.5	6.1	5.4	13.5	2.8
1980	7.1	13.5	-0.5	7.5	10.1	1.5	2.0	7.8	3.6	6.5	13.7	1.6	2.9	5.5	1.0	4.4	21.9	4.1	7.0	17.9	-2.2
1981	7.6	10.3	1.8	7.5	12.5	3.7	2.2	4.7	3.6	7.6	13.4	1.2	2.8	6.2	0.1	4.9	18.6	0.6	10.5	12.0	-1.3
1982	9.7	6.2	-2.2	11.0	10.9	-3.2	2.4	2.8	3.2	8.3	11.7	2.5	4.0	5.2	-1.1	5.4	16.5	0.2	11.3	8.5	1.7
1983	9.6	3.2	3.9	11.8	5.8	3.2	2.7	1.8	2.7	8.6	9.7	0.7	5.6	3.4	1.9	5.9	14.9	1.0	11.8	4.6	3.7
1984	7.5	4.3	6.2	11.2	4.4	6.3	2.8	2.3	4.3	10.0	7.4	1.3	6.9	2.4	3.1	5.9	10.6	2.7	11.8	5.0	2.3
1985	7.2	3.6	3.2	10.5	3.9	4.8	2.6	2.0	5.0	10.5	5.8	1.9	7.1	2.0	1.8	6.0	8.6	2.6	11.2	6.0	3.8
1986	7.0	1.9	2.9	9.5	4.1	3.3	2.8	0.7	2.6	10.6	2.6	2.5	7.2	-0.1	2.3	7.5	6.1	2.9	11.2	3.4	4.3
1987	6.2	3.6	3.1	8.8	4.4	4.2	2.9	0.1	4.1	10.8	3.2	2.3	6.6	0.2	1.5	7.9	4.6	3.1	10.3	4.2	4.8
1988	5.5	4.1	3.9	7.8	4.1	5.0	2.5	0.8	6.2	10.3	2.7	4.4	6.3	1.3	3.7	7.9	5.0	4.1	8.6	4.9	5.0
1989	5.3	4.8	2.5	7.5	5.0	2.4	2.3	2.2	4.7	9.6	3.5	4.3	6.3	2.7	3.6	7.8	6.6	2.9	7.3	7.8	2.2
1990	5.5	5.4	1.2	8.1	4.8	-0.2	2.1	3.1	4.8	9.1	3.4	2.5	5.7	2.7	5.7	7.0	6.1	2.1	6.9	9.5	0.4
1991	6.7	4.2	-0.6	10.3	5.6	-1.8	2.1	3.2	4.3	9.6	3.2	0.8	5.0	3.5	2.9	6.9	6.5	1.2	8.8	5.9	-2.0
1992	7.4	3.0	2.3	11.3	1.5	0.6	2.2	1.7	1.1	10.4	2.5	1.2	4.3	4.0	2.2	7.3	5.3	0.7	10.0	3.7	-0.5
1993	6.8	3.0	3.1	11.2	1.9	2.2	2.5	1.4	0.1	11.8	2.1	-1.0	4.6	4.1	-1.1	10.5	4.2	-0.7	10.4	1.6	2.0
1994	6.1	2.6	3.7	10.3	0.2	4.1		0.7	0.9		1.6	1.9	5.8	3.0	2.3	11.6	3.9	1.5	9.5	2.4	3.3

MACROECONOMIC PERFORMANCE IN SOME DEVELOPING NATIONS

from IMF, *International Financial Statistics Yearbook*, 1994; and World Bank, *World Development Report 1993*.

	GNP/capita	GNP/capita Avg. annual growth %	Population (millions)	Inflation Avg. annual %	Inflation Avg. annual %	Life Expectancy at birth, 1991	Govt. Spending (% of GNP)	Govt. Deficit (% of GNP)
	1991 $	1980-91	mid-1991	1970-80	1980-91	(years)	1991	1991
U.S.	22,240	1.7	252.7	7.5	4.2	76	25.3	4.8
Greece	6,340	1.1	10.3	14.5	17.7	77	60.0	26.2
Korea	6,330	8.7	43.3	20.1	5.6	70	17.3	1.7
Brazil	2,940	0.5	151.4	38.6	327.6	66	35.1	5.9
Argentina	2,790	-1.5	32.7	133.9	416.9	71	13.1	0.5
Chile	2,160	1.6	13.4	188.1	20.5	72		
Poland	1,790	0.6	38.2		63.1	71		
Turkey	1,780	2.9	57.3	29.4	44.7	67	30.4	7.6
Columbia	1,260	1.2	32.8	22.3	25.0	69	15.1	-2.0
Syria	1,160	-1.4	12.5	11.8	14.3	67	24.3	-0.4
Peru	1,070	2.4	21.9	30.1	287.3	64	8.8	0.5
Egypt	610	1.9	53.6	9.6	12.5	61	39.6	6.8
China	370	7.8	1149.5	0.9	5.8	69		
Nigeria	340	-2.3	99.0	15.2	18.1	52		
India	330	3.2	866.5	8.4	8.2	60	17.5	7.0
Ethiopia	120	-1.6	52.8	4.3	2.4	48		

Page numbers with an f indicate figures.

steady accumulation as the **national debt** has become a familiar and, to many, very disturbing presence. But just as a richer family can afford a larger mortgage, a richer nation can borrow more than poorer countries without endangering its future. Alternative and more informative measures of government borrowing, such as the **ratio of the deficit to gdp** and the **ratio of the national debt to gdp** (Figure 7), are far less alarming than the astronomical but deceptive raw numbers that we're used to seeing. Even so, the fact that these deficits are *postponed taxes* means that we can't ignore their implications for our standard of living in the years to come. For the past half-century, the events in these graphs have taken place against a backdrop of generally aggressive but sometimes erratic **monetary expansion** which has meant a persistent but uneven **climb in the overall price level** (Figure 8). This ongoing **inflation,** though much lower and less variable in the U.S. than in many nations, is factored into contracts by borrowers and lenders, savers and investors, and other capital market participants and thereby becomes a component of **market interest rates** (Figure 9).

While the U.S. remains among the most self-sufficient of major economies, the remarkable growth of its **foreign sector** in recent decades (Figure 10) reflects its participation in an expansion of trade that has brought steadily increasing economic flows across the borders of virtually every nation. This has obviously meant more *goods and services* moving across nations but also increased international transactions in *securities* (involving currencies, stocks, bonds and other earning assets). For the U.S. this has become a continuing *net inflow of goods and services* and a corresponding *net outflow of securities*, a pattern known as a **trade deficit** (Figure 11). The past 25 years of foreign sector growth, for most nations, has taken place within a framework of market-determined, flexible exchange rates across currencies. The ups and downs of the **international value of the dollar** (Figure 12) attract attention and concern, particularly from those in import- or export-sensitive industries.

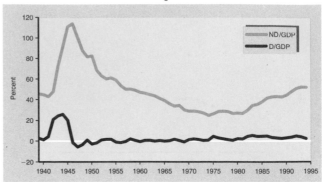

■ FIGURE 7

■ FIGURE 8

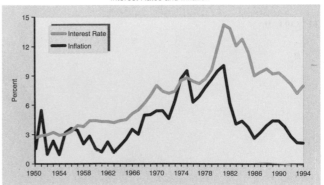

■ FIGURE 9